The Tao of Deception

The Tao of Deception

*Unorthodox Warfare in Historic
and Modern China*

RALPH D. SAWYER

With the collaboration of

MEI-CHÜN LEE SAWYER

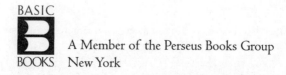

BASIC
BOOKS

A Member of the Perseus Books Group
New York

Books published by Basic Books are available at special discounts for bulk purchases in the United States by corporations, institutions, and other organizations. For more information, please contact the Special Markets Department at the Perseus Books Group, 11 Cambridge Center, Cambridge, MA, 02142, or call (617) 252-5298 or (800) 255-1514, or e-mail special.markets@perseusbooks.com.

Library of Congress Cataloging-in-Publication Data
Sawyer, Ralph D.
The Tao of deception : unorthodox warfare in historic and modern China / Ralph D. Sawyer With the collaboration of Mei-chün Lee Sawyer.
p. cm.
Includes bibliographical references and index.
ISBN-13: 978-0-465-07205-7 (hardcover : alk. paper)
ISBN-10: 0-465-07205-4 (hardcover : alk. paper) 1. Military art and science—China—History. 2. Deception (Military science)—History. I. Sawyer, Mei-chün. II. Title.
U43.C6S29 2007
355.4'1—dc22
2006031642

The paper used in this publication meets the requirements of the American National Standard for Permanence of Paper for Printed Library Materials Z39.48–1984.

10   9   8   7   6   5   4   3   2   1

In Memory of Li Kang

Contents

II MODERN THEORIES AND IMPLICATIONS

Preface

Our original idea for a brief primer on the intriguing concept of the un-orthodox in China, something more accessible to contemporary military strategists, historians, and others with a general interest in China or per-haps even the business application of core Chinese military concepts than a heavily footnoted, limited-circulation academic paper, quickly fell by the wayside as we presented focal materials to diverse audiences. Theorizing about the unorthodox across Chinese history has ranged from the simplis-tic to the highly esoteric, with the resulting strategic writings continuously reflecting the earliest fundamental assumptions. Equally important, a number of illustrative battles have been traditionally viewed as defining the nature and practice of the unorthodox.

Not unexpectedly, no single formulation—not even Sun-tzu's definitive articulation—nor individual battle adequately expresses or epitomizes the concept of the unorthodox. However, broad acquaintance with a wide range of theoretical formulations and numerous pivotal clashes can pro-vide an adequate basis for contemplation and assimilation. In addition, all these materials continue to be actively scrutinized in various PRC military and political think tanks as part of the highly motivated quest to create a contemporary military science with unique Chinese characteristics. Much of the Chinese populace has also become so familiar with at least some of them from mass media presentations that they have significantly affected the general strategic mindset.

Insofar as few materials, theoretical or historical, from the Chinese mil-itary tradition have been translated into English and few Sinologists seem interested in carrying forth the thrust initiated by Columbia University

Press some decades ago to provide Western readers with the fundamental Chinese writings in the style of the Loeb Classical Library, we felt compelled to provide somewhat more comprehensive coverage of the topic than otherwise. Thus, virtually all of the theoretical passages and nearly all the battles explicitly deemed unorthodox in the various manuals of China's vast military corpus have been included in their entirety. To the extent that the theoretical writings continuously build upon previous works and generally hark back to Sun-tzu or some other early articulation, some (and occasionally a lot of) redundancy is unavoidable.

However, rather than artificially abstracted and then interspersed among the various conclusions being presented, the thoughts of each era have been provided complete for scrutiny and pondering, including (for convenience) all the materials being integrated from previous works and centuries. Depending upon individual interest, the entire work may be read in detail, the theoretical or historical chapters studied separately, or materials in a particular historical period examined in isolation. (A comprehensive grasp of the relevance and impact of traditional unorthodox materials in contemporary PRC strategic thought may be achieved by perusing the chapters entitled "Sun-tzu's Definitive Formulation," "Han Dynasty Realizations," and "Sung Dynasty Theoretical Developments" before reading the two chapters in the Modern Theories and Implications section.)

The illustrative battles might easily have been multiplied simply by selecting additional examples from the dynastic histories that are discussed as essentially unorthodox in conception or execution by either the principle actors or the historian. However, apart from making an already substantial book somewhat unwieldy, they did not play a primary role in either Chinese theorizing or the general martial consciousness. Therefore, just as many that we viewed as paradigm implementations, they have not been included in order to essentially maintain the character of an internal study.

As originally conceived we had intended to examine the origins and evolution of the concept against early historical events; trace its peregrinations across the centuries in the theoretical writings, incorporating the illustrative battles cited in the latter in each section; and finally append a casebook of additional materials. However, perhaps because of Western absorption in chronological divisions and progression, some readers of our previous works found the Chinese penchant for "ahistorical" examination of the evidence to be confusing. Although strategists such as Li Ch'üan, Yeh Meng-hsiung, and Mao Yüan-yi were not ignorant of political developments nor insensitive to changes in military technology over the centuries, they moved seamlessly in their contemplations of military concepts and tactical principles among the centuries. Accordingly, if reluctantly, while not attempting to present a general military history of China, we have therefore abstracted all the illustrative battles and arranged them chronologically by era before presenting the corresponding theoretical discussions.

Not unexpectedly, this has occasioned criticism from one or two historical specialists who read parts of the work in manuscript because it forfeits to some degree the integrity of the illustrative materials of importance to any individual writer or text. However, readers with expertise in Chinese may easily consult the original, the incidents are all listed in abbreviated form in their original discussions, and the theoretical sources are also identified in the footnotes correlated to each battle account. (Many of the battles are only mentioned in abbreviated form in the theoretical discussions, so expansion could only be achieved by recourse to the historical writings in any event.) Several of the martial writings, such as the *Wu-ching Tsung-yao*, also contain illustrative chapters consisting solely of battle accounts and these have been similarly treated.

Three steps have been taken to make all the translated materials more accessible for readers unfamiliar with Chinese names and history. First, the historical illustrations have occasionally been abridged by deleting collateral events and omitting names of actors and especially honorific titles that do not add significantly to the core account. Second, theoretical and illustrative sections in the military compendia, especially the *Wu-ching Tsung-yao*, frequently contain erroneous characters and corrupted passages. Apart from comparing variant editions and emending where necessary (though generally without noting as this is not a work intended primarily for Sinologists, who can, in any event, readily examine the original materials and generally disparage the role or importance of military events in Chinese history), recourse for the historical incidents has primarily been to their original, expanded form in the dynastic histories, secondarily to the synthesized accounts in the *Tzu-chih T'ung-chien* and similar works. A certain amount of contextual information has also been provided for the historical illustrations, but only that minimally needed to understand the principles being discussed.

Although we normally keep our historical and contemporary work separate and rarely publish on modern Chinese military issues, we have diverged from our usual practice because of the importance of the traditional military writings to the ongoing formulation of PRC strategic and operational doctrine. The inclusion of certain implications was further stimulated by the preparation of a lecture for a May 2006 conference sponsored by the Centre for Military and Strategic Studies titled Continental Defense: Policies, Threats and Architecture. Portions of the accompanying paper, "Chinese Strategic Power: Myths, Intent, and Projections" (which should be consulted for further amplification), available in the September 2006 issue of the Centre's online *Journal of Military and Strategic Studies,* have been incorporated in the final chapter.

Finally, as in our previous works, while I am responsible for the historical content, writing, military texts, theorizing, and conclusions, Mei-chün has contributed immeasurably through our joint examination of a wide variety of historical records, especially contemporary materials. Chinese characters for the cover have once again been provided by Lee T'ing-rong.

Ralph D. Sawyer
Centre for Military and Strategic Studies
Spring 2006

A Note on Pronunciation

Unfortunately, neither of the two commonly employed orthographies makes the pronunciation of romanized Chinese characters easy. Each system has its stumbling blocks and we remain unconvinced that the pinyin *qi* is inherently more comprehensible to unpracticed readers than the older, increasingly discarded Wade-Giles *ch'i*, although it is certainly no less comprehensible than *j* for *r* in Wade-Giles. However, as many of the important terms may already be familiar, previous translations of Sun-tzu's *Art of War* have mainly used Wade-Giles, and for consistency with our other martial writings—as well as a minor protest against the perversities and political practices of the PRC regime—we continue to employ Wade-Giles here. (Most non-Chinese readers find the use of hyphens to indicate pronunciation breaks for the individual characters in compound words preferable to pinyin's run-on form.)

As a crude guide to pronunciation we offer the following notes on the significant exceptions to normally expected sounds:

t, as in *Tao*: without apostrophe, pronounced like *d* (pinyin "d")
p, as in *ping*: without apostrophe, pronounced like *b* (pinyin "b")
ch, as in *chuang*: without apostrophe, pronounced like *j* (pinyin "j" and "zh")
hs, as in *hsi*: pronounced like English *sh* (pinyin "x")
j, as in *jen*: pronounced like *r* (pinyin "r")

Thus, the name of the famous Chou (or Zhou in *pinyin*) dynasty is pronounced as if written "jou" and sounds just like the English name "Joe."

Dynastic Chronology

Legendary Sage Emperors	2852 – 2255 BCE	
Hsia (Xia)	2205 – 1766	
Shang	1766 – 1045	
Chou (Zhou)		
Western Chou (Zhou)	1045 – 770	
Eastern Chou (Zhou)	770 – 256	
Spring and Autumn	722 – 481	
Warring States	403 – 221	
Ch'in (Qin)	221 – 207	
Former Han (Western Han)	206 BCE – 8 CE	
Later Han (Eastern Han)	23 – 220	
Three Kingdoms	168 – 280	
Six Dynasties	222 – 589	
Sui	589 – 618	
T'ang (Tang)	618 – 907	
Five Dynasties	907 – 959	
Sung	960 – 1126	
Southern Sung	1127 – 1279	
Yüan (Mongol)	1279 – 1368	
Ming	1368 – 1644	
Ch'ing (Manchu) (Qing)	1644 – 1911	

PART ONE

Historical Experience and Formulations

Incipient Beginnings

What enable the masses of the Three Armies invariably to withstand the enemy without being defeated are the unorthodox and the orthodox. One engages in battle with the orthodox and gains victory through the unorthodox. Thus, anyone who excels at sending forth the unorthodox becomes as inexhaustible as Heaven, as unlimited as the Yangtze and Yellow rivers. In warfare, the strategic configurations of power do not exceed the unorthodox and orthodox, but the changes of the unorthodox and orthodox can never be completely exhausted. The unorthodox and orthodox mutually produce each other, just like an endless cycle. Who can exhaust them?

For many contemplating Sun-tzu's epochal definition, the unorthodox remained a mystery, tactically opaque and conceptually obscure, deliberately shrouded in fog and darkness, yet have others naively deemed it simplicity itself, reducible to merely "doing the opposite of what is expected." Ordinary commanders were content just to know that it existed and never burdened themselves with trying to understand or implement it, but extraordinary generals adopted the unorthodox through imagination and inspiration, employing unusual strategies and unexpected methods to forge great victories in improbable circumstances.

No episode has been more famous throughout Chinese history than T'ien Tan's innovative use of unorthodox measures to extricate the remnants of the state of Ch'i from a five-year siege at Chi-mo during the Warring States period.[1] In 333 BCE, the eastern state of Ch'i had exploited Yen's mourning to invade and seize some ten cities, an affront that continued to rankle even though they were eventually returned. Two decades later, civil war then caused such disaffection among Yen's populace that they refused to defend the state, allowing King Min of Ch'i to occupy it in 314 BCE. Persuaded not to annex it, in 312 BCE King Min supported the ascension of King Chao, who immediately committed himself to the task of reviving his vanquished state. Assiduously cultivating his Virtue in the prescribed fashion, he nurtured the people, sought out talented men, revitalized the military, and adroitly avoided conflict with other states. Finally, prompted by King Min's arrogance and his recent conquest of Sung, King Chao embarked upon a campaign intended to punish Ch'i for its predatory behavior.

Having recently defeated armies from Ch'u and the Three Chin, attacked Ch'in, destroyed Sung, and aided Chao in extinguishing Chung-shan, Ch'i possessed unsurpassed power and territory. Yen therefore cobbled together an allied force consisting of the states of Han, Wei, Chao, and Ch'in and invaded Ch'i in 285 BCE with Yüeh Yi as commander in chief. The coalition was disbanded shortly after they severely overwhelmed Ch'i's forces west of the Chi River, though Yen's armies continued to sweep through the countryside, seize the capital, subjugate several cities, and persuade others to voluntarily submit, all within six months. However, despite King Min having been slain, two Ch'i cities resolutely resisted demands to surrender as well as Yüeh Yi's promise of leniency.

Unwilling to needlessly incur heavy casualties, Yüeh Yi undertook a virtually interminable siege. However, detractors back in Yen assailed his failure to swiftly reduce the remaining cities and accused him of wanting to prolong his authority or even become king of Ch'i. Since King Chao of Yen perspicaciously disbelieved these slanders, the siege continued for nearly five years. However, when King Chao died in 279, T'ien Tan, who had been named commander at Chi-mo by popular acclaim, exploited the new monarch's flaws and inexperience to sow discord by employing double agents who successfully reiterated the same accusations, resulting in Yüeh's replacement by Ch'i Chieh.

T'ien Tan then embarked on a multi-stage, unorthodox effort to simultaneously undermine the enemy's will and rebuild the defenders' spirit. First, he created an "auspicious omen" by having food left out in the courtyards whenever the people offered sacrifice, thereby attracting flocks of birds, a phenomenon that puzzled Yen's soldiers. Second, he imparted a transcendent veracity to his measures by pretending to receive spiritual instruction. Third, correctly anticipating it would make his troops resolute, he ruthlessly sacrificed the well-being of prisoners held in Yen's camp by volubly worrying that Ch'i's spirit would be adversely affected if their noses were cut off. Fourth, he had double agents bemoan the severe consternation they would suffer if the outer graves were exhumed, thereby tricking Yen into enraging the populace when they burned the corpses. Fifth, his family led in the fortification work, he personally feasted his officers, and he nurtured Yen's overconfidence by concealing the able-bodied, visibly displaying only the weak and wounded. Finally, T'ien Tan not only exploited the antique ruse of a false surrender to induce laxity but further augmented its effectiveness by bribing Yen's generals.

As recorded in his *Shih Chi* biography, T'ien Tan then implemented his most famous unorthodox measure:

> T'ien Tan herded the thousand cattle within the city together and had them covered with red silken cloth decorated with five-colored dragon veins. Naked blades were tied to their horns and reeds soaked in fat bound to their tails. They then chiseled dozens of holes in the walls and that night ignited the reeds, releasing the cattle through them. Five thousand stalwart soldiers followed in the rear. When their tails got hot, the cattle angrily raced into Yen's army.
>
> Being the middle of the night, Yen's troops were astonished. The brightness from the burning torches on the cattle tails was dazzling. Everywhere Yen's soldiers looked there were dragon veins, everyone the cattle collided with died or was wounded.
>
> Accompanied by a great drumming and clamor from within the city, 5,000 men with gagged mouths exploited the confusion

to suddenly attack. The old and weak all made their bronze implements resound by striking them, the tumult moved Heaven
and Earth. Terrified, Yen's army fled in defeat.

Thus, through extended but innovative psychological operations and several unorthodox tactics in sequence, just 7,000 exhausted soldiers and another 10,000 inhabitants trapped in Chi-mo defied a siege force of
perhaps 100,000. Thereafter, aided by uprisings in the occupied cities,
Ch'i's reinvigorated armies drove Yen's disorganized forces out beyond the
borders, allowing Ch'i to reclaim its position, however weakened and tarnished, among the extant states. Not surprisingly, this episode has long
stirred the popular imagination and been justly considered the epitome of
imaginative command, accounting for its inclusion among the *Thirty-six
Strategies* and the *Hundred Unorthodox Strategies*, where it is cited as an
example of "estrangement."[2]

Historical Origins and Connotations

Ever since the late Spring and Autumn the character *ch'i* (*qi*), herein translated as "unorthodox" in a military context, has been employed to designate the unusual, unexpected, marvelous, strange, heterodox, and
sometimes eccentric. Because it does not appear in any of the Shang dynasty oracle writings, Chou dynasty bronze inscriptions, or even such historically sanctified Confucian classics as the *Book of Odes* (*Shih Ching*) or
Spring and Autumn Annals (*Ch'un Ch'iu*), its actual origins remain unclear.[3] Traditional Chinese dictionaries, citing examples from late Spring
and Autumn and early Warring States texts, classify the character under
"large" (which appears as the uppermost component) and explain it as basically meaning "different," what "differs from the ordinary" or from the
commonly seen and experienced.[4] The character also has a second reading, meaning "odd"—as in numbers being "even" and "odd" rather than
odd in the sense of "strange"—and venerable compendia also suggest it
indicates something that lacks a match or mate.[5]

In the sense of difference being a virtue, denoting distinctiveness, *ch'i* early on came to be employed in reference to people marked by superior appearance, superlative physical skills, surpassing behavior or demeanor, transcending personality, or incisive thinking that set them outside or beyond the realm of the pedestrian, common, and ordinary. Thus the Han dynasty *Shih Chi*, China's first synthetic history, occasionally records that powerful officials, upon first encountering hitherto unknown persons such as Han Hsin and Liu Pang, regarded them as "*ch'i*" and "*ch'i ts'ai*," "extraordinary" and "extraordinary talents," respectively.

Particularly unusual objects, spectacular scenes, and inspiring vistas similarly came to be designated as *ch'i*, a usage that continues to expand as uniquely shaped rocks command high prices as collectibles and highly visible personalities are termed *ch'i nü-jen* ("extraordinary" or "remarkable woman") or *ch'i-nan-jen* (a "remarkable man"), such as in a recent newspaper headline about a *hao-se ch'i-nan-jen*, essentially a "rake" or "Lothario."[6] Thus, the movie title *The League of Extraordinary Gentlemen* was translated as *T'ien-chiang Ch'i-ping* or "Ch'i Warriors Descended from Heaven" and troops of amazingly skillful Chinese acrobats routinely call themselves *ch'i-ping,* "unorthodox warriors."

As early as the Warring States period, the character was also used in an active sense, to "make something different or unusual." More intensively, it also conveyed a meaning of weird, extraordinary, and outlandish and was used to describe the mendicant persuaders who "made their clothes *ch'i*," "outlandish" or perhaps even "bizarre," as part of their effort to create an aura of distinctiveness and visibly suggest their disdain for normal constraints.[7] They were particularly noticeable or unusual in an era when the prescriptive materials subsequently codified in such ritual compendia as the *Yi Li* and *Chou Li* not only increasingly dictated conformity to certain rules and norms of behavioral propriety, but also emphasized "rectifying one's clothes" and generally prohibited "strange attire."

As the centuries passed and the term acquired more divergent and darker connotations, it acquired a sense of the mysterious, of something beyond ordinary comprehension, and it was therefore said that "things that cause people not to be able to fathom them are called *ch'i.*" (Its employment to designate a mode of warfare—*ch'i chan* or "unorthodox warfare"—emphasizes this aspect of being unfathomable.) Similarly, it further came to characterize the uncanny and occult, especially in reference to ethereal events and ghostly phenomena.

An interest in difference, what is uncommon or not yet known, underlies the contemporary term for "curiosity," *hao-ch'i* or "love of the unusual." However, Confucius declined to speak about three things—spirits, images, and death—in order to preclude distractions from the present. His pronouncement came to heavily impact China's official cultural orientation, consigning anything apart from the virtues, values, and rituals required to maintain social distinctions and court awesomeness not just to insignificance but to inimical status. However, from the Han dynasty onward, all things imaginative, esoteric, and supernatural, including ghost tales and bizarre stories, became popular among the realm's less pretentious members.

Largely in accord with the thrust of Confucian prejudice, stories and materials considered too unusual (*ch'i*) and irregular for inclusion in the orthodox dynastic histories came to be preserved in works such as the voluminous *T'ai-p'ing Kuang-chi* compiled in 977 CE, and in the late Ming many of the bizarre tales that had always fascinated the populace were assembled into collections of *ch'uan-ch'i* or sagas of heroes and "tales of the unusual." Although often bearing somewhat formalized titles such as *Observations on Ancient and Contemporary Oddities* (*Chin-ku Ch'i-kuan*),[8] they vividly preserve China's enthrallment with the esoteric and supernatural, with what is well termed *ch'i.*

In perhaps the ultimate acknowledgement of Confucianism's repressive impact, a work compiled by Yüan Mei in the Ming dynasty titled *What Confucius Didn't Speak About* (*Tzu Bu-yü*) assembles some 1,024 incidents of strange and ghostly phenomena, including wizards, outright magic, and witchcraft. To take just a single example, one tale involves a weird (*ch'i*) ghost with laser-like capabilities, an eye upon his back that emanates a light capable of killing! Other stories depict *ch'i nan* (odd men with unusual bodily powers) and *ch'i shu,* "rare skills" or "techniques," such as being able to predict events at a distance, including death.

In short, the term *ch'i* has always encompassed a fairly extensive range of intensities, all derived from the basic sense of difference. Many of them will be seen contributing to the fundamental sense of the "unorthodox" in unorthodox warfare, including being tinged with mysteriousness, not being normal or upright, and especially being unfathomable, though generally not bizarre.[9] It appears in a number of frequently used modern compounds[10] and has also become a key term in modern parlance and military circles, designating an unorthodox plan or strategy in the compound *ch'i-mou,* the reputed core of contemporary, surpassing PRC military thought.

Historical Vestiges

Chinese tradition has long held that the unorthodox tactics formulated by the T'ai Kung (Lü Shang)—the advisor, strategist, and confidant to the Chou dynastic founders, Kings Wen and Wu—enabled the ostensibly virtuous but sorely outnumbered peripheral state of Chou to surprisingly overthrow the long-reigning, tyrannical Shang and its perverse ruler.[11] According to the *Shih Chi,* "After King Wen was ransomed and returned from Yu-li, he secretly planned with Lü Shang and cultivated his Virtue in order to overturn Shang's government. The T'ai Kung's affairs were mostly concerned with military authority and the unorthodox, so when later generations speak about armies and the Chou's secret balance of power (*ch'üan*), they all honor the T'ai Kung for making the fundamental plans."

The *Shih Chi*'s appraisal is somewhat surprising because the unorthodox (*ch'i*) has traditionally been identified solely with Sun-tzu. However, the remarkable battle at Mu-yeh apparently turned upon an unexpected, concerted charge by 3,000 elite warriors that disrupted an overwhelmingly greater force. Moreover, rather than being an impulsive strike or extemporaneous tactic, it culminated decades of incrementally nurturing power, sequentially vanquishing contiguous states, consciously forging vital alliances, and imaginatively employing subversive measures. Once the conquest and subsequent brutal consolidation were concluded, the T'ai Kung was enfeoffed in the distant region of Shandong, no doubt as much to remove him as a military threat to the nascent dynasty as to stabilize the eastern perimeter. However, despite being an octogenarian, in true semi-legendary fashion he reportedly commanded troops and assisted in quashing the major protagonists when disaffected Shang elements rebelled against the Chou in conjunction with disaffected Eastern peoples.

Like many other early Chou enfeoffments, the incipient state of Ch'i was situated in a so-called barbarian area, one originally harboring the Eastern Yi and other indigenous peoples who had remained unsubmissive during the Shang's reign. A coastal state that early on was somehow associated with strange and marvelous doctrines, Ch'i would subsequently be the site of China's most famous hegemon, Duke Huan, and his advisor, Kuan Chung, otherwise known as Kuan-tzu from the book bearing his name.[12] Military studies burgeoned in Ch'i, Sun-tzu reputedly was a native, and Sun Pin implemented the famous, unorthodox doctrines that twice brought victory in the mid fourth century against the state of Wei. Not surprisingly, by the late Warring States period the T'ai Kung had come to be envisioned as the progenitor of Ch'i's vibrant military thought and was even honored in the T'ang dynasty with dedicated temples as the state's martial patron.[13]

Although the *Liu-t'ao* or *Six Secret Teachings*, the work attributed to the T'ai Kung, contains several important discussions of unorthodox tactics, the extant work probably dates to the middle to late Warring States period and was therefore compiled well after Sun-tzu's *Art of War*, the *Wu-tzu*, and possibly even Sun Pin's recently recovered *Military Methods*. Therefore, the *Art of War*, composed against a background of multiparty, internecine strife that saw conjoined chariot and infantry armies approaching 50,000 regularly engaging in campaigns that required weeks, even months, remains the conceptual progenitor.

Whether the *Art of War* was authored in large part by the legendary Sun-tzu at the end of the Spring and Autumn period or by his disciples or others in the early to middle Warring States period remains an intriguing but largely unresolved historical question.[14] However, it is not the focal concern of our broader examination of the theory and practice of the unorthodox in China. Rather, the degree to which unorthodox precursors may be found in the battles and tactics of the Spring and Autumn, particularly those found in the *Tso Chuan* that later writers have deemed to be realizations of the unorthodox and should predate the formulation of Sun-tzu's definitive paragraph, commands initial attention in the next chapter.

Early Military Context

Although our volume is not intended as a generalized history of Chinese warfare and limitations of space preclude extensively discussing Spring and Autumn (722–481 BCE) and Warring States (481 or 403 to 221 BCE) practices, a few salient characteristics will facilitate understanding the *Art of War*'s background, the examples to be cited in the *Tso Chuan* discussion, and certain other issues.[15] Named after the famous Confucian classic chronicling the era, the Spring and Autumn period witnessed the accelerated rise of state power, development of internecine strife, and annihilation and annexation of numerous minor political entities. At its inception, descendants of the various Chou feudal lords still ruled in most states, but the ongoing evisceration of Chou authority effectively freed them from all but minimal vestiges of subservient status. In fact, while they sometimes sought to justify or sanctify their actions in the name of the Chou, they willfully embarked on a path of mutual extermination.

As a result of the predatory campaigns of the stronger states, the scope of warfare in the Spring and Autumn period increased dramatically, necessarily involving greater numbers of peasants as integral elements, primarily as infantry and in logistical support. Sustained combat on open terrain was centered on infantry-supported chariot units, though the chariot's actual battlefield role apart from command and archery platform functions and its efficacy remain problematic. Initially, the aristocratic warriors were expected to adhere to the ritualized prescriptions of battle, the *li*, but the conscripted infantry seem to have escaped such constraints.

However, within a century only the foolish were burdened by the old code of ethics, and the ancient style of individual combat—despite personal challenges still offered to instigate battles—had become outmoded.

Campaign armies early in the Spring and Autumn might include several hundred to a thousand chariots accompanied by perhaps ten to twenty thousand men. However, by the end of the Spring and Autumn period in 481 BCE, the powerful states of Chin, Ch'in, and Ch'i could each reputedly field approximately 4,000 chariots supported by some 40,000 or more infantrymen, and coalition armies soared accordingly. Sieges and city assaults, though costly and still highly disadvantaged, proliferated but the cavalry remained unknown.

Compound, reflex bows and a long handled weapon to which was affixed a dagger (known as the *ko* or dagger-axe) comprised the era's most common weapons, though spears and daggers (but no swords until the Warring States) were also carried. Throughout the Eastern Chou, metalworking skills continued to advance, resulting in stronger, sharper, larger, and ever more deadly combat tools. Yet bronze technology remained the norm, with the newly discovered processes of iron and steel technology (in the late Spring and Autumn period) confined largely to agricultural implements.

Battles frequently arose and even the most powerful state, should it fail to prepare its defenses and train its soldiers, could be vanquished. Consequently, the recognition and retention of individuals proficient in the military arts became essential, and rewards for valor, strength, and martial achievements were initiated. Basic physical qualifications for members of the standing army and for those selected to more elite units were maintained. Administrative reforms that empowered centralized authority were accompanied by the evolution of political theory, bureaucratic staffs, and defined practices, all of which, in the context of nearly continual warfare, suddenly made military science necessary.

The pace of events accelerated significantly at the beginning of the Warring States period in 403 BCE. Spring and Autumn conflicts had segmented China among seven powerful survivors—Ch'i, Yen, the Three Chin (Han, Chao, Wei), Ch'u, and Ch'in—plus the emerging states of Wu and Yüeh, each intent upon not just enduring but dominating the realm through aggressive measures and preying upon some fifteen weaker states that had managed to precariously survive. Sustained by increasing agricultural productivity and expanding material prosperity, the scale of conflict surged phenomenally during the Warring States period.

The weakest of the nine major states could easily field an army of 100,000, while Ch'in, eventually the strongest, reportedly maintained a million-man standing army near the end of the period and reportedly mobilized 600,000 for a single campaign. (Although early, traditional figures are notoriously unreliable, the true degree of exaggeration remains uncertain, though reducing to a half or at most a third may be appropriate. Because of strong administrative and organizational measures the individual states were easily capable of levying such numbers, but sustaining them in the field would be another matter.)

In one decisive battle between Ch'in and Ch'u, the total combatants apparently exceeded a million, an astounding figure of several hundred thousand even when discounted by a factor of two or three. Numerical strength had become critical because in the previous campaign 200,000 soldiers from Ch'in had suffered a severe defeat. Naturally, casualties also escalated rapidly, with 100,000 from Wei reportedly dying at the battle of Ma-ling in 341 BCE; 240,000 in the combined forces of Wei and Han perishing at Yi-ch'üeh in 295; and 450,000 men of Chao reported as having been slaughtered at Ch'ang-p'ing in 260.

Campaigns of such magnitude doubtlessly required lengthy periods for logistical preparation, mobilization, and engagement. Instead of a few days or weeks on the march and perhaps a couple of days in battle, months were necessary and the battles raged intermittently for tens of days, while stalemates and sieges reportedly persisted for a year or more. Great expertise was required to manage such vast resources, plan for the army's deployment, and sustain the forces once in the field.

The peasants had long been subjected to military training on a seasonal basis and conscripted for combat when needed. However, this rapid expansion in force size required the army's core to be composed of trained officers and disciplined soldiers. Drill manuals, deployment methods, and the tactics they would be designed to execute suddenly became indispensable.

An extensive body of military theory appeared, stimulated not only by battlefield and training requirements but also by new political theories and individual philosophies.

Strategy and battlefield direction became so complex that the replacement of a general could result in an army's defeat and the nation's endangerment. The civilian realm became increasingly estranged from the realities of warfare and although rulers continued to meddle in army matters, often with catastrophic results, professional officers who specialized solely in military affairs normally assumed planning and command responsibilities.

During the Shang and early Chou periods, because battles had been fought on agricultural and otherwise open, undefended terrain, advancing armies encountered only scattered cities. Thick fortifications such as the famous Neolithic and Shang dynasty stamped-earth walls seem always to have existed, but forces in maneuver could essentially roam through the countryside unhampered. However, in the Warring States period the feudal lords expanded their border defenses, constructing "great walls," ramparts, forts, and guard towers at strategic points such as passes and road intersections to defend against incursion. Warfare's objectives changed because states no longer sought to capture prisoners or plunder for riches, but focused on vanquishing their enemies by exterminating their armies, annexing their lands, and subjugating their populace.

Fortified cities, previously military and administrative centers, grew enormously in significance as industry, trade, and population all flourished, and they became focal points in the road network. Accordingly, whereas in the Western Chou and Spring and Autumn periods it was advisable to circumvent these isolated cities rather than to waste men and resources besieging and assaulting them, capturing or destroying them now assumed critical importance. Techniques for assault and defense simultaneously advanced, with siege engines, mobile shields, battering rams, catapults, mobile towers, and similar mobile devices appearing in substantial numbers, and Sun-tzu's condemnation of assaulting cities, if not outdated, was readily ignored.

The growth of mass infantry armies was also accompanied by the per-
fection and widespread use of the crossbow during the fourth century; by
further developments in articulation, deployment, and maneuvering capabilities; and by the reluctant adoption of barbarian practices to create
the cavalry, also late in the fourth century. However, though the cavalry
came to constitute the third component force in the third century, both
actually and theoretically, their numbers remained few and their role was
largely confined to reconnaissance and harassing activities.

2

Spring and Autumn
Precursors

Although many consider the *Ch'un Ch'iu* or *Spring and Autumn Annals* purportedly edited by Confucius himself to be the era's definitive work, it is fundamentally constrained in being the chronicle of the single state of Lu and far too cryptic to allow reconstructing the period's history.[1] Thus, recourse has traditionally been to three independent works long viewed (however incorrectly) as deliberate commentaries upon the *Ch'un Ch'iu*—the *Tso Chuan*, the *Ku Liang*, and the *Kung Yang*—supplemented by the far less reliable *Dialogues of the States* (*Kuo Yü*) and the controversial *Bamboo Annals*.[2] Accordingly, despite significant questions, the analysis that follows assumes that the events depicted in the *Tso Chuan*, although sometimes heavily stylized and recast, are based on earlier, essentially reliable records. The dialogues, however, while perhaps capturing the gist of earlier conversations, should be regarded as much enhanced, subsequent reconstructions, if not outright creations.

Just as it was being increasingly disparaged during the Ming and Ch'ing as a worthless repository of outmoded tactics and martial concepts by Western-oriented critics, the *Tso Chuan* ironically became the focus of vibrant interest as the very progenitor of critical, classical military thought. In the Ming dynasty Ts'eng Yi composed a work entitled *Tso Strategies* (*Tso Lüeh*); Ch'en Yü-mo compiled the comprehensive, more categorically oriented *Tso-shih Ping-lüeh (Mr. Tso's Military Strategies)*, which includes extensive, comparative commentary from other texts; and Wei Hsi, a Ming adherent who retired to obscurity after the Ch'ing's ascension, created the *Ping Mou (Military Plans)*, an analytical work that dissects thirty-two essential categories of *mou* (strategic plans) identifiable within the *Tso Chuan*. (For Wei, the concept of *mou*, normally understood as encompassing strategic planning and complex plots, actually entails a number of fundamental concepts such as "harmony," though not the unorthodox.)

In the Ch'ing dynasty Li Yüan-ch'un compiled the *Tso-shih Ping-fa (Mr. Tso's Art of War* or *Military Methods)*, a work that abstracts and then appends illuminating commentary to nearly 200 military incidents from the *Tso Chuan*. Somewhat more surprisingly, recent decades have seen a vernacular edition of this work produced in the Peoples' Republic of China titled *Shallow Explanations of Tso's Art of War (Tso-shih Ping-fa Ch'ien-shuo)*, thereby revitalizing and making it accessible to a broad contemporary audience. Ironically, another work under the same title was produced at almost the same time by Chu Pao-hsing, who, though tangentially aware of the *Tso Lüeh*, apparently was ignorant of the *Tso-shih Ping-fa* itself.[3]

While not oblivious to changes in weaponry, component forces, and organization, these dedicated works all envision the origins and very foundation of Chinese military science in these early military tactics. Moreover, the authors assume that the concepts and essential tactical principles retain a timeless validity, that the lessons can be studied and appropriated. Of particular interest, in the preface to his book Li Yüan-ch'un asserts that Spring and Autumn commanders employed unorthodox (*ch'i*) tactics throughout the period. Furthermore, since the era's events all preceded the historical Sun-tzu and Wu-tzu, he believes that the theoretical writings known as the *Art of War* and the *Wu-tzu* were in fact based upon the reality of the experiences preserved in the *Tso Chuan*:

> Confucians certainly cannot avoid knowing about military affairs. The contemporary world asserts that the essence of military art (*ping-fa*) is fully encompassed by the *Seven Military Classics*, but I don't believe so.[4] Among the seven, the T'ai

Kung's *Liu-t'ao* comes first, but some knowledgeable people believe it is a forgery. Sun-tzu's thirteen chapters and Wu-tzu's six, which come next, certainly contain reliable material, but as they were all written after the *Tso Chuan*, the *Tso* is certainly the progenitor of military tactics (*ping-fa*). The *Tso* likes to speak about military conversations and affairs, often in exhaustive detail, thereby allowing people to see both the form (of events) and strategy, so it must be written in this fashion.

The *Tso* also discusses the secrets of military affairs such as found in the now lost *Chün-chih* [*Military Rescripts*], what has not necessarily been passed down through the ages. In recording what was transmitted, it preserves the intentions and extemporaneous means employed by famous generals on the battlefield in detail for posterity. Accordingly, how can it be said that Sun-tzu and Wu-tzu didn't take them as their basis?

In chronicling the more than 200 years of the Spring and Autumn period, the *Ch'un Ch'iu* [*Spring and Autumn Annals*] often speaks about generals and not infrequently about military events. In warfare, those who speak about the military do not invariably engage in warfare, but how can those who discuss military affairs amidst warfare not be comprehensive? Thus, how can the discussions in the *Sun-tzu* and *Wu-tzu* not be appropriate? However, their discussions are merely empty words, but what the *Tso* speaks about has been attested in experience. Those who subsequently excelled in employing the military knew that their tactics came out of Sun-tzu and Wu-tzu, but none realized they actually originated in the *Tso*.

Let's briefly examine some major issues. The military esteems employing the unorthodox, while among unorthodox measures none exceeds T'ien Tan's fire oxen. Sun-tzu and Wu-tzu never really speak about this sort of method, but the incendiary elephants in the *Tso* preceded him. Nothing was more unorthodox than Tsung Ch'üeh fabricating the appearance of lions or Ti Ch'ing's bronze mask. Sun-tzu and Wu-tzu never

manifestly discuss this sort of technique, but cloaking horses
precedes them in the *Tso*. . . . [5]

Li subsequently analogizes the study and employment of military tactics to the process of writing an essay, an act that, while creative, is necessarily founded upon detailed knowledge: "Those who excel at employing
the military read antique military works, calculate the means to achieve
decisive victory, and then, without imitating the visible aspects of ancient
plots, create unorthodox measures themselves. Without reading the ancient chapters and pouring over the ancient military books, it would be
impossible." However, he also adds that "what is not explainable is of
course *shen ch'i*," the "numinously" or "spiritually unorthodox."

Before we survey the chief unorthodox measures that evolved in the
Spring and Autumn in some detail, it is instructive to look at Li's initial
examples. As already seen, T'ien Tan's enormously famous fire oxen were
employed as a desperate but carefully calculated unorthodox measure to
extricate the long besieged city of Chi-mo. However, it and other animal
delivery systems were prefigured in 506 BCE when the king of Ch'u employed similarly motivated elephants to thwart Wu's onrushing forces that
had penetrated to the capital of Ying following several successive victories.
Immediately after crossing the Sui River, whether by tying fire brands to
their tails or using torches to enrage them, the fleeing king stampeded several elephants into his pursuers, disrupting them sufficiently to escape.[6]

The *Tso Chuan* records two incidents of cloaking horses to achieve an
effect much magnified beyond simple armor protection. The first incident, one in a series of clashes between Lu and the contiguous states of
Ch'i to the northeast and Sung to the southwest, unfolded in 684 BCE, early
in the Spring and Autumn period, when Lu was being threatened by the
allied forces of Ch'i and Sung.[7] It thus closely followed Ch'ang-chuo, the
famous battle that arose in the first month of the year at which not only
did the Sung prevail over Ch'i but the doctrine of debilitating the enemy's
ch'i, later adopted by Sun-tzu, was first articulated. In the second month
Lu made an incursion into Sung, prompting Sung and Ch'i to respond by
fielding a coalition force that encamped at Lang in the sixth month:

Armies from Ch'i and Sung halted at Lang where they were opposed by the duke of Lu. Kung-tzu Yen remarked, "Sung's army
is not well ordered and can be defeated. If Sung is defeated, Ch'i
will certainly return home. I suggest we launch a sudden attack." The duke refused permission.

Kung-tzu Yen then stealthily departed out through Yü gate,
draped his horses with dazzling (tiger skins), and went forth
against the enemy. The duke followed (with Lu's forces) and
they inflicted a major defeat on Sung's army at Ch'eng-ch'iu.
Ch'i's army then withdrew homeward.

Contrary to the impression furnished by the narrative, Kung-tzu
(prince) Yen would almost certainly have been accompanied by his personal followers rather than have rushed forth alone. Though no doubt an
extremely small contingent, the fervency of their onslaught proved sufficient to create disorder. Although Yen thus clearly contravened the ruler's
intent, historically his success has been seen as validating his impetuosity.
More important, within the context of an era that still stressed orderly
battlefield developments and imposed ritual and other formal constraints
upon rulers and warriors alike, suddenly exploiting a momentary opportunity created by the enemy's disorder can only be deemed unorthodox.

The second incident actually occurred in 632 BCE at the outset of the
pivotal battle of Ch'eng-p'u between the established, northern Chou states
and the "semi-barbarian" state of Ch'u in the south.[8] Hsü Ch'en, who had
cloaked the horses on his chariots with tiger skins, initiated Chin's ultimately successfully attack on Ch'u with an onslaught that directly targeted
the weaker allies of Ch'en and Ts'ai, causing them to collapse. Nevertheless, in neither case does the Tso suggest that the use of tiger skins (which
follows the Shang and early Chou tradition of decorating combat shields
with fierce animal visages) had any unexpected or overawing effect.

However, the two subsequent episodes cited by Li Yüan-ch'un very much
turn upon the enhanced effects of terrifying images just as the dragon
veins painted on the fire oxen at Chi-mo augmented the enemy's terror. In
446 CE the ruler of the small contiguous kingdom of Lin-yi, Fan Yang-mai,

mobilized all his forces and attacked (Northern) Sung.[9] Although rebellions against the Sung's nominal suzerainty were not uncommon, this attack was distinguished by the king employing heavily armored elephants as
his assault force. Among those deputed in response, Tsung Ch'üeh mused
that as the lions found in foreign countries reportedly had the power to
overawe all the other animals, they should somehow give their horses the
appearance of lions. Remarkably, since they had no knowledge of real lions, the ploy worked and the startled elephants ran off, creating the opportunity to inflict the severe defeat that followed. Despite having been born
into a Confucian-oriented family, Tsung was an astute practitioner of unorthodox techniques who frequently resorted to night attacks, roving unorthodox forces, and similar measures during his heroic career.

Ti Ch'ing, another of the Sung commanders distinguished by great
courage and heroic efforts, reportedly employed a bronze face mask and
left his hair disheveled when he plunged into Hsi Hsia "barbarian" forces
at the forefront of his cavalry regiment in 1040 CE, causing them to regard
him as some sort of spirit. A great fighter, he was also noted as an astute
practitioner of the unorthodox, conceiving and exploiting clever techniques as well as swift cavalry in unorthodox maneuver.[10]

The *Tso Chuan* itself never explicitly identifies any tactical inception as
unorthodox nor does it employ the concept either abstractly or concretely. In fact, as already noted, the character never appears apart from in
a personal name. However, from the T'ang onward certain innovative and
unexpected measures recorded in the *Tso Chuan* have been characterized
as unorthodox or employed to provide illustrations for important theoretical writings discussing the nature and employment of the unorthodox.
As their theories will be pondered in subsequent sections, the discussion
here focuses upon those incidents in which the commander's ingenuity
resulted in irregular and unexpected—that is, "unorthodox"—tactics.

An examination of the measures singled out as unorthodox within the
era's context by Li Yüan-ch'un and others shows that they were still fairly
simple, consisting of ambushes, feigned retreats, night attacks, *ch'i* manipulation, deliberately constructed ruses and misperceptions (subsequently known as "feinting east and striking west"), and a few localized

innovations such as the unexpected use of elephants. Other measures include feigned surrenders, creating deceptive facades by dragging brush and displaying multiple flags, and simple dissembling. Poison was also employed for the first time, water resources cut, flooding undertaken, and incendiary measures deliberately exploited. Most of these innovations exploited the enemy's expectations and thus essentially realized the *Art of War*'s crucial principle of being unexpected, the latter often achieved by employing every means and method possible to confuse, manipulate, and befuddle the enemy.[11]

Ambushes and Feigned Retreats

According to a passage from the Ming dynasty *Essential Strategies from a Grass Hut*, ambushes realize the Tao of deceit because "those who excel at ambushes can be expected to be victorious, those caught in them to suffer defeat."[12] Moreover, despite being frequently implemented from antiquity onward, they continued to be considered essentially unorthodox throughout Chinese military history. The first *Tso Chuan* occurrence, dating to 714 BCE, in fact illustrates not only that the best way to destroy the enemy in antiquity was through an ambush, but also the value of a well-executed, feigned retreat.[13]

> When the Northern Jung mounted an incursion into Cheng, the Duke of Cheng actively resisted them. However, he was troubled by the Jung army because "it is composed of infantry whereas we are on chariots. I am afraid that they will maneuver around behind us and launch a sudden attack."
>
> Prince T'u suggested, "We should have some courageous but irresolute men provoke the invaders and then quickly flee. Meanwhile, you should establish three ambushes to await them. The Jung act hastily and are not well ordered. They are greedy and lack close feelings.[14] In victory they will not yield to each other, in defeat will not rescue each other. When those in the forefront see potential gain they invariably concentrate on

advancing. When they advance and encounter our ambushes, they are sure to speedily run off. Since those to their rear will not rescue them, the conflict will not be sustained, resolving the difficulty."

The duke heeded his advice. When the Jung advance forces encountered the ambushes and ran off, Chu Tan pursued and isolated them before mounting a swift strike both front and rear, utterly destroying them. The remaining barbarian contingents fled in great haste.

In another incident a coalition force was mobilized to move eastward to attack the state of Cheng in reprisal for an earlier clash at Pi. However, having anticipated their line of march, Cheng ambushed and defeated them, thereby not only ending the invasion, but also providing an early example of the tactical principle enunciated in the *Hundred Unorthodox Strategies'* chapter on "Harm": "Whenever you and your enemy defend a common border, if they make incursions to plunder and disrupt your settlers in the contiguous region, you can establish ambushes at critical points and erect obstacles to block and intercept them. Then the enemy will not recklessly advance. A tactical principle from the *Art of War* states, 'What can cause the enemy not to come forth is the prospect of harm.'"[15]

The core, sedentary states of China that prided themselves on being highly civilized in contrast to the "barbaric" steppe peoples who lived nomadic lifestyles in the contiguous semi-arid regions suffered repeated incursions by the latter virtually from the inception of the Shang. Over the centuries only aggressive military campaigns and extensive defensive preparations kept them at bay, any flagging becoming an immediate enticement for more substantial invasions. In addition, the unsubmissive peoples still dwelling within the larger border states in the Spring and Autumn period were always ready to exploit any local misfortune or weakness in local government, as seen in this example dating to 611 BCE:[16]

As the state of Ch'u was suffering from an extensive famine, the Jung attacked in the southwest, advancing as far as the capital at

Mount Fou before encamping at Ta-lin. They also mounted attacks in the southeast, advancing as far as Yang-ch'iu and encroached upon Tzu-chih. Officers from Yung then led a collection of indigenous Man clans in a revolt against Ch'u and the Chün similarly assembled the Pai-p'u at Hsüan in preparation for attacking Ch'u. At this time (semi-independent state towns) such as Shen and Hsi kept their northern gates shut (to prevent incursions from the well established northern states that might exploit Ch'u's consternation).

Ch'u's officials were planning to shift the capital to Fan-kao but Wei Chia said, "We cannot, for wherever we can go, the invaders can also go. It would be better to attack Yung because the Chün and Pai-p'u attacked us on the assumption that the famine will preclude our fielding an army. If we send our army forth they will certainly be frightened and withdraw. The various Pai-p'u dwell separately and will race off to their own towns. How will they have any leisure to plan against anyone else?"

They therefore dispatched the army and within fifteen days the Pai-p'u had desisted. Proceeding outward from Lu, they relied upon the local granaries with all the men eating alike until they encamped at Kou-shih (on Ch'u's western border). They also had Lu Chi-li attack Yung where Lu advanced as far as the city of Fang-shih before being heavily pressed.

Tzu-yang Ch'uang was captured but escaped after three nights. Returning to his own forces, he reported that "the Yung have numerous troops and several Man clans have joined them. It would be better for us to rejoin our main force. Once the king's troops have been mobilized we can join them and then advance."

However, Shih Shu replied, "It's not possible. When we encounter them again in a little while, let's make them arrogant. If they become arrogant while our forces are enraged, we will be able to conquer them. This was the way our ancestral ruler Fen Mao subjugated the Hsing-hsi."

Accordingly, over the next several encounters they all ran off. Only the Pi, T'iao, and Yü actually pursued them while the men of Yung remarked that "Ch'u wasn't worth fighting with" and no longer made any defensive preparations. The earl of Ch'u raced forth and assembled the army at Lin-p'in before splitting off two operational contingents. Tzu Yüeh approached the enemy from Shih-hsi and Tzu Pei from Jen in order to attack the Yung. Troops from Ch'in and Pa joined Ch'u's main force and a number of Man clans reached an accord with the earl. Ch'u subsequently extinguished the state of Yung.

In traditional warfare, routs and retreats exposed the vanquished to vicious onslaughts and withering fire, resulting in innumerable casualties and decimation of armies. However, in their haste to exploit the moment, the victorious often fell into severe disorder and ignored the possibility of a fatal ambush, whether previously arranged as in the Northern Jung example, or brought about because they penetrated the enemy so deeply as to be naturally enveloped. Accordingly, Sun-tzu would warn commanders not to pursue feigned retreats or "swallow an army acting as bait,"[17] initiating consciousness of this problem in the military writings.[18]

Deceit and Deception

One of the earliest examples of deceit and deception, the very core of the unorthodox in most conceptions, was realized though disguising both appearance and intention in 520 BCE, when Hsün Wu mounted a surprise attack that extinguished the minor state of Ku.[19] The *Tso Chuan*'s laconic account merely states that "in the sixth month, Hsün Wu exercised the army in Tung-yang (near the contiguous state of Ku). He then had a contingent (of troops) disguised as traders buying grain momentarily rest outside the gate to Hsi-yang with their armor concealed on their backs. They subsequently mounted a sudden strike upon Ku and extinguished it."

Even though Ku's defenders failed to penetrate a simple deceit, their laxity should never have extended to allowing numbers of men to loiter outside their walls, however innocuous the latter's appearance or apparent intentions, nor should they have neglected the general defensive measures increasingly required by the era's developments. (However, even if they had recognized them as troops from Chin rather than itinerant grain traders, they might still have failed to take more stringent action because in addition to foraging and plundering, the era's armies bartered and purchased the provisions necessary to sustain them in the field.) Somewhat surprisingly, rather than focusing upon the use of disguise, later commentators such as Li Yüan-ch'un characterized the sudden strike as an unorthodox technique.[20]

This incident is actually somewhat more complex than it first appears, because Chin had subjugated Ku some seven years earlier.[21] At that time, Hsün Wu had besieged Ku, a Hsien-yü subject state, as an integral part of Chin's campaign against the Hsien-yü. Some of the inhabitants clandestinely offered to betray the city, but Hsün Wu resolutely refused to accept such an easy resolution, despite protestations by his officers, because he felt it would encourage the populace to similarly revolt against them later, as well as provide a negative example for the inhabitants of other states.

Some three months later he had similarly refused a formal offer of surrender because their provisions had not yet been exhausted and even admonished them to repair their walls and remain defiant, again to encourage resolute behavior. (Such decisions were completely contrary to the shifting practice of warfare, then increasingly emphasizing the exploitation of any wavering in the defender's spirit or commitment.) Only when their supplies were completely exhausted did he acquiesce, thereby subjugating Ku without a single casualty and realizing Sun-tzu's ideal of fighting with the aim of preservation. Hsün Wu even restored the local ruler to authority after a nominal visit to Chin before finally departing.

However, as the *Tao Te Ching* would subsequently opine, this sort of vaunted, moralistic emphasis upon virtue and righteousness reflects its growing absence.[22] In concord with a rapid escalation in warfare's scope and intensity, the end of the Spring and Autumn witnessed the culmination of a trend toward ruthlessness and Sun-tzu's characterization of warfare as the Tao of deceit. Despite the appearance of Confucius right at the end of the sixth century and beginning of the fifth, this sort of idealistic approach had not only become irrelevant but actually detrimental, as the Duke of Sung's ignominious defeat at the battle of Hung River in 638 BCE had proven. Furthermore, despite their benevolent treatment, the Ku still rebelled, ironically reverting their allegiance back to the ever threatening Hsien-yü, compelling Hsün Wu to resort to more underhanded methods.

Another rather simple incident arose during the internal strife that beset the antique state of Lu as its great clans battled for authority near the end of the Spring and Autumn period. In 501 BCE Yang Hu led an armed struggle but was vanquished and ultimately fled to nearby Ch'i, where he sought external aid to fulfill his quest for power. Ch'i's ruler was inclined to acquiesce but was dissuaded by one of his chief ministers, resulting in Yang Hu being loosely confined within Ch'i:[23] "The duke of Ch'i seized Yang Hu and was about to have him confined in the eastern quarters of the state. But when Yang Hu expressed his willingness to go to the east, he was imprisoned in the western suburbs. There he managed to borrow all the local chariots and almost completely filed through the axles before (covering the cuts) with hemp bindings and returning them. He then concealed himself in a vegetable wagon and escaped." Unstated in this quotation is the fact that Yang Hu wanted to be sequestered in the western area so as to more easily escape inland, since the eastern part of Ch'i fronted the sea. (Obviously he was not actually imprisoned or even confined to a specific building, but just generally restricted to an area, befitting his noble status.) No doubt the *Wu-ching Tsung-yao* compilers included this incident just to illustrate the simplicity and effectiveness of misdirection.[24]

A slightly earlier clash saw a much more complex deception perpetrated against the state of Ch'i, whose ruler had been acting belligerently despite the presence of Yen Ying, one of antiquity's great political savants and righteous advisors:[25]

> In the autumn the marquis of Ch'i mounted an invasion that reached Lu's northern suburbs. Subsequently, in the tenth month Chin and several other minor states convened at the side

of the Chi River in Lu to mount a joint attack on Ch'i in accord with the covenant of Ch'ü-liang.

The marquis of Ch'i then mounted his defense at P'ing-yin (in Shandong) where they excavated a moat around their main defensive gate about a *li* across.[26] Su Sha-wei advised, "If we cannot fight here, it would be better to defend the ravines (in the nearby mountains)" but was not heeded. Warriors of the feudal lords attacked the gate and many men from Ch'i died.

Fan Hsüan-tzu (of Chin) said to (the high Ch'i official) Hsi Wen-tzu, "As I know you, would I dare conceal the real situation? Officials from Lu and Chü have both requested permission to invade Ch'i from their respective positions with a thousand chariots each.[27] If they penetrate your borders, your ruler will certainly lose his state. You should plan against it." Hsi Wen-tzu advised the marquis who immediately grew fearful. When Yen Ying heard about it he commented, "Our ruler really has no courage. Now that he has heard this, he will not be able to long persevere."

The marquis of Ch'i ascended Mount Wu in order to observe Chin's army from a distance. However, Chin had ordered its commanders to establish outposts throughout the difficult terrain in the hills and marshes and even deploy regimental flags in areas where they would not emplace troops. Moreover, they manned their chariots with real warriors on the left but dummies on the right, set up large flags at the front of the chariot forces, and had other chariots dragging brush follow on. Observing this and fearing their large numbers, the marquis of Ch'i abandoned the field and returned to Ch'i.

After Ch'i's armies hastily retreated, Chin's forces scored repeated victories and pressed forward until they reached Ch'in-chou, where they reportedly "hewed down the catalpa trees around Yung Gate." A day later "they burned Yung Gate together with the western and southern quarters. Liu Nan and Shih Juo led the armies of the feudal lords in burning the

trees and bamboo around Shen-ch'ih. On the sixth, they burned the eastern and northern quarters and Fan Yang assaulted Yang Gate." Within a
few more days they had advanced in both the east and the south and finally pursued the vanquished Ch'i army right back to the capital of Lin-
tzu, where they torched the outer suburbs before withdrawing, ending the
first campaign known to have punitively exploited fire.[28]

Through one of the first recorded instances of deliberate disinformation, the marquis of Ch'i (who seems to have already been known for his
lack of courage) was psychologically primed to accept a basic facade as a
fearsome reality. The compound, unorthodox deception thus consisted of
two parts, each capable of significantly impacting the enemy's mindset
and actions. Subsequently the episode's clarity prompted its selection to
illustrate the means and importance of misleading the enemy in the *Hundred Unorthodox Strategies*, where the tactical discussion for "Daylight"
states: "You must set out numerous flags and pennants whenever engaging
an enemy in battle during daylight to cause uncertainty about your forces.
You will be victorious when you prevent the enemy from determining
your troop strength. A tactical principle from the *Art of War* states: 'In
daylight battles make the flags and pennants numerous.'"[29]

As discussed in our *Tao of Spycraft*, early armies actually implemented
numerous techniques besides deploying flags and multiplying drums to
deceive their enemies and prevent them from gathering accurate military
intelligence, including dragging brush, increasing or reducing the number
of cook fires, employing dummies, and undertaking disinformation operations. On a larger scale, major operations were even undertaken to mask
plans, such as when Yüeh blatantly attacked Ch'u in order to deceive Wu
as to their intentions to invade and exterminate them, twin objectives accomplished the very next year at the end of the Spring and Autumn
period.[30] Broadly construed, their first campaign constituted a form of
misdirection, a variant of the unorthodox technique subsequently elabo-
rated in the *Unorthodox Strategies*' "Utterances in Warfare": "In general, in
warfare what is termed 'utterances' refers to making some specious statement. For example, if you speak about attacking the east but instead strike

the west, if you target those but attack these, you cause the enemy's forces not to know where to prepare their defenses. Therefore, the location you attack will inevitably be undefended. A tactical principle from the *Art of War* states: 'When someone excels at attacking, the enemy does not know where to mount his defense.'"

Another famous incident that unfolded on the strategic level later provided the basis for the *ch'eng-yü* (formulaic phrase) "Having a nearby objective yet making it appear distant," also known as "the Marquis of Chin borrowed a passage through Yü."[31] Minor states such as Yü and Kuo had to be adroit politicians, forge viable alliances, and devote enormous energy to the agricultural and economic activities necessary to sustain an effective military and thereby survive during the Spring and Autumn period. According to the *Tso Chuan* account, the overall sequence of events required two campaigns and three years, but from the outset powerful Chin's sole intent was the annexation of both Yü and Kuo, the latter lying to the far side of the former:

> In 658 BCE Hsün Hsi suggested that Chin "borrow" an access route through Yü to attack the state of Kuo by offering the superlative horses from Ch'ü and Ch'ui-ts'e's jade. When the duke retorted that they were his treasures, Hsün replied: "If we gain permission to pass through Yü, it will be like having stored them in an external treasury."
>
> The duke said, "Ch'i-chih-kung is still there." Hsün replied, "Ch'i-chih-kung is timid and incapable of strongly remonstrating. Furthermore, as he grew up with the ruler, they are overly familiar. Even if he objects, he will not be heeded."
>
> The duke then had Hsün Hsi go to request the passage from Yü, saying "The state of Chi has violated the Tao and attacked the Three Gates of your poor state from Tien-ling. Since Chi has exhibited such perversity, our actions will not be solely for our own ruler's benefit. Moreover, Kuo has also violated the Tao and established citadels and troop dispositions along the routes into

Yü to facilitate mounted incursions into your capital's southern suburbs. We therefore request permission to pass through in order to charge Kuo with its offenses."

The duke of Yü not only assented but also requested permission to be in the forefront in attacking Kuo. In conjunction with an army from Yü, that summer Li K'o and Hsün Hsi led Chin's two armies in attacking Kuo and annihilating Hsia-yang.[32]

Kuo's behavior shortly after their defeat is noted in the *Tso Chuan* as portending their imminent demise: "After the duke of Kuo defeated a Jung force at Sang-t'ien, the diviner Yen said, 'Kuo will certainly perish. Even though they lost Hsia-yang, they remain unafraid and have gained achievement. Heaven has snatched away their mirror and is increasing their illness. They will certainly disregard Chin and fail to focus on the people's welfare. Kuo cannot last beyond five harvests."

Slightly more than three years later Chin mounted their second campaign against Kuo with the clandestine purpose of annexing Yü's territory. Ch'i-chih-kung repeated his futile remonstrance, pointing out the inevitability of their demise once Kuo perished. However, despite the inimical nature of the events swirling about them, the ruler remained unswayed because he was convinced that no harm would befall him as they were all descendants of the Chou and he had been generously propitiating the spirits. When his retort suggesting that the spirits only favored virtue and would not sustain him similarly went unheeded, Ch'i-chih-kung "departed with his entire clan saying that Yü would not see the solstice, that it would be the last time Chin would act."

Prior to besieging Kuo's capital of Shang-yang, the Duke of Chin queried his diviner whether he would be successful and was assured (based upon a children's ditty) that he would prevail "in the interstice between the ninth and tenth month." Events proceeded as Ch'i-chih-kung had foretold because once Chin extinguished Kuo, they encamped in Yü en route home before suddenly attacking and extinguishing them. The duke of Chin subsequently remarked that although the jade was unaffected by its storage in Yü, the horses had aged.[33]

Night Maneuvers and Strikes

Though it is difficult to imagine a complete lack of tribal precursors in the Neolithic or early dynastic periods, night maneuvers and the more dramatic variant of night attacks are only known from the Spring and Autumn, coincident with written records. In an era whose battles had previously been somewhat circumscribed, even formalized clashes undertaken in daytime against properly arrayed forces, night encounters would have been unimaginably problematic. Simply moving across level ground without either the men or the horses suffering incapacitating injuries from the innumerable ruts, holes, undulations, and mounds would have constituted a monumental task. Less than a full moon would have compounded their difficulties enormously, and on the darkest nights even well trained, cohesive forces probably found it virtually impossible to recognize the terrain or distinguish friend from foe. Accordingly, the night actions undertaken by the "night thieves" of later centuries (including incendiary raiders who wrecked havoc prior to attacks or during sieges) have always been considered crafty, innovative measures and therefore highly unorthodox.[34]

When Ch'u was about to suffer an allied assault in 701 BCE, a strategist advised mounting a surprise attack against their nearby enemies because they were negligently awaiting the arrival of coalition members and, secure in the might of their fortifications, lacked the will for battle.[35] Confidentially eschewing any prognosticatory consultations, he thus proposed a strike that not only shattered their forces but also deterred their allies from coming forth, thereby thwarting the invasion.

When a force from Ch'in attacked the state of Juo in the autumn of 635 BCE, Ch'u provided assistance by undertaking the defense of Shang-mi with troops from the satellite states of Shen and Hsi.[36] Because the invaders had to pass a river bend near the secondary city of Che en route to Shang-mi, Ch'in bound up some of their troops, disguising them as if they were prisoners that had been seized from Che, then approached Shang-mi at dusk. During the night they dug a sacrificial pit, consecrated it with blood, and displayed a document purporting to be a covenant between themselves and the Ch'u commanders at Shang-mi. The populace within, afraid that Che had been betrayed and already succumbed, surrendered to the Ch'in army without further resistance.

Ch'in's ingenious deception was premised upon the indistinctness of objects in dusky light. The disguised troops were adequately perceived to convey the impression that they were prisoners, but not in such detail as to allow the deception to be penetrated. Moreover, in a precursor to the common use of falsified documents to entangle and subvert, Ch'in fabricated a covenant and buried it with due ceremony in a sacrificial pit outside the walls where their actions could be seen by torch light and the document subsequently recovered, thereby solidifying the impression that Shang-mi's allies had betrayed them. Although Ch'in's behavior appears almost too blatant to have been believable, it succeeded in creating the fear that the defenders had become isolated, that they had no hope of survival or rescue. Since they abandoned further resistance, the episode well illustrates how alliances might be balked and victory achieved without wasteful assaults on well ensconced forces, just as Sun-tzu would subsequently advocate.[37]

In another nighttime action that arose in consequence of Ch'in escorting a claimant to the Chin throne back home in force, Chin made preparations to preemptively strike on the basic principle that "one who precedes others seizes their minds."[38] The troops therefore sharpened their weapons, ate, and fed their horses early in the night before clandestinely moving out under the cover of darkness in order to catch the enemy unprepared. They then secured an easy, devastating victory that caused Ch'in to forego further attempts at intercession.

Having failed in an attempt to invade Lu in 557 BCE, the next year Ch'i attacked the capital's northern suburbs and besieged the towns of T'ao and Fang.[39] Confucius' father, a stalwart figure despite his son's decidedly antimartial attitude, and two officials led 300 men in breaking through the defenses at Fang, extricating the prince, and striking the army before returning. Reeling in confusion from the unorthodox night assault, Ch'i withdrew both prongs of their expeditionary force.[40]

En route back from an incursion into Chin, Ch'i's ruler mounted a surprise attack on the minor state of Chü.[41] Despite being wounded, he still deputed two commanders to traverse bypaths that night and come up under Chü's outer wall, whereupon the ruler tried to bribe them not to engage in a "death struggle." However, finding his attempt rebuffed, he personally led an attack and achieved a localized victory before subsequently surrendering. Although this was an odd sequence of events, the *Tso-shih Ping-fa* still characterized Chin's flawed nighttime action as an unorthodox tactic.

One of numerous clashes between the antique state of Chin in the north and the so-called barbarian upstart Ch'u in the south, the nighttime clash at Jao-chiao turned upon a defector's advice:

> Duke Hsi fled to Chin during the chaos fomented by Tzu Yi in Ch'u. He was assigned a chariot just behind the ruler and made responsible for planning their strategy. At the Battle of Jao-chiao when Chin was about to withdraw he advised, "Ch'u's army is insubstantial and easily provoked so it will be easy to cause them to shake and tremble. If we have our many drums beat in unison and press them with our entire army during the night, Ch'u's regiments will certainly retreat." The men of Chin followed his advice and the armies of Ch'u collapsed in the darkness. Chin subsequently invaded Ts'ai; mounted a sudden attack on Shen, capturing its ruler; defeated the forces of Shen and Hsi at Sangsui; and captured Shen-li before returning home. Thereafter Cheng did not dare face south (to heed Ch'u).[42]

Although this particular account is embedded in a *Tso Chuan* discussion dating to 547 BCE about the impact of Ch'u defectors throughout the realm, the clash actually unfolded in the winter of 585 BCE, when Chin moved to relieve Cheng, which had been invaded by Ch'u the previous autumn for their perfidious inclination to Chin.[43] (Caught between two great powers, Cheng's allegiance frequently shifted over the decades and they suffered repeated invasions in consequence. If anyone had needed an unorthodox strategy in the Spring and Autumn period, it was certainly Cheng.) Ch'u then withdrew their forces, though the account does not speak about an actual battle or the defector's role in it.

Although the selection has been included in various military manuals because of Chin's boldness in mounting a night attack when retreat would have been the normal, prudent course, Duke Hsi's strategy was based upon thorough knowledge of Ch'u's forces. Even though the employment of defectors would always remain somewhat unorthodox because of the dangers of duplicity and the prejudices inherent in a system that esteemed loyalty, "local guides" or "local spies" (in Sun-tzu's terminology) would subsequently have a long tradition.[44]

Wu and Ch'u similarly engaged in decades of essentially unresolved conflict before Wu successfully mounted an invasion that penetrated to the very capital of Ying. A lesser clash in 525 BCE required Wu to resort to a famous nighttime deceit to recover their lost command ship:

> Ch'u's commander died when they engaged Wu in battle at Ch'ang-an but Ch'u's armies sustained the effort and severely defeated Wu's armies, capturing their command boat Yü Huang. They had the forces from Sui and those who came up last protect it, cutting a ditch all about into which they drained a spring. They then filled in the water accesses with charcoal and deployed to await further orders.
>
> Prince Kuang of Wu suggested to his troops, "Losing the former king's command boat is not just my offense, but also yours. Let's gather our strength and seize it in order to rescue ourselves from death." The troops assented. He then had three men with long beards submerge themselves in secret at the sides of the boat, instructing them that "When I call out 'Yü Huang' you should reply and the army will follow you in the night."
>
> He called out three times and all of them replied in turn. Ch'u's forces followed their sound and killed them. However, Wu's forces took advantage of the chaos to inflict a severe defeat on Ch'u's army and retake Yü Huang before returning to Wu.[45]

The boat's successful recapture turned upon three stalwart warriors disguised as men from Ch'u—hence the beards, not commonly found among Wu's forces—penetrating the defenses and preparing what appeared to be an inner response to Wu's attack. In the darkness of the night their actions sufficiently destabilized the defenders to allow the swift strike that successfully reversed the previous defeat.

Finally, the Spring and Autumn period essentially ended with Wu's defeat at the famous battle of Li-che River, a nighttime clash in which Yüeh astutely employed feints to outmaneuver the opponent's superior, well-entrenched forces on the opposite bank:[46]

> During the Spring and Autumn period the state of Yüeh attacked the state of Wu. Wu's forces mounted a defense at the Li-che river so both sides deployed hard along the river. Yüeh had the armies arrayed on the left and right flanks alternately beat their drums, set up a great clamor, and advance across the river. When Wu divided its forces to resist them, Yüeh's central army secretly forded the river, confronted Wu's central force, and only then beat their drums. Wu's forces were thrown into chaos, and Yüeh went on to destroy them.

The battle of Li-che River was considered so pivotal that the author of the *Hundred Unorthodox Strategies* twice employed it to illustrate tactical principles:

> Whenever engaging an enemy in a night battle, you must employ numerous fires and drums to change and confuse their eyes and ears. If you befuddle the enemy so that they cannot make preparations against your tactics, you will be victorious. One who has caused the enemy not to know where to prepare for his tactics will be victorious. A tactical principle from the *Art of War* states: "In night battles make the fires and drums numerous."[47]
>
> Whenever you or an enemy deploy on opposite banks of a river, if you want to attack them close by your position, you should, on the contrary, show them that you are going to attack far off. You must establish the facade of numerous troops

preparing to ford the river both upstream and downstream. The enemy will certainly divide their forces in response, and you can then secretly launch a sudden attack with your nearby hidden forces, destroying their army. A tactical principle from the *Art of War* states: "When an objective is nearby, make it appear as if distant."[48]

In this clash Yüeh managed to throw Wu's forces into chaos with a deliberately noisy, nighttime river crossing that suddenly threatened Wu's unguarded flanks with a double envelopment, compelling them to rush reinforcements to the perimeter. Yüeh's core forces then easily exploited Wu's destabilization and chaos to silently mount an unexpected, well-focused attack upon the now weakened center to achieve the overwhelming victory that ensured Wu's eventual extinction.

Tactical Innovation

By the Spring and Autumn period China's sedentary core had already been battling the peripheral tribal peoples for more than a millennium. Suppressive campaigns centered on chariot forces augmented by infantry had been routinely mounted in the Shang and continued into the early Chou. Many of the steppe peoples similarly fielded chariot based forces, but others relied solely upon infantry, as in the Northern Jung example from 714 BCE already discussed. Although asymmetric confrontations probably recurred throughout the Spring and Autumn and would be duplicated in the Warring States period (though as chariot-centered infantry forces opposing mounted steppe riders), the next recorded instance unfolded in 541 BCE.[49]

The *Tso Chuan* account reflects the dual realization that chariots unsupported by infantry units are susceptible to infantry attacks and, as subsequently discussed in the *Six Secret Teachings*, confined terrain will hinder chariot movement. The *Ch'un Ch'iu* simply states: "In the sixth month, Hsün Wu of Chin led the army in defeating the Ti at Ta-lu (T'ai-yüan)." However, as usual the *Tso Chuan* provides a more expansive account:

Hsün Wu of Chin defeated the Wu-chung and several other Ti tribal peoples at T'ai-yüan by stressing foot soldiers. When they were about to engage in battle Wei Shu advised, "They are composed of infantry forces and we will be encountering them in a narrow pass. If they encircle each of our chariots with ten men, they will certainly overcome us. Moreover, since the narrowness of the pass will put us in difficulty, they will again be victorious. I suggest that we all act as foot soldiers, beginning with me."

He then discarded their chariots in order to form ranks of infantry with the staff from every five chariots making up three squads of five. One of Hsün Wu's favorite officers who was unwilling to serve as an infantryman was executed as an example to the others. They then deployed into five dispositions, forming a deer like configuration with two contingents in the front, five to the rear, one at the right point, three at the left, and a narrow force acting as the vanguard in order to entice the enemy.[50] Laughing, the Ti failed to deploy, allowing Hsün Wu to mount a sudden attack and severely defeat them.

Although the significance and meaning of the terms for the various contingents in the deployment have occasioned much debate over the centuries, their relative sizes are fairly clear. From the *Tso*'s depiction it appears that Hsün Wu had come forth with a fast, roving force similar to the large chariot expeditions mounted against the Hsien-yün by the early Chou. Lacking infantry to disperse along the walls of the pass or protect the chariots from disabling attack, they would have been doomed to defeat without Wei Shu's suggestion and the highly unorthodox deployment they exploited. Since this was essentially a chariot formation best suited for open terrain, the arrangement, fewness of their numbers, and decision to fight dismounted prompted derisive laughter among their opponents. However, levity being tantamount to laxity, it provided a sufficient momentary opportunity for the unexpected Chin assault that swiftly vanquished them.

An experienced border fighter who would inflict another severe defeat on a complacent, unprepared Hsien-yün force a few years later, Hsün Wu obviously was adept at field command and knew how to embrace tactical flexibility.[51] However, being a singular incident, this extemporaneous change from chariot-based forces to infantry arrays never affected the already rapid evolution of infantry forces, particularly not in the way that Chao Wu-ling's forceful adoption of barbarian dress facilitated the cavalry's development, and therefore cannot constitute the sort of military revolution often claimed.

In a precursor from 704 BCE to the famous battles of Ch'eng-p'u and Chi-fu, the ruler failed to heed sagacious tactical advice to go contrary to normal, ritualized tradition and focus on the enemy's weak point. The attack's motivation was Ch'u's umbrage at Sui's failure to attend a conclave that they had convened:[52]

> The earl of Ch'u shifted his army to the area between the Han and Huai Rivers in order to attack Sui. In Sui, Chi Liang suggested that they submit because if Ch'u didn't accept their offer and they subsequently engaged in combat, Sui's forces would be angry while the invaders would have become lax. However, Sui's lieutenant commander said to the marquis of Sui, "We need to fight quickly. Otherwise, we will lose the opportunity of attacking Ch'u's army."
>
> The marquis of Sui then went forth to observe Ch'u's deployment. Chi Liang commented, "Ch'u's army has always esteemed the left, so you should position on our left rather than encounter their king. Moreover, attacking their right flank where they don't have any good men will certainly lead to their defeat. The defeat of one flank will entangle the rest of the forces."
>
> But the lieutenant commander responded, "If we don't oppose their king, we will not be their equals!" The marquis did not listen to Chi Liang and when they engaged in battle at Su-chi, Sui's army was badly defeated and the marquis fled. Tou Tan of Ch'u captured the marquis' war chariot and the subcommander who had occupied the position on the right.

The epochal Battle of Ch'eng P'u previously mentioned, in which a coalition of older, northern states severely defeated formidable Ch'u's initial thrust into the Chinese heartland, took place early in the spring of 632 BCE. From the sketchy description that has been passed down it is clear that, contrary to the vanquished leader of the last incident, Chin's commanders adopted unorthodox measures such as targeting the weakest components:[53]

> When they had finished cutting down the trees, Chin's forces deployed north of Hsin. Hsü Ch'en, in his role as assistant commander for Chin's Lower Army, deployed opposite the forces from Ch'en and Ts'ai (allied with Ch'u).
>
> When Tzu Yü, accompanied by six companies of Juo-ao clan troops, assumed command of Ch'u's Central Army, he said: "Today will certainly see the end of Chin!" Tzu Hsi was in command of Ch'u's Army of the Left and Tzu Shang their Army of the Right.
>
> Hsü Ch'en covered their horses in tiger skins and initiated the engagement by assaulting the troops from Ch'en and Ts'ai. Their troops fled and Ch'u's right wing crumbled.
>
> Hu Mao (of Chin) set out two pennons and withdrew his forces. Meanwhile Luan Chih (of Chin) had his chariots feign a withdrawal, dragging faggots behind them. When Ch'u's forces raced after them, Yüan Chen and Hsi Chen cut across the battlefield to suddenly strike them with the Duke's own clan forces. Hu Mao and Hu Yen (of Chin) then mounted a pincer attack on Tzu Hsi's army that resulted in Ch'u's left wing being shattered and Ch'u's forces decisively defeated. Tzu Yü gathered his clan forces and desisted from further action, avoiding personal defeat.

Two actions shaped the battle's course and determined its outcome. First, Hsü Ch'en's elite warriors initiated contact with an unexpected,

concentrated thrust while the final deployments and preliminary postur-
ing were probably still underway. Their surprising fervency shattered
Ch'u's insecure allies on the right wing, giving Chin's forces uncon-
stricted mobility and exposing the field to flanking attacks. Second, coordinated feigned retreats by Chin's right wing and elements of the left
wing that had not participated in the initial thrust, masked by clouds of
dust that were deliberately created by the branches that had been cut
down and attached to the rear of the chariots, easily drew the overconfident Ch'u armies forward in a disordered attack. Presumably Ch'u's central forces, under Tzu Yü's personal command, also moved forward to
exploit Chin's retreat and engage any remaining center forces; otherwise,
the *Tso Chuan* account would need not state that Tzu Yü "gathered his
personal forces and *desisted*."

Later writers such as Li Yüan-ch'un characterize the famous Battle of
Chi-fu that occurred more than a century later (and thus shortly before
Sun-tzu reputedly assumed an advisory role in Wu) as an unorthodox
clash.[54] Highly sophisticated in both conception and execution, Wu's tactics in this pivotal engagement turned upon the deliberate sacrifice of "expendable" troops to achieve a greater goal, a remarkably ruthless measure
in the context of limited resources and evolving theory that emphasized
the humanistic treatment of troops.

The battle unfolded in 519 BCE on the northeastern side of the mountain
range falling between Ch'u in the west and Wu in the east. Although Wu
apparently ferried some chariots upriver with their riverine forces, their
infantry was vastly outnumbered by Ch'u's formidable armies and the six
smaller states that Ch'u had hurriedly coerced into participating in a coordinated campaign. Wu had no alternative but to manipulate and destabilize the enemy before taking advantage of the resulting confusion.

Fortuitously for Wu, Ch'u's commander-in-chief died while the armies
were en route, throwing their central command into turmoil. Since his replacement was decidedly less capable and the officers and soldiers felt his
death boded ill, they became dispirited and disorganized. As retold in a classic *Tso Chuan* account that has been assiduously studied by military commanders for 2,000 years, Ho-lü astutely exploited these developments:[55]

Ch'u led the armies of several feudal lords to rescue the minor state of Chou-lai when Wu attacked. Ho-lü observed: "There may be many feudal lords following Ch'u but they are all small states that cannot avoid coming because they fear it. I have heard that in military affairs when awesomeness conquers love, even though small one will certainly be well-ordered. The rulers of Hu and Shen are young and extremely reckless; Chen's highest ranking official is experienced but stupid; the states of Tun, Hsü, and Ts'ai detest Ch'u's government; and Ch'u's commander is held in little esteem but has many favorites so Ch'u's administrative orders are not unified.

Although these seven states have undertaken a joint military effort, they are not united in mind. Since Ch'u's commander is slighted and unable to order the troops, his commands lack majesty and Ch'u can be defeated. If we segment our regiments and initially attack Hu, Shen, and Chen, they will certainly be first to run off. When these three states have been defeated, the armies of the other feudal lords will be shaken. With the feudal lords in confusion and disarray, Ch'u will certainly be badly defeated and race off. I suggest we first send forth some insignificant, little prepared troops while simultaneously making the formations at the rear dense and ensuring the regiments are well ordered." The king followed his advice.

On *hsü-ch'en*, the last day of the moon, they fought at Chi-fu. Wu initially employed 3,000 convicts in an assault on Hu, Shen, and Chen whose troops fought with them. Wu then divided its forces into three armies in order to follow behind the initial thrust and mount an attack. The king assumed command of the center army, Ho-lü that of the army on the right, and the other regiments were deployed on the left flank. Some of Wu's convict forces fled, others stood and fought. The forces of the three states were thrown into confusion and Wu's regiments pressed the attack, eventually defeating them and capturing their rulers. Wu then released the recently captured prisoners from Hu and

Shen so that they might flee back into the armies of Hsü, Ts'ai,
and Tun and proclaim that their rulers were dead.[56] Clamoring
and shouting, the soldiers from these three states followed them
in fleeing the battlefield. When these armies had run off, Ch'u's
army was in turn engaged and routed.

Rather than directly confronting Ch'u's approaching might at Chou-lai,
Ho-lü withdrew to more conducive terrain and then structured the battle
according to a carefully crafted assessment based upon accurate military
intelligence. Eschewing the precipitous assault directly on the main enemy
body that contemporary practice and self-respect normally dictated, he instead targeted the vulnerable armies of the coerced states. Furthermore, he
perversely (and thus unorthodoxically) decided to attack on the last day of
the lunar calendar, traditionally a time when armies remained quietly encamped because military activities were regarded as highly inauspicious.

Ho-lü deliberately disrupted Ch'u's defensive posture by employing a
vanguard of 3,000 ill-trained convicts, correctly anticipating that they
would probably be repulsed and draw at least part of the defenders forth
in disorganized pursuit when they fled in panic. Finally, he had numerous prisoners released whose false reports augmented the enemy's growing trepidation and whose fear proved contagious. The rout they
provoked probably caused at least some of the fleeing forces to collide
with Ch'u's core armies, blocking and disordering them, thereby facilitating the main attack.

Given Wu's tactical ingenuity and the success of the "few defeating the
many, the weak overcoming the strong," it is hardly surprising that the
Hundred Unorthodox Strategies employed the battle as the historical illustration for the topic of "Disorder in Warfare": "Whenever engaging an enemy in battle, if the enemy's rows and formations are disordered while
their officers and men clamor and shout, send the army forth to strike
them, for then you will be victorious. A tactical principle from the *Art of
War* states: 'Create disorder in their forces and take them.'"

Other precursors of successfully induced, irremediable disorder appear
in the *Tso Chuan*, though the formulations lack the perspicacious res-

oluteness of Ho-lü's approach. Not surprisingly, "attacking disordered forces" to wrest an easy victory, a basic method for multiplying combat power, became a much advocated principle in the classic Warring States military writings. For example, the *Six Secret Teachings* lists disorder among the fourteen vulnerable conditions that can be exploited; the *Wu-tzu* describes several such manifestations that might be fortuitously assaulted; and Sun Pin includes disarray and disorder among thirty-two fatal command flaws.

Shortly thereafter Ho-lü usurped the throne by assassinating King Liao in 515 BCE and Wu initiated a series of nearly annual, highly successful attacks against Ch'u.[57] With each attack they subjugated additional Ch'u client states, sometimes permanently absorbing them, at other times merely freeing them from Ch'u's dominance. At the same time Wu expanded their already extensive fortifications and undertook aggressive, preemptive assaults on the small but powerful contiguous states capable of mounting a surprise attack on their homeland while they might be engaged in far-reaching expeditions.

However, the campaign against Ch'u wasn't designed simply to annex territory or cower Ch'u's military into inaction, but rather to enervate the administration and dissipate the state's significantly greater military and fiscal resources through a deliberately crafted temporizing strategy. According to the *Tso Chuan*, this new (and therefore unorthodox) concept was formulated by the famous Wu Tzu-hsü when Ho-lü inquired of his advisor whether they could now attack Ch'u, the state from which Wu Tzu-hsü had defected:[58]

> Wu Tzu-hsü replied: "Those who hold the reins of government in Ch'u are numerous and at odds with each other. None of them is willing to undertake responsibility for resolving Chu's misfortunes. We should create three armies to harass them for when a single one of them arrives at Ch'u's border, all of Ch'u's troops will certainly come forth. When they come forth our army should withdraw; when the enemy retires, we should again go forth. Ch'u will certainly be fatigued from moving back and

forth over the roads. Do this several times to exhaust them, employ many methods to bring about misjudgment. If we follow up with our three armies after they are exhausted, we will certainly achieve a major conquest."

Wu therefore divided their forces into three field armies, each dispatched to engage the enemy in turn but never become involved in protracted battles or decisive confrontations with superior forces. Wu further employed the terrain's constraints and the superiority of its riverine forces to tactical advantage, spread the enemy out, chose their objectives carefully, and suddenly concentrated their forces where unexpected. Mobility and maneuver were emphasized in effecting a long-term campaign of harassment that not only disrupted Ch'u's command, spawned doubt, and nurtured dissension, but also rendered their leadership largely incapable of coping with the continuing threats. In consequence, Wu successfully mounted an invasion in 506 BCE that penetrated to the very capital, easily vanquishing all the armies futilely arrayed before them.

Desperate Actions, *Ch'i* Manipulation, and Fatal Terrain

Unfortunately for the inhabitants of the antique but minor state of Sung, they were located in a pivotal area contested by several contiguous powers, including Chin to the northwest and Ch'u to the south. Frequently invaded and otherwise coerced, Sung had to constantly revert their allegiance from one state to the other merely to survive. According to the *Ch'un Ch'iu*, Ch'u besieged Sung in the ninth month of 595 BCE and the two parties concluded a peace accord in the fifth month of 594.[59] However, the highly melodramatic *Tso Chuan* account suggests Ch'u deliberately provoked Sung into an inflammatory act that might be exploited as a pretext for invasion:

> The king of Ch'u instructed Shen Chou not to request permission to pass through Sung when he dispatched him on a diplomatic visit to the state of Ch'i. Similarly, he sent Kung-tzu Feng

on a mission to Chin without requesting Cheng to acquiesce in Feng's passage.[60]

Shen Chou hated Sung because of a previous incident involving Meng Chu in Sung. He said to the king, "Cheng is perspicacious but Sung is obtuse. Your emissary to Chin will not be harmed but I will certainly die."

The king replied, "If they slay you, I will attack them."

After seeing his son Hsi, Shen Chou set off.[61] When he reached Sung he was stopped by their officials where Hua Yüan said: "To pass through our state without requesting permission is an insult. To be so insulted is to perish. If we kill their emissary, Ch'u will certainly attack us. If they attack us, we will certainly perish. Either way, we perish." So they slew Shen Chou.

Learning of his death, the king of Ch'u shook his sleeves, rose up, put his shoes on in the throne room, donned his sword outside the door to the inner chambers, and ascended his chariot in the marketplace of P'u-hsü. In the ninth month, autumn, he besieged the capital of Sung.

In the fifth month, summer, of the next year Ch'u's army was about to depart from Sung but Shen Hsi, knocking his head to the ground in front of the king's horses, said: "Even though my father knew he would die, he didn't disregard your orders. You are betraying your promise to him." The king was unable to reply but Shen Shu-shih, his driver, said, "We should build huts and return to farming.[62] Sung will then certainly submit to our demands."

Terrified, the people of Sung had Hua Yüan penetrate Ch'u's encampment one night. He climbed up onto Tzu Fan's bed before rousing him and saying: "My ruler has ordered me to report our extremity, that 'In our debilitated city we are exchanging our children and eating them, and cracking the bones for kindling.' Nevertheless, we are unable to submit to any covenant forced upon us in our debilitated condition. If you depart 30 *li*, we will accept your edict.'"

Greatly afraid, Tzu Fan made an agreement with him and
then informed the king. After they withdrew 30 *li*, Sung and
Ch'u concluded a peace accord. Hua Yüan served as a hostage
while their covenant stated that "We (Ch'u) will not deceive
you, you will not be troubled about us."

Even though Ch'u's actions constituted an affront according to the era's
diplomatic and ritual conventions, it is somewhat surprising that Sung so
lacked imagination as to be this easily manipulated. Conversely, in mobilizing for an assault the provocateurs hardly occupied high moral ground
but apparently felt emotionally justified because the ruler could cite
Sung's transgression to motivate his troops. Following the incident's resolution Sung remained defenseless, having been enjoined by the
covenant not "to be troubled" about Ch'u or, in other words, to forego
defensive preparations.

All the accounts agree that Sung's situation had grown desperate after
nine months of being besieged. They had appealed to their nominal protector, Chin, for help, but Chin's strategists, cognizant of Ch'u's might
and Sung's valuable role as an obstacle to Ch'u's upward thrust into the
old Chinese cultural heartland, had prevailed upon the ruler to merely issue an indefinite promise of future aid while encouraging them to remain resolute.

Although Ch'u's withdrawal was essentially a facade, it sufficiently satisfied the era's emotional and ritual constraints for Sung to pretend not to
be under duress. In the view of Ho Shou-fa, the late-sixteenth-century author of the *T'ou-pi Fu-t'an*, it was Hua Yüan's honest reporting of the condition that prompted the retreat rather than the coercive dagger at Tzu
Fan's throat. However, other commentators tend to express admiration for
Tzu Fan, who adamantly kept his promise even though it had been elicited
under threatening circumstances.

King Chuang of Ch'u, known as a willful and irascible ruler, probably
accepted this outcome because he sought to escape from the entanglements of an unexpectedly long siege. The *Kung Yang*, another repository
of information about the period, retells the episode quite differently, as-

serting that Ch'u's army only had seven days of provisions remaining. Moreover, it depicts the departure as having resulted from a normal interchange of information between Tzu Fan, who had ascended an observation mound to ascertain Sung's true condition, and Hua Yüan, who had come forth to meet him.

After Hua candidly described the hopelessness of their destitution and appealed to Ch'u as gentlemen who should actively sympathize with their plight, Tzu Fan responded by informing them that they had only seven days of food and had already decided to decamp. This naturally enraged the king of Ch'u, but as Tzu Fan refused to continue in his command role, the king finally acquiesced in withdrawing so as to conclude a peace accord. In terms of merely providing information to the enemy and thereby balking their plans, this version clearly coheres more closely with Ho Shou-fa's formulation, though not with the succinct depiction of the incident in his book.

Although singular, bold actions including assassination might have major repercussions, the course of events was normally determined by organized battlefield encounters. Traditional ritual practices required the opposing armies to deploy on the chosen battlefield before beating the drums to signal the attack's onset, coincidentally rousing the troops to maximum fervor. However, a strategist in the 684 BCE clash at Ch'ang-chuo insightfully restrained his commander, thereby initiating the vital Chinese military science of *ch'i* or spirit manipulation and the tactic of waiting for the enemy's fervor to abate before engaging them:[63]

> The state of Ch'i attacked the state of Lu. Duke Chuang, in command of Lu's forces, was about to commit the army to battle when Ts'ao Kuei requested permission to join him. The Duke had him ride in his chariot as they went into battle at Ch'ang-shao. The duke was about to have the drums sound their advance when Ts'ao Kuei said to him: "Not yet." After Ch'i's drums had resounded three times Ts'ao said: "Now." They beat the drums and engaged in combat. Ch'i's army was severely defeated.

The duke inquired why Ts'ao Kuei had delayed the drums. Ts'ao replied: "Combat is a matter of courageous *ch'i*. A single drumming arouses the soldiers' *ch'i*, with a second it abates, and with a third it is exhausted. They were exhausted while we were vigorous, so we conquered them."

Even though astute commanders had no doubt been haranguing their troops and employing rewards and other incentives to motivate them for combat from the earliest organized clashes, based upon this *Tso Chuan* entry the concept of *ch'i* apparently had not evolved until the middle of the Spring and Autumn period.[64] If so, a single *Art of War* passage provides the earliest analysis to be found in the military manuals: "The *ch'i* of the Three Armies can be snatched away; the commanding general's mind can be seized. For this reason in the morning their *ch'i* is ardent; during the day their *ch'i* becomes indolent; at dusk their *ch'i* is exhausted. Thus one who excels at employing the army avoids their ardent *ch'i* and strikes when it is indolent or exhausted. This is the way to manipulate *ch'i*."[65]

Thereafter, the classic Warring States military writings developed a martial motivational science centered upon the concept of *ch'i* that articulated numerous measures and methods for modulating the army's fervor and controlling the soldiers' commitment.[66] Although determination, intention, and "will" were not overlooked, the core premise was that *ch'i* empowers the effort and must be stimulated, nurtured, and controlled if armies are to be successful. Thus the *Wei Liao-tzu* states: "The means by which the general fights is the people, but the means by which the people fight is their *ch'i*. When their *ch'i* is substantial they will fight; when their *ch'i* has been snatched away they will run off." Two centuries earlier Wu Ch'i had already noted that because *ch'i* ebbs and flourishes, success in combat depends upon it reaching a zenith just at the moment of battle.

The *Ssu-ma Fa* added a crucial insight: "In general, in battle one endures through strength and gains victory through spirit. One can endure with a solid defense, but will achieve victory through being endangered. When the heart's foundation is solid, a new surge of *ch'i* will bring victory." Combining this insight with a growing understanding of the effects of topographical constraints, particularly configurations of terrain or positions that apparently doom an army, the *Art of War* conceived the idea of deliberately exploiting "fatal terrain" to elicit maximum effort from the troops. As it has precursors identified as unorthodox in the Spring and Autumn (retold below), the critical passage merits note: "Cast them into positions from which there is nowhere to go and they will die without retreating. If there is no escape from death, the officers and soldiers will fully exhaust their strength."[67]

A Spring and Autumn incident that arose during Sun-tzu's lifetime amidst the clan friction besetting the period and that illustrates the effectiveness of resorting to "fatal terrain" coincidentally shows how external forces can become entangled in internal political affairs. In 521 BCE Ch'i came to the assistance of Sung's beleaguered ruling clan only to be opposed by forces from Wu that were acting in alliance with the divisive Hua clan. By the time of the extract, Sung had scored a victory over Wu and the Hua clan troops with Ch'i's aid, but shortly thereafter Hua Teng's remnant forces managed to vanquish Sung and press forward:[68]

> Hua Teng led the Wu army to defeat Sung. The duke of Sung wanted to flee but an officer named P'u from the Sung town of Ch'u said to him, "I can die in your service but cannot send off a vanquished ruler. Please await the outcome." Then he went around the city saying, "Raise your pennons if you support the duke." The masses followed him.
>
> Having observed the response from atop the Yang gate, the ruler descended and conducted a tour of inspection among them, saying "If the state perishes and the ruler dies it will be your shame as well, not just due to my offenses alone."
>
> Wu Chih-ming of Ch'i said: "When employing small numbers nothing is better than everyone being determined to die. If we are all determined to die, nothing is better than abandoning defensive measures. Since they have numerous soldiers, let's use swords against them."

The Hua clan fled and were pursued. P'u of Ch'u put a head
in a sack and carried it about on his back, proclaiming: "I have
Hua Teng's head!" They then went on to defeat the Hua clan at
Hsin-li.

Ping being the Chinese character for both "soldier" and "weapon," commentators have long understood the clause "they have numerous soldiers"
as "they have numerous weapons." However, insofar as "swords" were
merely long daggers at the end of the Spring and Autumn period, Wu
Chih-ming's suggestion actually constituted an unorthodox measure. By
abandoning their long weapons, including the six- to twelve-foot dagger-
axes then prevalent, the few remaining troops inescapably committed
themselves to a death-defying struggle at close quarters in a sort of precursor to Sun-tzu's "fatal terrain." Although the dagger's short thrusting
range would be advantageous in heavily crowded circumstances, courage
alone certainly determined the outcome.

While Wu was rousing the people's spirit, P'u sought to depress the enemy's *ch'i* by claiming that Hua Teng had been slain, leaving them leader-
less. The impact of his actions turned upon the simple ruse of claiming
the head in a sack was Hua Teng's, though he augmented it by racing
about in obvious triumph, displaying convincing confidence in perpetrat-
ing his unorthodox trick.

Finally, another action intended to induce psychological shock and dramatically impact the enemy's *ch'i* arose in 505 BCE, the year following Wu's
conquest of Ch'u. Yüeh invaded Wu for the first time in the summer, while
Wu's armies were still preoccupied with pillaging Ying and had become entangled with a rescue force from Ch'in. When the king of Yüeh died in 496
BCE and was succeeded by his son Kou-chien, King Ho-lü of Wu perceived
an opportunity in Yüeh's temporary discord and extended mourning
period to blunt its growing prowess by launching a sudden strike:[69]

Wu attacked Yüeh in the summer. Kou-chien, king of Yüeh,
went forth to resist them and deployed his forces at Tsui-li. Being troubled by Wu's disciplined order, he had death defying

soldiers twice try to obtain captives from among them but Wu did not stir. Kou-chien then had three rows of military criminals, holding swords at their own throats, say before Wu's ranks: "Although our two rulers are engaged in martial affairs, we violated the commands of the flags and drums. Having been negligent in the face of our ruler's deployment, we dare not flee from punishment, but venture to repay him with our deaths." They then cut their own throats.

While the eyes of Wu's entire army were transfixed, King Kou-chien attacked and severely defeated them. Ling Ku-fu suddenly struck King Ho-lü with a halberd, wounding his big toe and taking a boot. Wu's forces then turned back and King Ho-lü died at Hsing, some 7 *li* from Tsui-li.

Military breaches of discipline could often be redeemed in antiquity through courageous battlefield action and Warring States military theorists subsequently advised grouping previous offenders into special, even suicidal, contingents because they were likely, but not invariably, to be highly motivated. However, the sort of concerted, dramatic self-extinction witnessed in this episode, undertaken without even engaging the enemy, was unheralded. Not surprisingly, their action so mesmerized Wu's troops that they became oblivious to further developments. Kou-chien's highly unorthodox psychological ploy thus induced a momentary lapse that was quickly exploited with a fervent assault.

Other Innovative Tactics and Events

The first known use of poison in China to inflict causalities, stir consternation, cause chaos, and deny water supplies dates to 559 BCE.[70] The *Tso Chuan* simply states that "When an army from Chin attacked Ch'in, Ch'in's troops poisoned the upper reaches of the Ching River and many troops died." Naturally the situation was much more complex because Chin had assembled a somewhat reluctant coalition force that had been marked by dissension early on. Although the poison's effects quickly dissipated in the

flowing waters except in the stagnant marsh area, its sudden impact sufficiently disorganized their efforts and exacerbated their mutual animosity
that the armies withdrew even before striking at their objective. Although
denying water supplies became a fundamental tactic in the Warring States
period, Sung and Ming military writers still deemed poisoning water
sources to be an unorthodox measure.[71]

Finally, Ming and Ch'ing analysts identified a number of Spring and
Autumn tactical developments and behavioral modes as unorthodox that
merely require mention. Foremost among them might be Ch'u's creation
of a naval force to attack Wu[72] and the king of Wu apparently initiating
aquatic warfare in 512 BCE by employing a flooding attack.[73] The *Tso-chih
Ping-fa* comments that Wu Tzu-hsü, through his final warning against
Yüeh's perfidy and his method of self-sacrifice, clearly acted in an unorthodox manner,[74] while Fu Ch'ai, by employing a chorus to constantly
remind him of his father's death, adopted an unusual method. To these
might be added the inception of incendiary warfare, first articulated as
doctrine in the *Art of War* and subsequently deemed unorthodox by various writers, though no real Spring and Autumn incidents are ever cited.[75]

3

Sun-tzu's Definitive Formulation

T he attribution of a new concept is invariably tenuous, particularly when the historical evidence is sparse and dubious. The unorthodox's origins remain nebulous, though speculation has sometimes associated it with the conflation of ideas that eventually crystallized as Taoism. Conversely, since the interrelationship of *ch'i* (unorthodox) and *cheng* (orthodox) mirrors that of *yin* and *yang*, others have envisioned the concept of the unorthodox somehow being derived from divinatory practices, especially the *yin-yang* principles underlying the *I Ching*, in which case the orthodox might be expected to be correlated with *yang*, the firm and visible, and the unorthodox with *yin*, the dark and yielding. However, later commentators surprisingly contravene expectation to associate the unorthodox with *yang* and orthodox with *yin*.

Several of the *Tao Te Ching*'s concepts—including that reversal characterizes the natural world and that things, while remaining in complementary, dynamic tension, revert to their opposite after reaching their pinnacle or extreme—resonate most closely with Sun-tzu's dynamic characterization of the unorthodox turning into the orthodox and the orthodox into the unorthodox. Moreover, during the middle Warring States period when the *Art of War* probably attained final form, in accord with the well-known *Tao Te Ching* dictum, "With the orthodox govern the state, with the unorthodox employ the army," the military (in contrast to the civil) was generally regarded as unorthodox.[1]

Insofar as the *Art of War*, the earliest of the remnant Warring States military writings, preserves the first passage to actually discuss the unorthodox, its putative author—Sun-tzu—should be considered the first known proponent of unorthodox methods and perhaps even the concept's progenitor. However, in reflecting upon centuries of combat memory, the pronouncements of experienced commanders, and earlier writings, vestiges of which remain in the *Art of War* and other works such as the *Tso Chuan*, Sun-tzu may have merely adopted a preexisting concept, modified its role, given it a new orientation, or advanced a more comprehensive and sophisticated articulation. Although this is a historically important question, one inseparably related to the existence and role of the historical Sun-tzu (who is hereafter spoken about as the *Art of War*'s author, if only nominally), it remains irresolvable as well as irrelevant to subsequent military developments.[2]

A number of other tactics and concepts embedded in the *Art of War* were remarkably innovative in the context of Spring and Autumn warfare, particularly those integrally connected with the unorthodox's implementation. Some of them well cohere with Spring and Autumn inceptions characterized as unorthodox by later writers, others appear truly revolutionary and are therefore often cited as reflecting Warring States developments. Although it would be absurd to deem virtually every paragraph unusual or innovative, changes in orientation, emphasis, concepts, and operational practices certainly exist. Accordingly, to facilitate understanding the salient characteristics of the unorthodox and orthodox and the conceptual context, it might be useful to succinctly examine the general nature and thrust of the *Art of War*.

Narrow bamboo strips provided the recording medium in the late Spring and Autumn and Warring States periods. Their limited capacity of perhaps twenty to thirty brush written characters, sufficient only for cursive notes or the essence of complex thoughts, clearly accounts for the cryptic, often enigmatic nature of many pronouncements in the *Art of War* and in the *Analects* attributed to Confucius, both supposedly dating to the very end of the Spring and Autumn period.[3] Being cumbersome and easily disordered, the medium's very nature thus imposed enormous constraints on written expression, necessitating complex feats of memory as well as heavy reliance upon verbal instruction and oral transmission.

Despite the probably extensive manipulation of subsequent editors and compilers who may have drastically reordered the bamboo strips and perhaps discarded many, the *Art of War* still frequently seems to be nothing more than a pastiche of discrete pronouncements. However, close examination and sufficient pondering reveals that a core vision—which might be summarized as "the ruthless practice of efficient warfare," reflecting Sun-tzu's view that "warfare is the greatest affair of state"—underlies the numerous concepts, particularized observations, and individual tactical principles.[4]

Because every military engagement undertaken amidst the turmoil of the late Spring and Autumn period, successful or not, seriously endangered the state, the *Art of War* stresses a thoroughly analytical approach to employing the army. A comprehensive strategy based upon sound military intelligence and careful calculation should be formulated before initiating a campaign or engaging in battle. The primary objective should be to subjugate other states without actually engaging in armed combat, in itself a highly unorthodox concept, through diplomatic coercion, thwarting the enemy's plans and alliances, and frustrating their strategy to achieve the idealized form of complete victory.

The government should resort to armed combat only if threatened by aggressor forces or if battlefield enemies refuse to submit. Even then, every expedition should strive for maximum results with minimum fiscal exposure and manpower risks, limiting as far as possible the destruction to be inflicted as well as suffered. Faced with disadvantageous force ratios, a strong defensive stance should be adopted rather than the normal options of retreating or foolishly engaging the enemy, thereby conserving strength and exploiting the inherent advantages of fortifications.

Sun-tzu's basic strategy entails manipulating the enemy in order to create the opportunity for an easy victory and then applying maximum power at the appropriate moment. Somewhat prefiguring the current concept of shaping the battlefield, the *Art of War* classifies the types of terrain and their utilization;[5] advances numerous tactics for probing, manipulating, and weakening the enemy; stresses precision, speed, and surprise;[6] and emphasizes the necessity of avoiding prolonged conflicts, interminable sieges, and precipitous citadel assaults. Operationally, the enemy should be compelled to suffer the constraints of terrain; lured into untenable positions with prospects of gain;[7] enervated by being wearied and exhausted before the attack; and fervently penetrated by forces that are suddenly concentrated at gaps and other vulnerable points. Even when assuming a defensive posture, commanders should always seize the initiative in order to gain control of the situation and create the tactical imbalance of power that will ensure victory.

Deception, defined by the *Art of War* as the very essence of warfare, is vital to manipulating the enemy and achieving all these objectives. As succinctly expressed in the book's most infamous passage: "Warfare is the Tao of deception. Thus although capable, display incapability. When committed to employing your forces, feign inactivity. When your objective is nearby, make it appear as if distant; when far away, create the illusion of being nearby." Sun-tzu also added that "the army is established by deceit, moves for advantage, and changes through segmenting and reuniting." In the context of the Spring and Autumn's ritualized combat and set-piece deployments, this was highly unorthodox, as many writers subsequently emphasized.

False measures, feints, prevarications, specious troop deployments, dragging brush, feigning chaos, disinformation measures, and other such acts all evolved amid the quest to deceive the enemy, whether to simply cause confusion or compel them to respond in a predetermined way. When imaginatively created and effectively implemented, the enemy knew neither where to attack nor what formations to employ and was accordingly condemned to making fatal errors, thereby providing the army with an exploitable advantage.

Nevertheless, the most imaginative and skillful deceptive measures invariably prove futile without complete secrecy. Contrary to the modern emphasis upon conveying the commander's intent to the subordinate commanders, Sun-tzu believed that the commanding general should be obscure and unfathomable not just to the enemy, but even to his own troops.[8] Moreover, he considered deception and manipulation, deemed by the later military writings to be essential enablers for the unorthodox, to be aspects of form (*hsing*) and the formless (*wu hsing*).

Massive armies being highly visible even without air- and space-based reconnaissance capabilities, their movements and deployment invariably evoke a number of reactions in the enemy. Whether they modify their original estimates and projections, change their tactics, or simply view the events as confirming a preconceived battle plan depends upon their evaluation of the unfolding situation. Warfare in this period was neither as rigid nor as predictable as in the Early Chou, yet the commander's intentions and the attack's thrust could generally still be predicted with a high degree of accuracy.

Probably because of this relative transparency, Sun-tzu developed a sophisticated theory of the "deceptive and formless." While not truly "formless" in the sense of being entirely amorphous or invisible, the best way to be unfathomable or effectively formless—that is, to lack discernible and therefore predictable (and predicable) form—is creating facades and displaying false appearances. Although commentators over the centuries would frequently fail to realize that the formless is attained through creative deceit and would therefore artificially and erroneously isolate deception from the formless, foes can be manipulated and vital secrecy preserved simply by integrating them.

While unstated, there is an essential continuum that ranges from concrete deceptive methods that create false appearances to being completely formless. Feints and facades are primarily designed to create exploitable gaps at intended points by structuring the enemy's actions, compelling them to act ineffectively and assume disadvantageous positions. In contrast, being formless and therefore unfathomable—something akin to the current concept (or non-concept) of "strategic ambiguity"—compels the enemy either to anticipate the most likely tactics and react accordingly or to disperse their forces to cover every possibility, resulting in fissures and localized imbalances in power: "If I determine the enemy's disposition of forces (*hsing* or form) while I have no perceptible form, I can concentrate (my forces) while the enemy is fragmented. If we are concentrated into a single force while they are fragmented into ten, then we can attack them with ten times their (localized) strength. Thus we are many and the enemy is few. If we can attack their few with our many, those whom we engage in battle will be severely constrained."[9]

Over the subsequent centuries the question of whether deliberately deceptive behavior or formlessness might be inherently more effective would occasionally be raised. Theoreticians emphasized Sun-tzu's vision of the formless, often in highly esoteric discussions that folded the formless into the discrete and discernible, but battlefield commanders struggling with problems of control and topography tended to favor concrete deceptive measures, including misdirection and disinformation.

The critical, highly complex concept of *shih* ("strategic power") that figures prominently in the *Art of War* and underlies all subsequent military theorizing and much political thought presumably originated in the martial realm. A wide variety of terms has been used to approximate it in translation, including circumstances, force, force of circumstances, energy, latent energy, combined energy, shape, strength, momentum, power, tactical power, influence, positional advantage, and purchase. Comparative analysis of the term in the *Art of War*, classic military writings, and pre-Ch'in philosophical works indicates that the concept entails the idea of advantage, often temporarily realized and circumscribed, resulting from superior position coupled with skillfully deploying significant forces or raw military power in the most advantageous array.[10] Moreover, in addition to strength and numbers, the concept of "power" necessarily integrates such aspects as endurance, spirit, discipline, equipment, command, and physical condition. Accordingly, we have long translated *shih* as the "strategic configuration of power," though "strategic power" is an acceptable abridgement in most circumstances.[11]

Sun-tzu analogized strategic power with logs and stones perched atop a hill that, although temporarily stabilized, retain great potential energy that can be explosively effective once unleashed:[12] "One who employs strategic power commands men in battle as if he were rolling logs and stones. The nature of wood and stone is to be quiet when stable but to move when on precipitous ground. If they are square they stop, if round they tend to move. Thus the strategic power of one who excels at employing men in warfare is comparable to rolling round boulders down a thousand-fathom mountain. Such is the strategic configuration of power." Sun-tzu further imagized it in another famous passage by asserting that "the strategic configuration of power (is visible in) the onrush of pent-up water tumbling stones along." These analogies and the concept's configurational aspect have prompted a few writers, especially contemporary Westerners, to rapturously ponder its semi-mystical transformational possibilities. However, their suggestion that merely positioning the army to accord with a situation's latent potential will allow it to emerge victorious without any significant effort lacks historical substantiation and is not countenanced by contemporary PRC theoreticians.

Rather, Sun-tzu sought to actively maneuver the army into a position where it enjoyed such great tactical advantages that the impact of its attack, the impulse of its strategically configured power, would be like the sudden cascade of water racing down from mountain peaks. Exploiting advantages of terrain, deploying the troops into a suitable configuration, creating a localized imbalance of power, concentrating the army's lethality upon a well-defined target, stimulating the men's spirits, and other arduously implemented measures would all be directed toward this momentary, decisive objective.

The Unorthodox

Sun-tzu deemed the unorthodox and orthodox integral to creating the conditions required for the highly constrained but presumably unexpected onslaught achieved by strategically configured power. In fact, the sole passage defining their nature and role appears in a chapter titled "Strategic Military Power," parts of which have already been cited. The key paragraphs run as follows:

In general, commanding a large number is like commanding a few. It is a question of dividing up the numbers. Fighting with a large number is like fighting with a few. It is a question of configuration and designation.

What enable the masses of the Three Armies invariably to withstand the enemy without being defeated are the unorthodox (*ch'i*) and orthodox (*cheng*).

If, wherever the army attacks, it is like a whetstone thrown against an egg, it is due to the vacuous and substantial.

In general, in battle one engages with the orthodox and gains victory through the unorthodox. Thus one who excels at sending forth the unorthodox is as inexhaustible as Heaven and Earth, as unlimited as the Yangtze and Yellow rivers.

What reach an end and begin again are the sun and moon. What die and are reborn are the four seasons. The notes do not exceed five, but the changes[13] of the five notes can never be fully heard. The colors do not exceed five, but the changes of the five colors can never be completely seen. The flavors do not exceed five, but the changes of the five flavors can never be completely tasted.

In warfare, the strategic configurations of power (*shih*) do not exceed the unorthodox and orthodox, but the changes of the unorthodox and orthodox can never be completely exhausted. The unorthodox and orthodox mutually produce each other, just like an endless cycle. Who can exhaust them?

Prior to dissecting this seminal chapter it should be noted that the *Art of War*, as indeed all the military writings that follow, always order the unorthodox (*ch'i*) and orthodox (*cheng*) as *ch'i* and *cheng* rather than the conventional Western practice of orthodox and unorthodox. Against a historically prevailing consciousness of ritual correctness and uprightness, prioritizing the unorthodox clearly emphasizes its distinctiveness and importance.

As a preliminary definition it can be posited that "orthodox" tactics employ troops in normal, conventional, "by the book" expected measures while stressing order and deliberate movement such as undertaking massive frontal assaults. In contrast, the "unorthodox" is primarily realized through tactics that employ forces, especially flexible ones, in imaginative, unconventional, and unexpected ways. Therefore, in the context of Spring and Autumn warfare unorthodox tactics would consist of mounting flanking thrusts instead of direct chariot attacks. Instead of frontal assaults, indirect routes would be followed to stage unexpected, behind-the-lines forays; nighttime raids employed; and the terrain's configuration exploited while manipulating the enemy and taking advantage of deceit and obfuscation.

Although we initiated the translation of *ch'i* and *cheng* as unorthodox and orthodox nearly twenty years ago, over the past century Western scholars have employed a number of other terms. For example, General Samuel Griffith, a Marine officer with extensive World War II battle experience who had long studied Mao Zedong's military thought and was unsurpassed in his knowledge of strategy and tactics, states that *cheng* forces engage, or engage and fix the enemy, while *ch'i* forces defeat him, often through flanking and rear attacks.[14] He further characterizes *cheng* forces as the normal or direct and *ch'i* forces as extraordinary or indirect, as operating to fix and flank (or encircle), respectively, or "the force(s) of distraction and the force(s) of decision,"[15] and stresses that *ch'i* operations are always strange and unexpected. Finally, he notes the reciprocal relationship between *ch'i* and *cheng* and adds the crucial observation that they may be realized on strategic levels rather than confined to just tactical ones.[16]

As opposed to invariably identifying *ch'i* and *cheng* with forces, non-military scholars have emphasized their abstract nature and suggested that they might best be translated as "straightforward" and "crafty";[17] concluded that *cheng* refers to military operations that pin down or "spike" an enemy, *ch'i* to maneuvers that force the enemy off balance, bringing about his defeat;[18] or designate "normal" versus "extraordinary,"[19] "regular" as contrasted with "irregular."[20]

While they are initially dependent upon normal expectation within a particular context, the orthodox and unorthodox are situationally defined and inherently constrained by an opponent's ongoing assessment rather than unalterably fixed. Being a pair in polar tension, mutually defining, mutually transforming, and circular in essence, to the extent that the enemy's evaluations and assessments might change or be manipulated, so-called orthodox measures may be exploited in unorthodox ways. (An orthodox attack would be deemed unorthodox precisely because an orthodox attack was unexpected, while a flanking or indirect assault in such a context would be considered normal and therefore orthodox. A feint by a force too ponderous to possibly execute flexible maneuver, designed to distract or entice an enemy, would also then be unorthodox.)

Unorthodox attacks may become orthodox with repeated usage over time or because they have been anticipated. This can lead to chains of projecting and countering, to "I know that you know that I know" games carried to two or three levels, as well as stupefying self-delusion and paralyzing psychological complexity. Not surprisingly, throughout Chinese and now recent Western history the concept has often been misunderstood and even dismissed as nonsensical.

However, in essence the unorthodox remains a descriptive tool for tactical conceptualization, for characterizing and manipulating forces within and by exploiting an enemy's matrix of expectations, rather than a transformational mode to be actualized in the concrete reality of men and weapons solely through designating contingents and deploying formations. Even though later commentators frequently oversimplified or muddled the issue, there is nothing mysterious, mystical, or innately confusing about *ch'i* and *cheng* or their mutually productive, mutually defining dynamic interrelationship. Rather than a technique for balking the enemy's plans and wresting victory through spectacular but apparently easy victories, this insightful conceptualization frequently obstructed clear thinking, with inimical consequences.[21]

According to Sun-tzu's definitive passage, among the salient features of the unorthodox, variability (which well coheres with Sun-tzu's emphasis upon being flexible and thus unfathomable)[22] and inexhaustibility rank foremost. However, it is a well-reasoned, carefully chosen variability, not an accidental manifestation of confusion and chaos. In fact, extreme order and virtually draconian control are always necessary to employ forces in an unorthodox mode, to be able to segment and reform within the swirl of battle and create a facade of chaos. Thus, somewhat echoing the opening paragraph, the chapter goes on to assert that "(Simulated) chaos is given birth from control; (the illusion of) fear is given birth from courage; (feigned) weakness is given birth from strength; order and disorder are a question of numbers."

The Art of War's famous pronouncement on the critical role of deceit concludes with an equally important assertion: "The army is established by deceit, moves for advantage, and changes through segmenting and reuniting." Dividing and reuniting, which are themselves premised upon Sun-tzu's vision of articulation, effective command and control, and independent contingent maneuver, thus provide not just the means to realize unorthodox measures and conceptions, but also the military's very operational foundation.

The changes required by the unorthodox being manifold, the army must not only be able to divide, but also assume diverse formations, execute pre-designated battle plans, and flexibly respond to the commander's direction (as conveyed by drums and signal flags) in the heat of combat. Depending upon strength ratios, it may need to segment into discrete operational forces, some being held in reserve while others, appropriately chosen for maximum effectiveness, engage the enemy or execute unorthodox tactics.[23]

Although the entire thrust of a campaign or the tactics of a single battlefield effort may be unorthodox in conception and execution, generally speaking historical clashes would see unorthodox measures executed by one or more discrete contingents in maneuver. In consequence, although never asserted in the *Art of War* itself, two ideas arose over the centuries: first, large armies that fail to segment off and employ unorthodox forces are likely to be defeated, and second, forces can be designated as unorthodox not just prior to engagements, but even before mobilizing for campaigns.

The first no doubt originated in Sun-tzu's emphasis upon the unorthodox and the thrust of his assertion, albeit applicable to mismatched forces, on flexibility that "a small enemy that acts inflexibly will become the captives of a large enemy."[24] Nevertheless, while Sun-tzu apparently believed that the unorthodox would *generally* provide the key to victory in the context of Spring and Autumn warfare—thereby implying its necessity—he never asserted that it was the sole means nor mandated its employment. Rather, both the orthodox and the unorthodox have a role, accounting for such statements as "If your strength is ten times the enemy's, surround them; if five, attack them; if double, divide your forces; and if you are equal in strength to the enemy, you can engage them."[25]

The second idea, generally identified with Ts'ao Ts'ao, while perhaps suggesting units with special training for ranger and subversive operations to contemporary readers, was often vociferously condemned for being rigid and artificial and thereby undermining the commander's ability to freely designate and employ all his units in an unorthodox manner at the time of battle. Yet it would prove difficult to shake off the idea that fixed portions should be allotted to executing unorthodox measures as the *Hundred Unorthodox Strategies* would advise:[26]

> Whenever engaging an enemy in battle, if you are numerous while they are few, you should select level, easy, broad, and expansive terrain for the engagement in order to be victorious. If you are five times the enemy's strength, then three fifths of your forces should execute orthodox tactics and two fifths should implement unorthodox ones. If you are three times the enemy's strength, two thirds of your forces should execute orthodox tactics and one third should implement unorthodox ones. This is what is referred to as one segment opposing their front while another attacks their rear. A tactical principle from the *Question and Replies* states: "One who doesn't divide when he should divide entangles the army."

Further Observations

Insofar as the key paragraphs will be the subject of extensive discussion throughout our systematic review of later formulations, they need not be examined here in excruciating detail. However, in the light of the foregoing observations, a few comments might provide a useful orientation for subsequent peregrinations. In addition, it should be remembered that the unorthodox and orthodox are intellectual entities, a means of conceiving and designating the mode of employment of otherwise neutral or plastic formations, forces, and deployments. Even though highly trained special operations contingents are normally employed in essentially unorthodox ways and missions, it is the commander's intent and interpretation within the context of the battlefield and normal practice that render the tactics and operations orthodox or unorthodox, not some innate characteristic of the contingents themselves.

In terms of the concept's historical development, the *Art of War*'s definition is already complex and sophisticated. Rather than being confined to a simple tactical principle or the execution of some unusual maneuver or trick that, in contrast to normal practices, will provide a temporary tactical advantage and allow turning the battle, it already envisions the unorthodox and orthodox being dynamically coordinated, interdependent, and constantly changing, marked by an inherent ability to transmorph and be transformed into their counterparts. Just as the five flavors and colors can produce myriad shades, tones, and tastes, or the waters of the great Chinese rivers flow on inexhaustibly, the permutations and variations of the orthodox and unorthodox are unlimited, and the unorthodox can become the orthodox in concrete realization. As stressed by the *Art of War*, this transformational ability provides commanders with the requisite flexibility to constantly vary their tactics and be unfathomable, even though limited to a few formations and basic tactical possibilities.

Despite the escalating scope of warfare and increasingly moribund battlefield that tended to impede the execution of unorthodox measures on an operational scale, the *Art of War* envisions the unorthodox as generally being the key to victory, yet (as noted) the orthodox hasn't been denigrated or displaced. However, there is a sequential sense: the unorthodox is implemented to radically affect the course of battle only after the engagement has commenced in orthodox fashion with perhaps the bulk of the troops. The possibility of employing all the troops in a purely unorthodox fashion from the outset, although inherent in the concept's dynamics, would actually not arise for more than a millennium.

The definition's key paragraphs equally integrate two chief components of Sun-tzu's vision for the ruthless practice of efficient warfare: (1) the strategic configuration of power and (2) vacuity and substance. The modes of disposition for strategic power are either orthodox or unorthodox, the intent being to forge so great a tactical imbalance that victory is incipient. This is accomplished by manipulating the enemy through deception and enticements so as to create vacuities (voids, gaps, or fissures) that might be struck by concentrated forces, imagized as a whetstone crushing an egg.[27] In contrast to the era's dominant practice of courageously but simply attacking force on force, this was highly revolutionary, certainly the concept's first known enunciation. Victory achieved without combat would subsequently be envisioned as the highest realization of the unorthodox.[28]

4

Warring States
Commanders

U northodox measures would not see their true fluorescence until
the forthcoming extended conflict between Liu Pang and
Hsiang Yü that established the Han. Nevertheless, they rapidly
multiplied during the Warring States period coincident with the initial cir-
culation of unorthodox theory, the increased frequency, scope, and lethality of battles, the inception of the cavalry, and the proliferation of plots and
intrigue at every level.[1] Depending upon how previous practices are defined, many of the era's tactics and actions might well be deemed unorthodox, but only a few definitive battles (including T'ien Tan's fire episode),
several exemplary unorthodox strategists such as Sun Pin and Pai Ch'i, and
Ch'in's subversive program attracted the attention of later writers.

Sun Pin

Other than Ch'ang-p'ing, the most famous battles of the Warring States
period were undoubtedly the consecutive clashes at Kuei-ling and Ma-ling
in the middle of the fourth century BCE. Sun Pin, a shadowy figure whose
long lost *Ping-fa* (*Military Methods* or *Art of War*) was recently recovered
from a Han dynasty tomb and whose life has provided the basis for leg-
ends, stories, and even contemporary movies and television serializations,
has traditionally been credited with formulating Ch'i's victorious strategy.[2]

The idea of manipulating the enemy—enervating the rested, destabilizing the composed, stirring chaos in the well-ordered—had been emphasized as early as the *Art of War*, which states: "One who excels at warfare
compels men and is not compelled by other men. Go forth to positions to
which he must race, race forth where he does not expect it."[3] It also asserts:
"If the enemy is numerous, disciplined, and about to advance, first seize
something that they love, for then they will listen to you."[4]

While serving as a strategic advisor in Ch'i, Sun Pin applied Sun-tzu's
basic precepts to extricate the allied states of Chao and Han when they
were successively besieged by Wei. Rather than directly attacking Wei's
armies, the normal response, and perhaps compressing them between internal and external forces, Sun Pin adopted the unorthodox strategy of
threatening Wei's capital of Ta-liang in order to destabilize them and render them vulnerable. He also strongly advocated temporizing until the
two factions had decimated each other, thereby undermining any potential threat from their nominal allies while drastically weakening their actual opponent:

> The state of Wei attacked Chao. Being sorely pressed, Chao re-
> quested aid from Ch'i. T'ien Chi wanted to lead the army into
> Chao but Sun Pin said, "To untie confused and tangled cords,
> do not strike them with clenched fists. To disengage two com-
> batants, do not strike them with a halberd. While they stand op-
> posed to each other you should hit their vacuities. Then the
> difficulty will automatically be resolved because their disposi-
> tions will counter each other and their strategic power will be
> mutually blocked.
>
> "Now Wei and Chao are attacking each other, so Wei's light
> troops and elite soldiers must all be deployed outside their state,
> only the old and weak remaining within. Wouldn't it be better
> to lead the troops on a forced march to Ta-liang, occupying
> their roads and striking their newly vacuous points? They will
> certainly release Chao in order to rescue themselves. With one
> move we will thus extricate Chao from its encirclement and

reap the benefits of Wei's exhaustion." T'ien Chi followed his plan and Wei indeed abandoned Han-tan to engage Ch'i in battle at Kuei-ling where Ch'i extensively destroyed their army.

Thirteen years later Wei and Chao attacked the state of Han. Han reported the extremity of its situation to Ch'i. Ch'i ordered T'ien Chi to take command and proceed straight to Ta-liang. When general P'ang Chüan of Wei heard about it, he abandoned Han and embarked on his return. Ch'i's army had already passed by and was proceeding to the west. Sun Pin said to T'ien Chi, "The soldiers of the Three Chin (Han, Wei, and Chao) are coarse, fearless and courageous, and regard Ch'i lightly. Ch'i has been termed cowardly. One who excels in warfare relies upon his strategic power and realizes advantages from leading the enemy. As the *Art of War* notes, 'one who races a hundred *li* in pursuit of profit will suffer the destruction of his foremost general; one who races fifty *li* in pursuit of profit will arrive with only half his army.' Upon entering Wei's borders have our army light 100,000 cooking fires. Tomorrow make 50,000, and the day after tomorrow start 30,000 cooking fires."

After advancing for three days, P'ang Chüan elatedly said: "Now I know for certain that Ch'i's army is terrified. They have been within our borders for only three days but more than half the officers and soldiers have deserted." Abandoning his infantry, he covered double a normal day's distance with only light, elite units in pursuit of Ch'i's forces. Estimating his speed, Sun Pin calculated that he would arrive at Ma-ling at dusk.

The road through Ma-ling was narrow while to the sides were numerous gullies and ravines where troops might be set in ambush. Sun Pin hewed the bark off a large tree until the white showed and then wrote on it "P'ang Chüan will die beneath this tree."

He then ordered 10,000 skilled crossbowmen to wait in ambush on both sides, instructing them to "arise and shoot together at dusk, when you see a fire." P'ang Chüan indeed arrived in the evening at the debarked tree. He saw the white trunk with the writing, struck a flint, and lit a torch. Before he finished reading the message 10,000 crossbowmen fired en masse. Wei's army fell into chaos and mutual disorder. P'ang Chüan knew his wisdom was exhausted and his army defeated so he cut his own throat, exclaiming "I have established this clod's fame!" Ch'i proceeded to exploit the victory by completely destroying Wei's army before returning home with Prince Shen as their prisoner.

Sun Pin's strategy of an indirect strike that twice destabilized and manipulated Ch'i's enemies has been deemed one of the early period's most successful unorthodox innovations by such important military writings as the *Wu-ching Tsung-yao*.[5] His exploitation of P'ang Chüan's expectations is also regarded as a prominent example of the unorthodox and the episode was adopted by the *Hundred Unorthodox Strategies* to illustrate the tactical discussion of "Knowledge in Warfare" because of the conclusive nature of the onslaught in the valley at Ma-ling.[6]

Pai Ch'i and the Battle of Ch'ang-p'ing

Although the *Shih Chi* provides but a sparse account of his career, in noting that Pai Ch'i's "reputation shook the realm" Ssu-ma Ch'ien praised him for his surpassing skill in "analyzing the enemy, uniting and changing, and inexhaustibly conceiving unorthodox (operations)."[7] Thus, even though Ssu-ma Ch'ien was not a military thinker and Pai Ch'i proved unable to extricate himself from fatal vituperative attacks, insofar as the *Shih Chi's* biographies constitute the only depictions of such early commanders as Sun-tzu, Sun Pin, and Wu Ch'i, Pai Ch'i's inclusion canonized him as a consummate general and practitioner of the unorthodox.

Without doubt the most successful of the famous Warring States commanders, Pai Ch'i (died 257 BCE) served the king of Ch'in as he inexorably amassed power and territory during the first half of the third century. Moreover, although he is best known for the unorthodox measures adopted at the Battle of Ch'ang-p'ing, Ch'in themselves were already embarking upon a program designed to systematically subvert the other states through bribes, rumors, slander, coercion, assassination, debauchery, and estrangement techniques (as discussed in the concluding chapters). The scope and intensity of warfare had long been escalating and by Pai Ch'i's era field forces commonly exceeded 200,000 with campaigns requiring several months or more. The cavalry was just evolving into a component force and military command had become highly specialized, resulting in leadership changes easily turning near victors into the vanquished. Because courage, character, and acumen had all become essential, the smallest flaws were sought out and exploited.[8]

Despite being relatively well protected by mountainous terrain, the state of Chao still suffered formidable pressure from northern steppe tribes ("barbarians") and from Ch'in to the west. Around 295 BCE it was also beset by internal strife, creating an ideal opportunity for aggressors. Ch'in's subjugation of major towns in 295 and 294 and continued assaults on others, including Han's capital of Hsin-ch'eng, which had come under siege by forces initially commanded by Pai Ch'i, finally prompted a conjoined attempt by Han and Wei to extricate Hsin-ch'eng in 293.

Pai Ch'i was deputed to lead a Ch'in counter-attack that approached from the west and maneuvered behind the now ensconced coalition armies before attacking. Crushed between interior and exterior lines, the enemy's troops crumbled before being compressed onto nearby mountainous terrain and decimated, some 240,000 experienced warriors reportedly perishing in what became known as the Battle of Yi-ch'üeh. Pai Ch'i then went on to seize five more cities before peace was finally restored when Han and Wei each agreed to formally cede 200 *li* of territory to Ch'in. Nevertheless, Ch'in once again mounted sweeping strikes in 289 and 287 that seized several cities from Wei, including the vital secondary capital of An-yi, when Wei failed to take advantage of the strategic advantages provided by their terrain.

Exploiting Han's submissiveness, Ch'in later mounted a three-pronged attack against Wei's capital of Ta-liang under Wei Jan, who served as commander in chief. Pai Ch'i, who directed the southern component, initiated the campaign in 276 by quickly seizing several border towns, prompting

Chao to forcibly annex a few for self-protection. The next year Wei Jan advanced with the Central Army and defeated a Han counter-attack in which he inflicted 40,000 casualties and another Wei force before capturing additional cities en route to Ta-liang. The year after, Ch'i belatedly dispatched a rescue force that fared little better as the conjoined forces from Ch'i and Wei were defeated by Wei Jan north of Ta-liang, suffering another 40,000 casualties. Chao finally interceded by striking Wei Jan's forces encamped at Hua-yang a year later. Ch'in responded by having their armies deployed in the north and south converge and crush the combined armies from Chao and Wei, reportedly slaying some 130,000 troops. Pai Ch'i also pursued Wei's remnants to the Yellow River, where another 20,000 perished, mostly from drowning. Wei was therefore forced to cede additional territory in order to survive.

Ch'ang-p'ing unfolded within the final series of battles undertaken by King Chao-hsiang to gradually subjugate Chao and expand into central China. Intent upon securing a corridor to strike Han-tan, Ch'in attacked through the T'ai-hang mountains in 270 BCE, besieging the fortifications there. Since Lien P'o alone believed a favorable outcome could be achieved by fighting courageously, he was appointed commander of the relief force. Well versed in Sun-tzu's analysis of *ch'i* (spirit), he advanced out from Han-tan just thirty *li* before establishing a fortified encampment and then proceeding to frustrate the enemy by affecting no interest in marching onward. Nevertheless, some twenty-eight days later, just after spies were known to have departed, he raced his armies through the night to assume a position fifty *li* from the startled enemy, compelling them to sally forth in great disorder. His forces also occupied the nearby mountains, where they successfully repelled a strong enemy attack prior to Lien's forces launching a counterattack that garnered a major victory. Nevertheless, Ch'in attempted a second crushing attack on Chao the next year only to have it similarly repulsed, prompting them to redirect their attention to the weaker states of Han and Wei.

In 268 Ch'in attacked Wei and then in 265 once again attempted an assault on Chao only to be thwarted by a Ch'i relief force. However, Pai Ch'i's invasions of Han in 264 and 262 succeeded in capturing significant territory, prompting the now endangered, vital area of Shang-tang to change its allegiance to Chao. Unfortunately, Chao shortsightedly failed to fortify it against invasion and Ch'in quickly subjugated it in 260, compelling the inhabitants and vanquished troops to seek refuge in Ch'ang-p'ing. Ch'in then launched a concerted assault on Ch'ang-p'ing that was initially resisted by Lien P'o's 300,000 troops, though another 150,000 reinforcements arrived shortly thereafter. After Ch'in gained several limited victories, a standoff ensued from the fourth to the eighth month because Lien focused upon strengthening their fortifications and consistently refused to be drawn into battle despite repeated taunts, provocations, and even the loss of their western citadel:[9]

In 260 BCE general Wang Ho of Ch'in attacked Han and seized the area of Shang-tang which caused much of the populace to flee to the state of Chao. Chao's army encamped at Ch'ang-p'ing in order to bring the people from Shang-tang under control. In the fourth month Wang took advantage of the situation to attack Chao and Chao responded by having Lien P'o assume command. Chao's officers and troops repulsed Ch'in's reconnaissance forces but the latter managed to slay a sub-general named Ch'ieh. In the sixth month Ch'in forces penetrated Chao's army, seizing two strongpoints and four colonels. In the seventh month Chao's army erected massive fortifications and assumed a defensive posture. Ch'in again assaulted these fortifications and took two colonels, smashed their formations, and captured the western citadel. Lien P'o solidified his fortifications against Ch'in and although Ch'in repeatedly tried to provoke him into battle, Chao's troops did not go forth.

Several times the king of Chao upbraided him for his passive stance. Meanwhile, Ch'in's prime minister, the marquis of Ying, also dispatched emissaries to Chao with a thousand weight of gold to act as double agents and say that, "Among the things that Ch'in hates, they only fear Chao She's son Chao Kua. If he replaces Lien P'o, they will in fact surrender." Upon hearing the

words of these double agents, the king of Chao, already angry
that Lien P'o's army had suffered extensive losses, been defeated several times, and merely solidified their fortifications
without daring to engage in battle, had Chao Kua replace Lien
P'o and lead an attack against Ch'in. As soon as Ch'in learned
that Chao She's son had assumed command, they secretly had
Pai Ch'i assume the position of supreme commander and
shifted Wang Ho to assistant commander, issuing an edict that
anyone in the army who dared leak word of Pai Ch'i's appointment would be executed.

Immediately after reaching the army Chao Kua launched a
sudden attack. Ch'in's forces feigned defeat and retreated before unleashing two unorthodox forces to repress Chao's thrust
even as Chao's army, seeking to exploit their apparent victory,
mounted a pursuit right up to Ch'in's fortifications. However,
the walls proved solid and the enemy's resistance impossible to
penetrate. Meanwhile, Ch'in's 25,000 unorthodox troops severed the rear of Chao's main force and another 5,000 cavalry
cut off the forward element's retreat back to their own fortifications, sundering Chao's forces into two and severing all access to provisions.

When Ch'in then attacked with light troops and Chao found
themselves at a disadvantage, they erected temporary fortifications and opted to maintain a solid stance while awaiting a rescue force. Upon hearing that Chao's provisions had been cut
off, the king of Ch'in personally came up to Ho-nai, advanced
everyone by one rank, and mobilized all those fifty and above
to go to Ch'ang-p'ing to repress any rescue force or forwarding
of supplies.

Having not eaten for forty-six days, by the ninth month
Chao's troops were secretly killing and eating each other. Finally
they launched a series of attacks on the Ch'in fortifications, but
even though they divided into four contingents and attempted
four or five thrusts, were repulsed each time and unable to es-

cape. Commanding general Chao Kua personally led an elite force into combat but was killed by arrows from the Ch'in encampment. When his contingent was defeated, the remaining 400,000 men surrendered to Pai Ch'i.

Pai Ch'i calculated that "when Ch'in seized Shang-tang, the populace was unhappy to be part of Ch'in and turned their allegiance to Chao. Chao's troops are similarly uncommitted, so if we don't slay them all, I'm afraid they will cause chaos." Then, through pretense, he gathered them in a valley and slaughtered them, sending just 240 young boys back to Chao. The people of Chao were greatly shaken.

Whether Pai Ch'i was directly responsible for the formulation of this two-part plan or not, it immediately entered the virtual catalog of unorthodox techniques and became closely associated with his name. Moreover, it was a complex effort clearly based upon intelligence and an assessment that Chao Kua, despite his reputation for martial knowledge, would prove incompetent and reckless enough to be manipulated into seeking a decisive battle. (A massive clash would be much to Ch'in's advantage because, as an invader, they could simply withdraw if circumstances turned inimical, but a defeat for Chao, fighting on home territory, would have dire consequences.)

Kua was not only inexperienced but also so flawed that his father had earlier warned against entrusting him with command, and his mother, as well as other officials, tried to dissuade the king from appointing him.[10] Chao quickly displayed his incompetence by radically changing the command structure, regulations, and important officers before mounting a vigorous but ill-conceived frontal attack on Ch'in's deployments, resulting in perhaps the greatest debacle in Chinese military history.

This pivotal battle in which a staggering number of surrendered troops from Chao were slain despite the usual practice of integrating enemy troops into victorious armies effectively ended Chao as a military power and rendered them incapable of withstanding Ch'in's unremitting onslaughts. Apart from the highly successful estrangement measures, Pai

Ch'i also employed unorthodox troops to harass and shape the battlefield while manifesting an appearance of apparently having been routed. Since the military manuals, especially the *Ssu-ma Fa*, had long been warning against being enticed by feigned retreats, Kua should have been alert to the possibility.

Although Chao Kua's name thus became synonymous with "armchair general," Pai Ch'i's success paradoxically resulted in the campaign against Chao being temporarily suspended when he was subverted by jealousy and court intrigue in part instigated by the infamous Su Ch'in. Realizing his position had become untenable, Pai Ch'i declined subsequent command assignments and was eventually forced to commit suicide despite a masterly command of the unorthodox and having achieved five major victories that reputedly inflicted a million casualties. Ironically, even though Chao ceded territory to secure a temporary respite, Pai Ch'i's replacement failed in several battles at the end of 259.

Contemplating his fate prior to committing suicide with a sword sent by the emperor, Pai Ch'i reportedly lamented, "I truly deserve to die. At the battle of Ch'ang-p'ing I deceived and entombed several hundreds of thousands of surrendered troops from Chao. This is enough to die for." For this act, one that violated even the conventions of the brutal Warring States era but would not remain the only such example in early Chinese history, Pai Ch'i earned everlasting historical condemnation.[11] However, estrangement techniques and the exploitation of command flaws, having proven dramatically effective, while ever after still regarded as unorthodox measures, moved from the realm of the infrequent to the almost expected in concert with Ch'ang-p'ing's rising fame and the subsequent citation of his achievements in numerous military discussions.[12]

Li Mu and the Hsiung-nu Threat

In discussing the need to segment massive forces and designate a large portion as unorthodox, the Ming dynasty *Ts'ao-lü Ching-lüeh* cites General Li Mu's success in thwarting the escalating Hsiung-nu threat during the late Warring States era as a successful example.[13] Moreover, because Li's methods along Chao's northern border area ran distinctly contrary to normal practice, the incident is included in the *Wu-ching Tsung-yao* and his career is also reprised as the historical illustration for the topic of "The Strong in Warfare" in the *Hundred Unorthodox Strategies*.[14]

During the Warring States period General Li Mu of Chao long held command responsible for defending Yen-men against the nearby Hsiung-nu. He stressed convenience in assigning his officers to posts and had all the taxes and duties brought directly into their military headquarters and expended for the troops. Every day he would have several cattle butchered for his officers' enjoyment. He drilled the troops in horsemanship and archery, strictly regulated the signal fires, and employed numerous spies. Thereafter he constrained the soldiers with specific orders: "Whenever the Hsiung-nu launch a raid, quickly assemble in the fortress and protect it. Anyone who dares to fight the enemy will be beheaded."

Events unfolded as dictated for several years without them suffering any losses or deaths. Accordingly, the Hsiung-nu thought Li Mu was afraid and even Chao's own border soldiers felt their commander was a coward. The king of Chao upbraided him but Li Mu persisted in his policies. The king then summoned Li Mu back to the court and replaced him with another general.

For slightly more than a year the border forces went out to engage the Hsiung-nu in battle every time they came forth but repeatedly suffered extensive losses. Throughout the area farming and herding became impossible. The king therefore once again asked Li Mu to assume responsibility for its defense but he declined on account of illness, shut his doors, and did not go out.

The king again earnestly entreated Li Mu to undertake command of the army. Li Mu said: "If you want to employ me, I must proceed as before; only then will I dare accept your mandate." The king assented, so Li Mu went forth to his post. Immediately after arriving, he imposed the same restrictions on his forces as before.

Whenever the Hsiung-nu appeared they failed to seize anything and concluded that Li Mu was afraid. Meanwhile, the border soldiers all wanted to fight because they received their daily pay and other rewards but were unused. Li Mu then picked the best 1,300 chariots, 13,000 cavalrymen, and some 50,000 other elite warriors "worth a hundred catties of gold each" as well as 100,000 skilled archers. He had them assemble somewhat further away for additional combat training and also had all the livestock released to graze. The common people filled the wilds.

When a Hsiung-nu raiding party came he pretended to be defeated and abandoned the few thousand holding troops to them. Once the khan heard about it, he led a massive number of horsemen to invade the border. Li Mu employed numerous unorthodox formations, extended his left and right flanks in order to assault them, and inflicted a severe defeat, killing more than 100,000 Hsiung-nu cavalrymen. The khan fled and for more than ten years thereafter the Hsiung-nu did not dare to encroach on Chao's border.

Even in the Warring States period the Hsiung-nu and other northern steppe peoples had already been mounting armed forays into the long established Chou states and terrorizing the peripheral area itself, raiding and plundering essentially at will. King Wu-ling of Chao reputedly created the first Chinese cavalry in 304 BCE at least partly in response, though only by overcoming the acrimonious opposition that arose when he compelled his warriors to abandon their "civilized" long coats and adopt barbarian style trousers and tunics. (The cavalry was created as much to facilitate Chao's westward campaigns of aggression as to counter the mobility of horse-mounted steppe warriors.) Although Chao succeeded in conquering the Tung Hu (Eastern Hu), other ethnicities and splinter groups continued their border incursions.

The Hsiung-nu were known to prefer low-risk, lucrative raiding and shun hopeless battles and entanglements with superior foes. Li emphasized the use of spies and forward reconnaissance and stressed discipline in the use of the signal fires that would sufficiently warn of approaching contingents to bring the local inhabitants and collected livestock into the fortifications. Being denied easy gains, the raiders would have to either abandon the effort or engage the local, well-ensconced defenders. The former would waste their resources and energy, the latter entailed high casualties with little prospect of gain.

Because Li Mu possessed a decided, though localized advantage in numbers and firepower, including the crossbow, the era's most advanced weapon, he also had to conceal their ability and feign disinterest, even a fear of battle, to entice Hsiung-nu negligence and laxity. He therefore coupled a policy of denial intended to reduce their ongoing losses with apparent cowardice, a form of deceit necessary to lure the enemy into committing their forces prior to unleashing Chao's strategic power. As the tactical discussion in the *Hundred Unorthodox Strategies* notes, this was an approach that reflected Sun-tzu's principle of "although capable, display incapability": "In general, if you want the enemy to engage your stronger, more numerous troops in battle, you should feign fear and weakness in order to entice them into it. When they carelessly come forth you can suddenly assault them with your elite troops and their army will invariably be defeated. A tactical principle from the *Art of War* states: 'Although capable, display incapability.'"

His strategy demanded patience, determination, and a willingness to endure taunts and humiliation, as well as the deliberate sacrifice of a few thousand men to tantalize the khan, an act for which he was vociferously condemned in later historical writings despite the *Wei Liao-tzu*'s assertion that ruthlessness underlies martial success.[15] He exploited unorthodox battlefield tactics by initially deploying his forces in an extended horizontal array before maneuvering to turn the khan's flanks, producing the double envelopment that allowed his crossbows to slaughter an incredible number of highly mobile cavalrymen. Although the details remain unknown, the *Ts'ao-lü Ching-lüeh* concluded, "Even though Li Mu's troops were numerous, he was able to create unorthodox formations in order to mount sudden attacks in sections," and contrasted his capability in this regard with Fu Chien, who didn't know how to segment and create unorthodox units, leading to the debacle at Fei River.

5

Warring States
Explications

I rrespective of whether the *Art of War*'s unorthodox passages date to the very end of the Spring and Autumn period or the early Warring States period, roughly the early fifth to early fourth centuries BCE, Sun-tzu's formulation clearly reflected the escalating scope of warfare and the increasingly moribund nature of the era's ever-expanding, massive infantry forces. In fact, in many ways it essentially reverts to chariot-centered principles founded upon the tactics of mobile warfare rather than originating in the increasingly frequent extended clashes between ponderous armies deployed across virtually interminable terrain against whom a highly mobile arm, in maneuver, would enjoy an insurmountable advantage. However, the theoretical presumptions equally resemble the operational modes characterizing the era's steppe combatants then just transitioning between chariot-based but comparatively swift contingents and cavalry. Suggestions have been made that Sun-tzu's views were in fact derived from sedentary China's centuries of bitter experience with tribal raiders and invaders.

Despite the importance and irrefutable influence of the *Art of War*'s paradigm expression, without doubt the unorthodox's philosophical culmination appears in the final chapter of the *Sun Pin Ping-fa*. Attributed to the brilliant but ill-fated strategist Sun Pin, reputedly a lineal descendant of Sun-tzu and therefore thoroughly versed in the family military doctrine, the *Ping-fa* or *Military Methods* was in fact lost during the Han dynasty and only recovered a few decades ago. Sun Pin's theorizing essentially bridged the gap between Sun-tzu's initial theoretical conceptualization and the many fundamental tactics necessary for actualizing the concepts, including those subsequently embedded in the *Liu-t'ao* (*Six Secret Teachings*). The key elucidation appears toward the end of a chapter now titled the "Unorthodox and Orthodox":[1]

> The patterns of Heaven and Earth, [*yin* and *yang*], reach an extreme and then reverse, become full and are then overturned.[2] In turn flourishing, in turn declining, these are the four seasons. The five phases have those they conquer and those they do not conquer. The myriad things live and die. The myriad living things are capable and are incapable.
>
> Form and strategic power have that which is surplus and that which is insufficient. Thus, as for the disciples of form, there are none that cannot be named. As for the disciples that are named, there are none that cannot be conquered. The Sage conquers the myriad things with the myriad things; therefore, his conquering is not impoverished.
>
> In warfare, things with form conquer each other. There are not any forms that cannot be conquered, but no one knows the form by which one conquers. The changes in the forms of conquest are coterminal with Heaven and Earth and are inexhaustible.
>
> As for the forms of conquest, even the bamboo strips of Ch'u and Yüeh would be insufficient for writing them down.[3] Those that have form all conquer in accord with their mode of victory.[4] Employing one form of conquest to conquer the myriad forms is not possible. That by which one controls the form is singular; that by which one conquers cannot be single.
>
> Thus when those who excel at warfare discern an enemy's strength, they know where he has a shortcoming. When they dis-

cern an enemy's insufficiency, they know where he has a surplus. They perceive victory as (easily) as seeing the sun and moon. Their measures for victory are like using water to conquer fire.

When form is employed to respond to form, it is orthodox. When the formless controls the formed, it is unorthodox.[5] That the unorthodox and orthodox are inexhaustible is due to differentiation. Differentiate according to unorthodox techniques, exercise control through the five phases, engage in combat with [three forces]. . . . [6] Once differentiations have been determined, things take form. Once forms have been determined, they have names. . . .

Things that are the same are inadequate for conquering each other. Thus, employ the different to create the unorthodox. Accordingly, take the quiet to be the unorthodox for movement; ease to be the unorthodox for weariness; satiety to be the unorthodox for hunger; order to be the unorthodox for chaos; and the numerous to be the unorthodox for the few.

What has been initiated is orthodox, what has not yet been initiated is unorthodox. When the unorthodox is initiated and is unresponded to, it will be victorious. One who has a surplus of the unorthodox will attain surpassing victories.

This reconstructed chapter clearly embodies Sun-tzu's initial conceptualization and even echoes his images and terminology, the cyclic character of natural phenomena again being chosen to analogize the ever-changing, dynamically tensioned tactics of the unorthodox and orthodox. The passages not only provide explication but also systematize and advance the unorthodox and orthodox, integrating them with Sun-tzu's concept of the formless and the *Tao Te Ching*'s cosmogenic philosophy. Although the chapter may well be a synthesized compilation authored by his disciples, the *Ping-fa*'s formulation thus transcends the original and this incisive chapter remains the most comprehensive discussion to be found among China's martial writings.

The concept of naming probably stems from the *Tao Te Ching*, even though it also appears in other writings from the period. The *Tao Te Ching* opens with these famous words:

> *The Tao that can be spoken of is not the ineffable Tao;*
> *The name that can be named is not an ineffable name.*
> *The nameless is the beginning of Heaven and Earth;*
> *The named is the mother of the myriad things.*

Embracing the terminology, if not necessarily the full philosophy of the then still evolving *Tao Te Ching*, Sun Pin melded Sun-tzu's concept of the formless with the Taoist perspective on names in the passage that reads: "Thus, as for the disciples of form, there are none that cannot be named. As for the disciples that are named, there are none that cannot be conquered." The key is the nature of the visible, of that which has attained form. Once something is visibly formed, it can be described; once describable, characteristics can be appended, predications become possible, and plans may be formulated. Military deployments being visible and tangible, they can be conquered by other concrete forms (deployments) and the formlessness of tactics.

The normal penchant in the West, one reputedly stemming from the Greek tradition, has been to oppose force with force and launch strength against strength. In contrast, Sun Pin advocates determining and then employing the compliment to any manifestation, what he identifies as the "unorthodox" here and in earlier chapters that deprecate the direct application of force as wasteful and often futile. Although examples of complimentary dispositions found in several immediately preceding chapters (such as "quiet" and "movement") are reiterated here, they are now explicitly identified as unorthodox counterparts.

The principle of employing the unorthodox to achieve victory is the "singular" principle referred to by the sentence, "That by which one controls the form is singular; that by which one conquers cannot be single." It is only necessary to develop the tactics appropriate to any particular battle, to find the form or disposition among the myriad things whose strength will naturally counter and overwhelm the enemy. Although the unorthodox is overtly addressed only in this single chapter, the tactical principles encompassed by the core of his work, including segmenting the troops, mounting flank and encircling attacks, and generally manipulating the enemy, are all designed to render them vulnerable to unexpected measures and allow the implementation of unorthodox techniques.

Sun-tzu had stressed being formless in order to prevent the enemy from discerning one's intentions and disposition, thereby thwarting the development of effective tactics for either attacking or defending:[7] "Thus if I determine the enemy's disposition of forces while I have no perceptible form, I can concentrate my forces while the enemy is fragmented. The pinnacle of military deployment approaches the formless. If it is formless, then even the deepest spy cannot discern it or the wise make plans against it." Sun Pin, while obviously embracing his doctrine, makes the formless even more comprehensive and explicit through the arguments developed in the several middle paragraphs, concluding that "when the unorthodox is initiated and is not responded to, it will be victorious. One who has a surplus of the unorthodox will attain surpassing victories." Naturally this primarily applies to situations in which strengths are equal or one is outmatched, rather than those in which the enemy is outnumbered by a significant factor and more "orthodox" tactics, such as convergent attacks, would be advisable.

Other Formulations

The *Ssu-ma Fa*, a classic military text that purportedly preserves Western Chou political and martial thought but was certainly composed in the Warring States period, does not employ the word "unorthodox," yet the concept of employing forces in an irregular manner is clearly present, particularly smaller-sized contingents. Thus it states: "With a small force it is advantageous to harass the enemy; with a large mass it is advantageous to use orthodox tactics."[8]

The *Wu-tzu*, a text nominally attributed to the great general Wu Ch'i that should predate Sun Pin's *Military Methods* and is generally said to contain numerous expressions of the unorthodox, actually includes only one real use of the term:[9]

> Marquis Wu asked: "If we encounter the enemy in a vast, watery marsh where the chariot wheels sink down to the point that the shafts are under water, our chariots and cavalry are floundering, and we haven't prepared any boats or oars, so can't advance or retreat, what should we do?"
>
> Wu Ch'i replied: "This is referred to as water warfare. Do not employ chariots or cavalry, but have them remain on the side. Mount some nearby height and look all about. You must ascertain the water's condition, know its expanse, and fathom its depth. Then you can conceive an unorthodox stratagem for victory. If the enemy begins crossing the water, press them when half have crossed."

Although the *Shih Chi* ascribed the origination and implementation of unorthodox stratagems to the T'ai Kung and the lengthy *Liu-t'ao* or *Six Secret Teachings* includes numerous extemporaneous, inherently unorthodox techniques for extricating contingents suddenly trapped in disadvantageous situations, the book contains little explicit theorizing. Nevertheless, consciousness of the unorthodox's importance pervades the book, and chapters such as "Cloud and Crow Formation in the Mountains" occasionally describe obviously unorthodox tactics even though not explicitly so identified. Moreover, the last few chapters, including "Dispersing and Assembling," essentially amplify the principle that "One who cannot divide and move cannot be spoken with about unorthodox stratagems." Clearly, it was felt that the fundamental basis is segmentation and maneuver, synonymous with flexibility in controlling and employing forces.

According to "The King's Wings," historically the first chapter to specify the requirements for a general staff, three Officers of Authority were tasked with the "responsibility for implementing the unorthodox and deceptive; for establishing the different and unusual, things that people do

not recognize; and for putting into effect inexhaustible transformations."
(Note that the deceptive and the unusual, normally viewed as having an
innate connection with the unorthodox, if only as prime means of facili-
tation, are still distinguished and enumerated separately.) Furthermore,
the crucial idea of "transformation" once again appears because deception
and thus the unorthodox can only be achieved through transformation.
In fact, transformations realized through the flux of apparent turmoil and
dynamic change constitute its very essence and possibility.

As in the *Art of War*, strategic power and the unorthodox are insepara-
ble in the *Liu-t'ao*:[10]

> Strategic power is exercised in accord with the enemy's move-
> ments. Changes stem from the confrontation between the two
> armies. Unorthodox and orthodox tactics are produced from
> the inexhaustible resources (of the mind). Thus the greatest af-
> fairs are not discussed and the employment of troops is not
> spoken about. Moreover, words which discuss ultimate affairs
> are not worth listening to. The employment of troops is not so
> definitive as to be visible. They go suddenly, they come sud-
> denly. Only someone who can exercise sole control, without be-
> ing governed by other men, is a military weapon.
>
> If (your plans) are heard about, the enemy will make counter
> plans. If you are perceived, they will plot against you. If you are
> known, they will put you in difficulty. If you are fathomed, they
> will endanger you.
>
> Thus one who excels in warfare does not await the deploy-
> ment of forces. One who excels at eliminating the misfortunes
> of the people manages them before they appear. Conquering
> the enemy means being victorious over the formless. The supe-
> rior fighter does not engage in battle. Thus one who fights and
> attains victory in front of naked blades is not a good general.
> One who makes preparations after (the battle) has been lost is
> not a Superior Sage! One whose wisdom is the same as the

masses is not a general for the state. One whose skill is the same as the masses is not a State Artisan.

In military affairs nothing is more important than certain victory. In employing the army nothing is more important than obscurity and silence. In movement nothing is more important than the unexpected. In planning nothing is more important than not being knowable.

To be the first to gain victory, initially display some weakness to the enemy and only afterward do battle. Then your effort will be half, but the achievement will be doubled.

The Sage takes his signs from the movements of Heaven and Earth; who knows his principles? He accords with the Tao of *yin* and *yang* and follows their seasonal activity. He follows the cycles of fullness and emptiness of Heaven and Earth, taking them as his constant. All things have life and death in accord with the form of Heaven and Earth. Thus it is said that if one fights before seeing the situation, even if he is more numerous, he will certainly be defeated.

One who excels at warfare will await events in the situation without making any movement. When he sees he can be victorious he will arise; if he sees he cannot be victorious he will desist. Thus it is said he doesn't have any fear, he doesn't vacillate. Of the many harms that can beset an army, vacillation is the greatest. Of disasters that can befall an army, none surpasses doubt.

One who excels in warfare will not lose an advantage when he perceives it nor be doubtful when he meets the moment. One who loses an advantage or lags behind the time for action will, on the contrary, suffer from disaster. Thus the wise follow the time and do not lose an advantage; the skillful are decisive and have no doubts. For this reason when there is a sudden clap of thunder there isn't time to cover the ears; when there's a flash of lightning there isn't time to close the eyes. Advance as if suddenly startled, employ your troops as if deranged. Those who oppose you will be destroyed, those who come near will perish. Who can defend against such an attack?

Now when matters are not discussed and the general preserves their secrecy, he is spirit like. When things are not manifest but he discerns them, he is enlightened. Thus if one knows the Tao of spirit and enlightenment, no enemies will act against him in the field, nor will any state stand against him.

Another focal chapter, aptly entitled "The Unorthodox Army," includes several unorthodox measures among its numerous practices and techniques for achieving important objectives. Many of them seem exceedingly simple, others so complex and unrealistic as to have been unrealizable. However, just as by exploiting fatal terrain, the astonishing might be accomplished by deliberately taking advantage of the bizarre and unexpected, especially if the enemy becomes dispirited:[11]

The ancients who excelled at warfare were not able to wage war above Heaven nor could they wage war below Earth. Their success and defeat in all cases proceeded from the spiritual employment of strategic power. Those who attained it flourished, those who lost it perished.

Now when two armies, opposing each other, have deployed their armored soldiers and established their battle arrays, releasing some troops to create chaos in the ranks is the means by which to fabricate deceptive changes.

Holding defiles and narrows is the means by which to be solidly entrenched. Marshy depressions and secluded dark areas are the means by which to conceal your appearance. Mountain forests and dense growth are the means by which to come and go silently. Deep grass and heavy vegetation are the means by which to effect a concealed escape.

Valleys with streams and treacherous ravines are the means by which to stop chariots and defend against cavalry. Narrow passes and mountain forests are the means by which a few can attack a large force.

Setting up ingenious ambushes and preparing unorthodox troops, stretching out distant formations to deceive and entice the enemy, are the means by which to destroy the enemy's army and capture its general.

Dividing your troops into four and splitting them into five are the means by which to attack their circular formations and destroy their square ones.

Taking advantage of their fright and fear is the means by which one can attack ten. Taking advantage of their exhaustion and encamping at dusk is the means by which ten can attack a hundred.

Unorthodox technical skills are the means by which to cross deep waters and ford rivers. Strong crossbows and long weapons are the means by which to fight across water.

Distant observation posts and far off scouts, explosive haste and feigned retreats are the means by which to force the surrender of walled fortifications and compel the submission of towns.

Drumming an advance and setting up a great tumult are the means by which to implement unorthodox plans.

High winds and heavy rain are the means by which to strike the front and seize the rear.

Disguising some men as enemy emissaries is the means by which to sever their supply lines. Forging (enemy) commands and orders, and wearing the same clothes as the enemy are the means by which to be prepared for their retreat.

Thus it is said, "One who does not know how to plan for aggressive warfare cannot be spoken with about the enemy. One who cannot divide and move about cannot be spoken with about unorthodox strategies. One who does not have a penetrating understanding of both order and chaos cannot be spoken with about changes."

Obviously many of the possibilities are fundamental, not even a minimal challenge for the conceptually and tactically competent. Nevertheless, darkness, vegetation, disguise, and vile weather, among others, all facilitate the successful implementation of the battlefield measures that underlie or constitute the unorthodox.

The only other significant statement on the unorthodox appears in "Battle Chariots," where it is specifically linked with the cavalry that did not emerge as a viable component force until the end of the Warring States period: "The infantry values knowing changes and movement; the chariots value knowing the terrain's configuration; the cavalry values knowing the side roads and the unorthodox Tao." In addition, "The Few and the Many," which proposes assault options for outnumbered forces under duress, emphasizes employing the cover of terrain to mount ambushes and "setting out specious arrays and false enticements to dazzle and confuse their general" as well as other actions to "stir chaos among their forward and rear units."

More broadly, the *Liu-t'ao*'s most infamous chapters, "Civil Offensive" and "Three Doubts," outline an extensive program for subverting other governments through a series of concrete measures. Although thereafter vociferously condemned as immoral, dastardly, evil, and pernicious, in the context of the era's ruthless warfare it was inevitable that corruption would be aggressively practiced and that bribery, estrangement, licentiousness, and duplicity would become fundamental adjuncts to military offensives, particularly as the powerful state of Ch'in conspicuously employed them. Subsequent theorists generally regarded them (and assassination) as unorthodox and often neglected them, but many rulers and commanders adopted certain techniques and consistently resorted to them, as will be discussed in the concluding chapter.[12]

No doubt compiled at the end of the Warring States period from two dissimilar works, the *Wei Liao-tzu* stresses the reality of military intelligence, condemning any reliance upon divination and omens.[13] Moreover, perhaps because many of the chapters focus upon issues of administration and control and even incorporate extensive Ch'in ordinances, the unorthodox is rarely mentioned. Even then, despite the late composition date and increasing prevalence of unorthodox measures, it is simplistically reduced to a question of sequential order:[14]

> Now one must make decisions early and determine plans beforehand. If plans are not first determined, if intentions are not decided early, then neither advancing nor retreating will be ordered. When doubts arise defeat is certain. Thus an orthodox army values being first, an unorthodox army values being afterward. Sometimes being first, sometimes being afterward, (this is the way) to control the enemy. After receiving a mandate to advance, over the ages generals ignorant of this method, relying upon courage alone, initiated an attack. All were defeated.

This limited but subsequently pervasive view is reiterated in another chapter that comments: "Those who excel at repulsing the enemy first join battle with orthodox troops, then (use unorthodox ones) to control them. This is the technique for certain victory."[15]

Surprisingly, the *Three Strategies of the Duke of Yellow Rock* (*Huang-shih Kung San-Lüeh*), often considered a martial expression of Huang-Lao thinking, makes almost no mention of the unorthodox even though it would seem to constitute the most transcendent and esoteric strategy.[16] Rather, while still deemed necessary, its role is succinctly reprised only in the section known as "Middle Strategy":

> If your state's Virtue and strategic configuration of power are the same as those of the enemy so that neither state has the means to overcome the other, you must win the minds of the valiant, share likes and dislikes with the common people, and only thereafter attack the enemy in accord with changes in the balance of power. Without stratagems you will have no means to resolve suspicions and settle doubts. Without rumor and the unorthodox you will have no means to destroy evildoers and stop invaders. Without secret plans you will have no means to be successful.

That the unorthodox had already been significantly affecting battle-field results and thus impacting doctrine even during the Warring States period can be seen from the trepidation caused by its practitioners. A sentence in "Nine Changes" in the traditionally received *Art of War*—"There are roads that are not followed; there are armies that are not at-tacked"—has been amplified by recently recovered bamboo strips: "As for armies that are not attacked, suppose our two armies have intercepted each other and encamped and we have calculated that our strength is suf-ficient to destroy their army and capture their general. However, assess-ing it from a long-range perspective, there are those who excel in unorthodox strategic power and skillful tactics among them and the army manifests the will of the general. In such cases, even though the army can be attacked, do not attack it."[17]

Nevertheless, there is an undercurrent that suggests while unorthodox tactics had to be respected, they could be thwarted or exploited if recog-nized in time through defensive or even aggressive counter measures. Well-known dialogues attributed to King Ho-lü and Sun-tzu that appear in the *T'ung Tien* (and thus are virtually undatable) provide evidence of such concerns.[18] For example, to thwart an enemy on fatal terrain an ap-pended conclusion observes: "The *Art of War* also states: 'When the enemy is on fatal terrain, the *ch'i* (spirit) of their officers and troops will be courageous. The strategy for striking them is to seemingly accord with them and not resist. Secretly guard against their advantageous positions and sever their supply routes. If you are afraid that they have undetected, unorthodox troops in concealment, have our bowmen and crossbow men guard against their positions.'"

Similarly, in grappling with the highly topical problem of being sur-rounded and attempting a break out, it is noted that the enemy's prepara-tions may thwart an unorthodox thrust:

> The king of Wu asked Sun Wu: "Suppose the enemy arrives
> first on 'contentious terrain,' occupies the strategic positions,
> and holds the advantageous ones with selected troops and
> well-trained soldiers.[19] Some of them go forth, others assume

defensive positions, thereby being prepared against our un-orthodox tactics. What should we do?"

Sun Wu replied: "The rule for fighting on contentious terrain is that one who yields will gain while one who fights will lose. If the enemy has gained a position, be careful not to attack it. Draw them away by pretending to go off. Set up flags, beat the drums, and move swiftly toward what they love. Drag wood to raise clouds of dust, befuddle their ears and eyes. Divide up our superior troops and secretly place them in ambush. The enemy will certainly come forth to rescue (what is endangered). What others want we will give them, what they abandon we will take. That is the Tao to fight for land that (they occupy) first.[20]

6

Han Dynasty Realizations

T he titanic struggle between Liu Pang and Hsiang Yü to succeed the Ch'in not only launched China upon its dynastic course but also stirred the imagination for two millennia thereafter. The subject of stories and operas as often as that of historical writings, their conflict substantially affected China's identity and provided inspiration for politicians and revolutionaries alike. Ranging widely, their battles fostered a new consciousness of regional geopolitical characteristics and the need for localized campaign strategies and operational tactics. Although Liu Pang's biography does not credit him with any unorthodox innovations, three of his prominent associates excelled in formulating them: Chang Liang, Ch'en P'ing, and Han Hsin. Despite self-confidently boasting of his ability to control and utilize these men, the Han's dynastic progenitor was still compelled to acknowledge that their knowledge, skills, and expertise far exceeded his. However, Liu Pang reputedly excelled in adopting the advice of his strategists whereas Hsiang Yü had a reputation for being self-reliant and disregarding ingenious counsel, often with serious consequences.

Although several Warring States theorists pondered the unorthodox and a few commanders were clearly practitioners, the interstice between the Ch'in and Han witnessed a more thorough and extensive application. In fact, this turbulent period provided such an impetus to the unorthodox that through frequent application many unorthodox techniques became virtually orthodox. Numerous, often critical incidents preserved in the *Shih Chi* subsequently became canonical when they were adopted as paradigm illustrations by T'ang and later military writings. Because the *Shih Chi* was equally read for pleasure and extensively studied over the ensuing centuries, almost every interesting episode also came to enjoy a degree of notoriety and many furnished inspirational materials for generations of storytellers.

Chang Liang

The case of Chang Liang exemplifies the traditional Chinese sense that insightful wisdom has an arcane basis and, in consonance with a broadly based cultural attitude that reveres antiquity, tends to be transmitted down through the mists of time. Chang Liang became famous for his role as Liu Pang's primary strategist during the multi-year conflict that saw Hsiang Yü vanquished and the Han established. However, unlike the T'ai Kung, whose sagacity had reputedly been well established before he ventured to the incipient Chou, Chang Liang was in fact an assassin whose vengeful but righteously motivated attempt to slay the Ch'in emperor for extinguishing his native state of Han had failed.

A descendant of a hereditary ministerial family, he had expended the family wealth to find a qualified assassin and personally participated in the attack but their strike with an extraordinarily heavy iron cudgel went awry because they mistakenly targeted an attendant's carriage. Forced to adopt a peripatetic existence, he spent some ten years as a *yu hsia* or "wandering knight," hardly the lifestyle of a cultured gentleman but common enough during the dissolute final years of the Ch'in.[1] Fortunately, he encountered a mysterious, abrasive figure from whom he received a manual of strategic wisdom in an archetypical episode in which the talented but brash somehow qualify for initiation into the realm of martial studies:[2]

> Once when Chang Liang was leisurely strolling across Hsia-p'ei
> Bridge he encountered an old man wearing the poor garb of a

retired gentleman. When the old fellow reached the place where Chang was standing he deliberately lost a shoe over the side of the bridge. Looking at Chang he commanded, "Young fellow, go down and fetch my shoe." Startled, Chang Liang wanted to beat him soundly but repressed his impulse because of the man's age.

Chang went down below the bridge and got the shoe. Upon returning the old man ordered him to put it on his foot. As Chang had already gone and retrieved the shoe, he formally knelt down and put it on. Once he was wearing the shoe, the old man smiled and departed. Quite surprised, Chang Liang continued staring at him. After the old man had gone about a few hundred yards he returned and said, "Son, you can be taught. Meet me here at dawn five days from now." Although he found this strange, Chang Liang knelt and assented.

Five days later, Chang went to the bridge at dawn. However, already there, the old fellow upbraided him: "When you make an appointment with an old man, how can you arrive after him?" He then departed saying, "In five days we will meet even earlier." Five days later, when the cock first crowed, Chang Liang went there. However, once again having arrived first the old fellow angrily shouted, "How can you come after me?" As he departed he yelled, "In five more days come again, even earlier!"

In another five days, before the night was half over, Chang Liang went to the bridge. In a little while the old man also arrived and happily said, "This is the way it should be." Then, taking out a book, he continued: "If you read this, you can become a teacher of kings. Ten years from now you will flourish. In thirteen years you will see me on the northern bank of the Chi River. The yellow rock at the foot of Ku-ch'eng Mountain will be me."[3] He then departed without another word, never to be seen again. In the morning Chang Liang looked at the book and discovered it to be T'ai Kung's military strategy. Regarding it as something exceptional, he constantly studied and worked over the book.

Chinese tradition is filled with such stories and tales of famous figures in many disciplines who actively pursued books of esoteric knowledge, the wisdom or secret teachings that will allow them to surpass all others, perhaps even wrest control of the empire. In this case tradition holds that the old man may have somehow been connected with the state of Ch'i and had access to secret teachings that had been passed down for generations. Moreover, the contents were immediately attributed to the T'ai Kung himself, supposedly being the aging sage's mature pronouncements as king of Ch'i, though with allowance for subsequent systematization and compilation.

Many questions surround the *Three Strategies*, and the extant work almost certainly was composed late in the Warring States period or even in the Former Han. Suggestions abound that Chang Liang in fact received the *Six Secret Teachings*, a far more extensive text focused in part on the work of revolution, one with numerous immediately applicable tactical principles and concepts. Adding to the mystery was its deliberate obscuration because he reportedly ordered that the *Three Strategies* be buried with him since the Han had now restored peace and stability to the realm. Since there is an absence of bibliographic references he was apparently successful, the text being lost until recovered from his tomb in the Wei-Chin period, though it may well have been preserved in secrecy because it was an arcane military work replete with dangerous political implications. Irrespective of the exact contents, tradition holds that Chang Liang's measures exemplified the book's teachings and substantially contributed to the founding of the Han.[4]

However, a close examination of the historical records reveals only a few so-called unorthodox plans among Chang Liang's notable contributions. He reportedly encountered Liu Pang early on and expounded the T'ai Kung's strategy before they both joined Hsiang Liang, whereupon Chang attempted to resurrect the Han but was thwarted by superior Ch'in strength. He then rejoined Liu Pang just as he was commencing the rapid, though occasionally halting, westward thrust that would vanquish all the Ch'in forces not caught in a stalemate with Hsiang Yü in the north. Chang even commanded an army on his behalf that conquered a number of cities, thereby gaining actual command and battlefield experience. However, he first resorted to such unorthodox tactics as bribery and duplicity during their attempt to defeat enemy forces well ensconced in a town located near Mt. Yao:[5]

> When armies were raised throughout the realm at the end of the Ch'in dynasty, Liu Pang entered Wu-kuan pass in order to strike Ch'in's forces at Yao-kuan Pass. Chang Liang said: "Ch'in's army is still strong and cannot be taken lightly. I have learned that their generals are mostly descended from butchers and merchants so it will be easy to tempt them with profits. I suggest we remain among the cliffs for now."
>
> He then deputed a party to go forward and visibly make preparations to feed 50,000 men while also increasing the number of flags and pennants that the army displayed in order to feign greater troop strength. Separately, he dispatched Li Sheng and Lu Chia to entice them with bribes. As expected, Ch'in's generals wanted to agree to a peace treaty and Liu Pang similarly wanted to heed them.
>
> However, Chang Liang advised that "It is only their generals who want to revolt against the Ch'in; perhaps the officers and troops will not be so inclined. We should take advantage of the generals' laxity to suddenly attack." Liu Pang then led his soldiers forth in an attack on Ch'in's army and essentially destroyed them.

Unmentioned in this account but recorded in the *Shih Chi* biography was that Liu Pang intended to undertake the assault with just 20,000 men. Thus, Chang Liang not only increased the allotment, but also created a much magnified appearance by employing the classic "unorthodox" ploy of multiplying the flags and pennants, just as advised by the *Six Secret Teachings* and Sun Pin's *Military Methods*: "Spreading out the pennants and making flags conspicuous are the means by which to cause doubt in the enemy."[6] Or, as summarized under the topic of "doubt" in the *Hundred Unorthodox Strategies*, "Whenever occupying fortifications opposite an enemy, if you want to launch a sudden attack against them, you should gather large amounts of grass and different branches and make your flags and pennants numerous in order to create the appearance of a populated encampment. If you force the enemy to prepare in the east and then strike in the west, you will inevitably be victorious."[7]

These physical measures merely facilitated the conquest, the crux being the employment of bribes to subvert the command structure preliminary to attacking.[8] Although Chang Liang ostensibly exploited the greediness attributed to members of the generally despised merchant class by enticing them not just with bribes but also the prospect of joining the onrushing campaign, he may well have planned the sequence from the outset, making it an example of the tactic of luring the enemy into a fatal complacency with prospects for a peace accord. Such is the rationale for choosing it to illustrate "Peace Negotiations in Warfare" in the Unorthodox Strategies, the tactical summary for which states: "Whenever about to engage an enemy in battle, first dispatch some emissaries to discuss a peace treaty. Even though the enemy assents to the talks, the way you each understand the language of the proposals is invariably not the same. Then, relying upon their indolence and laxity, select elite troops and suddenly strike them because their army can be destroyed. A tactical principle from the Art of War states: 'One who seeks peace without setting any prior conditions is executing a stratagem.'" Despite Sun-tzu's warning, T'ien Tan had managed to exploit the same ploy at Chi-mo and another chapter of the Hundred Unorthodox Strategies reexamines it in the context of feigned surrenders.

Upon conquering Ch'in's capital of Hsien-yang, Chang Liang counseled Liu Pang to forego conspicuously enjoying the capital's luxuries because many officials and much of the populace had been enticed to submit by his ostensibly righteous and humanitarian policies. The empire having been temporarily settled, Liu Pang was consigned to Szechuan contrary to the agreement that the first commander to reach Hsien-yang would be enthroned there. Chang Liang returned east but when Hsiang Liang reneged on his promise to resurrect the former state of Han and enthrone a new king, being a Han loyalist Chang shifted his allegiance to Liu Pang. This set the stage for his second famous unorthodox action, deliberately misleading Hsiang Yü as to the threats facing him. In fact, almost as if in anticipation, he had previously advised Liu Pang to burn the wooden cliffside roadways into Szechuan to manifest a firm resolve not to return to central China or challenge Hsiang Yü. To facilitate Liu Pang's resurgence he therefore suggested that the king of Ch'i was planning to revolt, prompting Hsiang Yü to divert his military forces eastward. A classic case of misdirection, it temporarily caused Hsiang Yü to be oblivious to the potential danger posed by Liu Pang, who was then apparently confined within almost impenetrable mountains and obstructed by three former Ch'in generals entrusted with guarding the interceding region.

Apart from formulating unorthodox tactics for an attack on Tai, the conquest of Ma-yi, and counseling that Han Hsin be allowed to assume the title of king in order to placate him and retain his loyalty at a crucial moment, Chang's accomplishments were all in the service of the emperor's household. By attracting and conspicuously attaching four reclusive worthies to the heir apparent, he managed to preserve him despite Liu Pang's determination to change the succession. He also deterred Liu Pang from appointing the youthful, inexperienced prince to a doomed command against the powerful rebel Ch'ing Pu, just as he had earlier dissuaded him from enfeoffing multiple kings and thereby undermining his own cause. However, while ultimately affecting the course of the Han and certainly falling within the purview of Chinese doctrine of motivation, none were of direct military significance.

Ch'en P'ing

Although never the recipient of extensive recognition in subsequent historical and fictional media, Ch'en P'ing played a vital role at crucial moments in the rise of the Han.[9] (His craftiness should have stirred the imagination of storytellers, but over the centuries his close identification with unorthodox and disparaged techniques instead subjected him to derisive comments and even outright condemnation by the hypocritically self-righteous.) Nevertheless, the *Shih Chi* devotes a chapter to his biography and the *Wu-ching Tsung-yao* includes two of his ploys among the examples cited in its definitive "Ch'i Ping" ("Unorthodox Armies") section, though Han Kao-tsu's extrication from Hsiung-nu entrapment is cited because of the Hsiung-nu's effective display of incapability rather than Ch'en's ingenuity. However, the judicious employment of rumor and innuendo to cause Hsiang Yü to doubt his most capable subordinates is a masterful example of exploiting character flaws and preexistent disaffection instead of concocting some ruse or ingenious trick.

Ch'en P'ing, who ended his career as a kingmaker and by subverting Han Hsin, is noted as early on having loved the techniques (*shu*) of the Yellow Emperor and Lao-tzu, the twin pillars in the amalgamation and transformation of Taoist (or Huang-Lao) thought underway late in the Warring States period. Whatever their intellectual fidelity, Taoists were commonly associated with the arcane and bizarre, and a background in such texts invariably suggests unusual views and an unorthodox approach to the problems of mundane reality. Paradoxically, near the end of his life Ch'en remarked, "I formulated numerous hidden plots (*yin mou*), what the Taoists proscribe. Isn't it appropriate that my generation is already in decline and finished? In the end our clan will be unable to effect a resurgence because of the misfortune brought about by my many *yin* activities."

His reputation was also augmented by having conceived the unorthodox tactics that empowered Liu Pang to six successive victories in a consolidation campaign. His fief was increased after each clash, but despite the prominence of his success, according to the *Shih Chi* the substance of his plans remained unknown due to their secret nature. However, Ssu-ma Ch'ien concluded Ch'en's biography with the comment that "he frequently formulated unorthodox plans (*ch'i chi*), resolved difficult entanglements, and rescued the state from misfortune."

More concretely, in 204 BCE he devised and implemented the unorthodox ploy that allowed Liu Pang to finally escape extended besiegement at Jung-yang and almost certain defeat. Although accounts differ, it turned upon disguising 2,000 women as warriors and sending them out the west gate during the night, creating the impression that Liu Pang was attempting to punch through with an elite force. When their thrust elicited a disorganized attack in response, a double then riding in an imperial carriage announced that as their food supplies were exhausted, the "king of the Han" was surrendering. As news of his pronouncement quickly spread, the besiegers elatedly rushed to the eastern side even though the city was still defended by substantial forces, allowing Liu Pang and a small continent of cavalry to escape through the now deserted western exterior into the dark countryside.

Naturally the ruse was soon uncovered but to no avail. By creating a deceptive facade and exploiting a tendency to nighttime laxity they had thus successfully manipulated the enemy into movement before finally throwing the enemy into chaos by the feigned surrender that played upon their desire and expectations for an imminent resolution to the impasse. Although the city, then on the point of starvation, was subsequently reduced and the imitation king executed, from the Han dynasty's point of view Ch'en P'ing's unorthodox extrication plan had proven a resounding success.

Ch'en P'ing's reputation was much enhanced by conceiving of the infamous estrangement technique that caused Hsiang Yü to abandon and possibly even murder one of the chief architects of his success.[10] Liu Pang consulted Ch'en P'ing, still only a minor advisor, while they were isolated in Jung-yang in a famous exchange that, even if largely fabricated, reflects Ch'en's unorthodox approach and conception:

> Liu Pang said to Ch'en P'ing: "The whole world is so confused and turbulent, will it ever be settled?"
>
> Ch'en P'ing replied: "Hsiang Yü, king of Ch'u, is respectful and loves men so the realm's incorruptible, constrained, and well-mannered warriors have all given their allegiance to him. But when it comes to rewarding achievement, granting rank and fiefs, his parsimoniousness causes disaffection. Now because you, great king, are haughty and rude, the incorruptible and constrained do not come. However, as you, great king, are also generous in enfeoffing men and granting rank, the unscrupulous, covetous, and shameless give their allegiance to the Han. If you could truly eliminate such shortcomings and garner

these strengths, the realm might be settled just as easily as waving a pennant. But as my king loves to insult people, he remains unable to gather incorruptible warriors.

"I observe that there is some prospect for throwing Hsiang Yü's camp into confusion. He has only a few highly favored confidants such as Fan Tseng (Ya-fu), Chung Li-mei, Lung Chieh, and Chou Yin-chih. If only you could sacrifice forty or fifty thousand pieces of gold to employ double agents, we might cause the king and his ministers to become mutually estranged and doubtful. Moreover, being plagued by doubt and suspicion, Hsiang Yü easily believes slanderers so they will certainly begin killing each other. If you then mobilize your forces and attack, Ch'u's destruction will be inevitable."

Feeling this to be true, Liu Pang provided Ch'en P'ing with 40,000 pieces of gold to dispose of as he wished, never inquiring how. Ch'en P'ing then used most of it to insert double agents among Ch'u's forces who spread talk that Ch'u's generals, such as Chung Li-mei, having achieved great success but not been granted any fiefs or kingships, were inclined to unite with the Han forces, destroy Hsiang Yü, divide his land, and become kings. As expected, Hsiang Yü began to distrust his generals.

Already doubtful, Hsiang Yü dispatched an emissary to Liu Pang. Liu Pang appeared to be preparing a great feast with the best meats when, seeing the emissaries, he pretended to be surprised and exclaimed: "I thought that Fan Tseng had dispatched you, but you are Hsiang Yü's emissary." He then had the feast removed and vulgar, ordinary food brought in for Ch'u's ambassador. When the ambassador returned to Ch'u and reported everything to Hsiang Yü, the king became very suspicious of Fan Tseng.

Fan Tseng wanted to urgently assault and subjugate the city of Jung-yang but Hsiang Yü didn't trust him and was unwilling to heed his strategy. Hearing of Hsiang Yü's doubt, Fan Tseng was enraged: "The great affair of emperorship is largely settled!

Let my lord finish it himself. I just want to take my old bones home." Just outside P'eng while en route home he was hit in the back with a poison arrow and died.[11]

Ch'en P'ing's stratagem not only became a famous exemplification of how to employ clandestine agents for estrangement operations, but also the inspiration for novels, stories, and romances.[12]

In another famous incident that unfolded just after he had consolidated control over the realm, Liu Pang (Emperor Han Kao-tsu) foolishly succumbed to a desire for revenge and raced out onto the steppe, despite the bitterly cold weather, to assault the Hsiung-nu for their perfidious behavior:[13]

When King Han-hsin revolted in the seventh year of the Former Han dynasty, Emperor Kao-tsu personally led the army forth to strike him.[14] Reaching Ching-yang he learned that Han-hsin was planning to attack his army in alliance with the Hsiung-nu. Enraged, the emperor dispatched emissaries to the Hsiung-nu. However, the Hsiung-nu concealed their stalwart warriors, stout horses, and cattle so that all they saw were the old, the weak, and emaciated livestock. Ten emissaries in a row came back and reported that the Hsiung-nu could easily be attacked.

Emperor Kao-tsu then dispatched Liu Ching as an emissary to the Hsiung-nu. Upon his return he reported: "Two countries about to engage in battle ought to diligently display their strength. However, out there I saw nothing but emaciated livestock and the weak and the old. This certainly is an example of displaying weakness while concealing troops in ambush in order to gain an advantage. I humbly believe that the Hsiung-nu cannot be attacked."

By this time the emperor's forces, more than 300,000 strong, had already crossed through Chü-chu and his soldiers were advancing. The emperor angrily cursed Ching: "Son of the despicable Ch'i, you obtained your position through your tongue, yet you now wantonly use it to impede our army!" He had him tied up and left at Kuang-wu before proceeding onward.

When they reached P'ing-ch'eng the Hsiung-nu sent forth unorthodox troops and surrounded the emperor at Pai-teng. Kao-tsu only succeeded in escaping seven days later. When the emperor reached Kuang-wu he pardoned Ching, saying: "I failed to heed your words and thus suffered the difficulty at P'ing-ch'eng. I previously sent out ten emissaries, all of whom had concluded they could be attacked." He then enfeoffed him with 2,000 households as a lord within the pass and changed his title to Chien-hsin.[15]

The tactical discussion from the *Unorthodox Strategies* chapter "The Strong in Warfare" (which also employs the incident as a historical illustration) summarizes the unorthodox tactical measure employed here as follows: "In general, if you want the enemy to engage your stronger, more numerous troops in battle, you should feign fear and weakness in order to entice them into it. When they carelessly come forth, you can suddenly assault them with your elite troops and invariably defeat their armies. A tactical principle from the *Art of War* states: 'Although capable, display incapability.'"[16]

In the ongoing confrontation with peripheral border peoples, military intelligence was acquired through informers, prisoner interrogation, and traders, as well as probing missions carried out by official emissaries under various guises. Forewarned of the latter's meandering approach, the highly mobile steppe peoples could easily shift their best warriors and divert their livestock to less visible areas. Since the Hsiung-nu successfully obfuscated ten observers in succession, it would have been remarkable if Liu's perspicacious warning had actually been heeded!

The incident is remembered for more than just Liu Pang's error, which not only saw him humiliated by being encircled after allowing himself to be lured forward by a feigned retreat, but also caused many of his troops to perish from a lack of food and the cold, with a third of the 320,000 reportedly suffering severe frostbite. Instead, it is Ch'en P'ing's innovative extrication of Liu Pang from certain death that commands attention. Although his exact methods at Pai-teng remain unknown, he apparently augmented the promise of great gifts by exploiting the insecurity and jealousy of the Shan-yü's consort by persuasively suggesting she would be displaced once the Shan-yü subjugated the Han and became enamored of its elegant princesses. (Some commentators suggest that Ch'en P'ing had portraits of idealized women painted to create a stronger impression.) His presumed method was sufficiently well-known from the Han onward to be frequently included in various compendia of clever, even unorthodox techniques, and to attract the condemnation of such self-assured moral exemplars as Huan T'an:[17]

Someone said: "Ch'en P'ing succeeded in extricating Han Kao-tsu from the siege of P'ing-ch'eng but the records state the affair was secret so subsequent generations have not succeeded in learning about it. Was it successful because of subtle techniques and transcendent skill and accordingly concealed and hidden without being passed down? Can you, through weighing the factors, penetrate the nature of this affair or not?"

Huan replied: "On the contrary, his plan was skimpy, lowly, stupid, and odious; therefore it was concealed and not leaked out. When Han Kao-tsu had been besieged for seven days, Ch'en P'ing went and persuaded Yen-shih, the Shan-yü's consort, to release him. She in turn spoke with the Shan-yü who sent out Kao-tsu. Accordingly, we can deduce the substance of his persuasion.

"Ch'en P'ing certainly told her that the Han has such surpassingly beautiful women that no one in the world is capable of describing their appearance. Under the difficulty of his present extremity the emperor had already dispatched an emissary to race back, seek out, and obtain them because he wanted to present them to the Shan-yü. Were the Shan-yü to gaze upon these women he would certainly favor and love them. When he became enamored, Yen-shih would be increasingly estranged from the Shan-yü. Therefore it would be better to effect the emperor's departure before they arrive. Once released he would not forward the women.

"Yen-shih, a woman marked by an extremely jealous nature, would have certainly abhorred the prospect of being neglected and wanted to eliminate this possibility. This sort of persuasion is uncouth but effective. When he managed to successfully employ it, Ch'en P'ing wanted to make it seem mysterious and extraordinary, so they concealed it rather than let it leak out."

Such, of course, was the deprecatory attitude of the self-professed Confucian literati toward warfare in general, as well as unorthodox techniques and stratagems.

Stalemate Resolution

As already noted, in the fourth month of 205 BCE, well into the multi-year conflict between Hsiang Yü and Liu Pang to dominate the realm, Liu Pang was surprisingly vanquished by Hsiang Yü's swift cavalry attack at P'eng-ch'eng. His initial force of perhaps 300,000 having been decimated, he was compelled to flee westward and retrench where he could be sustained by the remaining bastions of Szechuan and Kuan-chung. After reassembling the paltry remnants of his armies at Jung-yang and deploying Han Hsin's army as a blocking force, Liu Pang managed to persuade Ying Pu to revolt and P'eng Yüeh to mount unorthodox marauding attacks in Hsiang Yü's rear.

Han Hsin was then entrusted with maintaining the defensive line anchored at the crucial strongpoints of Jung-yang and Ch'eng-kao while Liu Pang returned to Kuan-chung in the fifth month to solidify its security, returning just three months later. Han Hsin was then sent northward, where significant victories were scored in Liang and Yen. Liu also had two mountain strongholds established near the vital granary at Ao and took other means to strengthen his position in the surrounding territory, such as erecting palisades to protect his supply corridors.

Nevertheless, their situation became untenable when Hsiang Yü's attacks severed their supply lines, compelling Liu to seek an agreement to divide the empire. Balked by Fan Tseng, Liu Pang initiated the subversive techniques that successfully cast suspicion upon Fan's loyalty and caused the estrangement of other generals, but Hsiang Yü's unrelenting pressure persisted and he even assaulted Jung-yang in the fourth month of 204. Hungry and endangered, Liu ignominiously employed an impostor and 2,000 women clad as warriors to distract the besiegers and escape to Ch'eng-kao in the fifth month, as previously retold. Although Jung-yang continued to hold out, Hsiang Yü conquered Ch'eng-kao, though not before Liu again fled.

Forced to withdraw to Kuan-chung, Liu deliberately fragmented Hsiang's forces by moving south while Han Hsin went north, Ying Pu mounted attacks in Ch'u, and P'eng Yüeh thrust at P'eng-ch'eng. Once Hsiang Yü shifted to quash P'eng's threat, Liu briefly retook Ch'eng-kao before Hsiang, having repulsed P'eng, returned in the sixth month to recapture it and finally subjugate Jung-yang as well. (Although repeatedly successful, Hsiang was compelled to employ his armies almost continuously to quell these threats, often moving them great distances.) Reduced to a handful of troops, Liu Pang stealthily seized control of Han Hsin's highly successful northern army before dispatching him to attack Ch'i and sent Chang Erh to Chao. Reinforced by 20,000 troops operating on a second front, P'eng Yüeh recommenced his devastating incendiary attacks on Ch'u's supply lines in the eighth month.

In the tenth month an incident at Ch'eng-kao cited by the *Wu-ching Tsung-yao* as an illustration for "Unorthodox Armies" ("Ch'i Ping") unfolded despite Hsiang Yü having explicitly instructed his generals not to be provoked into leaving their fortifications to engage Liu Pang's forces.[18] Because of the devastating loss of Ch'i to Han Hsin's onslaught and other developments to his rear that fragmented his forces, Hsiang Yü was compelled to personally lead his main armies in a retrograde conquest effort, though he promised to return east within fifteen days. At this time Liu Pang, following the advice of his strategists, remained ensconced in their fortifications across the river from Ch'eng-kao, apparently either incapable or unwilling to mount a wasteful assault on Ch'eng-kao, which had already changed hands more than twice.

Once Hsiang Yü departed, Liu Pang had soldiers harass the forces in Ch'eng-kao and after several days of repeated taunts and insults the chief commander Ts'ao Chiu became enraged. Despite universal admonitions against such a blunder in the classical military manuals he personally led his troops across the Ssu River in an amphibious assault. As expected, they were attacked when halfway across and vanquished, causing Ts'ao Chiu and his subcommanders to cut their own throats in consternation rather than surrender. Liu Pang's army then went on to reoccupy the fortified city of Ch'eng-kao and acquire a vast store of jade, gold, and other valuables, as well as gain access to the crucial Ao granary.

Revitalized, Liu Pang immediately struck eastward, besieging much battered Jung-yang, but had to seek refuge in the hills when Hsiang Yü returned in strength. Only after an eleven-month stalemate (and shooting Liu Pang with an arrow in the chest, though Liu remarkably feigned a foot wound) did Hsiang Yü, who was suffering a shortage of provisions and facing threats from many directions, suggest a truce and reluctantly agreed to split the empire. However, Liu's strategists persuaded him to ignore the agreement and exterminate Hsiang Yü's tired armies, though this would require nearly another year and recovery from further reversals.

Han Hsin

Three famous, essentially definitive episodes have traditionally been associated with Han Hsin, Liu Pang's most resourceful tactician and successful field commander, making his name essentially synonymous with unorthodox tactics. One of them, an unexpected river crossing achieved by lashing spears and large jars together preliminary to vanquishing Wei's perfidious ruler at Lin-chin, is cited by several military manuals as an example of employing imaginative expedients in order to avoid foolhardy, direct assaults.[19]

Shortly after Liu Pang's sudden complacency resulted in the horrendous defeat at P'eng-yüeh that reversed all their gains and inflicted upwards of 200,000 casualties, the ruler of an area named after the ancient state of Wei renounced his allegiance and severed communications. According to the retelling in the *Unorthodox Strategies*:

> At the beginning of the Han dynasty, King Pao of the newly reestablished state of Wei at first submitted to the Han and was staying in the capital, but then requested permission to go back to his state because of a close relative's illness. Once he reached Wei he severed the passes and fords and instead signed a peace treaty with the state of Ch'u. Liu Pang dispatched an ambassador to persuade him otherwise, but King Pao would not listen.
>
> Liu Pang then appointed Han Hsin as Counselor-in-Chief of the Left with orders to mount a sudden strike on King Pao. King Pao deployed his forces throughout P'u-pan and blocked Lin-chin. Han Hsin then augmented the number of troops he had initially assigned to deceive the enemy and arrayed his boats as if he wanted to ford the river at Lin-chin. However, he actually drew his troops away to cross the river from Hsia-yang by employing earthenware jars lashed to ridgepoles to ferry them over. After effecting the crossing they suddenly struck An-yi. Startled, King Pao led his army to counter Han Hsin but ended up being defeated and captured. Thereafter the area east of the Yellow River was settled.

River crossings, even when unopposed, always entailed great risk because any army caught in the midst of fording would be an extremely vulnerable target. Tactical doctrine from the *Art of War* onward thus admonished commanders to minimize their exposure while simultaneously exploiting any opportunities that might arise. Imaginative techniques being virtually demanded, the *Liu-t'ao* commented that "unorthodox technical skills are the means by which to cross deep waters and ford rivers" and Sun Pin noted that "unusual movements and perverse actions are the means by which to crush the enemy at fords."[20]

According to the tactical discussion in the *Hundred Unorthodox Strategies*: "In order to ford the river far off when opposing an enemy along opposite banks of a river you should prepare numerous boats and oars, thereby showing that you intend to cross nearby. The enemy will certainly mass troops in response, allowing you to cross at some vacuous point. If you lack boats and oars, you can employ such things as bamboo, reeds, large wine vessels, cooking utensils, or spears and lances lashed together to serve as rafts and thereby cross the river. A tactical principle from the *Art of War* states: 'When your objective is distant, make it appear as if nearby.'"

Coming forth to reestablish nascent Han authority, Han Hsin chose to deceive the defenders rather than waste his limited resources in a costly amphibious assault across the Yellow River's expanse. Although initially discussed in the T'ang dynasty *T'ai-pai Yin-ching*, the first illustrations of these extemporaneous devices—often highly effective despite their sometimes comical appearance, which of course contributed to their unexpectedness and made them even more unorthodox—are found in the *Wu-ching Tsung-yao* and subsequent compendia.[21]

Han Hsin's subjugation of the rebellious king of Chao occurred immediately after the thrust against Wei and completed the conquest of the north and northeast, thereby confining Hsiang Yü to an increasingly untenable position even though he and Liu Pang were still locked in a stalemate. Part of this vibrant campaign was subsequently employed in the *Hundred Unorthodox Strategies* as the historical illustration for the tactical concept of a "guest" and the entire episode continues to be viewed in the PRC as a paradigm example of unorthodox measures:[22]

(In early winter, at the end of 205 BCE), Han Hsin and Chang Erh, in command of several tens of thousands of soldiers, having conquered T'ai-yüan wanted to move eastward down through Ching-hsing gorge to attack the state of Chao. Upon learning that Han Hsin was about to launch an assault, the king of Chao and Ch'en Yü assembled their troops, said to number about 200,000 men, at the mouth of the gorge. Li Tso-ch'e spoke to Ch'en Yü: "I have heard that when Han Hsin crossed the Yellow River and went west, he made a prisoner of Wei Pao, captured Hsia Yüeh, and once again saturated the ground of Yen-yü with blood.[23] Now that he has obtained Chang Erh's assistance, they are discussing a campaign against us that will exploit their previous victories but carry them far from their state to engage in combat. Thus, their front cannot be withstood.

"However, I have heard that when provisions are transported a thousand miles the soldiers have a famished look and that when they light their cook fires only after gathering firewood, the army does not sleep on a full stomach. At present the road to Ching-hsing cannot accommodate two chariots side by side nor cavalry properly deployed several abreast. Since they must travel several hundred *li*, their supplies and provisions will certainly lag behind them.

"Therefore, I would like your majesty to loan me 30,000 unorthodox troops so as to proceed by a bypath and sever their supply lines. Meanwhile, your majesty should deepen the moats, heighten the fortifications, and solidify your encampment without engaging them in battle. They will then be unable to advance and engage in battle or retreat and withdraw. Moreover, having severed their rear, our unorthodox troops will prevent them from foraging in the wilds and before ten days have elapsed, you will be able to suspend the heads of these two generals beneath your pennants. I would like your majesty to pay heed; otherwise, you will be captured."

Ch'en Yü, being a Confucian, constantly proclaimed that righteous troops do not employ false stratagems or unorthodox plans: "According to the *Art of War*, 'if you have ten times the enemy's strength, you should surround them, but if double you should engage in battle.'[24] Although Han Hsin's forces reportedly number several tens of thousands, in actuality they do not exceed a few thousand.[25] Just having been able to venture out

1,000 *li* to attack us must have caused extreme exhaustion. If we now avoid this sort of paltry force rather than attacking, how will we confront a larger one? The feudal lords will consider me cowardly and readily come forth to assault us." Thus Li Tso-ch'e went unheeded and his plan unused.

Elated to learn from his spies that Li's plan had been ignored, Han Hsin resolved to lead the army down through the gorge. Thirty *li* from the mouth they stopped and encamped. However, that night he circulated an order that 2,000 light cavalry, each man carrying a red pennant, should proceed by a concealed route and exploit the mountain's cover to observe Chao's army, instructing them that "When Chao sees us run off, they will certainly empty out their citadel to pursue us. You should then hastily enter it, take down their flags, and erect our red pennants." He also ordered his subordinate generals to distribute a basic ration, saying "Today, after we have destroyed Chao, we will gather and eat." None of his generals felt confident but they feigned assent.

He explained to his officers, "Chao has preceded us in occupying and fortifying the advantageous terrain. Moreover, until they see my personal flags and drums, they will not be willing to strike our vanguard out of fear that I will proceed only as far as the ravine and then turn about."

Han Hsin then had an army of 10,000 men first proceed out and deploy with their backs to the river. Watching them, Chao's troops all laughed uproariously. At dawn, Han Hsin set up the commander-in-chief's flags and drums, and then drummed their advance out the gorge's mouth. Chao's armies opened their citadel and attacked, resulting in a fierce battle that raged on for some time. Eventually Chang and Han feigned abandoning their drums and flags and raced to the troops deployed alongside the river whose ranks dispersed to accept them, after which intense combat resumed. As expected Chao's forces emptied the citadel to compete for the Han drums and flags and pursued Han Hsin and Chang Erh. However, after Han and Chang entered the riverside troops, their forces all fought with death defying intensity and could not be defeated.

Upon observing that the citadel forces had emptied out and were intently pursuing battlefield profits, the 2,000 unorthodox cavalry previously dispatched by Han Hsin raced into the citadel, took down all of Chao's flags, and erected 2,000 red Han pennants. Being unable to wrest victory or capture Han Hsin, Chao's armies wanted to return to their bastion but were startled to find that the walls all flew red Han pennants. Assuming that Han forces had already captured the king and other generals, they chaotically fled and could not be stopped even though Chao's generals executed some of them. The Han forces then concluded the clash with a pincer attack that destroyed Chao's armies and made prisoners of the remnants. Ch'en Yü was slain at the Ch'ih River and the king of Chao captured.

The *Shih Chi* account notes that because Han Hsin wanted to question Li Tso-ch'e about strategy, he ensured his capture by offering an enormous reward. More importantly, not only does this incident constitute one of China's most famous exemplifications of unorthodox operational tactics, it is also replete with important historical military information. While all the aspects cannot be pursued in detail, they merit at least summary discussion if only to orient his tactics within a broader context. Fortunately, Han Hsin's explanations for those measures that clearly violated fundamental precepts already espoused by the *Art of War* have apparently been preserved. Whether late fabrications or not, they certainly reveal early Han dynasty thinking about unorthodox measures and show how their success was founded upon contravening definitive military expectations:

After they had counted the heads of the dead, enumerated the enemy prisoners, and offered their congratulations, the generals asked Han Hsin: "According to the *Art of War*, one should deploy with one's back to the mountains and water or marshes to the front left.[26] Today when you ordered us to deploy with our backs to the river and said that we would eat after destroying the enemy, we didn't concur. Yet, we proved victorious. What sort of technique was this?"

Han Hsin responded: "This is also in the *Art of War* but clearly you failed to investigate it. Doesn't the *Art of War* say, 'Cast them into hopeless positions and they will live, have them penetrate fatal terrain and they will survive'?"[27] Moreover, I lacked experienced, familiar troops and was compelled to 'chase men from the market and fight with them.' If I had not thrown them onto fatal terrain, causing every man to fight to the death, but instead emplaced them on sustainable terrain, they would have all fled, so how would I have been able to employ them?"

The generals were compelled to acknowledge the wisdom of having employed a different operant principle, one already well explicated in Sun-tzu's "Nine Terrains." The manipulation of *ch'i*—the soldiers' vital spirit and their commitment to battle—was a complex subject much meditated upon in both the classic and later military writings, including the *Art of War* and *Military Methods*. It was generally believed that emplaced forces, particularly those defending home territory, could not withstand, not to mention repulse, an animated enemy arriving from afar.[28] (Contrary views that troops rushing forward would leave their baggage train behind, and that those at ease would easily defeat the tired and weary, were also frequently enunciated, reducing situational assessments and tactical specification to a matter of perspicaciousness.) In a prime pronouncement Sun-tzu said, "One who excels at employing the army avoids (the enemy's) ardent *ch'i* and strikes when it is indolent or exhausted."[29] And the *Hundred Unorthodox Strategies* succinctly added, "If the enemy's *ch'i* abates while yours surges, their defeat will be certain."[30]

Nevertheless, within the psychology of manipulating the soldiers' spirit and eliciting a death-defying commitment to fight on, Sun-tzu also provided the crucial insight that fatal terrain could be deftly exploited: "Cast them into positions from which there is nowhere to go and they will die without retreating. If there is no escape from death, the officers and soldier will fully exhaust their strength."[31] Because his best troops had just been confiscated by Liu Pang, Han Hsin was compelled to fight with unfamiliar and undisciplined troops, making motivation and command and control nearly impossible, though of course simultaneously magnifying his achievements.

Among the many chapters in the *Hundred Unorthodox Strategies* that focus upon questions of *ch'i* (spirit), the tactical discussion for the topic of "host" provides the most focused summary: "When engaging in warfare, if the enemy is cast in the role of the host while you are acting as the guest you should concentrate upon penetrating deeply. When you have made a deep penetration of their borders, the enemy, being the host, cannot be victorious because you will have attained the situation of the terrain being heavy for the guest and dispersive for the host. A tactical principle from the *Art of War* states, 'When you penetrate deeply, the troops will be unified.'"[32] Although the feigned retreat was crucial to drawing Chao's troops forward, it was the marked discrepancy in fervor that allowed the Han's paltry forces to prevail.

Historically, Ching-hsing gorge was a pivotal passageway for troops moving out from the interior as well as western invaders seeking to penetrate the state of Chao. No assault that exploited it should have been unexpected, so only overconfidence can explain Ch'en Yü's surprising failure to follow classical doctrine and deploy external defenses that could have readily exploited the narrows and constrictions to thwart Han Hsin's advance. Moreover, in summarily rejecting unorthodox measures, Ch'en Yü imitated the Duke of Sung who centuries earlier had been oblivious to changes in the practice of warfare and mistakenly believed that as righteousness would prevail, irregular tactics should always be eschewed. Perhaps Ch'en was provoked into blatantly assuming this naive, self-righteous stance by his animosity toward Chang Erh, formerly a devoted friend and early revolutionary compatriot who had vociferously condemned him for failing to mount a rescue attempt while he and the King of Chao had been besieged at Chü-lu by vastly superior Ch'in forces prior to Hsiang Yü's bold resolution of the impasse.[33]

The *Shih Chi* notes that although Hsiang Yü dispatched several "un-orthodox" forces against Chao, Chang Erh and Han Hsin were able to consolidate their gains and bring the entire state under their control. However, Han Hsin's most notable success was yet to be achieved. Having also neutralized Yen to the north, he was deputed to subjugate Ch'i, a daunting task rendered even more difficult by Liu Pang again seizing his now minimally experienced army. Accompanied by 30,000 hastily gathered, undisciplined troops assembled from the remnants of local armies and previously unlevied men, Han Hsin moved against the capital of Lin-tzu and easily captured it with an unexpected, swift cavalry strike that again exploited the laxity consequent to peace overtures, though not of his making.[34] Enraged, the self-proclaimed king of Ch'i appealed to Hsiang Yü, despite their personal antagonism, for a rescue force. In response, Lung Chü, perhaps Hsiang Yü's most experienced and successful general, was dispatched with a combined force of infantry and cavalry totaling some 200,000 men under a mandate to summarily vanquish Han Hsin. Unperturbed by these overwhelming odds, Han Hsin resorted to an ingenious, unorthodox variation of the feigned retreat premised upon exploiting Lung Chü's arrogance, laxity, and misperceptions:[35]

> During the Han dynasty, the Han high official Li Sheng attempted to persuade the king of Ch'i to give his allegiance to the Han, but every day the king and Li Sheng debauched themselves with wine while the king neglected his defensive preparations. When K'uai T'ung advised Han Hsin of the situation, he forded the river with his army and then suddenly attacked and destroyed Ch'i's forces. Thinking that Li Sheng had sold him out, the king of Ch'i had Li boiled in oil before fleeing to Kao-mi and begging Ch'u to rescue him.
>
> Ch'u dispatched Lung Chü to Ch'i in command of a rescue army. Someone said to him: "Since Han's troops are fighting far from their state, they are desperate invaders whose front cannot be withstood. In contrast, both Ch'i's and Ch'u's armies will be

fighting in their homeland, so when they engage in battle our soldiers will easily be defeated and scatter. Accordingly, it would be best for us to augment our fortified walls. If you have the king of Ch'i order his loyal subordinates to summon all those from the ravished cities, they will certainly revolt against the Han upon hearing that their king has sought Ch'u's aid. When Han's forces, occupying cities in Ch'i and Ch'u some 2,000 miles from their land, find that everyone has turned against them and that even with their power they are unable to obtain any food, they will surrender without fighting."

Lung Chü said: "I have always felt Han Hsin to be inconsequential. He relied on a washer woman for food so he never made any plans to support himself. He was insulted by having to crawl between a man's legs so he lacks the courage to confront people. He is not worth worrying about. Moreover, what will we achieve if Ch'i is rescued without any fighting? But if we now engage them in combat and conquer them, we will gain half of Ch'i, so why should we desist?" He then proceeded to join battle with Han Hsin.

Both sides deployed along opposite banks of the Wei River. That night Han Hsin ordered a contingent of men to make more than 10,000 sacks and solidly stuff them with sand and stones in order to block the river's flow upstream. The next day he led half his troops across the river to strike Lung Chü. However, once they clashed, he feigned being unable to wrest victory and instead turned his forces about and fled. Elated, Lung Chü exclaimed, "I knew Han Hsin was a coward!" He ordered his army to ford the river and pursue Han Hsin's forces.

Upstream, Han Hsin had his men break the temporary sandbag dam, sending a torrent of water down. More than half of Lung Chü's troops could not ford the river while Han Hsin attacked those who had, killing Lung himself. The remaining troops all scattered and fled. King Kuang of Ch'i also fled, so

Han Hsin pursued him north to Ch'eng-yang and captured him. Ch'u's troops all surrendered and Han Hsin eventually pacified Ch'i.

This highly dramatic incident is well-known not only for Han Hsin's manipulation of Lung Chü's expectations and foolish commitment to achieving victory through a glorious, decisive battle, but also for the innovative employment of a water ram.[36] Hardly a measure that might be concocted at a moment's notice, it required planning, systematic execution, communication, and timeliness to successfully implement. Even though Lung Chü's inexplicable failure to dispatch roving patrols and reconnaissance forces upriver, despite warnings from the *Art of War* onward against possible manipulation and riverside dangers, no doubt facilitated the achievement, it was still a brilliant stroke that exploited water's latent power and the terrain's configuration.

The episode subsequently defined the concept and execution of the water ram, prompting the Ming military writer Yeh Meng-hsiung to comment on Han Hsin's unorthodox methods as well: "On the whole Han's employment of military opportunities are all similar. This can be seen from his arraying his forces with their backs to the river at K'uai-kai. In later ages Chu-ko Liang and T'ang T'ai-tsung were enlightened by Han Hsin. But one should change and transform in accord with the enemy in order to seize victory."[37] Even as early as the Sung the *Hu-ch'ien Ching* was already advising readers that "If your troops are about to ford a river that sometimes flows quite full and sometimes diminishes, do not cross because some sort of temporary sandbag dam has certainly been erected upstream as part of an unorthodox strategy" and stressed the importance of controlling upstream areas.[38] Furthermore, the *Hundred Unorthodox Strategies* adopted it as the historical illustration for the topic of "River Warfare," assuring enduring recognition of the water ram as an unorthodox technique.

Han Hsin's biography essentially concludes with K'uai T'ung futilely admonishing Han Hsin to assert his independence rather than clash with Hsiang Yü, thereby permanently sundering the realm into three and preserving himself. (K'uai, who has no biography of his own, clearly had a predilection for unorthodox, even "unacceptable" thinking by the standards of his day, having previously advised Han Hsin to disregard Li Sheng's achievement.) His advice had been prompted by overtures instigated by Hsiang Yü, who was desperately seeking new allies in order to withstand Liu Pang though they were summarily rejected. However, Han's own survival and the tripart division of China, a geopolitical situation that would be realized for a century or so during the subsequent Three Kingdoms period, could only have been achieved through a strategy that Ssu-ma Ch'ien termed "an unorthodox plan designed to stimulate and move him." Despite his acumen, tactical imagination, and predilection for the unorthodox, Han Hsin unfortunately wavered. Subsequently accused of treachery and plotting to revolt, he was twice thwarted even before resolving his own doubts and perished just as many other successful generals would throughout China's turbulent history once peace was restored and their fame and threat potential outstripped their utility. Moreover, even though Ssu-ma Ch'ien depicted Han Hsin's career in a way that manifest his innocence, as a semi-official Han spokesman he could only condemn his treachery rather than lament the power politics that saw so many meritorious officials slandered, demoted, and slain.

Other Han Paradigm Examples

After the empire was settled, several decades of relative peace ensued because the government practiced generally beneficent policies and refrained from external campaigns. However, few Chinese courts were ever free of internecine strife and political intrigue and outright revolt eventually arose. Ironically, the following episode—a virtual replay of Han Hsin's engagement at Chao—was subsequently cited by Li Ch'üan in his comments upon Sun-tzu's definitive passage not for the brilliance of the unorthodox measures employed, but for a deliberate refusal to employ them:[39]

> During the reign of Emperor Ching in the Former Han dynasty, seven states, including Wu and Ch'u, revolted against imperial

authority. The emperor appointed Chou Ya-fu as Defender-in-Chief and entrusted him with the mission of going east to attack Wu, Ch'u, and the other states.

Chou personally made a request to the emperor: "Ch'u's soldiers are nimble and light so it will be difficult to engage their front in battle. I would like to employ the minor state of Liang as a lynch pin. If we then sever the enemy's supply lines, we can gain control over them."

Since the emperor assented Chou Ya-fu proceeded to the assembly point for his forces at Jung-yang. Wu had just mounted an attack against Liang, prompting the king of Liang to request that Chou Ya-fu rescue them. Chou led his forces northeast, rushing to Ch'ang-yi where he established solid fortifications and set up his defenses. The king of Liang dispatched an emissary to request that Chou take action, but he simply maintained his defenses and made appropriate improvements without going out to rescue them.

The king of Liang then submitted a memorial to Emperor Ching who in turn directed Chou to rescue Liang. Chou did not obey the mandate, but instead strengthened his walls without going forth. However, he did order the marquis of Kung-kao and others, in command of light cavalry, to sever the supply routes behind Wu and Ch'u's forces. Soon the armies of Wu and Ch'u lacked provisions, became hungry, and wanted to withdraw. Several times they tried to provoke battles with Chou's forces but he always refused to be drawn into an engagement. That night the soldiers within his army were frightened and disordered, fighting with each other outside his tent. As Chou was sleeping soundly he did not get up and the disorder shortly settled down by itself.

Wu's forces raced to the southeast corner of the walls, but Chou ordered his troops to prepare in the northwest. When they had finished, Wu's soldiers indeed raced to the northwest but failed to gain entrance. Wu and Ch'u's armies were famished so they withdrew their soldiers and retreated. Thereupon Chou Ya-fu dispatched his elite units to pursue, attack, and extensively destroy them.

The king of Wu suddenly abandoned his army and fled with several thousand stalwart soldiers to ensconce himself at Tan-t'u south of the Yangtze River. The Han forces, continuing to exploit their victory, pursued and attacked them, in the end capturing or killing them all but the king, forcing their provinces and commandaries to surrender. Chou Ya-fu issued an edict that stated: "Whoever obtains the head of the king of Wu shall be rewarded with a thousand catties of gold." In slightly more than a month a native of Yüeh beheaded him and reported it. In all, their defense and attacks lasted seven months, but Wu and Ch'u were completely pacified.

The complex political events that prompted the king's revolt stemmed as much from the Han's inherent structural weakness as the usual political and imperial family machinations. Liu P'i, a grandson of the founding emperor, had inherited one of the kingdoms originally parceled out to Liu Pang's brothers at the dynasty's inception as a reward for his courage in supporting Pang's suppression of Ch'ing Pu's revolt, these enfeoffments in themselves having been an attempt to stabilize the empire. (All the fiefs awarded to non-family, meritorious ministers such as Han Hsin and P'eng Yüeh had early on been reabsorbed, ostensibly because their holders were planning to revolt against Liu Pang.) Liu P'i's fief was located in the old Warring States territory of Wu and Yüeh, an area rich in natural resources such as copper and salt, yet remote from imperial court supervision. After P'i's son was killed over a chess match by the future Emperor Ching, P'i essentially remained ensconced within his kingdom, showing conspicuous disdain for the court while nurturing his populace and military power.

However, even Emperor Ching's ascension did not instigate his rebellion. Rather, it was the much hated prime minister Ch'ao Ts'o's advocacy of reducing the size and independence of the remaining kingdoms through various pretexts that prompted Liu P'i and several other local rulers, all of whom feared being displaced or even executed for minor offenses. Prior to initiating their campaign in 154 BCE, they rejected both a suggestion by T'ien Po-lü—that they not just move westward en masse but deploy a secondary, unorthodox force—and one by a young general, who advised undertaking a segmented strike toward Luoyang and thereby seizing control of the empire's lynch pin while avoiding mismatched battles between their powerful infantry forces and the Han's chariot and cavalry centered forces. (Wu's coalition forces exceeded 200,000, but from the Spring and Autumn period onward the area's highly wet character had always favored infantry and riverine forces while impeding mounted warriors.) However, his plan was considered too rash and the king's son opposed fragmenting their power in order to ensure that they could personally consolidate all the gains while precluding the possibility of a revolt should any subcommander become too powerful.

Conversely, from the outset Chou Ya-fu was determined to employ an attritional strategy, a belief that was reinforced by strategic advice he received in the field. Accordingly, he not only waited for rebel's sharp spirit to abate by persistently refusing battle, but also enervated them by severing their supply lines. To further entangle them he assumed a fortified position in Ch'ang-yi and temporarily sacrificed the Liang area, where the enemy blunted itself in repeated assaults. Despite orders from the emperor to engage the enemy, consistent with his earlier insistence upon the commander's independence in the field, he resolutely awaited the proper moment before moving to vanquish the rebel forces.

Although Li Ch'üan saw the episode as an incontrovertible example of failing to employ the unorthodox, Chou's actions came to furnish a prime illustration of adopting an attritional, defensive posture that can similarly be deemed unorthodox because far more dramatic actions were ordered and expected. As summarized in the *Hundred Unorthodox Strategies*: "In general, in warfare what is meant by defense refers to knowing oneself. When you know that you do not yet have the strategic power to forge victory, you should solidify your defenses and await the moment when the enemy can be destroyed. If you then send the army forth to assault the enemy, you will always be victorious."

During Han Wu-ti's reign, eleven extensive campaigns under such famous generals as Wei Ch'ing, Huo Ch'ü-ping, and Li Kuang-li had focused on the Hsiung-nu, China's nemesis during the Former Han. Although martial measures were also supplemented by marriage alliances, treaties of friendship, and subversion, numerous minority peoples were also targeted for attacks as the Han strove to project its might out into Central Asia. Forays by small contingents, including Pan Ch'ao's handful of troops in the Later Han,[40] continued throughout the imperial period with sometimes surprising success. However, several hundred thousand troops sustained by major logistical efforts, including in the Han, T'ang, and Ming, were generally required to achieve noticeable impact. Conversely, not only did such massiveness make them highly visible, their very ponderousness meant even the most aggressive thrusts could easily be avoided by elusive steppe enemies. In fact, from the Han onward the greatest success was achieved by swift, highly mobile cavalry contingents under commanders oblivious to adverse weather and topographical conditions that swiftly moved across the terrain to attack where unexpected, especially in snow and rain.[41]

Confident that imperial power could never affect them, the nomadic peoples and semi-nomadic tribes ensconced in rudimentary, fortified cities ignored, insulted, obstructed, and sometimes murdered Chinese emissaries over the centuries. Imperial response ranged from angrily mobilizing major forces to naively dispatching doomed emissaries to upbraid the miscreants for their inconceivable arrogance, duplicity, and heinous behavior. Being an intrigue-filled area where spies and subversives were almost as numerous as traders and raiders, overwhelmed generals who often lacked vital government support were compelled to employ audacious measures and unorthodox tactics merely to survive. Fu Chieh-tzu initially undertook just such a mission, one ostensibly entrusted with conveying an imperial reprimand, though the second venture, conceived upon his own initiative, was simply a dedicated assassination operation designed to extinguish Hsiung-nu influence and thereby end the menace of perfidious behavior:[42]

In the Former Han, when Fu Chieh-tzu, Supervisor of Superlative Horses, was to be sent as an emissary to Ta-yüan (Ferghana) in a quest for more mounts, he was summoned by the emperor and ordered to reprimand the statelets Lou-lan and Kuei-tsu en route.[43] When Chieh-tzu reached Lou-lan he castigated the king for having allowed Hsiung-nu troops to intercept and slay Han ambassadors, adding that "A large Han army will soon arrive, so do not advise the Hsiung-nu. If any Hsiung-nu ambassadors should pass by on their way to other states, be sure to speak of it."

The king submissively acknowledged his offense and advised, "A Hsiung-nu diplomatic contingent recently passed and should be arriving at the Wu-sun. Their march will have passed Kuei-tsu." Chieh-tzu then went on to Kuei-tsu and reprimanded their king who similarly acknowledged his offense. Later, when Chieh-tzu returned from Ta-yüan to Kuei-tsu, the king reported that the Hsiung-nu ambassador[44] had returned from the Wu-sun and was presently there. Chieh-tzu then led his diplomatic staff and military officers to execute the emissary, beheading him. When Chieh-tzu returned and presented his report, the emperor appointed him as a Palace Attendant and shifted him to be Supervisor of the P'ing-leh stables.[45]

Chieh-tzu advised Supreme Commander Huo Kuang, "The kings of the Lou-lan and Kuei-tsu are vacillating. If we don't execute them, the problem will remain uncorrected. When I last went by Kuei-tsu, I noted that the king brings people close to him. It would be easy to get near him. I would like to go and assassinate him in order to manifest our awesomeness to the other states."

The Supreme Commander replied, "The road to Kuei-tsu is far so you should put this into effect at Lou-lan." Then he simply sent him off. As a pretext Chieh-tzu and his officers prepared gold and silk and spread rumors that they were going to present them to foreign states. When they reached Lou-lan, the king of Lou-lan did not want to see Chieh-tzu. Chieh-tzu then made a show of departing but when he reached their western border he informed the translator that "As ambassador from the Han, I have brought gold and silks to present to the various states. If the king does not come to accept them, I will go out to the states in the west." Then he showed the gold and silks to the translator who then returned and reported to the king. As the king coveted the Han goods, he came out to give an audience to the Han ambassador.

Chieh-tzu sat drinking with him and displayed the items. After they were both drunk with wine, Chieh-tzu said to the king, "The Son of Heaven entrusted me with a personal communique for you." The king got up and followed Chieh-tzu into the tent for a private discussion, whereupon two stalwart officers followed behind and stabbed him. Their blades pierced his chest, he died immediately, and his attendants all fled. Chieh-tzu then proclaimed that "the king offended the Han so the Son of Heaven dispatched me to execute the king. You should install the heir-apparent who is presently a hostage in the Han as king. A Han army will shortly arrive. Do not move, for if you move, they will extinguish your state." Then he departed back through the various passes, bearing the king's head.

Although Fu Chieh-tzu achieved fame for accomplishing this imperially sanctioned task, Ssu-ma Kuang, renowned author of the great *Tzu-chih T'ung-chien*, vehemently condemned his actions:

In dealing with foreign peoples, the [true] king punishes the rebellious and releases those who submit. Because the king of the Lou-lan was executed after he acknowledged his offense, it will be impossible to bring future rebels back into the fold. If it were necessary to extirpate him for his offense, the army should have been deployed and the mission's intent formally declared, thereby publicizing his offense. But after having sent an ambassador to entice him with gold and silks and then slain him, will future emissaries to the western states have any credibility? Moreover, with the strength of the great Han, to have plotted like rebels and brigands against the various barbarians, isn't this shameful! Aren't discussants who praise Chieh-tzu for unorthodox achievement mistaken!

Such moralistic thinking well coheres with the antique concept of formalized punitive campaigns just as they were outlined by the *Ssu-ma Fa* early in the Warring States period.[46] First, the miscreant is to be clearly identified and isolated, thereby sparing the people from complicity and diffusing their animosity wherever possible; allies must be gathered for the effort; the cause properly publicized; appropriate oaths sworn before Heaven and the ancestors; and finally the army mobilized to swiftly extirpate him. It is against the expectation that a proclamation should be issued and a major force deputed to vanquish the perverse that Fu Chieh-tzu's actions can be defined as unorthodox and were thus included in a *Wu-ching Tsung-yao* chapter devoted to the subject.[47]

The next incident stems from near the end of several years of complex, multiparty conflict to dominate the empire that had been instigated by a nearly universal desire to overthrow the short-lived dynasty of the much hated Han usurper Wang Mang, whose policies, coupled with severe weather, had produced increasingly greater poverty, starvation, and social unrest.[48] Although the Keng-shih armies had established a nominal emperor (Liu Hsüan) by battling northward and inflicting horrendous damage on the populace and infrastructure, the Red Eyebrows remained unsubdued and a secondary Keng-shih army under Liu Hsiu—ultimately progenitor of the Later or Eastern Han—continued their independent quest in the Northern Plains to vanquish the Red Eyebrows. (The Red Eyebrows acquired their distinctive name from their custom of marking their foreheads with red in order to distinguish themselves from their enemies in battle. A peasant army that arose largely under the duress of economic conditions, they are generally understood to have been seeking to survive rather than achieve any grandiose objective. Although theoretically subject to draconian discipline, they lacked true military organization, the formal accouterments of unit designation, and literate, qualified leaders versed in military tactics.)

The debacle referred to in the illustration resulted from the impetuosity of a commander, Teng Yü, who was reportedly embarrassed at his own lack of field success, cajoling Feng Yi, then caught in a standoff with a large Red Eyebrow force, into precipitously attacking with their conjoined forces. One of the future emperor's earliest supporters, Feng Yi was also Emperor Kuang-wu-ti's most effective commander, a victorious leader whose efforts underpinned his rise to power.[49] At this point Feng had been given a mandate to pacify the area but keep the people's welfare paramount in marked contrast with the Red Eyebrows, whose generals had been pillaging and plundering despite their avowed claim to be acting in the people's interest.

Feng Yi's forces battled Red Eyebrow armies in the area of Hua-yi for some sixty days and managed to subjugate several important generals and bring about the surrender of some 5,000 enemy troops in the course of several dozen clashes. In the spring of 27 CE Teng Yü and Teng Hung brought up their forces and immediately pressed Feng to undertake a joint offensive that he felt to be ill conceived because the enemy remained strong. Although he argued for implementing a more positive policy designed to gain further submissions and then splitting their forces to occupy positions on the enemy's eastern and western flanks before finally mounting a strike, Teng Hung mounted a major offensive the next day. Coming under Teng Hung's frontal assault, the Red Eyebrows feigned a withdrawal, leaving behind a baggage train that deliberately included numerous heavy wagonloads of soybeans and other grains. As Teng's troops were also famished, instead of exploiting the retreat and guarding against a ploy, they fell to fighting among themselves over the provisions. The Red Eyebrows then reversed course to mount a sudden attack, inflicting heavy casualties amidst the now rampant chaos. Only a fervent effort by the united forces of Feng Yi and Teng Yü managed to compel a slight Red Eyebrow draw back.

At this juncture Feng Yi suggested they stand down to rest their hungry and tired troops, but Teng Yü insisted upon reengaging after they suffered a not unexpected major defeat and 3,000 casualties. Yü managed to extricate himself and withdraw to Yi-yang while Feng Yi's survivors abandoned their horses and fled on foot along the Hui-hsi-pan rise—low cliffs astride a small, several-kilometer ravine about 20 feet wide and 25 feet deep—back to their encampment. (In accord with traditional martial theory, the ravines constituted difficult terrain for mounting a pursuit, yet easy ground for controlling an aggressive enemy.)

Even more ignominious than the defeat was the stratagem underlying it because the conspicuous piles of beans were mere chimera, a coating applied atop mounds of sand. A trick repeatedly implemented to great effect in later eras, they thereby created the appearance of substantiality where none existed. Even though constantly termed illiterate, unstudied, and therefore not knowledgeable or practiced in the theory of warfare, the Red Eyebrow commanders thus successfully baited their enemies not once, but twice. First, they feigned a retreat to draw Teng Hung forward, then reinforced their manipulation of the enemy with the tantalizing prospect of provisions, virtually stopping them in their tracks and converting them into an easy target.

The military writers frequently speak of offering "bait" in contexts where profits potentially exist for only a fleeting moment, compelling hasty decisions within rapidly evolving circumstances. The possibility of capturing an enemy's supplies always proved particularly alluring since most campaign armies suffered from constant deprivation. Accordingly, Sun-tzu advised "displaying profits to entice them" and Sun Pin added, "Deliberate tactical errors and minor losses are the means by which to bait the enemy."

The incident could easily have been chosen to illustrate the *Unorthodox Strategies'* topic of "Bait in Warfare": "In warfare, what is referred to as bait does not mean that the army poisons the food and water, but rather any situation in which profit entices an enemy into action. When two fronts clash, perhaps the enemy will let loose teams of cattle and horses, abandon material goods, or leave provisions and supplies behind. In every case you should not seize them, for if you do, you will certainly be defeated. A tactical principle from the *Art of War* states: 'Do not take an army acting as bait.'"[50]

Although the episode ends here, Feng Yi's subsequent unorthodox actions to stem the enemy's momentum and retake the initiative are perhaps even more interesting. After regrouping his forces, he augmented the solidity of their fortified camps before setting a time to meet the enemy in battle. Next, he created an ambush force, cloaked them in the same uniforms as the Red Eyebrows, and had them deploy along the sides of the enemy's route of attack.[51] On the morning of the clash when the Red Eyebrows launched their initial assault against Feng Yi's front with 10,000 troops, Feng's tepid response—designed to exploit the classic tactical principle of displaying weakness where substantial, thereby luring the enemy in with apparent profits—emboldened them to over-commit and attack in full force.

Feng Yi's troops then fully responded, engaging the enemy in a widespread clash. As the day wore on and the enemy's spirit flagged, Feng finally released the troops concealed in ambush. Caught by unexpected flanking attacks and unable to distinguish friend from foe, the Red Eyebrows broke and fled. The Han armies exploited their collapse by mounting a strong pursuit and destroying them at Yao-ti. Although no casualty figures are reported, some 80,000 men and women surrendered and another 100,000 eventually submitted at Yi-yang.

The final incident not only depicts the successful execution of an unorthodox measure, but also shows that the lessons of history were neither lost nor slavishly followed by innovative commanders:

> During the Later Han dynasty, the Ch'iang (barbarians) revolted and invaded Han territory as far as Wu-tu. Empress Dowager Teng, in control of the government, felt that Yü Hsü possessed the tactical planning skills of a commanding general and therefore dispatched him to assume the post of Grand Protector for Wu-tu.
>
> The Ch'iang then led several thousand troops forth to intercept him at the strategic pass of Yao-ku in Chen-ts'ang commandery. Yü Hsü halted his chariots, ceased his advance, and publicly announced that he had submitted a request to the

central government for troops and would await their arrival before again setting out.

When the Ch'iang heard about it they divided up to plunder the nearby districts. Taking advantage of their scattering, Yü Hsü proceeded forward day and night at double the normal pace, covering more than a hundred miles a day. He also had his officials and officers each light two cookfires and then doubled them each succeeding day so the Ch'iang did not dare press him.

Someone asked him: "Sun Pin reduced his cookfires but you increase them. Moreover, according to the *Art of War*, an army on the march should not exceed thirty miles a day, yet today you have advanced a hundred miles. Why is this?"

Yü said: "The enemy's troops are numerous while our soldiers are few. When the barbarians see our fires increasing daily, they will certainly interpret it as evidence that local troops from the commandery are joining us. Believing that our numbers are many while our speed is quick, they will hesitate to pursue us. Sun Pin manifested weakness but I now display strength because our relative strategic power is different."[52]

Masking to cause misperception, while an ancient technique, turned upon a necessary measure of bravado, one equally witnessed in Li Ling's retreat and the "empty city ploy" developed by Chu-ko Liang and subsequently included among the *Thirty-six Stratagems*.

7

Three Kingdoms

T he Three Kingdoms period saw the territory formerly controlled by the Han segmented into three domains: Ts'ao (subsequently called Wei) in the north, Wu in the southeast, and Shu in the southwest, including the inhospitable Szechuan area. Ts'ao Ts'ao was essentially the north's progenitor and was followed by Ssu-ma Yi; Sun Ch'üan ruled the southeast, including the old regions of Wu and Yüeh; and Liu Pei, aided by his famous strategist Chu-ko Liang and two famous generals, Chang Fei and Kuan Yü, tenaciously defended Shu with the proclaimed objective of restoring the Han.

Because the three states would intermittently battle for about a century, the Three Kingdoms period acquired a romanticized reputation as an intrigue-filled era and its chronicle, the *San-kuo Chih*, provided the basis for the expansive Ming dynasty novel, the *San-kuo Yen-yi*.[1] Although campaign forces could run as high as 200,000 men, much was accomplished with more mobile armies of 30,000, including substantial cavalry components. These smaller forces allowed greater maneuver and the execution of the unorthodox strategies for which the era became famous, but the latter were far less frequent than reputation would suggest. However, a few became particularly well-known while others, although imaginatively fabricated by later pundits and storytellers, were also attributed to the era.

Early Expansion of Wu

In the swirling, multi-party chaos of the early Three Kingdoms period, as part of his effort to expand Wu's territory, Sun Ts'e marched against K'uai-chi, Yüeh's ancient bastion in 196 CE:[2]

Sun Ts'e was about to seize K'uai-chi but local clan leaders such as Yen Pai-hu (White Tiger Yen), each of whom had forces numbering over 10,000 men, were variously encamped throughout Wu. Sun's generals therefore advised first attacking Yen but he retorted that "Groups like the White Tigers are merely bands of brigands, they have no great ambitions and will simply become our prisoners." He then led the army across the Che River.

The Minister of Works at K'uai-chi advised Provincial Governor Wang Lang to avoid Sun Ts'e because he excelled in employing the army, but instead of heeding him, Lang dispatched an army to resist Ts'e at Ku-ling. Sun Ts'e mounted several amphibious assaults but was unable to gain a victory. His uncle therefore quietly advised: "It will be extremely difficult to suddenly extract Lang as he is relying upon the fastness of his fortifications for defense. It would be advantageous to advance and occupy Ch'a-tu which lies several tens of *li* to the south. This would be what is termed 'attacking where they are unprepared, going forth where they do not expect it.'"

Following his advance, that night Sun Ts'e had numerous torches set out to create the facade of emplaced troops but dispatched the majority along the route to Ch'a-tu to mount a sudden strike on the old encampment at Kao-ch'ien. Startled, Lang dispatched the former provincial governor of Tan-yang, Chou Hsin, and others to lead the army in a counter-attack. Sun Ts'e destroyed Hsin and executed them. Protected by his officials, Wang Lang fled by boat out into the China Sea and down to Tung-yeh. Sun Ts'e mounted a pursuit, suddenly struck, and severely defeated them, compelling Lang to surrender.

Although some later commentators term the troops that resolved the stalemate by mounting the attack on Kao-ch'ien *ch'i ping*, from the *Ch'ien K'un Ta-lüeh*'s perspective the key unorthodox element was the deceptive facade that initially held the army in place while they rushed against an interior target to "seize what they love," thereby destabilizing the enemy in imitation of Sun Pin's famous strategy for defeating Wei several centuries earlier.

Ts'ao Ts'ao

The collapse of the Later Han dynasty, although hastened by the Yellow Turban uprising, was largely precipitated by a clash between the eunuchs and the imperial family. Forces of every size and type, both locally spawned and government engendered, arose out of the rebellion's chaos and its suppression. Powerful leaders emerged and later others such as Chu-ko Liang, Kuan Yü, and Chang Fei became heroes.

After achieving prominence in subjugating the Yellow Turbans, Ts'ao Ts'ao seized authority for himself when his army was defeated in a clash with the eunuchs. Thereafter, for some seventeen years he repeatedly battled regional opponents of every variety and strength in his generally successful quest to consolidate power north and south of the Yellow River. Surrounded by enemies and plagued by defections, Ts'ao Ts'ao continuously enlarged his forces by absorbing vanquished enemies, allies, volunteers, clan members, local officials, and even hundreds of thousands of subjugated rebels. Famous for "knowing men" and employing them irrespective of any personal enmity, perverse background, or character flaw, he also attracted important defectors, strategists, and other talented individuals from throughout the empire. Meanwhile, confronted by widespread famine and a dire economic situation, he strove to reestablish order, settle migrant peoples, and stimulate agriculture while simultaneously nurturing the military field system in order to ameliorate logistical problems.

Despite his well-deserved fame for his many surpassing military achievements, diverse talents, courage, and resiliency, Ts'ao Ts'ao has been vilified far more often than praised over the centuries.[3] The subject of numerous biographies, he battled Liu Pei, Kuan Yü, Sun Ch'üan, Chang Fei, Lü Pu, and other larger than life figures for more than three decades and established the foundation for the subsequent Wei and Chin dynasties. Although he ruled most of China's traditional or "civilized" core (in contrast to the smaller states of Wu and Shu lying in formerly "barbarian" areas), he was never accorded the approbation accorded Chu-ko Liang or Liu Pei, nor raised to the status of a titular deity like the great warrior Kuan Yü. Instead, Chinese popular culture has long portrayed him as a brutal martial hero who, though often outnumbered, wrought great victories amidst a fragmented, turbulent age through acumen, wisdom, and unorthodox techniques.

In contrast to Chu-ko Liang, who came to be seen as the era's surpassing strategist without any justification, Ts'ao Ts'ao was a real innovator and astute commander. He excelled at fathoming strategic situations, frequently formulated unexpected tactics, generally exploited situational possibilities, and always manipulated the enemy. According to Ch'en Shou, compiler of the *San-kuo Chih* or *Chronicle of the Three States* (generally called *Three Kingdoms* in translations), Ts'ao Ts'ao combined Shang Yang's and Shen Pu-hai's administrative acumen with Han Hsin's and Pai Ch'i's insightful practice of *ch'i ts'e* or "unorthodox plots." Although collateral materials indicate that advisors such as Hsün Yü and Kuo Chia, both noted for their unorthodox plans, formulated many of these tactics and strategic measures, Ts'ao Ts'ao ultimately relied upon his own judgment and persevered in his decisions despite fervent remonstrance and outright opposition.[4]

Ts'ao Ts'ao was also a martial thinker who reputedly wrote commentaries to at least five military texts, though only his notes to Sun-tzu's *Art of War* survive. (It has been suggested that he drastically cut the *Art of War*'s original materials, reducing a massive volume of eighty-two chapters to just thirteen, an act that has earned him considerable condemnation.) He also composed several original works, though only fragments remain; authored several lengthy rescripts and explanations; and created a number of poems, though his son's fame as a poet would exceed him.

His *San-kuo Chih* biography contains several examples of unorthodox operations, two of which—the campaign against Ma Chao and the clash at Kuan-tu—were thereafter much studied and widely regarded as outstanding exemplifications of the unorthodox. His assault on Ma Chao and the other generals then occupying the vital Kuan-chung area unfolded with a ploy in the spring of 211 CE:[5]

> In the third month Ts'ao Ts'ao dispatched Chung Yao to extirpate Chang Lu and had Hsia-hou Yüan lead the Western Expeditionary Army forth from Ho-tung to join Yao. Quartermaster Kao Jou objected: "If we send a large army westward, Han Sui and Ma Chao will suspect it intends to suddenly attack them and will certainly incite each other to rebel. It would be better to first assemble our forces at San-fu (in Kuan-chung), and when San-fu has been pacified, you can simply issue a summons (to Chang Lu) and thereby easily settle the Han-chung area." Ts'ao Ts'ao didn't heed him.
>
> The generals dispersed throughout Kuan-chung indeed grew suspicious. Some ten of them, including Ma Chao and Han Sui, with over 100,000 troops rebelled and gathered to occupy the area about the pass at T'ung-kuan. Ts'ao Ts'ao deputed Ts'ao Jen to supervise the forces resisting them but instructed him to secure their fortifications and not engage in battle. He separately ordered Ts'ao Pi to continue to occupy the city of Yeh and appointed general Ch'eng Yü to consult with Ts'ao Pi on military affairs. Camp supervisors Kuang Ling and Hsü Hsüan were appointed to command an army in support on the left while Yüeh An and Kuo Yüan, both senior government officials, took charge of occupation matters (in Yeh).
>
> In autumn, the seventh month, Ts'ao Ts'ao personally led the army forth to mount a sudden strike against Ma Chao and the others. Several dissenters said that "the soldiers west of the pass are experienced in long spears, so they can not be opposed without an elite, picked vanguard." Ts'ao Ts'ao retorted, "Engaging in

combat lies with me, not with these brigands. Even though they are experienced in long spears, I'll make sure they are unable to stab anything. You only have to watch and see!"

Ts'ao Ts'ao reached T'ung-kuan in the eighth month and assumed a position opposite Ma Chao's forces outside the pass. Then, while resolutely maintaining a defensive posture, he clandestinely dispatched Hsü Yü and Chu Ling with a combined force of 4,000 infantry and cavalry to ford the river at P'u-fan-chin and occupy the western bank of the Yellow River.

The next month, Ts'ao Ts'ao moved northward across the Yellow River from T'ung-kuan. When the troops crossed over, Ts'ao Ts'ao remained alone on the southern bank with slightly more than a hundred tiger warriors to sever the rear. Ma Chao, in command of some 10,000 infantry and cavalry attacked and the arrows fell like rain.

Ts'ao Ts'ao still remained seated on a small stool, unmoving. Hsü Ch'u finally assisted him in boarding their boat, but all the deckhands had been slain by arrows. With his left hand Ch'u shielded Ts'ao Ts'ao with a saddle, with his right he pushed the boat away with an oar. Colonel Ting Fei released all their horses and cattle as bait, throwing the brigands into chaos when they raced about to seize them. Ts'ao Ts'ao was then able to cross the Yellow River and later recross into Ho-hsi, the area west of the Yellow River, at P'u-fan.

Thereafter, the armies followed the river downward, creating a passage as they went southward. Ma Chao and the others retreated (westward) to resist them at the junction of the Wei and Yellow Rivers. Ts'ao Ts'ao deployed numerous false troops and clandestinely employed boatloads of soldiers to enter the Wei where they constructed a floating bridge.

That night he divided these troops into encampments along the southern bank of the Wei River. Chao's coalition forces launched a night attack against them but were repulsed by a sudden assault by troops already deployed in ambush. Chao then similarly encamped on the southern bank before dispatching emissaries with an offer to cede the land west of the Yellow River in order to achieve a peace accord, but Ts'ao Ts'ao declined.

In the ninth month Ts'ao Ts'ao advanced his (remaining) armies across the Wei River. Ma Chao attempted to provoke them into battle but Ts'ao Ts'ao refused, so Ma persistently sought to cede territory and even offered to provide his son as a hostage, prompting Ku Hsü to suggest that they could feign acceptance. Queried by Ts'ao Ts'ao as to his plan, Hsü replied "It's just to cause dissension." Ts'ao Ts'ao then exclaimed that he understood.

Han Sui requested a meeting with Ts'ao Ts'ao. As they were longtime acquaintances, when their horses met they spoke about past times without ever mentioning military affairs. But when they spoke about their early days together in the capital, Ts'ao Ts'ao patted his hand and they laughed together. At this time as the Ch'in and Hu troops were crowded together about them, Ts'ao Ts'ao laughingly said, "Do you want to see Ts'ao Ts'ao? He's also a man and doesn't have four eyes and two mouths, but just knows a lot more!"

After they separated, Ma Chao asked Han Sui what they had discussed. When he replied nothing at all, Ma grew suspicious. Another day Ts'ao Ts'ao sent Han a letter that had numerous erasures and corrections, as if Han Sui had made some changes to it, causing Ma to increasingly doubt him. On the day set for the battle, Ts'ao Ts'ao initially sent his light troops forth to provoke them. Only after they had fought for a long time did he release his tiger cavalry to suddenly strike both flanks, shattering them and killing several subordinate commanders. Han Sui and Ma Chao fled to Liang-chou, others raced to An-ting.

Since the ostensible attack on Chang Lu had been predicted to precipitate a revolt of the independent, though still nominally court-recognized generals in the Kuan-chung region, Ts'ao Ts'ao may well have been deliberately seeking a pretext to extirpate them and consolidate power within that relatively isolated and well-protected area. He achieved his fundamental objective through a variety of techniques ranging from misdirection intended to entangle their forces through estrangement designed to cause dissension and thereby subvert their readiness:

> Ts'ao Ts'ao's generals queried him, "At the outset, when the brigands occupied T'ung-kuan and the area north of the Wei River was bereft of troops, why didn't you proceed through Ho-tung and strike Feng-yi rather than mounting a defense at T'ung-kuan, only fording to the north days later?"
>
> Ts'ao Ts'ao replied: "The brigands were defending T'ung-kuan, but if we had entered Ho-tung they would certainly have shifted their forces to occupy the fords and we would have been unable to cross over west of the Yellow River. I therefore deliberately flourished our troops at T'ung-kuan to draw them southward. When the defenses of the West Ho area emptied out,[6] you two generals were able to take possession of it.[7] I then shifted our forces to the north as the brigands were unable to contend with us for the West Ho region because of your two armies. Linking our wagons and setting up palisades we made a passage southward, what is referred to as 'being unconquerable,' and moreover displayed weakness.
>
> "We made the enemy arrogant by establishing fortifications and refusing to come forth after we crossed the Wei. Thus, rather than erect any fortifications, the brigands simply sought to yield some territory (to secure peace). I verbally accorded with their requests and apparently matched their intent in order to make them feel secure and not undertake any preparations. By nurturing the strength of our officers and troops, one morning we were able to strike them so swiftly that it was like 'being unable to cover one's ears at a sudden thunderclap.' There is not a single Tao for the army's changes and transformations."[8]

Rather than fearing their coalition army, Ts'ao Ts'ao actively structured the generals' response to attain the troop concentration required for a decisive battle, thereby avoiding a lengthy campaign against dispersed but well-entrenched troops:

> At the outset, when all the generals within Kuan-chung arrived, Ts'ao Ts'ao surprisingly had a pleased look. Queried by his generals as to the reason, he replied, "The area within Kuan-chung is long and distant. If these brigands were to occupy all the ravines and defiles, even a year or two would not be sufficient to subjugate them. Once they assembled, even though their troops were numerous, no one was willing to submit to anyone else, so the army lacked a director. To have the opportunity to extinguish them with a single effort, a remarkably easy task, made me happy."

Insofar as the classic military writings emphasize actively dispersing the enemy's forces so as to leverage strength and then exploiting the resulting tactical imbalance of power to either vanquish or cower them into surrendering without fighting, Ts'ao Ts'ao's approach was truly unorthodox. Nevertheless, by "deploying into a configuration to which the enemy must respond" he "excelled at moving the enemy" and thus implemented a fundamental principle from the *Art of War*.[9]

Under the topic of "Estrangement" the *Hundred Unorthodox Strategies* states: "Whenever engaging an enemy in warfare, you should secretly await the appearance of discord among their rulers and ministers, for then you can dispatch spies in order to estrange them further. If a ruler and his subordinates become mutually suspicious and doubtful of each other, you can employ elite troops to exploit the opportunity and inevitably gain your desires. A tactical principle from the *Art of War* states: 'If they are united, cause them to be separated.'" More specifically, the *Art of War* observes: "In antiquity, those who were referred to as excelling in the employment of the army were able to keep the enemy's forward and rear forces from connecting; the many and few from relying upon each other;

the noble and lowly from coming to each other's rescue; the upper and lower ranks from trusting each other; and the troops to be separated, unable to reassemble, or when assembled, not to be well ordered."[10]

Rather than employing spies and double agents, Ts'ao Ts'ao personally undertook the effort. His innocuous meeting with Han Sui in which they only recounted former experiences would have been dubious enough without deliberately reinforcing the desired impression of collusion with boisterous, laughing behavior. The actual events were more readily transformed into an apparent facade because Ma Chao's father and Han Sui had previously been bitter enemies prior to their tenuous reconciliation. Only because the ten generals commanded independent, localized forces were Han Sui and Ma Chao, both beneficiaries of powerful family heritages, forced into an otherwise undesirable, temporary coalition. This multiplicity of contending forces prevented the cohesiveness necessary to act effectively, precluding any one leader from making stringent demands on the other members of a multi-party coalition marked by ever-shifting alliances and loyalties.

Although it was relatively easy for Ts'ao Ts'ao to initiate this estrangement plot, he ensured its success by subsequently dispatching an innocuous letter marred by multiple corrections. Since no gentleman, let alone Ts'ao Ts'ao, would have been so impolite as to dispatch a missive without either personally rewriting it or having it rewritten, it readily created the appearance that Han Sui had altered the characters to prevent others from becoming aware of the original, presumably damaging contents. (Equally possible, Ts'ao Ts'ao's intent might be interpreted as marking certain characters that convey a secret message.) Although the sequence seems somewhat improbable, its success was probably assured because Sui's receipt of a personal letter from Ts'ao Ts'ao would probably have become common knowledge and he could not possibly avoid being queried about the contents.[11]

Ts'ao Ts'ao facilitated his manipulation of the enemy by deferentially refusing battle to foster arrogance just as the Art of War early on advised and the Hundred Unorthodox Strategies would restate under the rubric of "arrogance": "Whenever the enemy's forces are exceedingly strong and you cannot be certain of defeating them, you must speak humbly and cultivate obsequious behavior in order to make them arrogant. Wait until there is some political pretext that can be exploited, then with a single mobilization you can destroy them. A tactical principle from the *Art of War* states:[12] 'Be deferential to make them arrogant.'" Ts'ao Ts'ao reinforced this impression of weakness by only employing ordinary troops at the outset of the final clash and retaining his elite forces until the enemy had grown weary. Once committed, they easily overwhelmed their overconfident opponents, though Ma Chao escaped and subsequently joined Liu Pei before eventually dying from illness.

Ts'ao Ts'ao displayed the great courage for which he is noted by resolutely but somewhat foolhardily not moving during the rear action covering their withdrawal. Only an unorthodox ploy—the release of the oxen and horses, rewards far too valuable to be ignored—saved the day, though not because he ordered it. However, another episode from Ts'ao Ts'ao's career that unfolded just prior to the clash at Kuan-tu was subsequently adopted as the historical illustration for "Bait" in the *Hundred Unorthodox Strategies*:

> During the fifth year of Emperor Hsien's Chien-an reign period in the Later Han Dynasty, Yüan Shao dispatched an army to attack the city of Pai-ma. Ts'ao Ts'ao attacked and defeated them, killing Yüan's general Yen Liang and breaking the siege of Pai-ma. Ts'ao Ts'ao then moved the city's inhabitants westward, but Yüan Shao pursued them. When the army and people reached the south bank at Yen ford, Ts'ao Ts'ao established a holding force within wooden palisades on the southern slopes and then ordered his cavalrymen to remove their saddles and release their horses.
>
> At this time their baggage train from Pai-ma was just arriving and Ts'ao Ts'ao's generals thought that because the enemy's cavalry were numerous, it would be best to return to the protection of the encampment. Hsün Yü said: "This is what is referred to as an army acting as bait, so how can we abandon our exposure?"
>
> Yüan Shao's two cavalry generals, in command of five or six thousand cavalrymen, arrived in succession. Ts'ao Ts'ao's generals

advised that they should mount their horses, but Ts'ao Ts'ao resisted. After a while the number of enemy cavalry had increased
even further. Someone among the enemy yelled out, "Divide
and go after the baggage train," so Ts'ao Ts'ao shouted "Now!"
They all mounted their horses and loosed the attack, severely
defeating them.

Finally, Ts'ao Ts'ao displayed a mastery of both traditional and innovative tactics in the campaign against Ma Chao with his actions along the
Wei River. First, he augmented the apparent size of his troops and disguised their displacement by employing numerous flags and other measures, just as previously seen in the Han and advised across the ages. Next,
he moved swiftly and unexpectedly, entering the Wei region and establishing a crossing at a difficult and therefore unanticipated point by cobbling
together a pontoon bridge. Then, rather than becoming overconfident, he
established precautionary ambushes, allowing a devastating and no doubt
astonishing response to Ma Chao's nighttime strike. Thoroughly frustrated, rather than risk further defeats, Ma sought to conclude a peace accord that would allow him to retain control of at least part of the disputed
territory, only to be rebuffed and compelled to seek a battlefield resolution essentially on Ts'ao Ts'ao's terms.

Ts'ao Ts'ao's second famous exploitation of unorthodox measures, the
most famous incendiary raid in Chinese history, occurred while he was
besieged by Yüan Shao's vastly superior armies at Kuan-tu.[13] Prior to this,
while Ts'ao Ts'ao had been vanquishing various challengers from 197
through 198 CE, the powerful military aristocrat Yüan Shao had gained
control of much of the north and could thus field at least 100,000 infantry
and nearly 20,000 cavalry in the campaign against him. However, Yüan
Shao's troops were little unified, constantly suffered from a shortage of
provisions, and were exhausted after three years of combat. Moreover,
they had to penetrate perimeter defenses deployed along the Yellow River
and defeat a primary, highly animated holding force at Kuan-tu just to
reach Ts'ao Ts'ao's bastion at Hsü-ch'ang.

Rather than seeking a swift, essentially preemptive victory, Yüan secured his rear and proceeded in measured fashion, apparently ensuring a continuous flow of supplies by employing 10,000 wagons for transport. He also neutralized external threats with judicious alliances and improved the army's command and control, but generally ignored the cavalry and the possibility of maneuver to concentrate his superior numbers rather than segment them for multiple strikes, contrary to Sun-tzu's advice. Conversely, still threatened by leaders such as Liu Piao and Chang Hsi, heavily embattled Ts'ao Ts'ao could only field 30,000 men precariously close to starvation. However, his advisors discerned critical flaws in Yüan Shao's character—they considered him greedy, ignorant, cowardly, jealous, and suspicious.

Ts'ao Ts'ao dispatched 20,000 troops to Li-yang, deployed numerous small contingents to key areas and strong points on the flanks and rear, and shifted 10,000 soldiers to Kuan-tu, where he mounted his primary defense because Yüan's forces would be compelled to undertake an amphibious attack across the Chi River. In the second month, 200 CE, Yüan finally launched his southern offensive with perimeter strikes that saw Ts'ao Ts'ao withdraw from Li-yang, but also one of Yüan's generals defeated and killed in a collateral action at Pai-ma:[14]

In the fifth year of the Chien-an reign period at the end of the Later Han dynasty, Ts'ao Ts'ao and Yüan Shao were locked in a stalemate on opposite sides of the river at Kuan-tu. Yüan Shao dispatched his lieutenant generals Kuo K'uo, Ch'un Yeh-ch'eng, and Yen Liang to attack Ts'ao Ts'ao's general Liu Yen, Grand Protector for the Eastern Commandery, at the city of Pai-ma. Yüan Shao himself led his troops to Li-yang and prepared to cross the Yellow River.

In the fourth month of summer (June), Ts'ao Ts'ao was about to proceed north to rescue Liu Yen at Pai-ma when Hsün Yü offered this advice: "Right now our soldiers are few and not a match for the enemy. However, it will become possible if we can segment their strategic power. If my Lord proceeds to Yen-chin and then fords the Yellow River to move toward Yüan Shao's rear, he will certainly respond by moving west. Then your light forces can suddenly strike Pai-ma, surprising them where they are unprepared and general Yen Liang can be captured." Ts'ao Ts'ao adopted his advice.

Hearing that Ts'ao's troops were about to cross the Yellow River, Yüan Shao divided his forces and went west in response. Ts'ao Ts'ao then led his own army on a double pace advance to race to Pai-ma. Before they had proceeded ten miles, Yen Liang, greatly startled, came forth to counter-attack. Ts'ao Ts'ao deputed Chang Liao and Kuan Yü to move forward and attack them. They destroyed Yen's forces, beheaded Yen himself, and subsequently extricated the city of Pai-ma from its siege.

Exemplifying his frequent use of varying and imaginative tactics, Ts'ao Ts'ao managed to ambush Yüan's pursuing forces to gain another unexpected victory. Yüan Shao then gingerly attempted to exploit his numerical advantage by deputing secondary forces in maneuver down through the west, dispatching Liu Pei to strike toward the capital and a second force to proceed in a smaller arc. Perhaps because their numbers were insufficient, both were summarily defeated by highly motivated troops under Ts'ao Jen and others.

Seeking a decisive confrontation, Yüan then moved the bulk of his forces south in the eighth month, by which time Ts'ao Ts'ao's situation had deteriorated further. Although suffering constant shortages, increasing defections among his own and allied troops, and even the risk of subversion, Ts'ao Ts'ao maintained his defensive posture because retreat meant extinction. Fortunately, the six-month standoff was resolved when one of Yüan's frustrated commanders defected and provided detailed knowledge of their supply depot roughly forty *li* to the north, where some 10,000 wagons and an equal number of troops were concentrated but no perimeter defenses or scouting operations had been undertaken.

Ts'ao Ts'ao immediately mounted a night assault with 5,000 disguised cavalry flying the enemy's banners. Proceeding by an indirect route and deflecting all challenges by claiming they had been sent to reinforce the camp against sudden attack, they mounted an incendiary attack and then exploited the succeeding chaos to slaughter the defenders and complete the destruction. As succinctly retold in the *Hundred Unorthodox Strategies* under the topic of "Provisions":

At the end of the Later Han dynasty, Ts'ao Ts'ao and Yüan Shao were locked in a stalemate on opposite sides of the river at Kuan-tu. When Yüan Shao wanted to dispatch provisions to his army he had Ch'un Yeh-ch'eng and four others, in command of more than 10,000 troops, escort them. They encamped about forty miles north of Shao's position.

Hsü Yu, Shao's chief-of-staff, was covetous and greedy. As Yüan Shao did not employ him in a way that satisfied him, he fled to join Ts'ao Ts'ao and then encouraged him to take action: "Right now Yüan Shao has more than 10,000 provision wagons nearby but they lack strong defensive preparations. If you should suddenly strike them with light troops and incinerate their accumulated supplies, in less than three days Yüan Shao will have defeated himself."

Ordering Ts'ao Hung to remain behind to guard their encampment, Ts'ao Ts'ao then personally took command of more than 5,000 infantry and cavalry. They all carried the flags and pennants of Shao's army, even gagged the soldiers' and horses' mouths, and went forth at night along back roads. Someone carrying a bundle of firewood they passed along the way queried them, to which Ts'ao Ts'ao replied: "Duke Shao, being afraid that Ts'ao Ts'ao might plunder our rear army, has dispatched these troops to augment their preparedness." The wood carrier believed it to be true. In this fashion they arrived at their destination without incident, surrounded the encampment, and set extensive fires. The soldiers in the camp were frightened and confused, and Ts'ao Ts'ao inflicted a severe defeat.

Yüan Shao found himself in a dilemma upon learning of Ts'ao Ts'ao's un-expected raid: whether to immediately attack Kuan-tu en masse since its de-fenses had been significantly depleted or dispatch a large force to rescue the supply depot and vanquish the attackers. Essentially he attempted both, or-dering a massive, direct assault on Kuan-tu despite having failed to reduce it for some six months while also dispatching cavalry to the supply depot. Aware of the latter's imminent arrival, Ts'ao Ts'ao concentrated upon de-stroying it before defeating the onrushing reinforcements and then hasten-ing back. Meanwhile, realizing he was doomed for failing to overrun the bastion at Kuan-tu, the assault commander simply surrendered with all his troops and equipment. Ts'ao Ts'ao then counterattacked Yüan Shao's re-maining, dispirited troops and achieved total victory. Yüan barely escaped with just 800 men while his forces suffered upwards of 70,000 casualties.

The turning point at Kuan-tu was of course the nighttime raid that ex-ploited both disguise and intelligence, though the latter was fortuitously obtained from a greedy defector. The enemy's provisions were destroyed with a single effort mounted by minimal troops and an apparently in-evitable outcome reversed. The incident loomed so large in the Three Kingdoms period that, as just noted, it would be adopted as the historical illustration for the topic of "provisions," whose tactical discussion states:

Now when your forces and the enemy are maintaining fortified positions in a standoff, with victory and defeat still undecided, whoever has provisions will be victorious. Accordingly, you must vigorously augment the protective measures for your own supply lines, fearing that the enemy's troops might seize your provi-sions. Moreover, you should dispatch elite troops to sever the en-emy's supply routes. Then, since the enemy lacks provisions, their troops must withdraw and an assault on them will produce victory. A tactical principle from the *Art of War* states: "An army without provisions and foodstuffs is lost."[15]

The Clash at Ch'ih Pi

The Battle of Ch'ih Pi or Red Cliffs unfolded in 208 CE, when Ts'ao Ts'ao, who had been amassing power in the north of China, defeated Liu Piao and, after integrating his forces, particularly the naval units, moved to crush both Eastern Wu and Liu Pei, then tenuously based in the southwest but relying for his very survival on Eastern Wu and its ruler, Sun Ch'üan.[16] According to early historical records, prior to the actual battle Ts'ao Ts'ao deployed some secondary forces to fragment Sun Ch'üan's power, but the thrust of the campaign was simply the direct movement of both naval and infantry forces down the Yangtze River. However, despite an overwhelming superiority in numbers—perhaps a minimum of 150,000 against 30,000 (compared with the traditionally claimed 800,000 against 50,000)—Ts'ao Ts'ao failed to seize the initiative and even negligently ensconced his forces in port after suffering minor naval setbacks. Moreover, he not only abandoned the aggressor's role but also sacrificed his mobility by lashing his hundreds of vessels together and then erecting wooden catwalks across them and his land encampments on the northern side of the Yangtze River at Ch'ih Pi. Presumably intended to facilitate training and accommodating northern troops who were already beset by illness in the damp south and found the rocking motion uncomfortable, these catwalks were quickly noticed when archers were observed practicing upon them.

Immediately realizing that a fire would rapidly spread throughout the closely packed wooden boats, Huang Kai advised Chou Yü, Wu's commanding general, to mount an incendiary attack. The carefully planned assault employed ten large vessels filled with combustible materials soaked in oil and a number of small, swift boats intended for the troops to escape, their unimpeded approach being made possible by the key ruse of a feigned surrender.

Having commented extensively on the *Art of War*, Ts'ao Ts'ao should have been familiar with Sun-tzu's warning that peace talks and proffered surrenders might be exploited to induce negligence and laxity, yet he permitted himself to be persuaded that Huang wanted to surrender and should be allowed to approach with his forces. The wind fortuitously grew stronger after Huang launched their boats, magnifying the force of their impact and the intensity of the ensuing fires. A great conflagration ensued, land-based attacks increased the casualties, and Ts'ao Ts'ao's forces were decimated, compelling him to flee with just cavalry remnants. Apart from the horrendous losses inflicted by the fires, drownings, and enemy blades at Red Cliffs itself, thousands of disorganized, sick troops later perished on the road or were slaughtered by the southern forces. Even the Heavens themselves turned vengeful by inundating them with torrential rains, rendering the roads impassable.

Ts'ao Ts'ao's defeat at Red Cliffs virtually ensured the empire would be sundered into three for decades and thus significantly altered the course of Chinese history. However, the *San-kuo Yen-yi* dramatically expands the episode, adding several levels of intrigue and a penultimate scene in which Chu-ko Liang mounts a specially constructed altar to compel a change in the wind's direction so that their fireboats would be blown into, rather than away from, Ts'ao Ts'ao's immobilized flotilla. (His success terrifies Chou Yü into attempting to assassinate him with a company of troops, a move Chu-ko Liang had anticipated, allowing him to successfully escape.) The differences greatly enhance Chu-ko Liang's reputation, diminish Chou Yü's stature, and further nurture the sense that cunning and unorthodox plots will allow the disadvantaged to yet prevail.[17]

Several of the novel's dramatic embellishments not only magnify Chu-ko Liang's perspicacity but also create the impression that strategic wisdom and unorthodox techniques can be invincible even in the most disadvantageous circumstances. For example, despite their intrigue-filled relationship, Chu-ko Liang and Chou Yü are portrayed as having simultaneously realized that nothing other than an incendiary attack could prove effective against Ts'ao Ts'ao's massive forces. Chou Yü therefore persuaded a well-known local recluse, P'ang T'ung, to act as a feigned defector and inveigle Ts'ao Ts'ao into lashing his vessels together. P'ang accomplished his mission by persuading Ts'ao Ts'ao that linking the boats into larger aggregates would increase their stability, easing the misery of his nauseous troops. When Ts'ao Ts'ao tested the technique and found it beneficial, he ordered all the vessels to be lashed into units of five and interlinked, precluding their dispersal during a conflagration.

Ts'ao Ts'ao is warned of the danger of incendiary attack in the *San-kuo Yen-yi* but is portrayed as contemptuously dismissing the possibility because the seasonal winter winds were constantly blowing away from the fleet. (Surprisingly, he remains untroubled when the winds suddenly shift.) He also initially attempted to persuade Chou Yü to defect by dispatching an old friend, but during a carefully staged drinking bout Chou tricks him into apparently discovering and stealing a forged letter purportedly containing an offer from Ts'ao Ts'ao's two most effective naval commanders to defect and describing their measures to render the northern navy vulnerable. (Highly experienced riverine commanders who had previously been on Liu Piao's staff, the two had been specifically targeted by Chou Yü to undermine Ts'ao Ts'ao's naval capabilities.) Despite his familiarity with the *Art of War*'s chapter on spies, upon learning of this letter Ts'ao Ts'ao precipitously has them executed only to soon regret his folly.

Unfazed, Ts'ao Ts'ao then sends two false defectors into Chou Yü's camp. However, they are isolated and fed contrived information, including that two other important commanders are willing to defect. In addition, they confirm that Huang Kai, who had offered to defect through an intermediary, had been beaten for the minor offense of speaking out against Chou Yü, thereby validating his cover story and motivation as a disgruntled defector. In addition, his imminent surrender was made even more appealing by his promise to bring over recently received provisions. Finally, in perhaps the most egregious deviation from the conservative historical sources, Chu-ko Liang has an altar specially constructed in order to change the wind's direction to drive their fire boats into the northern fleet. Then, in accord with his arcane knowledge, he performs a lengthy ritual that raises a favorable wind on the third day before escaping to avoid being assassinated by troops dispatched by the now terrified Chou Yü.

Defeat of Ts'ao Jen

A simple clash between Eastern Wu and the nascent state of Wei early in the Three Kingdoms period has historically been cited to illustrate the advantages that can be realized by anticipating the enemy's route.[18] After inflicting a defeat on Ts'ao Ts'ao, who was then engaged in amassing the foundation for his incipient state, generals Chou Yü and Lü Meng from Wu surrounded Ts'ao Jen at Nan-chün. Chou Yü ordered Kan Ning to advance against Yi-ling but Ts'ao Jen dispatched forces to attack him, causing Kan, who was caught in the throes of a siege, to request that troops be sent to extricate them. Although most of Chou Yü's generals felt their forces were too few to act, Lü Meng—a commander traditionally recognized as skilled in formulating unorthodox plans—persuaded Chou Yü that victory could be achieved within ten days.[19]

Lü advised that 300 men be split off to fell trees in the nearby ravines prior to engaging the enemy, thereby clogging the roadway. They then advanced directly to Yi-ling, where half the enemy's troops were slain in the initial encounter. That night Ts'ao Jen's remaining forces tried to escape under the cover of darkness but had to dismount and lead their horses on foot upon encountering the logs. This made them vulnerable to ambushes from troops already pre-positioned along the sides, resulting in the capture of 300 horses.

Chou Yü scored another victory over Ts'ao Jen's main force ensconced in Nan-chün shortly thereafter, compelling him to abandon the city and retreat. Lü Meng's suggestion had thus exploited the terrain's constricted configuration to control the enemy's movements by emplacing obstacles that physically impeded their movement. It wasn't just that the retreating enemy was further decimated, but that the army's basic strength was augmented by capturing the extremely valuable horses that would be vital to any future thrust against Ts'ao Ts'ao in the north.

Defeat of Chu-ko Tan

Chu-ko Tan's rise and defeat occurred during the Three Kingdoms period just when Ssu-ma Yi was usurping power in the northern state of Ts'ao, soon to be renamed Wei by his heirs. The tripart division of China into Shu, Wu, and Wei created tempting possibilities for the era's powerful generals, particularly those operating in the various border regions, should they become disaffected and choose to ally themselves with a contiguous state or, remembering the perverse fate of many successful generals across history, fear execution because of doubt and innuendo.

A loquacious commander who enjoyed "characterizing men," Chu-ko Tan was deputed by Ssu-ma Yi to lead a suppressive campaign against Wang Ling when the latter revolted in the southeast.[20] Despite being less than successful, he was subsequently appointed as a regional commander in southern Wei and entrusted with crushing a revolt in the Shou-ch'un (modern Yang-chou) area just south of the Huai River. Although initiated by his close colleague Wen Ch'in and others, he executed their emissaries and spurned their secret entreaties to join their rebellion. Once he vanquished the rebels, Chu-ko Tan quickly moved his armies toward Shou-ch'un and easily occupied the city because Wang Ch'in and the 100,000 inhabitants had already fled to the hills, marshes, and nearby state of Wu out of fear of reprisal.

Chu-ko Tan was then elevated to the post of southern commander for Yang-chou in order to stabilize the region just in time to confront a Wu force sent to exploit the chaos in southern Wei and overawe them into turning back without conflict. Exploiting the opportunity, he immediately dispatched a pursuit force that readily inflicted significant losses on the retreating army and slew one of their generals, further enhancing his standing with Wei's rulers. Nevertheless, perturbed by the fate of his friends and cognizant of the turbulence around him, Chu-ko Tan expended his personal wealth to attract and retain several thousand skilled warriors that he molded into a deadly personal force.

Exploiting the urgency of a pending attack by Wu, he also requested reinforcements for the defense of Shou-ch'un and the staffing of a series of citadels to be erected along the Huai River that would secure the area. (Traditional sources perhaps prematurely attribute these actions to his desire to simply augment his power and create an impregnable bastion. Such measures, often implemented in later eras, were essential to obstructing any invasion along the Huai.) As always, there was no shortage of detractors back in the court to carp, cast aspersions, and accuse him of planning to revolt. These accusations prompted his preemptive recall to assume the post of Director of Works, but as he realized his loyalty had become suspect and his fate sealed, Chu-ko Tan revolted in the fifth month of 257 CE.

He first neutralized nearby enemies, then assembled some 160,000 men, gathered food supplies for a year, and ensconced himself in the fortified city of Shou-ch'un. The state of Wu enthusiastically supported his independence and professed shift in allegiance by granting appropriate titles and dispatching 30,000 troops under the escaped rebel Wang Ch'in in support. Though hardly a small contingent, they managed to slip through the ever-tightening noose around Shou-ch'un and enter the city without any losses. Strangely, Chu-ko Tan ensconced them all in Shou-ch'un rather than disperse a major portion of his combined forces among the various choke points and citadels, make any attempt to occupy a broad swath of nearby territory, or fortify the area along the Huai River. Thus, Wei's 260,000 men under Ssu-ma Chao were able to approach unimpeded, surround the city, erect several rings of high fortifications, and excavate supplemental moats, totally isolating the rebels. Roving contingents patrolled against any breakouts and a separate relief force dispatched from Wu was repeatedly repulsed at the Li-chiang River, ending any hope of quickly defeating Wei's overwhelming strength.

As the stalemate progressed even Chu-ko Tan's closest associates became troubled and soldiers began to defect in ever increasing numbers. The high-ranking officers were reemployed by Ssu-ma Chao as estrangement agents and they proved effective in encouraging several thousand more men to abandon the city. Attempting to break out of their encirclement, Chu-ko Tan finally constructed numerous siege engines designed to overcome the external fortifications and launched several intense assaults over a period of days in the first month of 258. However, his attacks were always repulsed, the siege equipment being set aflame by incendiary arrows and the men slain by arrows and boulders.

In view of their failure and the prospect of inevitable starvation, several tens of thousands of former Wei troops deserted. Wang Ch'in therefore proposed that the remainder of Chu-ko Tan's forces also depart, thereby conserving their nearly depleted provisions for Wu's more resolute Wu troops. This naturally caused heated conflict because Chu-ko Tan wouldn't relinquish his forces or hopes and he eventually murdered Wang Ch'in. Surprisingly, rather than seeking immediate revenge, Wang's two sons defected to Wei, where they were pardoned and immediately exploited as part of ongoing psychological operations intended to undermine the allegiance and fighting spirit of the remaining rebels.

In the second month, 258 CE, Ssu-ma Chao's forces suddenly launched a massive surprise attack from all four sides that so startled the remaining defenders that they offered no resistance. The rebellion was then formally quashed when Chu-ko Tan was slain while trying to escape along with a few hundred core supporters who loyally refused to surrender and were killed. From the outset Ssu-ma Chao had refused to accede to admonitions that he exploit their numerical superiority to immediately assault the city, feeling it to be wasteful and potentially self-defeating because the enemy was strong, well-organized, adequately provisioned, and ensconced in a solid bastion. Even though they repulsed several breakout attempts he steadfastly maintained this resolve until finally unleashing the surprise attack that exploited not only Shou-ch'un's severely deteriorated condition but also the defenders' belief that he wouldn't attack, thereby enhancing its impact. By thus refusing to take advantage of their superior strength and the city's isolation, he implemented an unorthodox operational strategy and simultaneously heeded Sun-tzu's admonition to refrain from wasteful assaults.[21]

As the tactical discussion for "Slowness" in the *Hundred Unorthodox Strategies* states: "In general, assaulting fortified enemy cities is the lowest form of strategy, to be undertaken only when there is no alternative. However, if their walls are high and their moats deep, their people many and supplies few, while there is no prospect of external rescue and you can thoroughly entangle and take the city, then it will be advantageous. A tactical principle from the *Art of War* states: 'Their slowness is like the forest.'"

When Wei's forces finally assaulted Shou-ch'un the conditions of "numerous soldiers but few supplies" and "high walls and moats but no prospect of rescue" had both been achieved, but only because he had employed temporizing tactics. Conversely, Chu-ko Tan's failure to take aggressive action (such as attacking when the enemy was just deploying outside Shou-ch'un), make the area impregnable, force his enemies to wade through numerous strongpoints and disperse their forces, and generally obstruct and thwart every attempt to reach and besiege their key bastion is astonishing. Despite having been a successful field commander, he not only vacillated but also ensured the victor's success.

Extinction of Shu

One of the fundamental principles repeated throughout China's martial writings for achieving victory is "Attack where they are unprepared, go forth where they will not expect it."[22] The tactical discussion for the *Hundred Unorthodox Strategies*' crucial chapter on unorthodox warfare essentially makes the latter synonymous with its execution: "In general, in warfare what is referred to as the unorthodox means attacking where the enemy is not prepared and going forth when they do not expect it. When engaging an enemy, frighten them in the front and overwhelm them in the rear, penetrate the east and strike in the west, causing them never to know where to mount defensive preparations." Teng Ai's deliberately unorthodox tactics in conquering Shu, the last bastion of the remnant Han dynasty, in 263 CE, is adopted as the chapter's historical illustration:[23]

> During the Three Kingdoms period, in the fourth year of the Ching-yüan era the emperor of Wei summoned his generals to undertake a punitive campaign against the kingdom of Shu. The Grand General of the Army Ssu-ma Hsüan Wang dispatched General Teng Ai to thoroughly entangle Shu's forces under General Chiang Wei in Yung-chou. Meanwhile, Inspector Chu-ko Hsü cut across behind them, preventing Shu's return homeward.
>
> Teng Ai in turn dispatched Wang Ch'i and others to directly assault Chiang Wei's encampment; Ch'ien Hong to press his for-

ward positions; and Yang Hsin to go to Kan-sung. When Chiang Wei learned that Chung Hui's armies had already entered Han-chung commandery, he retreated. However, Wang Ch'i's forces ascended through a mountain pass and badly defeated Chiang Wei, forcing him to flee with his remaining troops.

Subsequently hearing that the Regional Inspector for Yung-chou, Chu-ko Hsü, had already blocked the roads and encamped at Ch'iao-t'ou, Chiang Wei embarked the road to the north through K'ung-han valley in order to come out behind Yung-chou commandery. When Chu-ko Hsü discovered it, he withdrew some thirty miles. After Chiang Wei had himself advanced on the northern road about thirty miles he learned in turn of Chu-ko Hsü's withdrawal and passed through Ch'iao-t'ou. Chu-ko Hsü raced to intercept him but spent the day without making contact.

Chiang Wei subsequently retreated to the east and took up a defensive position at Chien-ko where he was attacked by Chung Hui who proved unable to defeat him. Grand General Teng Ai submitted a memorial to the emperor stating: "Now that the enemy brigands have been pushed to the breaking point, it would be appropriate to go from Yin-p'ing by way of the wretched roads passing through Te-yang-t'ing in Han-chung and race to Fu district, venturing west a hundred miles from Chien-ko and more than 300 miles from Ch'eng-tu so that our unorthodox forces can penetrate their very heart. The defenders at Chien-ko must return to Fu and our forces at Chien-ko can then follow their tracks and advance. If the army deployed at Chien-ko does not return to Fu, Fu will have few troops to respond to our unorthodox attack. The *Military Pronouncements* states: 'Attack where they are not prepared, go forth where they do not expect it.' Now if we can overwhelm their voids and vacuities, we will certainly destroy them."

General Teng Ai advanced more than 700 miles from Yin-p'ing through deserted territory, hacking out a passage through the mountains and building bridges and timber roadways. The mountains were high and the valleys deep, the going extremely arduous. Their supply train was almost exhausted and they were frequently endangered and threatened. Wrapping himself in a coarse blanket, Teng Ai pushed and shoved his way forward. Climbing among the trees and scrambling along the cliffs, his officers and warriors negotiated the mountain trail one after another.

When they reached Chiang-yu, the general in charge of Shu's defense, Ma Miao, surrendered. Shu's imperial guard commander Chu-ko Chan returned to Fu through Mien-chu and arrayed his troops to await Teng Ai. Teng Ai dispatched his son Teng Chung to go forth on the right and Ssu-ma Shih-ch'i on the left. After unsuccessfully engaging the enemy and withdrawing, Chung and Ch'i proclaimed that the brigands could not yet be conquered.

Enraged, Teng Ai, retorted: "The difference between survival and extinction lies in this battle. How can they not be defeated?" Cursing them and the others, he was about to have them both beheaded. However, Chung and Ch'i galloped back, courageously reengaged the enemy in fervent combat, and inflicted a severe defeat. They slew Chu-ko Chan and advanced the army to Ch'eng-tu. Liu Shan then dispatched an emissary with an offer of surrender and the kingdom of Shu was extinguished.

Well protected by numerous mountains, the fertile Szechuan valley was situated in a natural bastion whose sole access apart from the Yangtze River was through narrow passes, often on wooden plankways constructed over the decades at great effort. (Szechuan rulers who wished to temporarily augment their impregnability often burned them just as Liu Pang had in order to conspicuously show his resolve not to return to China's heartland.) A few strategically ensconced stalwart units could thwart any invasion provided that their spirits didn't flag and they met the enemy at forward positions.[24]

Shu's government had been deteriorating after Chu-ko Liang's death even as the great general Ssu-ma Yi was consolidating power in Wei to the north. In addition, Shu shortsightedly withdrew their troops from the vital mountain choke points to effect a new strategy premised upon enticing any invaders onto the interior plains where they could be vanquished. At the end of 263 Wei launched a three-pronged attack whose western and central strike forces each numbered 30,000 men while the eastern arm, itself divided into three prongs, encompassed 120,000. Rapidly transiting the undefended mountains, these forces easily overwhelmed the initial contact defenses, whose total numbers amounted to only 50,000, though another 40,000 remained in reserve about the cities.

Surprisingly, despite the defensive strategy's flaws and the tardy response of secondary forces, their resolute effort temporarily blocked the main advance, exposing Ts'ao-wei's troops to flank and rear attacks and rendering their supply lines untenable. However, Teng Ai's minor 10,000-man aggressor force negotiated a difficult circuitous route and suddenly materialized in Shu's rear, stunning many of the unprepared defenders into surrendered without fighting. Another quick victory brought them to Ch'eng-tu's very walls, whereupon the emperor meekly surrendered.

8

Northern and Southern Dynasties Exemplars

T he so-called Northern and Southern dynasties period that followed the consolidation of the Three Kingdoms, also referred to as the Sixteen States period, saw the realm split into northern and southern principalities before fragmenting even further as the north was subjugated by steppe peoples, dynasties fractured, and new challengers continually arose in the chaos. Several vigorous, innovative practitioners of the unorthodox appeared among the steppe peoples and the martial aristocracy that came to populate the northern part of China despite centuries of effort to deny knowledge of the concepts and principles of Chinese military science to non-Han minorities. Smaller kingdoms necessarily encompassed more limited resources, compelling the leaders to resort to maneuver, cleverness, and innovative battlefield tactics to survive. Several astute generals achieved surprising victories through the use of unorthodox tactics, and a few such as Shih Le, Liu Yü, and Yü-wen T'ai amassed great power and even founded short-lived dynasties.

Late in the third century the northern state of Wei (soon to be renamed Chin), seeking to reunify the realm and dominate All under Heaven, undertook the final conquest of Wu in the southeast.[1] Tu Yü, a remarkable administrator, strategist, and commander who had not only been instrumental in persuading the ruler to initiate the campaign, but also subsequently built canals, reclaimed lands, and taught military science because he feared the principles would be forgotten during peacetime, directed much of the action:

> After Wang Jui had broken through Wu's riverine defenses and vanquished several cities, Tu Yü dispatched Chou Chih in command of 800 unorthodox soldiers to cross the Yangtze at night on light boats and launch a surprise attack on Le-hsiang. After crossing over they set out numerous flags and pennants, ignited fires on Pa mountain, and went forth from the strongpoints in order to seize the rebels' minds.
>
> Terrified, Sun Hsin, Capital Supervisor for Wu, sent a missive to Wu Yen stating that "Several armies have come down from the north and flown over the Yangtze." Meanwhile, more than 10,000 men and women from Wu surrendered. Chou Chih set up ambushes outside Le-hsiang. Then, when the army that Sun Hsin had dispatched to resist Wang Jui returned after being badly defeated, Chou Chih's forces, still held in ambush, followed them into the city. Sun Hsin was unaware of them until they reached his tent and captured him. This is an example of combining the hidden with the visible and employing them together.

Shih Le

Shih Le's (274–333) personal history is the remarkable, though not unprecedented, story of the impoverished descendant of a minor Chieh pastoral clan chief in Shanhsi, on the periphery of Chinese civilization, ascending to emperorship.[2] Marked by an unusual (*ch'i*) aura early on, he survived famine and escaped enslavement to play a key role in terminating the Western Chin dynasty and establish the Later Chao in the western part of fragmented China. A skilled rider and archer, he began his revolt against the Chin (one of whose officials had captured and enslaved him) with a renowned band of sixteen cavalrymen, but readily attracted adherents in an era beset by poverty, starvation, and conflict. Although he quickly achieved several victories, the defeats he also suffered soon persuaded him to align himself with Liu Yüan, then king of the Han.

Through unorthodox techniques, rapid strikes with limited numbers, great personal courage, and good luck his increasingly victorious forces eventually participated in the conquest of Emperor Huai of Chin at Luoyang, reportedly inflicting more than 100,000 casualties in the course of their campaigns. Having occupied Hsiang-kuo (in Hopei), he adopted it as his bastion for future expeditions upon the advice of his strategist Chang Pin. However, he came under attack late in 312 CE by Wang Chün, a brutal and ruthless figure who controlled a major portion of Chin's military might and harbored pretensions to emperorship, but whose antagonization of the populace and his own troops would ultimately undermine him. After suffering several defeats at the hands of Wang's 50,000 troops under their field commander, Shih was compelled to employ Chang Pin's strategy of basically remaining ensconced in their fortifications to avoid disadvantageous, open field clashes. However, they were hardly quiescent, for Shih Le's swift cavalry unexpectedly sprang forth from some dozen concealed sally ports to overwhelm their negligent enemy, blunt the latter's advance, and drive them off, taking several important prisoners and a large amount of weapons and armor. Shih then not only arranged a treaty with the field commander but also converted him into an ally by repatriating prisoners and granting generous gifts, thereby temporarily resolving the siege situation.

Although Wang Chün's power had been declining due to defections, defeats in other conflicts, and the effects of flooding, he remained a major threat. Having learned of Wang's vulnerability through spies and agents, in the tenth month of 313 Shih Le adopted the unorthodox strategic ploy of pretending to acknowledge Wang Chün as his ruler and offered to support his ascension to emperorship. Along with the promise of a formal visit in the near future, he reinforced his protestations of fealty with generous gifts for both Wang and his consort. Meanwhile, to preclude an attack by Wang's sole military rival, Liu K'un, on his vulnerable base or any attempt to rescue Wang once he commenced his onslaught, Shih clandestinely offered to support Liu and subjugate Wang Chün as an expression of loyalty.

In accord with ancient precedent, Shih bribed Wang and his various emissaries, subverted many members of his staff, and early on attracted the allegiance of key generals and officers. He also concealed his elite troops and displayed only minimal numbers of old and tired soldiers so that any observers, corrupted or not, would depict him as weak and non-threatening. Moreover, to persuade them of the depths of his loyalty, he resorted to the melodramatic trick of hanging Wang's missive upon the wall and pretending to be too awestruck to lift his eyes up to view it. He also had his spokesmen persuade Wang that even though he was not without imperial ambitions himself, Shih realized that as a "barbarian" he could never achieve such an exalted objective. Nevertheless, he was like Han Hsin, a kingmaker whom Hsiang Yü had sorely needed but lost, and therefore crucial to Wang's own ambitions. Thus, despite strong assertions by his generals that this "barbarian" could not be trusted, the self-assured Wang allowed himself to be persuaded of Shih's fidelity and utility.

In the third month of 314 Shih Le came east to Yu-chou, site of Wang's palatial encampment, to personally profess his loyalty and deliver valuable gifts. Even as he advanced to the Yi River, Wang Chün—secure in his destiny and the certainty of his power—continued to reject every warning and admonition and angrily had remonstrators executed. To thwart the possibility of an ambush Shih let loose several thousand head of cattle and sheep ostensibly brought as tribute upon reaching the city gates, thereby effectively blocking all movement within the city. He then released his own troops to plunder the city before forcing his way into the palace and seizing the pretender. After castigating him in time-honored, retributive fashion for his offenses and for hoarding massive amounts of grain while the people starved, he sent Wang off for execution, burned the palace, and slew 10,000 of Wang's elite cavalry.

Having quashed the main threat, Shih Le continued to augment and consolidate power in the north, attracting the allegiance of many disaffected steppe peoples in the contiguous regions. He soon betrayed and vanquished Liu K'un[3] and extinguished Former Chao before finally founding Later Chao, assuming its kingship in 319, and proclaiming himself emperor in 329 before dying in 333, after several turbulent decades of colorful, though brutal, military life. Although, contrary to the *Wu-ching Tsung-yao,* Shih Le never "enfeoffed" Wang Chün, he did manipulate his arrogance and successfully vanquish him through the ploy of supposedly supporting his enthronement as self-proclaimed emperor.

Liu Chü

In 317 CE, after his forces had attacked and subjugated Ch'ang-an, extinguishing Western Chin, Liu Ts'ung continued his consolidation efforts by attacking Liu Chü, a highly popular local official who had gained the people's allegiance through his efforts to ameliorate their hardship during a period of famine:[4]

> In the second month Liu Ts'ung, ruler of Han-Chao, dispatched his cousin Liu Ch'ang with 30,000 troops to attack Provincial Governor Liu Chü at Jung-yang. After encamping about 7 *li* from an ancient Han dynasty citadel, Ch'ang sent an emissary with a surrender demand to Chü. As Ch'ang's troops had suddenly arrived, Chü hadn't had any time to prepare. He therefore dispatched a high official to falsely advise that they would surrender. Accordingly, without undertaking any preparations, Ch'ang held a great feast at which all his commanders got drunk.
>
> Liu Chü wanted to mount a surprise attack during the night but his officers and troops were too terrified. He therefore ordered Kuo Sung, his commanding general, to go and pray at Tzu Ch'an's temple where he had the shaman loudly proclaim that "Tzu Ch'an has instructed that he will send spiritual troops to provide assistance." Everyone leapt with enthusiasm upon hearing his pronouncement and competed to go forward.
>
> Liu Chü selected a thousand men of courage and daring who cut across and mounted a surprise attack on the encampment under Sung's leadership, killing several thousand. Only Ch'ang managed to escape.

· Although the ploy of a false surrender, warned against as early as the *Art of War*, was sufficient to encourage the necessary laxity, it was a repetition of T'ien Tan's "spiritual assistance" scenario that provided the confidence necessary to stir Liu Chü's men into decisive action. Accordingly, it is not surprising that despite his military acumen and martial skills, Shih Le also found himself thwarted by Liu Chü in a repetition of the antique "bait" ploy:[5]

> When Liu Chü was in charge of the defense of Ying-yang, Shih Le personally led an army to mount a sudden attack. Liu had the old and weak all enter the mountains and had those remaining disperse the cattle and horses. He then established ambushes and awaited the enemy. When Shih Le's troops were competing with each other to seize the horses and cattle, the forces lying in ambush sprang forth, letting out a unified yell that shook the mountains and valleys before going on to severely destroy Le's forces, capturing and executing a great many. Shih Le then withdrew.

Liu Yü

Among the more ruthless and successful aspirants to power during the Northern and Southern dynasties period was Liu Yü, a powerful Chin commander who eventually declared himself emperor of the early Sung dynasty, which should be distinguished from the more famous Sung dynasty that succeeded the T'ang. The *Wu-ching Tsung-yao* cites several incidents from his life as examples of unorthodox strategies and measures, the earliest of which occurred early in his career while he was serving as commander in chief of Chin's forces.

In 410 CE Liu Yü mounted an expedition northward, leaving a military vacuum in the capital region of Chien-k'ang that could be exploited by such rebellious commanders as Hsü Tao-fu and Lu Hsün, then ensconced in the mountains of Kuantung where large numbers of disaffected populace had augmented their core military forces. Although located in the deep south, they merely had to traverse the local river to reach the Yangtze and exploit its current to advance downstream into Chin's interior.[6]

> Eastern Chin's commander in chief Liu Yü went northward on a campaign against Kuang Ku. The Ling-nan general Hsü Tao-fu cajoled his superior, Lu Hsün: "Today's opportunity absolutely cannot be lost. Once we conquer the capital, even if Liu Yü returns he will be unable to do anything." Lu Hsün acquiesced.
>
> Hsü had earlier secretly wanted to construct warships, so he had ordered that suitable timbers be cut in the area around Nan-k'ang mountain, saying he was going to sell them in the capital. But claiming he lacked the means to forward them, he then sold them off cheaply in Shih-hsing for a fraction of the normal price. The local inhabitants, being destitute, even sold their clothes to buy them for resale. However, because the river current was extremely fast and it was difficult to put boats out they ended up accumulating it all. He did this several times so that the timbers really piled up, yet the common people did not grow suspicious.
>
> When Tao-fu raised his troops (in rebellion), he requisitioned it all, none remained hidden. Bringing it all together, he started building his ships and completed them in ten days. He then mobilized their troops and (sailing down the Yangtze) invaded the districts of Nan-k'ang, Lu-ling, and Yü-chang. The local defensive commanders all abandoned their posts and fled.

Hsü's persuasion of Lu Hsün emphasized their inability to indefinitely hold their limited region in the face of the Li Yü's growing might despite being well ensconced in the mountains. Although reluctant, Lu acquiesced because he couldn't dissuade Hsü. Taking advantage of Hsü's unorthodox method (and his realization that the current would preclude small traders from shipping the wood out), they quickly accumulated the materials necessary to construct the indispensable boats without the ever-present government spies realizing their intent and reporting it back to the capital in time for the latter to make defensive preparations or mount a preemptive strike.

Their cleverness and foresight provided the transport basis for a multi-pronged invasion into the contiguous provinces that initially achieved considerable success. Victories were scored over forces commanded by Ho Wu-chi and Liu Yi, causing much trepidation in Chin. However, within a few months they were repulsed by Liu Yü and ultimately perished early the next year, reportedly in part because Lu Hsün was a man "of many plans but little resolution."

Liu Yü and Liu Yi had originally been close associates, but they grew apart at the end of the Chin as Yü became more powerful. When he felt incapable of tolerating further affronts from the increasingly rebellious Liu Yi, Liu Yü initiated a campaign against Yi's stronghold of Chiang-ling in 412 CE. Just before they mobilized, Wang Chen-eh proposed that a rapid thrust be launched by a small contingent that would exploit a disinformation effort designed to make it appear that Liu Fan, one of Liu Yi's staunch allies, was coming up with his army:[7]

> When Emperor Wu (Liu Yü) of the Sung was planning an extirpation campaign against Liu Yi, Wang Chen-eh suggested: "If you want to go west to Ch'u, please give me a hundred boats to race ahead." The emperor appointed Wang as overall military commander and K'uai En as commander of the hundred ships acting as an advance front. The emperor ordered that, if possible, they should attack the enemy; otherwise, they should burn the enemy's boats and wait at the perimeter.
>
> Wang set forth as soon as he received his orders, traveling at a double pace both night and day, simultaneously spreading word that Liu Fan's army was proceeding upstream. Liu Yi, who regarded the reports as creditable, didn't realize he was about to be suddenly attacked.
>
> When he was 20 *li* from the city of Chiang-ling, Wang abandoned the boats and advanced with his infantry, though K'uai En still acted as commander of the vanguard and Wang fol-

lowed behind. Back at the shore he left behind one or two men per boat, instructing them to set their flags and drums up on the shore and then beat the drums in good order just when he was about to reach Chiang-ling so as to create the impression of a large army to the rear. He also ordered men to go and burn Liu Yi's boats at Chiang-chin.

While Wang was proceeding directly toward the city to mount a sudden attack, the people all said that Liu Fan's army was coming up, a report that wasn't doubted. Just when Wang was about to reach the city, general Chu Hsien-chih raced out to inquire where Liu Fan might be. The soldiers replied that he was at the rear, but when he reached the rear and saw that Liu Fan wasn't there, noticed their ships were on fire in the distance, and could hear the strong beat of drums, he knew it wasn't Fan advancing and reared up his horse to race and inform Liu Yi.

Although he yelled out to close the gates behind him, Wang (and a small contingent) raced in with him and then exploited the wind to set fire to the city's southern and eastern gates. Battling the troops within the larger confines, by noon the Sung troops had defeated and scattered the defenders. Wang punched through into the central citadel—the golden city—and then sent men to present the emperor's edict and a handwritten letter to Liu Yi. Liu Yi burned them all without looking at them and engaged Wang's forces with his remaining commanders.

Initially no one within the city had believed that the emperor was actually coming, but during the conflict, as fathers battled sons and relatives clashed, they learned the truth and became frightened. By nightfall all the previously obedient soldiers had scattered and the loyal commanders had been killed. Yi and his remnant forces remained barricaded in the eastern and western towers and continued to resist.

Fearing that his troops would wound each other in the darkness, Wang Chen-eh led them in surrounding the inner citadel but left the south side open. Suspecting that there would be an ambush on the south side, Liu Yi opened the north gate and rushed out in the middle of the night at the head of about 300 men. He raced to the Niu-mu temple and sought refuge but was denied because he had previously slain another general who had similarly sought refuge there, as well as the monk who had been protecting him. Realizing the hopelessness of his situation, he then hanged himself.[8]

The force that so easily penetrated Liu Yi's perimeter and then crushed the city gained entrance by exploiting the inhabitants' expectation and employing disinformation to induce laxity and inaction. Rather than mounting a large, riverine-based campaign and undertaking a lengthy, debilitating siege, they were thus able to employ surprise and a small contingent to overcome a severe tactical imbalance of power.

Shortly thereafter, in 414 CE, T'an Chih, one of T'an Tao-chi's older brothers, astutely employed his understanding of the enemy together with a clever ruse to thwart raiders:[9]

> During the Sung when T'an Chih was serving as minister in Kuang-ling, the fugitive Ssu-ma Kuo-p'an brothers gathered several hundred troops along the northern border in Hsü-chou and then secretly crossed the Huai River. Taking advantage of the darkness of a moonless night, they led more than a hundred men to climb the walls of Kuang-ling. Gaining entrance, they yelled out that they should go directly to the administrative chamber.
>
> Startled, T'an Chih arose and went out the door to resolve the situation but the brigands shot him with an arrow that deeply penetrated his thigh. He then secretly said to his attendants, "The brigands gained entrance in the darkness and attacked when we were not prepared. But when the fifth watch comes they will fear the dawn and certainly withdraw." When the brigands heard the beating of the drum and thought dawn was breaking, they fled and scattered. T'an's soldiers pursued and attacked them, capturing or slaying them all.

Although unstated, the unorthodox measure of prematurely beating the drum frightened the bandits into a hectic, easily exploited retreat, extricating T'ao Chih and the others from their dire situation.

A precursor to the famous "empty city ploy" found in the *Thirty-six Stratagems* that unfolded in 431 CE features T'an Chih's brother, the renowned but ill-fated T'an Tao-chi, who frequently employed multiple ruses and deceptions to manipulate the enemy, as in this example in which he created a facade of "deliberately feigned" substantiality and employed the old chimera of ample provisions:[10]

> When T'an Tao-chi supervised the campaign of rectification, he fought more than thirty engagements with Wei's forces, emerging victorious in most of them. However, when the army reached Li-ch'eng their supply lines were exhausted so he turned back. Some of his troops surrendered to Wei and reported that their provisions and foodstuffs were depleted and that the officers and troops, troubled and fearful, lacked resolution. That night Tao-chi had sand sacked up and then put their remaining grain atop the sacks. At dawn, when Wei's forces learned that he had a surplus of provisions, they no longer pursued them and also beheaded the deserters for making false reports as an example.
>
> At this time Tao-chi's troops were few and weak and everyone within the army was afraid. Tao-chi therefore ordered them to dispense with their armor and mount the wagons unencumbered before leisurely going forth out of the encirclement. Wei's armies feared an ambush and dared not press them, enabling them to return. Although Tao-chi didn't conquer Honan, he returned with his entire army.

Going back slightly to 417 CE, at the outset of a campaign to expand Chin's territory, Liu Yü's forces were proceeding westward along the Yellow River to attack Later Ch'in at Ch'ang-an when he was compelled to simultaneously battle the To-ba or Northern Wei ensconced north of the

Yellow River.[11] The To-ba dispersed as many as 100,000 roving cavalrymen along the northern banks to guard against potential Chin subterfuge and incursions. The actions of a subordinate general, Chu Chao-shih, proved crucial in deflecting the threat:[12]

> A force of several thousand cavalry from Wei shadowed the fleet's progress as it moved westward from the northern bank. Because the Sung army was pulling their boats from the southern bank with 100 *chang* long ropes, whenever the wind and waves grew intense a few boats floated across to the northern bank where the occupants were immediately slain by Wei's soldiers. Liu Yü dispatched troops to attack them but they ran off whenever Sung cavalry ascended the bank, only to return once the Sung contingent departed.
>
> In the fourth month, summer, Liu Yü ordered Ting Wu, commander of his "hundred stalwarts," to lead 700 warriors and a hundred wagons across to the northern bank where they were to advance inland about a hundred paces and then deploy in a crescent formation. The end vehicles were to abut the river bank and be guarded by seven warriors each. He was to raise a white pennant once their deployment was complete.
>
> None of Wei's forces moved because they did not understand the actions mounted by this small contingent. Yü had previously ordered the commander of the crescent deployment, Chu Chao-shih, to rigorously prepare and lead 2,000 men to race over to them as soon as the pennant was raised. They also brought one hundred large crossbows (that were dispersed one to a wagon), augmented each of the wagons with twenty men, and set defensive screens up on the axles. Seeing that an emplacement had been established, Wei advanced and besieged it.
>
> Because Chu initially employed weak bows and small arrows to shoot at them, Wei's forces closed in from every direction. After Chang Sun-sung of Wei brought another 30,000 cavalry up in support, they launched human wave attacks from all four

sides. Chu then had the hundred crossbows fire in unison but Wei's forces were too numerous to control.

When they had set out Chu had brought along a thousand long spears, so he had hatchets used to hack them down to a length of 3 or 4 feet. Each spear then penetrated three or four of the enemy. Wei's army could not withstand them and crumbled.

Although the text does not specify how these improvised weapons were employed, they must have functioned as giant bolts and been fired from the large, undoubtedly wagon-mounted crossbows. The hatchets were also reportedly used to flatten out the spear tips, increasing their penetrating ability. Although a remarkable achievement under the duress of battle, the crescent deployment that temporarily mystified the enemy and allowed the Sung forces to gain a foothold was equally unorthodox, as was the initial use of weak bows to deliberately lure the enemy closer. Only through the integrated use of all three were the Sung able to overcome the severe tactical imbalance and terrain disadvantages confronting them.

The unorthodox nature of the assault mounted at the end of the campaign against Later Ch'in also attracted the attention of subsequent military writers. The following incident, which centers upon the actions of Shen T'ien-tzu, a Chin commander who earlier in the year had scored two significant victories against Hou Ch'in's campaign forces, is featured in Wang Yü-yu's theoretical introduction to his chapter "Decisive Warfare Is Foremost":[13]

As Shen T'ien-tzu and Fu Hung-tzu advanced through Wu-kuan pass in the seventh month of autumn, Later Ch'in's troops all abandoned the cities and fled. They continued their advance until encamping near Ch'ing-ni. Yao Hung, Later Ch'in's ruler, had Yao Ho-tu encamp at Yao-liu to resist them. In the eighth month Liu Yü shifted his forces to Min-hsiang while Shen and Fu prepared to attack Yao-liu.

Yao Hung wanted to personally take command of the army and go forth to oppose Liu Yü's main army but feared that

Shen would mount a sudden strike on his rear. He therefore decided to attack and eliminate Shen before overturning the state to go eastward against Liu. Accordingly, he led several tens of thousands of infantry and cavalry to intercept Shen's forces at Ch'ing-ni.

Having been basically intended to act as a diversion, Shen T'ien-tzu's force only amounted to slightly more than a thousand men. When he heard that Yao Hung had come up, he wanted to attack him but Fu Hung-chih opposed him because their numbers were too few to match the enemy.

Shen T'ien-tzu then said, "The army esteems employing the unorthodox, not just masses. Today we are not a match for the enemy in terms of numbers so both powers cannot endure. If they manage to solidify their encirclement we will have nowhere to escape. It would be better to exploit their recent arrival, their encampment and fortifications not having yet been established, to attack them first. In this way we can achieve success." He then led those under his command off in an advance and Fu followed on.

The forces from Ch'in surrounded them several layers deep. Shen T'ien-tzu inspired his men and officers by saying "You have all come from afar and braved danger just for today's engagement. Life and death will be decided in one encounter, opportunity for enfeoffment lies here." The officers and troops enthusiastically beat the drums and shouted, took up their short weapons and fervently struck, and Ch'in's army was badly defeated. Shen's army slew over 10,000 of the enemy and captured the emperor's chariot, clothes, and insignia. Yao Hung, Later Ch'in's ruler, fled back to Pa-shang.

The *Tzu-chih T'ung-chien* adds that "because Shen's troops were few, initially Liu Yü had dispatched Shen Lin-tzu in command of another army from Ch'in-liang to assist him, but by the time he arrived Ch'in had already been defeated. He therefore joined with Shen T'ien-tzu in pursuing them and many of the districts within the pass secretly sent supplies to T'ien-tzu."

Shen's decision to attack even though vastly outnumbered rather than adopt the normal defensive response of ensconcing oneself in a fortified position in a desperate attempt to survive was a bold, unorthodox measure. He thus not only deliberately cast them onto "fatal terrain," but also proved to be a skillful motivator in a tradition of Chinese martial psychology that dates back to Sun-tzu and Sun Pin's *Military Methods*.[14]

Although not cited in any of the military manuals, Wang Chen-eh's immediately subsequent actions provide another example of concretely actualizing Sun-tzu's principle of exploiting fatal terrain to elicit maximum effort from otherwise doomed troops through unorthodox measures:[15]

> Wang requested permission to lead a riverine force up the Yellow River into the Wei River in order to race to Ch'ang-an and Li Yü agreed. General Yao Nan of Ch'in withdrew his army westward and Wang Chen-eh pursued him. Later Ch'in's ruler Yao Hung withdrew his army from Pa-shang and encamped at Shih-ch'iao (Stone Bridge, over the Wei) in order to support him. The general in charge of northern defenses, Yao Chiang, and Yao Nan united their armies and encamped above the Ching River in order to resist Wang. Wang had Mao Te-tsu advance in an assault, destroying them. Yao Chiang died and Yao Nan fled to Ch'ang-an.
>
> (After some Ch'in redeployments), Wang Chen-eh proceeded up the Wei River against the current. As the sailors were all concealed within small, covered assault vessels and Chin's observers saw the boats advancing upstream without any sailors, they were startled and thought they must be some sort of spirits.[16] On the morning of *jen-hsü*, Wang reached Wei-ch'iao (Wei Bridge) and ordered the army's warriors to eat their fill then take up their staves and ascend the bank, the last to ascend to be executed. When they finished clambering up the bank, all the boats floated away in the rapid current and their

positions were soon unknown. At that time Yao Hung still had several ten thousand men.

Wang Chen-eh harangued his officers and troops, "Our homes are in Chiang-nan (south of the Yangtze), 10,000 *li* away from Ch'ang-an's northern gate. Our boats and oars, clothes and provisions have already floated away. Today, if we advance and are victorious, our achievements and fame will be glorious. If we are not victorious, our bones will not be returned. There is no alternative, you must all exert yourselves!"

Then he personally led the officers and troops forward. Everyone fervently competed to be in the forefront and they severely defeated Yao P'i at Wei-ch'iao. When Yao Hung withdrew his army to rescue them, they were trampled by Pi's defeated troops and collapsed without fighting. Numerous commanders perished while Hung was alone able to return to the palace on a single horse.

Though Liu Yü would not yet assume regency of the Chin, this battle ended the short-lived Later Ch'in dynasty. Spurning his eleven-year-old son's admonition to commit suicide, Yao Hung fled on to Shih-ch'iao then finally surrendered, though his son flung himself off a palace wall and died.

Other Notable Unorthodox Commanders

When Northern Wei experienced internal strife in 531 CE, Ho-pa Yüeh was designated to lead the court's suppressive response. Fearing an ill outcome whether he succeeded or failed, Ho-pa managed to have T'ien Kuang named overall commander while he assumed a somewhat subordinate title, though he actually played the most active role in the campaign. Just prior to the aspects reprised by the *Wu-ching Tsung-yao*'s "Unorthodox Plans" ("Ch'i Chi"), with just 2,000 cavalry he managed to tempt a subordinate enemy commander and his 20,000 troops into crossing the Wei River at a shallow place in pursuit of a meager hundred riders, whereupon he sprung an ambush that struck them before the full force had crossed and inflicted a severe defeat. By thus exploiting the enemy's arrogance and the ruse of feigned retreat he not only captured some 3,000 cavalry, but also 10,000 infantry and the enemy commander:[17]

> During the Northern Wei period, Mo-ch'i Ch'ou-nu instigated a revolt in the Kuan-yu area. General Ho-pa Yüeh went forth to repress him. When the army was positioned between the P'ing and Wei Rivers, he announced near and far that "as the weather is gradually getting hotter, it's not the time for an expedition. We will wait until the fall when the weather cools and then plan to advance and seize them."
>
> Learning of this and taking it to be genuine, Mo-ch'i Ch'ou-nu had his generals disperse their encampments and begin farming at Wang-ch'uan some 100 *li* north of Mount Ch'i. He also had Hou-fu-hou Yüan-chin lead 5,000 troops to fortify the ravines and had contingents of fewer than a thousand men set up defensive palisades in several other places so that they could simultaneously farm and defend themselves.
>
> Knowing that Mo-ch'i had fragmented his power, after carefully making strict preparations late one day, Ho-pa Yüeh secretly dispatched light cavalry to initially go forth and sever the various routes before releasing the bulk of his troops. In the murkiness of early morning he surrounded and attacked Yüan-shin's palisades, seizing them, but then released all the captives. This prompted the remaining outposts to surrender.
>
> When Yüeh then announced that he was going to employ a shortcut to take Ching-chou, the censor in control of the city also surrendered. Ch'ou-nu abandoned P'ing-t'ing and fled.

The intent of this unorthodox strategy was simply to delude the enemy into dispersing their troops, a step they thought vital to acquiring the provisions necessary to sustain them through the summer months. Although unstated in the succinct *Wu-ching Tsung-yao* reprisal, its effectiveness was assured by a spy who had been unknowingly converted into a disinformation agent. Released after having been caught within the camp, he reported the well-staged and widely discussed summer stand down, initiating the dispersal and accompanying laxity that allowed them to be surprised and defeated in detail. Ch'ou-nu was captured soon thereafter.

Yü-wen T'ai (507–556), a member of the Hsien-pei, began his military career in the service of the To-ba or Northern Wei dynasty at an early age, rose to a minor generalship by eighteen, and rapidly achieved military prominence thereafter, often through the use of unconventional methods. Although his operational tactics were never formulated in consciously unorthodox terms, he is one of the few commanders praised for having excelled in the unorthodox by the contemporary, multivolume PRC military history, the *Chung-kuo Chün-shih T'ung-shih*.

Yü-wen T'ai had been named commander in chief in Northern Wei to protect the emperor as much as the state just before it was sundered by internal strife into two parts known as Western and Eastern Wei in 534 CE. The fracture, precipitated by Prime Minister Kao Huan's usurpatious exercise of military power, compelled the emperor to flee westward into the Kuan-chung area and seek refuge in the ancient capital of Ch'ang-an, though he soon succumbed to poisoned wine. Thereafter, having enthroned a new puppet emperor in the east, Kao Huan repeatedly mounted massive, menacing campaigns westward to subjugate his so-called rebellious enemies.

The years 537 and 538 saw two noteworthy clashes unfold in which Kao Huan's forces were summarily defeated, ensuring Western Wei's precarious preservation. In both cases Yü-wen T'ai carefully assessed the strategic situation, premised his actions upon evaluating the character and emotional state of the opposing commanders, and adopted unorthodox tactics over the objections of many of his subordinates. At the end of 536 CE Prime Minister Kao had advanced at the head of a three-pronged, massive force to P'u-fan in Shanhsi on the eastern bank of the Yellow River, where he commenced constructing three floating bridges. In the first month of the succeeding year the weather was still very cold and a year of drought and famine had seen a high percentage of the populace in the Kuan-chung area perish despite having resorted to cannibalism.

Yü-wen T'ai reportedly addressed his commanders at their camp at Kuang-yang, saying:

> The enemy has horned us in on three sides and is constructing floating bridges to show that they will certainly cross the Yellow River. Kao is taking this action because he wants to entangle our army and allow Tou T'ai to advance westward. Whenever Kao has mobilized his forces and come forth, Tou T'ai has always acted as commander of the vanguard. His officers and troops are all elite forces and he has won numerous victories and become arrogant. If we attack him now, we will certainly conquer his army. If we conquer them, Kao Huan will depart without engaging in combat.[18]

Appalled by the recklessness of his proposed course, Yü-wen T'ai's generals reacted by emphasizing that abandoning their position to mount a sudden attack far off could prove disastrous because of the proximity of other, major enemy forces. Moreover, if they encountered any difficulty, there "wouldn't even be time for regret." Therefore, the usual (conservative) operational measure of dividing the available troops and opposing the enemy at multiple places was thought to be wiser. However, Yü-wen T'ai justified his plans by saying "During the two previous attacks at T'ung-kuan our armies did not depart from Pa-shang. So now, having raised a large army and come forth, Kao Huan assumes we will once again simply preserve ourselves and thinks lightly of us. If we exploit his disdain to mount a sudden strike, why should we have any worries about not conquering? Even though the enemy is building floating bridges, they are still unable to directly cross, whereas in less than five days we can certainly seize Tou T'ai."

Perceiving the danger of finding themselves being attacked from both within and without, at least one of his advisors concurred. Moreover, he similarly advised that they should move stealthily forward to strike the enemy because Tou T'ai had come forward in great haste and would certainly be seeking a quick, decisive battle, contrary to common wisdom that dictated allowing the enemy's spirit to abate before engaging.

To increase the effectiveness of their efforts Yü-wen T'ai conspicuously announced that they were moving back to a defensive position but then stealthily advanced eastward until they reached Hsiao-kuan. When Tou T'ai heard that Yü-wen T'ai's army had come up, he hastily crossed the army over the Yellow River at Feng-ling. Yü-wen T'ai then sallied forth from the marshes at Ma-mu, launched a sudden strike, and smashed him. Finding that his officers and nearly 10,000 troops had been almost completely annihilated, Tou T'ai committed suicide. In view of these astonishing developments and his inability to dispatch a rescue force because the bridges were still incomplete and the ice too thin, Kao Huan destroyed them and withdrew.

The second clash became inevitable when, following a successful Western Wei foray into Eastern Wei that temporarily augmented the former's territory, Eastern Wei responded by mounting a massive invasion with 200,000 men in the main thrust under Kao Huan and 30,000 in a southern, corollary strike. Because famine had long plagued the area, the severely outmatched Yü-wen T'ai could only raise about 10,000 men in response. However, contrary to the normal policy of allowing the spirited invader's initial fervor to dissipate, he was again convinced that a swift response was required. A floating bridge was therefore constructed across the Wei River so that they could move northward to cut off Kao Huan, whose thrust had already forded the Yellow River and was advancing. Abandoning any hope of seizing a granary and taking only three days' provisions, they raced to a position within 60 *li* of the enemy, an action that caused all the subordinate generals apart from Yü-wen Shen to become fearful.

Shen's analysis is instructive because it ran counter to prevailing wisdom: "Kao Huan has pacified the area north of the Yellow River and gained the allegiance of the people. As long as he was relying on this, it wasn't easy to plan against him. But now, only because he is ashamed of Tou T'ai's loss, he has risked his entire army by crossing the Yellow River. Because of their reluctance, he had to strongly persuade the troops to advance so they are what might be termed a resentful army. He can be captured in a single clash."

Yü-wen T'ai also employed deep reconnaissance to determine the exact nature and disposition of Kao Huan's army. Three light cavalrymen disguised in uniforms identical to the enemy were dispatched and surreptitiously learned all the necessary passwords and then penetrated the camp to test their gaps and vacuities. Although Kao Huan was counseled by his commanders to simply avoid battle or at least split his forces rather than attacking on muddy, difficult terrain—especially as the enemy was weak from famine—he ignored the advice, preferring to listen to claims that they could easily prevail if only every hundred of their troops would seize but one of the enemy. (He was also seduced by the propaganda value of capturing T'ai alive, and therefore rejected the idea of burning the fields to destroy them.)

Yü-wen T'ai adopted the suggestion that, being so inferior to the enemy, they should avoid combat on the open plains and instead avail themselves of terrain about a severe bend in the Yellow River. T'ai therefore segmented his troops into three contingents, pre-positioning a third each on the east and western flanks while the remainder deployed in the middle with their backs to the river. To ensure the enticement value of this small, visible force, he had the soldiers conceal their long-handled dagger-axes and similar weapons in the tall grass rather than wave them about in the sky.

The ruse worked so well that Kao Huan's troops recklessly moved forward until they were suddenly attacked by the forces lying in ambush and thrown into complete chaos. In addition, a transverse attack split them into two, preventing any coordinated action whatsoever. Badly vanquished despite individual heroic efforts, the retreating elements were pursued as far as the Yellow River, where they were further decimated. Casualties reportedly amounted to 80,000 men and a vast amount of armor and weapons was lost. Although T'ai's results in subsequent years were less stellar, he greatly improved the state's economy and established the *fu-ping* military system, strengthening its military posture and ability to resist further inroads. Shortly after his death his son seized power, established the Chou dynasty, and honored his father as the first emperor.

Despite ambushes having been repeatedly employed across the centuries, the Sung and later military writings still continued to consider them an essentially unorthodox measure. Ho-juo Tun, a well-known Northern and Southern dynasties commander who reputedly excelled in employing ambushes, thus attracted their attention:[19]

In 558 CE General Ho-juo Tun of Later Chou led 6,000 cavalry across the Yangtze River to seize Hsiang-chou in Ch'en. General Hou Chen came forth to extirpate him, cutting Ho-juo's route across the Yangtze. With their provisions severed, the soldiers became fearful at the danger. Ho-juo therefore deputed troops to plunder and forage in order to supplement their supplies. However, fearing that Hou would learn that their provisions were low, he had dirt mounded up in the encampment and then covered the mounds with grain before summoning some nearby villagers on the pretext of having something to ask them. While they were there, he arranged that they saw the piles from outside the encampment before sending them off.

When he heard about their repleteness, Hou Chen proceeded to occupy the passes and strategic points in order to exhaust them. Meanwhile, Ho-juo Tun repaired and augmented their fortifications and had grass huts built to show that the army planned to encamp for a long time.

Several times deserters fled on horseback to join Hou and were, in every case, accepted. Ho-juo therefore had some horses led onto a boat where sailors then came out and whipped them. After two or three times the horses feared the boat and wouldn't go aboard. Subsequently, he secreted men in ambush along the river bank and then dispatched men riding the skittish horses in order to entice Hou's army forth. Because the riders pretended to want to shift their allegiance, Hou deputed a contingent to meet and accept them. However, when they tried to lead the horses onto the boat, they were too terrified to board. (Exploiting the confusion), Ho-juo launched their ambush and completely exterminated the enemy contingent.

Troubled that trappers on the Hsiang River were employing light boats to bring rice and grain together with ducks in baskets to feed Hou's men, Ho-juo disguised some men similarly and then hid ambushers in the boat. Seeing the boats, Hou's troops assumed more supplies were coming and competed with each other to get them. Ho-juo's armored troops then jumped out and captured them all. Thereafter, whenever supply boats or deserters approached Hou's position, it was assumed that they were participating in a ruse and, contrary to previous times, beaten off rather than accepted. After the two generals had maintained their relative positions for more than a year, Hou proved unable to control the outcome.

Eventually Ho-juo Tun accepted Hou Chen's offer of a safe passage across the river, ending the standoff but resulting in Tun's demotion for having lost valuable terrain. However, as he had penetrated deeply into enemy territory with a minor force and immediately found himself cut off from support and supplies, his actions might have been viewed more favorably in a less vituperative court. In fact, the anonymous author of the *Hundred Unorthodox Strategies* cited these very accomplishments as the illustration for the topic of "Hunger in Warfare," though from the perspective of an invader's problematic logistical requirements. (The *Unorthodox Strategies* version adds the important facts that Ho-juo Tun's provisions had been severed by heavy autumnal rains and that once their commitment to remaining was seen, the people caught in the region between the two armies abandoned agriculture and fled, precluding both sides from foraging for grain.)

Facades also remained highly functional across history. For example, Yü-wen Hsien, realizing that the enemy was bringing up overwhelmingly superior forces, in 576 CE perspicaciously had one of his subordinates prepare a substantial facade:[20]

During the Northern and Southern dynasties period, when Emperor Wu of the Chou went east on a punitive campaign, he employed Yü-wen Hsien as his vanguard to defend Chüeh-shu

Pass. At that time Ch'en Wang-ch'ün was encamped at Shih-li-ching, Grand General Yü-wen Ch'un was encamped at Chi-hsi-yüan, and Grand General Yü-wen Sheng was defending Fen River Pass.

Yü-wen Hsien, who was serving as overall Regional Commander, secretly said to Yü-wen Sheng: "Warfare is the Tao of deception. In erecting your present encampment, instead of setting up tents, you should cut down some cyprus trees to construct huts as this will show it will be more than just a temporary camp. Then when your army departs and the brigands arrive, they will still be doubtful."

At that time the king of Ch'i segmented an army off toward Shih-li-ching and dispatched the bulk of his forces through Fen River Pass. He himself led a large contingent to confront Yü-wen Ch'un. The latter reported that Ch'i's army was making a fervent attack so Yü-wen Hsien personally led a force to rescue them, but even after their armies joined together, they were defeated and pursued by Ch'i. That night Yü-wen Ch'un evacuated his position and retreated. However, Ch'i thought the cyprus huts indicated a fully manned defensive position and therefore dared not advance until the next morning when they realized they had been deceived.

Although the unorthodox manipulation of the enemy is clear, as summarized in the *Wu-ching Tsung-yao* account, the incident is somewhat cryptic. Yü-wen Hsien initiated the campaign by seizing two of the enemy's cities before their advance was stymied by the incineration of an important bridge. In the next clash, Yü-wen Sheng was nearly defeated until Yü-wen Hsien came to his rescue and they managed to turn the tide, inflicting a localized defeat of Ch'i's forces. Then Yü-wen Ch'un in turn came under pressure, again requiring Yü-wen Hsien—who frequently defied large enemy forces with just a hundred or so cavalry—to assist him. After both armies stood down, in response to the ruler's edict Yü-wen Hsien led their forces away in the middle of the night without the enemy ever suspecting the still-standing encampment had been abandoned.

Yü-wen Sheng's foresight in the face of an overwhelmingly superior force thus well accords with the tactical discussion for the subject of "Doubt" in the *Hundred Unorthodox Strategies*, which in fact cites the incident as its historical illustration: "Whenever occupying fortifications opposite an enemy, if you should want to retreat, create some false, empty deployments that can be left behind when you withdraw, for then the enemy will never pursue you." In addition, his actions epitomize the basic tactics embodied by another of the *Thirty-six Stratagems*, "The Cicada Sheds its Shell."

In another example of the disastrous effects that can be brought about by court competition and jealousy, Chou Fa-shang repeatedly clashed with the emperor's son in the minor state of Ch'en, prompting the latter to falsely accuse Chou of planning to revolt. The emperor seized Chou's brother in 579 CE and was just mobilizing an army to move against him when Chou and his personal troops sought refuge in the state of Northern Chou, though only after much soul searching because his father had been a high military official in Ch'en. Esteeming him greatly, Northern Chou's ruler gave him a combined appointment as a general and high regional official:

> The emperor of Ch'en dispatched Fan Meng to cross the Yangtze and extirpate Chou. Chou had Han Lang, one of his subordinate commanders, pretend to betray him. Han raced to Fan Meng's camp where he falsely claimed that "Chou's forces are unwilling to submit to Northern Chou. If you conduct a campaign against them, they won't have any will to fight and will certainly invert their weapons in their positions."
>
> Taking it to be true, Meng led his forces rapidly forth against Chou who then feigned great fear and ensconced himself at Chiang-ch'ü (a famous bend in the Yangtze River). Meng's formations rapidly pressed forward but Chou had already em-

placed light boats for ambush amidst the marshes along the banks and deployed elite, highly animated troops north of the old village. He then flourished his flags and, moving contrary to the river's current, went forth to oppose Meng.

After several clashes Chou pretended to retreat, ascended the bank, and sought refuge in the old town. When Meng had his forces abandon their boats in pursuit, Chou hastily fled another several ten *li* inland until he united with the ambush forces north of the village, turned and fronted Meng, and launched a sudden attack. Meng retreated back to the refuge of their boats only to discover that the ambushers had come forth, taken down all of Meng's flags, and set their own up on the boats. Meng's troops suffered a severe defeat, almost 8,000 troops were captured, and only he managed to escape.[21]

Although not identical, this essentially riverine encounter largely echoes Han Hsin's strategy in the famous battle at Chao castle. A feigned retreat was first employed to lure a superior enemy away from their bastion, then their refuge was easily seized by a force lying in ambush, confounding their plans and deflating their spirit. Misled by a false defection that augmented the credibility of a disinformation agent, Meng raced forward improperly prepared and thus fell into the same trap as the state of Chao, which had succumbed to Ch'in's campaign to name Chao Kua battlefield commander, resulting in the debacle at Ch'ang-p'ing. Several unorthodox techniques were thus used in combination, their sequence converting what had been expected to be certain victory in an essentially simple riverine clash (because Meng's forces were upstream in an almost invincible position) into defeat.

9

Sui and T'ang Conflicts

T he Sui dynasty was founded by Yang Chien, a powerful general who usurped the Northern Chou throne before reunifying China through widely ranging campaigns in the south, including northern Vietnam. His achievement thus reimposed centralized administrative control over north and south for the first time in nearly four centuries. Sui Wen-ti was soon succeeded by his son, Yang-ti, who seized the throne by killing both his father and his brother in 604. Even more energetic than his father, he undertook enormous public works projects, including the construction of canals linking the main rivers and capitals, partly to control the south and indulge himself in southern pleasures, partly to economically integrate the country and sustain the badly decimated north with southern agriculture products. (The canals also had a fundamental military intent, just as in the ancient state of Wu.) However, these projects, defensive border work, and three massive invasions of Korea caused great consternation and suffering among the people.

Historians have frequently remarked upon the thoroughness, complexity, and unorthodox nature of the program formulated by the Sui to alter the tactical imbalance of power and conquer the state of Ch'en south of the Yangtze River, accounting for different aspects of it being cited in two *Wu-ching Tsung-yao* focal chapters.[1] Obfuscation and deceit were employed to manipulate and debilitate the south, to mislead and disperse their defenses. Only time-worn, decrepit vessels were displayed across the river until the last minute while a vast armada was conspicuously constructed

upstream to induce Ch'en to shift troops in anticipation of their onslaught, thereby creating gaps and fissures in the lower reaches where amphibious assaults were planned. Other specious activities and facades were
also employed downstream to disrupt the enemy's preparations and dull
their reactions, including the use of dummies and repeated parades along
the river to wear out Ch'en's defensive response, and a display of old
horses to make their preparations appear laughable. Misdirection and disinformation steps were taken to suggest disinterest in invading, putting
Ch'en's ruler at ease and causing laxness in their border defenses until
Yang Su and Ho-juo Pi led the major thrust in the winter of 588 that led to
Ch'en's subjugation the next year.

Although Ch'en initially had significant forces available, they were thus
rendered largely ineffective through such means as the manipulation of
boats and horses:[2]

> Under the guise of pacifying Ch'en, the Sui initiated a policy of
> supposedly acquiring horses. This caused Ch'en to become fear-
> ful and seek horses themselves for the purpose of battle. How-
> ever, the area south of the Yangtze River, being very damp, was
> especially unsuitable for horses and in less than a year they
> would all die without having been used. But Ch'en Shu-pao (the
> ruler) had numerous boats constructed to exchange for horses.
> Only after they had shipped many northward did they realize
> that horses weren't suitable and desisted.
>
> In the Sui, Kao Chiung requested that all the boats they ac-
> quired be used to supply rice in support of Shou-yang. He also
> had a large pond dug out, supposedly for fishing and pleasure
> boating, but actually used it to train for riverine warfare. Ho-
> juo Pi was appointed general commander for Shou-chou and
> through these measures they eventually pacified Ch'en.

The technique of trading decrepit horses for viable boats, usually attributed to Ho-juo Pi, was but one of many measures that exploited the
ruler's laxity to enervate and debilitate Ch'en. As horses were in fact

equally necessary in the south for both logistical and cavalry purposes, their acquisition was not as foolish as the text suggests. However, Ch'en's stupidity in exchanging watercraft for them and thereby undermining their main defense—the rapidly flowing expanse of the Yangtze River—is astonishing, as is their numerous intelligence failures and general misperception of the situation.

The *Wu-ching Tsung-yao*'s "Unorthodox Plans" takes note of another, more concrete measure subsequently employed in preparation for the conquest:[3]

> During the K'ai-huang reign period (581–601), Emperor Wen of the Sui held discussions about the feasibility of attacking Ch'en. All his generals doubted it would be possible because the Yangtze was broad and distant and their troops were not experienced in naval warfare. Even if they managed to ascend the southern cliffs, a single enemy soldier could oppose a hundred invaders.
>
> The duke of Hsiang-yi, Ho-Juo Pi, presented ten plans, one of which suggested that numerous boats be built, though after a number had been completed the brigands would certainly harden their defenses. Moreover, as the south lacked horses, all those twenty or older from the contiguous areas along the river should be levied. Since the pure sand of the area was not conducive to shaping with tamped earth construction techniques, his general Lou Po-tzu advised: "Now that the weather is cold we can use sand to create a wall by first soaking it with water. In a short time it will freeze and be as solid as iron or rock. Before the next light, a hundred sections will have been erected whose solidity will surpass that of metal walls and roiling moats." The duke followed his suggestion and by light they were complete.[4]

Although creating temporary fortifications and crossing rivers by exploiting low temperatures became a well-known technique after it was first employed by Ts'ao Ts'ao in the Three Kingdoms period, in the Sung it was still regarded as comparatively unorthodox, accounting for its inclusion in the *Wu-ching Tsung-yao*.

Even as it was expanding its domain and consolidating power, the Sui was troubled by Turkish and Khitan steppe forces that mounted raids and occasional deep incursions. Conversely, some tribal elements nominally recognized the dynasty's authority, including 90,000 Turks who surrendered in 601 CE. Over the centuries many peoples were settled along the frontier to provide a buffer force against more aggressive groups further out onto the steppe, although this was not entirely without risk because it induced disruptive elements within the borders or even within the walls against whom there could be little preparation. However, in 605 continued raids prompted Emperor Sui Yang-ti to dispatch Wei Yün-ch'i to suppress the Khitan. Wei in turn employed some 20,000 Turkish cavalry:[5]

> When Wei Yün-ch'i conducted a punitive campaign against the Khitan, he (exploited the fact that) the Turks and Khitan had a harmonious relationship and that the Khitan had never had occasion to doubt or shun the Turks. Therefore, when he entered their border (in command of the Turkish force), Yün-ch'i had the Turks falsely state that they were proceeding toward the city of Liao in order to trade with the Korean kingdom of Kao-li. He also ordered that they never mention the presence of a Sui emissary within their camp, with anyone who dared leak the information being beheaded.
>
> The Khitan made no defensive preparations. When the Turks were 100 *li* from the main Khitan encampment they made a pretense of turning south and crossing the river but returned that night, encamping about 50 *li* away. The Khitan were still unaware of these developments. Then, when light broke, the Sui launched their cavalry all at once to race forward in a sudden attack that completely overwhelmed the Khitan, resulting in the capture of some 40,000 men and women. Half the women, children, and animals were given to the Turks, but all the men were

slain. Greatly elated, Sui Yang-ti assembled all his officials and exclaimed, "Yün-ch'i used the Turks to pacify the Khitan!"

The *Tzu-chih T'ung-chien* adds the operational information that Wei, who served as overall commander, employed segmentation, one of the fundamental enabling techniques of unorthodox warfare. The entire force was dispersed among twelve encampments whenever they halted and their advance employed four routes. Contrary to the random, exuberant activity that characterized most tribal forces, discipline was strictly maintained, turning the mass into a single, effective weapon. Although operational stealth facilitated the creation and execution of the main deception—the unorthodox element that changed the balance of power—it succeeded only because the Khitan made the mistake of trusting the Turks. Although this sort of duplicity could work only once (and historically drew the condemnation of the more ethically upright), from the Chinese standpoint it had the additional advantage of "employing barbarians to fight barbarians," a time-honored technique that propitiously stirred animosity and promoted dissension.

Another border clash included in the *Wu-ching Tsung-yao* that dates to the last year of the Sui dynasty, just before revolts wracked the land, depicts the T'ang progenitor Li Yüan (T'ang Kao-tsu) displaying great courage in imaginatively thwarting a large Turkish invasion force:[6]

> When the Turks penetrated the frontier, Sui Yang-ti ordered T'ang Kao-tsu and Wang Jen-kung, the Provincial Governor of Ma-yi, to lead a large force in preparation to the border. It happened that the raiders invaded the Ma-yi area and Wang had a troubled countenance because his few troops were not a match for the enemy.[7]
>
> Kao-tsu said to him, "Now the imperial offices are far away while all support to this isolated city has been cut off. It will be difficult to emerge intact if we do not engage in a death struggle." He then personally selected 2,000 elite cavalrymen to go forth as a roving army. In their moving and encamping, food

and drink they followed the water and grass just like the Turks. When they saw Turkish reconnaissance cavalry, they simply continued to race about shooting and hunting, deliberately showing that they regarded them lightly.

When they encountered a Turkish force, they split into two wings and deployed into formation, selected the best archers to comprise a separate contingent, and set out their rush mats to await the enemy. Being unable to fathom their actions, the Turks did not dare engage in a decisive battle. Kao-tsu then released his unorthodox troops to suddenly strike and drive them off. They slew the enemy by the thousands and ten thousands and even captured T'ieh-le's superlative horses.

The border situation required the commander to elicit fervent efforts from otherwise doomed men just as on Sun-tzu's fatal terrain. Copying nomadic methods to create a roving guerrilla force to counter the vast hordes then descending upon the border exemplified the use of imaginative, unorthodox tactics. Moreover, this irregular force, being highly mobile and completely distinct from Sui and T'ang heavy cavalry or moribund infantry, was unorthodox in its very nature, particularly since its numbers were so limited. Such special forces invariably relied upon surprise, mobility, and consternation not just to succeed, but even to survive.

The last vicissitudes of the Sui saw locally powerful commanders including Li Mi (582–618) rapidly ascending to power. A famous strategist and military leader known for his textual knowledge and insightful planning, Li eventually established his own small state of Wei in conjunction with Ti Hsiang, a local strongman, and battled Wang Shih-chung before eventually succumbing after briefly turning his allegiance to the incipient T'ang. The *Ch'ien K'un Ta-lüeh* cites two episodes from his life in its "The Tao of Decisive Warfare Lies in Conceiving the Unorthodox and Establishing Ambushes." The first depicts a clash that unfolded after Ti Hsiang adopted Li's advice to consolidate his control over the local area before starvation rendered his adherents too weak to stave off the enemy or caused them to disperse:[8]

After Li Mi persuaded Ti Hsiang to subjugate the several districts subordinate to Yung-yang in Honan, the Sui dispatched Chang Hsü-ta to extirpate them. Having previously been defeated by Chang a number of times, Hsiang grew fearful when he learned of his approach and thought to avoid him. However, Li Mi said, "Hsü-ta is courageous but lacks plans. Moreover, having scored repeated victories his troops are arrogant and quarrelsome. They can be captured in a single battle."

Shortly after Li had split off somewhat more than a thousand men to set up an ambush amidst the woods to the north, Hsü-ta, regarding them lightly, deployed his forces and advanced. Ti Hsiang engaged him but found his position untenable and retreated. Exploiting the opportunity, Hsü-ta pursed them more than 10 *li* northward. Li Mi then released the forces lying in ambush to intercept and defeat Hsü-ta's army. Although Li Mi, Ti Hsiang, and other generals surrounded them, Hsü-ta broke through and escaped. However, as not all his subordinates managed to get out, he spurred his horse and returned to rescue them, penetrating and escaping the encirclement four times before he died fighting. His subordinates wept for several days without ceasing and the area of Honan was greatly saddened.

Although this incident was ostensibly chosen to illustrate the importance of ambushes, it equally gives evidence of Li's perspicacity. Thereafter, facing continued famine and hardship, the next year Li advised Hsiang to seize the granary at Hsing-luo in order to sustain their forces and provide relief to the populace, thereby solidifying their strength. This prompted another Sui response:[9]

The government in Luo-yang dispatched the commanding general of the Tiger Warriors, Liu Ch'ang-kung, and Fang Tz'e in command of 25,000 infantry and cavalry to extirpate Li. At the time all the officials in Sui's capital assumed that Mi had stolen rice from the government granary because they were merely a loose band of starving brigands and would therefore be easy to destroy. People of every rank, including princes, scholars, imperial relatives, and other nobles, all competed to answer the summons to participate in the campaign. Their clothes were luxuriant and ornate, their pennants and drums were flourishing.

Liu Ch'ang-kung's forces occupied the fore while Fei Jen-chi was dispatched with the troops under his command to go forth along the Ssu River and intercept Li Mi from behind. They arranged to converge south of the granary's city on the eleventh. However, Mi and Hsiang knew their plan in detail.

Although the officers and troops had not yet eaten breakfast, when the imperial forces first arrived Ch'ang-kung pressed them to cross the Luo River and proceed to deploy west of Shih-tzu-ho along a line some 10 *li* from north to south.

After selecting the bravest and swiftest from among their men and dividing them into ten contingents, Mi and Hsiang had four contingents conceal themselves in ambush beneath the peaks of the nearby mountains to await Fei Jen-chi and deployed 6 *li* east of Shih-tzu-ho. Seeing that Mi's forces were few, Liu Chang-kung regarded them lightly. Hsiang engaged them first in battle but fell into difficulty whereupon Mi led his forces to intercept the enemy. Hungry and weak, the Sui army suffered a severe defeat. Liu Ch'ang-kung and the other commanders cast aside their clothes and escaped by clandestinely burrowing out of the chaos before racing back to the eastern capital. Their losses amounted to fifty or sixty percent of their original force.

Even though the victory resulted as much from the carefully nurtured conceit of the Sui commanders as the use of concealed troops in ambush, exploiting the enemy's hunger and controlling the battlefield also contributed significantly. Li Mi's fame and forces grew consequent to this victory and he was persuaded to assume their overall leadership, as well as the title of Duke of Wei.

The T'ang

Under the leadership of Li Yüan, a distinguished Sui military commander from a northern Turkish or Hsien-pei aristocratic clan who controlled the virtual bastions of Shaanhsi and Shanhsi, the T'ang displaced the Sui after a multi-year conflict (617–624). Although purporting to redress imperial perversities, Li simply acted before others could achieve irreversible success in the era's chaos. Managing to preclude interference by the Turks, he proclaimed himself emperor in the summer of 618 upon Sui Yang-ti's death. However, several years were required to consolidate control over the empire's territory and T'ang T'ai-tsung (the second emperor) was compelled to confront the Eastern Turks who had long plagued northern China and continued to invade with forces exceeding 100,000, threatening the capital. The T'ang quickly prevailed but apparently more through bribes and subversion than military action, turmoil having fortuitously roiled its enemies.

The early T'ang also had to contend with other Turkish threats. Li Ching (571–649), who will be seen in his role as expert adviser in the *Questions and Replies* in a subsequent section, was not only one of the few key generals in Li Yüan's campaign to overthrow the Sui, but also one of T'ang T'ai-tsung's earliest associates and supporters. He commanded T'ang troops in suppressing both internal and external challenges, the conquest of the Western Turks (for which he became justly famous), and the pacification of the south. His biography, here somewhat abridged, summarizes his unexpected and therefore unorthodox actions in subjugating the powerful Hsiao Hsien:[10]

> Li Ching, a native of San-yuan in the Metropolitan prefecture, was tall, elegant, and thoroughly versed in the classics and histories. Nevertheless, he once said to those about him, "Since men want to attain wealth and rank in this life through accomplishments, why must we compose passages like the Confucians?" He eventually accompanied T'ang T'ai-tsung on his campaign to pacify Wang Shih-ch'ung and was appointed a commander for his achievements.

Hsiao Hsien occupied Chiang-ling so the emperor issued an imperial edict for Ching to pacify the area. Accompanied by a few light cavalrymen he crossed to Chin-chou where he confronted several tens of thousands of Man [barbarian] Teng-shih-luo bandits encamped in the mountain valleys of the region. King Yüan of Lu-chiang had failed to be victorious, so Ching planned an attack for him that forced the enemy to withdraw. They then proceeded to Hsia-chou where they were blocked by Hsien's army and could not advance. The emperor assumed that he was procrastinating and issued an imperial edict to the Supervisor-in-Chief Hsü Shao for Ching's beheading. However, Shao entered a plea on Ching's behalf and he was spared.

The Man tribesmen in K'ai-chou under Jan Chao-tse then invaded K'uei-chou. Hsiao-kung, King of Chao Commandery, engaged them in battle without gaining any advantage. Ching led 800 men to destroy their encampment and strategic defiles, establishing an ambush that resulted in the beheading of Chao-tse and the capture of 5,000 prisoners.

Li Ching subsequently planned the strategy for ten campaigns against Hsien. By imperial edict Ching was appointed as Commander-in-Chief of the Campaign Army, concurrently serving as Aide to Hsiao-kung's Campaign Army, with both armies' administrative matters all entrusted to him. In August of the fourth year of the Martial Virtue reign period (621 CE) he reviewed the troops in K'uei-chou. It was the time of the autumn floods, with heavy waves on the vile, overflowing waters of the Yangtze River. As Hsien believed Ching would be unable to descend, he did not establish any defenses.

Ching's generals also requested that they wait for the river to calm before advancing. Ching said: "The most critical affair for the army is spiritual speed. The men have just assembled while Hsien does not yet know it, so if we take advantage of the water to attack his fortifications, it will be like being unable to cover one's ears at a thunderclap. Even if he can suddenly summon his troops, he will lack the means to oppose us and we will certainly capture him."

Hsiao-kung followed his plan and in the ninth month the navy attacked Yi-ling. Hsien's general Wen Shih-hung encamped at Ch'ing-chiang with several tens of thousands of troops. Hsiao-kung wanted to attack him, but Ching said: "You cannot! Shih-hung is a stalwart general and his subordinates are all courageous men. Having newly lost Ching-men they will all be full of ardor to oppose us. This is an army that can rescue the defeated and cannot be opposed. It would be better to go to the southern river bank and wait for their *ch'i* to abate before taking them."

Instead of listening, Hsiao-kung personally went forth to engage them in battle, leaving Ching behind to guard the encampment. After being soundly defeated, he returned. The bandits then employed boats to disperse and plunder the countryside. Seeing their disarray, Ching let his army loose to destroy them. They seized more than 400 vessels and 10,000 of the enemy drowned.

Leading a vanguard of 5,000 light cavalry, Li Ching then raced to Chiang-ling. They besieged the city and encamped before finally destroying Yang Chun-mao and Cheng Wen-hsiu and taking 4,000 armored soldiers prisoner. Hsiao-kung continued the advance and Hsien was terrified. He summoned troops from throughout the Chiang-nan region but surrendered the next day when they didn't arrive. When Ching entered their capital his orders were quiet but strict and the army was prohibited from looting.

In order to reward the army, some (of Ching's subordinates) suggested that they confiscate the wealth of Hsien's generals as punishment for their opposition. Li Ching replied: "The army of a True King has sympathy for the people and seizes the guilty. They were coerced into coming, so if we confiscate their wealth because the army opposed us, something they fundamentally did not wish to do, we make no allowance for the real rebels.

Now that we have just settled Ching and Ying, we should display generosity and magnanimity in order to pacify their hearts. If they surrender and we confiscate their wealth, I am afraid that from Ching south they will strengthen their walls and increase their emplacements. Forcing them into a desperate defense is not excellence in planning." He stopped their actions and did not confiscate their wealth. Because of this the cities lying between the Chiang and Han Rivers competed with each other to submit.

Among the various measures employed in this somewhat expansive episode, Li Ching's use of boats would subsequently be noted by the *Wu-ching Tsung-yao* in its section "Ch'i Ping" or "Unorthodox Armies." In reflecting upon a famous *Art of War* principle, it commented that "'By creating disorder and taking them,' Li Ching mounted light boats and destroyed Hsiao Hsien."

Before he became emperor even T'ang T'ai-tsung, a resolute and heroic battlefield commander from an early age, personally commanded small, unorthodox contingents against the Turks and other steppe groups:[11]

T'ang T'ai-tsung selected a thousand elite cavalry to comprise an unorthodox army. They all wore deep black clothes and black armor and were divided into left and right regiments. Each company carried large flags and had (well-known) cavalry generals assigned to command them. Every time they confronted invaders, the T'ai-tsung donned his black armor and personally assumed leadership of the vanguard. He awaited the vital moment to advance and wherever they ventured, they shattered the enemy and annihilated them. He normally attacked superior forces, yet the brigands were terrified.

Although these special forces, tasked with highly mobile missions of harassment and penetration, did not deliberately imitate nomadic ways, they intimidated their opponents through their decisiveness and the awesomeness of their somber black clothing and armor. Anchored by the T'ai-tsung's personal courage, these unorthodox cavalry contingents clearly reflected the Li family's so-called semi-barbarian heritage as northern military aristocrats, its members all being as well practiced in actual martial techniques as military tactics. Of particular interest is the *Wu-ching Tsung-yao*'s recognition of the critical point (*chi*), the subtle moment of incipient change when appropriately vigorous actions can achieve dramatic results. A crucial but insufficiently discussed concept of Chinese military science, it also appears in the compound character *chi-mou*, which might be rendered "subtle plans" or "stratagems," the means and method by which an astute commander can defeat any enemy, ranging from the inconsequential to the vastly superior.

The Western border also witnessed considerable turbulence in the T'ang's early decades, not only from the Turks but also from the T'u-fan (Turfan), an amalgamated steppe people then evolving in lower Inner Mongolia but now generally identified as Tibetan because they came to populate the area of modern Tibet. Never subjugated in this era, they were blunted and contained only through strenuous, extensive, and very expensive efforts. Certain imaginative commanders specialized in border issues, often remaining in one area for years or being systematically shuffled to the latest trouble point. (Long-term, remote service spawned the growth of independent military fiefdoms and personal power, particularly after the central government began employing foreign generals to avoid nurturing powerful contenders to imperial authority. However, the policy failed abysmally because it enabled An Lu-shan to amass control over some 200,000 troops and three regional defense areas before launching his infamous rebellion that nearly destroyed the T'ang.)

Not surprisingly, in the *Essential Strategies from a Grass Hut* (*Ts'ao-lü Ching-lüeh*) the definitive chapter on "Unorthodox Warfare" includes an episode from 714 CE among its few examples. Although it pivots upon a very small force exploiting the darkness of night to mount a surprise attack, its success significantly derives from the impact of pre-deployed, deceptive troops. In the early summer the T'u-fan (Turfan) mounted a massive 100,000-man incursion into the Lan-chou region of Kansu. Wang Chün, a military official who would spend some thirty years in border assignments and develop extensive military agricultural colonies to help the T'ang project power into Central Asia, was one of the sub-commanders participating in the response under Hsieh Na. The clash preserved in the *Ts'ao-lü Ching-lüeh* finally unfolded at the end of the year, under brutal conditions:[12]

> One hundred thousand elite, armored Turfan troops invaded Lin-t'ao. Wang Chün led the 2,000 men under his command at a double pace to join with the two armies at Lin-t'ao so that they might unite their power and resist them. After the invaders en-camped at the mouth of Ta-lai valley, the Turfan general P'en-ta-yen continued to lead troops there in unbroken succession.
>
> Wang then selected and sent forth 700 unorthodox warriors disguised in Turfan clothing to mount a sudden nighttime strike. He also deployed numerous drums and horns some 5 *li* to the enemy's rear so that when his main component met the enemy amidst great shouting, the men in the rear responded with drums and horns. Greatly frightened and suspecting that there were raiders among them,[13] the barbarians inadvertently started wounding and killing each other. The dead were counted by the tens of thousands.[14]
>
> Shortly thereafter Hsieh Na led the main T'ang armies forth to intercept the Turfan with a sudden attack. The Turfan then shifted to Wu-hen valley, about 20 *li* from Ta-li valley, a position between Wang and Hsieh, and were thus stretched out for sev-eral tens of *li*. Wang Chün once more sent his stalwart warriors forth with gagged mouths to mount a sudden nighttime assault whereupon the Turfan again crumbled. He then united with Hsieh's army to compress the remnants, compelling them to race to the T'ao River. The number killed and captured was be-yond counting.

Not only did the sudden nighttime appearance make the Turfan think they were being ambushed from the sides as well as attacked front and rear, but it also caused them to flee toward the main T'ang force some 20 *li* away and become caught between the two.[15] While they hesitated and before they managed to detect his limited strength, Wang Chün was able to mount the second, silent night strike with his few troops, causing them to completely crumble and flee to the T'ao River, where a concerted T'ang attack inflicted a third defeat. T'u-fan casualties reportedly amounted to forty or fifty thousand men.

The military writings attribute the T'ang's surprising success against vastly superior forces to the quick, unexpected action by Wang's 2,000 unorthodox cavalry. The use of disguise, a prominent unorthodox technique, to achieve dramatic results in highly disadvantageous situations should particularly be noted since most military conventions condemn it and generally mandate execution for those caught wearing enemy uniforms. Yet it was a ploy not infrequently employed, such as by Ts'ao Ts'ao when he destroyed Yüan Shao's massive food depot with an incendiary attack just prior to the battle of Kuan-tu. Other battles, such as the Sung defense of Shun-ch'ang, saw raiders successfully penetrate enemy camps at night, especially under rainy conditions, prompting the occupants to decimate each other, though without the critical use of disguise.

Wang's technique in the first assault replicated Pan Ch'ao's actions during his famous mission out among the Hsiung-nu during the Later Han, when he similarly deployed drums outside a small enemy encampment before mounting a nighttime incendiary attack. Multiplying drums and fires (at night) had been advocated from antiquity not only to ensure errorless communication, but also to create awesomeness and befuddle the enemy, confusing them as to the strength and deployment of troops. Being often employed over the centuries multiplying the drums might well be classified as an orthodox technique, but it was still considered unorthodox because of its surprise and effectiveness. Moreover, the dramatic effect of the drums' sudden pounding rendered the startled temporarily susceptible to sudden onslaughts, an effect presently achieved with massive aerial bombardments in "shock and awe" campaigns.

The situation in the steppe and other contiguous border regions being constantly in flux, even the most formidable steppe powers constantly waxed and waned. (From west to east, around the upper bend of the Yellow River, the T'ang's major enemies included from the Turfan, Uighurs, Turks, Khitan, and Hsi.)[16] The various clan and tribal groups frequently joined in irregular alliances with each other and sometimes with the T'ang, but they also readily betrayed their allies for the least advantage. Although the T'ang generally sought to exploit these shifting conjunctions, they still suffered deep incursions whenever their intelligence failed or their border defenses evinced any signs of weakness.

However, one episode noted by the *Wu-ching Tsung-yao* that unfolded shortly before An Lu-shan's rebellion saw a measure of success achieved through assassinating the chief evildoer, a Khitan *Ya-kuan* (commander in chief) who had amassed sufficient power to become a king maker:[17]

During the T'ang, the Khitan and Hsi (Tatabi) caused trouble along the border year after year. The Khitan *Ya-kuan* K'o-t'u-yü was skilled, courageous, and excelled in planning and numerous barbarian tribes therefore submitted to him.[18] After reaching his post Chang Shou-kuei quickly mounted several strikes against the Khitan, emerging victorious in every clash. Ch'ü-ts'e, chief of the Khitan, and K'o-t'u-yü were afraid, so they sent emissaries for permission to surrender. However, when Shou-kuei investigated he found that their submission was a sham.

Chang Shou-kuei therefore dispatched Wang Hui, secretary-general of the Right Cavalry Guards, to go and resolve the problem. When Hui reached Ch'ü-ts'e's encampment he discovered that the tribesmen never had any intention of surrendering. Furthermore, they had secretly dispatched an emissary to have nearby Turks slay Hui and join them in revolting.

It happened that another Khitan commander, Li Kuo-che, had been contending for authority and was in conflict with Ch'ü-ts'e. Hui clandestinely enticed him into killing Ch'ü-ts'e and K'o-t'u-yü at night and slaying all their clan before leading the remnants to surrender. Shou-kuei then brought his army forth and encamped at Tzu-meng-ch'uan where he reviewed the troops and rewarded the generals and officers. Finally he had the heads of Ch'ü-ts'e and K'o-t'u-yü sent to the eastern capital.

K'o-t'u-yü, who had wielded decisive power among the Khitan for some two decades, was an avowed T'ang enemy. Prior to this confrontation the Khitan had suffered a major defeat and escaped only by shifting somewhat northeastward. However, gathering allies and mounting incursions K'o-t'u-yü had led a resurgence and even defeated a T'ang commander sent to extirpate them. Chang Shou-kuei, whose success against the Tibetans was known even to K'o-t'u-yü (no doubt precipitating the fear noted in the account), was therefore deputed to exercise command over the punitive expedition. Although it successfully eliminated the leadership and thus the immediate threat, the campaign failed to suppress the greater danger because the Khitan soon amassed sufficient power to dominate the fractured T'ang and eventually establish the Liao dynasty over northern China. Thereafter, they continued to mount frequent invasions until finally being quashed by another rising steppe group, the Jurchen.

Another officer who became famous for his frontier achievements was Wang Chung-ssu, a commander whose unorthodox practices and control methods attracted the attention of the *Wu-ching Tsung-yao*'s compilers. Wang Chung-ssu not only excelled in border clashes, but also came to bear responsibility for two administrative areas (Tao or circuits) extending over 1,000 *li*. In this capacity he supervised the fortification of strong points, erection of forts, establishment of military agricultural colonies, and military efforts to thwart incursions and defeat invaders, and also served for a time in the central government:[19]

> Wang Chung-ssu was already courageous and self-reliant even when young. When he became a military commissioner responsible for maintaining security along the border, he always said to people: "A general's only duty when the state is at peace is to comfort the people. I do not want to exhaust China's strength in order to craft a name for achievement." However, he constantly trained his officers and troops, providing whatever was deficient,

and had a lacquered bow with a pull weight of 150 *chin* that was always stored in its case to show it was not being used.

Amidst the army he thought night and day about potential invaders and sent forth numerous agents in order to spy out gaps in the barbarians, striking them from time to time with unorthodox troops. His officers thus took pleasure in being employed and the army was invariably victorious.

Several foreign-born generals such as Kao Hsien-chih were also intentionally appointed to powerful border positions prior to An Lu-shan's rebellion in a futile attempt to prevent native Chinese from acquiring a power base sufficient to mount an imperial challenge. Even though the Turfan had recently suffered significant reversals and serious losses, they still sought to diminish, even negate, T'ang influence in the region. Slightly more than a decade after the last incident, the heroic Kao, originally a Korean, was entrusted with reversing the satellite status of Shao-po-lü close to the Chinese border after it had been suborned by the Turfan through a marriage alliance:[20]

While Kao Hsien-chih was serving as Assistant Protector-general for An-hsi, the Turfan brought the king of the Shao-po-lü under their influence by wedding him to one of their princesses. The Turfan thus controlled more than twenty statelets in the northwest area. Tribute from these statelets no longer reached the T'ang nor were the many plans of Military Commissioners T'ien Jen-wan and Kai Chia-yün at all successful. Emperor Hsüan appointed Kao Hsien-chih as Military Commissioner in command of a mobile brigade consisting of 10,000 horse and infantry to go forth and extirpate them. At that time all the infantry had their own horses.

After setting out and traveling for more than a hundred days they arrived at T'ieh-le-man-ch'uan, site of the statelet of Wu-shih-ni-kuo. Hsien-chih then divided his army into three and had them proceed by three routes to assemble in the early morning on the thirteenth of the seventh month at the Turfan citadel of Lien-yün-pao which stood along the Tzu-le River. The citadel itself held a thousand troops while palisades that exploited the mountains located 15 *li* to the south were manned by 8,000 to 9,000 soldiers.

It happened that the river was rising and could not be crossed. Hsien-chih sacrificed three ritual animals to the river then ordered his generals to select their men and horses, prepare three days of dry provisions, and quickly assemble at the bank. As the water was already difficult to cross the generals and officers all thought that he was mad. But when they finished fording the river and deployed neither the flags carried by the men nor the reins of the horses had gotten wet.

Elated, Hsien-chih said, "We would have been finished if the enemy had come up while we were half across. Heaven has made a present of these brigands." He then ascended the mountains and arrayed his forces for a sudden strike. Within a couple of hours he had smashed the enemy and by nightfall had killed some 5,000 fleeing troops and captured a thousand, the rest having all scattered. He also obtained more than a thousand horses and uncountable provisions and implements.

Because the men were reluctant to proceed further he had one of his commanders remain behind to hold the city with 3,000 weak and ill troops while he led the remainder ahead on a three days march to the Tan-chü mountain range and some 40 *li* down the outer slopes. Assessing the situation, Hsien-chih said, "If the A-nü-yüeh barbarians come forth right away to greet us, it will show their good intentions." Moreover, as he feared his troops would be too afraid to descend, he first had some twenty cavalrymen don A-nü-yüeh barbarian clothing [and sneak away in preparation for] ascending the hill to meet them.

When the army reached the Tan-chü-ling peak area the troops were indeed afraid to descend, asking "where do you want us to go?" Before they had finished speaking, Hsien-chih had the twenty come forth to meet them and say to his men, "We A-nü-yüeh tribesmen sincerely welcome you.[21] The So-yi River rattan bridge (to Turfan territory) has already been severed." Hsien-chih, pretending to be elated, ordered all his troops to descend the mountain. However, the So-yi River being the old Jo River, it could neither sustain grass nor herds.

Three days after they descended the mountain, representatives from A-nü-yüeh city actually came to meet them. The next day before he went to A-nü-yüeh city he ordered his subcommanders to repair the bridge road before advancing the army. He also ordered Hsi Yüan-ch'ing to take a thousand cavalry and first inform the king of the Shao-po-lü, "We won't seize your city or destroy your bridges, but are borrowing the road to Ta-po-lü."

The five or six leaders within the city who had supported the Turfan fled. However, Hsien-chih had instructed Hsi Yüan-ch'ing, "The leaders and common people will all flee into the mountain passes when you first approach. Proclaim the emperor's edict and entice them with gifts. When the leaders come forth, bind them all and wait for me."

When Hsi Yüan-ch'ing arrived he acted just as Hsien-chih had instructed, trussing up the leaders. The king and Turfan princess escaped by fleeing into a cave and couldn't be caught. Hsien-chih then beheaded the five or six Turfan sympathizers and urgently dispatched Yüan-ch'ing to destroy the rattan bridge that was still 60 *li* away. It was dusk before they were able to cut it down. Shortly thereafter a large Turfan army arrived but it was already too late and they couldn't cross. The span covered the flight of an arrow so it took a full year to rebuild it.

The Shao-po-lü had perfidiously loaned this route to the Turfan and thus this bridge had been built. At this time Hsin-chi gradually persuaded the king of the Shao-po-lü and his princess to surrender and also subjugated his state.

Kao's biography adds that he not only succeeded in bringing the king back but also brought about the submission of some seventy-two tribal groups to the T'ang. Ironically, despite his great success in thwarting the Tibetans, penetrating the steppe region as far as Ferghana and eventually Talas (where he was ultimately defeated by an Arab force), and having been among the very few commanders who managed to stem the onslaught of An Lu-shan's armies, he was eventually executed by the dissolute Emperor Hsüan-tsung for failing to defeat the rebels.

An Lu-shan's Rebellion entailed nearly eight years (755–763) of intermittent but often intense fighting that segmented T'ang authority and ultimately precipitated the dynasty's eventual collapse. Operational forces ranged from 30,000 to 150,000 men, casualties numbered in the tens of thousands, and entire field armies were virtually annihilated as the balance of power repeatedly shifted. Although the actual fighting was confined to two main corridors, the localized destruction and depopulation was immense while collateral revolts exploited the chaos to impact the land.

In 757 CE, just after An Lu-shan had been assassinated, government troops went forth to retake Ch'ang-an. The combined force, although expected to continue benefiting greatly from the participation of steppe cavalry components such as the Uighurs, who had proven critical to the government's resurgence, surprisingly allowed itself to be lured forward by a feigned retreat and then overwhelmed by the enemy's resurgence despite their enormous numbers. Only swift action by a single commander prevented a complete rout as this much simplified *Wu-ching Tsung-yao* version shows:[22]

The T'ang commander in chief, the king of Kuang-p'ing, led an army of 150,000 Han and Turfan troops to advance and reseize Ch'ang-an. They engaged in combat at Hsiang-chi Temple where their troops were deployed across some 30 *li*. The rebel general Li Kuei-jen pummeled the T'ang armies, throwing them into chaos.

The T'ang commander Li Ssu-yeh rashly raced about, capturing more than ten of the rebel's cavalry before the T'ang lines were stabilized. Uighur unorthodox cavalry then went forth behind the enemy and the T'ang forces mounted a convergent attack, slaying some 60,000 of the enemy.

The victory turned upon two events: first, Li Ssu-yeh's quick response (which is depicted in his biography and the *Tzu-chih T'ung-chien* rather differently because he supposedly threw off his armor and his clothes, grabbed a large halberd, and began chopping down the advancing enemy in order to stabilize the T'ang forces). Second, the Uighur cavalry, distinct in form and function from T'ang cavalry, were deployed (apparently at Li's instigation) as an irregular force of maneuver that quickly operated behind the enemy's lines, sufficiently harassing and disrupting them to create an opening for a successful convergent attack.

In the aftermath of An Lu-shan's rebellion local commanders exploited the T'ang power vacuum to seize peripheral authority, often in alliance with the Turks and Khitans, though the latter also continued their incursions. Jung-chou in Kuang-hsi near the center of southern China had thus been lost and the people still ensconced in their fortified towns were suffering unremitting predations. However, Wang Hung managed to vanquish vastly superior numbers with a truly minuscule force:

In the midst of the Ta-li period (771 CE) Wang Hung was appointed Military Commissioner for Jung-chou. Following An Lu-shan's rebellion the Yi and Liao in the Hsi-tung area had continuously caused chaos, penetrating numerous cities and towns and occupying Jung-chou. The ousted military commissioners were temporarily administering T'eng-chou and Wu-chou. When Wang arrived he addressed them all: "I am the prefect for Jung-chou so how can I expect to act as a foreign administrator in any other region? I must get back Jung-chou, that's all."

Wang then used his own wealth to recruit warriors and any-one who achieved merit was made a temporary lictor. The men therefore acted fervently and before many months had killed Ou-yang Kuei, an enemy commander.

Wang then went to Kuang-chou where he requested the assis-tance of the Military Commissioner, Li Mien, in fielding an army and uniting their strength. Mien refused, saying "Barbar-ians have long penetrated Jung-chou and the Liao are strong. To mount a distant attack now would only result in defeat."

Wang Hung replied, "If you will not send forth an army, I would like to circulate an announcement throughout the provinces and districts advising that we need soldiers to aid in the effort. I hope to thereby achieve the impossible." Mien assented.

Accordingly, Hung sent a missive to the prefects in Yi-chou and T'eng-chou who both agreed to advance in an effort to ex-tirpate the enemy. He then engaged the enemy with their 3,000 troops in heated battle for several days running before meeting with an urgent order from Mien to stand down that he simply concealed. The battle grew more intense and his troops de-stroyed the barbarians, capturing Liang Jung-ch'ien and recover-ing all of Jung-chou's former terrain. When his victory was reported Wang was summoned and transferred to Shun-chou in order to settle the remnant chaos. In more than a hundred en-gagements Wang Hung captured some seventy enemy leaders.[23]

Apart from the bold actions (including concealing an order to desist) that caused it to be included in the *Wu-ching Tsung-yao*'s examples, this episode coincidentally shows the dissension that repeatedly plagued T'ang and Sung campaigns because the central government often fragmented responsibility and authority for major expeditions and crucial riverside defense among two or more generals of equal rank to preclude threats to the ruler.

Theory in the Three Kingdoms and Early T'ang

Apart from vestiges preserved in the general compendia and two somewhat dubious, reconstructed works—Chu-ko Liang's *Ping-fa* and the *Wo-ch'i Ching*—all the theoretical manuals written in the interval between the Warring States and the T'ang, including those attributed to Ts'ao Ts'ao and other prominent strategists, have now been lost. However, early in the T'ang Li Ch'üan penned an esoteric contemplation titled the *T'ai-pai Yin-ching*; the immediately subsequent *T'ung Tien* includes a lengthy military section; and a book claiming a T'ang origin known as the *Question and Replies between T'ang T'ai-tsung and Li Wei-kung* eventually appeared. In addition, a synthetic work culled from T'ang and later materials, including the *T'ung Tien*, titled *Li Wei-kung's Art of War* was compiled in the Ch'ing dynasty but certainly suffers from revisions and lacuna.

As Sun-tzu's earliest known commentator, Ts'ao Ts'ao's notes always appear first in the Sung dynasty *Ten Commentaries* (*Sun-tzu Shih-chia Chu*) edition of the *Art of War* and are often incorporated in subsequent annotations. Normally the most concise, he never appends any historical illustrations and generally expresses himself in a sentence or two. Nevertheless, two of his three remarks on the vital unorthodox passage are much cited by later military manuals, including the *Questions and Replies*: "Going forth first to engage in warfare is orthodox, going forth afterward is unorthodox. The orthodox oppose the enemy, unorthodox troops attack the unprepared from the flanks."[1]

Chu-ko Liang Ping-fa

Although Chu-ko Liang was not the first nor the most effective strategist, popular imagination over the centuries magnified his few historical encounters and accorded him virtual primacy of place for strategic inventiveness and imaginative tactical ploys. Unfortunately, his martial writings were all lost during the centuries of fragmentation that followed the demise of the Three Kingdoms, the work now appearing under his name having been synthetically created by Ch'ing dynasty scholars from remnants preserved in other works and encyclopedias, supplemented by inferences drawn from *San-kuo Chih* historical materials. How much of this smoothly reading book is authentic remains problematic, making any realistic evaluation of his thought and contributions nearly impossible.

Nevertheless, because it has recently enjoyed both scholarly and popular reprints in the PRC and a variant is included in the PLA's corpus of military writings, a few observations are justified. First, the unorthodox appears in but a single discussion in a chapter titled "Controlling the Army" and even then the text merely reiterates the idea that the unorthodox and orthodox mutually produce each other in an inexhaustible cycle. More important, knowledge and preplanning are emphasized because they ensure victory before engaging in battle, well in accord with Sun-tzu's concept. (Somewhat more interestingly, Chu-ko Liang is quoted as attributing the very possibility of military planning to Sun-tzu.)

Surpassing knowledge is foremost in determining the army's strategy while the unorthodox provides the substance of plans. Moreover, his assertion that "the unorthodox and orthodox are taken as the beginning" emphasizes their dual importance, though he never suggests initiating with the orthodox and then implementing the unorthodox. Finally, insofar as the possible modes of military employment are generally drawn from the classic martial writings, he makes such observations as "the army is able to be flexible and firm, to be weak and hard, to survive and perish. Its speed is like the wind, its expansiveness like the rivers and seas, its stability like Mount T'ai. It is as difficult to fathom as *yin* and *yang*, it is as inexhaustible as Earth, as full and replete as Heaven."

T'ai-pai Yin-ching

Composed by Li Ch'üan about 750 CE or just before An Lu-shan's rebellion nearly sundered the T'ang, the extensive and generally comprehensive *T'ai-pai Yin-ching* is the earliest surviving, post-classical military manual. As might be expected because his comments on the *Art of War* are included in the famous Sung dynasty *Ten Commentaries* edition, Li's thinking and concrete formulations are solidly grounded in Sun-tzu's principles and conceptions. Accordingly, throughout the book he generally eschews brute force in favor of manipulating the enemy, employing subterfuge and deceit, and gaining victory through wisdom and imaginative plots. Although the *T'ai-pai Yin-ching* evinces a pervasive *yin-yang* orientation and includes numerous chapters devoted to such esoteric matters as prebattle prognostication, it preserves highly significant materials that reflect contemporary military conceptions, tactical principles, and siege and defense practices.

Cobbled together, Li Ch'üan's succinct observations on the definitive *Art of War* passage in the *Ten Commentaries* edition constitute an incisive commentary:[2]

> Directly opposing the enemy is orthodox, going forth on the flanks is unorthodox. Lacking unorthodox troops, no Three Armies commander has ever been able to contend for advantage.
>
> During the Former Han, King Wu gathered his troops in preparation for invading Ta-liang. General T'ien Po-lü advised: "Since all our troops have assembled and encamped to the west, it will be difficult to gain any achievement without some unorthodox method. I would like to be assigned 50,000 men and move upward along the Yangtze and Huai Rivers, consolidating

the areas south of the Huai and in Ch'ang-sha before penetrating Wu-kuan pass, whereupon I can rejoin your majesty. This
would be an unorthodox method." The king didn't heed him
and was defeated by Chou Ya-fu. This then is a case of just being
orthodox, of lacking the unorthodox.[3]

If you engage in warfare without employing deception, it will
be difficult to gain victory over the enemy. (As for one who
sends forth the unorthodox "being as inexhaustible as Heaven
and Earth"), it's a question of movement and rest. (The great
rivers) penetrate and flow without being severed, the unorthodox changes like the sun and moon, the diminishment and
flourishing of the four seasons, and the ceaselessness of cold
and warmth. (The five notes of) *kung, shang, chia, wei, yü* comprise eight tones, but the melodies performed from them can
never be exhaustively heard. (The colors) are blue, yellow, red,
white, and black. The flavors are sour, acrid, salty, sweet, and
bitter, but in cooking the chef brings about the changes of the
five flavors in the kitchen cauldrons. Assaults, severing, cutting
off, and sudden strikes, the strategic power of myriad routes,
cannot be completely exhausted. The unorthodox and orthodox, relying on each other for their birth just like an endless cir-
cle, cannot ever be exhausted.

Despite the expertise visible in Li Ch'üan's explication of Sun-tzu's initial
formulation, none of the *T'ai-pai Yin-ching* chapters ever really amplify the
nature and role of the unorthodox and orthodox. Nevertheless, in conjunction with his emphasis upon knowledge, strategic planning, and *yin*
and *yang* in subjugating the enemy, he imputes a crucial role to them:[4]

Those who excelled at employing the army could not have established themselves without trust and righteousness; achieved
victory without *yin* and *yang*; realized advantages without the
unorthodox and orthodox; nor engaged in battle without deceit
and subterfuge.

Plans are concealed in the mind, but affairs are visible in external traces. One whose thoughts and visible expression are identical will be defeated; one whose thoughts and visible expression differ will be victorious. Warfare is the Tao of deception. When capable, display incapability. When about to employ the army feign that you are not.[5] When your mind is filled with great plans display only minor concerns. When your mind is planning to seize something, feign being about to give something away. Obscure the real, cast suspicion upon the doubtful. When the real and doubtful are not distinguishable, strength and weakness will be indeterminable.

Be profound like the Mysterious Origin free of all images, be an abyss like the unfathomable depths of the sea. When you attain this, *yin* and *yang* can no longer be employed to calculate your intentions, ghosts and spirits will be unable to know them, techniques and measures unable to impoverish them, and methods of divination unable to fathom them, so how much more so mere enemy generals!

Although the passage opens by asserting the importance of being unfathomable, the discussion proceeds to link critical material from Sun-tzu in an integrated discussion that not only illustrates how these concepts flow from one to another, but also indicates the close association of the unorthodox with deceit and manipulation. In concord with the theme of the first excerpt quoted above, it reasserts the impossibility of achieving success without the unorthodox, the very reason the king of Wu's defeat was inevitable. Insofar as he raised a rebellious force against the Han itself, Li Ch'üan's chosen illustration might seem somewhat puzzling. However, it recurs in several military discussions, always being cited as an example of failing to employ unorthodox strategies.

Surprisingly, given his broad orientation to esoteric and deceptive measures, Li apparently felt that the orthodox and unorthodox would be realized in the concreteness of deployments and had to invariably be sequenced orthodox, then unorthodox, rather than the reverse. (Purely unorthodox measures are equally not a possibility.) Thus, in one of several chapters discussing the famous legendary *Wo-ch'i Ching* (*Classic of Grasping the Unorthodox*), he asserts:[6]

> The classic states: "From a single (unified) deployment they disperse to create eight formations, the eight formations then rejoin to make one." Listening to the sound (of the drums and gongs), watching the pennants (in the distance), they put forth the four unorthodox formations termed Flying Dragon, Tiger's Wings, Birds Soaring, and Snakes Coiling, and four orthodox formations of Heaven, Earth, Wind, and Clouds.
>
> One who excels at warfare engages with the orthodox and wrests victory with the unorthodox.[7] The mutual production of the unorthodox and orthodox is just like an endless cycle. Who can exhaust them? The unorthodox is *yang*, the orthodox is *yin*. When *yin* and *yang* intermix, the four seasons proceed.
>
> The unorthodox is the firm, the orthodox is the flexible. When the firm and flexible gain each other, the myriad things are completed amidst them. Through employing the unorthodox and orthodox the myriad things are all conquered. What is referred to as "joining" is the joining of the eight unorthodox and orthodox formations to be one.

Surprisingly, contrary to common views that regard normal tactical efforts as *yang* and irregular ones as *yin*, this passage identifies the unorthodox as *yang* and the orthodox as *yin*. Accordingly, the unorthodox is also viewed as being "firm" and the orthodox as "flexible," again contrary to normal expectation but fully consonant with the theory and imagery of the *Yi Ching*, wherein *yang* or solid lines are firm, *yin* or broken ones yielding and flexible. Although the implications remain to be explored, the initial interaction of *yin* and *yang* was conceived as a vital step in the *Tao Te Ching* and in other Warring States cosmogenic schemes, and the firm and flexible were commonly envisioned as continuously producing the myriad things.

Finally, several *T'ai-pai Yin-ching* prognosticatory chapters are devoted to determining the proper geospatial orientation and the day's appropriateness before engaging in battle. In general, three of the ten Heavenly stems that produce the sixty-day cycle in the conjoined permutation of the ten stems and twelve Earthly branches are designated as unorthodox. Subject to the activity of the sun, moon, and Venus,[8] they are all fundamentally auspicious for initiating military activities, especially for going forth on campaign.[9] Depending upon their relationship with these unorthodox days, additional days may be rendered auspicious by erecting an "unorthodox gate" (*ch'i men*) and observing proper directional orientations at the outset. In addition, when days with these three unorthodox designations are identified with *yang*, the army should assume the role of a "guest," but when with *yin*, that of a host.[10] However, to what extent these prescriptions were ever followed in the quest to achieve a hundred victories in a hundred encounters remains an open question.[11]

Wei Kung Ping-fa

Duke Wei's Art of War (referring to Li Ching, also known as Li Wei-kung) is a synthetic work cobbled together by Wang Tsung-yi in the Ch'ing dynasty from materials apparently preserved in the encyclopedias and fragments and quotations found in earlier military writings. Surprisingly, it has little in common with the *Questions and Replies* and virtually ignores the core concept of the unorthodox that receives so much focal attention in the latter. However, the text acknowledges (rather than emphasizes) that generals need to have a working knowledge of the unorthodox and orthodox, noting that "those who do not establish a selected front and do not divide into the unorthodox and orthodox will be defeated."

In addition to the long established idea of engaging with the orthodox and achieving victory with the unorthodox, the text adds that "one moves the enemy with the unorthodox and controls them with the orthodox." However, rather than offering a sophisticated formulation, it essentially reverts to the traditional idea of pre-designated contingents, though they are assigned a critical role in effecting the ambushes necessary to turn the battle.

Questions and Replies

Without doubt, the text known as *Questions and Replies between T'ang T'ai-tsung and Li Wei-kung* (*Li Wei-kung T'ang T'ai-tsung Wen-tui*), one of the seven books included in the official eleventh-century compilation known as the *Seven Military Classics* (*Wu-ching Ch'i-shu*), contains the most extensive discussion of unorthodox theory and practice embedded in China's numerous military writings.[12] Ostensibly a dialogue between Li Ching, one of the three commanders who distinguished themselves during the T'ang's vanquishment of the much maligned Sui, and T'ang T'ai-tsung, the second emperor, the discussion's sophistication suggests it actually stems from the tenth century, though certainly before the famous eleventh-century *Wu-ching Tsung-yao*.[13] Moreover, rather than simply espousing a series of tactical principles, the discussants review a wide range of earlier theories, assessing their applicability and contradictions.

Although he probably instigated the revolt against the Sui and certainly usurped the throne by murdering his older brother and displacing his father in 627, T'ang T'ai-tsung had apparently received a Confucian education, was thoroughly versed in the classics and histories, and even developed an interest in divination near the end of his life. Renowned for his martial skills, he commanded troops by age fifteen, fought heroically at the head of elite cavalry contingents during the Sui's overthrow, and subsequently repulsed numerous challenges to the incipient dynasty. Stories of his prowess and famous horses abound in popular Chinese history and the subsequent *Hundred Unorthodox Strategies* adopted several episodes from his life for its historical illustrations.

Li Ching's (571–649) biography indicates that he began his military career in the northwest under the Sui but eventually joined the nascent T'ang forces just after the fall of Ch'ang-an to become one of T'ang T'ai-tsung's earliest associates. He subsequently commanded imperial troops in campaigns to suppress both internal and external threats, the remarkable conquest of the Western Turks, and pacification of the south.

Although the *Questions and Replies* seems to be a pastiche of particularized observations, their joint examination of the unorthodox and orthodox evidences a degree of internal development. As the unorthodox can only exist and be defined over and against the orthodox, the initial section emphasizes and grounds the orthodox. Thereafter, the discussion ponders the role and function of orthodox troops and the simplistic concepts commonly identified with the unorthodox before finally reverting back to Sun-tzu's sophisticated articulation.

An early exchange indicates that Li Ching believed the orthodox provided the means for controlling the movement of expeditionary forces over great distances. Constraint and measure had been emphasized as early as the *Wu-tzu* but the issue required revisiting because the T'ang was about to undertake a long-range expedition into Korea despite the Sui having perished partly because of three massive, ill-conceived campaigns:

> T'ang T'ai-tsung inquired: "Koguryo has repeatedly encroached upon Silla. I dispatched an emissary to command them to desist but they rejected our edict. As I am about to send forth a punitive expedition, how should we proceed?"
>
> Li Ching replied: "According to what we have been able to determine, Kai Su-wen relies upon his personal knowledge of military affairs. He has contravened your mandate because he believes that China lacks the capability to mount a punitive expedition. I request an army of 30,000 men to capture him."
>
> The T'ai-tsung said: "Your troops will be few but the place distant. What strategy will you employ to approach them?"
>
> Li Ching said: "I will use orthodox troops."
>
> The T'ai-tsung said: "You employed unorthodox troops when you pacified the Turks, so why do you now speak about orthodox troops?"
>
> Li Ching said: "It was just this Tao that allowed Chu-ko Liang to capture Meng Hu seven times.[14] He employed orthodox troops, that's all."

Extended campaigns out into the steppe against highly mobile nomadic peoples, undertaken to a limited extent as early as the Shang and then massively from the Han onward, had required similar constraints and forceful measure:

> The T'ai-tsung said: "When Ma Lung of the Chin dynasty conducted a punitive campaign against Liang-chou, it was also in accord with the Diagram of Eight Formations and he built narrow chariots.[15] He employed encampments of deer-horn chariots when the terrain was broad, and built wooden huts and placed them upon the chariots when the road was constricted so that they could both fight and advance. I believe that the ancients valued orthodox troops!"
>
> Li Ching said: "When I conducted the punitive campaign against the Turks, we traveled west for several thousand *li*. If they had not been orthodox troops, how could we have gone so far? Narrow chariots and deer-horn chariots are essential to the army. They allow controlling the expenditure of energy, provide a defense to the fore, and constrain the regiments and squads of five. These three are employed in turn. This is what Ma Lung learned so thoroughly from the ancients."[16]

In Li Ching's view, the orthodox is not just a prerequisite for unorthodox maneuvering; rather, only strictly and systematically implemented orthodox constraints can ensure the resiliency essential to highly attritional campaigns across hostile terrain. More than a millennium earlier, among numerous detailed measures for disciplined control, Wu Ch'i had already outlined the essential principles in a section titled "Controlling the Army": "In general, the Tao for commanding an army on the march is to not contravene the proper measure of advancing and stopping; not miss the appropriate times for eating and drinking; and not completely exhaust the strength of the men and horses. These three are the means by which the troops can undertake the orders of their superiors."

The next topic of concern derives from the equally ancient practice of the feigned retreat, much discussed in such early military classics as the *Ssu-ma Fa* and generally regarded as an unorthodox technique, though successfully practiced so frequently in famous incidents over the centuries as to diminish its effectiveness and even render it an expected device.[17] The discussion itself ponders an initial collapse that was prevented from becoming a rout and then surprisingly converted to a victory only through T'ang T'ai-tsung's heroic efforts. Insofar as the sequence was not a deliberate ploy but accidentally unfolded, the T'ai-tsung wondered whether it could be considered an unorthodox tactic:

> The T'ai-tsung said: "At the battle in which I destroyed Sung Lao-sheng, when our fronts first clashed our righteous army retreated somewhat. I then led our elite cavalry in racing down from the southern plain, cutting across in a sudden attack on them. After severing Lao-sheng's troops to the rear, we severely crushed them and subsequently captured him. Were these orthodox troops? Or unorthodox troops?"
>
> Li Ching replied: "Your majesty is a natural military genius, not one who learns by studying. I have examined the art of war as practiced from the Yellow Emperor on down. First be orthodox and afterward unorthodox; first be benevolent and righteous, afterward employ the tactical balance of power and craftiness. Moreover, at the battle at Huo-yi the army had been mobilized out of righteousness, so it was orthodox. When Prince Chien-ch'eng fell off his horse and the Army of the Right withdrew somewhat, it was unorthodox."[18]
>
> The T'ai-tsung asked: "At that time our slight withdrawal almost defeated our great enterprise, so how can you refer to it as unorthodox?"
>
> Li Ching replied: "In general, when troops advance to the front it is orthodox, when they retreat to the rear it's unorthodox. Moreover, if the Army of the Right had not withdrawn somewhat, how could you have gotten Lao-sheng to come forward? The *Art of War* states, "Display profits to entice them, create disorder and take them."[19] Lao-sheng didn't know how to employ his troops. He relied upon courage and made a hasty

advance. He didn't anticipate his rear being severed nor being captured by your Majesty. This is what is referred to as using the unorthodox as the orthodox."

This interchange incidentally raises two brief formulations that purportedly distinguish the orthodox from the unorthodox and were, despite being simplistic, given widespread credence: "First be orthodox, and afterward unorthodox" and "In general, when troops advance to the front it is orthodox, when they retreat to the rear it's unorthodox."

Li Ching's tactful approbation apart, the feigned retreat had been a favorite ancient ploy because of its effectiveness in the fervency of battle, an irresistible lure to commanders seeking to exploit apparent victory prior to the advent of cavalry and their greater mobility. (As the *Liu-t'ao* states, "One who excels in warfare will not lose an advantage when he perceives it or be doubtful when he meets the moment.")[20] But feigned retreats, although generally unorthodox, must be distinguished from true routs:

> T'ang T'ai-tsung inquired: "Can every army withdrawal be considered unorthodox?"
>
> Li Ching replied: "No. Whenever soldiers retreat with their flags confused and disordered, the beating of the large and small drums not responsive, and their orders shouted out clamorously, this is true defeat, not an unorthodox strategy.
>
> "If the flags are ordered, the drums respond to each other, and the commands and orders seem unified, then even though they may be retreating and running, it must be a case of unorthodox strategy rather than a defeat. The *Art of War* says, 'Do not pursue feigned retreats.'[21] It also says, 'Although capable, display incapability.'[22] Both of them refer to the unorthodox."

In these lines Li Ching thus introduces the essential relationship between deception and the unorthodox. However, rather than pursue this new topic, T'ai-tsung rephrases his earlier query about the events that unfolded at Huo-yi:

The T'ai-tsung asked: "When the Army of the Right withdrew somewhat at the battle of Huo-yi, was this a question of Heaven? When Lao-sheng was captured, was this due to the efforts of man?"

Li Ching replied: "If our orthodox troops hadn't changed to unorthodox and unorthodox to orthodox, how would you have gained victory? Thus for one who excels at employing the army, unorthodox and orthodox lie with man, that's all. Because they changed in spiritlike fashion, they are attributed to Heaven."

Postponing further development of the idea of their interchangeability to slightly later, the discussion then raises a key question that baffled commentators over the centuries: how and when the orthodox and unorthodox are determined. Rather than a mode of employment applicable to all forces, by the Three Kingdoms some troops were being simplistically defined as unorthodox, essentially meaning that only they were predisposed to mobility and maneuver. In opposition, Li Ching reaffirms the complexity of Sun-tzu's fundamental vision, but not before detouring through more mundane terrain:

The T'ai-tsung asked: "Are the unorthodox and orthodox distinguished beforehand or are they determined at the time of battle?"

Li Ching replied: "According to Ts'ao Ts'ao's *New Book* (*Hsin Shu*), 'If you outnumber the enemy two to one, divide your troops into two, with one section being orthodox, and one section being unorthodox. If you outnumber the enemy five to one, then three sections should be orthodox and two sections unorthodox.' This states the main point.[23]

"However, Sun-tzu said, 'In warfare, the strategic configurations of power do not exceed the unorthodox and orthodox, but the changes of the unorthodox and orthodox can not be completely exhausted! The unorthodox and orthodox mutually produce each other, just like an endless cycle. Who can exhaust them?' This captures it. So how can a distinction be made beforehand?"

Perhaps because the *Hsin Shu* fragment undermines Ts'ao Ts'ao's reputation for strategic acumen, Li Ching immediately provides an ameliorating context:

> "If the officers and troops are not yet trained in my methods nor the subordinate generals familiar with my orders, their training must be broken into two. To teach battle tactics, the soldiers must learn to recognize the flags and drums, dividing and combining in turn. Thus Sun-tzu said that 'dividing and combining are changes.'[24] Such are the techniques for teaching warfare.
>
> "Only after their instructions and evaluation have been completed and the masses know my methods can they be raced about like a flock of sheep, following wherever their general points.[25] Who then makes a distinction of unorthodox and orthodox? What Sun-tzu refers to as 'giving shape to others but being formless ourselves' is the pinnacle in employing the unorthodox and orthodox. Therefore any distinction beforehand is merely for the purpose of instruction. By determining the changes at the moment of battle, they become inexhaustible."

Naturally the T'ai-tsung affirmed Li Ching's appraisal by commenting, "Profound indeed! Ts'ao Ts'ao must have known it but the *Hsin Shu* just teaches what he conveyed to his generals, not the fundamental method of the unorthodox and the orthodox."

Another simplified view that may have originated during the Three Kingdoms period imposed constraints on unorthodox troops, often by sequence as much as behavior. Queried by the T'ai-tsung about Ts'ao Ts'ao's assertion that "unorthodox troops attack from the flank," Li Ching replied, "I recall that, in commenting upon *Sun-tzu*, Ts'ao Ts'ao said: 'Going out first to engage in battle is orthodox, going out afterward is unorthodox.' This is different from his discussions about flank attacks. I ignorantly refer to the engagement of great masses as orthodox, and those that the general himself sends forth as unorthodox. Where is the restriction of first, or later, or flank attack?"

In response to these apparent limitations, Li Ching offers a vision of the unorthodox as a mode of employment undertaken by contingents in flexible maneuver, troops capable of immediately responding to the commander's intent. Despite the opacity of his previous questions, the T'ai-tsung insightfully refocuses their discussion in terms of Sun-tzu's original thrust: "If I cause the enemy to perceive my orthodox as unorthodox and cause him to perceive my unorthodox as orthodox, is this what is meant by 'displaying a form to others'? Is employing the unorthodox as orthodox, the orthodox as unorthodox, unfathomable changes and transformations, what is meant by 'being formless'?"

After having his articulation confirmed, he continues with a more operationally focused question that elicits what might be termed the crux of unorthodox:

> The T'ai-tsung said: "If dividing and combining are changes, wherein lie the unorthodox and orthodox?"
>
> Li Ching replied: "For those who excel at employing troops there are none that are not orthodox, none that are not unorthodox, so they cause the enemy never to be able to fathom them. Thus with the orthodox they are victorious, with the unorthodox they are also victorious. The officers of the Three Armies only know the victory, none know how it is attained. Without being able to fully comprehend the changes, how could anyone attain this? However, only Sun-tzu was capable of comprehending the origins of dividing and combining. From Wu Ch'i onward, no one has been able to attain it."

Li Ching's reply deliberately echoes a well-known *Art of War* pronouncement on the nature of strategic command: "In accord with the enemy's disposition we impose measures on the masses that produce victory but the masses are unable to fathom them. Men all know the disposition [or form] by which we attain victory, but no one knows the configuration through which we control the victory. Thus a victorious battle strategy is not repeated, the configurations of response are inexhaustible."[26]

Immediately preceding this paragraph the *Art of War* states that the "pinnacle of military deployment approaches the formless" and subsequently adds a few brief comments on the crucial role of amorphousness phrased in terms of the vacuous and substantial:

> Now the army's disposition of force is like water. Water's configuration avoids heights and races downward. The army's disposition of force avoids the substantial and strikes the vacuous. Water configures its flow in accord with the terrain, the army controls its victory in accord with the enemy. The army does not maintain any constant configuration of power, water has no constant shape. One who is able to change and transform in accord with the enemy and wrest victory is termed spiritual. Thus none of the five phases constantly dominate; the four seasons do not have constant positions; the sun shines for longer and shorter periods; and the moon wanes and waxes.

Nevertheless, the basic insight is simply that being "formless" precludes the enemy from anticipating and preparing for any single tactic and thus compels them to contemplate every probability: "If I determine the enemy's disposition of forces while I have no perceptible form, I can concentrate while the enemy is fragmented. If we are concentrated into a single force while they are fragmented into ten, then we attack them with ten times their strength. Thus we will be many and the enemy few. If we can attack their few with our many, those who we engage in battle will be severely constrained." Unfortunately, despite the importance of the concept in the *Art of War* and subsequent theoretical manuals, Sun-tzu offers nothing more.[27]

The mention of Wu Ch'i's name initiates a series of exchanges on the essence of historic practices replete with details for training and deploying special contingents capable of executing unorthodox tactics. (Depending upon the context and stage of operations, a certain amount of inconsistency creeps into Li Ching's formulation.) Although much of the material will mainly interest historical specialists, none is irrelevant to gaining a more pervasive sense of the nature of the unorthodox. Prompted by the T'ai-tsung's query as to what Wu Ch'i's strategy was like, Li Ching comments:

> "Permit me to speak about the general points. Marquis Wu of Wei asked Wu Ch'i about two armies confronting each other. Wu Ch'i said, 'Have some of your low ranking, courageous soldiers go forward and attack. When the fronts first clash, have them flee. When they flee, do not punish them, but observe whether the enemy advances to take the bait. If they crouch and arise as one and do not pursue your fleeing troops, the enemy has good strategists. If all their troops pursue your fleeing forces in disordered fashion with some advancing and some halting, the enemy is not talented. Attack them without hesitation.'[28] I think that Wu Ch'i's strategy was generally of this sort, not what Sun-tzu would refer to as an orthodox engagement."

The remnants of the *Wu-tzu* contain several passages devoted to evaluating the enemy, to both passively and actively "ascertaining the enemy's voids and strengths and then racing to exploit his endangered points."[29] Many exploitable situations result from enemy movement, difficult terrain, the army's overall condition, and the men's spirit, but others arise from deficiencies in command and control that may be determined by probing attacks, feigned retreats, astute reconnaissance, and observation. Rather than simply engaging the enemy in a straightforward attack, Wu Ch'i counseled cautious assessment and deliberate action to manipulate their forces, affect their commander, degrade their capabilities, and fathom their plans, resulting in Li Ching's somewhat grudging approbation.[30]

Against the "inexhaustible changes of the unorthodox and orthodox," the next exchange reveals Li Ching's view on the evolving nature of military tactics and his rather low estimation of certain famous historical commanders:

The T'ai-tsung continued: "When the ancients approached enemy formations and then sent forth unorthodox troops to attack where unexpected, were they also using the method of mutual changes?"

Li Ching said: "In earlier ages most battles were a question of minimal tactics conquering those without any tactics, of some minor degree of excellence conquering those without any capabilities. How can they merit being discussed as the art of war? An example is Hsieh Hsüan's destruction of Fu Chien. It probably resulted from Fu Chien's incompetence rather than Hsieh Hsüan's excellence."

Fu Chien's defeat at Fei River quickly became a legendary example of tactical stupidity and was even cited as the historical illustration for the topic of "Large Numbers" in the *Hundred Unorthodox Strategies:*[31]

In 383 CE, during the T'ai-yüan reign period of the Eastern Chin dynasty, Emperor Fu Chien of the rival Ch'in advanced his army and encamped at Shou-yang. Thereafter he deployed his forces along the Fei River, resulting in a stand-off with Chin's general Hsieh Hsüan. Hsieh Hsüan addressed Fu Chien: "You have come from afar, crossed our border, and are now deployed along the river, indicating that you do not quickly intend to do battle. We request that you withdraw somewhat to allow our generals and warriors a little space to put their feet, after which we will bludgeon ourselves against you exalted gentlemen. Wouldn't it be pleasant to relax your constraints a little and observe it?"

Fu Chien's staff officers all objected: "We should stop them at the Fei River. Do not let them ascend the embankment! We are numerous while they are few and must fully preserve our strategic power." However, Fu Chien said: "If we withdraw but a little and let them cross, with our several hundred thousand resolute cavalrymen we can press them toward the river and then exterminate them." His brother Fu Jung thought similarly, so they signaled their soldiers to withdraw.

The troops became disordered and were unable to halt. Thereupon Hsieh Hsüan, Hsieh Yen, Huan Yi, and others, accompanied by 8,000 elite cavalrymen, forded the Fei River. Chang Hao, commanding the army on the right, fell back somewhat. However, Hsieh Yüan and Hsieh Yen continued to advance their soldiers and engaged Fu Chien's army in a major battle on the south bank of the Fei River. Fu Chien's massive forces were shattered.

Having ensconced his troops along the river in order to exploit the immense advantages enjoyed by protected troops employing bows and crossbows against forces bogged down in an amphibious assault, Fu Chien should never have belatedly adopted Sun-tzu's advice to deploy slightly upland to entice the enemy. Once ordered into motion his massive hordes could no longer be controlled and were thus easily shattered by an elite though vastly outnumbered cavalry unit. (However, it should be noted that the underlying dynamics have long been disputed in PRC military circles, and in recent decades historians have questioned the battle's very actuality, the vehemence of their arguments even approaching battlefield intensity.)[32]

Following their review of the Fei River debacle, the T'ai-tsung diverts their attention onto the semi-legendary, unorthodox *Wo-ch'i Ching* with an explanation that coincidentally illustrates how titles tend to multiply and become confused:

The T'ai-tsung inquired: "The Yellow Emperor's *Art of War* has been transmitted by previous generations as *The Classic of Grasping the Unorthodox* and as *The Classic of Grasping Subtle Change*. What do you have to say about this?"

Li Ching replied: "The pronunciation of the character *ch'i* (unorthodox) is the same as that for one meaning 'subtle change' (*chi*). Thus some transmitted the title as the latter but the meaning is the same. If we investigate the actual writing it says: 'Four are orthodox, four are unorthodox. The remaining forces are for 'grasping subtle change.' Here the character *ch'i* (unorthodox) means 'excess' and is therefore pronounced *chi*. My foolish opinion is that there is nothing that is not subtle, so why stress 'grasping' in speaking about it? It ought to be 're-mainder,' then it would be correct.

"Now orthodox troops receive their (mission) from the ruler, while unorthodox troops are ordered forth by the general. Sun-tzu said, 'If orders are consistently implemented so as to instruct the people, then the people will submit.'[33] These are received from the ruler. He also said, 'The employment of the troops cannot be spoken of beforehand' and 'there are commands from the ruler which are not accepted.'[34] These are issued by the general himself.

"As for generals, if they employ orthodox tactics without any unorthodox ones, they are defensive generals. If they employ unorthodox tactics without any orthodox ones, they are aggressive generals. If they employ both, they are generals to preserve the state. Thus 'grasping subtle change' and 'grasping the unorthodox' are not fundamentally two methods. Students must thoroughly understand them both!"

Following this brief digression their discussion becomes briefly enmired in the broad details of early encampment and deployment methods:

The T'ai-tsung said: "According to *The Classic of Grasping Subtle Change*, 'The number of formations is nine, with the excess in the center being under the control of the commanding general. The four sides and eight directions are all regulated therein. Within the (main) formation, formations are contained; within the platoons, platoons are contained. They can take the front to be the rear, the rear to be the front. When advancing, they do not run quickly; when withdrawing, they do not race off. There are four heads, eight tails. Any place that is struck is made the head. If the enemy attacks the middle, the (adjoining) two heads will both come to the rescue. The numbers begin with five and end with eight.' What does this all mean?"

Li Ching replied: "Chu-ko Liang set stones out horizontally and vertically to make eight rows. This is the method for the square formation. When I instructed the army, we invariably began with this formation. Its rough outline is probably included in *The Classic of Grasping Subtle Change* passed down through generations."

Whatever the exact array, its essential responsiveness entailing multiple changes thus provides the possibility of unorthodox measures.[35]

Although Sun Pin's *Military Methods* initiated the discussion of military formations and their employment, the earliest known deployments actually date back to the Shang. Thus, by the T'ang military thinkers had long been contemplating how to exercise command and control on the battlefield, often conceived in terms of predetermined formations and their potential adaptability in rapidly changing circumstances, with Chu-ko Liang, who repeatedly employed numerous variations to thwart Shu's more powerful enemies, being anointed as the true master. Accordingly, the later military compendia contain focal chapters replete with diagrams, many of them obviously more theoretical than practical, reflecting centuries of effort. Unfortunately, despite the recent appearance of numerous books dedicated to reconstructing their evolution, little original material seems to have been transmitted, and even the latter posed questions as early as the T'ang:

The T'ai-tsung inquired: "What is the meaning of the eight formations known as Heaven, Earth, wind, cloud, dragon, tiger, bird, and snake?"

Li Ching said: "An error was made in their transmission. The ancients craftily created eight names in order to secretly conceal their methods. The eight formations were originally one that divides into eight.

"Heaven and Earth originated in the flag designations, wind and cloud in pennant names. Dragon, tiger, bird, and snake originated in the distinctions made in platoons and squads. Later generations erroneously transmitted them. If they had been cleverly creating formations in the image of animals, why would they have stopped at just eight?"

Despite Li Ching's explanation, formations and fighting techniques with these names are readily found in the later martial writings and skill manuals, and were apparently circulating in the era of the *Questions and Replies*. Moreover, as will be seen later, Li Ching was in favor of deliberately perpetuating such mysteries so as to maintain control among a core of elite "knowers" and thereby obfuscate enemies and possible revolutionaries. But more mundane organizational questions, of interest only to the extent that they aid in envisioning what Li Ching deemed unorthodox within the context of their military capabilities, are first contemplated:

The T'ai-tsung said: "The numbers begin with five and end with eight, so if they were not set up as images, then they are really ancient formations. Would you please explain them for me?"

Li Ching said: "I observe that the Yellow Emperor governed the army according to the methods by which he first established the 'village and well' system. [Within the village, the basic unit organized around the well] was created by the intersection of four roads, and eight families occupied it.[36] Its shape being essentially that for the Chinese character for 'well,' nine squares were thereby opened.

"(Employing it on the battlefield), five were used for formations, four were empty. This is what is meant by 'the numbers begin with five.' The middle was left vacant to be occupied by the commanding general, while the various companies around the four sides were interconnected, so this is what is meant by 'ending with eight.'[37]

"As for changes and transformations to control the enemy: 'intermixed and turbulent, their fighting [appears] chaotic but their method is not disordered. Nebulous and varying, their deployment is circular but their strategic power is not dispersed.'[38] This is what is meant by 'they disperse and become eight, reunite and again become one.'"

While emphasizing the possibility of change and transformation, Li Ching clearly believes the method was based upon China's famous "well field" system, an idealized projection of village order based upon eight families arrayed around the outside squares of a nine-block array created by the intersection of two horizontal and two vertical paths identical to a contemporary tic-tac-toe board. When adopted on the battlefield, functions of command and flexible reaction are exercised from the central block, the contingents in the eight outer squares being manipulated in a variety of ways. Options range from single-force, directed responses to reciprocal interaction and coordinated, multiple-unit, predetermined deployments.

Certain historically witnessed practices, although apparently more rigid, remain viable when imaginatively employed to realize unorthodox tactics. In illustration Li Ching relates an incident already raised in our introductory material, one often cited by contemporary military historians as evidencing a revolution in military affairs as well as being an early example of unorthodox thinking:

The T'ai-tsung asked: "During the Spring and Autumn period, when Hsün Wu attacked the Ti, he abandoned his chariots to make infantry lines. Were they also orthodox troops? Or unorthodox troops?"

Li Ching said: "Hsün Wu used strategy for chariot warfare, that's all. Although they abandoned their chariots, his strategy is still found therein. One force acted as the left flank, one force acted as the right flank, and one resisted the enemy in the front. Dividing them into three units, this is one tactic for chariot warfare. Whether a thousand or ten thousand chariots, it would be the same.

"I observe that in the period from the Han to the Wei five chariots composed a squad under a Supervisor. Ten chariots formed a company under a Chief Commandant. For a thousand chariots a general and lieutenant-general were assigned. Even if more chariots were added, their organization still followed this pattern. When compared with present methods, our probing force is the cavalry; our frontal assault troops are half infantry and half cavalry; and our holding force goes forth by employing combined chariot tactics.

When I went to the west to rectify and punish the Turks we crossed several thousand *li* of treacherous terrain. I never dared change this system because the constraints and regulations of the ancients can truly be trusted."

Finding himself confronted by non-chariot warriors and facing entrapment on confined terrain, Hsün Wu had faced a formidable challenge. Two centuries later Wu Ch'i would postulate that "For one to attack ten, nothing is better than a narrow defile" and despite the *Liu-t'ao* having asserted that "on difficult terrain one chariot is equivalent to forty infantry-men," it also recognized that such circumstances as Hsün Wu encountered meant death for chariot forces.[39] Thus, it is not surprising that in a subsequent discussion Li Ching acknowledges that Hsün did indeed employ unorthodox tactics: "When Hsün Wu of Chin attacked the Ti he abandoned their chariots and had their personnel form rows as infantry. In this case numerous cavalry would have been advantageous. He only concentrated upon employing unorthodox forces to gain the victory and was simply not concerned with resisting and defending."

Conflict between the comparatively mobile contiguous peoples and sedentary China characterized every dynasty, even the conquest eras, as the victors gradually found themselves embroiled with newly arisen or recently resurgent powers. Despite deploying massive numbers of troops and expending vast sums to construct "great walls," over the centuries the border remained essentially porous to both localized incursions and sweeping invasions. Even the T'ang perished partly because its rulers futilely relied upon foreign generals to staff the border region, hoping to prevent Chinese commanders from amassing troops and instigating a revolt. (Ironically, it was a Sogdian, the infamous An Lu-shan, whose rebellion temporarily sundered the empire and dramatically eroded imperial authority thereafter.)

In this context, the two discussants in *Questions and Replies* were no doubt compelled to ponder the nature of border defenses, external campaigns, and other issues critical to preserving the state's integrity, aspects and practices of which are inherently linked with the unorthodox. In their first joint contemplation Li Ching emphasized that any advantages derived from operational distinctiveness are essentially forfeited when the contingents can be identified. To prevent predictability, enemy observers must be deliberately obfuscated:

> The T'ai-tsung reported: "At present the northern regions are all at peace but groups of barbarians and Han Chinese dwell intermingled with one another. What long-term method can we employ to settle and preserve them both?"
>
> Li Ching said: "I believe it is appropriate for Han forces to be trained in one method and barbarians in another. Since their instruction and training will be different, they should not be intermixed nor treated the same. The moment we experience an incursion by any other group, you can secretly order the generals to change their insignia and exchange their uniforms and employ unorthodox methods to attack them."
>
> The T'ai-tsung then inquired, "For what reason?"
>
> Li Ching replied: "This technique is termed 'manifesting many methods to cause misperception.' If you have barbarians appear to be Han Chinese and Han Chinese masquerade as barbarians, the enemy will not be able to distinguish between barbarians and Chinese. Then, no one will be able to fathom our plans for attack and defense. One who excels at employing an

army first strives not to be fathomable, for then the enemy will
be confused wherever he goes."

Since their tactical methods differ and their relative strengths and weaknesses diverge, obscuring their respective identities through disguise in
accord with Sun-tzu's fundamental dictum to cause misperception and
deceive the enemy creates the twin possibilities of surprise and errant expectation. In fact, the *Ts'ui-wei Pei-cheng Lu* subsequently advocated routinely obscuring the identity of commanding generals to frustrate enemy
reconnaissance and anticipation.[40] However, Li Ching continues by stressing that within the context of the unorthodox, their basic capabilities and
fighting characteristics should not artificially constrain their modes of
employment:

> The T'ai-tsung said: "Barbarian armies simply rely upon their
> strong horses to mount a fervent assault. Are they unorthodox
> forces? Han armies primarily rely on their strong crossbowmen
> to hamstring the enemy. Are they orthodox forces?"
>
> Li Ching said: "According to Sun-tzu, 'Those that excel in
> employing the army seek victory through the strategic configu-
> ration of power, not through relying upon men. Therefore they
> are able to select men for positions and employ strategic
> power.'[41] 'Selecting men' means engaging in battle in accord with
> the respective strengths of the barbarians and Han.
>
> "Barbarians excel in the use of horses and horses are advan-
> tageous in fast-moving fights. Han troops excel in employing
> crossbows and crossbows are advantageous in slow-paced bat-
> tles. Each of them naturally relies upon their strategic power,
> but they are not distinguished as unorthodox and orthodox.
> Previously I discussed how barbarian and Han contingents
> ought to change their insignia and exchange their uniforms, a
> technique in which the unorthodox and orthodox mutually give
> rise to each other. Horses also have orthodox tactics, crossbows
> similarly unorthodox employment. What constancy is there?"

The T'ai-tsung said: "My lord, please discuss the technique again in detail."

Li Ching replied: "First manifest a form and cause the enemy to follow it. This is the technique."

The T'ai-tsung commented: "Now I understand it. Sun-tzu said, 'For the army, the pinnacle of military deployment approaches the formless' and 'in accord with the enemy's disposition we impose measures upon the masses that produce victory, but the masses are unable to fathom them.'[42] This is what is meant!"

Li Ching's comment on manifesting a form of course represents but a partial, perhaps lower-level approach within an ascending continuum of reality, false appearances, and the formless. However, it should be noted that the military writers not only differ but also generally vacillate between viewing "deception and misdirection" designed to compel the enemy into undertaking disadvantageous actions and "formlessness," necessitating a complete dispersal of resources, as more efficacious. However, the formless can also be concealed within false appearances, so that being formless does not necessarily mean being amorphous.

Following another brief discussion of border issues, Book II of the *Questions and Replies* commences with Li Ching's explication of the unorthodox in terms of a common, though sophisticated, concept prevalent in their era, "vacuity and substance." Creating gaps in the enemy's defenses and then exploiting them, a fundamental operational necessity, although phrased in terms of Sun-tzu's vacuity and substance, inescapably depends upon the primacy of the unorthodox:

The T'ai-tsung said: "I have looked through all the military books but none surpass Sun-tzu. In Sun-tzu's thirteen chapters there is nothing that surpasses the 'vacuous' and 'substantial.' Anyone who recognizes the strategic power of the vacuous and substantial when employing the army will always be victorious. But contemporary generals are only able to talk about avoiding the substantial and attacking the vacuous. When they approach the enemy, few of them recognize the vacuous and substantial, probably because they are unable to compel the enemy but are, on the contrary, compelled by the enemy. How can this be? My lord, please discuss all the essential details with our generals."

Li Ching replied: "It is possible to first instruct them about the techniques for changing the unorthodox and orthodox into each other and then tell them about the form of the vacuous and substantial. Many generals do not yet know how to use the unorthodox as the orthodox or the orthodox as the unorthodox, so how can they recognize when the vacuous is substantial and the substantial vacuous?"

The desirability of avoiding strength and attacking fissures and weakness was certainly one of the earliest insights in the development of combat thought. Despite its sparseness, the *Art of War* chapter "Vacuity and Substance" raised it to the level of sophisticated doctrine by conceiving it in terms of the "vacuous" and "substantial," though many of the book's other sections are also premised upon manipulating the enemy through deception and formlessness, causing them to disperse their forces and become insubstantial. Subsequent military writers universally embraced it as a tactical principle but rarely offered any explicit theorizing or focal discussion. Instead, singular statements are found scattered throughout their works, such as the T'ai Kung's admonition, "When you see vacuity in the enemy you should advance; when you see substance you should halt" or Wu Ch'i's assertion that "In employing the army, you must ascertain the enemy's voids and strengths and then race to take advantage of his endangered points."

Three tactical discussions in the *Hundred Unorthodox Strategies* suggest methods to operationally realize this concrete objective:

Whenever engaging an enemy in battle, if their troops are extremely numerous you should establish a vacuous form in order to cause them to segment their strategic power because they will not dare to not divide their soldiers in order to prepare for you. When the enemy's strategic power has been fragmented, their soldiers at any single point will invariably be few. Thus, if you concentrate your troops into a focused unit, they will naturally be more numerous at any chosen point. You will always be victorious when you attack the few with the many. A tactical principle from the *Art of War* states: "Determine the enemy's disposition of force while we have no perceptible form."[43]

If, when you engage an enemy in battle, your strategic power is vacuous, you should create the facade of a substantial disposition to make it impossible for the enemy to determine where you are vacuous, where substantial. You can preserve your regiments and protect your army when the enemy does not dare recklessly engage your forces. A tactical principle from the *Art of War* states: "If the enemy does not dare engage us in battle, it is because we thwart his movements."[44]

Whenever you engage an enemy in battle, if their strategic power is substantial you must rigorously deploy your troops in order to prepare against them, for then the enemy will certainly not recklessly move. A tactical principle from the *Art of War* states: "If they are substantial, prepare for them."[45]

The tactical discussion for "Compulsion in Warfare" in the *Hundred Unorthodox Strategies* further notes that "Whenever you compel an enemy to come forth and engage in battle, their strategic disposition of power will usually be vacuous so they will be incapable of going into combat while your strategic power will always be substantial. If you employ many methods to compel the enemy to come forward while you occupy improved terrain and await them, you will always be victorious. A tactical principle from the *Art of War* states: 'Compel others; do not be compelled by others.'"

Again in the dialogues in the *Questions and Replies*, the still-puzzled T'ai-tsung raises several methods from the *Art of War*'s "Vacuity and Substance" for actively assessing the enemy:

The T'ai-tsung said: "Make plans against them to know the like-lihood for gain and loss. Stimulate them to know their patterns of movement and stopping. Determine their disposition to know what terrain is tenable, what deadly. Probe them to know where they have an excess, where an insufficiency.[46] Accordingly, do the unorthodox and orthodox lie with me, the vacuous and substantial with the enemy?"

Li Ching said: "The unorthodox and orthodox are the means by which to bring about the vacuous and substantial in the en-emy. If the enemy is substantial, then I must use the orthodox. If the enemy is vacuous, I must use the unorthodox. If a general does not know the unorthodox and orthodox, even though he knows whether the enemy is vacuous or substantial, how can he attain them?

I respectfully accept your mandate (to teach them), but will first instruct the generals in the unorthodox and orthodox and afterward they will realize the vacuous and substantial by themselves."

Insofar as unorthodox maneuvers had previously been postulated as the chief means to manipulate and defeat the enemy, Li Ching's advocacy of orthodox actions against substantial armies—essentially a force on force scenario—and unorthodox ones against vacuous (or highly dispersed) enemies is somewhat surprising. However, it no doubt reflects the realiza-tion that "inherently" unorthodox forces, generally being mobile and lightly armored, would normally be wasted against solidly entrenched or-thodox deployments until the latter can be manipulated and emptied. Nevertheless, the T'ai-tsung immediately reaffirms that they are amor-phous and essentially controvertible:

The T'ai-tsung said: "If we take the unorthodox as the orthodox and the enemy realizes it is the unorthodox, then I will use the orthodox to attack him. If we take the orthodox as the unorthodox and the enemy thinks it's the orthodox, then I will use the unorthodox to attack him. I will cause the enemy's strategic power to always be vacuous and mine to always be substantial. If you teach these methods to the generals, it should be easy to make them understand."

Li Ching said: "A thousand essays, 10,000 sections, do not go beyond 'compel others, do not be compelled by them.'[47] I ought to teach this to all the generals."

Although obviously a variant of the indefinitely extendible tactical conundrum "I know that you know that I know," China's battlefield realities generally precluded more than simply reverting to orthodox measures when unorthodox deviations had been fathomed. But highly disciplined troops being necessary to even contemplate these variations, the idea of dividing one's forces (however arbitrarily and artificially) into unorthodox and orthodox components for training purposes inevitably resurfaces:

The T'ai-tsung said: "Our old generals and aging troops are exhausted and nearly all dead. Our armies are newly deployed so they have no experience in assuming formations against the enemy. If we want to instruct them, what would be most essential?"

Li Ching said: "I would instruct the soldiers by dividing their activities into three steps. They must first be organized into squads according to the method of five. After this organization into squads of five is complete, organize them into brigades and armies. This is one step.

"The method for organizing into brigades and armies is to build from one to ten, from ten to a hundred. This is another step.

"Entrust them to the command of subordinate generals who will unite the platoons in each brigade. Then assemble and instruct them with the diagrams for the various dispositions. This is another step.

"The commanding general examines the instructions in each of these three steps and conducts maneuvers to test and evaluate their deployment into formation and their overall organization. He divides them into unorthodox and orthodox, binds the masses with an oath, and implements punishments. Your Majesty should observe them from on high, and all measures should be possible."

The antique, so-called method of five, initially expounded in such classic military writings as the *Ssu-ma Fa* and *Liu-t'ao*, was also favored by Shang Yang and other social engineers. The foundation of China's draconian military discipline across the centuries, it generally entailed the imposition of obligations of mutual responsibility that were strictly reinforced by severe penalties on all members of the group for any infraction or failure committed by any one of them.[48] Although not the only form of organization—the state of Ch'in formerly employed a decade-based hierarchy and Ch'u had another, somewhat obscure variant derived from units of fifteen—as chariots were displaced from their formerly central role it came to predominate in the Warring States period and continued on through the imperial era. Nevertheless, continued confusion over the idealized form of military organization and its relationship with the unorthodox prompted Li Ching to provide a brief overview:

The T'ai-tsung said: "There are several schools of thought on the method of five. Whose is the most important?"

Li Ching said: "According to the *Tso Chuan*, 'First the battalion (of chariots), afterward the squads of five (in the gaps).'[49] Moreover, the *Ssu-ma Fa* states, 'Five men make up the squad of five.'[50] The *Wei Liao-tzu* has a section entitled 'Orders for Binding the Squads of Five.' Han military organization had one foot long (wooden strips) for records and insignia (for the squads). In later ages the records and insignia were done on paper, whereupon they lost the organization.

"I have studied and contemplated their methods. From the squad of five men they changed to twenty-five. From twenty-five men they changed to seventy-five comprised of seventy-two infantrymen and three armored officers. When they set aside chariots and employed cavalry, then twenty-five infantrymen were equivalent to eight cavalrymen. This then was the organization of 'five soldiers matching five.'[51]

"Thus among the military methods of the various strategists, only the method of five is important. In the minimal arrangement there are five men, in the largest twenty-five. If the latter are tripled, they become seventy-five. Multiplied by another level of five, one obtains 375. Three hundred are orthodox forces, sixty are unorthodox (with the remaining fifteen being the armored officers). They can be further subdivided into two orthodox companies of 150 men and two unorthodox platoons of thirty men, one for each flank. This is what the *Ssu-ma Fa* means by 'five men composing the unit of five, with ten squads of five being a platoon,' what we have relied upon until today. This is its essence."

Following a brief discussion of the techniques for training the troops in various formations, Li Ching provides an example of the fundamentals of battlefield manipulation phrased in terms of another of Sun-tzu's famous concepts, the precision of constraints:

The T'ai-tsung said: "Sun-tzu's words are profound indeed! If one doesn't determine the terrain as near or distant, the shape of the land as wide or narrow, how can he regulate the constraints?"

Li Ching said: "The ordinary general is rarely able to know what constraints are. 'The strategic configuration of power of those that excel in warfare is sharply focused, their constraints are precise. Their strategic power is like a fully drawn crossbow, their constraints like the release of the trigger.'[52] I have practiced these methods.

"Thus standing infantry platoons are ten paces apart from each other, holding platoons (of chariots) twenty paces from the main army (of infantry). Between each platoon one combat platoon is emplaced. When advancing forward, fifty paces is one measure. At the first blowing of the horn all the platoons disperse and assume their positions, not exceeding ten paces apart. At the fourth blowing they position their spears and squat down. Thereupon the drum is beaten, three strikes to three shouts, and they advance thirty to fifty paces (each time) in order to control the changes of the enemy.

"The cavalry comes forth from the rear, also advancing fifty paces at a time. The front is orthodox, the rear unorthodox. Observe the enemy's response, then beat the drum again, with the front (changing to be) unorthodox, and the rear orthodox. Again entice the enemy to come forth, discover their fissures and attack their vacuities. The Six Flowers Formation is generally like this."

Infantry and chariots mounting a coordinated, mutually protective advance may of course be likened to the interdependence of mid-twentieth-century tanks and ground troops. This highly constrained (and no doubt idealized) performance was not only envisioned as underlying the possibility of combat success, but also transforming the initial orthodox and unorthodox nature of the various components. However, battlefield control being largely a matter of flags and pennants, Li Ching is compelled to dispel the notion of any fixed identification:

The T'ai-tsung said: "Ts'ao Ts'ao's *Hsin Shu* states, 'When you deploy your formations opposite the enemy, you must first establish the pennants, drawing the troops into formation according to the pennants. When one brigade comes under attack, any other brigade that does not advance to rescue them will be beheaded.' What sort of tactic was this?"

Li Ching said: "Approaching the enemy and then establishing the pennants is incorrect. This is a method applicable only when you are training men in the tactics of warfare. The ancients who excelled at warfare taught the orthodox, they did not teach the unorthodox. They drove the masses just as if driving a herd of sheep. The masses advanced with them, withdrew with them, but they did not know where they were going.[53] Ts'ao Ts'ao was arrogant and loved being victorious. Contemporary generals have all followed the *Hsin Shu* without anyone daring to attack its shortcomings. Moreover, wouldn't setting up pennants when about to engage the enemy be too late?"

The T'ai-tsung then asked: "Are the flags in the colors of the five directions for orthodox forces? Are the pennants and banners for penetrating the enemy for unorthodox forces? Since dispersing and reforming are changes, how is an appropriate number of platoons realized?"

Li Ching replied: "I have examined and employ the methods of old. In general, when three platoons combine, their flags lean toward each other but they are not crossed. When five platoons combine, the flags from two of them are crossed. When ten platoons combine, then flags from five of them are crossed. When the horn is blown the five crossed flags are separated and the combined unit disperses into ten platoons. When two crossed flags are separated, the contingent disperses to form five platoons. When the two flags leaning toward each other, but uncrossed, are separated, the single unit will again disperse to form three platoons.

"When the soldiers are dispersed, uniting them is unorthodox; when they are united, dispersing them is unorthodox. Give the orders three times, explain them five times. Have them disperse three times, have them reform three times. Then have them reform the orthodox configuration, after which the 'four heads and eight tails' (of the Eight Formations

diagram) can be taught to them. This is an appropriate training method for the platoons."

Flags and drums were of course the crux of command, the very possibility of successful warfare prior to the development of electronic communications. Tactically, the fundamental idea of transformation is
achieved through the two complimentary modes of disposition: "When
the soldiers are dispersed, uniting them is unorthodox; when they are
united, dispersing them is unorthodox."

The nature of warfare having fundamentally changed over the centuries, the applicability of earlier tactics invariably arises:

> The T'ai-tsung said: "Ts'ao Ts'ao had fighting cavalry, assault
> cavalry, and roving cavalry. What elements of our contempo-
> rary cavalry and army are comparable?"
>
> Li Ching said: "According to the *Hsin Shu*, 'fighting cavalry
> occupy the front, assault cavalry occupy the middle, and roving
> cavalry occupy the rear.' If so, then each of them was established
> with a name and designation, so they were divided into three
> types. Generally speaking, eight cavalrymen were equivalent to
> the twenty-four infantrymen accompanying the chariots, and
> thus twenty-four cavalrymen to seventy-two infantrymen. This
> was the ancient system.
>
> "Infantrymen accompanying chariots were normally taught
> orthodox methods and cavalrymen unorthodox ones. Accord-
> ing to Ts'ao Ts'ao, the cavalry in the front, rear, and middle are
> divided into three covering forces but he did not speak about
> the two wings, so he was only discussing one aspect of the tac-
> tics. Later generations have not understood the intent of the
> three covering forces so they assume fighting cavalry must be
> placed in front of the attack cavalry. How then would the roving
> cavalry be employed?
>
> "I am quite familiar with these tactics. If you turn the forma-
> tion about, then the roving cavalry occupy the fore, the fighting

cavalry the rear, and the assault cavalry respond to the changes of the moment to split off. These are all Ts'ao Ts'ao's methods."

The T'ai-tsung laughed and said: "How many people have been deluded by Ts'ao Ts'ao?"

Since the T'ang still retained battle chariots despite giving priority to the infantry and especially cavalry, the question remained whether any of them might be inherently predisposed to orthodox or unorthodox functions:

The T'ai-tsung said: "Chariots, infantry, and cavalry, these three, have one method. Does their employment lie with man?"

Li Ching said: "According to the Yü-li formation recorded in the *Spring and Autumn Annals* (*Ch'un Ch'iu*), 'First the battalions (of chariots), afterward the squads of five (in the gaps).' Thus, in this case they had chariots and infantrymen, but no cavalry. When it refers to the left and right resisting, it is speaking about resisting and defending, that's all. They didn't employ any unorthodox strategy to attain victory.

"When Hsün Wu of Chin attacked the Ti he abandoned their chariots and had their personnel form rows as infantry. In this case numerous cavalry would have been advantageous. He only concentrated upon employing unorthodox forces to gain the victory, and was simply not concerned with resisting and defending.

"I have weighed their methods: in general, one cavalryman is equivalent to three infantrymen; chariots and infantrymen are similarly matched. When intermixed they are governed by a single method, their employment lies with man. How can the enemy know where my chariots will really go forth? Or where my cavalry will really come from? Or where the infantry will follow up?"

Their mode of employment being a matter of the commander's intent rather than any inherent characteristic, any battlefield role assigned to any single contingent or component can be readily changed and transformed just as the overall operational tactics may be orthodox or unorthodox. However, the prevalence of esoteric concepts from China's more heterodox tradition adds to the confusion:

The T'ai-tsung said: "Li Chi speaks about male and female, square and circular tactics for ambush. Did they exist in antiquity or not?"

Li Ching said: "Male and female methods come out of popular tradition. In actuality they refer to *yin* and *yang*, that's all. According to Fan Li's book, 'If you are last use *yin* tactics, if you are first use *yang* tactics. When you have exhausted the enemy's *yang* measures, then expand your *yin* to the full and seize them.' This then is the subtle mysteriousness of *yin* and *yang* according to such strategists.[54]

"Fan Li also said, 'Establish the right as the female, increase the left to be male. At dawn and dusk accord with the Tao of Heaven.' Thus left and right, dawn and dusk, differ according to the time. They lie in the changes of the unorthodox and orthodox.

"Left and right are the *yin* and *yang* in man, dawn and dusk are the *yin* and *yang* of Heaven. The unorthodox and orthodox are the mutual changes of *yin* and *yang* in Heaven and man. If one wished to grasp them and not change, then *yin* and *yang* would both deteriorate. How can one preserve only the shape of the male and female?

"Then, when you display an appearance to an enemy, show the unorthodox, not the orthodox. When you conquer, employ the orthodox to attack the enemy, not the unorthodox. This is what is meant by the orthodox and unorthodox changing into each other.

"An 'army in ambush' does not only mean forces lying in ambush in the mountains, valleys, grass, and trees, for hiding them away is the means to effect an ambush. Our orthodox should be like the mountain, our unorthodox like thunder. Even though the enemy is directly opposite our front, no one can fathom where our unorthodox and orthodox forces are. At this point what shape do I have?"

Despite *yin* and *yang* normally being employed to characterize differentiated phenomena and thus having an inherent orientation, Li Ching nevertheless concludes with another affirmation of plasticity and again raises the issue of obfuscation within the ultimate context of the formless. Coincidentally, despite the *Art of War*'s and *Wei Liao-tzu*'s vehement rejection of divination and non-human agency, both official and unofficial prognosticatory practices had not only continued to flourish but paradoxically were also codified and included in the military manuals commencing with the *T'ai-pai Yin-ching*. Li Ching contemptuously dismissed these practices yet perceived them to be a means for occluding the enemy as well as mystifying subordinate staff, thereby preserving the army's secrecy and formlessness. Although not directly conceived in terms of the unorthodox, it was clearly an unorthodox technique and an appropriate conclusion to our lengthy explication of their vital conceptualizations:

The T'ai-tsung asked: "What are the Five Phase formations?"

Li Ching said: "The name was originally established from the colors of the five quarters, but in reality the formations all derive from the terrain's configuration as square, round, curved, straight, and angular. In general, if the army doesn't constantly practice these five during peacetime, how can they approach the enemy? 'Deception being the Tao of warfare,'[55] they resorted to naming them the Five Phases and described them according to the ideas of the School of Techniques and Numbers regarding the patterns of mutual production and conquest.[56] But in actuality the army's form is like water which controls its flow in accord with the terrain.[57] This is the main point."

The T'ai-tsung said: "The four animal formations are also symbolized by the notes *shang, yü, wei,* and *chiao.* What is the reason for this?"

Li Ching said: "It is the Tao of deceit."

The T'ai-tsung inquired: "Can they be dispensed with?"

Li Ching said: "By preserving them one is able to dispense with them. If you dispense with them and don't employ them, deceitfulness will grow ever greater."

The T'ai-tsung asked: "What do you mean?"

Li Ching said: "They obscured the names of the four formations with those of the four animals together with the designations of Heaven, Earth, wind, and clouds, and moreover added the notes and associated phases of *shang* and metal, *yü* and water, *wei* and fire, *chiao* and wood. This was the cleverness of the ancient military strategists. If you preserve them, deceitfulness will not increase further. If you abandon them, how can the greedy and stupid be employed?"

The T'ai-tsung commented: "My lord should preserve this in secrecy, not let it leak outside."

11

Sung Dynasty Theoretical Developments

A lthough the tradition of literate military texts continued into the Ming, most thinkers still illustrated their tactical observations with well-studied, pre-Sung examples. This is somewhat puzzling because warfare in the Sung, first with the Khitan, then the Jurchen and Mongols, although sporadic, was horrific in both scope and consequences. While the focus of these often eclectic compilations continued to evolve, the absence of later episodes may simply reflect the authors' familiarity with the readily available histories, especially the *Tzu-chih T'ung-chien*, coupled with records of more contemporary events, apart from personal chronicles not being readily accessible.

The realm had once again fragmented into several discrete political entities largely created by regional military commanders along old fault lines following the collapse of the long faltering T'ang. Rather than simply harboring their resources and nurturing their population and wealth, these large kingdoms engaged in almost unremitting conflict, providing the *Wu-ching Tsung-yao* editors and later thinkers with extensive materials for contemplation. Border clashes from the chaotic period known as the Five Dynasties period, such as this one in approximately 947 CE, offered virtually unlimited opportunity to implement unorthodox techniques:[1]

When Han Kao-tsu (Liu Chih-yüan) was at Chin-yang, Kuo Chin
went and threw in his lot with him. Han Kao-tsu admired his talent. It happened that the northern invaders butchered the populace of An-yang so he dispatched Chin to attack and recover it. The
Khitan fled so Kao-tsu appointed him as regional inspector for
Fang-chou. When the Khitan leader died, Kao-tsu sent a major
force forth through Ching-ching pass (in the T'ai-hang mountains) while Kuo Chin ventured through narrow byways with unorthodox troops, entering Luo-chou before they pacified Ho-pei.

In this case, although unorthodox troops are employed, it was the unexpected strategy that dispatched them through the difficult T'ai-hang
mountains that merited the episode's inclusion in the *Wu-ching Tsung-yao*.

Continuing a vibrant clandestine tradition, during the period secret
agents were employed not just to garner information, but also to create
doubt in the enemy:[2]

During the Five Dynasties period the founding emperor of the
Hou (Later) Liang encamped his armies at Ch'i-hsia. Hou Chin
forces stealthily mounted a sudden attack upon Chiang-chou,
retaking it. Liang's forward armies lost ground and Chin's army,
relying upon their strategic power, attacked Lin-fen. However,
Shih Shu-tsung had made rigorous defensive preparations.
Moreover, from among the army he selected two warriors with
deep eyes and beards, men whose appearance resembled that of
the local Sha-t'o tribesmen, and had them herd horses alongside
a road out in the countryside.

When the Chin "barbarian invaders" saw them they were
not at all suspicious. The two were subsequently able to inter-
mix with Chin's troops and soon discovered their gaps. They
then each captured a prisoner and returned to the besieged
city. Startled, Chin's commander suspected there might be
troops lying in ambush (among them) and therefore withdrew
to occupy P'u-ch'eng.

Shih's ingenuity in deploying just two spies thus resulted in the dispropor-
tionate effect of the enemy actually withdrawing, certainly an unexpected
but highly fortuitous development.

The classic unorthodox ploy of the feigned retreat also continued to be
exploited to advantage, as in this example in which it was directed toward
defenders resolutely holding a well-fortified city rather than an opposing
army in open-field combat.[3]

> During a campaign mounted by Hou Liang, Chu Chin was at-
> tacked at Yen-chou. When the city didn't succumb, Hou Liang's
> emperor deputed Ko Ts'ung-chou to besiege it. Chu Chin shut
> their gates and refused to come forth.
>
> Ts'ung-chou widely announced that rescue forces were com-
> ing and then visibly withdrew to Kao-wu to supposedly avoid
> them. However, that night he stealthily returned to their origi-
> nal position outside the city walls. Meanwhile, assuming that
> Ts'ung-chou had already departed, Chu Chin dispatched troops
> to retake the outer ditches. Ts'ung-chou closed and struck with
> a sudden attack that killed more than a thousand men.

Although forged by the martial conflict that ended two centuries of
fragmentation, the Sung would never be free from the dark specters of
invasion and rebellion. First they battled the Khitan, later the Jurchen
who conquered the former and then compelled the Sung to abandon
K'ai-feng for the south whose rivers and marshes could impede mounted
steppe invaders. Finally they were extinguished by the Mongols, who vanquished the Jurchen before becoming the first steppe power to occupy all
China.

Traditionally championed as the pinnacle of civilization, an era in which
civil virtue prevailed over martial values, the Sung has equally been excoriated as cowardly, debased, self-indulgent, and myopic for suppressing the
military, undermining its valiant armies, and readily concluding "disgrace-
ful" peace settlements. Being a battle-hardened commander, the founder's
paranoia compelled him to thwart potentially threatening military prowess

and thus bequeathed a heritage of peripheral weakness, fragmented commands, and frustrated missions.[4]

Sung warfare was characterized by the fuller exploitation of night attacks; ruse and deception; incendiary strikes; distant maneuver; conjoined infantry and cavalry forces; the targeting and seizure of enemy supplies; lengthy, technically and tactically complex sieges; square infantry formations; and the deliberate exploitation of terrain configurations. Gunpowder weapons that exploited gunpowder's incendiary capability more than its explosive power first appeared. Primitive, tubed gunpowder devices were also developed that emitted flames, gasses, and even arrows and ceramic fragments, though explosive projectiles were still hurled by catapults and trebuchets.

Negatively, whether civil officials or experienced commanders, Sung generals displayed a tendency to flee and defect, often before engaging in battle, though many outnumbered subcommanders performed heroically and died resolutely. (The calumny and distrust pervading the court, disinterest in defending the state, active opposition to martial achievement, and dire fate of many successful field officers encouraged them to accept the tantalizing rewards offered by the enemy.) Military intelligence played an important role and the steppe powers repeatedly profited greatly from defectors who provide crucial tactical and defensive information.

Sung T'ai-tsu's strategy for conquering the seven independent entities initially confronting him over sixteen years of campaigning embraced two fundamental principles: attack the south while defending to the north, strike the easy before the difficult. Throughout he implemented unorthodox measures on the strategic and operational levels coupled with unorthodox tactics that emphasized night attacks, swift assaults, and incendiary warfare in the watery terrain of the south. (As none of the theoretical military writings cite them, they are only noted in passing.)

Although beset by the Khitan throughout their existence, the Northern Sung still felt compelled to divert border resources to battling Hsia incursions. Horrendous losses had been sustained in the eleventh century during aggressive campaigns to suppress the Turfan, whose Hsia state generally encompassed the northern parts of Kansu and Ninghsia, as well as territory within the Ordos region and lower Inner Mongolia. About 1116, just a decade before the Sung would be vanquished by the Jurchen and forced south of the Yangtze merely to survive, Chung Shih-tao was among the generals assigned to protect the borders and quell the barbarian threat. An astute and resourceful commander, he had previously advised Emperor Hui-tsung (reigned 1101–1126) that they "should first make themselves unconquerable and then respond to the enemy upon their arrival. Wanton activity and untried plans would not be a (viable) strategy."[5]

> Chung Shih-tao, in command of the Wei-chou area (in eastern Kansu), had the troops from the military circuits under his supervision fortify Fu-k'ou. When the enemy subsequently came up and established a solid bastion at the Hu-lü River (in Ninghsia), Shih-tao deployed his forces along the river's margins as if about to engage in a decisive battle. However, he secretly dispatched lieutenant general Ch'ü Wan-ching to go forth across the heights and conspicuously speak about troops coming. The enemy was just looking about in fear when Yang-shih K'o's clandestine army assaulted their rear. Yao P'ing-ching then mounted a surprise attack with elite troops and the enemy crumbled. They killed 5,000 opposition troops and completed the fortified city before withdrawing. He thus combined and coordinated the employment of front and rear, hidden and visible.

Despite the difficulty of their circumstances, several prominent Sung dynasty commanders such as the Wu brothers, Han Shih-chung, Li Kang, and others have not only retained their importance across the centuries but continued to grow in stature, even being lionized by the generally anti-historical Chinese Communist Party and regarded as superlative practitioners of the unorthodox. Preeminent among them is Yüeh Fei, whose lengthy biography in the *Sung Shih* depicts his resourcefulness, imaginative tactics, patriotism, fervor, courage, and resoluteness. Excelling in personal combat, Yüeh frequently plunged into the enemy to single-handedly slay opposing commanders, stir consternation, and induce chaos, causing the enemy's forces to crumble. Despite generally disdaining book learning, he was known for having studied the *Tso Chuan*, Sun-tzu, and Wu-tzu, and employs terminology from the *Art of War* such as "vacuity and substance" in his extemporaneous remarks.

Wo-ch'i Ching

Although the military writings contain a variety of highly formalized, often esoteric and needlessly complex formations that can only be viewed skeptically, they reflect the quest to develop methods to deploy, maneuver, and control functional contingents amid the chaos of the battlefield. Sun Pin's *Military Methods* provides evidence that numerous, though still singular formations not only were being employed by the middle Warring States period, but had already become the subject of theorizing and evaluation. Unique (or simply more easily executed) configurations could already prove to be the difference between victory and defeat, survival and death.

Although the *Military Methods* extensively discusses some twenty or more formations and their appropriate use, the issue of change and transformation is not yet explicitly raised. Moreover, the formations are generally straightforward, characterized by single adjectives indicating their shape, such as "angular" or "geese," or their density as dispersed or concentrated. This does not mean that battlefield commanders were not confronted by the need to employ more complex arrays with greater capabilities or change from one form to another (as depicted in contemporary media), but that no theorizing has been transmitted to posterity. In fact, it would not be until Chu-ko Liang's eight formations that change and transformation would be seriously studied.

The mysterious, semi-legendary work known as the *Wo-ch'i Ching* reflects this quest for battlefield mastery. The origins of the text are obscure, the earliest attribution being to a Lord Feng (Lord of the Wind), reputedly one of the Yellow Emperor's powerful ministers, and even to the Yellow Emperor himself, whom many have viewed as warfare's progenitor as well as the virtual creator of order and civilization because he vanquished Ch'ih Yu's forces of chaos.

The *Liu-t'ao* refers to two of the formations, suggesting that the book existed in at least prototypical form just before the Han, while Han Wu-ti's chancellor Kung-sun Hung supposedly penned the first commentary, one still seen in most versions. Nevertheless, only a few myopic traditionalists assume the extant text predates the T'ang and many skeptics claim it didn't appear until the Sung.[6] However, although decidedly not an antique work, based upon substantial quotations in the *Questions and Replies*, the inclusion of a partial text in the *Hu-ch'ien Ching*, and some materials in the *Wu-ching Tsung-yao*, including a tentative reconstruction of the previously unseen core diagram, it seems likely that the current version probably existed by the middle T'ang.[7]

The title exists in two main variants, prompting discussions on whether the second character wasn't originally *chi*, "subtle moment," as Li Ching discussed, or *ch'i*, "unorthodox" or "excess / remainder." Moreover, it is debated whether *wo*—"to grasp"—should be another character somewhat similar in appearance and similarly pronounced meaning "tent." If so, the basic idea would then be that the general should keep the subtle or unorthodox in his tent, that is, secreted away in his own mind, as the martial texts always advocate.

As the *Wo-ch'i Ching*'s utilization of the unorthodox has already been thoroughly discussed by Li Ch'üan and Li Ching, further explication may be sought from Ma Lung, a Chin dynasty commentator who added a series of succinct appraisals that he initiated with the observation that: "One controls the army through credibility but seeks sagaciousness with the unorthodox. Credibility cannot be changed, warfare lacks constant guidelines. What can be grasped should be grasped, what can be implemented should be implemented so that through a thousand changes and ten thousand transformations the enemy is incapable of knowing them."

Ma Lung also notes that "when in movement one should be unorthodox, when quiet deploy formations" and praises Han Hsin for having used limitless transformations, preventing others from fathoming him. However, most importantly he observes that "In antiquity, unorthodox troops were placed within the deployment, but modern men place them outside the deployment. The army's body should be formless because they will certainly crumble if their form is exposed. Through careful investigation and application, in a hundred battles you'll never be mystified." No doubt commanders had come to feel that pre-positioning the forces entrusted with unorthodox actions outside the main deployment facilitated their flexibility and responsiveness, though probably at the greater cost of constraint and limitation.

In the context of searching for transformable methods on the battlefield, note might also be taken of Kao Ssu-sun's comments in the Sung: "The subtle mysteriousness of the *Feng Hou Wo-ch'i Ching*'s 384 characters lies in the unorthodox and orthodox mutually producing each other, in unfathomable changes and transformations." Theorists were enamored of this text because the basic formations coupled with the method of transformation, powered by the mutual productivity of the unorthodox and orthodox, would allow multiple modes of responsive deployment, ensuring flexibility and the controlled realization of ever changing tactics on the battlefield itself.

Hu-ch'ien Ching

Hsü Tung compiled the *Hu-ch'ien Ching* at the turn of the millennium (1004 CE), just when escalating steppe threats were making the importance of military knowledge increasingly apparent. Surprisingly, despite being a comprehensive work that integrates extensive materials from the T'ang dynasty's *T'ai-pai Yin-ching* and *T'ung Tien*, he not only warns against slavishly following ancient methods, but also advocates deliberately contravening them in order to shed inimical constraints and avoid predictability. As his iconoclastic attitude and irreverent suggestions orient his discussions solidly within the unorthodox and expand the concept's domain of applicability, several theoretical passages merit contemplation.

Numerous passages from the *Art of War* are seamlessly melded into the *Hu-ch'ien Ching*'s thematic discussions. However, the book never devotes any chapters to the unorthodox itself nor does Hsü ever comment upon Sun-tzu's definitive passage, though parts of it are quoted.[8] Instead, he emphasizes rigorously assessing the enemy, manipulating their forces, and formulating detailed plans. Nevertheless, because he cites Sun-tzu's assertion that "armies engage with the orthodox but achieve victory through the unorthodox" he clearly deems the unorthodox to be crucial.[9] Deceptive measures and subversive programs are thus considered critical components in the commander's repertoire, the latter being labeled unorthodox for the first time.[10]

However, it is not just in specifics that the unorthodox is visible. Rather, the spirit of the unorthodox pervades the work and underlies several dedicated chapters such as "Contrary Employment of Configurations of Terrain" and "Contrary Employment of Ancient Methods."[11] While the former summarily rejects the normal tactical constraints imposed by topography, the latter provides a better illustration of Hsü's overall approach and identifies methods that should be considered unorthodox:

> Those who study military theory and employ the martial generally assume ancient methods are empowering. However, this is no different from trying to play the lute after gluing up the tuning stops. It has yet to be seen!
>
> Advantage for military strategists lies in determining whether the response to momentary opportunities should be concordant or contrary. Accordingly, while still mobilizing your armies you should investigate whether the enemy's commander is talented or not. If he is incapable of adopting military methods to employ his troops and simply relies upon his own courage and daring, you can resort to ancient tactics to deal with him. But if he excels at using ancient tactics, you should employ methods contrary to those of old against him.
>
> In the military's unorthodox employment nothing is more unorthodox than establishing ambushes. In establishing ambushes, nothing is more unorthodox than new wisdom. However, it's not that new wisdom doesn't take antiquity as its teacher, but rather that it contravenes the old.
>
> The ancients assessed their enemies upon their initial approach. In order to determine victory or defeat before their

formations engaged, they provoked them with some inferior but courageous troops and then observed whether the orders and commands conveyed by the flags and drums were ordered or chaotic; whether the officers and horses were strong or weak; the encampment and deployments balanced or distorted; the rows and columns correct and composed or dispersed and chaotic; and their speech clamoring or subdued.

The ancient methods state: "If their troops approach yelling and screaming, their flags and pennants in confusion, some of their units moving of their own accord and others stopping, some weapons held horizontally and others vertically, and they pursue fleeing forces as if afraid they will not be able to catch them, or seeing advantage fear not being able to gain it, the general certainly lacks plans. Even if they are numerous, they can be taken."[12] In this way the ancients gained success. Accordingly, when others evaluate us, we should (apparently) cohere with their assessment and deploy troops in ambush to control them. Display facades, wait for them to send their armies forth, and then spring your ambush to attack them.

The ancient methods state: "Those who stand about leaning on their weapons are hungry, who go for water and drink first are thirsty, who encounter advantage but do not pursue it are fatigued. If the army is turbulent, the general lacks severity. Those whose flags move about are in chaos. Those whose officers are resentful are tired. Those who hang up their cook pots without encamping are exhausted invaders. Those whose troops congregate in small groups, whispering together, have lost the masses. Those who frequently look about have lost their organization. Those who seek accommodation want to rest."[13]

Although the ancients used these methods to evaluate the enemy, today it is different. Elite officers and spirited soldiers should be dispersed in ambush at the strategic points and intersections. Meanwhile, create a facade that accords with the enemy's assessment by having your visibly fatigued, wounded, and or otherwise incapacitated soldiers appear to be hungry and thirsty troops who have seemingly lost their unitary organization. Have some repeatedly shift and shake their flags; frequently startle and stir up the masses, have the officers and soldiers clamor and shout. Then, if the enemy sends their army forth in a surprise attack, you can clandestinely launch your forces lying in ambush to unexpectedly attack them.

The ancient methods state: "When the enemy has just arrived from afar and their battle formations are not yet settled, they can be suddenly attacked. When they have covered a great distance and the rear guard has not yet had time to rest, they can be suddenly attacked. When they are traversing hillocks and crossing ravines, half concealed and half exposed, they can be suddenly attacked. When they are fording rivers and are half way across, they can be suddenly attacked. Along narrow and confined roads, if their pennants and flags move about chaotically, they can be suddenly attacked. When the component formations move and shift, they can be suddenly attacked."[14]

Our case is different. When the lines and formations are not yet settled we can establish ambushes on the four sides. When we are traversing a long route without rest, we can establish ambushes. When we are half hidden, half exposed, in woods or muddy valleys, we can establish ambushes. When fording rivers and half way across, we can establish ambushes along the banks and on nearby hillocks. Along narrow roads and confined ways we can establish ambushes to the front and rear. When our flags chaotically move about and our formations frequently stir and shift, we can establish ambushes to the front and rear. But when our armies do not dare pursue a vanquished enemy in flight, it is to prevent being ambushed.

The ancient methods state: "Where birds take flight there is an ambush. If large numbers of trees move enemy forces are coming."[15] Even in such circumstances, it's not invariably true that there is an ambush or that troops are coming because they may simply be trying to create the illusion of troops. When we have run off or disengaged, we should implement numerous measures such as having our old and weak soldiers shake lots of trees and startle the birds.[16]

It's also said that "one who seeks peace without setting any prior conditions is executing a stratagem" and that "one whose troops half advance and half retreat is enticing you."[17] But it may also be that their main forces have clandestinely moved off and that they are trying to cause doubt out of fear that they will be pursued.

When assessing the enemy through various criteria you should extensively ponder acting contrary to ancient methods. Contemplate numerous variations to gain your objective, employing them in the world of men. Thus military tactics may be compared to a wagon carrying things. The wagon's turning in any direction depends upon the wheels, but employing the wagon to go north, south, east, or west all depend upon man. Thus, the impossibility of simply gasping and employing ancient tactics is clear.

The *Hu-ch'ien Ching* chapter "Five Differences" enumerates several other deceptive techniques designed to overcome powerful enemies, expanding Sun-tzu's basic idea of encouraging blinding self-confidence and arrogance and thereby inducing carelessness and laxity. Given a sound understanding of common tactical wisdom, virtually any situation can be advantageously structured through manipulating the enemy's perceptions and projections. The more regular and defined the circumstances, the greater the opportunity for resorting to deceptive, irregular, and unorthodox techniques, including acting contrary to normal methods:

The T'ai Kung said: "One whose wisdom is the same as the masses is not a commander for the army, one whose skill is the same as the masses is not an artisan for the state. No movement is more spiritual than being unexpected, no victory greater than being unrecognized."[18] Sun-tzu said: "The strategic power of those who excel in warfare is sharply focused and their constraints are precise."[19]

"Leading" means being different from the ordinary. For this reason those who excel at employing the military act distinctively in five circumstances: The first is constrained terrain; the second, lightness; the third, danger; the fourth, stupidity; and the fifth, fear.

Exhausted roads and deep valleys, fatal and severed terrain, ruined fortifications and moats, all places normally raced through are ordinarily taken by the masses as constricted and to be avoided. However, in contrast you should make your deployments internally solid while externally manifesting an appearance of disorder in order to entice the enemy. Internally you should be strict with your troops while externally appearing afraid in order to make the enemy arrogant. Then, when they fail to recognize the true situation, oppress them with changes, assault them with troops. This is the Tao for utilizing constricted terrain.

When they are numerous but you are few, your strength is ruined and supplies exhausted, and the power for victory lies with them, you should swear a blood oath with your warriors, strictly order generous rewards, and advance and retreat as if certain to die. Also select a small number of soldiers to suddenly mount a fierce defense against them. The enemy, being more numerous, will assume you are light, but lightness has its employment. Passing through exhausted terrain on which the gate to life has been shut will convert lightness into decisiveness. This is the Tao for employing lightness.[20]

When a strong enemy mounts such a fervent attack that your soldiers are trembling, the masses will assume you are endangered but you should not become agitated or chaotic. In employing perilous conditions your orders must be strict, your preparations thorough. Encourage the officers and troops with thoughts about the will of Heaven, externally close off your appearance, and internally grasp the vital moment to covertly employ unorthodox tactics in sending your troops forth. This is the Tao for employing danger.

When the enemy employs agents to spy upon you, pretend you do not realize it and receive them. When the enemy sends spies into your encampment, pretend you are unprepared but establish ambushes to await their forces. The enemy will assume that you are stupid, but employing the method of apparent stupidity is, on the contrary, wise. This is the Tao for employing stupidity.

When you see the enemy's army approaching, retreat and concentrate behind defensive walls. When you see the enemy's emissaries approaching, speak deferentially and act dispirited, as if you hope to be reconciled with them. The masses will assume you are afraid. When utilizing fear you should withdraw and contract, establish ambushes, and then attack, employing unorthodox tactics to penetrate them. Act as if you want to be reconciled, move them with profits, and make them arrogant through your humility. This is the Tao for employing fear.

These five are contrary to the methods of the masses. When the masses assume we are constricted, we employ the advantages. When they assume we are light, we employ it to be decisive. When they assume we are endangered, we utilize their sense of security. When they assume we are stupid, we employ their wisdom. When they assume we are afraid, we employ their courage. Thus the T'ai Kung said: "One who cannot extend and move his troops about cannot be spoken with about the unorthodox."[21] This is what he meant.

The *Hu-ch'ien Ching* further advanced and expanded Sun-tzu's concept of misdirecting the enemy's perceptions on the battlefield within the parameters of the orthodox and unorthodox:[22]

Warfare is the Tao of deception. Deception can make the empty appear full. Thus, when (the objective) is distant, make it appear nearby; when nearby, make it appear distant. There are six methods for employing the deception of the far and near.

First, those who excel at attacking the enemy cause them to be alert to the front and then assault their rear, they speak of the east then strike the west. They go forth where the enemy will not race, and race where the enemy does not expect. They lure them with profits, causing the settled to move, the rested to labor, and the sated to become hungry. They observe where they are unprepared and suddenly exploit it.[23]

When your army approaches the edge of a deep canyon with a deep river running through it that you cannot suddenly cross, temporarily deploy your army and erect bastions. Then cut down trees and hew out wood, constructing boats across a broad area to show that you will certainly cross. In the middle of the night secretly order elite troops to silently use rafts to cross at some other place and mount sudden strikes.[24] Have your defensive deployments wait along the river until the enemy's masses are in chaos, then your main army can follow up on rafts. This is the second technique.

When the enemy has severed every route of approach to your intended target, your main force should go forth and then return in order to deceive the enemy. When they hear about it, they will assume it's true and neglect their preparations. Then secretly order light, agile fighters to proceed by bypaths, using hanging ladders and bamboo ropes to continuously advance and rapidly cross the terrain to appear where unexpected. Thereafter, race your main force forward in response. This is the third technique.

When your armies have deployed across from each other and the enemy beats the drum and clamors for battle, do not respond. Wait a long time, then gradually withdraw.[25] If the enemy is moving forward to assault your deployments, quickly send forth elite, courageous fighters to attack their heart. Your rear army should expand out to the flanks and follow them. This is the fourth technique.

When the engagement has become intense, secretly segment off unorthodox troops out onto the left and right flanks and have both of them proceed out from behind your deployment to mount sudden strikes, causing their exterior to collapse and their interior to tremble. This is the fifth technique.

While engaged in combat with the enemy, have elite troops prepare an ambush behind the main battlefield. Do not display any pennants or drums, only take strong crossbows, swords, shields, dagger-axes, and metal staves that can be concealed on one's person. Set the ambush up in a mountain forest or in deep grass. When the main force encounters difficulty, open your lines and have the concealed troops first shoot them with their strong crossbows. Thereafter, have the front ranks gradually press the enemy but then pretend to be defeated and lure them into pursuing. The ambush should move (in coordination) and pound them. This is the sixth technique.[26]

These six all display objectives being nearby but gain victory far off. Such are the strategies of the unorthodox and orthodox. Sun-tzu said: "Armies engage in battle with the orthodox and gain victory through the unorthodox." This is what he meant.

Hsü Tung's numerous tactical suggestions obviously depend upon a common, shared military science that can be viewed as applicable to basic situations but that he believes should not be slavishly followed. Its concepts and principles provide fertile ground for exploitation, for taking advantage of probable enemy actions and acting contrary to their expectations, which must somehow be fathomed. Hsü was clearly a sophisticated military thinker, well versed in the era's theories and practices. Nevertheless, his battlefield measures consist largely, though not exclusively, of creating facades and then taking advantage of the enemy's misdi-

rection. Ambushes, especially concealed flank attacks, realized both by regular and unorthodox troops still dominate, with the ancient ruse of a
feigned retreat being the prime lure. However, throughout the emphasis is
upon acting contrary to previous practice, a vision subsequently embraced
by Shih Tzu-mei, who regarded ancient techniques as ossified constraints.

With the flourishing of military thought in the T'ang dynasty and subsequent efforts in the Sung to compile the military classics and create integrated compendiums of tactical teachings, off the battlefield strategists
began to address the question of how spies might be employed rather than
simply categorizing and describing them. However, only Hsü Tung seems
to have pondered their non-military utilization, describing their role and
functions in two chapters of his *Hu-ch'ien Ching*, "Employing Spies" and
"Deceiving the Enemy." Although only the second articulates practices
deemed unorthodox, all eight methods for employing covert agents described in the former provide important contextual information and illustrate the concrete employment of unorthodox measures:

> The officials described in the ancient *Rites of Chou* who traveled
> about the feudal states and reported their plans back to the king
> were actually spies. Thus Sages have always valued the Tao of
> spycraft. If you would utilize the army to determine victory, you
> must also employ agents. If you use agents to fathom internal
> affairs, you must be secretive. Apart from the very wisest, who
> can attain this?
>
> In general, a spy's activities depend upon the situation. There
> are eight basic techniques:
>
> First, when your troops are locked in a standoff with the en-
> emy at the border, pretend to be tired, in difficulty, and fearful.
> Clandestinely leak out word that you will generously provide
> gifts to the enemy's favorites so as to attain what you seek there.
> Next, dispatch emissaries with jade, silk, boys and girls, car-
> riages, superlative horses, and subtle adornments to apparently
> seek a reconciliation. When you observe the enemy becoming
> arrogant and insulting, secretly select and dispatch elite troops

by several routes, having them press their advance both early and late in order to exploit the enemy's laxity and negligence.

Second, when you capture enemy prisoners, leak false plans to them and secretly allow them to escape, thereby causing the enemy to trust in their validity. Since your actions will differ, you will thus be employing the enemy's soldiers as your agents.

Third, when enemy agents come to spy on you pretend not to realize it, instead allowing them to acquire information about a fake plan. Thereafter unexpectedly attack their forces, thereby turning their agents around so that they speak as if they were your own.

Fourth, when enemy agents come, bribe them generously to compel them to betray their missions, thereby spying on the enemy while converting their agents into your own.

Fifth, when engaged in battle with the enemy, feign a minor defeat and urgently withdraw the army into a deep fortress, displaying a terrified countenance. Then select men whose speech is rustic and blunt, of little knowledge or thought, to act as emissaries to the enemy. Have them magnify and exaggerate your army's flourishing strength, causing the enemy to know that they are agents. They will certainly conclude that you are afraid since you have sent agents who speak boldly and spy upon them. After they have departed, mobilize your unorthodox troops to follow on with a surprise attack. This is employing visible agents as spies.

Sixth, when there are favorites in the enemy's court, have your confidants ply their families with gold and jewels so that they might clandestinely learn the enemy's secret affairs. This is employing court favorites as agents.

Seventh, to subvert the enemy's strategists secretly bribe the ruler's confidants with gold and gifts to have them slander them in the court. Then appropriately respond to the slanders from outside the state, causing the ruler and his strategists to grow mutually suspicious, instigating them to ruin and harm each other. This is using slanderers as agents.

Eighth, seek out those that the enemy trusts with their affairs, copiously satisfy their desires, and then secretly ferret out information about the enemy's movements and rest, words and speech. This is employing local people as agents.

Accordingly, we know that agents are the critical essence of the military theorists. But without sagacious wisdom and moral worth one cannot employ agents. Thus the Tao for employing agents lies in the subtle, secretive, clandestine, and submerged, all of which have long been stressed by the best generals.

Although the first two methods intended to spread misinformation apply exclusively to military situations, several expound fully developed counter-intelligence practices that convert enemy agents to useful assets, whether knowingly or not, while the remainder are designed to acquire essential knowledge by subverting enemy officials. In this context the chapter titled "Deceiving the Enemy" advances two brutal, specifically unorthodox techniques designed to spread disinformation that may be seen as continuing Sun-tzu's thought on the critical importance of deceiving the enemy and employing "unconscious" or "expendable" agents:

Warfare is the Tao of deception. Even Heaven and Earth, ghosts and spirits cannot fathom the myriad changes of condensing and expanding. Thus there are two methods for deceiving the enemy:

When an enemy emissary comes to you, privately treat him as if he were a powerful minister, generously plying him with treasures and showing him great gifts. Converting doubts with manifest sincerity is the technique for tying up emissaries. When you have thus convinced him to believe you, when he has no further doubts, you can then delude him by apparently leaking state secrets. Contrary to the enemy's original intent, you will secretly entangle their estimations, yet they will never doubt their veracity. Then, in accord with the information thus passed on to the enemy's ruler, to encourage an internal response show that you are mobilizing troops at the time and place designated. But act unexpectedly when the moment arrives, employing your elite troops to pound their vacuities and press them from outside. This is the first technique.

Select a courageous and daring officer as an attendant, then suddenly pretend to be angry and have him beaten with a bamboo whip until blood is visible. Afterward, secretly let him sneak away to the enemy. In addition, imprison his wife and children so that when he hears about it he will be angry and certainly transmit any secret affairs he formerly heard to the enemy, speaking about your attack at a certain place and time. You should then act as foretold at the right moment, but then secretly send forth elite troops to strike where unexpected. This is the second technique. These are both examples of employing the unorthodox to conquer, the essential Tao of the military. You can never be too knowledgeable about them!

The first case simply advises how to exploit diplomats who, being mesmerized by riches and superlative treatment, can readily be manipulated into believing and confidently reporting whatever is desired. However, the second provides an example of how rulers might ruthlessly manipulate their subordinates into unconsciously acting as expendable agents. Just as described in the now well-known *k'u-jou chi* or "stratagem of suffering flesh" in the *Thirty-six Stratagems*, the individual's conspicuous suffering attests to his veracity. (Yi Yin, China's legendary spy, many of the early assassins, and Huang Kai employed cover stories whose veracity was attested by their physical suffering.) Although Hsü Tung obviously learned from historical practice and is simply embracing Sun-tzu's advocacy of employing expendable agents, his approach has become even more ruthless, no doubt reflecting the Sung's precarious position and an unremitting escalation in the intensity and consequences of warfare. In so doing he has integrated deception and the practice of spycraft into the realm of the unorthodox, at that time expanding from basic military issues to encompass the realm of intelligence and statecraft.

Wu-ching Tsung-yao

The *Wu-ching Tsung-yao* was compiled by imperial directive about 1040 CE amid increasing external threats in part because the emperor had been persuaded that his military officials lacked an understanding of the definitive martial writings and military practices. Its comprehensive theoretical sections were therefore highly regarded and enjoyed widespread, even necessary familiarity, while the examples embedded in the topical discussions and arrayed in the supplementary or second half of the work came to be disproportionately important. Although some of the battles were already well-known, others were unique events dating from more recent centuries of disruption and all acquired new interpretations from within the purview of the unorthodox.

Thorough familiarity with the *Wu-ching Tsung-yao*'s examples, which range from terse references through complete reprisals, is a prerequisite to any penetrating understanding of the highly nebulous concept of the unorthodox.[27] Some of the chapters, such as "Unorthodox Plans" ("Ch'i Chi"), are simply collections of case studies showing how astute commanders manipulated and deceived their enemies through unorthodox techniques. Others, with somewhat enigmatic titles such as "*Ch'üan Ch'i*"—literally "tactical imbalance of power" plus "unorthodox"—depict unorthodox measures that were implemented when confronted with an overwhelming tactical imbalance (*ch'üan*) in power.[28] Although often quite limited, being imaginative and unexpected they invariably had sufficient impact to reshape inimical circumstances or turn the battle.

Another chapter, "Ch'u Ch'i" ("Conceiving the Unorthodox"), draws most of its examples from the T'ang dynasty, focusing upon several generals who spent most of their careers in onerous frontier service.[29] Particularly when the *Wu-ching Tsung-yao* was being compiled, being essentially porous and constantly in flux despite extensive efforts to stabilize and defend it, the border area demanded unorthodox thinking and tactics just to survive. The speed and mobility of mounted steppe peoples (derisively termed "barbarians" or "brigands" in court discussions and official records) presented an almost insurmountable challenge to sedentary Chinese forces confined to forts and strongpoints, dispersed in moribund agricultural colonies, and concentrated in massive cavalry commands.

Although they normally avoided the intense summer heat to attack in autumn and winter when there was adequate grass and water and were therefore somewhat predictable, the steppe peoples could strike at times and places of their own choosing. Even small contingents might exploit gaps and weaknesses with impunity, easily bypassing or overwhelming the local defenders and withdrawing before Chinese forces could mobilize and appear in strength. Forward reconnaissance and clandestine intelligence being vital, both sides continuously dispatched large numbers of spies to ascertain the enemy's status and probable intent.

Two of the several chapters devoted to the unorthodox include extensive theoretical introductions. "Ch'i Ping" or "Unorthodox Troops," although heavily drawing upon and integrating passages from Sun-tzu's *Art of War*, succinctly outlines eleventh-century Sung views:

> Unorthodox troops are orthodox troops that have changed. Troops in ambush are another form of unorthodox troops. Without the orthodox, the unorthodox would have nothing to rely upon; without the unorthodox, the orthodox could not seize victory. Thus those who mount sudden, unanticipated strikes are referred to as "unorthodox" (*ch'i*) troops; those who conceal their shape before acting are referred to as troops in ambush. Their substance is one. A historical survey of the intentions of generals who formerly commanded a million troops shows that whenever two armies were deployed opposite each other for battle anyone who failed to employ the unorthodox inevitably suffered the misfortune of defeat. Thus, troops which are not unorthodox will not be victorious.

Now the plans through which their troops were deployed and maneuvered to achieve victory were invariably based in the unorthodox. Han Hsin destroyed Chao through an unorthodox maneuver but his forces were orthodox. Fu Chien's defeat by Chin was due to Fu's troops being solely orthodox. Even when Hsiang Yü, who excelled at employing troops, had only twenty-eight cavalrymen left at the Wu River, he still divided them into unorthodox and orthodox components, so how much more so should this be the case when your masses are numerous!

The *Ping-fa* states: "When deploying a major formation, always employ thirty percent as unorthodox and ambushing forces."[30] For example, if you have 10,000 men, 1,500 will comprise two unorthodox contingents, 1,500 two ambush contingents. Unorthodox troops are like hands, ambush troops like feet, and orthodox deployments like the trunk. The three are commanded as a single body so that they can alternately rescue and sustain each other. In combat, they mutually advance and withdraw in a never ending cycle.

Thus the *Art of War* asserts: "Troops engage with the orthodox and gain victory through the unorthodox. One who excels at sending forth the unorthodox is as inexhaustible as Heaven and Earth, as unlimited as the Yangtze and Yellow Rivers. The unorthodox and orthodox mutually produce each other just like an endless cycle." This means that the unorthodox is also orthodox, the orthodox is also unorthodox. "When the troops unite to occupy a position they are orthodox, but when they go forth and disperse, they are unorthodox." This refers to taking advantage of the enemy's lack of foresight to suddenly strike.

Through the deceptive Tao of going in and out and the false strength of racing about, strategic power has a myriad changes. Thus the *Art of War* states: "Although capable, display incapability. When committed to employing your forces, feign inactivity. When your objective is nearby, make it appear as if distant;

when far away, create the illusion of being nearby. Display profits to entice them, create disorder and take them. If they are substantial, prepare for them; if they are strong, avoid them. If they are angry, perturb them; be deferential to foster their arrogance. If they are rested, force them to exert themselves. If they are united, cause them to be separated.[31] If they are well fed, make them hungry. If they are rested, force them to exert themselves.[32] Attack where they are unprepared. Go forth where they will not expect it."[33] This is what the *Art of War* refers to as spiritual.

An example of "being capable but displaying incapability" was the Hsiung-nu luring Han Kao-tsu onto the steppe and surrounding him at Pai-teng.

A case of "being about to employ troops but feigning inactivity" was Li Mu keeping his army ensconced at Yün-chung and thereby severely defeating the Lin Hu (steppe tribe).

Having a distant objective yet making it appear nearby was Han Hsin deploying his boats at Lin-chin but crossing at Hsien-yang.

Having a nearby objective yet making it appear distant was the Marquis of Chin attacking Kuo after borrowing a passage through Yü.

The revolutionary Red Eyebrows abandoning their baggage train as bait for Teng Hung is an example of enticing others with profit.

By creating disorder and taking them, Li Ching mounted light boats and destroyed Hsiao Hsien.

As for "if they are substantial prepare for them," when Kuan Yü extirpated the city of Fan he left numerous troops behind in preparation for Liu Pei securing the southern commanderies.

"If they are strong, avoid them," so in the Spring and Autumn period Chi Liang of Sui did not engage the ruler of Ch'u.

In accord with "if they are angry, perturb them," when Han troops attacked Ts'ao Chiu they didn't suffer any calamity at Ssu River.

"Act deferentially to make them arrogant" is illustrated by Shih Le enfeoffing Wang Ling.

In accord with "if they are at ease, tire them," Wu Tzu-hsü severely stressed Ch'u's army to wear them out.

"If they are united, separate them," so Han Kao-ts'u treated Hsiang Yü's emissary rudely and caused Fan Ts'eng to be doubted.

"If they are well fed, make them hungry," so Chin Wen put Chu-ko Tan into difficulty and seized Shou-ch'un.

"If they are rested, move them"; thus Ch'i's army went to Ta-liang and caused Wei's army to withdraw [from Han-tan].

What is referred to as "attack where they are unprepared," by controlling people through what they did not expect Nan Yen was defeated.

"To go forth where they did not expect it" Teng Ai followed vile byways and raced to Chien-ko.

These sixteen all exemplify the experience of former generations. However, there are also cases of changing in accord with the terrain's configuration. The *Methods* states: "When an army on campaign approaches the enemy's border, the commander in chief must carefully ascertain the configuration of the mountains, rivers, plains, and ravines and mentally calculate where troops might be concealed in ambush."[34] Generally speaking gorges and valleys, ravines and defiles are the means to stop and defend against chariots and cavalry. Narrow passes and deep forests are the means to employ a few to attack many. Depressions, marshes, caves, and darkness are the means to conceal shape.

Speed as explosive as a flowing arrow, strikes as sudden as releasing a trigger[35] are the means to smash the most stalwart and elite forces. Deceitful ambushes and distant enticements are the means to capture enemy generals. Segmenting into four and dividing into five is the way to suddenly attack circular formations and destroy square ones.

Taking advantage of their being startled and frightened is the way for one to attack two. Exploiting their terror and fatigue is the way for ten to attack a hundred. Narrow roads and deep grass are places to conceal ambushes. Employing ingenious devices is the way to cross great rivers such as the Yangtze and Yellow. High winds and heavy rain are the means to pummel the front and launch a sudden attack on the rear. Falsely pretending to be an enemy emissary is the way to sever provisions and food, mislead orders and commands. Mountain forests and natural vegetative screens are the means to silently come and go.[36]

"The army is established through deceit and moves for advantage."[37] "Keeping the enemy's forward and rear forces from connecting, upper and lower ranks from trusting each other, generals and troops from rescuing each other, the many and few from relying upon each other"[38] may be likened to a bee or wasp coming out of your sleeve or a fierce fire breaking out in a thatched hut. Even stout fellows and fierce officers are startled and perturbed. This is what is known as being able to exploit an advantage to control them.

The reading of the initial line, literally "Now unorthodox troops are orthodox troops that have been changed," should be understood as meaning unorthodox troops are orthodox troops that have *functionally* changed because all troops are amorphous unless they have been equipped for a particular fighting style or mission. (Plasticity does not extend indefinitely, but is constrained by the original definition.) Troops equipped with standard infantry weapons such as the *chi* (long-handled, spear-tipped dagger-axe) and heavier armor, having sacrificed mobility for stability and being trained for fairly moribund formations, were inherently limited in their flexibility and combat capabilities and thus expected to engage the enemy in orthodox fashion, in set piece battles and forward-oriented clashes.[39] In contrast, troops equipped for highly mobile action with short armor, light bows, and swords, innately lacking the substantiality necessary for massive direct conflict, would be predisposed to undertaking the maneuver warfare that would constitute their orthodox employment. However, even the heaviest, most orthodox troops can be employed in irregular fashion such as by suddenly collapsing to feign a retreat, segmenting for angular attacks, or launching concealed incendiary or similarly unexpected, technologically facilitated strikes, thereby operating in unorthodox fashion and being considered functionally unorthodox troops.

The next line, "Without the orthodox, the unorthodox would have nothing to rely upon (or means by which to be established), without the unorthodox the orthodox could not seize victory," somewhat surprisingly reaffirms the traditional conception that the orthodox provides the basis for victory but the unorthodox achieves it. The authors thus reiterate the view that the former confronts, opposes, immobilizes, and ties down the enemy while the unorthodox component maneuvers and flanks, penetrates gaps, and acts unconventionally and unexpectedly to wrest victory over the now entangled foe. In this conception purely unorthodox forces and operations would be precluded.

Over the centuries the initially unorthodox combination of suppressive fire and maneuver gradually became common practice and thus increasingly orthodox rather than spectacular and unexpected. Conversely, within this continuum maneuver, reconnaissance and other forces (simplistically) designated as unorthodox that traditionally undertook limited missions and irregular actions began to mount conventional assaults and steadfast defenses (such as by exploiting constricted terrain), thereby transcending their apparent constraints to execute orthodox tactics and thus act in an unorthodox manner. However, given the importance of deception and facades in leveraging combat strength and the possibility that either (artificially defined) orthodox or unorthodox forces might be feigning an appearance to manipulate the enemy, characterizing them apart from the context of concrete circumstances is impossible.

Another theoretical chapter, "Attacking the Many with a Few," focuses upon the unorthodox:[40]

When attacking the many with a few, it is advantageous to initiate unorthodox (methods). Three are discussed in the *Ping-fa*:

First, press them in ravines; second, strike the chaotic with the well ordered; and third, exploit the setting sun. Generals who understand these three can employ one to strike ten and a thousand to strike ten thousand. Even the strategic power of an extremely numerous enemy can then be easily overturned. I have therefore reprised the sayings of earlier strategists below.

When the enemy is numerous and we are few, we must avoid them on easy terrain and press them into constricted spaces where one defender can thwart the approach of a thousand men. If we encounter each other in a ravine or defile and our troops beat their drums, set up a clamor, and rise up, even though the enemy's masses are extremely numerous, their front ranks will certainly be startled and fearful. We can exploit their reaction to suddenly attack them and destroy them as their power diminishes.

It is also said that if we occupy woody hills or forested mounds, we can set out flags and pennants and emplace numerous drums and cymbals, scattering them about as "doubtful" troops. The enemy will certainly divide their armies in order to prepare against us, allowing our elite troops to go forth in a sudden, unorthodox strike. However, if we cannot gain an advantageous situation, we can rest in dark woods or along a river, spreading out our formations with our archers and crossbowmen deployed at the front to oppose them. Then we can wait for late night to swiftly strike them.

Whenever a small formation encounters a major deployment, prolonged contact will not be advantageous. The enemy will certainly think lightly of us and not fear engaging in combat, providing an advantage that we should exploit to quickly advance. Being numerous, the enemy's troops will invariably be spread across an extensive area and be disordered. The sound of the gongs and drums will not be heard nor the color of their flags seen. The left will not be able to hear the right nor the right hear the left. The front will not hear the rear nor the rear hear the front. If we suddenly strike their masses with the united strength of our few forces, we will certainly be victorious.

If the enemy's encampment is not yet settled, the fortifications around their deployment incomplete, or their orders and rescripts not yet promulgated, we can urgently strike them.

The *Ping-fa* also refers to situations in which the enemy is numerous while we are few, saying that we should exploit an advantageous route that allows us to be surrounded in order to solidify the mind of the troops. When the enemy besets us on all four sides, our soldiers will (fervently) hold their terrain and engage in a decisive battle.[41]

Whenever we engage a massive enemy in combat, we should divide into three or four, some going west, some east, resting and fighting in turn. Some should beat the drums, shout, and advance while others should be silent and set up ambushes. Have our light cavalry forces race around our flanks to the left and right, then we can wait for the sun to set before striking. Every man should carry a torch, every two men a drum. Some will be illuminated, some in the darkness. Some will beat drums, some shout, and others, with gagged mouths, will silently but swiftly strike their two sides and penetrate their left and right flanks. Some will courageously pummel their formations with headlong attacks. Even though the enemy is numerous, their generals can be captured.

The use of constricted terrain to overcome severe strength discrepancies dates back to Sun Pin's *Military Methods* and Wu-tzu's idea of vital point of terrain and was incipiently embedded in the *Art of War*'s recognition of configurations of terrain. Most of the concrete measures are obvious or already familiar and thus need no further explication. However, the exploitation of environmental conditions such as the angle of the sunlight, darkness, and the concealment of vegetation bear note, as well as the emphasis upon swiftness, segmentation, misdirection through the creation of dubious troops, and taking advantage of the enemy's laxity in the face of paltry forces.

Four Innovative Commentators

A number of Sung martial thinkers who exerted significant influence in their own and subsequent eras are known more for their commentaries than stand-alone works. **Chang Yü** was one of the three individuals responsible for compiling the *Wu-ching Ch'i-shu* or *Seven Military Classics* that became canonical late in eleventh-century Sung China. Therefore, his views as a commentator to the *Art of War* presumably reflect hierarchical thinking and may well have affected official Sung dynasty interpretations of the *Art of War*, as well as doctrinal formulations derived from them:

> When the (enemy's) Three Armies are massive, the way to cause each and every man to withstand them and not be defeated lies in the unorthodox and orthodox. Explanations of the unorthodox and orthodox vary. The *Wei Liao-tzu* states: "Orthodox troops value being first, unorthodox troops value being afterward." Ts'ao Ts'ao said: "Going forth first to engage in battle is orthodox, going forth afterward is unorthodox." And Li Wei-kung noted: "Armies take the forward direction to be orthodox, rearward movement to be unorthodox."
>
> These views all take the orthodox to be orthodox and the unorthodox to be unorthodox and never speak about the meaning of change and circularity. Only T'ang T'ai-tsung said, "If we take the unorthodox as the orthodox but cause the enemy to perceive it as the orthodox, we will attack with the unorthodox. If we take the orthodox as the unorthodox but cause the enemy to misperceive it as the unorthodox, then we will suddenly strike them with the orthodox. Intermix them to be a single

method, keep the enemy from being able to fathom it."[42] This is
the most felicitous.

Despite Chang's emphasis upon the abstract dynamics of *ch'i / cheng*, in
explaining the final sentences of the critical passage—"in battle one engages
with the orthodox and gains victory through the unorthodox"—he surprisingly reverts back to a more limited, force-based implementation: "When
two armies approach each other, first send forth orthodox troops to engage
them, deputing the remainder as unorthodox troops. Some will pound their
flanks, others suddenly strike their rear in order to conquer them just like the
Duke of Cheng who, in resisting the hordes of Chao, employed his Three
Armies to confront them while clandestine troops attacked their rear."

More importantly, in commenting upon the intrusive sentence "If
wherever the army attacks it is like a whetstone thrown against an egg, it is
due to the vacuous and substantial" Chang unfolds the sequential links
that empower the adoption of unorthodox tactics:

> The next chapter ("Vacuity and Substance") states that "One
> who excels at warfare compels men and is not compelled by
> other men." This is the method of vacuity and substance in our-
> selves and the enemy.
>
> If we compel the enemy to come forth, their strategic power
> will always be vacuous. If we do not approach the enemy, our
> strategic power will always be substantial. Attacking the vacuous
> with the substantial is like picking up a stone and hurling it
> against an egg—the egg's destruction is certain!
>
> Now when combining the armies and assembling the
> troops, their division and numbers must first be settled.[43] Only
> after their division and numbers are clear can they be trained
> in configuration (formations) and designation (name). Only
> after configuration and designation are correct can they be di-
> vided into unorthodox and orthodox. Only after the unortho-
> dox and orthodox have been clearly illuminated can the

vacuous and substantial be perceived. Such is the sequence of these four affairs."

Or, as Ts'ao Ts'ao asserted, "one (thereby) attacks the most vacuous with the most substantial." However, surprisingly the "substantial" here essentially refers to a strongly defensive posture wherein the enemy is compelled into attacking and the innate advantages of an ensconced defense can be exploited, but the active role may easily be sacrificed. His interpretation clearly derives from Sun-tzu's ideas about compelling men and assuming a defensive posture to ensure strength will be more than adequate, but in so doing unnecessarily limits the possibilities.

Ho Ch'ü-fei, who held the civil title of Po-shih, apparently served throughout his professional military career in the Sung dynasty's newly established martial university, having been initially appointed around 1082 CE, near the end of the Northern Sung. Unknown apart from having participated in the editing of the imperially compiled *Wu-ching Ch'i-shu* (*Seven Military Classics*), his *Pei Lun* (*Complete Discussions*) was probably penned near the end of the eleventh century. Each of the extant twenty-six chapters reevaluates an important historical era or figure such as the Ch'in dynasty and Ts'ao Ts'ao. Throughout his views are heavily based upon the *Art of War* and he explicitly states that Sun-tzu's work provides the foundation for all military tactics. Nevertheless, he also believes that military tactics cannot be fully expressed in words, that (as might be said today) the commander's intent, formulated in the exigency of the moment, cannot be fully expressed. Moreover, he subscribes to the *Art of War*'s tenet that the commander's control of battlefield tactics should be transcendent, a matter of suddenly informing the troops of the requisite actions but not the underlying understanding. In this context deception is deemed a useful adjunct, the objective being one's own troops as much as the enemy.

Although the concept of the unorthodox is accorded a fundamental place in his thought and pervades the entire work, it's not overemphasized. Rather, it frequently reappears in scattered, individualized pronouncements that reflect his view that it's impossible to wrest victory without the unorthodox, that the army can never neglect the unorthodox. In fact, he cites the king of Wu's rebellion in the Former Han dynasty, previously discussed in conjunction with Li Ch'üan's *Art of War* commentary, as an illustrative example. Interestingly, Ho argues that despite friction and animosity, Liu P'i had effectively governed the potentially troublesome area of Wu (around modern Shanghai and Suzhou) for some forty years without overtly opposing the throne, and that the blame for the debacle should fall upon the prime minister, Ch'ao Ts'o.

Although Li Ch'üan, in following the *Shih Chi*'s basic account, had faulted the king for failing to adopt an unorthodox operational plan, Ho believes that neither what he terms the orthodox plan formulated by the older generals to simply mount a massive effort against Liang where imperial strength was concentrated nor the unorthodox method of a swift strike upward upon the ancient capital of Luo-yang, positioned in an area of grain supplies and great richness, would have succeeded by itself. Rather, the two were complementary, with the orthodox and unorthodox both being necessary, thereby preventing stagnation in their advance and loss of their supply lines. Ho therefore remarks that it was a good thing the king of Wu didn't understand military strategy; otherwise, the Han dynasty would have been overthrown.

In another development, Ho revisits Sun-tzu's doctrine of segmenting and reuniting, making capability in dividing the foundation of the unorthodox: "By establishing the unorthodox in accord with events it will be inexhaustible. The army is mobilized in accord with righteousness and conquers through wisdom. In warfare, one engages through concord but achieves victory through the unorthodox. Moreover, apart from wisdom, the essence of the unorthodox is the ability to divide. The army must be able to put forth the unorthodox, while the unorthodox constantly lies in dividing." This of course re-expresses the idea that one joins battles with the orthodox and gains victory through the unorthodox.

Historically, Ho is not surprised that large armies that failed to segment were defeated because they thereby acted just like a singular force and lacked responsiveness and flexibility. Ideally, the army should be as responsive as the snake from Mount Ch'ang made famous by Sun-tzu's *Art of War*: When the tail was struck, the head responded; when the head was struck, the tail responded; and when the middle was hit, the two extremities reacted. Accordingly, he concluded that "armies have many and few, strategic power has dividing and uniting. When you meet the many with a few, strategic power is appropriate to uniting, but when you meet the few with the many, strategic power is appropriate to divide."

In illustration he cites the astonishing defeat of Fu Chien's massive forces by a paltry enemy at Fei River, Fu having failed to segment his forces. (Ho also notes that reluctance to yield power and authority to another commander was an almost universal flaw.) Hsiang Yü's apportionment of his twenty-eight remaining cavalry into smaller groups, designating one of them as an unorthodox component, in his very last moment is also seen by Ho as further evidence of the importance of dividing. Thus he concludes that "Military tactics must stem from the unorthodox while the unorthodox always lies in segmenting."

Ho singles out Ts'ao Ts'ao (whom he notes was clever, deceptive, unorthodox, and constantly changing) and Han Hsin as surpassing generals whose success derived from their great capacity for effecting "inexhaustible changes." Similarly, the Former Han cavalry commander Huo Ch'ü-ping was innovative and flexibly responded to the moment even though he disdained the study of military texts.[44] (He therefore exemplifies Ho's view that the effective commander achieves a sort of innate, incommunicable understanding.)

Conversely, he vociferously condemns Chu-ko Liang—despite the latter's fame as the unorthodox's virtual progenitor—for refusing to use unorthodox methods when invading the Chinese heartland despite Wei Yen's cajoling. Because only one of the six campaigns exploited unorthodox tactics while Shu, though well-ensconced in the bastion of Szechuan, could not sustain the logistical requirements of 1,000 *li* supply lines through difficult, even impossible, terrain, they were doomed from the outset. Meanwhile, under Ssu-ma Chung-ta's brilliant command, the enemy simply adopted an attritional strategy and persistently refused to be drawn into battle despite the most egregious insults.

In the context of Shu's ruler, Liu Pei, having three times lost control of core terrain that could have constituted a pivot for recovering the empire, the famed retreat into Szechuan constituted a viable expedient that ensured temporary survival but could not be the sustainable basis for an overarching strategy. Moreover, in discussing Chu-ko Liang's strengths and weaknesses, Ho disparages his vaunted reputation: "He had the ambition to achieve success and the benevolence to bring the masses together, but not the knowledge to use the masses. He had the ambition to establish achievements but not the capacity to achieve success, he had the benevolence to unite the masses but not the knowledge to employ the masses."

Surprisingly, Ho believes that Ssu-ma Chung-ta surpassed all others in his achievements and excelled in self-control, yet was also a master of the unorthodox. "At the outset he controlled his army, putting forth the unorthodox and responding to change, coping with the hasty and sudden as if spiritual. There was nowhere he went that was not superlative." Finally, echoing his own evaluation, he cites Ssu-ma Chung-ta's reported perceptions: "Chu-ko Liang's ambition is great, but he doesn't perceive the subtle moment. He has many plots but is rarely decisive. He loves the military but lacks tactical power or authority. Even if he raises a mass of 100,000, he will still fall into my plans. It is certain that I will destroy him."

Apparently a late Sung martial official, **Ho Shih** is otherwise unknown, though his commentaries to the *Art of War* follow the T'ang practice of introducing historical examples to concretely illustrate abstract doctrine:

> In the confused and turbulent body of the army, amidst a myriad changes, there are no (troops) that are not orthodox, none that are not unorthodox. Troops raised in righteousness being orthodox, those that change when they engage the enemy are unorthodox. If we cause the enemy to perceive our orthodox as unorthodox and our unorthodox as orthodox, the orthodox will also be unorthodox, and the unorthodox orthodox.
>
> Generally, those who employed the military used both the unorthodox and orthodox. Victories gained without the unorthodox were lucky victories, the engagements wasteful. For

example, insofar as Han Hsin deployed his forces with their backs to the river and dispatched troops around the mountain to seize Chao's pennants and destroy their state, deploying with their backs to the river was orthodox, going around the mountain was unorthodox.

Han Hsin also massively approached Chin but attacked An-yi via Hsia-yang by using poles and jars and thereby captured King Pao of Wei. Their thrust toward Chin was orthodox while (crossing at) Hsia-yang was unorthodox. From this point of view, "withstanding the enemy without being defeated" refers to the unorthodox and orthodox. The *Wei Liao-tzu* states, "If you have the sharpness of the (famous sword) Mo Yeh, the solidity of rhinoceros armor, the masses of the Three Armies, and unorthodox and orthodox methods, no one under Heaven will be able to withstand you in battle."[45]

Ho Shih's assertion of the absolute need for the unorthodox to achieve victory evinces a view found in other later writers as well, one that envisions unorthodox techniques as both complimentary and essential. More importantly, he asserts the importance of causing the enemy to misperceive the tactics being employed, thereby (at least conceptually) converting one to the other, though he falls short of fully asserting their plasticity. However, his interpretation of Han Hsin's deploying with their backs to the river as orthodox is somewhat puzzling because Han himself understood the deployment on fatal terrain as contrary to normal practice and therefore unorthodox.

In the middle of the Southern Sung dynasty **Shih Tzu-mei** penned a series of commentaries to the *Seven Military Classics* so extensive as to merit the title of lectures. Much studied in both Japan and China over the centuries, they were the first to treat the *Seven Military Classics* as canonical, thereby showing the continuity of military thought from Sun-tzu's *Art of War* through Li Ch'üan's T'ang dynasty *T'ai-pai Yin-Ching* up into his own studies in the early thirteenth century. Not surprisingly, through considerable effort the lectures have even been reprinted in the contemporary PLA series of essential military works, attesting to their currency and probable locus of ongoing study as the PRC searches for inspiration amidst the records and texts of antiquity and reevaluates indigenous conceptions and tactical principles.

Shih Tzu-mei's explications almost seamlessly interweave quotations from previous writings to express his own viewpoint. As such, they provide a case study in the mastery of Chinese military manuals, as well as a penetrating understanding of the most esoteric doctrines.[46] In commenting upon the *Art of War*'s initial statement, "In warfare, one engages with the orthodox and gains victory through the unorthodox," Shih extensively paraphrases materials from both the *Methods* and *Questions and Replies*:

> If you do not display the orthodox, you will not have any means to bring the enemy forth. If you do not control them with the unorthodox, you will not have any way to bring about the enemy's defeat. Engaging in battle on a designated day and uniting your armies (on the battlefield) at a pre-announced time are orthodox. Making noise at the front but then suddenly striking the rear, visibly harassing the left flank but then seizing the right, are unorthodox. The *Methods*' assertion "First be orthodox and afterwards unorthodox" also expresses this idea.[47]
>
> At the battle of Huo-yi the army had been mobilized out of righteousness so they were orthodox troops. But when the right flank withdrew somewhat and Lao-sheng was captured, it was unorthodox. Insofar as the orthodox changed to the unorthodox and the unorthodox changed to the orthodox, they cannot be spoken of in a single way. Thus, in referring to Ch'in-hu, Li Ching commented, "How could Ch'in-hu know about the pinnacle of the unorthodox and orthodox?"

Shih then explicates the core section of Sun-tzu's definitive passage with a lengthy contemplation focusing upon the inexhaustible changes of the

unorthodox and orthodox, stressing their interdependence and convert-
ibility while deriding those who become enmired in viewing and employing them in isolation:

> Those who innovate strategic plans for decisive victory esteem
> bringing about minute, subtle opportunities while those who
> trust to things to make their ideas clear value the emblemiza-
> tions of profundity and depth. As for profundity, nothing is
> more profound than Heaven; as for the depths, nothing is
> deeper than the oceans. Conceiving the unorthodox and em-
> ploying wisdom, turning them about inexhaustibly, pondering
> them without exhaustion, these are what the *Fa* (*Methods*)
> refers to as "like the depths of Earth, like the secrecy of Heaven."
> Or again, "Like the rivers and oceans." Truly. The numbers of
> the sun and moon cannot be estimated, the four seasons cannot
> be encompassed by calendars.
>
> The basic flavors of sour, bitter, acrid, salty, and sweet can all
> be tasted individually, but if you change and employ them the
> flavors can never be exhausted. The individual colors of blue,
> yellow, red, white, and black can be observed, but when they are
> changed and employed they can never all be seen. The individ-
> ual notes of *kung, shang, chiao, wei,* and *yü* can be heard, but
> when they are changed and performed the melodies can never
> all be heard. The unorthodox and orthodox, being the normal
> configurations of power in warfare, can be exhaustively known,
> but if you change and extend them, they cannot be exhausted.
>
> Without doubt armies are employed through tactical meth-
> ods but tactical methods can only be employed on a basis of
> strategic power. There are subtle moments of appropriateness
> for all tactical measures, moments when minute changes allow
> penetration. The unorthodox and orthodox are techniques,
> their employment is a matter of a subtle moment. Tu Mu says,
> "Employing the military is like rolling a pearl around in a
> basin."

Whether horizontal or angled, curved or straight, plans are made extemporaneously. The *Questions and Replies* states, "Unorthodox and orthodox lie with man who changes them in spiritlike fashion, causing them to be attributed to Heaven." Moreover, in discussing Han Ch'in-hu, Li Ching said, "He only took the unorthodox as the unorthodox, and the orthodox as the orthodox. He never knew about the 'mutual change of the unorthodox and orthodox into each other, the inexhaustible cycle.'" And in discussing Ts'ao Ts'ao's *Hsin Shu*, added: "As Sun-tzu said, 'In warfare the configurations of power for achieving victory do not exceed the unorthodox and orthodox, but the change of the unorthodox and orthodox cannot be completely exhausted. The unorthodox and orthodox mutually produce each other just like an endless cycle.'" This expresses it.

Those in antiquity who excelled in speaking about the unorthodox and orthodox did not depart from this. But only Han Hsin understood their Tao. In capturing King Pao of Wei he used wooden poles and jars to cross at Hsia-yang; his slaying of Lung Chü was achieved by employing sacks of sand to sever the Ch'ih River; in suddenly striking Chao he deployed with their backs to the river; and he subjugated Yen with a (persuasive) letter speaking about Heaven. Didn't Han Hsin's unorthodox innovations thus inexhaustibly revolve and seize without limit? He must certainly have been like the dark depths of Heaven and Earth, the rivers and oceans. This is why Tu Yu similarly said, "The four seasons are in turn reborn, they arise and afterward decline; the sun and moon revolve about, they enter (the darkness) and then again come out."

Pai-chan Ch'i-lüeh

A focal work whose very title emphasizes the unorthodox, the *One Hundred Unorthodox Strategies* was probably compiled late in the Southern Sung after the court had been ignominiously driven into exile south of the

Huai and eventually Yangtze Rivers to commence a period of precarious existence plagued by predations by the Khitan, Jurchen, and finally Mongols, who ultimately conquered them. An anonymous book that has recently been reprinted in several formats, including cartoon versions, and republished under other titles in the PRC, it identifies one hundred fundamental martial concepts and tactical principles and provides a brief tactical analysis and an illustrative battle for each of them. Despite the title, the book does not transform them all into unorthodox strategies, but instead emphasizes flexibility in their understanding and adoption, often in terms of paired alternatives such as swiftness and slowness. Two focal chapters delineate the unorthodox and orthodox:[48]

> In general, in warfare what is referred to as the "unorthodox" means attacking where the enemy is not prepared and going forth when they do not expect it. When engaging an enemy, frighten them in the front and overwhelm them in the rear, penetrate the east and strike in the west, causing them never to know where to mount defensive preparations. In this fashion you will be victorious. A tactical principle from the *Questions and Replies* states: "When the enemy is vacuous, then I must be unorthodox."
>
> Whenever engaging an enemy in battle, if the roads are impassable, preventing the movement of provisions and supplies, your plans cannot inveigle the enemy, nor can proffered advantages and threatened harm confuse them, then you must employ orthodox troops.
>
> For an orthodox army you must train the officers and troops well, make the weapons advantageous, ensure that the rewards and punishments are clear, and make certain that edicts and commands are trusted. If you then engage in combat and advance, you will be victorious. A tactical principle from the *Questions and Replies* states: "Without orthodox troops, how can one venture out far?"

Both tactical discussions conclude with statements already familiar from the *Questions and Replies*. In Li Ching's synthesis of Sun-tzu's thought, exploiting the vacuous and avoiding the substantial provides the key to victory, while they in turn are realized through the crucial methodology of the unorthodox and orthodox: "The unorthodox and orthodox are the means by which to bring about the vacuous and substantial in the enemy. If the enemy is substantial, then I must use the orthodox. If the enemy is vacuous, then I must use the unorthodox." However, the *Pai-chan*'s disquisition on the vacuous and substantial, no doubt in accord with the perplexing problem of being weaker and thereby having to resort to defensive and unorthodox measures, stresses preparation against substantial enemy forces and "creating the facade of a substantial disposition to make it impossible for the enemy to determine where you are vacuous, where substantial."[49]

As we have already translated the *Unorthodox Strategies* in full and parts have been cited for convenience throughout our discussions, only a few key tactical principles that specifically fall within the unorthodox need be noted. Generally speaking, Sun-tzu's concept of manipulating the enemy through all available means, including enticements, deceits, and facades, provides the fundamental thrust. Thus, for example, "The Strong in Warfare" states: "In general, if you want the enemy to engage your stronger, more numerous troops in battle, you should feign fear and weakness in order to entice them into it. When they carelessly come forth you can suddenly assault them with your elite troops and their army will invariably be defeated. A tactical principle from the *Art of War* states: 'Although capable, display incapability.'"

Conversely, "if the enemy is numerous while you are few, if the enemy is strong while you are weak, you must set out numerous flags and pennants, double the number of cook fires, and display strength to the enemy. If you make it impossible for the enemy to determine your numbers as many or few or your strategic power as strong or weak, they will certainly not lightly engage you in battle. Thus you will be able to rapidly depart, thereby preserving your army and keeping harm distant.

A tactical principle from the *Art of War* states: 'Strength and weakness are a matter of disposition.'"[50]

Deceptive measures being a key component for executing unorthodox tactics, the *Pai Chan* elucidates them in several chapters, including "Utterances in Warfare," which suggests making specious statements to mislead the enemy, and "Doubt," which states:

> Whenever occupying fortifications opposite an enemy, if you want to launch a sudden attack against them, you should gather large amounts of grass and different branches and make your flags and pennants numerous in order to create the appearance of a populated encampment. If you force the enemy to prepare in the east and then strike in the west, you will inevitably be victorious. If you should want to retreat, create some false, empty deployments that can be left behind when you withdraw, for then the enemy will never pursue you. A tactical principle from the *Art of War* states: "Many obstacles in heavy grass is suspicious."

Similarly, "Daylight Warfare" advocates using specious displays of flags and pennants to cause misperceptions,[51] "Night Warfare" advises "employing numerous fires and drums to confuse their eyes and ears. If you befuddle the enemy so that they cannot make preparations against your tactics, you will be victorious." Intentions should be similarly concealed and misdirection employed to divert the enemy's attention and preparations to other sites, as advised in "The Distant in Warfare"[52] and "The Nearby in Warfare."[53]

False negotiations, particularly in times of duress, are considered highly effective: "Whenever about to engage an enemy in battle, first dispatch some emissaries to discuss a peace treaty. Even though the enemy assents to the talks, the way you each understand the language of the proposals is invariably not the same. Then, relying upon their indolence and laxity, select elite troops and suddenly strike them because their army can be destroyed. A tactical principle from the *Art of War* states: 'One who seeks peace without setting any prior conditions is executing a stratagem.'"[54]

Finally, in the tradition of early subversive programs the text strongly encourages the use of estrangement techniques: "Whenever engaging an enemy in warfare, you should secretly await the appearance of discord among their rulers and ministers, for then you can dispatch spies in order to estrange them further. If a ruler and his subordinates become mutually suspicious and doubtful of each other, you can employ elite troops to exploit the opportunity and inevitably gain your desires. A tactical principle from the *Art of War* states: 'If they are united, cause them to be separated.'"[55]

12

The Ming and Beyond

The Ming evolved out of the chaos of unremitting strife. As Yüan (Mongolian) control began to erode in the early 1350s following decades of onerous impositions exacerbated by years of horrendous weather, draconian government policies intensified smoldering animosity among the populace, prompting opposition and rebellion. Because Mongolian military officials bent upon repressing the numerous bands of brigands and religiously motivated rebel groups preyed upon the people and allowed their troops to ferociously plunder the land, unorthodox secret societies led by charismatic visionaries rapidly acquired adherents and power.

After early success as a northern Red Turban military commander, Chu Yüan-chang emerged victorious from years of conflict to establish the Ming. Because many of the key battles unfolded in the Yangtze River watershed, riverine clashes, amphibious assaults, and incendiary measures (including a famous attack implemented as part of a feigned defection at P'o-yang Lake) played a vital role.[1] Chu also employed complicated estrangement techniques and other subversive measures to undermine and eliminate his enemies before gradually retaking northern China, defeating the major Mongolian forces, and expelling the remnants.

The Ming then embarked on massive, aggressive steppe campaigns to control the still formidable Mongol groups on the periphery. However, when they turned disastrous despite several brilliant actions in cold and heavy snow, the dynasty reverted to what might be considered an unorthodox measure—the "Great Wall"—thereby resurrecting the antique *Art of War* concept that in defense strength will be more than adequate. (Although the Ming wall retains an imposing physical presence, the concept stressed the implementation of integrated measures, including strongpoints, dispersed forts, external watch towers, roving cavalry, and even military agricultural colonies. Ironically, a foreign dynasty—the Toba Wei—had also aggressively resorted to the comparatively unorthodox measure of wall building to deflect even more warlike steppe peoples just after the Three Kingdoms.)

About 1381 CE the founding emperor dispatched some 300,000 campaign forces into Yunnan to subjugate the nominal Mongolian stronghold of Ta-li and intervening areas.[2] Historically a difficult area for the central government to control because of its remoteness and topography, Yunnan was populated by strong, indigenous groups including the Tuan clan ensconced in their proto-kingdom of Ta-li, where they had long resisted imperial consolidation attempts. In its chapter on unorthodox warfare, the *Ts'ao-lü Ching-lüeh* cites the last portion of a campaign in which Mu Ying, one of the emperor's adopted sons, finally subjugates them:

> Mu Ying attacked Ta-li. At that time their remnant forces were relying on the solidity (of the area) where Tien-ts'ang mountain approaches the Erh River, including two previously constructed strongpoints known as Dragon's Head and Dragon's Tail. Learning that an imperial army would soon arrive, the local Tuan clan chieftain assembled 50,000 men to resist them below the fortified strongpoints.
>
> Mu Ying personally commanded the attack, but the strongholds could not be broken. He then ordered Wang Pi to take some troops and race eastward along the Erh River before going up above the barriers to form a two-pronged strategic configuration. Thereafter, he dispatched Hu-hai's army to follow an indirect route and cross the River at night, going around and coming out behind Tien-ts'ang mountain.
>
> Pulling on trees and clambering up embankments, they set out flags and pennants. At dawn the army below jumped up.

Shouting fervently, they broke through the strongpoint while
Hu Hai's army on the upper reach of the mountain attacked
downward. Caught between enemies front and back, the rebels
collapsed. This is the hidden and visible, dividing and uniting,
front and rear all being used together.

Although not included as an example, Mu Ying's strategy in defeating a
major Mongolian commander prior to this clash equally displayed his
readiness to resort to unorthodox actions. When the troops first approached an enemy force that numbered some 100,000 there was a heavy
fog and they couldn't see each other across the river. However, when it
lifted the Mongolian commander was astonished to find that the Ming
army had come up. Fu Yu-te, the imperial commander in chief, wanted to
attack immediately, but as their troops were exhausted Mu suggested that
they make a serious show of deploying as if preparing to cross but actually
have unorthodox troops sneak across down river prior to creating a false
deployment behind the enemy. Much like Wang Chün, by augmenting the
usual display of flags in the mountains and at the strongpoints with gongs
and horns, this advance force managed to create the impression that a
huge army was undertaking a surprise attack at the rear. Exploiting the
ensuing consternation, Mu Ying dispatched his best swimmers across the
river where they hewed out a beachhead with long-handled axes. The remaining Ming troops then immediately forded the river and engaged in
the lengthy, pitched battle that was won when their elite cavalry troops finally engaged the enemy. The dead were reportedly strewn across some 10
li, symbolic of the battle's swirling nature.[3]

Although rebellious forces in the Ch'ing such as the T'ai-p'ing employed
a few unorthodox tactics with considerable success, insofar as none of the
pre-modern military writings cite them, our final example stems from the
turbulent early Ming era known as the Ching-nan period (1399–1402).
(The term *ching-nan*, which means something like "pacifying difficulties,"
was chosen in a context of a rebel manifesto that accused the current emperor of egregiously disregarding Ming household rules, perverse actions
in eliminating the various princes, and allowing the pernicious influence of

corrupt and dastardly advisors.) One of the founding emperor's sons, Chu Ti (subsequently known as the Yung-lo Emperor), having been appointed to important military positions along the border, gradually amassed considerable power in the northeast just like An Lu-shan by paradoxically integrating the very Mongolian cavalry elements that his command had been entrusted with thwarting. Despite being a highly competent military commander in his father's mold, three years and several reversals were required before his forces could prevail, resulting in a significant victory important to consolidating control of the north:[4]

> During the Ching-nan period, Yang Wen, the general defending Liao-tung, led his troops in to besiege Yung-p'ing. Before dispatching Liu Chiang in command of a rescue force, Chu Ti instructed him: "When you reach Yung-p'ing, the brigands will certainly flee back to Shan-hai. You should then openly proclaim that you are going to return to Pei-p'ing. However, after you depart, roll up your flags and bag your armor and take advantage of nightfall to go back in. When the enemy hears that you have returned to Pei-p'ing, they will certainly reinvade the area. If you quickly go out and launch a sudden strike, you will certainly be victorious." Chiang did as instructed and defeated the Liao-tung army. In this case a withdrawal constituted an advance.

Final Formulations

The culmination of the unorthodox tradition is found not in such individualized, highly sophisticated Ming manuals as the *Yün-ch'ou Kang-mu*, the more prominent encyclopedic *Wu-pei Chih*, or even Ch'i Chi-kuang's esteemed writings, but instead the relatively obscure *Essential Strategies from a Grass Hut* (*Ts'ao-lü Ching-lüeh*). Rather than just a pastiche of earlier materials, the *Essential Strategies* is a highly thoughtful compilation of crucial tactical principles informed by a unified vision of warfare as active, aggressive, and invariably oriented to manipulating the enemy. Adopting a form similar to the *Hundred Unorthodox Strategies*, the anonymous author identifies and briefly discusses 152 tactical principles and concepts and illustrates each of them with examples drawn from as far back as the Spring and Autumn era. Although the summaries integrate important, though rarely identified, fundamentals from numerous earlier writings, especially the *Art of War* and *Questions and Replies*, they generally emphasize issues of operational realization, battlefield shaping, maneuver, and feasibility. Being a Ming dynasty compilation, the discussions and appended examples often reflect China's many centuries of utilizing water and incendiaries for assault, as well as its growing expertise with gunpowder weapons and explosives.

The unorthodox is not only singled out for focal discussion, but also pervades the work, being deemed a vital part of every commander's repertoire and frequently specified in conjunction with individual measures.[5] In addition to certain situations and terrains that are not only particularly conducive to their employment but virtually demand resorting to them, imaginatively conceived unorthodox measures should be routinely employed rather than being reserved solely for disadvantageous circumstances. Nevertheless, while essential and applicable at every level, there is little discussion about employing the unorthodox on the strategic level.

After reviewing previous definitions, the first of two chapters to explicitly ponder the subject, "Orthodox Armies," paradoxically concludes that orthodox forces have only limited validity because no force or measure is innately or inescapably either orthodox or unorthodox:

> Like the explanations for other military principles, those for orthodox armies are mostly confused. Some take assembling to be orthodox and segmenting to be unorthodox. Some take moving forward to be orthodox and retreating backward to be unorthodox. Others believe being the first to go forth and engage in combat is orthodox while responding is unorthodox, that orders received from the ruler are orthodox, those that the general issues himself are unorthodox.[6] Moreover, Ts'ao Ts'ao's *Hsin Shu* takes flank attacks to be unorthodox, those mounted against dead center to be orthodox. He also said: "If you are

double the enemy, employ one half in unorthodox tactics, one half in orthodox tactics. If you are five times the enemy's strength, then two parts should be orthodox and three unorthodox."[7] All these explanations are correct. Sun-tzu said that the unorthodox and orthodox mutually produce each other just like an endless cycle. How pointed were his words!

Li Ching regarded generals who only employ the orthodox, never the unorthodox, as defensive generals; those that only employ the unorthodox as aggressive generals. Moreover he said, "If the enemy is substantial then we must be orthodox, if the enemy is vacuous then we must be unorthodox." This once again distinguishes them upon issuing forth, not what Sun-tzu termed mutual production.

Probably for those commanders who excel at employing the military there are none that are not orthodox, none that are not unorthodox.[8] These explanations show the ordinary concept of the unorthodox and orthodox but Sun-tzu speaks about the changes of the unorthodox and orthodox. Without speaking about the ordinary it would not be possible to distinguish the unorthodox and orthodox, but without investigating their extremes, it is impossible to exhaust their subtlety.

Orthodox armies deploy in well-ordered fashion, their contingents are well regulated, their withdrawing is like a mountain moving, their advancing cannot be withstood. Their advancing and retreating are constrained, their left and right flanks respond to the pennants. Their troops can rest in turn and return to battle, they can reach distant objectives without becoming fatigued. They won't stir if enemy forces come up and provoke them; they will endure without becoming turbulent if the enemy secretly attacks. Accordingly, they unfathomably change and transform, their leisure and suddenness have no constancy. This is how the orthodox gives birth to the unorthodox. "Intermixed and turbulent, the fighting appears chaotic but they can-

not be made disordered; in turmoil and confusion their deployment is circular and they cannot be defeated."⁹ In this way the
unorthodox returns to the orthodox and the employment of the
unorthodox and orthodox are inexhaustible.

The passages obviously draw so heavily upon Li Ching's *Questions and
Replies* as to be virtually continuous. However, the *Ts'ao-lü*'s increased
emphasis upon the fundamental plasticity of all forces and the endless
possibilities of change and transformation carry Li's formulation to its extreme conclusion. (Li posits the essential controvertibility of all forces and
reverts to Sun-tzu's articulation, yet he also meanders in the more mundane and never thoroughly adopts the latter with finality.) Nevertheless,
the chapter's only illustration is Li Ching's highly constrained campaign
to subdue the Turks, itself discussed in the previous work.

The focal chapter titled "Unorthodox Armies" not unexpectedly stresses
the crucial role of the unorthodox, envisioning its realization in virtually
every military activity:

> The military is a matter of secret strategic planning.¹⁰ The places
> armies suddenly strike; whether they move slowly or rapidly;
> are segmented or united; retreat or advance; shift to the left or
> right, front or rear; act clandestinely or visibly; besiege or extri-
> cate; or move in the Nine Heavens above or bury themselves
> away in the Nine Sources below, they always responsively ex-
> ploit sudden opportunity and manifest changes through ten
> thousand beginnings. They generally stupefy and manipulate
> the enemy, perceive fissures and initiate action, attacking where
> they are not prepared, going forth where unexpected.
>
> The army will not be victorious without the unorthodox so
> generals will not engage in battle without it. This is what is
> meant by victorious armies first being victorious and then seek-
> ing to engage in battle.¹¹ Conversely, defeated armies first engage
> in battle and then seek victory. Their generals do not know how

to employ the unorthodox, they simply seek victory in battle-field clashes. Any success is therefore a matter of luck.

Those who excel in employing the army implement unortho-dox measures when they approach the enemy's deployment and wrest victory through responding to the enemy. Thus it is natu-ral that they do not have any constant configuration of power.[12]

Within the above parameters, a number of other pronouncements scat-tered throughout the text concerning the nature and application of the unorthodox deserve mention. The basic operational premise remains that closely ordered, strictly disciplined formations provide the basis for war-fare and that when they are realized, even though they may be attacked by commanders capable of adroitly employing unorthodox measures, will be difficult to defeat.[13] Moreover, it is repeatedly said that "one engages with the orthodox but seizes victory with the unorthodox. Display facades to the enemy but suddenly attack in obscurity."[14]

Just as Sun-tzu asserted, segmentation underlies the possibility of un-orthodox activities. Large concentrations of troops particularly require di-viding into coherent, operational units, many of them to be designated as unorthodox forces or operate in an unorthodox manner. Otherwise, the army's unwieldy nature coupled with communication difficulties will pre-clude reacting to the enemy's tactics in a timely manner, resulting in destabilization, chaos, and defeat, just as at Fei River.[15] In the simplest for-mat, the unorthodox component will be but one of the forces designed to segment the enemy's power and act flexibly:[16]

Irrespective of the deployment chosen, it is always appropriate to segment off two wings to await the clash. These two wings will split the enemy's strategic power. The central formation will assault the enemy with its elite soldiers while the rest will support them as provocateurs and as unorthodox, reserve, and ambush forces.

Provocateurs are soldiers who provoke the enemy and thus constitute a selected front. The unorthodox forces are employed to execute unorthodox tactics and thereby control victory; forces in ambush are employed to suddenly strike the two flanks; those in reserve establish ambushes to the rear in order to be prepared against the unexpected.

Other sections of the text advocate segmenting the army into as many as ten operational units and designating up to eight of them as unorthodox forces whose purpose will be to "harass the enemy's flanks, assault their very core, mount surprise attacks on their rear, sever their reinforcements, establish ambushes along their routes of retreat, raid their encampment and barriers, and confiscate their stores and provisions."[17] Naturally they can also provide protective resources but in the context of orthodox forces entangling the enemy, their function is primarily to harass, trouble, and balk the enemy, segmenting their power and confusing their response, both creating the possibility of victory and driving it home.

The unorthodox is both active and extemporaneous, unorthodox measures being decided on the tactical level at the moment of battle, rapidly changing and constantly being adopted to circumstances, yet always oriented toward manipulating the enemy as much as intended to effect decisive changes and strike crippling blows.[18] Although their realization and applicability are virtually unlimited,[19] at the simplest level unorthodox measures are frequently realized with troops in ambush, whether deployed as an integral assault component or pre-positioned against the eventuality of a forced retreat. Pre-deployed ambushes may be visible or invisible, the former designed to deter and shape the enemy's movements, the latter intended to mount a surprise attack that can repel advancing forces and inflict sufficient casualties to retake the offensive.[20]

Whether chosen for strategic reasons or simply under duress, unorthodox measures, including ambushes, often prove more valuable in defense, particularly when surviving might prove impossible without them.[21] Under siege or attack, unorthodox forces can harass the enemy, cut off their provisions, stir confusion, and mount flank attacks.[22] When reinforced with other deceptive measures and facades, they can break the enemy and thwart their plans.[23] Appearing lax and negligent can also create favorable circumstances for using unorthodox measures.[24]

Unorthodox troops provide the means to survive on confined terrain, particularly if the forces are segmented rather than unified and partially deployed along the ridge or behind the immediate horizon.[25] They are equally necessary and effective in exploiting the constraints of valleys and gorges where compression hampers movement, taking advantage of the topography and adverse weather conditions to attack from all directions,[26] even going around mountains to strike:[27]

> The ancients compared combat on the confined terrain of a gorge (or deep ravine) with two rats fighting in the entrance to a hole.[28] The courageous will be victorious. Even so, one cannot lack the unorthodox.
>
> While orthodox troops mount a defense to the fore, unorthodox troops should suddenly strike their flanks or their rear. Strong crossbows and tubed, explosive weapons should pour projectiles down like rain so that wherever they strike the enemy has no place to hide. If you then act expectedly, their strategic power will run off and scatter.
>
> Anciently, Hsün Wu destroyed his chariots to make up infantry ranks and formed his soldiers into squads because dispersed deployments facilitate advancing and retreating on constricted routes. When the battlefield is already narrow, the men and horses pressed together, it is probably difficult to look about alertly. If the enemy's *ch'i* is sharp and they are just racing forward, our unorthodox troops should divide to mount surprise attacks at the points of contact. When the topography is narrow and marked by high cliffs and the officers and troops clamoring and perturbed, dividing and uniting and advancing and retreating are not possible. But if the enemy just lacks the unorthodox, you will invariably control him.
>
> The methods for valley warfare are similar to those for gorges. First of all employ agile soldiers and resolute troops as

the front rows in your deployment and have solid shields and strong crossbows protect the left, right, and the rear in order to be prepared against the enemy. Segment and dispatch unorthodox troops to clandestinely go forth along the mountain ridges to the left and right and take advantage of the heights to attack from both sides. The way to certain victory will then be to have your orthodox troops assault them from the center.

The text includes a number of suggestions for facilitating the employment of unorthodox measures, some so fundamental as to provide the very possibility of their execution. Apart from exploiting adverse weather conditions, concrete deceptive techniques such as dragging brush, generating smoke, and employing deception are paramount. Although they are regarded as a minor skill—somewhat of a rebuke to those enamored of deceptive practices in themselves—they are crucial for manipulating the enemy just as Ch'en P'ing's six unorthodox schemes were in the early Han.[29] Naturally deploying flags and pennants to create the impression of large forces occupying deserted areas, an ancient ruse, can induce doubt and even immobilize the enemy sufficiently to allow strategic power to be brought to bear.[30] In short, every method and technique that can create momentary tactical advantages should be exploited in the quest to vanquish the enemy while never forgetting that "unorthodox forces and orthodox forces mutually act as exterior and interior."[31]

T'ou-pi Fu-t'an

Another late Ming dynasty work dating to the end of the sixteenth century, the T'ou-pi Fu-t'an was probably composed by Ho Shou-fa, who is also credited with the main commentary and explication. Deliberately divided into thirteen topics and otherwise heavily indebted to Sun-tzu, the T'ou-pi Fu-t'an represents the final stage of indigenous thought prior to the Jurchen conquest and establishment of the Ch'ing. Ho's observations on the unorthodox return to the Art of War's original formulation, stressing the concept's flexibility in application and the fundamental inter-convertibility of the unorthodox and orthodox:[32]

> In the methods for employing the military, host and guest have no constant behavior, offense and defense no constant shape, segmenting and reuniting no constant organization, advancing and retreating no constant measure, movement and quiet no fixed periods, and expanding and contracting no constant configuration of power. Conceiving changes and transformations that the enemy cannot fathom is referred to as the military's subtlety.
>
> Explication: Only when there is no constancy can the mysterious be preserved in the mind. Therefore it is called subtle.
>
> Thus those who take the unorthodox as the unorthodox and the orthodox as the orthodox are like musicians who glue up the stops to tune a lute. Those who take the unorthodox as the orthodox and the orthodox as the unorthodox are like disciples who copy calligraphy or imitate paintings.
>
> Those who are unorthodox but display orthodoxy to the enemy, or are orthodox but display the unorthodox, know victory. Someone who is unorthodox but the enemy does not know it is the unorthodox, or is orthodox but the enemy does not know it is the orthodox, knows victory within victory. Now when armies clash and formations are deployed, victory and defeat being decided in an instant, preservation and extinction settled in a moment, the unorthodox and orthodox must always be given form.
>
> Explication: This generally discusses the application of the unorthodox and orthodox. Gluing up the stops to tune a lute does not accord with change. Imitating calligraphy and copying paintings is not excelling at change. Only when you display the orthodox while being unorthodox and the unorthodox while being orthodox can you change. If the enemy does not discrim-

inate the unorthodox and orthodox, we can change and be spiritual! Those who are capable of doing this gain victory and are
preserved, those who are incompetent suffer defeat and perish.
It is all caused by the unorthodox and orthodox.

The chapter then goes on to elucidate ten applications and provide examples of the subtle moment when unorthodox measures allowed otherwise disadvantaged commanders to wrest victory:

> Thus those who excel at controlling the enemy stupefy them to
> cause them to believe things and lie to cause them to be suspi-
> cious. They conceal what they excel at and cause them to be
> amused. They expose their own shortcomings and cause them
> to be befuddled. They falsify orders and commands and cause
> them to be deaf. They change their flags and emblems and cause
> them to be blind.[33] They conceal what they detest in order to tie
> up their defenses. They accord with their desires in order to
> muddle their will. They inform them about their situation in
> order to entangle their plans. They frighten them with awe-
> someness in order to snatch away their *ch'i* (spirit).
>
> Explication: These ten are all places where subtlety is con-
> cealed and employed. *Thus those who excel at controlling the en-*
> *emy stupefy them to cause them to believe things and lie to cause*
> *them to be suspicious* just as Ch'en P'ing changed the banquet
> meats to coarse grass to stupefy and mislead Hsiang Yü. Hsiang
> Yü believed it and doubted Fan Tseng.
>
> *They conceal what they excel at and cause them to be amused.*
> *They expose their own shortcomings and cause them to be befud-*
> *dled* just as Han Hsin secretly dispatched red flags and deliber-
> ately deployed his armies with their backs to the river, causing
> Chao's forces to be amused and confused right into being de-
> feated and perishing.

They falsify orders and commands and cause them to be deaf just as Wu Mu who caught Li Ch'ing's spy and pretended to leak out that their provisions were exhausted, then released him in order to lure Li in coming to attack.[34]

They change their flags and emblems and cause them to be blind just as in the clash between Feng Yi and the Red Eyebrows wherein Feng changed their uniforms, inducing chaos and causing the Red Eyebrows to be unable to discriminate (the real and false).[35]

They conceal what they detest in order to tie up their defenses and accord with their desires in order to muddle their will just as the king of Yüeh hid his instructions and intentions to gain revenge and visibly exerted himself to be respectful and submissive, causing the king of Wu to become more arrogant and licentious every day and forget to make preparations.

They inform them about their situation in order to entangle their plans just like Hua Yüan did in straightforwardly reporting Sung's misery and starvation (under Ch'u's siege). Ch'u's army did indeed retreat.

They frighten them with awesomeness in order to snatch away their ch'i (spirit) just as Kuan Hsün assembled the (few) troops from several districts and blatantly pretended that Han Kuangwu's armies had arrived, causing Su Mao's formations to stir.[36]

These are all examples of where the subtle lies.

As in Sun-tzu, there is a close connection between techniques designed to obfuscate (and thereby facilitate manipulating the enemy) and vacuity, the emptiness that makes rapid penetration and combat success possible. The next paragraph in the *T'ou-pi Fu-t'an* chapter summarizes the advantages, though without any explicit connection with unorthodox theory:

Thus, when the enemy is substantial, I cause him to be vacuous. However, the enemy is unable to cause my substantiality to be made vacuous. I take advantage of the enemy's vacuity but the enemy is not able to take advantage of my vacuity.

If I make our substantial (appear) substantial, it is because I want to confront the enemy. If I make our vacuity (appear) vacuous, it is to cause doubt in the enemy. If I make our vacuous substantial, it's because we want to cause the enemy to shun us. When we make our substantial vacuous, it is because we want to draw the enemy in. The subtlety of the vacuous and substantial changes and is derived from the enemy. Only if even ghosts and spirits do not know the mysteriousness of its vastness and minuteness will you be able to twist the enemy and achieve success.

As the last lines indicate, in accord with Sun-tzu's admonitions the intent is to manipulate perceptions and thereby achieve great gains with minimal effort. On the premise that even minor skills may bring about dramatic results, the next chapter ("Fang Shu") emphasizes that every effort, even the fabrication of ghosts and spirits—the unorthodox within the unorthodox—should be made to distract and obfuscate the enemy. Confusing them and diverting their attention toward facades and simulated realities will create the misperceptions that allow the unorthodox to be employed.

Teng-t'an Pi-chiu

The *Teng-t'an Pi-chiu* by Wang Ming-ho, the third important late Ming dynasty (1599) compilation, includes a chapter titled "Compilation of Unorthodox and Ambush Theories" ("Chi-ch'i Fu-shuo") that essentially reformulates *Wu-ching Tsung-yao* material. However, the introductory paragraphs emphasize the need for unorthodox concepts even while decrying the possibility of exploiting them with the disorganized forces of his era:

Some commanders exercised measured constraint in employing their armies just as they did in antiquity, halting and reordering after every five or six paces and after five or seven blows. This is the theory of orthodox troops but we cannot really know about the battles that unfolded at Nan-ch'ao and Mu-yeh. In later generations armies have valued the Tao of deceit, taking advantage of being unexpected and attacking where the enemy is unprepared. Nevertheless, whenever armies have deployed into formation and erected fortifications opposite each other, no one has ever fashioned victory without the unorthodox and ambushes.

Thus the *Art of War* states, "Those who excel at sending forth the unorthodox are as inexhaustible as Heaven and Earth, as unlimited as the Yangtze and Yellow Rivers." Although Sun-tzu subsequently included instructions for cultivating the Tao and defense, the imperishable material still hangs within this chapter. Being orthodox yet unorthodox, unorthodox yet orthodox, this is the subtle tactical imbalance in employing the army, an unchanging definition for ten thousand generations.

Accordingly, we have the stratagems of Han Hsin who crossed the army upriver so that he could seize Chao Chih and the wisdom of Sun Pin who chopped the bark off a tree and left a message on its whiteness and thus slayed P'ang Ch'üan. Conversely, how can those who merely have Hsiang Yü's unorthodox expertise and Wang Hui's ambushes (expect to) achieve decisive victory in the marshes of Hsien and be lucky in luring (the Hsiung-nu) into Ma-yi?

Now at this time of conflict on the sea, we are levying troops from throughout the southeast, bringing them together as uselessly as crows. Unpracticed and untrained, they truly "hear the drum but do not advance, hear the gong but do not retreat." To still think of speaking about the Tao of the unorthodox and ambushes in such an urgent situation is like someone who excels at playing the lute being unable to play (a melody) on untuned strings or one who excels at being a general being unable to maneuver with untrained warriors. Those responsible for defense should give this their attention.

Late Ching Contemplations

Although widely regarded as a "sinicized" dynasty, the Ch'ing should probably be viewed as simply another of the alien groups that conquered China proper over the millennia.[37] With the cooperation of collaborators, Ch'ing rulership imposed a radically different organizational and command structure on the government and populace only to witness the forceful intrusion of Western powers in the last century of its domination. Whether this was a result of constraints imposed by traditional military thought or a failure to rigorously implement the latter's insights and practices unfortunately lies beyond the scope of our immediate study. However, the observations of three prominent Chinese thinkers on the complexity and importance of the unorthodox, articulated within the constraints of Jurchen dominance and the quest to integrate Western technology and Chinese culture, merit noting.[38]

All three—Ts'eng Kuo-fan (1811–1872), Hu Lin-yi (1812–1861), and Tso Tsung-t'ang (1812–1885)—came to prominence as a result of their efforts to suppress the T'ai-p'ing Rebellion that essentially extended from 1850 to 1864. Moreover, because Ts'eng and Hu's martial thoughts were subsequently compiled into a book early in the Republican period that became a text for the Huang-p'u (Whampoa) Military Academy in 1924 (primarily because it stressed the core concerns of structure, benevolent control, and village organization), their influence extended beyond the late Ch'ing.[39]

In order to cope with the T'ai-p'ing threat, Ts'eng Kuo-fan, formerly a high-ranking civil official, began to assiduously study the classic Chinese military writings about 1853. Although he is best known for his ideas on organizational issues and methods for command-and-control, his operational concepts were thus significantly influenced by Sun-tzu's *Art of War*. He was seconded in his command by Hu Lin-yi and Tso Tsung-t'ang, two famous generals who, in however disjointed fashion, formulated military doctrines of their own. Of the three, Hu Lin-yi was the most incisive and prolific martial commentator, but Tso Tsung-t'ang became well-known for his emphasis on defending Hsin-chiang (Xinjiang) and the contiguous western territories, where he achieved considerable success. Of course, all three were acting on behalf of the Ch'ing, tenuously regarded as the legitimate rulership, and the Chinese people benefited only indirectly, if at all, despite the commanders' avowed interest in reducing their suffering from the rebels.

Hu Lin-yi's brief comments stress the essential role of the unorthodox and orthodox and the need to rapidly shift between them:

> Sun-tzu said that "the masses of the three armies can be made to withstand the enemy without being defeated is due to the unorthodox and orthodox. In warfare one engages with the orthodox and achieves victory with the unorthodox. Strategic power in combat does not go beyond the unorthodox and orthodox while the changes of the unorthodox and the orthodox cannot be exhausted." This discusses the unorthodox and the orthodox in detail.
>
> Military affairs do not lie outside the orthodox and unorthodox. Probably those who have the orthodox without the unorthodox will be overturned when they encounter difficulty. But without the orthodox, the unorthodox will be thwarted by extreme power.
>
> If you take the orthodox as the orthodox and the unorthodox as the unorthodox, then the enemy will be able to anticipate them and make defensive preparations. Instead, you must be orthodox and then suddenly unorthodox, unorthodox and then suddenly orthodox. Only after the unorthodox and orthodox mutually give birth to each other just like an endless chain will the enemy not be able to fathom them.
>
> But in employing unorthodox troops you must act as suddenly as the whirlwind, anticipating where the enemy will go

and then acting unexpectedly. Do not adhere to the rules for formations, attack solidified fortifications, or get entangled by allied forces or the enemy's situation. Apart from an elite, well-trained army and commanding generals who can respond to changes and are self-reliant, it's impossible.

Armies that go forth in accord with the orthodox rather than the unorthodox allow the enemy to make preparations in advance.

Ts'eng Kuo-fan was more concerned with fundamentals, including what sort of troops might be considered unorthodox:

Many people who are able to speak about employing the army, about host and guest, the orthodox and unorthodox, are not necessarily capable of knowing them. Troops that are deployed in the interstice between two armies to respond to the enemy are orthodox troops. However, those that harass the enemy's left and right flanks are unorthodox troops.

Heavy troops that have temporarily halted, those with solid palisades or long encamped, and those involved in a standoff with the enemy are all orthodox troops. Guerrilla forces that are segmented off and dispatched, who hastily change and lack constancy, who rapidly attack any fissure they detect, are unorthodox troops.

When we anticipate intentions and mount a defense against invaders, the troops are orthodox. When we set out suspicious deployments and cause people to be unable to fathom us, the forces are unorthodox.

When our flags and pennants are detailed and clear, causing the enemy to not dare oppose us, the troops are orthodox. When we display worn out horses and fatigued troops, furl our flags and silence our drums, and are fundamentally strong yet show weakness, the troops are unorthodox.

When we set up our flags, beat the drums, and are like a lofty mountain peak in not lightly moving, the troops are orthodox. When we pretend to be defeated and feign retreat, setting up ambushes and drawing the enemy in, the troops are unorthodox.

If you can suddenly be the host, then suddenly the guest, suddenly be orthodox then suddenly unorthodox; can effect changes and movement without any fixed schedule, make turns and shifts without any set configuration of power; and are able to separate them area by area, you have already comprehended more than half in the Tao for employing the military.

Unless your troops are very stable on ordinary days, you cannot lightly employ them in danger. On ordinary days, apart from the Tao of the purely upright or orthodox, you cannot lightly employ unorthodox plans. Accordingly, stability is orthodox, it is what human endeavor puts into effect on ordinary days. Danger, the Heavenly mechanism that compels us to act in the exigency of the moment, is unorthodox.

Finally, two brief comments from Tso Tsung-t'ang, who recognized the need for unorthodox troops to be well disciplined:

When you are conducting guerrilla operations using only unorthodox troops, it is advantageous to be as sudden as the whirlwind and rapidly engage in combat. Without elite, trained, and experienced soldiers and talented generals capable of responding to change, it will be difficult for them to be preserved complete when thrust onto dangerous terrain. Even more so, they cannot be lightly tested.[40]

Attacking a visible enemy is excellent, but unexpectedly attacking a previously unseen enemy in accord with your estimations of where they must go is the pinnacle of excellence. Those who employ the unorthodox are like this.

Ch'ien K'un Ta-lüeh

The *Ch'ien K'un Ta-lüeh*, the last of what might be considered the Ming military writings, was compiled by Wang Yü-yu (1615–1684), a scholarly loyalist who lived in seclusion after the Ch'ing's ascension. The book consists of generally well-known battles selected from the *Examination of Battles* (*Chan-lüeh K'ao*) thematically grouped into ten chapters, though one has now been lost. In concord with previous interpretations, Wang envisions both the orthodox and unorthodox as invariably necessary, with the unorthodox and ambushes, especially ambushes set up by feigned retreats, furnishing not just the primary, but the essential means for achieving victory in battle. However, in a major theoretical development he surprisingly stresses the need to engage in decisive battle, as the following excerpts from the introductory passages to three key chapters show:[41]

> II "For the Army to Advance It Must Have Unorthodox Methods"
> Is there but a single Tao for the military? Certainly not. When the direction of events is already clear, then it is the orthodox Tao about which nothing further need be said. However, you cannot seize victory if you do not realize the unorthodox Tao to assist the orthodox. Only after Hsiang Yü did battle with Chang Han at Chü-li did Han Kao-tsu exploit the vacuity to enter the pass. Only after Chung Hui mastered Chiang Wei at Chien-ko was Teng Ai able to cross over the ravines and enter Shu.
>
> Accordingly, every deployment has its unorthodox Tao, every state has its unorthodox Tao, and the realm has its unorthodox Tao. Thus, sometimes the orthodox can be unorthodox and the unorthodox orthodox. But you must absolutely have them both. Now when an army advances that doesn't recognize the Tao of the unorthodox, it is because the ruler is stupid or the general obtuse. This is termed "casting away the army."
>
> In antiquity when Liu P'i attacked Ta-liang, Duke T'ien Lu (futilely) suggested that 50,000 men separately follow the Yangtze

and Huai Rivers to consolidate the area of Chang-an south of the Huai in order to facilitate their assemblage at Wu-kuan.

Conversely, when Ts'ao Ts'ao and Yüan Shao were stalemated at Kuan-tu, Ts'ao Ts'ao shifted his army as if wanting to move toward Yen-chin but stealthily mounted a sudden attack with light troops at Pai-ma.

Those who employ the army should be cautious not to say "Our army can proceed directly (to the target) by a single route without troubling about racing off to the side and following winding bypaths." This is the way people and states trust to luck! Avoid it!

III "When Recently Mobilized Armies First Encounter the Enemy, Decisive Warfare Is Foremost"

When the army is advancing, invariably passing cities and towns that do not submit, must they be attacked?[42] I would say it isn't that we take pleasure in war, but if war is unavoidable and we encounter the enemy, without combat we have no means to make them withdraw. When our army has already deeply penetrated their territory, the enemy will certainly unite all their strength and turn the country upside down to try to trample and shake us, fearing that our majesty will soon be complete. Accordingly, if we do not engage in fierce warfare and urgent fighting, the situation will be beyond rescue, becoming just like trying to take advantage of fish that have dispersed and birds that have been startled.

But if we are truly able to do something unexpected, frustrating their sharpness with one battle, then the enemy's masses will lose their courage while our army's *ch'i* will redouble! Only after our wills are settled and our awesomeness established can we attack, seize, and plan against the enemy. What the ancients referred to as a single battle settling All under Heaven lies in this. Han Kuang-wu at K'un-yang and T'ang T'ai-tsung at Huo-yi can be pondered in this regard.

In antiquity, when Shen T'ien-tzu encountered Yao Hung's masses of several ten thousand at Ch'ing-ni with just a thousand men he said, "The army esteems employing the unorthodox, not just masses. Today we are not a match for the enemy in terms of numbers. However, two strategic powers cannot both endure. If they manage to solidify their encirclement we will have nowhere to escape. It would be better to attack them." He then defeated Yao Hung. This is truly according with the crux of the moment, the unchanging Tao of a hundred ponderings.

IV "The Tao of Decisive Warfare Lies in Conceiving the Unorthodox and Establishing Ambushes"

Even when there isn't the slightest doubt about (the necessity of) engaging the enemy in battle, if you do not realize the Tao of warfare the disaster will be even deeper than if you did not engage in combat. Antiquity had a saying about a hundred battles, but from my point of view it isn't merely a hundred.

On what basis do I say this? I would say that when we (the Ming) initially engaged in combat (with the Jurchen), we opposed elite cavalry that chased the wind with men from the cities who were brought together like a flock of birds. We deployed into formations on the broad plains, all correct and in good order, and locked horns with them. It shouldn't have required any wisdom to predict the ensuing misfortune. How could any tactics other than conceiving the unorthodox and establishing plans been useful here?

Sun Pin destroyed P'ang Chüan with "fearful" troops, Han Hsin destroyed Ch'en Yü with city people. Li Mi destroyed Chang-hsü-ta with a collection of bandits. They employed small numbers to overturn masses and relied upon weakness for strength. The techniques for excelling in warfare are assuredly not limited to these, but if you focus on just these two your efforts will be correct every time. If not, you will certainly be defeated.

Wang's minimally veiled condemnation of the Ming court for failing to use imaginative, unorthodox tactics to thwart the highly mobile Jurchen is remarkable in the context of his heavily repressive era, even for a recluse hiding in the countryside.

PART TWO

Modern Theories and Implications

13

Traditional Wisdom
Revitalized

D espite the extensiveness of the foregoing materials, the nature
of Chinese warfare as practiced over the centuries is only im-
perfectly glimpsed. As we have written in other contexts, the
scope of warfare rapidly escalated from the Spring and Autumn period
until it engulfed the entire realm. Rarely a decade passed without major
combat or a century without cataclysmic upheavals, whether wars with
external peoples, millenarian rebellions, internecine conflict among the
tenuous political entities during periods of fragmentation, or dynastic upheavals.[1] The great military encyclopedias produced in the past decade
summarize thousands of battles of every size, hundreds of which drastically altered the political and economic landscape. Even the massive *Tzu-
chih T'ung-chien*, a comprehensive, orthodox examination of China's
history compiled by the great Ssu-ma Kuang in the Sung dynasty, devotes
much of its space to recounting this virtually unremitting struggle.

Despite admonitions to exercise restraint, the lethality of these conflicts
remains almost unimaginable, the destruction and casualties they inflicted incalculable. Even though he emphasized the ruthless practice of
efficient warfare, Sun-tzu also wrote of the need to fight with the aim of
preservation, an objective that numerous contemporary analysts have ab-
surdly identified as one of the defining characteristics of Chinese warfare.
Moreover, to the extent that armies motivated their troops with the

prospect of plunder and often incorporated surrendered enemy forces intact, needless destruction would be counter-productive.

However, whatever the commander's intention—or simply because of the raw emotions of battle—across the centuries victorious forces frequently slaughtered every survivor, including surrendered soldiers, all the local inhabitants, and even the animals before destroying the city. In addition to plundering the countryside and seizing all the food stocks to supply their logistical requirements (as advocated by Sun-tzu), they also razed much of the surrounding infrastructure. The development of aquatic and incendiary materials and methods extended the scope dramatically, with sixty to seventy percent of the populace in a besieged city normally perishing by its resolution, including several hundred thousand in K'ai-feng at the end of the Ming.

Rather than dwelling in an idyllic world in which the much vaunted Confucian values of Virtue, righteousness, deference, and self-cultivation held sway, the ordinary populace was tormented by violent groups ranging from local ruffians to bands of brigands who haunted the fringes of civilization. They were also plagued by battles that raged across their area and entangled by millenarian revolts mounted by groups such as the Yellow Scarves and Red Eyebrows that decimated the inhabitants and immersed the survivors in inescapable famine and suffering.

Contrary to the impression conveyed by the official histories and generations of Western scholars that China was a tranquil, high culture unmarked by the violence and excesses that plagued the West, civilization never constituted more than a thin veneer, social stability was frequently absent, and life always precarious for the ordinary people. In fact, even when not troubled by battles and bandits, they often suffered brutally at the hands of local landowners and government officials entrusted with governing, though rarely nurturing, them.

Despite claims to the contrary, this inescapable heritage of conflict spawned a popular martial culture that embraced heroes, strength, and violent action. Furthermore, even as combat evolved and new weapons and technologies were fervently pursued, knowledge (rather than courage) came to be emphasized. By the onset of the Warring States period military commanders had long been pondering their experiences with an eye to discerning tactical patterns, understanding basic concepts, and imposing battlefield control. Numerous military texts were compiled during the Warring States period, six of which eventually formed the core of a continuous literate tradition: the *Art of War*, *Ssu-ma Fa*, *Wu-tzu*, *Liu-t'ao* (*Six Secret Teachings*), *San-lüeh* (*Three Strategies*), and *Wei Liao-tzu*. Together with a T'ang dynasty manual, the *Questions and Replies*, they comprise the *Seven Military Classics* that eventually furnished the basis for the imperial military examinations established in the Sung.[2] Hundreds of writings from the T'ang onward still exist, with ten or so being of primary contemporary interest, both popular and defense related, and Sun Pin's *Military Methods* was rediscovered in a Han dynasty tomb four decades ago after being lost for more than two millennia.[3] However, many others, including works attributed to the famous Ts'ao Ts'ao and Chu-ko Liang, have disappeared.

Within the popular imagination the quest for lost manuals and hidden texts that will ensure battlefield domination or individual prowess has long been an important theme. This search not only reflects an unshakable belief in the power of knowledge but also a general sense of the difficulty of capturing superlative wisdom in mere words. Thus, in its famous opening line the *Tao Te Ching* states that "The Tao that can be spoken of is not the ineffable Tao" and subsequently adds that "The knowledgeable do not speak, speakers do not know."[4]

The desire for knowledge naturally ventured into more esoteric and arcane realms, producing complex divinatory systems and such prognosticatory writings as the *Yi Ching*, *Ling Ch'i Ching*, and *T'ai-hsüan Ching*.[5] Much in the tradition of the T'ai Kung and other early sages, famous savants such as Tung-fang Shuo and hidden recluses including Kuei-ku-tzu, who were thought to have achieved penetrating understanding, were therefore assiduously sought out for their wisdom. In fact, despite lacking a known military text or any historical traces, Kuei-ku-tzu, the "Master of Ghost Valley," has now become the most widely portrayed of legendary strategists. However unlikely, numerous stories and serializations depict such famous historical figures as Sun Pin and Li Ssu ferreting out Kuei-ku-tzu's mist-enshrouded dwelling to learn the strategic and martial secrets, particularly the nature of the unorthodox, that will empower them. An enigmatic text of obscure, possibly even Warring States, origin attributed to him has been synthetically reconstructed from quotations and fragments, and there is now a Kuei-ku-tzu society devoted to its study that has recently produced several volumes.[6]

Not simply an expression of romanticism, this faith in transcendent knowledge expresses a felt sense that these sages and superlative commanders were somehow more perspicacious, that they could penetrate to the essence of martial affairs just as the wise men who formulated the *Yi Ching* fathomed the universe at large. The resulting knowledge, being of surpassing character and incomprehensible to most, was thought to be easily misperceived and even provoke laughter among ordinary people:

> *When superior officers hear about the Tao,*
> *They exert themselves to practice it.*
> *When ordinary officers hear about the Tao,*
> *It sometimes seems to be present, sometimes absent.*
> *When inferior officers hear about the Tao,*
> *They uproariously laugh at it.*[7]

The classic Chinese military writings, particularly the *Art of War*, all stress the importance of the commander's plans and intent being unfathomable, beyond knowing. In addition, there was also a sense that true martial knowledge, the insights that made battlefield success possible and marked the greatest commanders, was generally beyond expressive ability. The *Liu-t'ao* states: "Unorthodox and orthodox tactics are produced from the inexhaustible resources of the mind. Thus the greatest affairs are not discussed and the employment of troops is not spoken about. Moreover, words that discuss ultimate affairs are not worth listening to." And in speaking about the *Liu-t'ao*, Li Ching commented: "I find that in the eighty-one chapters of the *Liu-t'ao* what is termed secret strategy cannot be exhausted in words."[8] Emperor T'ai-tsung added, "Probably military strategy can be transmitted as ideas, but cannot be handed down as words."[9]

The daunting nature of the task never prevented the ardent from undertaking the quest nor believing in its attainment while always hoping
they will be as fortunate as Chang Liang and perhaps receive another
Three Strategies. In a sense the current scrutinization of antique materials
for viable concepts and lessons mimics their search for superior wisdom,
reflects their confidence that advantageous insights will be discovered,
and continues the well-developed traditions of "crafty" or "insightful
knowledge."[10] Being part of the mystique embedded in the mindset, this
reverence and yearning for secret knowledge proves difficult to escape,
both consciously and unconsciously.

In fact, the traditional Chinese military writings, especially Sun-tzu's
Art of War, the *Six Secret Teachings*, *Hundred Unorthodox Strategies*, and
Thirty-six Stratagems, have recently enjoyed astonishing popularity
among the populace at large and now appear in many formats ranging
from vernacular editions through serialized television dramas and comic
book versions. Together with episodes from the famous martial novels—
Water Margin and *Three Kingdoms*—their teachings pervade contemporary Chinese consciousness and contribute immeasurably to the Chinese
mindset and body of common strategic and tactical knowledge. However,
these developments dramatically reverse the trend of much of the past 150
years, when European military thought largely reigned supreme.

Western military conceptions, organizational methods, and tactics
suddenly attracted notice about the middle of the nineteenth century,
when the Manchu Court's impotence in the face of paltry Western forces
and massive internal rebellion became apparent. In the martial realm
puzzlement over how the magnificent, indigenous military inventions of
earlier centuries, including the crossbow, gunpowder, incendiaries, and
proto-firearms, came to be surpassed quickly turned into consternation
and widespread rejection of traditional military writings and practices.
These unexpected events stimulated intense debate over the question of
whether indigenous cultural values could be preserved while integrating
Western science, technology, and industrial practices or the weighty heritage of tradition doomed China to everlasting inferiority and therefore
required thorough rejection. Naturally a few counter-voices zealously,

even violently (as exemplified by the Boxers) rejected everything Western as polluted, decadent, corrupting, and inferior.

In their quest for correctives at the end of the Ch'ing and in the Republic, martial authorities increasingly turned to Western military hardware and doctrine. German, French, Swedish, and especially Russian concepts and tactics all competed for preeminence, with Japanese advisors surprisingly being employed for a time despite lingering enmity.[11] However, they were in turn displaced by Mao's concept of people's warfare and the strategic defensive during the war with Japan and subsequent clash with the Kuomintang prior to the founding of the PRC, initiating a period of isolation and conservatism. Throughout the Cultural Revolution traditional military materials continued to be disparaged and their mere possession was often sufficient cause for self-criticism, incarceration, or execution.

However, with Mao's demise and the cessation of the devastating Cultural Revolution, both Western and traditional martial thought were rediscovered, with the former receiving considerable impetus from the startling developments witnessed in the first Iraq War. Naturally, burdened by the heritage of a strongly Marxist context, the theories formulated by Mao Zedong, Deng Xiaoping, Jiang Zhemin, and now Hu Jintao determine the confines and orientations of acceptability and orthodoxy. Nevertheless, since 1985, coincident with the founding of the National Defense University and the immediately subsequent publication of the initial volumes of the great Chinese military corpus (*Chung-kuo Ping-shu Chi-ch'eng*), Chinese strategists have been increasingly looking to their own martial tradition for theories and practices that will enable them to formulate a distinctive military science, one that will allow its practitioners not to just be imitators and therefore second-best in Western thinking and methods, but to surpass Western strategists and be unfathomable while yet incorporating all the latest advances in weaponry, command, and communications.

Accordingly, not only are historical military studies deemed one of the five divisions of military science, but their importance continues to grow.[12] The military think tanks include professors of traditional military studies who often hold significant posts in the strategy department; important historical battles and selected theoretical writings are regularly included in the core curriculum for officers and are the subject of numerous study groups; paradigm clashes are pondered for tactical principles and unorthodox techniques; conferences, especially those focusing on Sun-tzu's thought, are regularly held on integrating core theoretical concepts into contemporary practice; articles are routinely included in *China Military Science* (*Zhongguo Junshi Kexue*) and *National Defense* (*Guofang*), the authoritative theoretical journals published by the Academy of Military Science and National Defense University respectively;[13] books by esteemed military academicians exploring historical doctrine and its implications are constantly offered by the publishing arms of the military think tanks;[14] and the amount of historical material in the recently revised edition of the *Chung-kuo Chün-shih Pai-k'o Ch'uan-shu* (*China Military Encyclopedia*) has been greatly expanded.[15]

Rather than existing in isolation, these resurgent ideas have been integrated into an all-encompassing concept of "military science with unique Chinese characteristics" or "a revolution in military affairs with unique Chinese characteristics." Although virtually every article discussing these "unique Chinese characteristics" focuses upon indigenous weapons development and phrases the characteristics in terms of guidelines derived from the martial thought of recent leaders, traditional materials that provide many of the strategic concepts and orientations are equally expected to provide uniqueness to Chinese military science.[16]

Beginning in the late 1980s, but especially in 1991, coincident with the re-emergence of the classical military writings as viable subjects for investigation, there was a sudden surge of interest in strategy and stratagems (*mou-lüeh*). Numerous compendiums of uneven quality, variously organized and titled, encompassing a wide range of contents were published in succession. Some were astute collections of doctrinal pronouncements assiduously culled from the many military manuals with insightful commentaries and illustrative battles, others just enumerations of clever strategies and tactics from both the martial and the civil realms, often blended with heavy doses of machination and intrigue.[17]

In intent they range from simple exploitations of the popular fascination with clever tricks and unusual tactics to serious contemplations of fundamental theory and the concept of the unorthodox, often expanded with examples from recent Western military history. The largest, being well oversized and exceeding a thousand pages, physically attain coffee table book dimensions, but even the smallest paperbacks generally number 500 pages and include 200 or more "stratagems." Although they embrace the entire scope of Chinese history, plans and episodes from the Three Kingdoms period predominate, with one volume simply being titled *Three Kingdoms Strategies*.[18] In a sense these distillations represent a compromised attempt to ascertain and employ the surpassing knowledge of the master strategists as revealed in the particularity of concrete circumstances. Only the challenge (or perhaps insurmountable difficulty) of discerning the true nature of individual circumstances remains.

Insofar as these works, the numerous theoretical manuals, and selected historical battles in which paltry forces overcame vastly superior foes are being pondered for their tactical principles and conceptual breakthroughs, the unorthodox (and its facilitator, deception) can certainly be expected to comprise a crucial element in any revised military science. Nevertheless, over the past few years the concept has received little attention in the chief theoretical magazines, *National Defense* and *China Military Science*. Reliance therefore has to be upon vestiges, indications, and projections from the core role that the unorthodox has played in traditional military doctrine, particularly as embodied in historically oriented works including the comprehensive military histories and focal volumes on specialized topics, as well as the more broadly oriented monthly military publications such as *Chün-shih Shih-lin*.[19] In focusing upon what might be termed the "wisdom" tradition in China, the discussion that follows examines several historical materials that have prominently affected the mindset, become the subject of conscious contemplation, and comprise an ineradicable element of modern strategic culture.

Two famous heroic novels—the *San-kuo Yen-yi* or *Three Kingdoms* and *Shui-hu Chuan* or *Water Margin*—have long been recognized as contributing significantly to the contents of both the popular and defense-oriented strategic cultures. Recently, however, two other works that are reprinted in the massive PLA compendium of traditional military writings have dominated the popular press, the *Hundred Unorthodox Strategies* already cited in selected form in earlier sections, and the *Thirty-six Stratagems*. Under different titles both have appeared in a variety of vernacular translations, expansions, and even comic book editions, presumably destined for the general public but also found in the hands of PLA officers, evidencing their pervasiveness.

Shui-hu Chuan

Despite being a fictional creation, albeit one with a minor historical core, the *Shui-hu Chuan* (*Records of the Marsh*) has paradoxically assumed a critical place in China's strategic culture. Well-known in the West from Pearl Buck's translation as *All Men Are Brothers*, the highly formulaic *Shui-hu Chuan* purportedly depicts the struggles of a band of brigands that gathered in the Liangshan marsh near Mount T'ai and were active for a few years under Sung Chiang's leadership in the Shantung-Jiangsu border area until being summarily defeated by the Sung about 1121 CE.[20]

Even before their initial compilation as a novel early in the Ming, their adventures had long been the focus of numerous popular tales recited by street side storytellers and operatic plots. The embryonic novel recounts the individual stories of 108 bravos who, compelled by circumstances and perversity, gradually seek refuge in the marsh; their evolution into an organized bandit gang; their battle to survive against government forces dispatched to extirpate them; and finally their amnesty when imperial armies prove incapable of suppressing them. A more extensive edition later evolved that appends the subsequent adventures of the now rehabilitated members as they undertake an imperially mandated military campaign against aggressive Khitan border forces and then play a primary role in the suppression of the Fang La rebellion.[21]

Over the past decade the *Shui-hu Chuan* has appeared in numerous printed and televised cartoon versions, several book formats, and an immensely popular forty-three episode television serialization. Having become an essential part of the common culture and fundamental mindset, at least some of the tales and their embedded tactical lessons are known to virtually everyone, even the illiterate and those who never read it. In addition, the novel has served as a virtual source book of concepts, methods, and techniques for experts pondering the nature of irregular warfare and been the focus of numerous military seminars and articles in the PRC.

Even a cursory reading of the *Shui-hu Chuan* reveals that the outlaws who comprise the bandit gang fit the well-known mold of the Han dynasty *yu-hsia* or "wandering knights."[22] Men whose behavior was conspicuously unfettered by normal laws and constraints, who supposedly adhered to a higher standard of righteousness and loyalty, in reality they readily resorted to brute force to avenge supposed insults and redress personal wrongs. In fact, while manifesting a veneer of righteousness and mouthing platitudes about honor, they perpetrated many ruthless deeds, wantonly slaying scores of men, women, children, and servants, not to mention officials and soldiers.

This vaunted disdain for death—their own or others'—held a romantic appeal over the centuries for a populace suffering from government corruption, the inequities of radical class distinctions, constant exploitation, and interminable brutality. Helpless in the face of collusive authorities, the populace readily embraced the tales, suggesting that their renewed popularity bodes ill for the People's Republic of China insofar as injustice, corruption, repressive governmental measures, and economic disparity have spawned an astonishing resurgence of unrest and violent disorder.

In some episodes the heroes resort to spies, skill and cunning, disguise, subterfuge, ruses, and such heinous means as drugs and poison (including at an inn that specializes in rendering people into meat dumplings) to achieve surprise and explosively prevail in highly disadvantageous situations. Perhaps the best developed early tale recounts the plot for a major robbery that ironically pits several of the future brothers against each other as brigands and victim. The storyline's summary, "Yang Chih takes charge of the pole bearers conveying the gold and silver; Wu Yung seizes the birthday gifts through wisdom," emphasizes that wisdom (*chih*), although not explicitly unorthodox but certainly synonymous with subterfuge and plotting, rather than force (*li*) underlay their approach.[23]

A martial arts expert who had been incarcerated in a northern provincial prison for having slain an insolent local ruffian, Yang Chih was employed by the local governor to transport eleven trunks of jewels and other valuables—ostensibly a birthday gift but actually a bribe—to his father-in-law, a high court official. Yang had been selected because his demeanor and capabilities as a warrior were required to negotiate the lengthy, bandit-plagued route to the capital.

Rather than trust a contingent of possibly unreliable troops to protect the convoy, Yang surprisingly opted to employ a small band of soldiers disguised as porters. He assumed that they could proceed quickly along otherwise impassible mountain routes by carrying their load on balance poles and thus attract minimal attention. However, prompted by famine and poverty, seven famous thieves under Wu Yung (who would subsequently plot many of the marsh band's military operations) resolved to seize the treasure.

Even though they might have easily prevailed in an armed encounter with Yang and his exhausted bearers, Wu opted to employ deceit and trickery and therefore concocted a two-part plan. After Yang's soldiers had been on the road for several days and were laboring to ascend the mountains in overwhelming heat, they encountered several naked date merchants resting in a grove of trees. Initially suspicious, Yang was satisfied with their story and allowed his men, who were already rancorous and rebellious, to rest briefly.

Seemingly by chance, an itinerant wine merchant carrying two large wooden casks of wine suspended from a balance pole passed by. Naturally the bearers wanted to purchase some of his wine, but Yang, fearing that sedatives or poison may have been intermixed, loudly refused, provoking the wine vendor's wrath. The date merchants, hearing the commotion, wandered over and eventually prevailed upon the vendor to sell them a cask of wine that they rapidly drank with no ill effects, munching dates all the while. (This should have aroused further suspicion because merchants would be unlikely to consume such laboriously transported products.)

The key to the ruse then unfolded as Yang's soldiers continued to clamor for the wine. One of the date merchants surreptitiously took a ladle full from the other cask, drank some, and then ran off to finish it, all without apparent effect. Wu Yung then appeared with a ladle, dipped it into the bucket, and was about to drink, but the wine vendor snatched it away and dumped the remainder back into the cask. Having witnessed these developments, Yang finally relented and allowed the bearers to buy the second cask. Moreover, he even accepted a drink himself before they voraciously downed the entire quantity.

Suddenly, taunted by the date merchants, the bearers began to sink down to their knees and onto the ground. Even Yang himself felt increasingly paralyzed and finally collapsed only to witness the merchants throw away the date sacks, load the trunks full of treasure upon their wheelbarrows, and laughingly depart. Having consumed only a little wine, he remained conscious throughout the robbery and recovered his mobility first. Realizing the futility of proceeding further, Yang departed alone, thereby allowing the others to accuse him of acting in consort with the robbers and thus get him doubly condemned.

The cleverness, complexity, and preparation required to execute this imaginative stratagem have impressed readers for centuries. Wu Yung and his cohorts didn't employ brute force or simply poison the water along the way, but constructed a well-rehearsed scenario designed to convince their prey of the wine's innocuousness and purity. As revealed in the *Shui-hu Chuan*, its success turned upon Wu Yung introducing the hypnotic into the undrunken cask when he apparently dipped the ladle in to take a measure, for at that moment he actually poured in the previously prepared drug. This ensured that the wine would be untainted whichever cask was first opened. Thirst compelled the soldiers to accept a highly believable facade, resulting in the successful execution of a basically unorthodox stratagem.

The novel's earlier chapters also contain limited-scale, prototypical rehearsals for the major military clashes that follow after the band has become well-established and starts terrorizing the land. Maneuver and deception are employed in coordinated fashion against government enemies consisting of a few hundred troops rather than several divisions of ten thousand. For example, in chapter 34 the still embryonic bandit gang confronts a suppressive force of some one hundred government cavalry and 400 infantry under the noted commander Ch'in Ming. After initially stopping them by initiating single combat between Hua Jung and Ch'in Ming on an open plains area at the foot of some mountains, they vanish into the tangled mountainside vegetation in order to manipulate, harass, and control their enemies.

Government forces that try to pursue them up the irregular paths are pummeled by the era's defensive weapons of lime, stones, rocks, and logs. Small contingents then repeatedly pop up on every side to harass and harry them before suddenly disappearing without a trace. Ch'in Ming's infantry and cavalry quickly become exhausted from futilely racing back and forth and suffer numerous casualties without ever managing to engage the enemy in close combat.

The marsh forces continue their provocations into the night even after Ch'in Ming abandons the attack and encamps, employing the clanging of gongs, brightness of incendiary arrows, and thunder of cannon to frighten and disrupt them. When the beleaguered troops seek refuge in a nearby ravine for security, they are suddenly inundated by the release of two pent-up streams, drowning many, with the remainder being easily slaughtered in the entangling mud.

In another precursor to the large-scale marsh battles that later ensued, the government attempted to exterminate Wu Yung and his associates with 500 troops by requisitioning a hundred boats and advancing to capture them in their marsh side village.[24] However, right after abandoning their cavalry escort the troops are lured along winding paths further and further into the grassy wetlands by two boatmen in succession. By exploiting their detailed knowledge of the local topography and their superior swimming skills, the bandits are able to suddenly rise up out of the water to attack the now lost, hapless troops. Tipping the smaller craft over, they drown the non-swimmers, quickly overwhelm the remnant forces, and then exploit the panic of the confused officers to propel fire boats into their vessels from several directions, setting them ablaze. The remaining soldiers quickly abandon their failing vessels only to also find themselves enmired in heavy mud and easily slain with long-handled weapons.

The first of the major suppressive campaigns mounted under an overly confidant imperial commander employs a somewhat paltry but picked force of 3,000 cavalry and 5,000 infantry.[25] The marsh bandits respond by organizing their forces into two operational contingents and emphasizing "wisdom." However, they suffer an initial defeat on the far or non-lair side of the marsh under the onslaught of linked cavalry groups created by binding thirty horses each with chains into massive units whose advance cannot be broken simply by striking down individual riders or turning the horses aside with long spears.[26]

To thwart the government's newly arrived cannon expert, Ling Chen, the bandits resort to "lure and pounce" tactics. First they provoke Ling's small force then deployed along the marsh's edge into pursuing them toward some forty small boats tied along the shore. Then, as if they lack time to man the boats, they simply jump into the water and swim away, conspicuously abandoning the enticing vessels. Elated at this turn in events, Ling's contingent races onto them and rows out into the deeper channel waters in hot pursuit only to suddenly start sinking when underwater swimmers disable the rudders to prevent their escape and pull plugs temporarily sealing numerous pre-drilled holes in the bottom. The bandits then easily capture the immensely valuable Ling and even though many government troops drown, persuade him and numerous others to join them.

The challenge of linked cavalry is soon overcome by using long staves against the riders and forging new, hooked lances designed to undercut the horses' legs, as well as by training men in their employment. (Long-handled axes were in fact used by innovative Sung defenders against Khitan cavalry.) Moreover, before hacking the horses down and capturing the riders, they draw the enemy's cavalry into the tall grass and mucky terrain in order to compromise their mobility and obscure their vision. With the vanguard eliminated, the remaining isolated infantry are easily defeated, compelling a government retreat. Thus, although imperial innovation created almost unstoppable shock units, the bandits prove more adept at adopting unorthodox techniques. Moreover, despite having sufficient numbers to mount a concentrated attack against a relatively weak foe, they still segment their troops into smaller operational contingents—an unorthodox hallmark—and employ discrete tactical measures.

The government's second campaign, a much augmented effort entailing 100,000 men under T'ung Kuan, is launched after an ostensible amnesty mission turns into a fiasco.[27] Well organized, it is however once again flawed from the outset by the commander's overbearing self-confidence, a liability not only much exploited in historical China, but also emphasized in contemporary PRC military science. Wu Yung responds by once again dividing the bandits into multiple operational contingents. After two groups lure the imperial forces onto relatively flat terrain at the edge of the mountains, some 2,000 men deploy into the famous octagon formation, startling T'ung with their discipline and martial capabilities.

Not surprisingly, single combat between representative commanders initiates the confrontation. However, the rapid defeat of the government's illustrious warrior spreads consternation among the Sung troops that is quickly exploited in a force on force clash. Despite the paucity of their numbers, the emboldened marsh warriors easily prevail because the government forces quickly collapse and sustain some 10,000 casualties before being allowed to disengage.

After regrouping, the imperial armies decide to employ a concept initially articulated in Sun-tzu's *Art of War* and therefore array their troops in a linear formation known as the "ever responsive snake."[28] However, their progress is quickly halted by a simple but effective ploy: a single fisherman who repeatedly taunts them is assailed with arrows without effect because copper armor concealed under his hat and cloak harmlessly deflects them.

The frustrated Sung commander immediately orders fifty swimmers to eliminate this annoying provocation only to witness them being easily warded off and slain by the boatman. Even as he dispatches another 500, a separate contingent that has been lured toward the mountain suddenly encounters cannon fire. The main thrust then comes under repeated attack from regiments of 5,000 men while another bandit contingent cuts across the field in a standard disruptive maneuver, severing the government forces. Divided and in chaos, the density of their overwhelmingly superior numbers merely hampers the government's efforts, resulting in a massive slaughter that sees some two-thirds of the army lost before they can disengage.

The magnitude of their failure ensures another mission will be undertaken. This time 130,000 men consisting primarily of former bandits and other ruthless fighters under Kao Ch'iu are dispatched. Deeming a dual-front approach crucial, the army is accompanied by a large flotilla manned by 15,000 sailors and marines charged with coordinating their advance before eventually mounting an amphibious attack. The initial infantry clash compels the bandits to retreat but being stretched out some 10 *li* into the marsh, the Sung naval forces become susceptible to attack. In accord with traditional practice they are rapidly immobilized with logs, faggots, and other materials and then viciously assaulted by limited but widely dispersed forces piloting numerous small boats. Amidst panic and widespread desertion, heavy casualties are incurred from wounds and drowning and all the boats are captured.

Having lost their vital water-borne transport, Kao Ch'iu has the contiguous area scoured for usable boats and manages to confiscate some 1,500 that he converts into 500 floating infantry platforms capable of conveying about 100 soldiers each. Although Kao's cavalry protectively shadows them by synchronously advancing along the shore, the marsh bandits resort to the well-honed, highly effective weapon of fire boats. These are easily created by reinforcing the front of small vessels with metal plates and stuffing them with brush interlaced with sulfur and saltpeter, the basic components of gunpowder, for intensity. After pre-positioning, they merely have to be propelled with sufficient force to collide with the enemy's vessels to incinerate them.

The bandits also fabricate the appearance of a substantial encampment with flags and other props, including cannon, much in accord with classical Warring States deceptive methods in order to shape and control the nature of the encounter. With their first amphibious assault easily repulsed, the government vessels try to retreat but are quickly attacked by the fire boats and set ablaze. Heavy casualties are inflicted before a coordinated strike is launched against their main forces, now in retreat, ending the clash.

Troubled by the effectiveness of the bandits' small boats, the Sung designed large paddlewheel-powered vessels capable of simply overwhelming them in the tangled marshes. Three hundred behemoths with twelve wheels per side, well protected against arrows by bamboo screens and capable of carrying hundreds of marines each, are eventually constructed despite repeated sabotage efforts by night incendiary raiders.[29] Their advance is met with the usual skirmishers, who again prove the government's inability to slay their antagonists even before the warships are immobilized with logs and other materials that clog the paddlewheels.[30] Thereafter, they begin to sink even as they come under swarming attack because expert swimmers split apart the slats and chisel holes in the boats, essentially dooming the campaign of repression.

In the longer edition, the *Shui-hu Chuan*'s final forty chapters retell the heroic actions mounted by the now amnestied rebels as they participate in external campaigns undertaken by the beleaguered Sung government. First they are thrown against the increasingly aggressive Khitan in the semi-arid steppe region, then ordered to spearhead the suppression of Fang La's populist revolt in the more familiar and hospitable terrain of the moist south. In both cases they are depicted as emerging victorious, though only after great travail as the stalwart heroes perish one after another, frequently in almost impossible circumstances.

Vestiges in the historical records indicate that the marsh bandits did in fact participate in the Fang La campaign and some may also have served in the subsequent steppe conflict with the Khitan. However, apart from the sequence having been inverted for artistic purposes, details are lacking and the novel's depictions are purely fictional. Nevertheless, because they are forced to operate as a regular field force, the nature of the mission and the character of the conflict are markedly changed. Rather than being able to mount an aggressive defense at points of their choosing, exploit the terrain to their advantage, and manipulate enemies forced to attack, they are compelled to assault static enemy positions. With their innovative flexibility severely hampered, conventional open-field engagements and assaults on ensconced defenses inflict a heavy toll on men and contingents long accustomed to the freedom entailed by feint and maneuver.

Even in these circumstances they frequently vanquish their foes through subterfuge, particularly through exploiting logistical vulnerabilities, such as by disguising troops as grain carriers. Other unorthodox techniques include ferreting out indirect routes and bypaths; false defections and surrender; employing drugs and poisons to disable key defenders prior to slaughtering them; and infiltrating night incendiary raiders to cause confusion and create access to otherwise impregnable citadels. However, the individual heroes also suffer from overconfidence, the nemesis of all conventional commanders, and occasionally become negligent, to their undying regret.

While formulating their strategy for thwarting the government's linked cavalry by luring them into ambushes on difficult terrain, Sung Chiang notes that "Sun-tzu and Wu-tzu's tactics are advantageous in mountain forests and marshy expanses."[31] Although similar courses of action predicted upon "wisdom" or "soft" measures are often advanced, most of the novel's heroes embrace an ethos of direct action, of realizing objectives through force. Moreover, in many clashes force is initially employed to shock and thwart the enemy, with maneuver and irregular methods only being resorted to out of necessity. Despite Sung Chiang's deliberate cultivation of a reputation for righteous actions, for acting on behalf of Heaven, rather than compassionate disengagement, the final result is carnage on an immense scale, upwards of two-thirds of the enemy's forces perishing before they can escape. Such ruthlessness and brutality, even in fictionalized form, of course reflects the slaughter that accompanied many clashes across Chinese history and remains a core precept of contemporary PRC military science.[32]

Beset by Japanese invaders and Kuomintang troops with superior numbers and firepower, Mao Zedong enjoined his commanders to study the tactics of China's well-known mountain and marsh bandits, including those found in the fictional *Shui-hu Chuan,* and conduct a war of annihilation.[33] Although the geopolitical situation has dramatically changed, the burgeoning PRC is now focused upon projecting power and engaging adversaries on more distant terrain rather than confronting an invader on home territory, and much of Mao's thinking has been consciously rejected or discarded, many of the tactics retain interest for application in larger theaters, provided only that the battlefield can be suitably chosen and shaped.

Whether as concrete lessons to be learned, tactical principles, or simply impressions, certain aspects predominate. The initial chapters that portray the gathering band are replete with bold, courageous, swift, and decisively violent action, often undertaken by actors completely oblivious to the consequences and characterized by an extreme ruthlessness that results in women and peripheral personnel being gratuitously slain. Nevertheless, spirit, unwavering commitment, and supreme confidence fundamentally underlie their success, particularly when pitted against passive, often reluctant government armies.

Innovative tactics, subterfuge, and maneuver are all required once the encounters shift to circumstances in which heroic violence and simple carnage cannot prevail. Always outnumbered, the bandits must eschew direct, set piece, force on force confrontations for harassing campaigns, multiple prongs and sallies, and a variety of unremitting but never predictable measures to disorder and confuse the enemy. Nighttime raiders and internally mounted incendiary strikes terrorize the enemy and deny important resources; incessant noise and random missiles prevent rest; attacking shipments and seizing provisions impoverishes them while augmenting the army's own reserves, just as Sun-tzu advocated.

Although not explicitly stated, constricted and watery ground should always be chosen to leverage the power of the disadvantaged and dictate the terms of the engagement in accord with the fundamental concept of recognizing configurations of terrain and appropriately exploiting the characteristics. Local knowledge is crucial for exploiting highly specific topographical features that will disrupt the enemy's synchronization, sever their communications, and isolate units for defeat in detail.

Feigned retreats and other ruses should be employed to entice and manipulate the enemy, compelling them onto disadvantageous terrain while shattering their ability to act in a cohesive manner. Ambushes should be adopted on unfamiliar ground, with challenges and feints constantly fragmenting their concentration and exhausting their troops. Mobility should be thwarted, just as the logs and flotsam clogged the marsh waterways (with more modern but still simplistic variants being employed against contemporary fleets). Unexpected, locally applicable unorthodox techniques such as "frogmen" with chisels and drills attacking from below and drugs and poison contaminating apparently innocuous food should be introduced at pivotal moments for maximum effectiveness. More visible, inescapable weapons (such as incendiary devices) that can both destroy and terrorize should be exploited, particularly against confined or constrained enemies.

Many of the *Shui-hu Chuan*'s techniques and principles are not only found throughout the traditional Chinese military manuals, but actually received their original impetus from Sun-tzu's *Art of War:*

> If you are fewer than the enemy, you can circumvent them. A small enemy that acts inflexibly will become the captives of a large enemy.[34]
>
> Warfare is the Tao of deception. Thus although you are capable, display incapability to them. When committed to employing your forces, feign inactivity. When your objective is nearby, make it appear as if distant; when far away, create the illusion of being nearby.
>
> Display profits to entice them. Create disorder in their forces and take them. If they are substantial, prepare for them; if they are strong, avoid them. If they are angry, perturb them; be deferential to foster their arrogance.[35]

However, following these prescriptions and choosing to repeatedly employ unorthodox techniques rather than engage in direct confrontations may also allow the enemy commanders to feel and claim that they were not really defeated, but had merely been overcome by tricks, as illustrated by events in the novel itself.[36]

San-kuo Yen-yi

An even more majestic and sweeping treatment of epoch-making events than the *Shui-hu Chuan*, the *Romance of the Three Kingdoms* retells the largely historical events of China's Three Kingdoms period (168–280 CE) in highly dramatized and episodic fashion. Although closely based upon the chronicle known as the *Records of the Three Kingdoms* (*San-kuo Chih*), the novel assumed final form sometime in the early to middle Ming, many of the episodes having evolved and been embellished over the previous centuries by storytellers and operatic composers.[37] Just as *Water Margin*, it now appears in numerous formats, enjoys immense popular appeal, and has been transformed into a highly successful television serial.

The narrative begins by describing Han attempts to stem the popular unrest spearheaded by the Yellow Turbans that eventually sundered the realm into three parts. Ts'ao Ts'ao manages to gain control of the Han remnants in the north; Sun Ch'üan rules the kingdom of Wu in the southeast; and Liu Pei, theoretically a member of the Han ruling lineage, and Chu-ko Liang finally consolidate power in the southwest. Although very few permutations are possible, the strategic situation constantly changes because of the unremitting enmity among the three parties and intercession of numerous minor players.

A number of the characters have well-developed personalities, though others are simply the embodiment of extremized tendencies. Nevertheless, insofar as the protagonists are fighting for the greater glory of the realm, the drama surpasses the more circumscribed, personal conflicts of mere marsh bandits entangled by perversity and local constraints. Moreover, contrary to claims that China has no heroes, it would be impossible to find more dramatically forceful behavior than exhibited by the numerous exemplary commanders who readily throw themselves into individual combat, engage overwhelming foes out of a sense of righteous mission, and generally, though not invariably, adhere to a commonly espoused code of chivalrous behavior. Many of China's greatest warriors cross the stage, including the irascible and impetuous Chang Fei; the transcendent strategist Chu-ko Liang; the crafty but brutal Ts'ao Ts'ao; the powerful but flawed Kuan Yü, later apotheosized as the god of war, who fights as readily as he endures pain;[38] and generals such as Chou Yü and Chiang Wei. Conversely, as epitomized by Tung Chuo and Ts'ao Ts'ao, the novel abounds with examples of baseless, self-serving, brutal behavior.

Despite its somewhat romantic aura, the *San-kuo Yen-yi* actually depicts a ruthless world marked by deceit, brutality, and the slaughter not just of individuals, but of families, clans, and entire armies, including through aquatic and incendiary attacks. A strong theme of martial chivalry predominates, though it sometimes proves to be merely a veneer because the soon to be vanquished often resort to clandestine weapons, false flight, and archers concealed off the battlefield during heroic single combat. In addition, petty conflicts and severe character flaws ultimately doom many commanders and massive military efforts to failure, invariably at the expense of a populace unable to escape the swirling throes of war.

Although it remains just a novel despite its historical base, the *San-kuo Yen-yi* should not be underestimated in its role as a source of military wisdom and tactics applicable to the contemporary martial environment.[39] A number of the more famous incidents continue to have a strong impact upon the popular imagination and contribute critical components to the strategic mindset. Noting the similarity with the recent history of the major powers, particularly the shifting relations among the United States, Russia, and China, contemporary PRC strategists have long avidly studied the period for useful lessons and occasionally taken note of echoes in George Orwell's *1984*.

These lessons are not confined to strategic and geopolitical concepts and methods, but also envisioned in techniques of subversion and betrayal that may be advantageously implemented in both the political and the military arenas. No doubt the machinations of court officials, dynamics of jealousy, struggle for power among commanders, and other dramas of surpassing intrigue have accounted for its popularity over the ages in Japan and other Asian countries as well as China, and it is even claimed that the infamous Tai Li derived his inspiration for the Chinese secret service from it.[40]

The novel also shows the lunacy of repeatedly fighting over the same terrain, advancing at great cost before simply withdrawing and allowing the enemy to freely reoccupy it, as in Shu's numerous but futile campaigns into the north under Chu-ko Liang and then Chiang Wei. However, many pivotal events are newly dramatized, augmenting their already significant fame, including Ch'ih Pi and Kuan-tu. In fact, although the *San-kuo Yen-yi* rarely speaks about the unorthodox, during the stalemate at Kuan-tu Ts'ao Ts'ao is advised that it's "time to employ the unorthodox." Furthermore, people do speak about *ping chi*, "military stratagems" or what might be termed "clever military tactics"; a few recluses are known for their arcane wisdom; and several strategists are noted for having made many unorthodox contributions.

Selected tactics are repeatedly employed throughout the book, primarily those designed to manipulate the enemy, including the feigned retreat, estrangement techniques, disguise, false defectors, ambushes, night raids, incendiary attacks, and subversion. In the context of its depiction of late Han and Three Kingdoms period warfare, orthodoxy may be defined as the set battle. The two sides deploy in full array, often at a pre-designated time, before supposedly initiating the clash with single combat between their respective champions. One or another emerges victorious after repeated blows, leading to consternation in the enemy's troops and the initiation of full-scale combat, frequently resulting in the dispirited being overwhelmed.

The feigned defeat, generally manifest as a retreat designed to lure the enemy forward in disorganized fashion prior to springing an ambush, is employed so frequently that it must be considered an orthodox technique, yet it still manages to repeatedly ensnare the headstrong and unwary. By making it conspicuously artificial in order to deter pursuit when truly vanquished, much in the mold of the "empty city ploy" associated with subsequent *Thirty-six Stratagems* thinking, the feigned retreat comes to be employed in a newly defined, unorthodox manner.

Less actively, flags are conspicuously used to create the impression that troops occupy critical positions or are deployed in depth in order to fix enemy forces or prompt certain movements, thereby shaping the battle-field and preserving one's own forces when compelled to abandon a position. The original historical incidents no doubt reflected the advice of such classical writers as Sun-tzu and Sun Pin, but the novel's additional, fictionalized incidents may have been prompted by formulations appearing in the *One Hundred Unorthodox Strategies*. For example, Ts'ao Ts'ao manipulates Lü Pu by placing flags in the nearby woods to elicit his attack on what appear to be troops in ambush[41] while Chu-ko Liang increases the number of fires in the camps of his retreating armies in order to deter Ssu-ma Yi's attack.[42] He also multiples his flags during a snowstorm to create the appearance of numbers[43] and Chang Fei has brush dragged to raise dust, an antique ploy that continued to have value.[44]

More substantial versions of this ruse employ physical facades, earth-works, and palisades, occasionally augmented by decoys, for added realism. For example, to deter an attack by Ts'ao Ts'ao's massive forces, amidst heavy fog Hsü Sheng had false walls and towers staffed by straw soldiers constructed overnight along the river, astonishing the enemy with their numerousness and appearance when the heavy fog lifted and they suddenly became visible.[45]

Although commonplace, this technique can also be used in a truly un-orthodox fashion when the enemy commander is known to have sufficient expertise to fathom the ploy, thereby taking the sequence of anticipation and response to another dimension. For example, while assigning contingents from Liu Pei's limited forces to prepare ambushes at several positions along Ts'ao Ts'ao projected escape route prior to the incendiary attack at Ch'ih Pi, Chu-ko Liang instructs Kuan Yü to set fires on the side of a valley to ensure that Ts'ao Ts'ao will move through that constricted terrain.

When Kuan Yü inevitably protests that any sign of troop presence will deter even the most inexperienced commander from approaching, Chu-ko Liang utilizes Sun-tzu's concept of vacuity and substance to buttress his assertion that Ts'ao Ts'ao's tactical acumen will invariably prompt him to choose that very passage: "Haven't you heard of the tactical discussion of making the vacuous vacuous and the substantial substantial? Although

Ts'ao Ts'ao is a capable commander, this should be sufficient to delude him. When he sees the smoke arising, he will consider it a conspicuous manifestation of power at a point of emptiness and certainly pick this route to come forth."[46]

Two additional unorthodox variants turn on exploiting an undefended position to either draw or deter an attack. (Insofar as the latter is best known as the "empty city stratagem" it will be discussed in the next section on the *Thirty-six Stratagems*.) In the more mundane, former case, weakness in the form of few numbers, absence of preparation, lack of will, or simple abandonment is displayed in order to compel the enemy to advance and strike, rendering them vulnerable to flanking assaults, or lure them into a city where they can be trapped and slaughtered. Even Ts'ao Jen was caught in such a trap[47] and Teng Ai successfully employed this ruse by having the old and weak appear to be fleeing the city, thereby confirming its abandonment.[48]

Inanimate decoys constructed to mimic the appearance of specific individuals and doubles wearing recognizable garb are also used to divert attention and confuse the enemy. For example, Chang Fei deliberately allows spies to report on his plans to personally command a night raid but instead leads a contingent to attack the ambushers while their attention is temporarily transfixed by the imitation Chang Fei spearheading the vanguard.[49] Another time he tempts a nighttime attack by pretending to be drinking heavily in his tent, but when enemy raiders penetrate the deliberately accessible camp to cut him down, find only a straw dummy.[50]

The usually impulsive Chang Fei isn't the only commander to creatively exploit dummies for military purposes. Chu-ko Liang once virtually clones himself with three doubles, each seated in a replica of his well-known small carriage and accompanied by the usual contingent of black clad troops to mislead and mystify the onrushing enemy.[51] Even on his deathbed he orders a statue to be carved in his image and placed in his carriage after his demise so as to deter attacks while they undertake an orderly retreat.[52] His son subsequently imitates his example during a futile attempt to defend Ch'eng-tu against Teng Ai's forces, after the latter unexpectedly penetrate Szechuan's mountain barriers, and succeeds in momentarily astonishing them with the possibility that Chu-ko Liang was still alive![53]

Conversely, much in contrast to Liu Pang and other famous heroes who remarkably maintained a facade of normalcy after suffering painful wounds just to avoid adversely affecting the army's morale, a few commanders deliberately circulate rumors of their deaths after being wounded on the battlefield, apparently assassinated, or reportedly dying from illness. For example, the great Wu commander in chief, Chou Yü, has the entire camp visibly mourn him after being shot by a poisoned arrow. Convinced of his death, Ts'ao Jen mobilizes his northern forces and launches a surprise attack that, having been well anticipated, is decimated by a massive ambush.[54]

Even Sun Ts'e, who was instrumental in his family consolidating power over the area that became the kingdom of Wu, employs the ruse during an attack upon the fortified city of Mo-ling. Confronted by an obdurate defense after having been wounded in the thigh by an arrow, he feigns death, thereby luring the now overconfident defenders out of the city in a fervent attempt to exploit an apparent command void.[55] Conversely, fear that reports of Chu-ko Liang's death might prove false deters Ssu-ma Yi from precipitously committing his massive forces to any sweeping action against Shu's retreating armies.[56]

Although Sun-tzu early on warned against being taken in by peace talks and false surrenders, the novel repeatedly portrays the employment of these tactics by various commanders seeking time to regroup, subvert the enemy,[57] or induce laxity in the mode of T'ien Tan.[58] Despite being sometimes penetrated,[59] these remain among the most dangerous techniques in the modern arsenal of deception, rendered highly effective through playing upon a widespread desire for peace and vociferous but naive acceptance of even implausible utterances as credible.

On a personal level the well-recognized "false surrender ploy" (cha-chiang chi) underlies the employment of double agents. As Sun-tzu pointed out, accurate knowledge of the enemy's situation can only be gained through such human resources as spies, prisoners, and defectors, with the latter being especially valuable because they can often provide detailed maps and valuable insights into strategic thinking and military strength.[60] However, defectors always entail a problem of credibility, particularly when accompanied by large numbers of troops as sometimes occurred in traditional Chinese warfare. In the novel captured generals are often turned around, even employed to subvert their former comrades through surreptitiously gaining entrance to camps, cities, and citadels.[61] Defectors are also employed to induce others to defect (or at least abandon the enemy), thereby eliminating the wise and capable. Feigned defections are also used to manipulate the enemy into desired actions, such as a well-anticipated attack.[62]

The most effective method for legitimizing feigned betrayals and establishing the veracity of expendable agents on misinformation missions—the infliction of severe corporal punishment—is well depicted in two *San-kuo Yen-yi* incidents. In the most famous, Chou Yü first orders Huang Kai executed, then beaten instead, convincing Ts'ao Ts'ao that Huang's desire to defect is truly motivated, thereby setting the stage for the devastating incendiary attack at Ch'ih Pi. In another episode the irascible Chang Fei finds a pretext to beat one of his soldiers in a moment of apparent drunken anger, then promises to have him sacrificed before they conduct a night raid on the enemy. However, much as captured prisoners might be employed, he allows the aggrieved man to escape, knowing that the information will be convincingly conveyed to the enemy.[63] Forewarned of the impending assault, the enemy commander empties his camp and deploys his men in ambush around the external perimeter only to suffer a surprise attack himself after a token raiding party enters the camp to set fires, resulting in his defeat and capture.[64]

Another aspect of deception is disguise, a technique advocated as early as the Warring States period. But even if the classic military writings hadn't sanctioned the use of troops disguised as enemy forces, the success of Ts'ao Ts'ao's famous nighttime raid against Yüan Shao's grain reserves certainly provided sufficient impetus for disguise to become a prominent unorthodox technique. Apart from its employment by spies for a variety of intelligence missions, subversives exploit disguise to surreptitiously penetrate enemy citadels and camps (such as by appearing to be returning troops) and nighttime incendiary raiders repeatedly succeed in causing chaos and undermining the defenses of otherwise secure bastions. The *San-kuo Yen-yi* also depicts contingents in enemy garb creating the facade of friendly forces before suddenly surprising their opponents. Forged credentials, false letters, and stolen tallies are all employed to substantiate such deceptions.[65] Thus Chu-ko Liang, despite his vaunted reputation for unsullied virtue and close association with the pedantic Liu Pei, has no compunction about resorting to troops in disguise because he employs them on several occasions, including during the suppressive campaign mounted against the Man in the south.[66]

The most famous use of disguise in the *San-kuo Yen-yi* unfolds as part of Wu's well-orchestrated campaign to defeat Kuan Chung and retake the cities held by Shu. A well-developed episode with a solid historical basis, its retelling occupies almost two full chapters.[67] After Liu Pei subjugates the highly fertile area known as Yi—essentially modern Szechuan—through the unconventional measures depicted in the novel, he strives to forge a stable bastion to serve as a platform for conquering the north and reestablishing the Han. However, his seizure of Yi infuriates Sun Ch'üan, ruler of Wu, who had been deceived by specious arguments and was now forcefully blocked by Kuan Yü. (Liu Pei had originally acknowledged Sun Ch'üan's authority and even enjoyed close marriage relations with him, while Sun had ceded administrative control over two commanderies on the premise that Liu could unify the people in Ching-chou and thereby constitute an active bulwark against Ts'ao Ts'ao's strength. However, when Sun Ch'üan demanded that the commanderies be returned, Liu refused on the basis they were necessary for withstanding Ts'ao Ts'ao and immediately deputed Kuan Yü to occupy the potentially contested regions.) Armed conflict is only aborted when Wei's advance prompts a temporary reconciliation, the non–Wei-controlled portion of Ching-chou being split between them.

In 219 Liu Pei's forces manage to seize Han-chung, then Wu and Wei clash in the Huai-nan region in the seventh month, presenting Kuan Yü with an opportunity to attack the pivotal city of Fan-ch'eng. Heavy rains in the eighth month fortuitously inundate the northern encampments, forcing the surrender of seven Ts'ao-Wei armies totaling some 40,000 men. Kuan Yü then surrounds Fan-ch'eng and attacks the companion city of Hsiang-yang on the southern bank of the Han River. Kuan Yü has momentum and looks invincible but in moving north, he inadvertently leaves a vacuum to his rear.

Prudence dictates mounting a preventive defense against possibly perfidious Wu but Kuan Yü focuses all his efforts on the assault, allowing Ts'ao Ts'ao to persuade Wu to launch an unexpected strike. Wei then deviously releases Sun Ch'üan's secret letter of agreement to stimulate resolve in the beleaguered defenders and foster doubt in Kuan Yü's camp. However, wary of the latter's strength, rather than immediately undertaking a strike Lü Meng, the Wu commander, opts to obfuscate Kuan's wariness. Feigning illness, he arranges for the appointment of a subcommander (Lu Hsün), who sends laudatory letters of admiration that exploit Kuan Yü's vanity and put him so at ease that he fails to undertake any defensive preparations.

This idyllic rapport is shattered when Lu Hsün cleverly cloaks his assault on Ching-ling as a fleet of commercial vessels moving upriver by concealing the troops and dressing the sailors as ordinary boatmen. Traveling both day and night, they overwhelm all the lookouts before suddenly appearing on target and startling most of the local commanders into abandoning their posts without resistance, often through employing surrendered troops to aid their efforts. Venturing further westward, Lu seizes Yi-ling and subdues local resistance, cutting off Kuan Yü's retreat and exposing him to a northern strike that never materializes because Ts'ao Ts'ao hopes his two enemies will reduce each other's military capability.

In a classic manipulative effort, Wu's commander in chief Lü Meng then implements a conspicuously humanitarian policy in the newly occupied territory, treating the populace so well that the glowing reports of spies severely undermine Shu's fighting spirit. Refused external support by nearby Shu generals, Kuan Yü also experiences a high rate of desertion even as he moves to a more advantageous position. In the twelfth month he is finally captured and killed, an ignominious fate for a much glorified warrior who would subsequently be apotheosized as the god of war.

Battlefield commanders and powerful generals are also eliminated in the *San-kuo Yen-yi* through the implementation of particularly well-developed estrangement techniques. Two incidents stand out: the manipulation of Lü Pu (discussed in the next section on the *Thirty-six Stratagems*) and the subversion of Generals Li Chüeh and Kuo Fan. While Ts'ao Ts'ao is still out in the field amassing power during the early days of the Han's collapse, Li and Kuo gain control of the court and basically badger the emperor into subservience. Seeing no possibility of eliminating their conjoined forces, Yang Piao suggests an estrangement plot that effectively unleashes the power of jealousy to create animosity between them.[68]

Yang initiates the chain of events by having his wife suggest to Kuo's wife, a woman known for her jealousy, that her husband's late nighttime returns stem from his involvement in an illicit affair with Li's wife, a liaison that will endanger him if discovered. Although her precise emotional reaction—envy, anger, fear—is not described, she prevails upon her husband to remain at home rather than risk being poisoned, a possible turn of events given that both men are ambitious. When Li happens to send some food over, she exploits the opportunity to poison it and then expertly stages a scene in which she suggests that any food brought from outside should be tested for safety. The rapid death of the unfortunate dog that tastes it immediately confirms the presence of poison and of course attests to her sagacity.

Coincidence intervenes to further confirm the likelihood of a poisoning attempt when Kuo drinks to excess at Li's house after a court session and then develops a stomachache that is ameliorated only by an emetic provided by his wife after he returns home. This prompts him to prepare an armed strike but Li's spies alert him to the developments, allowing him to preemptively send his forces forth. The two armies clash in the capital's outskirts, plunging the countryside into chaos and inflicting enormous casualties on the populace before the antagonists finally reunite after having respectively kidnapped the emperor and court, only to be vanquished by Ts'ao Ts'ao.

Similar methods are employed to fragment external enemies, undermine battlefield generals, stir dissension within the government, provoke animosity among commanders, and cause the capable to defect or have them marginalized or executed if they cannot be induced or coerced into cooperating. The most common method, both historically and in the novel, is using rumors of betrayal and disloyalty to plant doubt. In an example already reprised but further expanded in the novel, Ts'ao Ts'ao deliberately splits Ma Chao and Han Sui by making it appear that Han Sui was about to shift his allegiance.[69]

In yet another famous *San-kuo Yen-yi* example Chu-ko Liang sets two closely allied enemy commanders against each other by concocting appearances that suggest they are plotting to betray each other and cleverly manipulating captured spies and prisoners to complete the illusion.[70] Chu-ko Liang also manages to subvert Chiang Wei with forged instructions and other means to make it appear that he willingly surrendered to Shu, thereby compelling him to defect to them.[71]

Just as T'ien Tan subverted Yüeh Yi by spreading rumors that the highly successful field commander was about to revolt, estrangement methods can also be employed on the strategic level to eliminate competent and therefore dangerous generals. In the novel a number of methods are employed, including letters purporting to cement new alliances,[72] but the most commonly encountered are rumors spread among the populace at large or conveyed to the ruler by bribed officials. For example, to subvert Ssu-ma Yi just after Ts'ao Jui assumes power, rumors that he is plotting to usurp the throne are circulated and forged proclamations posted under his name in the major cities, augmenting the effect.[73] Ssu-ma yi similarly uses the disaffected Kuo An to undermine Chu-ko Liang in the field by starting rumors he will usurp the throne, prompting his recall from a strong field position.[74] Despite this experience, the second Shu emperor is again persuaded to recall a commander on the verge of success when Teng Ai sows rumors in Ch'eng-tu that Chiang Wei is planning to revolt and ensures the emperor will be informed of them by bribing the eunuch Huang Hao, who controls imperial access.[75] Although defeated and a prisoner of Wei, Chiang Wei manages to exploit the animosity between Wei's two conquering generals Chung Hui and Teng Ai before exacting revenge on Teng by similarly causing Ssu-ma Chao to believe that Teng is about to revolt.[76]

A number of other basically unorthodox lessons and techniques are visible in the *San-kuo Yen-yi*. Perhaps foremost among them is the utility of incendiary attacks for subversive effects, destructive purposes, facilitating ambushes, restricting mobility, entrapping, and slaughtering, especially on constricted terrain.[77] Contrary to the normal practice of early warfare, raids and full-scale attacks are frequently mounted at night, often in conjunction with the employment of incendiary measures, with remarkable success.[78] Aquatic attacks, in some sense a corollary to incendiary strikes, are also successfully employed on several occasions, including against Ts'ao Ts'ao, while denying water debilitates a few notable armies, including those under Ma Su.[79]

Finally, whether directed toward individual commanders or complete armies, the entire thrust is focused on manipulating the enemy in order to wrest an easy victory. Although astute leaders such as Teng Ai are able to anticipate the enemy and shape the battle space prior to the enemy's arrival,[80] the emphasis is generally upon blunting spirit and inducing laxity, whether through unusual or ordinary means, such as simply refusing battle.[81] Laxity is induced to facilitate surprise attacks, arrogance nurtured to blind commanders to threats and cause them to heatedly reject threat assessments.[82] Traps and tricks are commonly used and even Ts'ao Ts'ao, despite his learning and experience, is lured into one with the promise of an internal response from within a citadel.[83] Duplicity marks most interstate relationships even to the extent of abandoning an "ally" despite promises of joint action.[84] Misinformation effectively muddles enemy planning and battlefield commanders constantly resort to facades and rumors to contort and confuse the enemy.[85] One commander, Chung Hui, even fools his own ruler by supposedly building boats to invade Shu when he really intends to strike Wu.[86] Finally, in accord with ancient Chinese tradition, women and pleasure are used to debauch others and estrange the capable from the dissolute, and even the ostentatiously virtuous Liu Pei is temporarily afflicted.[87]

Thirty-six Stratagems (*San-shih-liu Chi*)

Three of the purely martial writings—the *Art of War*, *Hundred Unorthodox Strategies*, and *Thirty-six Stratagems*—provide the essential theoretical core for the contemporary strategic mindset. (This in no way diminishes the importance of the *Shui-hu Chuan* and *San-kuo Yen-yi* materials nor the other theoretical writings and paradigm battles, though the last two generally require conscious study in military settings to be fully comprehended and consciously appropriated.) The *Thirty-six Stratagems* has enjoyed enormous popularity over the past decade, appearing in the usual array of formats including television serializations with titles such as *Sun Pin and the Thirty-six Stratagems* and extended cartoon features in newspapers.[88] Few people are not cognizant of at least some of the plots and ploys, even fewer unacquainted with the title and basic concept of a stratagem. The PLA has long made the book a subject of study and included it among its publications, and books specifically devoted to countering the thirty-six that often suggest employing the stratagems against each other have also begun to appear.[89]

The text's origins remain obscure, though it is generally thought to have been composed by a reclusive scholar near the end of the Ming and thereafter transmitted largely in secret, accounting for variations in the explanations and illustrations.[90] Although superficially evincing a unitary structure, the book actually builds on the tradition of strategic categories and identifiable plots while appropriating numerous pithy statements about tactical principles that date back to the fifth century CE.[91] The work also integrates materials from the *Yi Ching* that may have been subsequently appended in the Ming and often betray a sort of ad hoc character, fundamental concepts of *yin* and *yang*, numerous historical illustrations, and cryptic secondary explications.

Most versions of the text begin with the following assertion: "Six sixes, thirty-six. Within numbers there are techniques, within techniques there are numbers. The crux lies within *yin* and *yang*, the patterns of change. The crux cannot be established, for when it is established, it will not meet the situation." This enigmatic pronouncement has given rise to numerous interpretations, most of which understand the word *chi*, translated here as "crux," as "plans" (as in *chi-mou*) or "strategies," thereby advising against formulating or determining one's strategies in advance. However, despite the identical pronunciation it should be emphasized that this is not the same word as the character *chi* in the book's title, *san-shih-liu chi*, whose core meaning is "plan" or "stratagem" and thus "thirty-six stratagems."

A closer rendering of *chi* (crux) that well accords with the early concept of a world in flux yet marked by discernible tendencies and patterns would be "incipient moment," the subtle point when affairs begin to develop and action can and should be initiated for maximum ease and effectiveness. Not only do the *Yi Ching, Ling Ch'i Ching, T'ai-hsüan Ching*, and other prognosticatory texts all unfold and acquire meaning within this context, but essentially the same vision also pervades the *Tao Te Ching* despite various inconsistencies and contradictions within the text.[92] For example, in a chapter entitled "Act Actionlessly" it states:

> Plan against the difficult while it remains easy,
> Act upon the great while it is still minute.
> The realm's difficult affairs invariably commence with the easy;
> The realm's great affairs invariably arise from the minute.

Another chapter, "The Tranquil Is Easily Grasped," states:

> The tranquil is easily grasped,
> What yet lacks signs is easily plotted against.
> The brittle is easily split,
> The minute is easily scattered.

Among the classical military texts, the *Six Secret Teachings* particularly stresses the idea of timely action:

> When the sun is at midday you should dry things. If you grab a knife you must cut. If you hold an axe you must attack. If, at the height of day, you do not dry things in the sun, this is termed losing the time. If you grasp a knife but do not cut, you will lose the moment for profits. If you hold an axe but do not attack, then bandits will come. If trickling streams are not blocked, they will become great rivers. If you don't extinguish the smallest flames,

what will you do about a great conflagration? If you do not eliminate the two leaf sapling, how will you use your axe when the
tree has grown?

Although unstated, action at the incipient moment invariably exploits
the enormous tactical imbalance of power analogized by Sun-tzu's whetstone against an egg. Whether balking the enemy's plans or destroying
them on the battlefield, the application of overwhelming strategic power
simply requires releasing the trigger—another meaning of *chi* (crux),
which came to designate mechanisms in general—of a fully cocked crossbow. However, the thirty-six stratagems are conceived from the perspective of an inferior force necessarily striving to subvert and overcome just
such overwhelming strategic power. Nevertheless, even these inimical circumstances present pivot points or opportunities (*chi*) ranging from Ts'ao
Ts'ao's linked boats to total dependence upon modern communications
and net-centric warfare, the latter a sort of abstract technological analogy
to the boat entanglements at Ch'ih Pi.

Other interpretations of the chapter's initial lines have also been offered, including that the numbers refer to assessing the enemy or a situation as discussed in the *Art of War*'s opening chapter, "Initial Estimations."
However, perhaps the best rendering might simply be: "Six sixes produce
thirty-six. Within these numbers lie techniques, within techniques lie
numbers. The incipient moment for action lies within the changing patterns of *yin* and *yang*. This moment cannot be artificially determined, for
when it is forced, it will not accord with the situation."

The *Stratagems* imposes a broad classificatory system apparently based
upon increasingly difficult circumstances, apportioning the thirty-six
equally among six distinctive categories. Each of these categories is in turn
supposedly marked by an internal *yin yang* progression, though some of
the sequences seem disjointed and the entries misplaced, as might be expected in a pastiche work. Although often abstruse and esoteric (at least in
the original Chinese), they clearly are founded upon the basic concepts
and tactical principles of traditional Chinese military science, many of
them being derived from the *Art of War* even though unacknowledged.

These include *yin* and *yang*, firm and inflexible, advancing and retreating, deception, maneuver, manipulation, attack and defense, and the orthodox and unorthodox.

The six categories are broadly grouped into two categories of three that reflect different tactical imbalances in power. The first three encompass plans or stratagems applicable to advantageous situations, particularly when one's strength exceeds the enemy's: stratagems for achieving victory, battling a well-matched enemy, and attacking, generally through the use of plots and planning. The second category, premised upon being caught in disadvantageous circumstances, has a long tradition dating back to the *Six Secret Teachings*.[93] As generally described, its three groups consist of warfare in confused circumstances, techniques for seizing terrain, and efforts in the face of defeat, the most dire of all.

Space precludes an extensive discussion of the thirty-six despite their intriguing content and conceptual and tactical importance in the contemporary strategic environment. Nevertheless, the work's orientation and the integral nature of its unorthodox measures merit comment. As already seen, even the most orthodox maneuvers can be employed in unorthodox ways, yet within the context of warfare as traditionally practiced in China several of the thirty-six may be deemed inherently unorthodox. Surprisingly, contrary to traditional application and probable expectation, they are not confined to the last category, but spread throughout the book.

The more competitive and complex the relationships among the parties—be they commanders, politicians, officials, or armies—the greater the possibility of exploiting the often deliberately induced confusion and then maneuvering in the chaos, contrary to the enemy's expectations. In fact, their very success depends upon a relatively knowledgeable opponent who will make the usual assumptions in assessing the possibilities before coming to an "informed" and thus orthodox decision. Their first use is innovative and imaginative, but once they become part of the library of essential techniques, their unorthodox character diminishes somewhat despite further successful application.

Even though the entire work is generally felt to comprise a handbook of unorthodox techniques, in the strictest sense only a few of the stratagems can be considered unorthodox: "replacing the beams and changing the pillars" and "pulling firewood out from beneath the cauldron," two that essentially describe methods for subversion; "beautiful women," whose meaning is clear from the rubric; the "turned agent" or doubled agent, the most important of Sun-tzu's spies; "feint east and strike west," the basis of much battlefield duplicity and maneuvering; "non-being gives birth to being," a technique likely to see contemporary utilization; and especially the "empty city ploy," a stratagem that turns upon conspicuously displaying weakness. Although they all merit close scrutiny, only the three most imaginative are discussed below.

Mei-jen-chi (Stratagem of Beautiful Women)

As recounted in our *Tao of Spycraft*, the allure of beauty and pleasures of sex were extensively employed for a variety of subversive purposes beginning with the Spring and Autumn period. Whether individually or in groups, women were used to debauch the licentious and entice the virtuous, cause jealousy and antagonism, stimulate disaffection, engage in a variety of espionage tasks, undertake assassinations, and act as a diplomatic tool for enthralling external "barbarian" peoples and cementing marriage alliances. Being so fundamental, their employment greatly surpasses the notion of a stratagem. Nevertheless, in the particularity of application, whether in the political or personal domain, especially in desperate circumstances, the stratagem acquires sufficient concrete character to justify inclusion among the *Thirty-six*. Moreover, contemporary commentators have vastly expanded the scope of "beautiful women" to encompass all things esoteric and beautiful, including art objects, material goods, speech, and music.[94]

The text of the stratagem, although simple, entails extended connotations: "When the troops are strong, attack their general. When the general is wise, attack his emotions. When the general weakens and army disintegrates, their power will wither by itself. It will be advantageous to employ defenses against incursions and conducive to defend each other." The last line is a quotation from one of the *Yi Ching*'s sixty-four hexagrams, *Chien*, whose name (Chinese character) means "gradual" and is sometimes associated with the image of water soaking into the ground. Taking the act of a woman setting forth for marriage as the theme for its judgment and trees growing on a mountain as its image, the hexagram naturally counsels being firm and correct. However, the judgment for the line quoted here is somewhat contrary because it implies that morality has been lost, that a man who goes forth on a mission doesn't return (for unspecified reasons), and that misfortune is likely.

The core explication usually associated with the stratagem states:

> You cannot match up against (armies) whose troops are strong and generals wise. Their power requires that you serve them instead. However, serving them with land and thereby increasing their power as the Six States did in submitting to Ch'in (in the Warring States period) is the most inferior strategy. Serving them with silks and money and thereby augmenting their wealth in the way the Sung served the Liao and Chin is equally the lowest form of strategy.
>
> Only serving them with beautiful women in order to enervate their wills and weaken their bodies, thereby increasing the animosity of their subordinates, (will do). For example, when King Wen was incarcerated, (in order to ransom him) beautiful women, buildings, and horses were presented to Emperor Chou. Kou Chien employed (the famous beauty) Hsi Shih and immensely valuable treasures to ply Fu-ch'ai, King of Wu, with pleasure. In this way you can turn defeat into victory.[95]

Hundreds of tales, including a recent novel titled *Mei-jen Chi*, have focused upon the machinations and allure of beautiful women and the particularly famous example of Yang Piao's subversion of Li Chüeh and Kuo Fan in the *San-kuo Yen-yi* has already been recounted. But among the many illustrative possibilities, most editions of the *Thirty-six* include Tiao Ch'an's well-known (but fictional) role in the assassination of Tung Chuo, a brutally perverse general who had all but usurped the throne near the end of the Han dynasty, by a number of officials led by Wang Yün. According to the era's chronicle, a strongman named Lü Pu who had risen through the ranks and become closely attached to Tung Chuo as his chief protector was persuaded to participate in a murder scheme initiated by Wang Yün. Wang coerced and cajoled him simply by playing upon Lü's fears of his mentor's unpredictable behavior and his likely death if his illicit liaison with one of Tung's serving girls were to be discovered.[96]

Even though Lü might have been enamored of the woman, there is nothing in the traditional account to justify the episode's classification under *mei-jen chi*. In contrast, the novel unfolds a far more complicated plot that requires two chapters filled with poetic descriptions to recount and portrays Wang Yün craftily manipulating Lü into betraying Tung Chuo through the use of an enticing woman.[97] According to the tale, Wang Yün had Tiao Ch'an, an alluring girl of sixteen who had not only been essentially adopted by his family but also become highly accomplished in singing and dancing, enthrall Lü Pu and Tung Chuo in turn in order to sow dissension, jealousy, and hatred between them.

Out of gratitude the willowy Tiao Ch'an zealously plays the role of a fatal seductress in the comfort and seclusion of two consecutive dinner scenes. First Wang Yün invites Lü Pu to dine at his home and then, following a sumptuous meal accompanied by numerous cups of wine, draws him into the inner quarters. Wang soon has Tiao specially perform for Lü before suggesting that he would like to present her to the "great hero" as his concubine. Completely bewitched, Lü enthusiastically accepts the proposition and returns home to await an appropriate date.

Wang then similarly invites Tung Chuo to dinner and plies him with a combination of the best delicacies and obsequious flattery, even encouraging him to usurp the throne that only he deserves. After the meal and its accompanying entertainment, Wang similarly invites him to the inner quarters where he encounters Tiao Ch'an and enthusiastically accepts Wang's offer to present the girl to him.

Lü becomes enraged when he learns that Tiao Ch'an has been sent to Tung's house in a screened carriage, but Wang deftly deflects his anger onto Tung by saying that he had come to confirm the marriage arrangements and took her home with him. However, back at Tung's residence Lü is unable to learn anything about her whereabouts. Over subsequent days Tiao manages to entice Lü with shadowy appearances, sorrowful looks, and minor glances, but Tung notices Lü's obvious interest and becomes angry. In another incident Lü enters Tung's bedroom while he is lying ill and exchanges furtive signs with her, further enraging Tung, who notices them apparently flirting. However, the corpulent Tung is subsequently dissuaded from taking any action because he needs Lü's strength and protection.

A month later Tiao Ch'an finds an opportunity to lure the long-seething Lü into meeting her in the garden, where she roils his emotions by claiming that having been despoiled by Tung and kept from her true love she has no wish to live. He prevents her from drowning herself in the pond only to have his resentment further inflamed by her criticism of his irresolute behavior and failure to confront Tung Chuo. Just then Tung enters, finds them together, and rushes in; however, Lü flees, though Tung grabs and throws Lü's famously heavy halberd at him.

While Lü is left to reflect on these events, Tiao Ch'an complains to Tung Chuo that she was accosted and vehemently rejects Tung Chuo's feigned intention to give her to Lü, augmenting the enmity between the two stalwarts. The stage having been well set, Wang Yün then complains to Lü Pu that they have been disgraced and his daughter violated. At last enraged, Lü bemoans his inability to act because of his status as Tung's adopted son, prompting Wang to point out that not only are their surnames different, but Tung had tried to slay him with his own halberd. Convinced of his own blamelessness, he willingly joins the assassination plot that is implemented when Tung, despite several baleful omens, comes to the capital for the ceremony marking his ascension to the Han throne. Lü Pu then takes Tiao Ch'an as his concubine, ensuring her fame as another of China's femme fatales and concluding Wang Yün's well-conceived machination.

K'ung-ch'eng Chi (Empty City Stratagem)

The final section of the *Thirty-six Stratagems* contains six measures said to be designed for truly desperate situations, applicable when weakness confronts strength, though nothing prevents their exploitation in more hopeful situations. The most imaginative of them all is the unorthodox principle embodied by the "Empty City Ploy" whose initial lines enigmatically state, "Make the 'vacuous' vacuous, spawn doubt amidst doubt. In the interstice of the firm and flexible, the unorthodox is redoubled."

The stratagem turns upon the distinction between vacuity and substance, a pair of concepts apparently first raised in the *Art of War* but probably long employed by commanders throughout the late Spring and Autumn period. However, rather than defining them, Sun-tzu's "Vacuity and Substance" focuses upon manipulating and dispersing the enemy through movement, deceit, and being formless while striving to fathom the enemy's intent and disposition. Tactically, the implications are clear: strike vacuities while avoiding substantial deployments and impregnable surfaces. Thus, the T'ai Kung advised that "When you see vacuity in the enemy you should advance, when you see substance you should halt" and Wu Ch'i added that "In employing the army you must ascertain the enemy's voids and strengths and then race to take advantage of their endangered points."

Accordingly, astute commanders struggled to conceal their own weaknesses even as they sought to discern and exploit voids in the enemy, just as the tactical summary for the "vacuous" in the *Hundred Unorthodox Strategies* admonishes: "If your strategic power is vacuous when you engage an enemy in battle, you should create the facade of a substantial disposition to make it impossible for them to determine where you are vacuous, where substantial. When the enemy does not dare recklessly engage your forces, you can preserve your regiments and protect your army. A tactical principle from the *Art of War* states: 'If the enemy does not dare engage us in battle, it is because we thwart their movements.'"

Similarly, "The Weak in Warfare" counsels that "if the enemy is numerous while you are few, if the enemy is strong while you are weak, you must set out numerous flags and pennants, double the number of cooking fires, and display strength to the enemy. If you make it impossible for the enemy to determine your numbers as many or few, your strategic power as strong or weak, they will certainly not lightly engage you in battle. Thus you will be able to rapidly depart, thereby preserving your army and keeping harm distant."

Across Chinese history a strong show of bravado buttressed by such commonly exploited devices as dragging brush or deploying numerous battle flags to magnify the army's apparent size frequently proved successful.[98] In fact, the thirty-sixth and therefore last of the *Thirty-six Stratagems*, known as "Retreat Is Best"—flight being justified by the idea that to surrender would be a compete defeat, suing for peace terms a half defeat, but departing before engaging the enemy no defeat at all as it preserves the possibility that victory can be achieved another day—is often illustrated by the case of Pi Tsai-yü. (The incident also sometimes appears as the historical illustration for "The Cicada Sheds Its Shell" even though the latter is best interpreted as maintaining a positional facade to temporarily freeze the enemy while striking elsewhere.)

Typical of the resourceful commanders who became enthralled with military activities at an early age, Pi Tsai-yü was resolute, heroic, and excelled in archery. Moreover, he frequently commented that military victories are fashioned from unorthodox techniques. Unfortunately, both he and Yüeh Fei were caught up in the largely futile efforts to thwart the Chin onslaughts that repeatedly penetrated the Southern Sung's newly compressed territory south of the Huai River. Nevertheless, more than once he superbly defended beleaguered cities by employing the latest military technology in conjunction with unexpected measures, thwarting massive Jurchen assaults before escaping with the remnant troops.

Apparently well versed in Three Kingdom's military events, he once employed a variant of the arrow-gathering technique subsequently attributed to Chu-ko Liang by deliberately parading a double attired in his distinctive robes atop the parapets in order to draw sufficient arrow fire to replenish their depleted supply. As generally recounted as the "Retreat Is Best" illustration, when Pi wanted to extricate his badly outnumbered forces from a heavy Jurchen besiegement with minimum casualties, he implemented several traditional measures to create the appearance of an occupied camp, such as leaving their battle flags fully deployed. However,

rather than sacrificing a small contingent of men who would normally
have continued to march about, raise dust, maintain the fires, and generally create a clamor, he had some sheep suspended so that their front
hoofs rested upon various war drums.[99] When the sheep struggled to escape, they beat the drums fervently, creating a volume of sound sufficient
to preclude any suspicion that the camp had been abandoned.

The *Hundred Unorthodox Strategies* succinctly notes in its tactical summary for the topic of "doubt": "If you should want to retreat, create some
false, empty deployments that can be left behind when you withdraw, for
then the enemy will never pursue you." In illustration, it cites an episode
from the Northern and Southern Dynasties period:

> When Emperor Wu of the Chou went east on a punitive cam-
> paign, he used Yü Wen-hsien as his vanguard to defend Chüeh-
> shu Pass. At that time Ch'en Wang-ch'ün was encamped at
> Shih-li-ching, Grand General Yü Wen-ch'un was encamped at
> Chi-hsi-yüan, and Grand General Yü Wen-sheng was defending
> Wen-shui Pass.
>
> Wen-hsien, who was also the Regional Commander, secretly
> said to Wen-sheng: "Warfare is the Tao of deception. In erecting
> your present encampment, instead of setting up tents, you
> should cut down some Cyprus trees to construct huts to show
> that it will be more than just a temporary camp. Then when your
> army departs and the brigands arrive, they will still be doubtful."
>
> At that time the king of Ch'i segmented an army off toward
> Shih-li-ching and dispatched the bulk of his forces through
> Wen-shui Pass. He personally led a large contingent to confront
> Wen-ch'un. The latter reported that Ch'i's army was making a
> fervent attack, so Wen-hsien led a force to rescue them but even
> after their armies joined together, they were defeated and pur-
> sued by Ch'i.
>
> That night Wen-ch'un evacuated his position and retreated.
> However, thinking that the Cyprus huts indicated a fully manned

defensive position, Ch'i dared not advance until the next morning when they finally realized they had been deceived.

In dramatic, almost foolhardy contrast to creating a facade of strength, the Empty City Ploy carries vacuity to its extreme, creating the appearance of deliberately fabricated weakness by "making the vacuous (more) vacuous and spawning doubt amidst doubt." The stratagem was almost certainly inspired by a famous historical incident that unfolded during the Three Kingdoms period when Chu-ko Liang, China's most renowned strategist, found himself severely outnumbered by approaching enemy forces:[100]

During the Three Kingdoms period, General Chu-ko Liang of Shu remained in Yin-p'ing while Wei Yen and several other Shu generals assembled in the east and took their forces down river. Chu-ko Liang retained only about 10,000 men for the city's defense. Ssu-ma Yi of Wei, who was leading 200,000 troops to crush Chu-ko Liang, moved along a different route than Yen's field forces before stopping about sixty miles from Chu-ko Liang. One of his observers returned to report that there were few soldiers in Yin-p'ing and their overall strength was weak.

Chu-ko Liang knew that Ssu-ma Yi's armies would soon reach them and feared they would be severely pressed. Although he wanted to join forces with Wei Yen's army, they were too far apart and he lacked the strategic power to achieve it. Not knowing what the plan might be, his generals and officers all lost their composure. Nevertheless, Chu-ko Liang's determination and spirit remained unchanged.

Chu-ko Liang commanded that their battle flags should be furled, their drums set aside, and no one should irresponsibly go forth. He also ordered the four city gates thrown wide open and instructed that the grounds be swept and sprinkled with water. Ssu-ma Yi had always regarded Chu-ko Liang as a serious commander, so when he displayed a weak appearance, he suspected Liang of holding troops in ambush. Ssu-ma Yi therefore led his numerous troops in a retreat to the northern mountains.

By mealtime Liang and his assistants were clapping their hands and laughing. Liang said: "Ssu-ma Yi thinks I am deliberately displaying fear because I have troops in ambush, so he will go around the mountains and depart." An observer returned and reported that it was just as Liang had said. When Ssu-ma Yi subsequently learned of it, he hated him deeply.

Even as recorded in the *San-kuo Chih* this historical incident may already be exaggerated or simply apocryphal, a characteristic of many episodes originating in the Three Kingdoms period.[101] Nevertheless, it was accorded great credibility over the centuries, long before being adopted as the historical illustration for "The Vacuous in War" in the *Hundred Unorthodox Strategies* and further enhanced by the *San-kuo Yen-yi*'s depiction.[102] The latter's key passages unfold as follows:

Chu-ko Liang led 5,000 troops back to Hsi-ch'eng to transport provisions and fodder. Suddenly more than ten flying horsemen rode up in succession to report that "A massive army of some 150,000 under Ssu-ma Yi's command is swarming toward Hsi-ch'eng." At that time Chu-ko Liang didn't have any significant generals in camp, only some ordinary civil officials, and of the 5,000 men he had retained, half had already been deputed to transport provisions and fodder, so only 2,500 remained in the town. The officials all turned pale when they heard the news.

When Chu-ko Liang ascended the wall and looked out, he indeed saw the dust was rising up to Heaven. Wei's armies had divided into two columns and were ferociously advancing. He therefore circulated an order: "All the flags and pennons should be concealed and troops manning the internal guardhouses should execute anyone who wantonly moves about or talks in a loud voice. Fully open the four gates. Twenty soldiers disguised as ordinary inhabitants should sprinkle the streets with water and sweep them. If Wei's army arrives, no sudden movement is allowed, for I have a plan."

Chu-ko Liang put on his (famous) cloak of crane feathers and his silk kerchief and ascended the wall with two young boys who carried his zither. Reclining on a parapet in front of a watch tower, he burned incense and played the zither.

The image of Chu-ko Liang nonchalantly playing his zither while the incense burned with the two boys standing on either side in attendance is indelibly associated with this episode. Chu-ko Liang became so identified with the stratagem that Ssu-ma Yi's uncertainty of his death was similarly attributed to Liang's army maintaining the facade of his existence, giving rise to the saying that "even in death Chu-ko Liang was able to walk away from the living Ssu-ma Yi."[103]

Notwithstanding the traditional attribution of the empty city ploy to Chu-ko Liang, the renowned Han dynasty barbarian fighter Li Kuang appears to have been the first to knowingly exploit it. Equally famous for his courage and archery skills, Li successfully battled the Hsiung-nu and other contiguous peoples from 166 to 119 BCE before eventually perishing at his own hand rather than submit to an insulting inquiry from mere clerks following a battlefield miscue. Not long into his career, a court official sent to exercise a supervisory role over troop training happened to pursue a party of three Hsiung-nu who easily vanquished the twenty or thirty troops accompanying the official. The official managed to escape and return to their camp whereupon Li, surmising that they were eagle hunters, mounted a pursuit with a hundred cavalry. Roughly 30 or 40 *li* out into the steppe they finally caught them, slaying two of the three, whereupon Li noticed several thousand Hsiung-nu in the distance:[104]

Seeing Li Kuang and his cavalrymen, the startled Hsiung-nu assumed they were acting as a decoy and rapidly ascended a nearby mountain to deploy. Terrified, Li's hundred cavalrymen all wanted to turn around and race away. However, Li said: "As we are tens of *li* from our encampment, we will all quickly perish if our band of a hundred flees and the Hsiung-nu pursue us. But if we remain here, they will certainly assume that we are acting as a lure for a large army and not dare attack."

Li ordered his cavalry to advance until they halted about 2 *li* away from the Hsiung-nu formation. He then ordered them to dismount and release their saddles. The cavalrymen responded, "The barbarians are numerous and close, so if the situation becomes urgent, what would we do?"

Li responded, "These barbarians originally assumed we would go off, so if we release our saddles, thereby showing we are not going to depart, we will solidify their opinion (that we are acting as a decoy)." The Hsiung-nu did not dare launch a sudden attack.

When a general riding a white horse came forth to screen his troops, Li Kuang mounted his horse and with slightly more than ten cavalry raced out and shot him before returning and undoing his saddle. He then instructed the others to release their horses and lie down. In the dusk the puzzled Hsiung-nu still did not dare attack. In the middle of the night, still fearing the existence of a Han army lying in ambush on the flanks, they finally withdrew. The next morning Li returned to the main force which, not knowing where he had gone, had been unable to follow.

Classic versions of the *Thirty-six Stratagems* frequently include two more examples. The first arose about a century into the first half of the T'ang dynasty when powerful Turfan forces conducted massive raids against border settlements in the Kansu area, including the fortified town of Kua-chou in the winter of 727 CE.[105] The previous winter Wang Shou-huan, a local border area commander, had exploited harsh weather conditions, including cold and snow, to follow exhausted Turfan raiders who had been similarly pillaging and burning and inflict severe casualties. (He also took preemptive measures to deprive them of fodder by burning the grasslands en route and heroically crossed the frozen waters of Lake Ch'ing-hai to gain an advantage.) However, Wang was slain in a collateral clash with the Turfan a year later, just before they besieged and subsequently devastated most of Kua-chou.

Chang Shou-kuei, newly appointed to supervise the town's defense, had just undertaken the reconstruction of the wooden palisade when the Turfan returned, panicking the terrified inhabitants. Realizing that they were in a totally indefensible position, he adopted the nonchalant posture required by the empty city ploy, having the officers and troops conspicuously indulge in wine and music atop the skeleton walls, thereby causing the Turfan commanders to assume that some sort of fierce ambush awaited them. To stifle opposition to his plan and revive the spirit of his troops he explained that "They are numerous while we are few. Moreover, since we recently suffered heavy casualties, we cannot combat them with arrows and stones, but must control them through the Tao of stratagems."[106] Once the raiders commenced their retreat, Chang launched a successful attack before reconstructing the town and restoring order in the area.

A second, somewhat less satisfactory example is also commonly cited. In 573, during the period of fragmentation that preceded the establishment of the Sui, Tsu T'ing, a newly appointed Northern Ch'i commander, suddenly found himself threatened by a large Southern Ch'en force. Compounding his problems, local brigands were exploiting the chaos to rampage through the immediate area. Realizing the impossibility of his situation, he adopted an even purer variant of the empty city ploy. Leaving the city gates of Pei-hsü-chou open, he cleared the walls of troops, prohibited all movement on the streets, required complete silence from the populace, and ordered that all fires be extinguished to prevent telltale signs of smoke. Clandestine defenses were mounted along the interior alleys and he confined the populace and their animals inside closed quarters. When the newly arrived Southern Ch'en forces became puzzled by failing to detect any signs of life, Tsu exploited their momentary indecision to launch a surprise attack punctuated by a great uproar that startled them into fleeing.[107]

Even though the empty city ploy proved effective in these melodramatic incidents, because it entails irreversible exposure its adoption was no doubt accompanied, if not prompted, by a sense of desperation. Premised not just upon being marked by weakness but also upon the enemy detecting that weakness, it inherently compounds the original vulnerability. Surprisingly, the chances for success seem to be enhanced by overplaying nonchalance rather than emphasizing subtlety.

Nevertheless, Chin's failure to become suspicious at the incessant but random nature of the drums being beaten by the goats or detect the escaping troops remains puzzling. Minimally competent surveillance and reconnaissance techniques should have provided adequate information to accurately assess the situation. An aggressive commander or one who simply calculates that the opportunity is too good to waste, that a quick if localized victory might be achieved at reasonable cost—not to mention those now benefiting from modern satellite and UAV reconnaissance— may simply disregard the threat of an ambush and launch a penetrating attack. In fact, although the secondary literature that has arisen to formulate methods designed to penetrate and balk the thirty-six stratagems sometimes offers sophisticated sequences, the sort of direct measures first articulated in the *Wu-tzu* to counter the empty city ploy are generally recommended.[108]

Wu-chung Sheng-yu (Non-being Gives Birth to Being)

The inherent vulnerability of the empty city ploy has also been recognized in the *Thirty-six Stratagems* itself, being encapsulated in a discussion of *Wu-chung Sheng-yu*, a stratagem that can be seen as a variant form but remains distinctive. The somewhat enigmatic explication appended to "Non-being Gives Birth to Being" laconically states that "prevarication is not prevarication when the prevarication is made substantial" or, more colloquially, "facades are not facades when they become real."[109] Then, in referring to the three lines composing the *Ling Ch'i Ching* trigraph known as "Opening the Concealed," adds: "Minor *yin*, ultimate *yin*, ultimate *yang.*" (The Oracle associated with the trigraph states: "*Yin* extreme changes to *yang*. Torpid insects awaken and stretch.")[110]

In explanation, most editions of the *Thirty-six Strategies* note that "to make a display of having something despite lacking it is prevarication. Because prevarication cannot go on for long without being easily discovered, emptiness cannot remain empty in the end. Since being is given birth amidst non-being, the real is employed through prevarication and the substantial through vacuousness (emptiness). Although emptiness cannot defeat the enemy, through giving birth to being it defeats the enemy." Thus the empty city ploy can be seen as epitomizing the use of emptiness to temporarily fend off an enemy, yet being incapable of inflicting damage.

Only a single incident is cited in illustration: "Just as when Ling Hu-ch'ao besieged Yung-ch'iu, Chang Hsün fabricated more than a thousand men out of straw, clothed them in black, and then lowered them down outside the walls. Ling's troops competed with each other in shooting at them, resulting in Chang obtaining several tens of thousands of arrows in this fashion. Subsequently, when on another night he again lowered men down the enemy troops laughed and didn't make any preparations. He then employed 500 warriors willing to fight to the death to hack into the enemy's encampment, burn their fortifications and tents, and drive them off more than 10 *li*."[111]

The events actually unfolded during An Lu-shan's rebellion in the midst of the T'ang dynasty, when Chang Hsün took over Yung-ch'iu's defense in 756 CE, after the city had reverted to imperial auspices when the inhabitants rejected the local commander's surrender. An exemplary leader who shared every hardship with his troops and personally commanded highly successful forays outside the walls, Chang Hsün resolutely refused to allow his subcommanders to surrender despite being outnumbered and cut off from provisions. After successfully holding off overwhelming enemy strength through innumerable clashes over forty days—ironically mounted under the direction of their former commander, Ling Hu-ch'ao—the thousand or so beleaguered defenders had exhausted their supply of arrows and were confronted by the virtually insurmountable difficulty of halting swarming attacks at a distance, before they could reach and ascend the walls, prompting the use of straw men in the darkness. (Prior to gunpowder's inception and employment, only basic incendiaries, hot liquids, stones, and similar devices were available for close mounted defense.)[112]

Shortly thereafter, he similarly inspired the epic defense of Sui-yang that finally saw the bastion subjugated and Chang himself executed after the original 10,000 troops had been reduced to a few hundred badly wounded, starving survivors.[113] At Yung-ch'iu his compound tactic consisted of a successful initial ploy that satisfied their immediate needs for ammunition, but upon whose penetration the subsequent external sally depended. The vacuous or insubstantial was thus converted into the substantial, or in terms employed by the *Tao Te Ching*, which notes, "the myriad things under Heaven are all given birth in being, but being stems from non-being," non-being was thus turned into being.[114]

Chang's straw man technique apparently, though not actually, mimics a far more illustrious predecessor identified with the wily Chu-ko Liang that is reprised in a chapter of the *San-kuo Yen-yi* titled "By Using Unorthodox Stratagems, Chu-ko Liang Borrows Arrows."[115] One in a series of intriguing clashes with Chou Yü, the Eastern Wu field commander obsessed with eliminating him so as to preclude future harm, it does not appear in the *San-kuo Chih*. (Conversely, the latter does report that Sun Chien's nighttime amphibious reconnaissance of Ts'ao Ts'ao's camp resulted in numerous arrows being wildly fired at his boat and impaling the sides. Sun Chien thus depleted the enemy's arrow supply while replenishing his own and subsequently employed them to repel an attempted amphibious attack.) But the *San-kuo Yen-yi* incident, known by children and adults alike in recent centuries, is a well-developed, though relatively minor episode in the Ch'ih Pi narrative.

In their continuing battle of wits, Chou Yü assigns him the task of preparing 100,000 arrows for the coming clash with Ts'ao Ts'ao and apparently tricks him into guaranteeing their provision upon penalty of death. Claiming that the situation is too urgent, Chu-ko Liang surprisingly rejects the ten-day implementation period initially offered, opting instead for just three days even though fully aware that Chou intends to impede him by withholding the necessary workers and materials.

Two days pass without any visible action apart from Chu-ko Liang clandestinely persuading Lu Su, a high-ranking, supposedly sympathetic friend (who actually repeatedly betrays him) to secretly furnish twenty high-walled boats packed with bales of hay along the sides. Taking advantage of a heavy nighttime fog, Chu-ko Liang then mounts a deliberately noisy reconnaissance near the perimeter of Ts'ao Ts'ao's vessels. Their approach naturally prompts a hasty response during which thousands of bowmen chaotically shoot into the impenetrable mist. When the fog finally begins to clear, Chu-ko Liang turns the boats back and retrieves the undamaged arrows from the hay bales just as the deadline approached. Much to Chou Yü's astonishment, the number easily surpasses the requisite 100,000.

By the middle of the Ming dynasty this and similar incidents, created over the millennium between the *San-kuo Chih* and *San-kuo Yen-yi*, had become a constituent part of Chu-ko Liang's reputation, contributing to his image as the period's paragon strategist and sustaining the emotional belief, both conscious and subconscious, that wisdom and cleverness can prevail even in the most disadvantageous circumstances. Although more a question of cleverness than tactical acumen, the method was clearly unorthodox, and has always been deemed so.[116]

14

Modern Embodiments
and Implications

Despite notable historical examples such as Operation Fortitude to the contrary, Western culture has long been portrayed as deprecating deception in warfare as dastardly and condemning subversion and espionage as unrighteous and inappropriate. Moreover, because of the pristine heritage of early Greek warfare, ambushes, flanking attacks, and anything less than direct force on force clashes have often been considered "unsportsmanlike." However, although no explicit theorizing about the nature and effectiveness of irregular or improper measures is to be found in Greek or Roman works, later Greek warfare was hardly idyllic in nature or practice and many examples of so-called heinous behavior ranging from duplicity through brutality and perversion can readily be seen. Moreover, despite being comparatively infrequent, early Western warfare was not totally bereft of practices termed "unorthodox" by Chinese military thinkers, including the feigned retreat, false treaty, fire oxen, poisoning of water sources, incendiary attacks, and various types of ambush from the fourth century BCE onward.

Even though only vestiges are visible in the earliest defensive treatise by Aineias the Tactician, *How to Survive Under Siege*, composed around 350 BCE or just about the time of Sun Pin's *Military Methods*,[1] late in the first century CE Frontinus made a particular study of these essentially unorthodox tactics and measures, subsequently categorizing and compiling them in a work known as the *Strategemata*.² Originally a companion volume to his now lost *Art of War*, it had apparently been designed to illustrate the lesser aspects of military science, "stratagems" as opposed to "strategies." Not surprisingly, since Machiavelli is known for having advocated the ruthless prosecution of warfare and esteeming the use of deception in *The Discourses* and *The Prince,* he subsequently incorporated many of them into his treatise on war.³ Maurice's *Strategikon,* composed around 600 CE, also outlines a number of such techniques,⁴ though Vegetius never mentions them in his *Epitome of Military Science,* a purely tactical manual written two centuries earlier.⁵ However, Clausewitz, now revered as theoretical progenitor of modern warfare, essentially denies their utility in his section on "cunning."⁶

Similarly negative views toward unorthodox measures have been vociferously expressed in China as well, not just as the result of Confucian influence and the rise of the self-interested literati who sought to suppress the military, but also as a vestige of earlier eras when ritual strongly affected the battlefield. A famous incident occurred in 638 BCE during the Spring and Autumn period, a time when chariots still dominated field clashes but the ostensibly moral, somewhat constrained warfare of earlier centuries was morphing into vicious combat dedicated to exterminating the enemy.

Duke Hsiang of Sung sought the newly vacant role of hegemon even though it required thwarting volatile Ch'u's ambitions. When Sung besieged Cheng, one of Ch'u's client states, Cheng naturally sought Ch'u's aid. Being significantly outnumbered, Sung's forces had little hope unless they exploited brilliant tactics or momentary advantages. However, not unlike President Roosevelt, who refused to allow the employment of poison gas despite almost unanimous command approval at Iwo Jima, the Duke of Sung refused to abandon a lifelong practice of Virtue to wrest a quick victory:⁷

> Armies from Ch'u attacked the state of Sung in order to relieve the state of Cheng. That winter, in the eleventh month on the first day of the lunar cycle, the Duke of Sung and forces from Ch'u engaged in battle at the Hung River. Sung's armies had already deployed into formation before Ch'u's men finished ford-

ing the river. The Minister of War said: "They are numerous while we are few so we should suddenly strike them before they finish fording the river." The duke replied, "It is not permissible."

After Ch'u's forces had forded the river but not yet deployed into formation the Minister of War repeated his request but the Duke of Sung again demurred, repeating "It is not permissible."

After Ch'u's forces deployed into formation, Sung's troops attacked them only to be severely defeated. The duke himself was wounded in the thigh and his chief officers all perished. Sung's aristocrats excoriated the duke, but he countered: "A true ruler does not wound someone twice nor capture those showing gray hair. Ancient armies never exploited ravines and defiles, so even though we are merely the remnants of a ruined state, I will not drum an attack on disordered forces."

Tzu Yü said: "My lord still does not understand warfare. Whenever a fierce enemy is in a defile or not deployed in formation, Heaven is sustaining us. So even if they are in a ravine, shouldn't we still beat the drums for an attack? Even then we would fear not being victorious. Moreover, all these stalwarts are our enemies. Even if they are old and mature, if we can capture them alive we should seize them. What does gray hair matter? You should make clear the nature of shame and teach warfare. If you flinch at inflicting a second wound, it would be preferable not to wound anyone; if you have compassion for the gray haired, then it would be better to submit.

"The Three Armies are employed for advantage, gongs and drums raise the soldier's *ch'i* through their sounds. If the army is employed for advantage, then attacking an enemy in ravines and defiles is permissible. When the sound of the drums has stimulated their *ch'i*, signaling an attack on the disordered is appropriate."[8]

The Battle of Hung River has the dubious distinction of being famous not for the victor's courage or tactics, but the naively righteous practices of the vanquished. The duke subsequently died from his wounds, still maintaining his adherence to an idealized doctrine that is preserved in a Warring States work known as the *Ssu-ma Fa*:[9]

> In antiquity they did not pursue a fleeing enemy more than a hundred paces nor follow a retreating enemy more than three days, thereby making clear their observance of the forms of proper conduct [the *li*]. They did not exhaust the incapable and had sympathy for the wounded and sick, thereby making evident their benevolence. They awaited the completion of the enemy's formation and then drummed the attack, thereby making clear their good faith. They contended for righteousness, not profit, thereby manifesting their righteousness. Moreover, they were able to pardon those who submitted, thereby making evident their courage.

Eighteen hundred years later the incident was still remembered, being adopted as a counter example for the topic of "Initiative in Warfare" in the *Hundred Unorthodox Strategies*, whose tactical discussion admonishes commanders to exploit evolving enemy vulnerabilities: "Whenever engaging an enemy in battle, if after arriving they have not yet decisively deployed their power nor put their formations in order, if you urgently mount a sudden attack, you will be victorious. It is a stated principle that 'one who precedes others seizes their minds.'"

Duke Hsiang's refusal to act despite being badly outnumbered and strongly harangued by subordinates was not simply another example of the martial conservatism that often characterizes experienced generals who arrogantly dismiss new concepts, tactics, and weapons. (Such intransigence not only marred Chinese command across the centuries, but also painfully manifested itself in bizarre incidents such as the resurrection of ox-drawn chariots as part of suppressive measures mounted against An Lu-shan.) Instead, it was a manifestation of fervent belief in an inherited value system and adherence to an increasingly archaic ritual code inappropriate to the harsh demands of warfare.[10] Witnessed in Ch'en Yü's rejection of unorthodox methods in his confrontation with Han Hsin, it would frequently be visible in heated court denunciations of military activities, often to the detriment of China's ability to withstand such aggressive steppe powers as the Khitan, Jurchen, and Mongols.

Naturally this becomes a question of priority: whether survival and victory are to be achieved as efficiently as possible, or men and materials are to be sacrificed to preserve some transcendent virtue. Surprisingly, overwhelming power and material superiority tend to nurture spokesmen who embrace the latter viewpoint, inevitably fostering a tolerance for them among policy makers and other non-combatant interest groups. In China, although the Shang and Chou may have motivated the people partly by justifying their rebellions as inescapably required to extirpate evil oppressors, they were subsequently portrayed as Heavenly mandated victories achieved by great moral exemplars over debauched states led astray by perverse rulers.[11] Furthermore, the sole objective was explicitly stated as being to "restore life" to the many then suffering and dying under a cruel oppressor, the virtual incarnation of evil.

Thus, despite the carnage witnessed on the battlefield, post conquest it could be claimed that the enemy's troops lacked any enthusiasm for the fight, that they readily fled, were easily vanquished, or simply offered no opposition. The appeal of the Virtuous being so great, none would willingly raise arms against them. Instead they were warmly welcomed and campaigns could be, and were, fought "with the aim of preservation" as subsequently espoused in the Art of War. It was Mencius who, in condemning a graphic depiction in the revered Book of Documents of the slaughter at Mu-yeh, formulated what eventually became the watchword of the imperial literati: "The benevolent man has no enemies under Heaven. When the most benevolent attacked the most non-benevolent, how could the blood have floated pestles?"[12]

However, as revealed in other materials and sources, the reality is quite different. Not only was the Chou conquest achieved through an apparently horrific battle at Mu-yeh, but extensive campaigns of suppression and rectification were also required over the next decade.[13] Moreover, the Shang had long brutally mistreated the steppe and other contiguous peoples, enslaving and sacrificing some of their enemies in great numbers. Nevertheless, numerous works, including such classics military writings as the *Ssu-ma Fa* and *Three Strategies*, as well as the *Tao Te Ching* and Confucianism in general, all conceive of the passage of time merely marking a devolution from the peaceful Virtue of the high ancestors and cultural progenitors even though the Yellow Emperor is depicted as having smote the evil and perverse in extended conflicts.[14]

This view underpins the *Ssu-ma Fa*'s approach to warfare, being clearly articulated in several passages that outline an extensive ritual program for identifying the evil before proclaiming the military objective to solely be their extirpation while preserving the populace.[15] Subsequently, the *Three Strategies* succinctly asserted: "The sage king does not take any pleasure in using the army. He mobilizes it to execute the violently perverse and punish the rebellious. Now using the righteous to execute the unrighteous is like releasing the Yangtze and Yellow Rivers to douse a torch, or pushing a person tottering at the edge of an abyss. Success is inevitable!"[16]

In the third century BCE, with Ch'in increasingly dominating the realm and inexorably consolidating its power, military topics became the focus of court discussions and even entangled the era's noted Confucians, Mencius and Hsün-tzu. Best known for his "realistic" view that human nature is inherently selfish and (forcible) socialization therefore required to create obedient, if not, perfected citizens—traditionally oversimplified by his detractors to just "human nature is evil"—Hsün-tzu still espoused a belief in the efficacy of Virtue. The work bearing his name preserves a dialogue conducted during King Hsiao-ch'eng of Chao's reign (265–244 BCE) that, however unrealistic, reflects the conflicting viewpoints that often characterized the military and bureaucratic literati in traditional China as both battled for influence after the ruler no longer fulfilled a command role. Framed in response to the query "what is the crux of warfare," the Lord of Lin-wu focused upon battlefield management while Hsün-tzu stressed the foundation of warfare, embracing the idea that Virtue will prevail:[17]

The Lord of Lin-wu stated: "The chief principles[18] for employing the military are gaining the seasons of Heaven above, secur-

ing the advantages of Earth (terrain) below, observing the enemy's changes and movement, and arriving first even though issuing forth after them."[19]

Hsün-tzu retorted: "Untrue. According to what I know of the
ancient Tao for warfare, the foundation for employing the military in combat lies in unifying the people.[20] Had Archer Yi's bow
and arrows not been properly attuned, he would have been unable to hit any target. Had Tsao Fu's team of six horses been un-
matched, his chariot would not have been able to go far. If the
lictors and populace have not been attached, King T'ang of the
Shang and King Wu of the Chou would have been unable to
achieve inevitable victory. One who excels at attracting the
people's allegiance will also excel in employing the military. Accordingly, the crux of military affairs lies in being adroit in attracting the people, that's all."

The Lord of Lin-wu said: "Certainly not. What the military
esteems is strategic power and advantage, what it implements is
change and facade.[21] One who excels at employing the military
responds suddenly and reaches objectives in obscurity so that
no one knows where he came from. When Sun-tzu and Wu-tzu
employed them, no enemy under Heaven could withstand
them. Why must one wait until the people are attached?"

Hsün-tzu replied: "Not at all. What I have been speaking
about is the military of the benevolent man,[22] the intentions of
a true king. What you value are tactical imbalance, plots
(strategic plans), configuration of power, and advantage, and
what you would implement are assaults, seizures, changes, and
feigning, all affairs of the feudal lords. The ones that can be de-
frauded are the insolent and dilatory, the exposed and afflicted
whose rulers and ministers are estranged, whose leader tumul-
tuously departs from Virtue. When an evil despot like Chieh of
the Hsia attempted to deceive another Chieh it was a question
of skill and luck, but a Chieh trying to deceive a sage emperor
like Yao may be compared to throwing an egg against a stone,[23]

stirring water with a finger, or plunging into water or fire and thereby being burned or drowned."

Apart from believing that the virtuous cannot be deceived, Hsün-tzu felt that people would not oppose their best interests, "that even if they had emotions like Chieh or (the brigand) Chih, who would be willing to act on behalf of those they hate to harm those they love." Later, he similarly disparaged the great Spring and Autumn and Warring States heroes, men such as the renowned T'ien Tan: "Those commonly said to have excelled at employing the military, in their skill and clumsiness, strength and weakness still did not resemble a true ruler. Following the same Tao, they failed to reach the point of harmony and accord. They obfuscated and seized, spied and deceived, employed the tactical imbalance of power, plots, subversion, and overturning, so they cannot be regarded as other than brigand armies."

Moreover, in "Strengthening the State" he dogmatically asserts that "rulers who esteem the li (ritual forms of behavior) and revere the Worthy will become kings; who emphasize the laws and love the people will become hegemons; who love profit and are frequently deceptive will be endangered; and who exploit the tactical imbalance of power, plots, subversion, and overturning will be plunged into darkness and danger and perish."

Remarkably, despite the increased lethality of ever escalating warfare and the dramatic example of Ch'in's martial success, a sort of amalgamated Confucian position largely based upon Mencian views whose adherents were seduced by the idyllic prospects of Virtue frequently held sway in imperial China. (Hardly a vestige of ancient China alone, the past century has seen several examples of conquest being naively undertaken in the expectation that the populace, being liberated from oppression, would welcome their saviors, and that democracies will not engage each other in battle.) Moreover, amidst a multiplicity of views and perspectives ranging from the draconian Legalist approach of Shang Chün and Han Fei-tzu through Yang Chu's reclusive philosophy, the sort of deprecations iterated in Hsün-tzu's final paragraph against the tactical exercise of martial power and, more importantly, unorthodox and subversive techniques often predominated.

When "Confucian" or "Virtuous" prejudices prevailed and the unorthodox was disdained, a natural tendency to mirroring often resulted in a generalized failure to imagine the enemy might employ irregular tactics and subversive approaches. Conversely, overconfidence that the enemy is well-known, their intentions clear, or their forces constrained to behaving in highly orthodox, predictable ways similarly provide a fertile field for the implementation of unorthodox measures. (Superior strategic power buttressed by supreme confidence in signals intelligence and satellite data fosters such confidence in contemporary circumstances.)

The successful employment of unorthodox tactics across history such as at the repeatedly cited, epochal battle of Ch'ih Pi is seen as attesting to the validity of the unshakable Chinese belief that superior cunning and wisdom will always allow the disadvantaged to prevail, however dire and overwhelming the circumstances. While contemporary military thinkers certainly regard Chu-ko Liang's ability to shift the wind's direction prior to the battle of Ch'ih Pi as the stuff of legend, this episode and similar depictions of magical achievements by kung-fu practitioners and others possessing books of esoteric wisdom contribute to the confidence that surpassing powers can be derived from the unorthodox. This sense of invincibility is of course frequently seen, even deliberately nurtured, in those animated by religious fervor and dedicated to heinous acts, and was particularly witnessed in the I-ho Ch'üan's (Boxers') belief in their invincibility even in the face of bullets and gunpowder weapons.[24]

Systematic Programs

As already suggested and extensively discussed in our *Tao of Spycraft*, China has a lengthy heritage of conceiving and implementing systematic programs for subverting other states. Without doubt the most famous dates back to the late Spring and Autumn period, when Kou Chien, reduced to subsistence status in a small enclave after his state had been vanquished by Wu, adopted well-conceived, coherent measures to diffuse any

concern that Yüeh's remnants might pose a threat. He buttressed his syco-
phantic behavior by plying the court with bribes, causing the estrangement of loyal ministers, and debauching the ruler until his resurgent state
could mount the first of the vengeful invasions that astonished the king of
Wu and eventually led to the annihilation of his state.[25]

Notwithstanding this famous episode, the *Six Secret Teachings* (*Liu-t'ao*)
contains the first series of measures designed to systematically undermine
the enemy. In part because of its purported setting at the interstice of the
Shang and Chou dynasties (between 1050 and 1035 BCE) and its nominal attribution to the semi-legendary T'ai Kung, the book holds great interest for
PRC theoreticians. Just like the Ch'in and now the PRC, the Chou found itself in a subservient position, compelled to overcome the disadvantages of
markedly inferior technology, governmental organization, and manpower
as it strove to shed its status as an inferior peripheral state and emerge as
the dominant power. In fact, at the decisive battle at Mu-yeh the odds were
nearly insurmountable, reputedly being 700,000 to a paltry 35,000. (Although 700,000 is an impossible figure, whatever their respective forces, a
five to one ratio is not improbable.) Apart from stressing surprise, mobility, and deception, the Chou succeeded by rapidly concentrating their
forces and mounting a lethal, penetrating attack spearheaded by elite warriors and 300 chariots, originally a Shang implement.[26]

Being consistent with admonitions by Teng Hsiao-p'ing and others to
bide one's time and gradually amass power, the generations required to
reach the point when the Chou could in fact challenge the Shang are well
noted by Chinese theoreticians. Not only is the *Liu-t'ao* highly esteemed
in PRC military circles, it has also appeared in several popular guises and
formats, including widely circulated comic book versions, under a variety
of titles. Two of its sixty chapters, both frequently condemned in China
for their perversity and inhumanity over the centuries, formulate a number of unorthodox measures that, when concurrently implemented, comprise a systematic subversive program and become, as the text states, "a
military weapon."[27]

The first, "Civil Offensive," provides the essentials for twelve measures
directed toward the ruler but broadly effective against the ruling authori-

ties of any powerful state. Most of them involve currying favor, employing coercion, causing disaffection and estrangement, discrediting the capable, marginalizing the wise, generally acting submissive, nurturing licentiousness and dissolution, obscuring the truth, and fostering arrogance and laxity. Using potential profits as a lure and deliberately nurturing trust in order to end suspicion and undermine defensive preparations are also focal components.[28]

The second *Six Secret Teachings* chapter, "Three Doubts," expounds the preferred method for undermining enemy rulers, concretely conceived in terms of the hated Shang. Although abstract, the embedded techniques are considered highly applicable in the context of Chinese–American power discrepancies. According to the text, King Wu queried the T'ai Kung: "I want to overthrow the Shang but have three doubts. I am afraid our strength will be inadequate to attack the strong, estrange the close supporters within the court, and disperse their people. What should I do?" In reply, the T'ai Kung outlined another series of measures that, in addition to the usual lures and enticements designed to cause disaffection among allies, clearly reflect the Taoist penchant for attacking strength by strengthening it to the point that it becomes unstable and vulnerable:

> In order to attack the strong you must nurture them to make them even stronger and increase them to make them even more extensive. What is too strong will certainly break, what is too extended must have deficiencies. Attack the strong through their strength. Cause the estrangement of favored officials by using favorites, disperse the people by means of people.
>
> Thoroughness and secrecy are treasured in the Tao of planning. You should become involved with them in numerous affairs and ply them with temptations of profit. Conflict will then surely arise.
>
> If you want to estrange their close supporters, you must do it by using what they love, making gifts to those they favor, giving them what they want. Tempt them with what they find profitable, making them ambitious. Those who covet profits will be

extremely happy at the prospects and their remaining doubts will be ended.

Now without doubt the Tao for attacking is to first obfuscate the king's clarity and then attack his strength. Debauch him with beautiful women, entice him with profit. Nurture him with flavors and provide him with the company of female musicians. Then after you have caused his subordinates to become estranged from him, you must cause the people to grow distant from him while never letting him know your plans. Appear to support him and draw him into your trap. Don't let him become aware of what is happening, for only then can your plan be successful.

While the program's elements have to be recast for contemporary circumstances, the essentials of causing disaffection among the people and employing profit as a lure are clear. Moreover, the premise that the strong will inevitably have deficiencies reflects fundamental tenets of what might be broadly termed Warring States Taoist thought. Chapter 36 of the traditionally received *Tao Te Ching* states: "If you want to reduce something, you must certainly stretch it. If you want to weaken something, you must certainly strengthen it. If you want to abolish something, you must certainly make it flourish." Reflecting the assumption that what proceeds to extremity will invariably be unstable and revert, similar views are expressed in the late Warring States period *Three Strategies of Huang-shih Kung*.[29]

Exactly how this operational premise may be translated into active measures remains enigmatic. However, economic policies that temporarily cause the United States (or Taiwan) to apparently flourish even while fiscally impoverishing it and creating massive manufacturing dependency presumably fall into this category. Political gestures such as repeatedly threatening Taiwan and military actions including the selective development and acquisition of newly menacing weapons that compel the U.S. to augment and disperse its military power (much as the PRC perceives that the U.S. deceptively manipulated the U.S.S.R. into the arms race that ultimately exhausted it) would seem to be another possibility.

More concretely, contemporary military weapons are viewed as the epitome of complex systems while martial power is known to have become technologically and communications dependent. Having been recently documented by battlefield reports and the subject of ongoing discussions in professional military journals, their associated, innate weaknesses are well-known. In a Pacific conflict the logistical burden would be enormous and unwieldy, the supply lines severely extended and exposed, and power projection invariably spearheaded by increasingly vulnerable carrier groups. In a conceptually unorthodox approach, PRC theorists perceive great opportunity to exploit the instabilities inherent in such "overextension" and believe that they have discerned nodes of vulnerability that can be targeted in both normal and asymmetric fashion, particularly through the employment of unorthodox techniques. A number of indirect methods are therefore being discussed to directly thwart U.S. efforts and balk the execution of plans, including the blinding of down-looking sensors, distorting the GPS signal or eliminating it altogether with attacks by micro-satellites employed as kinetic weapons, disrupting communications, and sinking vessels with sabotage and other unorthodox measures.

Secrecy provided the essential foundation for all of the T'ai Kung's measures, with the draconian version practiced by the PRC merely being the latest embodiment of a lengthy tradition of conscious effort and complex theoretical pronouncements.[30] (The high degree of success of its policies is evident in the ignorance that prevails about basic issues and aspects of the state, as well as the bewildering range of assessments and projections offered by analysts.) Moreover, as initially conceptualized in the *Art of War* and explicated over the centuries, secrecy does not just entail being unfathomable and therefore unpredictable, but also creates the possibility of misinformation, deception, manipulation, and the unorthodox. Conversely, misinformation and deception reciprocally ensure the preservation of secrecy, misleading and obfuscating the enemy.

As just seen, in antiquity, an age that emphasized sincerity and veracity, misinformation and deliberately misleading the enemy were fundamentally unorthodox in both conception and implementation. However, despite repeated cries for truth and veracity in our troubled world, propaganda and misinformation have become so common that only their absence can be considered unorthodox. Important elements of contemporary PRC misinformation practice include revitalizing the specter of Confucianism as a fundamental Chinese value that naturally gives precedence to righteousness and tranquility, coinciding with their employment of the rapidly proliferating Confucius Institutes as propaganda organs; perpetuating and reemphasizing Western misconceptions that China has always esteemed cultural achievements and disparaged the martial, that it has been a static peaceful society unmarked by Western-style brutality and excessive violence; that it has no martial culture or heroes; and (in substantiation of their claim that they harbor no expansionist or aggressive intents, to allay fears and forestall counter-measures such as adversarial alliances), that China never mounted aggressive campaigns against anyone.

Although we have already demythologized these assertions in other works, it might again be noted that ever since its inception with the Shang, China has continuously and systematically conducted massive, externally directed campaigns out into Central Asia, down into Vietnam, and onto the Korean Peninsula in a quest to vanquish contiguous peoples and foreign states.[31] "New China" has similarly invaded and occupied Tibet, clashed with Soviet forces, and mounted incursions into India and Vietnam. Naturally, all the historic conquest expeditions, as well as the present occupation of Tibet and disputed territory bordering India, continue to be justified as "defensive" actions envisioned as necessary to preserve the state and ensure its "territorial integrity," a concept emphasized by Mao Zedong and much discussed in contemporary military journals.

Subversive Lessons

Although contemporary think tanks tend to emphasize the classical military manuals and selected battles, certain lessons in power politics derived from China's pre-imperial historical writings have also been deemed applicable to the PRC's contemporary geopolitical situation. Thus, once disparaged accounts of "corrupt feudalistic society" are being not only revitalized, but carefully scrutinized as well as employed to prove the complexity and sophistication of traditional Chinese culture as part of current worldwide propaganda efforts. Even the previously despised, ancient works recognized for over two millennia as the Confucian classics, including the *Book of Documents* (*Shu Ching*) and *Spring and Autumn Chronicle* (*Ch'un Ch'iu*), spuriously held to have been edited by Confucius himself, now receive occasional mention and the Master's sayings are being expropriated and publicized as a corrective to the rampant hedonism and corruption plaguing the land, including in articles in the major theoretical military journals.[32]

Three antique works have become the focus of conscious study: the *Tso Chuan*, which retells the historical events of the Spring and Autumn period when Chou imperial authority could no longer restrain its former fiefs, warfare suddenly burgeoned, and dozens of states perished; the *Intrigues of the Warring States* (*Chan-kuo Ts'e*), which describes various episodes from the Warring States period; and Ssu-ma Ch'ien's masterful *Shih Chi*, China's first synthetic history. All three, together with the *Kuo Yü* or *Discourses of the States*, which purportedly preserves important discussions from the Spring and Autumn period, have been not only assiduously studied through the centuries in China, but also pondered in Korea and Japan.

Although generally praised by the Confucian-oriented scholars and literati for more than two millennia and consciously examined for appropriate lessons in the practice of righteous government, these works were simultaneously recognized as dangerous handbooks of plots and intrigues, strategy, and tactics—both orthodox and unorthodox—that might be employed by foreign peoples or unscrupulous court members and imperial relatives for pernicious purposes.[33] Efforts were therefore intermittently made to prevent their dissemination and acquisition by potential enemies, no doubt coincidentally drawing attention to the "perversity" of their contents and enhancing their appeal among the disaffected.

As previously discussed, the Warring States period (481–221) saw warfare's lethality continuously escalate as the seven major states that survived the Spring and Autumn period interminably battled each other both politically and militarily until Ch'in emerged as the ultimate victor.[34] Originally an insignificant, semi-barbarian state lying on the periphery of the "civilized" Chou world, just like the Chou before it Ch'in had continuously nurtured its economic and military power until becoming capable of challenging, then finally vanquishing, the other states to unify the realm. Furthermore, its rise had similarly been facilitated by being located between vigorous steppe peoples and the civilization of sedentary China, from which it could acquire knowledge, tools, inventions, and advanced materials.

Largely ignored by the self-absorbed Chou fiefs, Ch'in also benefited from the strategic advantages provided by interceding mountains and easily defensible passes; its government was efficient, if draconian, and consistently exploited foreign talent; several successive kings pursued a deliberately gradual policy of expansion; it consciously nurtured a martial spirit and disdained the values promoted by Confucianism; it stressed agriculture and fundamental pursuits while the other states were more inclined to ritual, hedonism, and extravagance; and it trained and fielded a formidable army that generally incorporated the latest advances in weaponry and mobility, though the cavalry never really played any role in its ascension.

Given these dynamics, many contemporary PRC strategists perceive Ch'in's slow but astonishing rise as analogous to China's own emergence on the periphery of the highly advanced Western world. Rather than Han, Wei, Chao, and Ch'i, the enemy states figuratively arrayed to its east and conjoined in an inimical American alliance range from South Korea down through Japan, Taiwan, the Philippines, and finally Australia lying in the deep background. Recent announcements of increased U.S. military cooperation with Indonesia and Vietnam; logistical support from Singapore; growing rapprochement with India and Mongolia; extensive American military activities in Afghanistan and the appearance of U.S. bases in Central Asia; and finally Pakistan's reliability as an ally are also increasingly deemed problematic.

Within these geostrategic circumstances and the PRC's avowed determination to exclude the United States from the Pacific region, ultimately end American hegemony, and finally ascend to a position of dominance (such as by encircling the U.S. with bases in Panama, Cuba, Latin America, Egypt, and other choke points, much as in a game of *wei-ch'i*, better known under the Japanese name of *Go*), the multi-faceted Ch'in approach has great appeal as a comprehensive methodology.[35]

Even though the Spring and Autumn period saw the initiation of numerous perverse techniques such as bribery, rumors, assassination, and estrangement, they always remained ad hoc measures implemented when opportune or resorted to when desperately required. In contrast, Ch'in deliberately integrated their practice into its strategic doctrine and emphasized bribery as the foundation of their unorthodox practice of systematic subversion even though bribery's employment to further overt political purposes continued to be disparaged in a political context that still superficially esteemed ritual, sincerity, and righteousness. When utilized for such sinister purposes as thwarting policies, corrupting rulers or officials, and estrangement, bribery must therefore be regarded as an unorthodox measure.

A meeting convened by the other states for the purpose of forming an obstructive strategic alliance provided the initial impetus for Ch'in's formulation and adoption of monetary enticements. When it rapidly succeeded in causing disaffection and wrangling among the realm's officials despite the precariousness of their existence, similar measures were employed to subvert the lynchpin states of Han and Wei followed by a clandestine thrust into Yen and finally Chao, where agents sufficiently impugned the loyalty of Chao's last two capable generals to prompt displacement and execution.[36] Although subversion alone couldn't topple a strong state like Chao, Ch'in's mighty forces soon attacked and destroyed its army before extinguishing Chao itself.[37]

Given these impressive achievements further exhortations should not have been required. Nevertheless, about 237 BCE a foreign strategist known as Wei Liao-tzu advised the future Ch'in emperor to systematically employ bribes to weaken the feudal states and "confuse their plans."[38] Li Ssu, then serving as prime minister, not only concurred but lethally augmented the policy by instructing their agents to assassinate anyone who continued to oppose them (such as by advocating strong defensive measures), thereby paving the way for conquest by campaign forces.[39]

Coupled with the continuing implementation of these unorthodox measures, Ch'in's well-known martial spirit and awesome military power persuaded many states to abandon any thought of "provocative" military preparations and even adopt active policies of appeasement. Whether oblivious to the severity of the threat or fearful of antagonizing the king, they not only failed to conclude advantageous strategic partnerships, but also shortsightedly quarreled and fought among themselves, enervating their states and decimating each other's forces. Ch'in then went on to sequentially defeat the now isolated states with comparative ease.

In "Planning Offensives" Sun-tzu asserts that "The highest realization of warfare is to attack the enemy's plans; next is to attack their alliances; next to attack their army; and the lowest is to attack their fortified cities." Contemporary Chinese strategists openly admire Ch'in's success in balking enemy plans and disrupting inimical alliances and the PRC is obviously employing a number of unorthodox measures to achieve similar results.[40] Although space precludes a detailed discussion, a few possibilities might be noted.

As Sun-tzu stressed, the foundation of any martial program has always been thorough knowledge of the enemy, both military and non-military. Glimpses of extensive PRC intelligence efforts in the United States over the past decade, both clandestine and open source, have been revealed in a variety of formats and articles ranging from the COX report to *Time* magazine special investigations. Open source information is largely gathered by masses of amateurs, primarily the many students and businessmen presently in North America, though clearly supplemented by professionals who approach predetermined targets. Armies of the inquisitive thus siphon off the latest ideas and discoveries for PRC exploitation; front companies and major PRC entities gain access to proprietary information through a variety of means, including paid informants, defectors, and businessmen and others entrapped by female agents, especially in Asia; military specialists are targeted, particularly overseas;[41] military manuals and publications are combed for knowledge and weaknesses; and cyberwarfare specialists routinely filch vital data and plans through the pervasive internet.[42] Disinformation is also actively practiced, both by official spokesmen and by prominent American lobbyists, and academia infil-trated with congenial views and benign portrayals.[43]

Yet revelations about these practices in both topical pronouncements and specialist monographs are more frequently ignored than noted. Whether as a result of misinformation campaigns or blindness prompted by the lure of economic riches (just as formulated in "Three Doubts"), China is generally viewed as too incompetent to achieve real success in this sophisticated game or not constituting a perceivable threat; or the view is that the information being lost (despite being developed at the cost of millions of dollars and, more importantly, worker hours) is not worth being troubled about in the greater context of glowing Chinese–American relations. No doubt blind faith in America's ability to continue as the world's leading innovator in virtually every field, including military tech-nology, contributes to this complacency.

As a matter of such topical interest, it merely need be pointed out that (as analyzed in our *Tao of Spycraft*) the practice, and shortly thereafter, theory of intelligence gathering in traditional China dates well back into antiquity. Moreover, with the latter's inception with the infamous thir-teenth chapter of the *Art of War* on clandestine agents, intelligence activi-ties have always surpassed simple information acquisition, being oriented to actively carrying out intrigue, disinformation, and assassination. Nev-ertheless, despite being deemed a necessary but inherently improper ac-tivity, spying was not actually termed an unorthodox activity until the early Sung, when Hsü Tung offered a number of suggestions for compro-mising and doubling enemy agents in order to spread misinformation in his *Hu-ch'ien Ching*.[44]

Although the theoretical manuals counseled restraint, as already noted Sun-tzu's concept of what might be termed the "ruthless practice of effi-cient warfare" dominated the battlefield, often degenerating to total war-fare marked by ruthlessness in execution rather than deliberate efficiency.[45] When the fundamental idea of always attacking where unexpected, where the enemy is unprepared, is coupled with the *Art of War*'s emphasis upon the active nature of intelligence work, the extension of unorthodox war-fare beyond the battlefield to target logistics, the populace, and infrastructure itself, not just with troops but with lethal, clandestine methods such as poisoning the water supply and nighttime incendiary sabotage must be considered inevitable.

Not unexpectedly, the end of the last millennium saw the publication of a lengthy theoretical discussion reportedly prompted by the ongoing revolution in military affairs, *Unrestricted Warfare*, which falls squarely into the Chinese tradition of total warfare.[46] Based upon their determination that traditional forms of warfare have become outmoded and the battlefield no longer artificially confined, the authors conclude that conventional restraints should be ignored and every possible means systematically employed to wrest victory, with effectiveness being the only criteria for judging appropriateness. Accordingly, future warfare will be fought in many dimensions rather than restricted to any single domain, whether commercial, ecological, or informational, eroding all distinctions between the battlefield and the homeland, even between combatants and non-combatants.[47]

Destructive measures that target the financial sector, communications, and the core infrastructure components of electricity and transportation are postulated as certain to severely disrupt normal life, causing consternation and undermining any will to fight because Americans are perceived as lacking self-discipline, resilience, and the capacity to endure casualties. Moreover, in discussing the requisite measures to bring about "social panic, street riots, and a political crisis," they approvingly cite Sherman's advance toward Savannah in the Civil War because it was designed not to engage enemy forces in combat, but to destroy the economy and the South's will to resist. Accordingly, psychological warfare, weapons of mass destruction, and every means of corrupting and enervating society are to be deployed, ruthlessly causing disaffection and chaos in the manner of what we might term the "ruthless practice of efficient warfare."

Although the authors admit that waging war in this manner will not realize Sun-tzu's well-known ideal of achieving victory without combat, their overall approach well coheres with his emphasis upon manipulating the enemy and enervating their will by "seizing" (or in this case eliminating) what they value: "If the enemy is numerous, disciplined, and about to advance, first seize something that they love, for then they will listen to you."[48] These measures will also destroy the pervasive accord that Sun-tzu postulated as the foundation of warfare.[49]

Observers have tended to dismiss *Unrestricted Warfare* as a radical work without any real significance, yet many of the ideas have previously been expressed in key PRC military journals, albeit in truncated form.[50] Moreover, many Chinese strategists have realized that the conflict cannot be confined to the battlefield nor structured in the traditional manner if the PRC is to successfully confront America's overwhelming military power. Although the PRC has been visibly preparing to wage a "high tech war under localized conditions" (presumably over Taiwan or with contiguous states like Vietnam), the key to thwarting, if not defeating, the United States is therefore increasingly envisioned as severely affecting the homeland populace and logistical base. In fact, numerous articles thus speak of how Communist success in Vietnam was achieved solely through destroying the will of the people to sustain the military effort while others suggest that the extended supply lines may equally be attacked in the heartland, at their point of origin.

Because the overt employment of weapons of mass destruction would certainly result in costly reprisals, in accord with their interpretation of the American doctrine of proportionality and restrained escalation, recourse might well be had to guerrilla and other unorthodox measures in an asymmetric clash intended to achieve the desired objective without incurring inescapable self-destruction. Although many possibilities with varying prospects for success can be imagined, one possibility would be the coordinated implementation of low-tech, systematic sabotage and subversion (or "Triple S") on a vast scale.

Although low-tech, systematic sabotage and subversion is consistent with Mao's concept of people's warfare and Ch'in's subversive thrust, the initial impetus for this sort of program can be detected in another chapter of the *Six Secret Teachings*, in which the T'ai Kung advised that "the implements for offense and defense are fully found in ordinary human activity."

He then went on to detail how the various techniques and equipment employed in construction and farming might be used for destructive and other purposes in warfare.[51]

Battlefield technology and the civilian infrastructure have radically changed over two millennia, but for sabotage operations within the heartland neither the principle nor basic methods have altered. Although explosives may readily be acquired in rural areas and knowledge of bomb making is widely accessible, intelligently selecting the targets to exploit their inherent destructive potential and readily recognized nodes of vulnerability makes them unnecessary. Hacksaws and axes, flares and lighters, metal chains and long aluminum spikes, even rope and superglue, not to mention poisons, acids, Molotov cocktails, and the ubiquitous computer all provide sufficient, readily available means that arouse no suspicion yet can easily be employed with devastating effect. Little skill will be required to wield them effectively and only moderate courage as the risk of injury or detection would be minimal.

Two broad categories of unorthodox action based upon historical practice and well articulated doctrine may be envisioned: those that exploit the infrastructure and environment's latent potential and those that can be accomplished by simple, unobtrusive means that singularly would go almost unnoticed and be quickly forgotten, but en masse will have a devastating effect. Although the former entails possibilities ranging from attacking the environment's sustainability to the destruction of crops and livestock, water's dynamic power provides the most readily exploitable means because, as the *Wei Liao-tzu* asserts, "water is the softest and weakest of things, but whatever it collides with, such as hills and mounds, will be collapsed by it for no reason other than its nature is concentrated and its attack is totally committed."[52]

Over the past 2,500 years aquatic attacks have been ruthlessly employed in China to subjugate cities, annihilate armies, and inundate terrain.[53] Many were accomplished by diverting rivers or streams, others by building dams to back water onto designated targets or by destroying dams, resulting in an initial impulse that acted as a destructive ram before flooding the land. As in New Orleans, severe damage to the infrastruc-

ture, contamination and destruction of buildings, death and displacement of the inhabitants, and rampant social unrest all resulted, well attesting to their effectiveness.

More conveniently and therefore realistically, the power of flowing water may also be exploited by converting assets already found upon most
rivers into kinetic and incendiary weapons. Chinese military theory from
the T'ang onward formulated methods for exploiting both of them, while
common historical practice punctuated by pivotal battles such as Ch'ih
Pi extends back into the third century. However, Sun-tzu early on employed water's incredible force as an analogy for his pivotal concept of
shih or "strategic configuration of power" by saying that "The strategic
configuration of power is visible in the onrush of pent-up water tumbling stones along."[54]

Apart from employing vessels as rams in an "aim and release" mode,
terrifyingly random destruction can be realized simply by unleashing
them. However, by maintaining active control until just before impact
they can be directed against vital targets such as levees, bridge abutments,
piers, and loading facilities. Employed in coordinated fashion, these kinetic weapons can achieve strategic objectives such as severing the finite
number of bridges over the Mississippi River, thereby catastrophically disrupting the transport of industrial goods and agricultural products within
the United States.

Fire boats were initially simple affairs, merely derelict boats filled with
burning reeds set adrift in the current, but with the development of various incendiary concoctions, including early gunpowder formulations, they
became well-engineered, floating weapons. Most major rivers have virtually continuous barge traffic carrying highly flammable petroleum products that can easily be converted into fire ships, compounding the disaster
when they strike their intended targets. Moreover, once in motion there
would be inadequate response time, not to mention coordination and
methodology, to stop them, particularly if several vessels were simultaneously released in a limited area, as traditionally conceived and practiced.

The third well developed form of aquatic attacks, both theoretically and
historically, targets essential water supplies.[55] Although they may attempt

to directly introduce poisons or contaminants, such techniques have limited applicability, being effective only for well defined sources and low-flow volumes. More devastating and widely practiced has always been denying a locale's supplies by blocking the source, damaging or severing the conduits, or diverting the flow. This might easily be accomplished in many older North American cities because the systems often incorporate antique, highly fragile cast iron pipes, badly weakened valves, and inadequate or no redundancy. Many also depend upon a variety of aqueducts and oversized pipes to carry water dozens, if not hundreds of miles, and are therefore easily targeted in remote areas. Given their high flow volumes, an easily accomplished minor breach in the latter would quickly produce massive collapse and the probable erosion of nearby terrain, requiring a lengthy period to repair. In the absence of sufficient water even the smallest fires, being unextinguishable, would grow to all-consuming conflagrations while coordinated incendiary attacks launched throughout a city suffering water deprivation might inflict levels of devastation comparable to historically famous fires.

Because of fire's terrifying psychological impact and tendency to quickly spread once minimal temperatures are attained, igniting fires is the simplest, most unobtrusive, and potentially most devastating of all the acts of low-tech sabotage that might be contemplated, particularly given the virtually unlimited number of readily accessible targets. For example, a synchronized nighttime effort mounted by untrained agents could easily destroy all the retail gas stations in the United States or Canada. There would be little risk of identification or capture; the attacks could be accomplished with easily concealed means; and the fire response expected to be rapidly overwhelmed. The ensuing economic impact and psychological consternation wrought by the widespread destruction of gasoline distribution facilities in every aspect of contemporary life can hardly be imagined!

A number of other target categories suggested by *Unrestricted Warfare* capitalize on predispositions in the infrastructure and human dependence on provisions, services, and material goods, with railroads being particularly vulnerable to disruption or exploitation. Disrupting the electricity grid, whether by toppling high-voltage transmission towers in remote regions with high temperature torches or using cyber attacks, would have extended consequences and wreck great havoc. However, massive computer attacks, already being witnessed in limited situations, occupy the key role in overt theorizations, no doubt in part as the reincarnation of Mao Zedong's concept of people's warfare.

Contrary to spectacular but singular attacks that inflict significant casualties and localized damage but remain largely circumscribed in impact, a well coordinated program of low-tech systematic sabotage and subversion would thus devastate the economy, entangle the military forces, hinder the resupply of necessary war materials, provoke widespread social unrest, and produce chaos. The mere threat of its actualization could be coercively employed just as effectively as a threatened nuclear attack, deterring the United States from becoming embroiled in distant PRC military actions.[56] Moreover, these measures could be effected by amateur personnel selected from among the numerous students, tourists, illegal immigrants, and businessmen temporarily dispersed throughout the country, or even by the criminals, gang members, and religious dissidents that PRC analysts envision as readily exploitable for guerrilla warfare.

Systematic Assassination

Another prominent unorthodox measure whose practice extends back into the earliest centuries and received theoretical sanctification in the *Art of War*'s chapter on clandestine agents, assassination—now euphemistically termed "targeted killing" whenever one's opponents are somehow designated as enemies and assigned (often secretly and unilaterally) the status of combatants—may well play a significant role in any future conflict between the PRC and its enemies, whether indirect and clandestine or open and extensive. This strikes many as both surprising and unlikely in view of oft repeated claims that China has no martial culture, no appreciation of heroes, and always deprecated everything associated with power and brute force.

Contrary to such myths, the common people have always esteemed strength, bravado, martial skills, great fighters, and exemplary warriors.

Their military heroes have ranged from the purely cerebral such as Chu-ko Liang and the T'ai Kung through bold warriors whose prowess simply carried the field, including Kuan Yü. All of them became the focus of stories, operas, episodic tales, and novels, and now form the basis for serialized television presentations and movies.

More importantly, many of these traditional heroes were marked by a dark, brutal dimension. Chang Fei was a ruthless fighter and, as noted, many of the leading Sung dynasty rebels portrayed in the famous novel *Water Margin* impulsively slew servants, women, and children equally with those who offended them in so-called righteous rage. Historically, this sort of dramatically unbounded behavior struck a highly responsive cord among the downtrodden and suppressed, no doubt explaining the appeal of the wandering knights (*yu-hsia*), macho bravos with underworld connections who prominently roamed about in the Han.[57]

First made prominent late in the Spring and Autumn period, when the future king of Wu, Ho-lü, employed it to ensure his ascension to power, assassination assumed a much expanded role during the Warring States period when adopted by Ch'in as basic policy and otherwise used by generals and rulers to swiftly resolve inimical situations. Late in the era Prince Tan of Yen, noting that strong arm measures had historically succeeded in winning concessions, decided to employ an assassin against Ch'in in order to forestall extinction at the hands of the massive invasion force then being readied. The account of the entire episode, the longest in the *Shih Chi*'s focal chapter, so struck the Chinese mind that the name of the warrior chosen for the task, Ching K'o, became synonymous with "assassin."[58] Moreover, the timeless Chinese fascination with assassins and the possibility of significantly affecting circumstances through singular, violent action continues to be evident in two recent movies that lionize assassins, *Hero* and *Assassin*, as well as a lengthy television fictionalization of Ching K'o's life.

Insofar as the PRC still finds itself militarily in an extremely disadvantageous situation, assassination may be expected to have great appeal, whether for selectively targeting "obstructive" individuals (as in the Vietnam conflict) or systematically incapacitating enemy governments. Employing assassins in a preconceived plan, particularly if undertaken in the wider context of systematic sabotage and subversion, would not only fall into the unorthodox tradition, but also be easily accomplished because the physical offices and general movements of Western officials are generally well-known. Absent a betrayal by one of the perpetrators, an attack mounted with nerve agents or small but powerful explosives delivered by remotely controlled means would be virtually unstoppable. In addition, the prospects for success have been greatly enhanced by such lethal minia-turized technologies as rockets and unmanned aerial vehicles while the blame can be deflected or avoided by judiciously employing third-party contractors and high visibility dissident groups.

Although actual assassinations have proven relatively rare outside of in-surgencies, the ongoing conflict between the PRC and other nations con-stantly sees a more figurative form employed. Targeted individuals are frequently "removed" by marginalizing, discrediting, framing, blackmail-ing, or even coercing. Insidious terms such as "cold warrior mentality," "warmonger," "out of touch with reality," and bent on "demonizing China," frequently succeed in deprecating anyone who would venture to criticize PRC activities and intentions when coupled with the implemen-tation of the various measures suggested in "Three Doubts," particularly the lure of wealth, to create sycophants in Washington who self-assuredly assert that China not only poses no threat, but will invariably become a non-threatening democratic state and even a strategic ally.[59]

Purely military contexts will also see the creation and execution of un-orthodox measures both on the operational and on the tactical level. As documented in Pentagon and other reports, the PRC has been rapidly in-creasing the number of modern, though still conventional weapons such as submarines, torpedoes, and surface to surface weapons in its arsenal and emphasizing the development of indigenous versions with unique Chinese characteristics, particularly those with unexpected, "assassin"-like characteristics. Given that an immense disparity will still remain for the foreseeable future, despite the exhaustion of American forces and equip-ment in Middle East entanglements, many of them can be expected to see unorthodox employment. However, concrete discussions of Pacific and other conflicts must be left to other venues and more capable experts.

Notes

Chapter 1

1. The fundamental events of Chi-mo are scattered throughout the *Chan-kuo Ts'e* and condensed in T'ien Tan's biography in the *Shih Chi*. The entire episode is also reprised in the *Tzu-chih T'ung-chien*, "Chou Chi" 4, 279 BCE. (The inception and development of animal delivery systems are discussed in our *Fire and Water: The Art of Incendiary and Aquatic Warfare in China* [Boulder: Westview Press, 2003], and T'ien Tan's methods are reprised in further detail in our *The Tao of Spycraft: Intelligence Theory and Practice in Traditional China* [Boulder: Westview Press, 1998].)

2. It also numbers among the few examples included in the *T'ung Tien* (*chüan* 141, "Ping" 14) under the rubric *yin-chi she-ch'üan*. (References to *huo niu* ["fire oxen"] in the histories are not invariably to actual animals because straw versions—actually simply large bundles—were also fabricated for incendiary purposes. [For an example of their use, see *Tzu-chih T'ung-chien*, "T'ang Chi" 67, 869 CE.])

3. Even the highly esteemed *Tso Chuan*, traditionally regarded as the essential source for Spring and Autumn history, only employs it once in a variant edition in Duke Min's second year in conjunction with the term *mang* ("variegated") to describe something irregular, as in *mang ch'i wu ch'ang* or "strange and unusual," though it also appears in a personal name (Kun Chih Ch'i). Across the centuries it would continue to appear, though rarely, in personal names, including those of non-Han minorities. Historical examples include Yang Shih-ch'i, Han Pang-ch'i, and Ch'en Shih-ch'i; Wu Chung-ch'i, a calligrapher of minor repute who served as a PLA (People's Liberation Army) commander in the anti-Japanese War; and the modern *wu-hsia* (martial arts movie) actor Huo Cheng-ch'i.

4. For example, the *Ts'u-hai* and *Ts'u-yüan* cite a use in the "Chin-yü" section of the *Kuo Yü* (*Dialogues of the States*), where it states that *ch'i sheng kuai*—the "unusual gives birth to the weird."

5. Such as the *Shuo-wen Chieh-tzu Ku-lin*.

6. *Ch'i-shih* or "unusual rocks" are deemed fascinating not just because of their uniqueness or unusual appearance, but often because of their aura, because they suggest something larger or seem to embed or emanate transfigured power, *Te*. Extraordinary terrain, scenery, and locations described as *ch'i-t'e* ("unique" or "outstanding") or as *shen-ch'i* (spiritually *ch'i*) are also experienced as numinously empowered. (*Hao-se*

ch'i-nan-jen is definitely stronger than the modern sense of "playboy," for the emphasis is upon the extreme degree, perhaps something more akin to the colloquial "sex maniac.")

7. *Hsün-tzu*, "Fei Hsiang."

8. The *Chin-ku Ch'i-kuan* encompasses selections from three larger, late Ming works known as the *San-yen*.

9. The sense of not being upright or correct (but unorthodox rather than perverse or heterodox) is particularly witnessed in the *Chou Li*, a late Warring States or early Han compilation.

10. Although the term *ch'i* can be prefixed to almost anything, including books and the statue of a *ch'i-chi*, an unusual rooster created in 2005 for the year of the rooster from electronic components, it has long appeared in a number of common, fixed compounds connoting a basic sense of difference, uniqueness, and unexpectedness. For example, *ching-ch'i* refers to something to marvel at or something that causes surprise or astonishment; *ch'i-chi* is a miracle; and *ch'i-chen / chen-ch'i* are rarities. However, the common term for "strange" is actually quite weak compared with what might be expected because it is composed from *ch'i* and *kuai*, "unusual" and "bizarre."

11. For a discussion of the T'ai Kung and the late Warring States work—the *Liu-t'ao* or *Six Secret Teachings*—attributed, however spuriously, to him, see our translation and the accompanying introduction and notes in the *Seven Military Classics of Ancient China* (History and Warfare; Boulder: Westview Press, 1993).

12. Duke Huan's achievements as hegemon, long disparaged by the Confucians, have been substantially denied by the work of Bruce and Taeko Brooks. The *Kuan-tzu* is a massive, eclectic Warring states work. (For an annotated translation, see W. Allyn Rickett, *Guan-tzu*, 2 vols. [Princeton: Princeton University Press, 1985 and 1998].)

13. The T'ang dynasty *Questions and Replies*—a book purporting to be a dialogue between the dynasty's second emperor and the famous general Li Ching—reviews his career. However, somewhat unexpectedly, despite the unorthodox being a focal topic in the *Questions and Replies*, Li Ching just enumerates the T'ai Kung's orthodox achievements, praising him for having successfully copied the Yellow Emperor's methods, thereby pushing back the implied inception of unorthodox techniques to the legendary Yellow Emperor, who reputedly suppressed the forces of evil and chaos with chemical fog and marvelous devices. He then concludes: "When he deployed the army at Mu-yeh, with only a hundred officers the T'ai Kung controlled the army and established his military achievements. With 45,000 men he conquered King Chou's mass of 700,000. In the Chou Dynasty the *Ssu-ma Fa* was based upon the T'ai Kung. When the T'ai Kung died the people of Ch'i obtained his bequeathed strategies. When Duke Huan became hegemon over All under Heaven, he relied on Kuan Chung who again cultivated the T'ai Kung's methods. Their army was referred to as a restrained and governed force and all the feudal lords submitted." (*Questions and Replies*, Book I. The contents will be discussed in detail in a subsequent section. However, for an annotated translation and historical introduction, see *Questions and Replies between T'ang T'ai-tsung and Li Wei-kung* in our *Seven Military Classics of Ancient China*.)

14. For a brief discussion see *The Art of War*, trans. Ralph D. Sawyer with Mei-Chün Lee Sawyer (History and Warfare; Boulder: Westview Press, 1994).

15. The following paragraphs are essentially drawn from the introduction to our single-volume *Art of War*. More extensive discussion will be found in our forthcoming

work, *Early Chinese Warfare*, which focuses on warfare from antiquity through the rise of the Ch'in.

Chapter 2

1. However, for a contrary view, see the position and work of Bruce and Taeko Brooks, progenitors of the Warring States Project, as posted on the project's website: http://www.umass.edu/wsp.

2. Recent decades have seen several books and articles by David Nivison, Edward Shaughnessey, Yuri Pines, and others that discuss the dating, reliability, and veracity of these early texts that extensively revise Ch'ing dynasty views and supplement the appraisals found in Michael Loewe's *Early Chinese Texts: A Bibliographical Guide*, Early China Special Monograph Series, 2 (Berkeley: Society for the Study of Early China, Institute of East Asian Studies, University of California, Berkeley, 1993). (Complete translations of the *Tso Chuan* have been undertaken by James Legge and Bernhard Karlgren, while Burton Watson has provided a volume of selected passages.)

3. *Tso-shih Ping-fa* (Shaan-hsi: Jen-min Ch'u-pan-she, 1991).

4. Complete translations with historical introduction and commentary may be found in our *Seven Military Classics*.

5. Li assumes that Sun-tzu had access to records of these events, particularly the *Tso Chuan*. However, the relative compilation dates of the *Tso Chuan* and *Art of War* remain a somewhat problematic issue.

6. Recent archaeological reports have confirmed the existence of elephants south of the Yangtze, especially in Ch'u, during the Spring and Autumn.

7. *Tso Chuan*, Chuang Kung, tenth year. Also seen in the *Tso-shih Ping-fa* as an example of *ch'i* and included in the *Wu-ching Tsung-yao*'s "Ch'üan Ch'i."

8. *Tso Chuan*, Hsi Kung, twenty-eighth year.

9. The primary account, found in Tsung Ch'üeh's biography (*Nan-shih*, *chüan* 37) is replicated in the *Tzu-chih T'ung-chien*, "Sung Chi," 6. It is also found as an illustration in the *Wu-ching Tsung-yao*'s "Ch'üan Ch'i."

10. The incident is preserved in his biography in the *Sung Shih* (*chüan* 290) and also reprised in the *Hsü Tzu-chih T'ung-chien* under King Ting's first year.

11. It should be noted that arguments have been advanced that such sophisticated tactics reflect Warring States developments or that they characterize the mobile warfare of mounted steppe warriors.

12. *Ts'ao-lu Ching-lüeh*, "Fu Ping." The comments are also cited in the *Tso-shih Ping-fa*.

13. *Tso Chuan*, Yin Kung, ninth year.

14. This sort of appraisal of steppe "barbarians" would persist across Chinese history, even in the context of major invasions by the Khitan, Jurchen, and Mongols.

15. *Tso Chuan*, Ch'eng Kung, third year (588 BCE).

16. *Tso Chuan*, Wen Kung, sixteenth year. (The example is found in chapter four of the *Ch'ien K'un Ta-lüeh*, "The Tao of Decisive Warfare Lies in Conceiving the Unorthodox and Establishing Ambushes.")

17. "Military Combat."

18. Although the *Ssu-ma Fa* and other classic works discuss the danger of feigned retreats, the quintessential expression appears as the *Unorthodox Strategies'* tactical

discussion under the rubric of "Retreats": "Whenever you engage in pitched assaults with an enemy, you must carefully investigate it if they withdraw for no apparent reason. If their strength is really exhausted and their spirit spent, you can select elite, fierce cavalrymen to pursue them closely." And in discussing the question of "Pursuit" the text comments:

> Whenever racing after a fleeing enemy or pursuing a retreating one, you must distinguish real and feigned withdrawals. If their flags are well ordered and their drums responsive, while their commands and orders are unified, even though they appear to be retreating in chaos and confusion, it is not a true defeat but certainly an unorthodox tactic. You should ponder it for some time before taking any action. However, if their flags are confused and disordered and the response of their large and small drums discordant, while their commands and orders are shouted and clamorous and not at all unified, this truly is a defeated, terrified army that should be vigorously pursued.

19. *Tso Chuan*, Chao Kung, twenty-second year.

20. As Li Yüan-ch'un asserts in his *Tso-shih Ping-fa*.

21. *Tso Chuan*, Chao Kung, fifteenth year.

22. See "Superior Virtue Is Not Virtuous," chapter 38 of the traditionally received *Tao Te Ching*.

23. *Tso Chuan*, Ting Kung, ninth year. It is among the illustrations included in the *Wu-ching Tsung-yao*'s chapter "Ch'üan Ch'i."

24. Yang was actually captured during his first attempted escape despite having sabotaged the chariots of his pursuers and it was only upon his second attempt with another wagon that he eventually succeeded. (How he could have managed to "borrow" the chariots remains puzzling.)

25. The incident, which is included in chapter four, "Decisive Warfare," of the *Ch'ien K'un Ta-lüeh*, appears under Hsiang Kung's eighteenth year (555 BCE) in the *Tso Chuan*. (The conflict in the *Tso*, presumably the chronicle of Lu, is actually told from Lu's perspective.) It has been here somewhat abridged, deleting a dream of doom found in the *Tso* and additional material about certain heroic but irrelevant actions found in both the *Tso* and *Ch'ien K'un Ta-lüeh*.

26. Being between the Chi River and the sea, the site was apparently amply provided with water, obviating any need for a vast undertaking—merely improving depressions and ravines could channel the water, accounting for its astonishing width of nearly 2,000 feet in comparison with the normal 20 to 50. (One *li* is about a third of a mile.)

27. The specter of an additional thousand chariots from each of the states, no doubt psychologically devastating, was almost certainly a deliberate exaggeration, since neither of them probably had sufficient resources to field more than a few hundred.

28. The records for Duke Ling's reign in "Ch'i T'ai Kung Shih-chia" and Duke P'ing's in the "Chin Shih-chia" (both in the *Shih-chi*) emphasize that the populace was slain and the area thoroughly burned. (For further discussion of the evolution of incendiary warfare in this period, see our *Fire and Water*.) The incident finally concludes when the marquis' eldest son cuts the harness bindings on the chariot to prevent him from fleeing further away.

29. The tactical discussion for "Doubt in Warfare" notes how such deceits may be employed to shape enemy action and the battlefield:

> Whenever occupying fortifications opposite an enemy, if you want to launch a sudden attack against them, you should gather large amounts of grass and different branches and make your flags and pennants numerous in order to create the appearance of a populated encampment. If you force the enemy to prepare in the east and then strike in the west, you will inevitably be victorious. If you should want to retreat, create some false, empty deployments that can be left behind when you withdraw, for then the enemy will never pursue you. A tactical principle from the *Art of War* states: "Many obstacles in heavy grass is suspicious."

30. *Tso Chuan*, Ai Kung, nineteenth year.

31. The episode is reprised in numerous early Warring States and Han texts, including the *Han Fei-tzu, Shuo Yüan,* and *Ch'un-ch'iu Fan-lu,* generally being employed to illustrate shortsightedness; retold in the *Chan-kuo Ts'e* and *Shih Chi;* included in the *Thirty-six Strategies;* and numbers as one of the important examples in the *Wu-ching Tsung-yao* chapter "Ch'i Ping."

32. Hsia-yang was apparently the closest city to the state of Yü, so Kuo's ruler was forced to move his capital southward, perhaps even divide the state into northern Kuo and southern Kuo. (The *Tso* account has been somewhat abridged for clarity.)

33. *Han Fei-tzu,* "Shih Kuo."

34. Further discussion of night incendiary thieves may be found in our *Fire and Water.*

35. *Tso Chuan,* Huan Kung, eleventh year.

36. Hsi Kung, twenty-fifth year. (The *Tso Chuan* identifies the forces as coming from Ch'in and Chin, but the addition of "Chin" is clearly an error.)

37. See "Planning Offensives," in *Art of War.*

38. *Tso Chuan,* Wen Kung, seventh year.

39. *Tso Chuan,* Hsiang Kung, seventeenth year.

40. A similar example of a nighttime penetration occurred when Tzu Ch'an and Tzu Chan of Cheng, while attacking the capital of Ch'en, broke through the fortifications during the night. (See *Tso Chuan,* Hsiang Kung, twenty-fifth year.)

41. *Tso Chuan,* Hsiang Kung, twenty-third year.

42. *Tso Chuan,* Hsiang Kung, twenty-sixth year (547 BCE). It is also cited as an example in the *Ch'ien K'un Ta-lüeh's* "Chüeh-chan chih Tao Tsai-yü Ch'u-ch'i She-fu" or "The Tao of Decisive Warfare Lies in Formulating the Unorthodox and Establishing Ambushes."

43. See the *Tso Chuan,* Ch'eng Kung, sixth year.

44. The Duke of Shen and Wu Tzu-hsü, both of whom ventured to Wu and provided military and strategic advice, are two prominent examples of defectors who found Ch'u's despotic brutality and unremitting court strife intolerable.

45. *Tso Chuan,* Duke Chao, seventeenth year. This battle, and in particular the concept of an advantageous position upstream, furnishes the historical illustration for the chapter entitled "Amphibious Strategies" in the *Unorthodox Strategies* and it also appears in the *Wu-ching Tsung-yao* selections included in the chapter "Unorthodox Plans."

46. *Tso Chuan*, Ai Kung, seventeenth year. The clash and its precursors are extensively discussed in the section "The War between Wu and Yüeh" included in the historical introduction to our single-volume *The Art of War*.

47. "Night in Warfare."

48. "The Nearby in Warfare."

49. *Tso Chuan*, Chao Kung, first year. The episode is cited by Li Ching as an example of the unorthodox in *Questions and Replies*, as will be seen in the theory section.

50. More literally, "The squads were then deployed into five arrays set out apace, a *liang* to the fore, *wu* to the rear, a *chuan* at the right point, a *san* at the left point, and a *p'ien* to resist to the front in order to entice the enemy." Although the names of the five arrays have occasioned extensive commentary and divergent explanations, whether they specify various formations current in the Spring and Autumn or merely designate comparative numbers remains unresolved. (*Wu* basically means five and *san* means three, so they could simply mean five and three contingents of these ad hoc troops, whatever the number entailed by each contingent.)

51. *Tso Chuan*, Chao Kung, thirteenth year.

52. *Tso Chuan*, Huan Kung, eighth year. (It appears as an example in "The Tao of Decisive Warfare Lies in Formulating the Unorthodox and Establishing Ambushes" in the *Ch'ien K'un Ta-lüeh*.)

53. *Tso Chuan*, Hsi Kung, twenty-eighth year. The Battle of Ch'eng-p'u, which is included among the examples in the *Wu-ching Tsung-yao*'s "Ch'üan Ch'i," has been the subject of innumerable articles over the years and is extensively discussed in the two major Chinese military histories. Further explication in English may also be found in Frank A. Kierman Jr., "Phases and Modes of Combat in Early China" in *Chinese Ways in Warfare* (Cambridge: Harvard University Press, 1974).

54. "The Tao of Decisive Warfare Lies in Formulating the Unorthodox and Establishing Ambushes," *Ch'ien K'un Ta-lüeh*. (For further discussion of the battle and its consequences, see the introduction to our translation of the *Art of War*, from which the material here is abstracted.)

55. *Tso Chuan*, Chao Kung, twenty-third year.

56. According to the *Ch'un Ch'iu*, the rulers of Hu and Shen perished, but Chen's ruler was taken captive.

57. The story of the assassination accomplished by Chuan Chu is retold in the *Tso Chuan* under the twenty-seventh year of Duke Chao. (A more extensive account and discussion may be found in our *Tao of Spycraft*, pp. 68ff.)

58. *Tso Chuan*, Chao Kung, thirtieth year. The tactics are also cited in the *Ch'ien K'un Ta-lüeh*, chapter 4, "Decisive Battle," and "Ch'i Ping" of the *Wu-ching Tsung-yao*. Wu Tzu-hsü had fled the internecine strife that had long plagued the state of Ch'u and that proved responsible for many defectors playing pivotal roles as strategic advisors while in exile in other states, including the famous Duke of Shen, a military advisor who earlier had come to Wu at the behest of Chin. (The *Tso Chuan* incident in which the Duke of Hsi fled to Chin, included in this section, also reflects these circumstances. Further discussion and examples may also be found in our *Tao of Spycraft*, pp. 52–58.)

59. *Ch'un Ch'iu*, Hsüan Kung, fourteenth and fifteenth years.

60. There is a brief section in the *Yi Li* ("Ch'eng Li, Part Eight") about the proper ritual behavior to employ when a diplomatic mission crosses a state en route to an objective beyond, including the exchange of presents. (For an English rendering, see "The Ceremonial of a Mission" in *The I-Li or Book of Etiquette and Ceremonial*, trans. John Steele [London: Probsthain & Co, 1917], p. 193.)

61. Commentators generally interpret this as Shen Chou having introduced his son to the king—that is, the king seeing him in interview—but such an interpretation is forced and unnecessary.

62. There are various interpretations for this sentence, but he was obviously suggesting that they erect a more permanent looking encampment and assign part of their troops to the task of farming so as to provide for their food requirements and cower Sung with their determination.

63. *Tso Chuan*, Chuang Kung, tenth year. In "Military Combat" Sun-tzu asserts the basic principle: "One who excels at employing the army avoids (the enemy's) ardent *ch'i* and strikes when it is indolent or exhausted." Mao Zedong also emphasized the lessons provided by this *Tso Chuan* passage in propounding his strategy for defeating the Japanese in "Strategy in China's Revolutionary War."

64. Other interpretations have been advanced, but this sequence is highly plausible.

65. "Military Combat," in *Art of War*. Many of Sun-tzu's measures were designed to manipulate the enemy until they became physically and emotionally exhausted, until their spirit or "will to fight" had been so undermined that victory became certain. (As Li Ching would point out, the sequence of morning, noon, and night is simply an analogy for the pattern of growth and decline.)

66. See, for example, "Expanding Ch'i," in *Sun Pin Ping-fa* (*Military Methods*).

67. "Nine Terrains." A second passage adds that although they may weep, "if you throw them into a hopeless situation, they will have the courage of Chu or Kuei."

68. *Tso Chuan*, Chao Kung, twenty-first year. (As there are some discrepancies with the original *Tso Chuan* account, the *Wu-ching Tsung-yao* version included in the illustrative chapter "Ch'üan Ch'i" has been followed.)

69. *Tso Chuan*, Ting Kung, fourteenth year. (The clash is included in the *Wu-ching Tsung-yao*'s "Ch'üan Ch'i" while the definitive struggle between Wu and Yüeh is extensively discussed in the introduction to our *Art of War* and in the section on covert programs in our *Tao of Spycraft*.)

70. *Tso Chuan*, Hsiang Kung, fourteenth year. (For a brief discussion of the theory and practice of denying water resources and employing poison to incapacitate and slay enemy forces, see "Negating Water Sources," in our *Fire and Water*, pp. 317ff.)

71. The *Wu-ching Tsung-yao* includes the incident in its chapter "Ch'üan Ch'i," as does Yeh Meng-hsiung in his "Use Poison to Defeat the Enemy" found in the *Yün-ch'ou Kang-mu*.

72. *Tso Chuan*, Chao Kung, twenty-fourth year. (In his chapter "Aquatic Warfare" Yeh Meng-hsiung deems the use of water as a weapon to be unorthodox.)

73. *Tso Chuan*, Chao Kung, thirtieth year.

74. For the events, see Wu Tzu-hsü's biography in the introduction to our *Art of War* translation.

75. "Incendiary Attacks," chapter 12 of *Art of War*.

Chapter 3

1. Opening lines, Verse 57, *Tao Te Ching*. (For a discussion of the chapter's implications and another reading of the character for "orthodox" as understood by the T'ang martial theorist Wang Chen, see our *The Tao of War: The Martial Tao Te Ching* [originally published as *The Tao of Peace*, 1999; reprint: Boulder: Westview Press, 2002], pp. 174–77.)

2. For a discussion of the increasingly acrimonious debate over Sun-tzu's existence—long questioned by a number of traditional Chinese scholars as well—see the introduction to our *Art of War*, either in the *Seven Military Classics* or single-volume editions.

3. The chronologically layered, composite nature of the *Analects* has long been known. However, for a radical reevaluation see E. Bruce Brooks and A. Taeko Brooks, *The Original Analects: Sayings of Confucius and His Successors* (New York: Columbia University Press, 1997).

4. For a more systematic, extensive discussion of the contents, see the introduction to our single-volume *Art of War*.

5. The recognition that topography is fundamental to military tactics, the classification of terrain types, and the association of basic tactical principles with particular terrains are all generally attributed to Sun-tzu. Even though a cursory examination of the *Tso Chuan* will quickly indicate that effective commanders had long been implementing terrain-based tactics, and certain land configurations, such as sinkholes, were commonly known to be fatal to any disposition of forces, Sun-tzu was perhaps the first to systematically study these questions and develop a coherent body of operational principles. More importantly, as they evolved, so did the possibility of exploiting them and eventually employing them in ways contrary to normal practice.

6. "Strategic Military Power" states: "The (effect of) constraints (is visible in) the on-rush of a bird of prey breaking the bones of its (target). The strategic configuration of power of those that excel in warfare is sharply focused, their constraints are precise. Their strategic configuration of power is like a fully drawn crossbow, their constraints like the release of the trigger."

7. "One who excels at moving the enemy deploys in a configuration to which the enemy must respond. He offers something that the enemy must seize. With profit he moves them, with the foundation he awaits them" ("Strategic Military Power").

8. For example, in "Vacuity and Substance" Sun-tzu said: "In accord with the enemy's disposition we impose measures on the masses that produce victory, but the masses are unable to fathom them. Men all know the disposition by which we attain victory, but no one knows the configuration through which we control the victory." Such formlessness is virtually spiritual: "When someone excels at attacking, the enemy does not know where to mount their defense. When someone excels at defense, the enemy does not know where to attack. Subtle, subtle! It approaches the formless. Spiritual, spiritual! It approaches the soundless." Passages in "Nine Terrains" are even more explicit:

> It is essential for a general to be tranquil and obscure, upright and self-disciplined, and able to stupefy the eyes and ears of the officers and troops, keeping them ignorant. He alters his management of affairs and changes his strategies to keep other people from recognizing them. He shifts his position and traverses indirect routes

to keep other people from being able to anticipate him. At the moment the general has designated, it will be as if they (the troops) ascended a height and abandoned their ladders. The general advances with them deep into the territory of the feudal lords and then releases the trigger. He commands them as if racing a herd of sheep—they are driven away, they are driven back, but no one knows where they are going.

9. "Vacuity and Substance." Sun-tzu also said: "The location where we will engage the enemy must not become known to them. If it is not known, then the positions that they must prepare to defend will be numerous. If the positions the enemy prepares to defend are numerous, then the forces we engage will be few."

10. It should also be noted that *shih* (and *hsing* or "form") are also found in an important verse of the *Tao Te Ching* that may be translated as follows: "Tao gave them birth, *Te* (Virtue) nurtured them, things shaped them (*hsing*), power (*shih*) completed them" (Chapter 51 of the traditionally received text).

11. For a more extensive discussion and detailed analysis, see the introduction to our translation of the *Art of War*.

12. "Strategic Military Power."

13. Although the character *pien*, "change," is often translated as "transformation," we have opted to preserve the distinction between *pien* ("change") and *hua* ("transformation").

14. Samuel B. Griffith, *The Art of War* (New York: Oxford University Press, 1963), pp. 34–35.

15. Griffith, *The Art of War*, p. 42.

16. Griffith, *The Art of War*, p. 43. In general, unlike much Western military doctrine, the principles and concepts of Chinese military science are not rigidly constrained nor limited to one level or sphere of application, such as tactical rather than operational or strategic.

17. D. C. Lau, "Some Notes on the *Sun-tzu*," *Bulletin of the School of Oriental and African Studies*, 28, 1965, pp. 330–31.

18. Benjamin Wallacker, "Two Concepts in Early Chinese Military Thought," *Language* 42, no. 2, 1966, pp. 295–99. Wallacker further speculated that Sun-tzu's formulations were derived from cavalry experience. However, this would require revising the date of composition to roughly the dawn of the third century BCE, or pushing back the introduction of cavalry forces, not necessarily impossible and in fact occasionally claimed, but presently bereft of historical evidence.

19. See Christopher Rand, "Chinese Military Thought and Philosophical Taoism," *Monumenta Serica* 34, 1979–1980, p. 118.

20. Roger T. Ames initially distinguished the terms by translating them as "regular" and "irregular" deployments in his *The Art of Rulership: A Study in Ancient Chinese Political Thought* (Honolulu: University of Hawaii Press, 1983), p. 68. However, in his Sun-tzu and Sun Pin translations he employs "straightforward" and "surprise."

21. Recall that Sun-tzu said: "Perceiving a victory that does not surpass what the masses could know is not the pinnacle of excellence. Wresting victories for which All under Heaven proclaim your excellence is not the pinnacle of excellence. Those that the ancients referred to as excelling at warfare conquered those that were easy to conquer"

("Military Disposition"). Some commanders, as the examples will show, either misunderstood or disdained the unorthodox and suffered horrific defeats as a result.

22. For example, in "Vacuity and Substance" Sun-tzu states: "Victorious battle (strategies) are not repeated, the configurations of response are inexhaustible. The army does not maintain any constant strategic configuration of power, water has no constant shape. One who is able to change and transform in accord with the enemy and wrest victory is termed spiritual!"

23. "Planning Offensives" states: "If your strength is ten times the enemy's, surround them; if five, attack them; if double, divide your forces; and if you are equal in strength to the enemy, you can engage them. If fewer, you can circumvent them. If outmatched you can avoid them."

24. "Planning Offensives."

25. "Planning Offensives."

26. "Segmenting in Warfare."

27. Surprisingly, the chapter entitled "Vacuity and Substance" barely raises the topic.

28. For example, see Chang Yün-hua, *Lao-tzu Mou-lüeh-hsüeh* (Hong Kong: Chung-hua Shu-chü, 1996), pp. 112–20.

Chapter 4

1. Among the most remarkable tales at the individual level is how Lü Pu-wei, reputedly Ch'in Shih-huang's actual father, helped Shih-huang's presumed father secure the throne through an elaborate plot facilitated by knowledge, careful human assessment, ambition, and money that had to be carefully executed over time. Definitely unorthodox, the success of such plots contributed immensely to a general orientation toward their formulation and confidence in their possibilities, but space unfortunately precludes anything more than a few cursory comments.

2. For an analysis of Sun Pin's thought, the historical context, a translation of the reconstructed book attributed to him, and an extensive discussion of the two pivotal battles of Kuei-ling and Ma-ling, see *Sun Pin Military Methods*, trans. Ralph D. Sawyer with Mei-Chün Lee Sawyer (History and Warfare; Boulder: Westview Press, 1995).

3. "Vacuity and Substance."

4. "Nine Terrains."

5. It is included in "Ch'i Ping" or "Unorthodox Armies" with the summary: "'If they are rested, move them'; thus Ch'i's army went to Ta-liang and caused Wei's army to withdraw."

6. The tactical summary states: "Whenever mobilizing the army to attack an enemy, you must know where the battle will occur. On the day the army arrives, if you can compel the enemy's forces to advance at the right moment, you will be victorious when you engage in battle. When you know the day for battle, your preparations will be unified and your defenses solid. A tactical principle from the *Art of War* states: 'If one knows the field of battle and knows the day of battle, he can traverse a thousand miles and assemble to engage in combat.'"

7. *Shih Chi*, "Pai Ch'i Wang Chien Lieh-chüan." (A complete translation of Pai Ch'i's biography may be found in Burton Watson, *Records of the Grand Historian: Qin Dynasty*

[Hong Kong: Chinese University, 1993], pp. 121–26.) Ssu-ma Ch'ien's comment echoes the *Art of War*'s original formulation.

8. The tradition of identifying essential traits and flaws in commanders that commenced with Sun-tzu and the *Military Methods* would continue throughout the military writings. (For further discussion, see the section "Field Intelligence" in our *Tao of Spycraft*.)

9. The incident is preserved in Lien P'o's biography in the *Shih Chi, chüan* 81; reprised in Pai Ch'i's biography, *Shih Chi, chüan* 73; and summarized in the *Tzu-chih T'ung-chien,* "Chou Chi" 5.

10. Not only did Kua's mother oppose it, warning the king that his father had forecast doom, but the aging general Lin Hsiang-ju had also complained: "You are employing Kua solely because of his father's name, just like someone gluing the tuning stops but trying to play the lute. Kua only knows how to read his father's books, he doesn't have any idea how to effect battlefield segmentation and changes." Even Kua's father had reportedly said: "The army is a field of death yet Kua easily speaks about it. If our state never appoints Kua as a general that will be the end of it; otherwise, if they insist he serve as a commander, the one responsible for destroying Chao's forces will certainly be Kua."

11. Their vast numbers ostensibly precluded any possibility of integrating them into Ch'in's army, a common practice of the Spring and Autumn and Warring States periods. However, although unstated, the intent may also have been psychological, designed to strike terror into Chao's populace and overawe them into abandoning all resistance in the future, well in accord with Ch'in's overt campaign to create and manifest surpassing awesomeness.

12. For example, it is included in the *Wu-ching Tsung-yao*'s "Ch'u Ch'i."

13. "Yung Chung" or "Employing Masses."

14. Although the translation is taken from the historical illustration to chapter 19, "The Strong in Warfare," in the *Unorthodox Strategies,* the material is originally found in Li's brief biography in the *Shih Chi, chüan* 81. The episode is included in the *Tzu-chih T'ung-chien,* "Ch'in Chi" 1, assigned to the year 244 BCE, while the *Wu-ching Tsung-yao* ("Ch'i Ping") cites it as a case of "being about to employ troops but feigning inactivity."

15. "I have heard that in antiquity those who excelled in employing the army could bear to kill half their officers and soldiers. The next could kill thirty percent, and the lowest ten percent. The awesomeness of one who could sacrifice half of his troops affected all within the Four Seas. The strength of one who could sacrifice thirty percent could be applied to the feudal lords. The orders of one who could sacrifice ten percent would be implemented among his officers and troops" ("Army Orders, II").

Chapter 5

1. The key chapter appears in the second part of the reconstructed materials, all of which lack "Sun-tzu said," being more extended discourses on single topics than dialogue. This has prompted some scholars to assert that the chapter stems from other sources, possibly subsequent disciples, rather than Sun Pin, and future analysis or discoveries may in fact confirm this. Nevertheless, the explication marks significant developments and remains vital to any understanding of the unorthodox.

2. Extensive translation notes and some minor variations will be found in *Sun Pin Military Methods*. (Our reconstruction, as here, does not necessarily cohere with the views of any commentator. Items in square brackets are probable reconstructions for illegible or lost portions and therefore uncertain.)

3. Because paper did not appear until late in the Han dynasty, in ancient times writing was done on silk rolls and especially bamboo strips, such as the ones preserving Sun Pin's tomb text. Since the states of Ch'u and Yüeh were prime bamboo production areas, asserting that even all their strips would be inadequate to record the myriad forms of conquest is equivalent to stating the latter are virtually infinite.

4. That is, in accord with their particular strengths.

5. Accordingly, cyber and communications warfare can both be considered "unorthodox."

6. Here and in the next sentence the characters have been obliterated or the strip itself has disintegrated.

7. "Vacuity and Substance."

8. "Employing Masses."

9. "Responding to Change."

10. "The Army's Strategic Power." The paragraph is a response to the broad question, "What is the Tao for aggressive warfare?"

11. The selection has been slightly rearranged for clarity and abridged by eliminating many ordinary measures, such as large rewards (which are assuredly necessary to motivate men to undertake dangerous missions). A complete translation may be found in our *Seven Military Classics*.

12. Extensive discussion of the theory and practice of subversive measures and programs may also be found in our *Tao of Spycraft*.

13. A complete translation with historical introduction and commentary of the *Wei Liao-tzu* is included in our *Seven Military Classics*.

14. "Orders for Restraining the Troops."

15. "Army Orders, I."

16. A complete translation with historical introduction and commentary of the *Three Strategies* is included in our *Seven Military Classics*. The text is traditionally identified with Chang Liang, to whom are attributed a number of unorthodox strategies that proved essential to the rise of the Han dynasty.

17. Although found in the tomb at Lin-yi and generally included in most bamboo reconstructions of the text, the materials' explanatory nature suggests the sentence may well have been later commentary that became intermixed with the text. As such, the sentences might date to the middle or later Warring States period, and are only cited here as evidence of growing expertise in, and fear of, the unorthodox.

18. The *T'ung Tien*, compiled by Tu Yu in the eighth century CE, preserves numerous fragments and a few lengthy passages that reputedly derive from the *Art of War* or are otherwise identified with Sun-tzu's thought. Whether they were deliberately excised, simply dropped out of the text at an early date, constitute supplementary materials originating with Sun-tzu after he composed the thirteen section *Art of War* to capture King Ho-lü's interest, or (as is likely) are simply subsequent expansions by members of his school or military thinkers in the Warring States period or later centuries remains heavily debated. Of greatest importance are thirteen passages on configurations of ter-

rain correlated with battle tactics. Despite strongly resembling those found in the *Wu-tzu* and especially the *Six Secret Teachings*, it is highly unlikely that they were formulated by Sun-tzu himself. (Frequent references to the cavalry forces that would not appear for generations identifies them as revisions, if not later creations.) Nevertheless, tomb fragments of a series of questions raised by King Wu and Sun-tzu's responses have been seen as lending some credence to the traditional attribution. For our purposes, they may simply be seen as reflecting a consciousness of the unorthodox and need to react to unorthodox measures that arose in the early centuries of the first millennium BCE.

19. Sun-tzu states: "If when we occupy it, it will be advantageous to us, while if they occupy it, it will be advantageous to them, it is 'contentious terrain.'" As for the appropriate tactics: "On contentious terrain I race our rear elements forward" and "On contentious terrain do not attack" ("Nine Terrains").

20. This passage echoes Sun Pin far more than Sun-tzu. Another section on the same topic from the *T'ung Tien*, while not specifically speaking about the unorthodox, clearly advises how to thwart unorthodox measures:

> The king of Wu asked Sun Wu: "Suppose an enemy (on encircled terrain) is surrounded by our forces. They lie in ambush and make deep plans. They display enticements to us, they tire us with their pennants, moving all about as if in confusion. We do not know how to deal with this. What should we do?"
>
> Sun Wu replied: "Have a thousand men take up pennants, divide up, and block off the strategic roads. Have our light troops advance and try to provoke the enemy. Deploy our battle arrays but do not press them. Intercept them, but do not go off. This is the art of defeating stratagems."

Chapter 6

1. The *yu hsia* came from many backgrounds and ranged from powerful local landowners to outright brigands but basically were men of martial skill and bravado who esteemed courage and personal honor contrary to state- and Confucian-espoused values. Ssu-ma Ch'ien's biographical section includes a chapter of their portraits, "Yu-hsia Lieh-chuan," translated by Burton Watson in *Records of the Grand Historian of China*, vol. 2: *The Age of Emperor Wu, 140 to circa 100 B.C.*, as "The Biographies of the Wandering Knights" (Records of Civilization; New York: Columbia University Press, 1961). James J. Y. Liu's *The Chinese Knight-Errant* (Chicago: University of Chicago Press, 1967) still provides the definitive study of the *yu-hsia* tradition.

2. This probably apocryphal episode appears in Chang Liang's biography in both the *Shih Chi* ("Liu Hou Shih-chia") and *Han Shu* ("Chang, Ch'en, Wang, Chou Chuan"). A translation of his complete biography may be found in "The Hereditary House of the Marquis of Liu," in Burton Watson, trans., *Records of the Grand Historian of China*, vol. 1: *Early Years of the Han Dynasty, 209 to 141 B.C.* (Records of Civilization; New York: Columbia University Press, 1961).

3. According to his biography, Chang Liang indeed found this rock thirteen years later, exactly as predicted, while accompanying Liu Pang, now the first Han Emperor, through the area. It and the *Three Strategies* were reportedly buried with him.

4. The extant *Three Strategies* focuses on broader issues of organization and strategy but generally ignores such traditional topics as military command and tactics. (For a discussion of the various views on the text's origin and transmission, as well as a complete translation, see *The Three Strategies of Huang Shih-kung* in our *Seven Military Classics*.)

5. With a few emendations, the *Hundred Unorthodox Strategies* (translated here) adopted the *Shih Chi* account as the historical illustration for the subterfuge of "Peace Negotiations."

6. *Sun Pin Ping-fa* (Military Methods), "Kuan, 1" ("Offices, 1").

7. The creation of deceptive appearances to fix an enemy in place or cause doubt, thereby compelling them to spread their defenses, was fundamental to Chinese military science. As well as being raised by all the classic manuals, it is an underlying theme of most of the *Hundred Unorthodox Strategies*, three chapters of the latter—"Doubt," "Night," and "The Weak"—discussing flags and pennants in this role. (Additional examples of this practice may be found in the chapter on "Field Intelligence" in our *Tao of Spycraft*.)

8. Liu Pang learned this lesson well for he subsequently employed it, perhaps at Chang Liang's suggestion (thereby accounting for Chang's biography crediting him with plotting an unorthodox strategy for Tai), to subvert Ch'en Hsi's generals when Ch'en, who had been entrusted with the critical northern area of Tai, revolted.

9. Ch'en has a dedicated biography in the *Shih Chi* ("Ch'en Yung-hsiang Shih-chia") and the same material appears in the *Han Shu*'s "Chang, Ch'en, Wang, Chou Chuan."

10. It is included in the *Wu-ching Tsung-yao*'s definitive "Ch'i Ping" ("Unorthodox Armies") section under the heading, "'If they are united, separate them,' so Han Kao-ts'u treated Hsiang Yü's emissary rudely and caused Fan Tseng to be doubted."

11. "Ch'en Yung-hsiang Shih-chia," *Shih Chi*.

12. For further examples and discussion of the role of estrangement techniques in traditional China, see "Assassination and Other Techniques" in our *Tao of Spycraft*.

13. This incident is similarly included in the *Wu-ching Tsung-yao*'s "Ch'i Ping" ("Unorthodox Armies") section under the heading, "'Being capable but displaying incapability' was the Hsiung-nu luring Han Kao-tsu onto the steppe and surrounding him at Pai-teng."

14. Here we romanize Han Hsin's name, who had defected to the Hsiung-nu, as "Han-hsin" to distinguish him from the famous commander Han Hsin, closely identified with achieving the empire's subjugation, often through the exploitation of unorthodox strategies.

15. *Han Shu*, *chüan* 43, "Li, Lu, Chu, Liu, Shu, Sun Chuan." The *Han Shu* contains a cryptic entry in Han Kao-tsu's basic annals for his seventh year: "Han Kao-tsu went to P'ing-ch'eng where he was surrounded by the Hsiung-nu for seven days but through employing Ch'en P'ing's secret plan managed to escape." (*Shih Chi*, *chüan* 110, "Hsiung-nu Lieh-chuan." The chapter has been translated in full by Burton Watson in volume 1 of *Records of the Grand Historian of China*.) A similar but slightly longer entry appears in Ch'en P'ing's biography in the *Shih Chi*, *chüan* 56.

16. Contemporary PRC strategists particularly emphasize lessons such as these in advocating the minimization of visible power.

17. Huan's disparaging comments in the *Hsin Lun* subsequently became embedded in commentaries to the *Shih Chi* and *Han Shu* records of the episode.

18. The incident, together with purported dialogue of advisors, is recounted in "Kao-tsu Pen-chi" in the *Shih Chi* and "Kao-ti Chi" in the *Han Shu*. The *Wu-ching Tsung-yao*

notes: "In accord with 'if they are angry, perturb them,' when Han troops attacked Ts'ao Chiu they didn't suffer any calamity at the Ssu River."

19. It is employed by the early T'ang *Ch'ang-tuan Ching* to illustrate its extremely brief chapter "Ch'i Cheng" ("Unorthodox and Orthodox"); included in the *Wu-ching Tsung-yao's* "Ch'i Ping" ("Unorthodox Troops") under the rubric "Having a distant objective yet making it appear nearby"; and serves as the illustration for "The Distant in Warfare" in the *Hundred Unorthodox Strategies*.

20. "The Unorthodox Army" in the *Six Secret Teachings* (*Liu-t'ao*) and "Offices, I" in *Military Methods*, respectively.

21. For further discussion and illustrations, see *Fire and Water*.

22. A complete translation of Han Hsin's biography appears as "The Marquis of Huai-yin," in *Records of the Grand Historian of China*, vol. 1.

23. This of course refers to the events associated with the unorthodox river crossing.

24. Although apparently a quote from the section titled "Planning Offensives" in the *Art of War*, the original is slightly different, though it still carries the implication of engaging in combat: "If your strength is ten times theirs, surround them; if five, then attack them; if double, then divide your forces. If you are equal in strength to the enemy, you can engage them. If fewer, you can circumvent them. If outmatched, you can avoid them."

25. Since Han Hsin reportedly had 30,000 troops, including Chang Erh's newly integrated army, Ch'en Yü was either deluded or the victim of bad intelligence!

26. Similar, but not identical, tactical admonitions appear in the "Maneuvering the Army" section of the extant *Art of War*. The sentence has also been understood as asserting that watery terrain should be kept either to the front or to the left, though deploying with wetlands (or a river) to the front would emphasize its defensive function in deterring any enemy that didn't want to be entrapped, exactly its role if to the left flank, and perhaps precluding the very engagement for which the army has ventured forth.

27. Essentially a quotation from "Nine Terrains," in *Art of War*.

28. Further discussion of this fundamental topic may be found in the commentaries to our *One Hundred Unorthodox Strategies* (Boulder: Westview Press, 1996), especially under the rubrics of "Host," "Guest," and "Response," and a more systematic treatment in Ralph D. Sawyer, "Conception and Role of *Ch'i* in Chinese Military Thought," Chinese Military History Group Conference, March 1999.

29. "Military Combat," in *Art of War*.

30. "Spirit." The tactical discussion concludes, "A tactical principle from the *Wei Liao-tzu* states, 'When their *ch'i* is substantial they will fight, when their *ch'i* has been snatched away, they will run off.'"

31. "Nine Terrains," in *Art of War*. According to Sun-tzu, it is fatal terrain where, if "one fights with intensity he will survive, but if he does not fight with intensity he will perish." Sun-tzu obviously ignores the possibility of a complete collapse in the face of an impossible situation.

32. Han Hsin thus manipulated his troops just as advised in the tactical discussion for "Danger": "Whenever engaging an enemy in battle, if you should suddenly penetrate terrain where you are in danger of perishing, you should arouse your generals and officers, encouraging them to commit themselves to fight to the death, for you cannot seek to live and hope to be victorious. A tactical principle from the *Art of War* states: 'When the officers and soldiers have penetrated deeply they will not be afraid.'"

33. Both Chang and Ch'en had originally supported Ch'en She, but defected to seek control of Chao when Ch'en She behaved wantonly and irresponsibly. At Chü-lu Ch'en insisted their external forces should not be foolishly sacrificed even though associates asserted it would be preferable to die for honor. Ch'en Yü's "betrayal" of Ch'en She and his behavior in other battlefield actions significantly subvert his vaunted Confucian image.

34. For the complete incident, including Li Sheng's sacrifice and his canonization as a "fatal" or "expendable" spy, see the subsection on "Expendable and Double Agents" in our *Tao of Spycraft*, especially pp. 158–63.

35. Found first in Han Hsin's biography, "The Marquis of Huai-yin," in the *Shih Chi*, it is also reprised in the *Tzu-chih T'ung-chien* ("Han Chi" 2, Kao-ti fourth year, 203 BCE) and cited in numerous military manuals, including the *T'ung Tien*, "Shui Kung"; *Wu-ching Tsung-yao*, "Yung-shui Wu-ti"; *Hundred Unorthodox Strategies*, "Rivers"; *Chüeh-sheng Kang-mu*, "Shui Chan"; and *Wu Pien*, "Tu Shui." (This version appears as the historical illustration for the topic of "River Warfare" in the *Hundred Unorthodox Strategies*. It should be noted there are slight variations in the various accounts, including whether the king of Ch'i actually agreed to submit or was merely dithering.)

36. For the theory and practice of the water ram in China, see our *Fire and Water*.

37. *Yün-ch'ou Kang-mu*, "Chü-kao Tsung-shui" in "Shui Chan."

38. "Analyzing Rivers." Also found in the *Wu-pei Chih*, "Chi Shui."

39. This version, which is taken from the *Hundred Unorthodox Strategies*, where it is employed to illustrate the topic of "Defense," is essentially condensed from the *Shih Chi* biographies of the two critical actors, Chou Ya-fu and Liu P'i, king of Wu (found in *chüan* 57 and 106, respectively). Both are translated in full in Watson's *Records of the Grand Historian of China*, vol. 1.

40. Pan Ch'ao's mission is reprised in our *Fire and Water*, p. 50ff.

41. For example, the great Ming general Lan Yü achieved surprising success against the Mongols by exploiting heavy snowstorms at least twice.

42. Imperial authorities felt that as these peoples fell within their domain, they should not only behave submissively, but evince proper groveling and respect. (*Wu-ching Tsung-yao*, "Li Ch'i-kung." This incident is also reprised in the section entitled "Assassination and Other Techniques," pp. 256–57 in our *Tao of Spycraft*.)

43. One commentator to the *Han Shu* suggests the characters for Kuei-ts'u should be pronounced Ch'iu-ts'u.

This *Wu-ching Tsung-yao* passage essentially follows Fu Chieh-tzu's biography found in *chüan* 70 of the *Han Shu*. A summary is also found in the "Hsi Yü" ("Western Regions") section, *chüan* 96b; his achievements are cited in the "Basic Annals of Emperor Chao," *chüan* 7; and virtually the entire account is reprised by a *Tzu-chih T'ung-chien* entry for 77 BCE ("Han Chi" 15, Yüan Feng fourth year), where Ssu-ma Kuang also takes note of how the Han had routinely exploited and mistreated the Lou-lan. (Lou-lan was located in Hsin-chiang, about 250 miles west of Tun-huang. For background on the earlier missions see "Ta-yüan Chuan" in the *Shih Chi*, translated by Burton Watson as "The Account of Ta-yüan," in *Records of the Grand Historian of China*, vol. 2, pp. 264ff.)

44. Actually a military commander with a small contingent of troops.

45. Tantamount to control of all the cavalry.

46. The ritual formalities of a punitive campaign are outlined in the initial chapter of the *Ssu-ma Fa*, "Benevolence the Foundation." (A complete translation of the *Ssu-ma Fa*, with an extensive historical introduction and textual notes, will be found in our *Seven Military Classics*.)

47. Because Ssu-ma Kuang compiled the *Tzu-chih T'ung-chien* in the decades just after the *Wu-ching Tsung-yao*, a highly publicized imperially sponsored project, was completed, Ssu-ma Kuang may have been referring to its approbation even though Fu's accomplishment had long been considered an example of unorthodox tactics.

48. For background, see *The Cambridge History of China*, vol. 1: *The Ch'in and Han Empires, 221 B.C.–A.D. 220*, ed. Denis Twitchett and John K. Fairbank (Cambridge: Cambridge University Press, 1978), pp. 240–56. The *Wu-ching Tsung-yao's* "Ch'i Ping" notes that "The revolutionary Red Eyebrows abandoning their baggage train as bait for Teng Hung is an example of 'enticing others with profit.'"

49. For a full account, see Feng Yi's biography in "Feng, Ts'en, Chia Lieh-chuan," *chüan* 17, *Hou Han Shu*, or the summary reprisal in the *Tzu-chi T'ung-chien*, *chüan* 41 ("Han Chi," 33).

50. The historical illustration cites Ts'ao Ts'ao's waiting for Yüan Shao's forces to go after his baggage train before attacking and vanquishing them.

51. Disguising the troops in enemy garb fully accords with Li Ching's idea of interchanging the dress of T'ang-settled barbarian and Han troops, though in this case it was the enemy's garb that was employed. However, although sometimes discussed in the military texts, it seems to have been a ploy little used except in reconnaissance and raids, such as Ts'ao Ts'ao's famous nighttime strike during the stalemate at Kuan-tu. (See the historical illustration to "Provisions" in the *Hundred Unorthodox Strategies*.) However, the *Ch'ien K'un Ta-lüeh* includes it in the section titled "The Tao of Defensive Warfare Lies in Conceiving the Unorthodox and Establishing Ambushes."

52. The incident serves as the historical illustration for the *Hundred Unorthodox Strategies'* "The Weak in Warfare."

Chapter 7

1. Most of the important events depicted in the *San-kuo Chih*, after being reworked and romanticized over many centuries, were incorporated into the *San-kuo Yen-yi*, generally known as the *Romance of the Three Kingdoms*. Differences in the treatment of the various historical events in the two are systematically documented by Hsü P'an-ching and Chou Wen-yeh in their *San-kuo Yen-yi, San-kuo Chih Tui-chao-pen* (Nan-ching: Chiang-su Ch'u-pan-she, 2002).

2. Included in the *Ch'ien K'un Ta-lüeh's* "When the Army Advances It Must Have an Unorthodox Tao," the account here follows the *Tzu-chih T'ung-chien*, "Han Chi" 54, for the year 196.

3. For example, in his *San-kuo Yen-yi Ts'ung-heng T'an* (p. 246) Ch'iu Chen-sheng labels him as the leading villain of all time. (For an insightful discussion of how Ts'ao Ts'ao's reputation became increasingly tarnished and his historical image converted into the personification of brutality and evil despite his vision of acting as a hegemon or even imitating the Chou dynasty sage advisors, see Rafe de Crispigney, "Lun Ts'ao Ts'ao," *Shih-hsüeh Hui-k'an* 6, 1972.

4. Hsün and Kuo are included in several modern strategy compendia, including the *Chung-kuo Mou-lüeh-chia Ch'uan-shu*.

5. The episode's primary account appears in Ts'ao Ts'ao's biography, "Wu Ti Chi," the first chapter of the *Wei Shu* portion of the *San-kuo Chih*. Ssu-ma Kuang's somewhat expanded, synthesized *Tzu-chih T'ung Chien* version is found in "Han Chi" 58, Chien-an sixteenth year. The events are also briefly mentioned in Ma Chao and Han Sui's biographies in the *San-kuo Chih*, though without expansion since they were defeated.

6. Literally "became vacuous," Sun-tzu's term.

7. Thus, as the *Art of War* advises in "Nine Terrains," "stressing speed, taking advantage of the enemy's absence, traveling unanticipated roads, and attacking where they are not alert" as well as being unexpected.

8. The last phrase echoes Sun-tzu's original formulation of the unorthodox.

9. "Strategic Military Power."

10. "Nine Terrains."

11. From the Warring States' *Liu-t'ao* to the late Ming *Ping-fa Pai-yen*, forged letters always numbered among the techniques of subversion. Ts'ao Ts'ao, however, showed even greater ingenuity by employing innocuous reality to achieve the same ends. (Further discussion and examples may be found in several sections of our *Tao of Spycraft*.)

12. "Initial Estimations."

13. The basic source is Ts'ao Ts'ao's biography ("Wu-ti Chi") in the *San-kuo Chih*, while the *Tzu-chih T'ung-chien*'s well-known summary account appears in "Han Chi" 55, "Chien-an" 5. The clash is also included among the illustrative cases for "Huo Kung" in the *T'ung Tien*, *Wu-ching Tsung-yao*, *Ping-ch'ou Lei-yao*, *Yün-ch'ou Kang-mu*, and *Ts'ao-lü Ching-lüeh*; cited in the chapter on "Provisions" in the *Hundred Unorthodox Strategies* and *Chüeh-sheng Kang-mu*; included in the *Ch'ien K'un Ta-lüeh*'s illustrations in the chapter "The Tao of Decisive Warfare Lies in Conceiving the Unorthodox and Establishing Ambushes"; and extensively discussed in our *Fire and Water*. Apart from stories and television depictions, it has also been memorialized in paintings and with large, inlaid screens.

14. The passage is adopted from the historical illustration for "Disposition" in the *Hundred Unorthodox Strategies*.

15. The actual sentence found in the extant *Art of War* differs somewhat: "If the army does not have baggage and heavy equipment it will be lost; if it does not have provisions it will be lost; if it does not have stores it will be lost."

16. Apart from being discussed in virtually every Chinese work of military history and summarized in the *Tzu-chih T'ung-chien* (*Han Chi* 57, "Chien-an" 13, 208 CE), the Battle of Ch'ih Pi is also employed as an illustration in the subsection on "Incendiary Attack" in the *T'ung Tien* and numerous subsequent works, including the *Wu-ching Tsung-yao*, *Ping-ch'ou Lei-yao*, *Yün-ch'ou Kang-mu*, and *Teng-t'an Pi-chiu*, where it appears in "Shui Chan." It is also cited in the *T'ou-pi Fu-t'an*, "Ta Ch'üan," as an example of failing to take adequate precautions against surrenders and "T'ien Ching," illustrating the effects of wind on fire; "Huo" in the *Wu Pien*; and the *Huo-lung Shen-ch'i Ch'en-fa*. (Surprisingly, it does not appear in the *Hundred Unorthodox Strategies*.) Basic accounts are also found in the *San-kuo Chih* biographies of the various participants, including Ts'ao Ts'ao, Kuan Yü, and Chou Yü. Contemporary interest continues high, with a movie with that title scheduled for release in 2006 and a recent, book-length examina-

tion of the clash, *Ch'ih Pi chih Chan Yen-chiu* (*Research into the Battle of Ch'ih Pi*) by Chang Ching-lung (Chung-chou Ku-chi, 2004). However, others have also questioned whether the battle even occurred!

As this battle has been extensively discussed in our book *Fire and Water*, only a summary is provided here. However, for a full translation of the episode as portrayed in chapters forty-five to fifty in the *San-kuo Yen-yi*, see Moss Roberts, *Three Kingdoms: A Historical Novel* (Berkeley: University of California Press, 1991).

17. The *San-kuo Yen-yi*'s depiction of the epochal battle at Ch'ih Pi substantially differs from the sequence of events preserved in the primary historical records known as the *San-kuo Chih* and *Tzu-chih T'ung-chien*. The clash itself is essentially relegated to a secondary role in the novel because the six chapters unfolding the events focus upon the prolonged battle of wits between Chu-ko Liang and Chou Yü, Eastern Wu's field commander. Centuries of stories and plays have essentially transformed Chu-ko Liang from a mere advisor into a brilliant strategist and paradigm of wisdom known for his skill and acumen in assessing situations, anticipating others, and mystifying the enemy, and when questioned as to China's greatest strategist, most people in modern China will name him. However, although he occasionally exercised overall command of major expeditions, according to *San-kuo Chih* accounts he rarely distinguished himself as a commander nor is he included in any of the commonly circulating compendia of great generals such as the *Chung-kuo Li-tai Ming-chiang* published in 1987. Conversely, despite his numerous achievements, Chou Yü is depicted as a frustrated ploy, someone repeatedly thwarted in his efforts to subvert Chu-ko Liang, even have him assassinated to prevent his great abilities from being exercised against Wu in the future.

18. The incident, which is cited in the *Wu-ching Tsung-yao*'s "Ch'üan Ch'i" and thus included here, appears in Lü Meng's biography, *chüan* 54 of the *San-kuo Chih*. (The *San-kuo Chih* version is used instead of the compressed *Wu-ching Tsung-yao* account for clarity. A Spring and Autumn incident—the rescue of Yü-huang, the king of Wu's boat, from Ch'u already recounted—actually appears intermixed at the end of the previous example and also appears at the beginning of "Ch'u Chi.")

19. The *Hundred Unorthodox Strategies* cites incidents involving Lü Meng to illustrate four of its tactical principles, including his defeat of Kuan Yü, the subtle exploitation of a spy, and the good treatment he accorded the populace in occupied territories.

20. The main source for this incident is the fairly lengthy account found in Chu-ko Tan's biography (*San-kuo Chih*, *chüan* 28, "Wang, Wu-ch'ou, Chu, Teng, Chung Chuan") that coincidentally contains the biographies of the two rebels with which his career intersected, Wang Ling and Wu-ch'iu Chien. The incident is cited in the *Wu-ching Tsung-yao*'s "Ch'i Ping" or "Unorthodox Armies," which states, "'If they are well fed, make them hungry,' so Chin Wen put Chu-ko Tan into difficulty and seized Shou-ch'un." (Wei soon became Chin, accounting for the *Wu-ching Tsung-yao*'s reference to grand commander Ssu-ma Chao as Duke Wen of Chin.)

21. "Planning Offensives," in *Art of War*, states: "This tactic of attacking fortified cities is adopted only when unavoidable. Preparing large movable protective shields, armored assault wagons, and other equipment and devices will require three months. Building earthworks will require another three months to complete. If the general cannot overcome his impatience but instead launches an assault wherein his men swarm over the walls like ants, he will kill one-third of his officers and troops, and the city will still not

be taken. This is the disaster that results from attacking [fortified cities]." This passage is often cited by Western writers to claim that Sun-tzu opposed urban warfare, thereby overlooking the point that assaults against fortifications, although regarded as an unimaginative and wasteful strategy, were not completely excluded.

22. It first appears in "Initial Estimations," *Art of War*.

23. The *Wu-ching Tsung-yao*'s "Ch'i Ping" or "Unorthodox Armies" includes the incident, which it summarizes by saying "'To go forth where they did not expect it' Teng Ai followed vile byways and raced to Chien-ko."

24. The *Wu-tzu* characterizes such locations as "vital points of earth": "When the road is narrow and the way perilous; when famous mountains present great obstacles; and if ten men defend a place a thousand cannot pass, this is termed a 'vital point of earth'" (*Wu-tzu*, "The Tao of the General").

Chapter 8

1. Wang Jui's campaign and his measures to destroy the heavy iron chains stretched across the Yangtze to thwart invaders coming down river are described in our *Fire and Water*, pp. 230–32. As the *Ts'ao-lü*'s abridged version, which includes the incident in its focal chapter on unorthodox warfare, leaves out major actions necessary to understand the unorthodox nature of the example, the account reprised here is actually drawn from Tu Yü's biography in the *Chin Shu*, *chüan* 34. (Slightly abbreviated, it may also be found in the *Tzu-chih T'ung-chien*, "Chin Chi" 3, for 280 CE.)

2. Shih Le's life is the subject of a lengthy, two-chapter biography in the *Chin Shu* (*chüan* 104 and 105). The incident is also reprised in Wang Chün's biography (*Chin Shu*, *chüan* 39), and the history of their conflict from 312 to 314 is summarized in the *Tzu-chih T'ung-chien*'s "Chin-chi," 10. The incident discussed here is included in the *Wu-ching Tsung-yao*'s "Ch'i Ping" or "Unorthodox Armies," which states, "'Act deferentially to make them arrogant'" is illustrated by Shih Le enfeoffing Wang Chün.

3. One of the battles prompted by Liu's effort to suppress him serves as the historical illustration for "Fatigue" in the *Hundred Unorthodox Strategies*.

4. The *Ch'ien K'un Ta-lüeh* incident translated here, cited in "The Tao of Decisive Warfare Lies in Conceiving the Unorthodox and Establishing Ambushes," is drawn from the abbreviated *Tzu-chih T'ung-chien* account in "Chin Chi" 12, for 317 CE, rather than the more extensive version in his Liu's *Chin Shu* biography, *chüan* 63.

5. This episode, similarly found in Liu Chü's biography, though preceding it chronologically, immediately follows the previous one in the *Ch'ien K'un Ta-lüeh* chapter.

6. The account here closely followed the *Wu-ching Tsung-yao* text in "Ch'üan Ch'i," which is taken almost verbatim from Lu Hsün's biography in the *Chin Shu*, *chüan* 100, one of the four chapters on the Yi people. However, additional information may be found in the *Tzu-chih T'ung-chien*, "Chin Chi" 37.

7. This incident, included in the *Wu-ching Tsung-yao*'s "Ch'üan Ch'i" and here somewhat expanded to compensate for abridgement and corruption in the *Wu-ching Tsung-yao* text, is drawn from Wang's biography, *chüan* 16 in the *Nan Shih*. The campaign is also recounted in the *Tzu-chih T'ung-chien*, "Chin Chi" 38, for the year 412.

8. Based upon the *Tzu-chih T'ung-chien*, the last paragraph summarizes the developments and is not meant to be an exact translation. (The *Wu-ching Tsung-yao* text is not

only incomplete but also intermixes the story of rescuing the ship *Yü-huang* that appears in the section called "Ch'i Chi" or "Unorthodox Plans.")

9. The incident derives from T'an Chih's brief biography in *chüan* 15 of the *Nan Shih*. (The *Wu-ching Tsung-yao* incorrectly identifies him as T'an Yüeh. T'an Tao-ch'i appears in an incident in the *Wu-ching Tsung-yao*'s "Ch'i Chi" or "Unorthodox Plans." This incident is included in the illustrative section titled "Ch'üan Ch'i.")

10. Somewhat surprisingly, another of T'an's achievements is cited as the historical illustration for "The Orthodox" in the *Hundred Unorthodox Strategies*. Although included in the *Wu-ching Tsung-yao*'s "Unorthodox Plans" ("Ch'i Chi") chapter, the account reprised here is taken from T'an's biography in the *Nan Shih* (*chüan* 15) while the campaign is summarized in the *Tzu-chih T'ung-chien*, "Sung Chi" 4, for 431 CE.

11. Later Ch'in were so named because they occupied ancient Ch'in territory in the Wei River valley, centered on a capital at Ch'ang-an (modern Xian). At the time of the clash, they were ruled by the short-lived emperor Yao Hung.

12. This incident is included in the *Wu-ching Tsung-yao*'s illustrative chapter "Ch'üan Ch'i." However, the text has been supplemented from Chu Chao-shih's brief biography (*Nan Shih, chüan* 16) and the *Tzu-chih T'ung-chien* (*Chin Chi* 40, 417 CE) because it somehow became interspersed with another episode and is incomplete.

13. The account follows the *Tzu-chih T'ung-chien*, "Chin Chi" 40, for 417 CE but also appears in the *Ch'ien K'un Ta-lüeh*.

14. See *Sun Pin Ping-fa*, "Expanding Ch'i."

15. Wang Chen-eh has a brief biography in the *Nan Shih* (*chüan* 16), Shen has none. Both accomplished great battlefield achievements, but they were bitter rivals. (The incident is recounted in the *Tzu-chih T'ung-chien*, "Chin Chi" 40.)

16. Either rowers or pullers along the shore—both highly visible—would have been required to proceed upstream.

17. The *Wu-ching Tsung-yao* account being somewhat abridged from Ho-pa Yüeh's biography (found in the *Pei Shih, chüan* 49), it elides certain aspects recounted in both the biography and the *Tzu-chih T'ung-chien* summary ("Liang Chi" 10, 530 CE), including the fact that it was apparently T'ien Kuang who, after finally moving forward following Yüeh's major victory, announced the plan among their troops and the release of the enemy agent.

18. *Tzu-chih T'ung-chien*, "Liang Chi" 13; *Pei Shih, chüan* 9, "Chou-ti Chi."

19. The incident, which is found in the *Wu-ching Tsung-yao*'s "Unorthodox Plans" ("Ch'i Chi"), is preserved in Ho-juo Tun's biography, *chüan* 28 of the *Chou Shu*.

20. As frequently happened in China, he was unfortunately less perceptive about the threat posed by the next ruler, who, jealous of his prominence and power, had him executed. The events are summarized in the *Tzu-chih T'ung-chien*, "Ch'en Chi" 6, for 576 CE, as well as his—Yü-wen Hsien, known as King Hsien of Ch'i—biography in the *Chou Shu, chüan* 12, and also mentioned from Ch'i's perspective in "Ti Chi" 7, *Pei Ch'i Shu*. (As the *Wu-ching Tsung-yao* text for "Unorthodox Plans" ["Ch'i Chi"] where the selection appears is somewhat confusing and corrupt, the text from the historical illustration in the *Hundred Unorthodox Strategies*, "Doubt," which follows his biography, has been substituted.)

21. The *Ch'ien K'un Ta-lüeh* account (in "The Tao of Decisive Warfare Lies in Conceiving the Unorthodox and Establishing Ambushes") is essentially taken from Chou's biography in the *Shui Shu, chüan* 65. A laconic version also appears in the *Tzu-chih T'ung-chien*, "Ch'en Chi" 7, for 579 CE.

Chapter 9

1. It appears in "Ch'üan Ch'i" and "Ch'i Chi." All the standard military histories devote significant coverage to the eight-year campaign and it remains a model for contemporary study. (See *Chung-kuo Li-tai Chan-cheng Shih*, vol. 7, pp. 95–116, and *Chung-kuo Chün-shih T'ung-shih*, vol. 9, pp. 46–67). The *Tzu-chih T'ung-chien* also integrates extensive materials into its summary recounting, including many of the tactical suggestions, as do the biographies of the main participants, especially Kao Chiung (*Sui Shu*, *chüan* 41) and Ho-juo Pi (*Sui Shu*, *chüan* 52). Unfortunately, there are some discrepancies and contradictions as to how some of the aspects worked, such as concealing the existence of a flotilla while also visibly building it upstream. (Because the *Wu-ching Tsung-yao* accounts are somewhat confused, they have been emended and supplemented from more reliable sources.)

2. "Ch'üan Ch'i."

3. For a complete account, see *Tzu-chih T'ung-chien*, "Ch'en Chi" 10, for the years 587–590 CE. Some aspects are also preserved in Ho-juo Pi's brief biography in *chüan* 52 of the *Sui Shu*. (The exploitation of freezing weather to harden fortifications dates back at least to Ts'ao Ts'ao, whose success was subsequently noted by the *Yün-ch'ou Kang-mu* and incorporated in the *Thirty-six Stratagems*.)

4. This extremely condensed selection suffers from errors and distortions, such as attributing the ten suggestions to Ho-juo Pi alone rather than the several actual authors, especially Ts'ui Chung-fang. However, a memorial apparently submitted by Ho-juo Pi after the conquest describing the seven measures he proposed for conquering Ch'en no doubt contributed to the subsequent impression of his role as the major architect.

5. The *Wu-ching Tsung-yao* account found in Ch'üan Ch'i derives from Wei's biography, *chüan* 75, *Chiu T'ang Shu*. A slightly different recounting is found in the *Tzu-chih T'ung-chien*, "Sui Chi" 4, for 605.

6. *Wu-ching Tsung-yao*, "Ch'u Ch'i." Aspects of this conflict are found in Wang Jenkung's biography (*Sui Shu*, *chüan* 65), though only in summary form, and the *Tzu-chih T'ung-chien* (*Sui Chi* 7, "Ta Yeh" 12), but not Kao-tsu's basic annals. The portrait appears to be part of a subsequent effort to inflate Li Yüan's image and reputation. (According to Wang's biography, he assembled an elite contingent from the 3,000 under his command and then attacked a force amounting to some forty or fifty thousand with dramatic success.)

7. Somewhat odd since he had previously exhibited great courage in attacking overwhelmingly superior forces.

8. The incident is also found in Li Mi's extensive biography, *chüan* 70 of the *Sui Shu*, as well as Chang Hsü-ta's biography (in the section on meritorious officials, *chüan* 71 of the *Sui Shu*), and the *Tzu-chih T'ung-chien*, "Sui Chi" 7, for the year 616.

9. The *Tzu-chih T'ung-chien* account is followed because it includes some important information lacking in the *Ch'ien K'un Ta-lüeh*. (Ironically, the now deceased Chang Hsü-ta had once opened a granary upon his own accord, without imperial permission, to relieve the people.)

10. For the complete biography, see the introduction to *Questions and Replies* in our *Seven Military Classics*.

11. The depiction is included in the *Wu-ching Tsung-yao*'s "Ch'u Ch'i."

12. Wang Chün has a biography in both the *Chiu T'ang Shu* (*chüan* 93) and the *Hsin T'ang Shu* (*chüan* 111), but the incident is described only in the latter. (The *Chiu T'ang Shu* chapter also contains the biography of Hsieh Na, who appears in this episode.) The *Wu-ching Tsung-yao*'s "Ch'u Ch'i" also reprises the incident in greater detail, as does the *Tzu-chih T'ung-chien* in "T'ang Chi" 27 for the year 714 CE. (The latter two, rather than the *Ts'ao-lü* version, are employed here to reprise the incident.)

13. Some versions state "Startled and fearful because they thought a massive army had come up."

14. The *Ts'ao-lü Ching-lüeh* concludes: "This is using the hidden (clandestine) to attack."

15. Frontinus discusses the use of such methods in his *Stratagems*.

16. For a glimpse of the complexity and prolonged nature of the steppe problem, see the various sections of the *Cambridge History of China* volume *The T'ang and Alien and Border States*, vol. 6, *Alien Regimes and Border States, 907–1368*, ed. Denis Twitchett and John K. Fairbank (Cambridge: Cambridge University Press, 1978–2002), or *The Cambridge History of Early Inner Asia*, ed. Denis Sinor (Cambridge: Cambridge University Press, 1990).

17. The *Wu-ching Tsung-yao*'s "Li Ch'i-kung" essentially follows the *Tzu-chih T'ung-chien* account for 734 CE ("T'ang Chi" 30).

18. The *Tzu-chih T'ung-chien* gives K'o-t'u-yü's name as K'o-t'u-kan. The *Wu-ching Tsung-yao* wood block, being carelessly cut, gives it both ways.

19. Though Wang has an extensive biography in *chüan* 103 of the *Chiu T'ang Shu*, from which this is adopted, the incident is cited in the *Wu-ching Tsung-yao*'s "Ch'u Ch'i." A brief account is also found in the *Tzu-chih T'ung-chien*, "T'ang Chi" 31, for 745 CE.

20. Kao Hsien-chih's biography in the *T'ang Shu*, *chüan* 135, is the source for the *Wu-ching Tsung-yao* passages. (The summary found in the *Tzu-chih T'ung-chien* for 747 CE ["T'ang Chi" 31] is partially substituted here for obviously corrupted and problematic portions in the *Wu-ching Tsung-yao*'s "Li Ch'i-kung." Descriptive material enumerating the many places the campaign traversed and the names of incidental commanders have also been eliminated or simplified for the reader's convenience.)

21. The *Tzu-chih T'ung-chien* has them explicitly stating that they submit themselves to the T'ang.

22. The *Wu-ching Tsung-yao* version in "Ch'u Ch'i" is condensed from Li Ssu-yeh's biography, *chüan* 109 of the *Chiu T'ang Shu*. It is also reprised in the *Tzu-chih T'ung-chien*, "T'ang Chi" 36.

23. The *Wu-ching Tsung-yao* account in "Li Ch'i-kung" is taken from Wang Hung's biography in the *T'ang Shu*, *chüan* 230, though it is also reprised in the *Tzu-chih T'ung-chien*, "T'ang Chi" 40.

Chapter 10

1. His third merely notes that all the sentences following "as inexhaustible as Heaven and Earth" are simply analogies for the non-exhaustion of the unorthodox and the orthodox.

2. Found in "Strategic Military Power."

3. Li Ch'üan could also have chosen Han Hsin's battle with Chao, whose commander equally rejected the use of unorthodox methods and troops and thereby perished. (Chou Ya-fu's battle has already been reprised in the chapter on Han illustrative battles.)

4. "Submerged Plans" ("Ch'en Mou"). (For a translation of the complete passage, see our *Tao of Spycraft*, p. 205ff.)

5. A famous quote from Sun-tzu's "Initial Estimations."

6. "Ho-erh-wei-yi Chen-t'u" or "Diagram of Deployments for Uniting to Make One." ("Pu Shu" contains the *Wo-ch'i Ching* text.)

7. This principle is also cited in Li Chüan's introduction to the sixth subject category, "Ch'en T'u."

8. "San Ch'i" or "Three Unorthodox (Designations)."

9. "K'o Shih."

10. For example, see "T'ui yin-yang Ping-fa." Even the need for ambushes may be so determined ("T'ui-fu Ping-fa"). ("Guests" are generally, but not invariably, invaders, while "hosts" are normally ensconced defenders, often fighting on home terrain. The concept's earliest articulation is found in Sun Pin's chapter "Distinction between Guest and Host" and discussed in our translation of Sun Pin's *Military Methods*.)

11. For a discussion of the contradictory tendencies regarding the role of prognostication in Chinese martial thought, see "Historical Practices and Their Rejection" in our *Tao of Spycraft* and Ralph Sawyer, "Paradoxical Coexistence of Prognostication and Warfare." *Sino-Platonic Papers*, No. 157 (August 2005).

12. For a complete translation of the *Questions and Replies* together with additional commentary on the passages that follow and historical context, see our *Seven Military Classics*.

13. Whether the book was based upon preexisting notes or is a complete fabrication of the late T'ang or early Sung, its inclusion in the *Seven Military Classics* ensured that subsequent generations would assiduously study it. (References to Li Ching and T'ang T'ai-tsung in the discussion that follows should be regarded as merely nominal, a matter of convenience rather than an attribution of authenticity.)

14. Li Ching's reference to the semi-apocryphal capture of Meng Hu in the wilds of southern Szechuan is somewhat puzzling since, according to the *San-kuo Chih*'s laconic materials, he employed a number of different stratagems and the story is not fully developed until the *San-kuo Yen-yi*.

15. According to the historical records, "In 279 CE, during the Western Chin dynasty, Yang Hsin, Inspector General for Liang-chou commandery, fell into discord with the Ch'iang and Jung peoples and was slain. The region west of the Yellow River was then cut off. The emperor appointed Ma Lung as Protectorate General for Wu-wei commandery. Ma Lung then recruited men capable of using waist-drawn crossbows with a pull weight of thirty-six catties and set up targets to test them. Commencing early in the morning, by midday he had obtained 3,500 men, a number he pronounced sufficient for the task. Ma Lung then led his troops westward to ford the Wen River. Mu-chi-neng and other barbarian leaders, with more than 10,000 cavalry, took advantage of the ravines in order to intercept Lung's front, and established ambushes to cut off his rear. Then, in accord with the Diagram for Eight Formations, Ma Lung had rectangular chariots constructed. Where the

terrain was expansive, he employed deer-horn chariots; where the road was narrow he added protective wooden structures on top of the chariots. Thus he was able to fight and advance and wherever their arrows fell, for every draw of the bowstring a man dropped. Fighting running battles for a thousand miles, the dead and wounded were counted by the thousands. When Ma Lung arrived at Wu-wei, he captured the great barbarian leader Ts'ui-pa-han. Ch'ieh-wan-neng and others, leading more than 10,000 troops, then gave their allegiance. Thus the numbers that Ma Lung executed and killed, together with those who surrendered and submitted to Chin rule, were several tens of thousands. Moreover, he led friendly Jung leaders such as Mu-ku-neng to engage Mu-chi-neng and his allies in battle and slew him. Thereafter, Liang-chou was pacified." (The incident is employed to illustrate the topic of "Chariots" in the *Hundred Unorthodox Strategies*.)

16. This appraisal is essentially quoted in the *Hundred Unorthodox Strategies'* tactical discussion for "Chariots in Warfare."

17. In "Obligations of the Son of Heaven," the *Ssu-ma Fa* states: "In antiquity they did not pursue a fleeing enemy too far or follow a retreating army too closely. By not pursuing them too far, it was difficult to draw them into a trap. By not pursuing so closely as to catch up, it was hard to ambush them."

18. Li Chien-ch'eng, the T'ai-tsung's ill-fated elder brother, was eventually murdered prior to the T'ai-tsung displacing his father from the throne.

19. "Initial Estimations."

20. "The Army's Strategic Power."

21. "Military Combat."

22. "Initial Estimations."

23. Note that in "Planning Offensives," Sun-tzu states: "In general, the strategy for employing the military is this: If your strength is ten times theirs, surround them; if five, then attack them; if double, then divide up your forces. If you are equal in strength to the enemy, you can engage them. If fewer, you can circumvent them. If outmatched, you can avoid them."

24. "Military Combat."

25. The sheep analogy deliberately echoes a similar passage in "Nine Terrains," in *Art of War*.

26. "Vacuity and Substance."

27. Whether deliberate or simply by default (because of a lack of planning or decision making) so called strategic ambiguity can thus be considered a contemporary manifestation of formlessness.

28. This passage is essentially found in the *Wu-tzu* chapter titled "The Tao of the General," the actual premise being the somewhat more specific task of fathoming the enemy's general.

29. "Evaluating the Enemy." In recent decades the task of executing such probing attacks has been assigned to heavy reconnaissance units.

30. Further discussion of these and other evaluative methods may be found in the section titled "Field Intelligence" in our *Tao of Spycraft*. A complete translation of the *Wu-tzu* appears in our *Seven Military Classics*.

31. Accounts are found in Fu Chien's biography in the *Chin Shih* and the *Tzu-chih T'ung-chien*. (Fu Chien was emperor of what has historically been regarded as a sini-

cized "barbarian" state, one of many that arose in the turbulent centuries following the Han's disintegration.)

32. For a recent rebuttal to this denial see Sun Wei-kuo, "Fei-shui chih Chan: Ch'u T'ang-shih-chia-men de Hsü-kou?" *Wei Chin Nan-pei-ch'ao Sui T'ang-shih*, 2004:2, pp. 49–55. Although often claimed as 8,000 against a million, the strength of Chin and Ch'in are more realistically estimated at 80,000 and 300,000, respectively, still normally insurmountable odds. Chin's victory is attributed to astute planning and knowledge of Ch'in's long exposure in the field as well as a recent defeat that had depressed their spirits. (For example, see *Chung-kuo Chün-shih T'ung-shih*: vol. 8, *Liang Chin Nan Pei Ch'ao Chün-shih Shih*, pp. 498–99.)

33. "Maneuvering the Army," *Art of War*.

34. Essentially quotations from "Initial Estimations" and "Nine Changes," in *Art of War*, respectively.

35. The *Wu-ching Tsung-yao* and later martial compendia contain diagrams reputed to be Chu-ko Liang's deployments.

36. For clarity, the translation diverges from the text somewhat. (For further amplification, see the textual notes to our translation in the *Seven Military Classics*.) In theory, there was a well in the middle field, and the produce from that central field was designated for the government as the contribution of the eight families, though in practice they were taxed far more heavily and their burdens included labor and military service. However, it was a much idealized system, promoted by Mencius and others as a solution to onerous government and the numerous attendant problems of their age.

37. The four corners were initially left empty, the forces being deployed horizontally and vertically through the middle. However, the middle is not counted as "filled" because they are the "excess" or unorthodox troops under the commanding general's personal direction.

38. Essentially a quotation from the *Art of War*, "Strategic Military Power."

39. See "Equivalent Forces" and "Battle Chariots" in the *Liu-t'ao (Six Secret Teachings)* and "Responding to Change" in the *Wu-tzu*.

40. For additional examples and further discussion, see "Secrecy and Countermeasures" in our *Tao of Spycraft*.

41. "Strategic Military Power," in *Art of War*.

42. "Vacuity and Substance," in *Art of War*.

43. "Disposition in Warfare."

44. "The Vacuous in Warfare."

45. "The Substantial in Warfare."

46. All, except the first (which derives from "Initial Estimations"), are essentially quotations from "Vacuity and Substance," in *Art of War*.

47. "Vacuity and Substance," in *Art of War*.

48. Numerous examples, possibly including late Ch'in regulations, are preserved in the second half of the *Wei Liao-tzu*.

49. Huan Kung, fifth year (707 BCE). The statement is cited again below.

50. This sentence no longer appears in the extant *Ssu-ma Fa*.

51. A famous discussion of equivalent forces, presumably composed near the end of the Warring States, when cavalry were just beginning to play a role as a component force, is found in the *Liu-t'ao* chapter titled "Equivalent Forces."

52. "Strategic Military Power," in *Art of War*.

53. Essentially a paraphrase from "Nine Terrains," in *Art of War*.

54. Although none of his writings have survived, Fan Li apparently developed military theories based upon the concepts and interactions of *yin* and *yang* in the Spring and Autumn period.

55. "Initial Estimations," in *Art of War*.

56. The "five phases" (sometimes termed "elements") were systematically correlated with a wide variety of phenomena and envisioned as interacting through a number of productive and conquest relationships. (For a succinct introduction, see Joseph Needham, *Science and Civilisation in China*, vol. 2: *History of Scientific Thought* [Cambridge: Cambridge University Press, 1962], pp. 253–65.) Apart from numerous diagrams in the military compendia and secondary writings, a concise explanation of one possible set of configurations may be found in the section "Chiao Pu Chen" ("Teaching Unit Deployments") in the *Ts'ao-lü Ching-lüeh*.

57. Echoing Sun-tzu: "Water configures its flow in accord with the terrain, the army controls its victories in accord with the enemy." ("Vacuity and Substance," in *Art of War*.)

Chapter 11

1. The account in "Ch'u Ch'i" is essentially abstracted from Han Kao-tsu's biography in the *Han Shu* (*Wu-tai Shih*), "Kao-tsu Chi, Shang." The episode is also briefly mentioned in the *Tzu-chih T'ung-chien*, "Hou Han Chi" 1.

2. "Ch'üan Ch'i," *Wu-ching Tsung-yao*. The translation follows the *Wu-ching Tsung-yao* account, which is also found in Shih's biography *chüan* 43 of the *Wu-tai Shih* but not mentioned in the *Tzu-chih T'ung-chien's* recounting of contextual events for the year 902 CE. (The *Chung-kuo Jen-ming Ta-ts'u-tien* alone gives Shih Shu-tsung's name as Shi-shu Tsung.)

3. The *Wu-ching Tsung-yao* passage in "Ch'üan Ch'i" is extracted from Ko Tsung-chou's biography, *chüan* 21 of the *Wu-tai Shih*. The incident is also summarized in the *Tzu-chih T'ung-chien*, "T'ang Chi" 76, for 895 CE.

4. Recent years have seen a number of revisionist studies of the Sung's martial characteristics that emphasize the Sung's aggressive measures in border defense and the realism of their appeasement policies. However, evidence for the traditional view—such as commanders simply abandoning their posts and achievements being nullified by cowardly emperors—overwhelmingly supports a highly negative evaluation.

5. The incident is contained in the *Ts'ao-lü Ching-lüeh's* definitive chapter "Unorthodox Warfare." Chung's biography, which is found in *chüan* 335 of the *Sung Shih*, notes that on this campaign in semi-arid terrain, he was able to recognize telltale signs of water and a plentiful supply was found. (In "Military Disposition," the *Art of War* advanced the concept of first making oneself unconquerable.)

6. Chu Hsi attributed the *Wo-ch'i Ching* to Li Ch'üan while others, based on the title not appearing until the *Sung Shih's* "Yi-wen Chih," assume it is a Sung dynasty fabrication. (For a brief discussion, see Fu Lao-hu's comments, pp. 380–81, in the *Chung-kuo*

Ku-tai Chün-shih San-pai T'i, ed. K'ung-chün Cheng-chih Hsüeh-yüan [Shanghai Ku-chi, 1989] and the classic discussion in the *Ssu-k'u Ch'uan-shu* catalog.) The diagram, titled "Huang Ti Suo-ch'uan Feng Wo Hou Ch'i-ch'en T'u" may be found on pp. 327–28 of the *Chung-kuo Ping-shu Chi-ch'eng* edition of the *Wu-ching Tsung-yao*.

7. A clear, readily available version of the text may be found in the *Chung-kuo Ping-shu Chi-ch'eng*, vol. 1. Most of the great collections include a variant, as does the recent *Chu-tzu Pai-chia* paperback reprint series from Shanghai Ku-chi.

8. For example, in "Yüan Chin," which is translated below.

9. "Yüan Chin."

10. "Kuei Ti."

11. For a translation of "Contrary Employment of Configurations of Terrain," see "Hsü Tung's Contrary Practices" in our *Tao of Spycraft*, pp. 488–91.

12. The method and associated criteria are outlined in the last paragraph of "The Tao of the General" in the *Wu-tzu*.

13. All except the last two are from the *Art of War*, "Maneuvering the Army," with those pertaining to looking about essentially being from "Evaluating the Enemy," in the *Wu-tzu*.

14. Virtually all these conditions are among those identified as invariably rendering an enemy vulnerable to attack in *Wu-tzu*'s chapter titled "Evaluating the Enemy." (See p. 213 of our translation of the *Wu-tzu* for the complete passage, as well as the conditions on the preceding page.)

15. These are among the manifestations enumerated in "Maneuvering the Army," in *Art of War*.

16. "Maneuvering the Army," in *Art of War*. (For a discussion of these and many other field measures to deceive enemy observers, see "Field Intelligence" in our *Tao of Spycraft*.)

17. "Maneuvering the Army," in *Art of War*.

18. This statement is not found in the extant *Liu-t'ao* (*Six Secret Teachings*) but certainly echoes Sun-tzu's sentiments in "Military Disposition."

19. "Strategic Military Power," in *Art of War*.

20. Pronouncements such as these that emphasize unorthodox measures entailing a strong martial spirit component have particularly attracted PRC theoretical attention.

21. Essentially a quote from "The Unorthodox Army," in *Six Secret Teachings*.

22. "Yüan Chin" or "Far and Near."

23. This paragraph essentially reiterates a well-known portion of Sun-tzu's "Initial Estimations." However, other versions, including the one preserved among the forty-seven chapters in the *Wu-pei Chih*'s "Ping-chüeh-p'ing" section (such as found in vol. 27 of the *Chung-kuo Ping-shu Chi-ch'eng*) differ considerably in not including any of the Sun-tzu material, but instead stressing deceiving the enemy through exploiting captured prisoners who are allowed to return with false information. (The remaining five are essentially the same, with our translation reflecting the best reading among minor variations.)

24. Certainly an echo of Han Hsin's famous victory.

25. Thereby frustrating their intentions and deflating their initial enthusiasm, just as Sun-tzu and classic Chinese military doctrine advises.

26. Evidently a pulse technique that exploits the classic technique of a feigned withdrawal, applying force but then weakening, reapplying it then withdrawing to lure the enemy forward into the ambush. The ebb and flow no doubt catches the enemy up,

making them oblivious to the possibility of an ambush despite historical precedents and warnings.

27. All the examples, emended and expanded where necessary by reference to the primary historical writings, are incorporated in our casebook sections.

28. The text of this chapter is badly corrupted, with major portions simply being transposed or repeated.

29. The four examples in "Li Ch'i-kung" or "Establishing Unorthodox Achievements" also focus on steppe conflict, the first being a famous Han dynasty episode, the other three all unfolding in the T'ang. In each case a determined commander undertook a difficult assignment with minimal forces, deeply penetrated enemy territory, and through resolute action decisively achieved unexpected results.

30. This is not a quote from either Sun-tzu's or Sun Pin's *Ping-fa* (*Art of War* or *Military Methods*).

31. All material from "Initial Estimations."

32. From "Vacuity and Substance."

33. "Initial Estimations." "Vacuity and Substance" has slightly different text: "Go forth to positions to which they must race. Race forth where they do not expect it."

34. Not found in the extant *Ssu-ma Fa*.

35. A reference to Sun-tzu's analogy for the precision of actions executed in exploiting strategic power on the battlefield. (See "Strategic Military Power," in *Art of War*.)

36. Most of the tactical measures in these paragraphs appear in the classic military writings, especially Sun Pin's *Military Methods,* the *Wu-tzu,* and the *Liu-t'ao.*

37. "Military Combat," in *Art of War.*

38. Essentially a slightly reordered paraphrase of Sun-tzu's passage in "Nine Terrains": "In antiquity those who were referred to as excelling in the employment of the army were able to keep the enemy's forward and rear force from connecting; the many and few from relying upon each other; the upper and lower ranks from trusting each other; the troops to be separated, unable to reassemble, or when assembled, not to be well-ordered."

39. The *Wu-ching Tsung-yao* includes an example of perspicacious planning in deploying and retaining a large force (so as to secure the crucial core area of Ching) in its "Ch'i Ping" or "Unorthodox Armies" section. The summary states: "'If they are substantial prepare for them,' so when Kuan Yü extirpated the city of Fan he left numerous troops behind in preparation for Liu Pei securing the southern commanderies."

40. *Wu-ching Tsung-yao,* "Yi Kua Chi Chung."

41. This is certainly derived from Sun-tzu's concept of deliberately exploiting "fatal terrain."

42. Obviously this is not true because Li Ching clearly makes such assertions in the *Questions and Replies* and in fact the citation is essentially a quotation from *Questions and Replies,* Book II.

43. This reflects the chapter's initial paragraph, "In general, commanding a large number is like commanding a few. It is a question of dividing up the numbers. Fighting with a large number is like fighting with a few. It is a question of configuration and designation."

44. Huo's biography appears in *chüan* 111 of the *Shih Chi.*

45. "Martial Plans."

46. An illustrative example—his explication of the famous *Art of War* chapter on spies—may be found in the section "Nature and Theory of Agents" in our *Tao of Spycraft.*

47. It's unclear to what text the term *fa*, as in *ping-fa*, here translated as "methods," refers. The *Ssu-ma Fa* never mentions the unorthodox but the *Wei Liao-tzu* states: "An orthodox army values being first, an unorthodox army values being afterward" ("Orders for Restraining the Troops"). In "Army Orders I," it further notes that "Those who excel at repulsing the enemy first join battle with orthodox troops, then use (unorthodox troops) to control them. This is the technique for certain victory."

48. "The Unorthodox" and "The Orthodox." Other chapters such as "Chariots in Warfare" also contain references to the concept of the orthodox, where it tends to be defined as essential for mastering expeditionary situations and those circumstances in which order is foremost, just as Li Ching emphasized, with Li's explication and even his example of Ma Lung's campaign being cited.

49. "The Vacuous."

50. "The Weak in Warfare."

51. "Whenever engaging an enemy in battle during daylight, you must set out numerous flags and pennants to cause uncertainty about your forces. When you prevent the enemy from determining your troop strength, you will be victorious. A tactical principle from the *Art of War* states: 'In daylight battles make the flags and pennants numerous.'"

52. "Whenever you and an enemy oppose each other along opposite banks of a river, if you want to ford the river far off, you should prepare numerous boats and oars to show that you intend to cross nearby. The enemy will certainly mass troops in response and you can then effect a crossing at some vacuous point. If you lack boats and oars, you can employ such things as bamboo, reeds, large wine vessels, cooking utensils, or spears and lances lashed together to serve as rafts and thereby cross the river. A tactical principle from the *Art of War* states: 'When your objective is distant, make it appear as if nearby'" ("The Distant in Warfare").

53. "Whenever you or an enemy deploy on opposite banks of a river, if you want to attack them close by your position, you should, on the contrary, show them that you are going to attack far off. You must establish the facade of numerous troops preparing to ford the river both upstream and downstream. The enemy will certainly divide their forces in response, and you can then secretly launch a sudden attack with your nearby hidden forces, destroying their army. A tactical principle from the *Art of War* states: 'When an objective is nearby, make it appear as if distant'" ("The Nearby in Warfare").

54. "Peace Negotiations in Warfare."

55. "Estrangement in Warfare." (Extensive discussion of estrangement and subversion programs will be found in our *Tao of Spycraft*.)

Chapter 12

1. The epochal battle at P'o-yang Lake is discussed at length in our *Fire and Water*.

2. A map and brief account of the campaign may be found in *The Cambridge History of China*, vol. 7: *The Ming Dynasty, 1368–1644*, Part I, ed. Denis Twitchett and John K. Fairbank (Cambridge: Cambridge University Press, 1988), pp. 144–46.

3. See Mu Ying's biography, *Ming Shih*, *chüan* 126.

4. A summary account may be found in *The Cambridge History of China*, vol. 7, pp. 193–202.

5. "Yi Chan."

6. A view also expressed in passing by Li Ching in *Questions and Replies*.

7. The proportions are surprisingly weighed to the unorthodox and in fact reverse Li Ching's values in *Questions and Replies* despite the sentences obviously being drawn from the latter.

8. Another quotation from Li Ching's views in the *Questions and Replies*, where he concludes "so they cause the enemy not to be able to fathom them."

9. "Strategic Military Power," in *Art of War*.

10. An important term, *yin* (of *yin* and *yang*, meaning secret and hidden) and *mou*, which fundamentally means to plan, but with an emphasis upon conceiving and exploiting unexpected strategies.

11. Essentially a statement from Sun-tzu's "Military Disposition."

12. In "Vacuity and Substance," Sun-tzu states: "The army does not maintain any constant strategic configuration of power."

13. "Shang Cheng."

14. "Hsing Jen," "Yung Chung."

15. "Yung Chung."

16. "Chiao Pu-chen." Although the ambushing and unorthodox forces are here distinguished, forces in ambush are generally considered unorthodox.

17. "Yung Chung."

18. "Chih Jen" and "Nieh Ti."

19. "Yeh Chan."

20. For example, "Ch'ih Hou" states that one should employ unorthodox measures and establish ambushes so that "they cannot attack in daylight nor launch sudden raids in the darkness."

21. "Ch'u K'un" "Getting out of Difficulty."

22. "Chu Ping."

23. See "Chiu Yüan," "Rescues"; "Ying Tsu."

24. See "Hsieh Ti," which warns against the enemy doing this and also "Yi Ping" ("Doubtful Troops").

25. "Tu Hsien."

26. "Huo Kung."

27. "Yi Chan."

28. An analogy found in the *Hundred Unorthodox Strategies* under the topic of mountains, but originating in the Warring States period.

29. "Kuei Chü." Also see "Yen Chan."

30. "Yi Ping," "Yi Ti."

31. "Pu Fen." The *Ts'ao-lü Ching-lüeh*'s focal chapter on "Unorthodox Warfare" concludes with several examples from across the span of history, though the emphasis falls upon the Sung. They are all included in the illustrative examples found in our earlier chapters.

32. "Ping Chi."

33. Two possible ways, the first being to change your own, as Li Ching discussed, and thereby confuse the enemy, with the second being to adopt some of the enemy's attire

and emblems and then mingle with them on the battlefield, causing confusion. (Similarly, though less likely, falsifying orders and commands, presuming that the enemy's can be intercepted and changed.)

34. A commonly found disinformation technique, some examples already having been seen in the *Wu-ching Tsung-yao*'s "Unorthodox Plans." (Further discussion and additional illustrative cases may be found in our *Tao of Spycraft*.)

35. The Red Eyebrows were previously seen in the *Wu-ching Tsung-yao* example of attacking baggage trains.

36. A disproportionately important event in Han Kuang-wu's unexpected rise to power and his success in restoring the Han dynasty after Wang Mang's interregnums. The incident is recounted in Kuan Hsün's biography in the *Hou Han Shu*, *chüan* 16. Badly outnumbered, Kuan essentially tricked the enemy into thinking Han Kuang-wu's massive forces were arriving although it was only a paltry number under Feng Yi by beating the drums and yelling with joy from within the beleaguered city. Exploiting the momentary disorder, he then rushed forth to inflict a surprising victory on the startled enemy without.

37. The complex, intriguing question as to how this could have been accomplished and why the indigenous populace, who outnumbered the Manchu occupational forces by an almost inconceivable factor, did not overthrow and extinguish them perhaps remains unanswered.

38. Ts'eng and Hu's observations, scattered among their writings rather than any specifically martial work, were initially compiled by Ts'ai Eh under the title of *Ts'eng Hu Chih-ping Yü-lu*. (An edition may be found in volume 50 of the *Chung-kuo Ping-shu Chi-ch'eng* published by the PLA Press.) Only a single reference to the unorthodox appears in the two chapters on military theory included in this work, the other ten chapters being devoted to issues of command and control. Subsequently, in 1935 Wang Chih-p'ing compiled a much more comprehensive volume that included Tso Tsung-t'ang's thinking—the *Ts'eng Hu Tso Ping-hsüeh Kang-yao* that was reprinted in Taipei by Li-ming Wen-hua in 1988. Perhaps because the compiler may have been searching for materials based on Sun-tzu's original paired categories, a brief section containing several passages on the unorthodox and orthodox appears.

39. The *Ts'eng Hu Chih-ping Yü-lu*.

40. Tso, just like Sun-tzu, is obviously thinking of the emotionally cohesive effect that being thrust onto fatal terrain normally elicits.

41. For ease in comprehension, most of Wang's examples in these translated materials have been eliminated. However, the more unusual have already been reprised in the chronological sections.

42. Undoubtedly a reflection of contemporary operational issues as well as Sun-tzu's definitive assertion to avoid assaulting fortified cities, as well as the *Art of War* tomb text fragment that states "There are fortified cities that are not assaulted."

Chapter 13

1. For example, see the introduction to *Seven Military Classics*; Ralph D. Sawyer, "Chinese Warfare: The Paradox of the Unlearned Lesson" (*American Diplomacy Maga-*

zine, autumn 1999); and Ralph D. Sawyer, "Chinese Strategic Power: Myths, Intent, and Projections" (*Journal of Military and Strategic Studies*, September 2006).

2. For a discussion of the Chinese military writings, see Ralph D. Sawyer, "Military Writings" in *A Military History of China*, ed. David Graff and Robin Higham (Boulder: Westview Press, 2002); for a historical introduction and complete translation of the classic writings, see *Seven Military Classics*.

3. For a complete translation together with an extensive historical introduction and textual notes, see *Sun Pin Military Methods*.

4. Chapter 56 of the traditional text. (For a complete translation of the *Tao Te Ching* in a martial context, see our *Tao of War*.)

5. Numerous translations of the *Yi Ching* are well-known. However, for the *Ling Ch'i Ching* see *Ling Ch'i Ching: A Classic Chinese Oracle*, trans. Ralph D. Sawyer and Mei-Chün Lee Sawyer (Boulder: Westview Press, 2004 [1995]); Michael Nylan has translated Yang Hsiung's *T'ai-hsüan Ching* as *The Canon of Supreme Mystery* (Albany: State University of New York, 1993). Traditional China also produced many complex divinatory systems based upon temple sticks, natural phenomenon, and astrological interpretations, and the military corpus preserves extensive examples. (For a discussion of the nature and influence of omens in a military context, see Ralph D. Sawyer, "Paradoxical Coexistence of Prognostication and Warfare," *Sino-Platonic Papers*, no. 157, August 2005. For a recent textual example, see *Ch'i-men Wang-ch'i Shu* or *Techniques for the Unorthodox Gates and Observing Ch'i* by Ch'en Ying-lüeh, published by the Kuei-ku-tzu memorial society in 1983.)

6. For example, *Kuei-ku-tzu Ping-fa* or *Kuei-ku-tzu's Art of War*; *Kuei-ku-tzu Mou-lüeh* or *Kuei-ku-tzu on Strategy*; *Kuei-ku-tzu Ch'i-men Ping-fa* or *Kuei-ku-tzu's Unorthodox Gate Art of War*; *Kuei-ku-tzu Tou-fa Ch'i-shih-erh Pien* or *Kuei-ku-tzu's Seventy-two Fighting Variations*, *Kuei-ku-tzu Wu-tzu T'ien-shu* or *Kuei-ku-tzu's Non-textual Book of Heaven* (in both Chinese and Japanese versions), and the massive *Kuei-ku-tzu Ch'uan Shu* or *Complete Book of Kuei-ku-tzu* in 1,045 pages!

7. *Tao Te Ching*, chapter 41.

8. *Questions and Replies*, Book I.

9. *Questions and Replies*, Book II.

10. This sort of knowledge has been the subject of a work by Lisa Raphals that includes a section on strategic knowledge: *Knowing Words: Wisdom and Cunning in the Classical Traditions of China and Greece* (Ithaca: Cornell University Press, 1992). China also has a similar, insight-based practice known as "knowing men" that is extensively discussed in our *Tao of Spycraft*.

11. For a brief overview of the nineteenth century, see Yao Yu-chi and Chao Yi-p'ing, "Chong-kuo Ch'uan-t'ung Chün-shih Ssu-hsiang te Ch'en-lun yü Shan-pien" ["Deterioration and Change in Traditional Chinese Military Thought"], *Chün-shih Shih-lin*, 2005:11, pp. 38–41. For a more general discussion, see Liu Tzu-ming, *Chung-kuo Chin-tai Chün-shih Ssu-hsiang Shih* [Chiang-hsi: Chiang-hsi Jen-min, 1997] or Yü Hua-min and Hu Che-feng, *Tang-tai Chung-kuo Chün-shih Ssu-hsiang Shih* [K'ai-feng: Honan Ta-hsüeh, 1999].)

12. The importance of traditional, even ancient, military thought in current PRC military science is widely known, being, for example, mentioned in numerous contexts in Michael Pillsbury, *China Debates the Future Security Environment* (Washington: National Defense University, 2000). Pillsbury's *Chinese Views of Future Warfare* (rev. ed.;

Washington: National Defense University, 1998) also includes a translation of Cheng Wen-han's "Categories of Military Science" (pp. 205–12).

13. In addition to those cited in "Chinese Strategic Power: Myths, Intent, and Projections," among the more interesting of the historically themed articles recently published in *China Military Science (Chung-kuo Chün-shih K'o-hsüeh*, hereafter *CMS*) are Li Te-yi, "Chung-kuo Ku-tai Lien-meng Chan-lüeh Ch'u-t'an" ("Tentative Study of the Allied Strategy in Ancient China"), *CMS*, 2004:3, pp. 121–31; Huang Pu-min, "Ch'i Lu Ping-hsüeh te Wen-hua T'e-cheng yü Shih-tai Ching-shen" ("Cultural Features and the Spirit of the Times of the Art of War in Qi and Lu of the Zhou Dynasty"), *CMS*, 2003:2, pp. 111–18; Ch'ang Wan-ch'uan, "Chung-kuo Li-tai Chung-yang Wang-ch'ao Wei-hu Kuo-chia An-ch'uan te Fang-lüeh" ("Strategies of the Successive Chinese Central Dynasties in Safeguarding State Security"), *CMS*, 2005:1, pp. 98–101; Ch'ang Wan-ch'uan, "Chung-kuo Ku-tai Chih-chün Ssu-hsiang chi ch'i Ch'i-shih" ("Ancient Thought of Military Management in China and Its Inspiration"), *CMS*, 2004:1, pp. 127–36; and Wu Ju-sung and Kung Yü-chen, "Chung-kuo Li-shih-shang Kuo-chia An-ch'uan te Chi-pen Ch'i-shih" ("Basic Revelations for the Issue of National Security in Chinese History"), *CMS*, 2004:4, pp. 115–20. (English equivalent titles for articles from *CMS* exactly follow the appended English translations.) Dozens of articles appear annually on applying Sun-tzu's thought and numerous papers from the Sun-tzu conferences are reproduced, often in specially themed sections. There is also a monthly journal on military history titled *Chün-shih Shih-lin* and the other, less theoretical martial journals often include historically oriented articles.

14. To cite but two well-known examples: The PLA press published Wu Ju-sung's annotated commentary on the *Art of War (Sun-tzu Ping-fa Ch'ien-shuo)* in 1983 in its series of definitive editions of the early writings and in 2003 National Defense University's press put out Ch'en Hsiang-ling's *Wu-ching Ch'i-shu yü Tang-tai Chan-cheng Chan-lüeh* (*Seven Military Classics and Contemporary Military Strategy*). Numerous works focused on military strategy and special topics such as deception generally include extensive historical material, both theoretical and episodic.

15. However, it should be noted that there appears to be an unresolved tension between those who want only the newest theories and weapons and those who see Chinese culture as unique and entailing superior wisdom, planning, and resiliency of spirit. (For example, see Liu Pang-ch'i, "View of Military Creative Systems with Chinese Characteristics" ["Chung-kuo T'e-se Chün-shih Ch'uang-hsin T'i-ssu Ch'u-t'an"], *CMS*, 2004:5, pp. 65–73, or Ch'eng Pao-shan, "Issues on Emancipating the Mind and Creating New Military Theories" ["Kuan-yü Chieh-fang Ssu-hsiang Ch'uang Hsin-chün-shih Li-lun te Chi'ko Wen-t'i"], *CMS*, 2004:6, pp. 55–59.)

This tension has also been seen in the treatment of military writings over the centuries. Some commanders studied them carefully before adopting or revising the principles, others deliberately ignored them in favor of experience and battlefield improvisation. However, certain manuals became disproportionately important, including the *Art of War*, *Wu-tzu*, *Liu-t'ao*, *T'ai-pai Yin-ching*, *Hu-ch'ien Ching*, *Wu-ching Tsung-yao*, and *Pai-chan Ch'i-lüeh*. The modern fascination with early military thought and its applicability is witnessed in Taiwan strategy books such as *Sun-tzu San-lun: Ts'ung Ku-ping-fa tao Hsin-chan-lüeh* (*Three Essays on Sun-tzu: From Ancient Tactics to New Strategy*) by an elderly Taiwan professor being reprinted in simplified characters in the PRC (by Kuang-hsi Shih-fan Ta-hsüeh in 2003).

16. Extensive materials on the "RMA with unique Chinese characteristics" are included in Michael Pillsbury's *Chinese Views of Future Warfare* and *China Debates the Future Security Environment*. *Zhongguo Junshi Kexue* and *Guofang* include one or more articles on the subject in every issue.

17. Although the *Thirty-six Stratagems* verges well into the domain of despicable application, one of the most popular works that emphasizes the "dark side" has been *Chung-kuo Yin-mou-chia* or *China's Secret Strategists* (Beijing: Kuo-chi Wen-hua, 1992). Even though Chang Hsiu-feng, the author, denounces the practitioners of these stratagems as evil and perverse, base and despicable, and exhorts readers to fervently fight against such machinations, he still describes numerous plots attributed to thirty-six "dastardly" figures, including Po P'i and Yüan Shih-kai.

18. The oversized *San-kuo T'ao-lüeh* (Beijing: Chung-kuo Jen-min Ta-hsüeh, 1995) devotes nearly a thousand pages just to the strategies, tactics, and machinations of the Three Kingdoms period as recorded in the *San-kuo Chih*, the chronicle of the period rather than the novel. However, none of Chu-ko Liang's stratagems are termed "unorthodox."

Other, representative titles include Nan Kuan-yin, *Chung-hua Mou-lüeh Pao-k'u: Li-tai Chih-shih Yung-ping Ch'uan-shu* (Hai-k'ou: Nanhai, 1992), a thousand pages that largely explicate the strategies found in the classic military writings, including the fragments attributed to Chu-ko Liang, but also include an interesting interpretation of Sun-tzu's *Art of War* that emphasizes the context of water management; *Chung-kuo Mou-lüeh Ta-tien* (Beijing: Kuo-chi Wen-hua, 1993), also nearly a thousand oversized, double-column pages with selections from virtually every known work, including unexpected philosophers such as Confucius and Mencius, and a section on the strategists as well; *Chung-wai Kuei-mou Ch'uan-shu*, a 1992 compilation of nearly 500 pages that emphasizes craft and deception, attacking the mind, and using poison against poison, and includes selections from the *Thirty-six Strategies, Hundred Unorthodox Strategies*, and a significant number of cases from Western military history; and two massive works of over a thousand pages each that emphasize the "crafty" aspect of strategy by Fang Li-chung, *Kuei-ku-tzu Ch'uan-shu* (Beijing Hsüeh-yüan, 1995) and *Chiang T'ai-kung Ch'uan-shu* (1996). Others include the *Ts'ung-heng Ch'uan-shu* (1994); the early *Li-tai Ming-ch'en Ch'i-mou Miao-chi Ch'uan-shu* or *Unorthodox Strategies and Surpassing Plots of Famous Historical Ministers* (Ch'ang-ch'un: Chi-ling Wen-hua, 1986) by Ch'en Wei-li that has been reprinted numerous times; and Ling Kuang, *Wen-t'ao Wu-lüeh* (*Civil Secret Teachings and Martial Strategies*), subtitled *San-kuo Chih-hui Chin-yung* or *Contemporary Application of Three Kingdom's Wisdom* with Chu-ko Liang, Ts'ao Ts'ao, and Liu Pei being singled out for the three sections (Beijing: Chin-ch'eng, 2000).

Although several others have also been published, the most extensive contemplation and thorough historical study was written by a long-serving officer, Tzu Yü-ch'iu, whose 500-page *Mou-lüeh Lun* or *Discussion of Strategy* (Beijing: Lan-t'ien, 1991) dissects the *science of strategy*, analyzing its substance, history, theorists, philosophy, strengths, role, and weaknesses while envisioning it as a scientific endeavor crucial to contemporary military doctrine. (Tzu had just previously compiled another nearly 500-page, double-column compendium of stratagems from the military writings that was published under the title *Mou-lüeh K'u* [*Compendium of Strategic Plots*], and a third volume focusing on the strategists themselves simply named *Mou-lüeh Chia*.)

19. To cite but a single recent example, see Li T'ang-chieh, "Lun Chan-yi-hsüeh Chi-ch'u Li-lun T'i-hsi te Chien-li" ("On the Establishment of the System of Basic Theory of the Science of Campaigns"), *CMS*, 2004:1, pp. 144–56. *Chün-shih Shih-lin*, a journal that reviews worldwide military history for didactic purposes, often carries articles on the role of the unorthodox in Chinese history and sometimes even Western history. (For an example of the latter focusing upon Russian tactics employed in the plan known as Uranus during the Battle of Stalingrad in November 1942, see Liao Ch'ing et al., "Luo-chin Hsiao-chiang Ch'u-ch'i-ping Ch'iao-chuo Tun-h'o-ch'iao" ("General Luochin Sent Forth Unorthodox Troops to Skillfully Capture the Don River Bridges"), *Chün-shih Shih-lin*, 2005:8, pp. 58–59.

20. The novel has also been translated in its entirety by Sidney Shapiro under the title *Outlaws of the Marsh*, 2 vols. (Bloomington: Indiana University Press, 1981) and an earlier version by J. H. Jackson called simply *Water Margin* may still be found. (Shapiro's translation basically coheres with so-called [traditional character] *K'o-yü-t'ang-pen* reprinted by Shanghai Ku-chi in 1988.) Despite the passage of decades and numerous specialist studies, Richard Irwin's *The Evolution of a Chinese Novel* (Cambridge: Harvard University Press, 1966) still provides a highly useful examination of the novel's evolution and sources. (Although the marsh disappeared long ago, authorities are now trying to recreate the effect for tourists with a theme park.)

21. These heroic actions not only "justify" their amnesty, but also ameliorate the otherwise blatant conflict with Confucian ethical prescripts, thereby facilitating the publication of a book filled with insurrectionist values and inimical teachings in a context of draconian government censorship. The novel continues to be available in two primary forms, generally of 70 or 80 and 100 or 120 chapters.

22. The *yu-hsia* tradition has been the subject of a focal work by James Liu titled *The Chinese Knight-Errant. Water Margin* is discussed on pp. 108–16.

23. Chapter 16 in both the Shanghai Kuchi text and Shapiro's translation.

24. Chapter 19, "Ch'ao Kai Liang-shan Shao Chuo-po."

25. Described in chapters 55 through 57.

26. Even allowing for the fictional nature of the work, it seems that felling a horse or two should have entangled them. This idea of linking—premised upon solidity invariably producing massive crushing effects—reappears from time to time across Chinese history. Though sometimes highly effective, it often proved disastrous.

27. Chapters 75 through 77.

28. In "Nine Terrains" Sun-tzu states: "One who excels at employing the army may be compared to the *shuaijan*. If you strike its head the tail will respond; if you strike its tail the head will respond. If you strike the middle both the head and tail will react." (How the head or tail would effectively react once stretched across 10 *li* of difficult terrain remains puzzling.)

29. The use of bamboo screens was extremely ill conceived because dry bamboo, unless coated with mud, is highly flammable. (For a discussion of these and other riverine offensive and defensive techniques, see our *Fire and Water*.)

30. Similar low-technology techniques are envisioned as applicable for disabling American fleet vessels. In fact, in a remarkable eight-day campaign that unfolded in 1134 CE the great patriot Yüeh Fei defeated a large partisan force under Yang Yao that, after arising in opposition to the brutality of both Jurchen invaders and government forces,

had forcibly seized control of the general area around Tung-t'ing Lake and defeated Sung suppressive efforts over several years. Yüeh employed a combination of subversive methods and unorthodox tactics to defeat the rebel's large naval force, including lowering the water level on the lake, drawing the enemy into shallower marsh waters, and blocking their route of escape. However, the key measure was using grass, branches, and logs to disable the paddle wheels on the enemy's numerous, different sized boats, denying them the mobility needed to maneuver. (For a brief discussion, see Chang T'ieh-niu and Kao Shao-hsing, *Chung-kuo Ku-dai Hai-chün Shih* [Beijing: Pa-yi Ch'u-pan-she, 1993], pp. 103–6. The episode is also briefly recounted in Yüeh Fei's biography, *chüan* 365 of the *Sung Shih*.)

31. Chapter 57.

32. In "Army Orders," II, the *Wei Liao-tzu* states: "I have heard that in antiquity those who excelled in employing the army could bear to kill half their officers and soldiers. The next could kill thirty percent and the lowest ten percent. The awesomeness of one who could sacrifice half his troops affected all within the four seas. The strength of one who could sacrifice thirty percent could be applied to the feudal lords. The orders of one who could sacrifice ten percent would be implemented among his officers and troops."

33. Mao even cites an example from the *Shui-hu Chuan* in his "Strategy in China's Revolutionary War."

Insofar as his military thought may be defined by the volume *Selected Military Writings of Mao Tse-tung* (Beijing: Foreign Language Press, 1966) rather than the enormous number of specialized articles found in the professional military journals or by dedicated monographs on the topic (some of which are listed in the bibliography), it's clear from the few citations that Mao read Sun-tzu's *Art of War* and adopted some of the core concepts, including mobility and especially knowing, manipulating, and obfuscating the enemy. However, while advocating the selective or guided study of historical battles, especially those in which the inferior defeated the superior (such as in his "On Protracted War"), and previous military works, he rarely integrates them into his writings and surprisingly never speaks of the concept of the unorthodox despite emphasizing guerrilla warfare. (Mao's familiarity with the classic Chinese military writings has been a subject of some debate. Although he apparently learned many of the essential principles of Sun-tzu's *Art of War* while still a student, it is claimed he never actually read it until 1936. In contrast, it is generally emphasized that he read the *Shui-hu Chuan* as a youth and was familiar with the *San-kuo Yen-yi*, *Tso Chuan*, and the *Tzu-chih T'ung-chien*. [For a brief discussion, see Wei Lien-ti, "She-lun Mao Tse-tung Chün-shih Pien-cheng-fa tui Chung-kuo Ku-tai Chün-shih Pien-cheng-fa Yi-ch'an te P'i-p'an Chi-ch'eng" in *Mao Tse-tung Chün-shih Che-hsüeh Ssu-hsiang Ch'u-t'an* (Beijing: Kuo-fang Ta-hsüeh, 1991), pp. 28–35.])

34. "Planning Offensives."

35. "Initial Estimations."

36. A sentiment much expressed in the West over the centuries!

37. For a solid examination of the text's history, see the afterward of Moss Roberts' masterful translation, *Three Kingdoms*. There is an extensive literature in Chinese devoted to the *San-kuo Yen-yi* ranging from purely literary studies through random commentaries and extensive explications of the embedded tactics and strategies. (An example of the latter would be *San-kuo Yen-yi Ts'ung-heng T'an* by Ch'iu Chen-sheng. However,

the massive work titled *San-kuo T'ao-lüeh*, which includes a number of what the editors term "stratagems," is based upon the historical *San-kuo Chih* rather than the novel.)

38. In a famous episode, he serenely plays chess while the famous physician Hua T'o makes an incision in his arm and scrapes the poison deposited by an enemy arrow from his bone. (See chapter 75.)

39. There is an extensive secondary literature on the novel from every standpoint, including of course literary criticism and the novel's history. However, more important are the notes and substantive analyses of many of the episodes from a military standpoint, especially those oriented to contemporary understanding and application. Two particularly interesting examples by PRC authors have even been published in Taiwan in traditional characters: Ch'iu Chen-sheng, *San-kuo Yen-yi Ts'ung-heng T'an* (*Perspectival Discussion of the San-kuo Yen-yi*) and Kuo Chi-hsing, *San-kuo Yen-yi yü Ching-ying Mou-lüeh* (*Three Kingdoms and Business Strategies*), both published by Shao-yüan in Taipei in 1991.

40. Although spies are frequently mentioned as having brought vital information, the novel never discusses how to employ them and most of the intelligence reports simply derive from active field reconnaissance. The commonly circulated claim that Tai Li derived much of his inspiration and methods from the *San-kuo Yen-yi* apparently derives from his fascination with the work and consciously proclaimed identification with Chu-ko Liang. (For a recent study of Tai Li, see Frederick Wakeman, *Spymaster: Tai Li and the Chinese Secret Service* [Berkeley: University of California Press, 2003]. In an earlier, popular work—*The Chinese Secret Service* [New York: Ballantine, 1974]—Richard Deacon notes K'ang Sheng's interest in the novel.)

41. Chapter 13; Roberts, *Three Kingdoms*, p. 96. Additional examples are found in chapter 98, Roberts, *Three Kingdoms*, p. 755; chapter 51, Roberts, *Three Kingdoms*, p. 389; chapter 101, Roberts, *Three Kingdoms*, p. 783; and chapter 110, Roberts, *Three Kingdoms*, p. 857.

42. Chapter 100; Roberts, *Three Kingdoms*, p. 777.

43. Chapter 94; Roberts, *Three Kingdoms*, p. 723.

44. Chapter 41; Roberts, *Three Kingdoms*, p. 318.

45. Chapter 86; Roberts, *Three Kingdoms*, p. 638.

46. Chapter 49. The best explication of employing vacuity and substance in this manner is actually found in the *Hundred Unorthodox Strategies* under the respective rubrics.

47. Chapter 85; Roberts, *Three Kingdoms*, p. 645.

48. Chapter 115; Roberts, *Three Kingdoms*, p. 887.

49. Chapter 64; Roberts, *Three Kingdoms*, p. 487.

50. Chapter 70; Roberts, *Three Kingdoms*, p. 535.

51. Chapter 101; Roberts, *Three Kingdoms*.

52. Chapter 104; Roberts, *Three Kingdoms*, p. 806.

53. Chapter 117; Roberts, *Three Kingdoms*, p. 906.

54. Chapter 51; Roberts, *Three Kingdoms*, p. 390–91.

55. Chapter 15; Roberts, *Three Kingdoms*, p. 120.

56. Chapter 104. This incident also furnishes the historical illustration for the topic of "Security" in the *Hundred Unorthodox Strategies*, leading to the saying that "Even in death Chu-ko Liang was able to walk away from Ssu-ma Yi."

57. Chapter 92; Roberts, *Three Kingdoms*, p. 710.

58. Chapter 108; Roberts, *Three Kingdoms*, p. 840.

59. Such as by the astute Chu-ko Liang in chapter 102, Roberts, *Three Kingdoms*, p. 791.

60. Two incidents show defectors providing important, detailed maps. (Chapter 60, Roberts, *Three Kingdoms*, p. 458; and chapter 117, Roberts, *Three Kingdoms*, p. 905.)

61. For example, see chapters 33 and 62, Roberts, *Three Kingdoms*, pp. 255–56 and 475, respectively.

62. For examples, see chapters 97 and 109, Roberts, *Three Kingdoms*, pp. 750 and 846, respectively. In another incident (chapter 114, Roberts, *Three Kingdoms*, pp. 833ff.), Chiang Wei not only thwarts just such a plot but also turns it about.

63. Although not exactly an incident of *k'u-jou-chi* ("stratagem of suffering flesh") as explicated by the *Thirty-six Stratagems* (because it was not voluntarily suffered in order to accomplish the mission), it certainly accords with the traditional practices discussed in our *Tao of Spycraft*.

64. Chapter 22; Roberts, *Three Kingdoms*, p. 177.

65. For example, Wei Yan deceives the guards and takes the city of An-ting in chapter 92, Roberts, *Three Kingdoms*, p. 709.

66. Chapter 88; Roberts, *Three Kingdoms*, p. 672. (Other uses by Chu-ko Liang appear in chapters 100, 102, and 109 [Roberts, *Three Kingdoms*, p. 772, 794, and 845, respectively].)

67. Chapters 75 and 76. It is also recounted as the historical illustrations for chapters 21, 22, and 44 in the *Hundred Unorthodox Strategies*.

68. The incident is the subject of chapter 13, Roberts, *Three Kingdoms*, pp. 98ff. Much of the episode is derived from the *San-kuo Chih* account, though the plot's inception—a variant of the so-called turned spy or double agent—is attributed to Ts'ao Ts'ao. (The method actually echoes a famous Spring and Autumn episode recorded in the *Shih Chi* ["Chin Shih-chia"] in which the Duke of Chin's favorite concubine, in order to displace the heir apparent and ensure the succession for her own son, makes it appear the former had tried to poison the duke.)

69. Chapter 59; Roberts, *Three Kingdoms*, p. 446. For another incident involving Ma Chao, see chapter 65, Roberts, *Three Kingdoms*, p. 498.

70. Chapter 87; Roberts, *Three Kingdoms*, p. 662.

71. Chapter 93; Roberts, *Three Kingdoms*, p. 715.

72. Chapter 62; Roberts, *Three Kingdoms*, p. 473.

73. Chapter 91; Roberts, *Three Kingdoms*, p. 698.

74. Chapter 100; Roberts, *Three Kingdoms*, p. 776.

75. Chapter 113; Roberts, *Three Kingdoms*, p. 878.

76. Naturally they all perish. (See chapter 118, Roberts, *Three Kingdoms*, pp. 914ff.)

77. For example, see Chu-ko Liang's complex tactics in chapter 90, Roberts, *Three Kingdoms*, pp. 690–91. Chu-ko Liang and Chiang Wei both use grain wagons filled with incendiaries as fatal lures, and Chu-ko Liang anticipates this technique being used by the enemy. (For example, see chapter 114, Roberts, *Three Kingdoms*, p. 883.)

78. For example, see chapter 98, Roberts, *Three Kingdoms*, p. 758. Several astute commanders, including Chu-ko Liang, also employ the inimical conditions brought about by snow, rain, or fog to advantage.

79. Ssu-ma Yi's defeat of the overconfident Ma Su, already described in the historical section, is further enhanced in the *San-kuo Yen-yi*. (See chapter 95, Roberts, *Three Kingdoms*, p. 731. For another example, see chapter 107. Roberts, *Three Kingdoms*, p. 835.)

80. Awaiting Chiang Wei's return to the area about Mount Ch'i, Teng deliberately left an open space undefended in order to entice Chiang to encamp there. In addition, he had a tunnel leading to the general area dug in anticipation, then exploited it for a night raid into the very heart of the enemy. (Chapter 113, Roberts, *Three Kingdoms*, p. 876.)

81. For example, Teng Ai even succeeds in manipulating Chiang Wei by falsely accepting his challenges. (Chapter 112, Roberts, *Three Kingdoms*, p. 870; for some other examples, see chapters 71 and 72.)

82. Not only Kuang Chung, but also Liu Pei fell prey to this error. (See chapter 84, Roberts, *Three Kingdoms*, p. 639. Also see chapter 70, Roberts, *Three Kingdoms*, p. 538.)

83. Chapter 12, Roberts, *Three Kingdoms*, pp. 91–92. Among unorthodox tricks well discussed in such works as the *Hundred Unorthodox Strategies*, leaving animals, material goods, even treasures for the enemy to gather, thereby breaking their focus and unity, is commonly depicted. (For an example in the *San-kuo Yen-yi*, see chapter 72, Roberts, *Three Kingdoms*, p. 550.)

84. For example, in chapter 98 (Roberts, *Three Kingdoms*, p. 757) Wu promises to support Shu in their northern invasion but merely creates a facade of activity while waiting for the two parties to diminish each other.

85. For example, Chu-ko Liang sets up farming colonies to convey the impression that his forces will remain stationary, knowing that the enemy will eventually capture some of the soldiers. (Chapter 103, Roberts, *Three Kingdoms*, p. 799.)

86. Chapter 115; Roberts, *Three Kingdoms*, p. 892.

87. See chapter 55. Women are also employed to gather information. (For example, see chapter 57, Roberts, *Three Kingdoms*, p. 435.)

88. Several cartoon versions drawn by different artists have appeared in the PRC and other areas, including the highly detailed *Hua-shuo San-shih-liu Chi* (Beijing: Mei-shu, 1992) and Wang Hsüan-ming's (Xuanming) more famous and widely circulated Asiapac Comic Series edition titled *Secret Art of War: Thirty-six Stratagems* (Singapore, 1992) that includes an excellent English rendition.

Two significant English translations have appeared: Gao Yuan, *Lure the Tiger Out of the Mountains: The Thirty-six Stratagems of Ancient China* (New York: Simon & Schuster, 1991) and Harro von Senger, *The Book of Stratagems* (New York: Viking Penguin, 1991). Both illustrate the stratagems with contemporary examples, the former focusing on business, the latter incorporating a far wider range of contemplations. (Von Senger's work, originally published in German as *Stratageme*, only covers the first eighteen. The second German volume, consisting of the last eighteen, was never translated into English, but Von Senger released *The Thirty-six Stratagems for Business* in English in 1995, a book that has recently been reissued.) China's Foreign Language Press also published a compact paperback translation titled *The Wiles of War: 36 Military Strategies from Ancient China* in 1991.

89. Although not the first to print it, the PLA published an edition in 1962 and their great compilation, the *Chung-kuo Ping-shu Chi-ch'eng*, includes a variant of it in vol-

ume 40. The first known copy dates to the late Ming and the first printed edition was privately published in 1941 from a handwritten copy.

For an example of a "counter" work, see *Fan San-shih-liu Chi* or *Countering the Thirty-six Stratagems* (Beijing: Beijing Ch'u-pan-she, 1994); for an illustration of the strategies—in this case the "empty city ploy"—in contemporary thought, see "Strategic Deterrence" (in English) *CMS*, 2004:5, pp. 143–56.

90. For example, Pi Tsai-yü's cleverness (discussed below) appears as the illustration for two different stratagems in variant texts, suggesting the degree of flexibility that characterizes their interpretation as much as a period of evolution and different editors or commentators.

91. It's often noted that the thirty-sixth stratagem is associated with the great commander T'an Tao-ch'i, active in the Southern Sung (early fifth century CE), while others date back even earlier (such as "borrowing a road"), and they may all have been preexisting fixed sayings that were fleshed out by the compiler. (See, for example, Su Han, *San-shih-liu-chi Mi-pen Chi-chieh* [Taipei: Kuo-chia, 1991], pp. 1–4 and Li Han-ju, "Shem-ma Shih 'San-shih-liu-chi'" in *Chung-kuo Ku-tai Chün-shih San-bai T'i* [Shanghai: Shanghai Ku-chi, 1989], pp. 420–22.)

92. For a martial understanding of the *Tao Te Ching*, see our translation of Wang Chen's meditations on the text, *The Tao of War*. Numerous translations of the *Yi Ching* have been published over the past decades, but for the *Ling Ch'i Ching* see Sawyer and Sawyer, *Ling Ch'i Ching* and for the *T'ai-hsüan Ching* see Nylan, *The Canon of Supreme Mystery*.

93. For example, see the "Secret Teaching" categories titled "Tiger" and "Leopard" in our translation of the *Six Secret Teachings* (found in the *Seven Military Classics*).

94. For an example, see Yü Hsüeh-ping, *San-shih-liu Chi Hsin-chieh Hsiang-hsi* (Beijing: Chung-kuo Ching-chi, 1993), pp. 325–39.

95. Kou Chien's successful strategy to obfuscate and debauch Fu-ch'ai and the efforts of King Wen's ministers to ransom him through similar means are described in our *Tao of Spycraft*.

96. Lü Pu's brief biography is found in *chüan* 7 of the *San-kuo Chih*, Tung Chuo's in *chüan* 6. Tung was murdered in 192 CE.

97. However, rather than *mei-jen-chi* in the chapter title, the *San-kuo Yen-yi* employs the term *lien-huan-chi* or "connected ring plot," aptly translated by Moss Roberts as "double snare." (Chapters eight and nine, pp. 62–73 in Roberts, *Three Kingdoms*.)

98. A number of these techniques are discussed in the subsection "Concealment and Deception" in our *Tao of Spycraft*.

99. Surprisingly, this incident does not appear in Pi Tsai-yü's biography (*Sung Shih*, *chüan* 402), but is reprised in the *Hsü Tzu-chih T'ung-chien* for 1206 CE, as well as the *Chan-lüeh K'ao*. (For further examples of Pi's skills as an innovative commander, see our *Fire and Water*, p. 314.) In an earlier instance Pi deliberately frazzled his opponents before escaping by a recently constructed, undetected bridge.

100. The passage appears in Chu-ko Liang's biography in the *Shu Shu* (*Book of Shu*) in the *San-kuo Chih*.

101. Ch'iu Chen-feng, for example, sees its origins in a clash between Sun Ch'üan and Wen P'ing, who deliberately left fortifications collapsed by recent downpours unrepaired. (See "K'ung-ch'eng Chi te Lai-li" ["Historical Origins of the Empty City Ploy"] in *San-kuo Yen-yi Ts'ung-heng T'an*.)

102. Ironically, the *Pai-chan*'s tactical principle for this chapter emphasizes that self-preservation can be achieved when weak by displaying a substantial image, the converse of Chu-ko Liang's ploy of deliberately displaying weakness to foster a conclusion of substantiality: "If, when you engage an enemy in battle, your strategic power is vacuous, you should create the facade of a substantial disposition to make it impossible for the enemy to determine where you are vacuous, where substantial. When the enemy does not dare recklessly engage your forces, you can preserve your regiments and protect your army. A tactical principle from the *Art of War* states: 'If the enemy does not dare engage us in battle, it is because we thwart his movements.'" (The episode appears in chapter 95 of the *San-kuo Yen-yi*.)

103. The incident is cited as an illustration for the topic of "Security" in the *Hundred Unorthodox Strategies*. (For another example of deliberately employing this ploy, see *Tzu-chih T'ung-chien*, "Sung Chi" 3, for the year 430 CE.)

104. Abstracted from Li Kuang's lengthy biography in the *Shih Chi*, *chüan* 108 and *Han Shu*, *chüan* 54. A complete translation, titled "The Biography of General Li Kuang," may be found in *Records of the Grand Historian of China*, vol. 2, *The Age of Emperor Wu*.

105. Kua-chou's travails are recounted in the successive biographies of Wang Shou-huan and Chang Shou-kuei, *Chiu T'ang Shu*, *chüan* 103, and *Hsin T'ang Shu*, *chüan* 133.

106. *Ch'üan*, usually "tactical imbalance" but here "plots and stratagems."

107. The incident is recounted in Tsu T'ing's biography, *Pei Ch'i Shu*, *chüan* 33.

108. As discussed in "Responding to Change."

109. The character translated as "prevarication" appears in two variants among the common editions, both pronounced "*k'uang*." One (Mathews # 3599) is defined as meaning to "swindle or mislead," the other (Mathews # 3602) "to lie or deceive." (Sun-tzu's famous statement in "Initial Estimations," the *Art of War*, "Warfare is the Tao of deception," employs the character *kuei* [Mathews # 3626] meaning "to feign, to cheat, cunning, perverse.") All three actually have the "word" signifier as the left part of the character, perhaps implying a verbal rather than phenomenal basis at inception.

110. *Yin* extreme—i.e., the progression of *yin* from minor to extreme *yin*, referring to the top and second lines of the trigraph, respectively—then changes to *yang*. The description is cited for the connotations of the concealed now being revealed, the facade (associated with *yin*) changing to substance (associated with *yang*).

111. According to the *Tzu-chih T'ung-chien*, the rebels burn their own fortifications before fleeing, but being ashamed at their defeat, return shortly thereafter and remount the siege. (The primary account for the sieges at Yung-ch'iu and Sui-yang, mentioned below, are Chang Hsün's biography in the *T'ang Shu*, *chüan* 192, and the *Tzu-chih T'ung-chien*'s narrative for the years 755 through 757, "T'ang Chi" 33 through 35.)

112. For a discussion of incendiaries in siege assaults and defense, see Sawyer, *Fire and Water*, and for more general measures "Early Poliorcetics" by Robin Yates in Joseph Needham's *Science and Civilisation in China*, vol. 5, Part 6 (Cambridge: University Press, 1994), as well as Needham's masterful examination of the evolution of gunpowder in China in the section titled "The Gunpowder Epic" in vol. 5, Part 7 (1986).

113. However, Chang was also posthumously condemned for ultimately surrendering at Sui-yang and for allowing cannibalism, a not uncommon practice in these sieges, as well as the slaying and presentation of his own daughter for the troops' consumption. (The siege of Sui-yang is briefly described in our *Fire and Water*, pp. 189–91.)

114. The verse is found in the short fortieth section of the traditionally received *Tao Te Ching*, "Reversal Is the Movement of the Tao." (For a complete translation of the verse and the remainder of the *Tao Te Ching* in a martial context, see our *Tao of War*.)

115. "Yung Ch'i-mou, Kung-ming Chieh-chien."

116. For an overview of how Chu-ko Liang's image changed over the centuries through portrayals by storytellers and operatic composers, see the afterword of Roberts' full translation of the text, *Three Kingdoms*.

Chapter 14

1. For a translation, see *Aineias the Tactician: How to Survive Under Siege*, trans. David Whitehead (Oxford: Clarendon Press, 1990). For the definitive study of the origin of the word (and perhaps concept) "stratagem," see Everett L. Wheeler, *Stratagem and the Vocabulary of Military Trickery* (Leiden: E. J. Brill, 1988).

2. For a translation, see Frontinus, *The Stratagems, and the Aqueducts of Rome*, trans. Charles E. Bennett, ed. Mary B. McElwain (Loeb Classical Library 174; Cambridge: Harvard University Press, [1925] 1993).

3. Recent translations of Machiavelli's works include Neal Wood, *The Art of War* (New York: Da Capo, 1990); George Bull, *The Prince* (London: Penguin, [1961] 1995); and Bernard Crick, et al., *Niccolo Machiavelli: The Discourses* (London: Penguin, 1970).

4. For a translation, see George T. Denis, *Maurice's Strategikon: Handbook of Byzantine Military Strategy* (Philadelphia: University of Pennsylvania, 1984). The Byzantines have frequently been said to readily resort to what the Chinese term unorthodox measures and (in a virtual echo of Sun-tzu?) reputedly preferred winning without combat.

5. For a translation, see *Vegetius: Epitome of Military Science*, trans. N. P. Milner (Liverpool: University Press, 1993).

6. Chapter 10 of Book 3 in the classic Michael Howard and Peter Paret translation of Carl von Clausewitz, *On War* (Princeton: Princeton University Press, 1976).

7. This refusal to exploit the most appropriate weapon for subterranean warfare reputedly was a major factor in the 20,000 American casualties that resulted when naval and air bombardment failed to destroy the heavily ensconced defenders.

8. *Tso Chuan*, Hsi Kung, twenty-second year (638 BCE).

9. "Benevolence the Foundation," in *Ssu-ma Fa*.

10. The lesson has not been lost on PRC thinkers. Despite stressing the righteous motivation of China's fighters, Mao Zedong derisively cited the Duke of Sung's behavior as an example of a totally wrongheaded approach in "On Protracted Warfare." More recently, in his *Mou-lüeh Lun* Ch'ai Yü-ch'iu cites it in substantiation of his view that "benevolence" is inappropriate to the battlefield, prefiguring the views expressed in *Unrestricted Warfare*.

11. Chou epigraphic material confirms they had espoused this viewpoint immediately after the conquest, and early texts such as the "Shih Fu" chapter in the *Yi Chou-shu* tend to confirm it.

12. *Mencius*, VIIB3. His subsequent statement, "State rulers who love benevolence will not have any enemies under Heaven," would be repeatedly employed across history to dissuade rulers from martial activities. (In IVA14 Mencius also asserts that "those who excel at warfare should be subjected to maximum punishment.")

13. For further discussion, see Ralph D. Sawyer, "The Chou Conquest and the Battle of Mu-yeh," Society for Military History Conference, Calgary, 2001.

14. See, for example, "The Great Tao Abandoned" or "Superior Virtue Is Not Virtue," chapters 18 and 38 in the traditional *Tao Te Ching*, and "Benevolence the Foundation," in *Ssu-ma Fa*.

15. See "Benevolence the Foundation" and "Obligations of the Son of Heaven," pp. 126–33 in *The Methods of the Ssu-ma* in *Seven Military Classics*. Mencius emphasizes this point in trying to dissuade the king of Ch'i from military intervening in Yen despite the latter's internal chaos.

16. "Inferior Strategy."

17. For an annotated translation of the chapter, see John Knoblock, "Debate on the Principles of Warfare" in *Xunzi: A Translation and Study of the Complete Works* (Stanford: Stanford University Press, 1990), vol. 2, pp. 211ff. Under the title "Debating Military Affairs" it is also included in Burton Watson's earlier *Hsün-tzu* (New York: Columbia University Press, 1963), pp. 56ff. The question is essentially the same as posed by King Wu to initiate the chapter titled "The Unorthodox Army" in the *Liu-t'ao* (*Six Secret Teachings*), and the Lord of Lin-wu's replies resonate closely with the latter. (Commentators have generally assumed the Lord of Lin-wu to be an actual person, presumably a general in attendance at the Chao court, but his name means the "lord who governs the martial" and he may simply have been a literary artifice for an entirely fictional debate. This would help explain his failure to attack Hsün-tzu for constantly shifting the frame of reference and redefining the issues rather than rebutting his claims with more relevant retorts.)

18. The term is *shu*, broadly meaning "techniques" or even "numbers." Hsün-tzu may be using it in a pejorative sense to mean "techniques" as opposed to real "principles," but in this context it simply means "principles."

19. A clause found in "Military Combat," in *Art of War*, where methods rather than objectives are the actual focus: "In military combat what is most difficult is turning the circuitous into the straight, turning adversity into advantage. Thus, if you make the enemy's path circuitous and entice them with profits, although you set out after them, you will arrive before them."

20. As Sun-tzu and the other classical military writers all assert.

21. The term *cha*, here translated as "facade" in order to distinguish it from the technical term *kuei*, meaning deception throughout the *Art of War* and other military writings, encompasses the full range of facade, ruse, fraud, and deception.

22. *Jen*, "benevolence" or "humaneness" (being human), being one of the cardinal Confucian virtues.

23. Sun-tzu uses this analogy in "Strategic Military Power" but with the terms reversed: "If, when the army attacks, it is like a whetstone thrown against an egg, it is due to the vacuous and substantial."

24. Note that the T'ai-p'ing Rebels and the Boxers both employed unorthodox tactics with some success.

25. For a detailed discussion of Kou Chien's resolve, the measures employed, including a biological plot that decimated Wu's food supply, and the highly melodramatic story of Wu Tzu-hsü, who tried to prevent the debacle but was eventually shunned and executed for his efforts, see "Systematic Programs and Psychological Warfare" in our *Tao*

of Spycraft, pp. 232–43. For a contemporary discussion by a high-ranking PRC strategist, see Wu Ch'un-ch'iu, "The War between Wu and Yüeh for Supremacy: Grand Strategy and Strategists" ("Wu Yüeh Cheng-pa chih Chan: T'a Chan-lüeh yü Chan-lüeh-chia"), *CMS*, 2004:2, pp. 72–82. (Wu's views and his book *Grand Strategy* are discussed by Pillsbury in *China Debates the Future Security Environment*, pp. 207ff.)

26. For an overview of the Chou's rise and overthrow of the Shang, see the introduction to our translation of the *Six Secret Teachings* in our *Seven Military Classics* or the more extensive analysis in our single-volume *The Six Secret Teachings on the Way of Strategy* (Boston: Shambhala, 1997). (The conquest expedition and subsequent second campaign are analyzed in detail in Sawyer, "The Chou Conquest and the Battle of Mu-yeh.")

27. "Civil Offensive." Han Fei-tzu, another Warring States thinker, described numerous ways in which court officials manipulate the ruler that can similarly be employed for subversive purposes. (For a discussion, see "Political Intelligence" in our *Tao of Spycraft*.)

28. A complete translation of the chapter will be found in the *Six Secret Teachings* portion of our *Seven Military Classics*, as well as in the *Tao of Spycraft* section on subversive programs.

29. For further discussion of these Taoist concepts in a military vein, see the introduction to our *Tao of War*; for a complete translation of the *Three Strategies*, see our *Seven Military Classics*.

30. For further discussion, see "Secrecy and Countermeasures," in our *Tao of Spycraft*.

31. For further discussion of historic China's external campaigns, see Ralph D. Sawyer, "Preemptive and Punitive Strikes: China's Campaigns of Aggression," Society for Military History Conference, Washington, DC, 2004. (Much of the discussion that follows is adopted from Sawyer, "Chinese Strategic Power: Myths, Intent, and Projections" that appears in the September 2006 issue of *The Journal of Military and Strategic Studies*, available online, and may be consulted for further discussion and amplifications, particularly of potential sabotage targets and methods.)

32. See, for example (in addition to the references found in "Chinese Strategic Power"), T'ao Ming-pao, "Kuan-yü Wu-te Chia-chih-shuo te chi-ko Chi-pen Wen-t'i" ("On Basic Issues of the Idea of Value of Military Virtues"), *CMS*, 2005:4, pp. 116–25.

33. For examples and further discussion, see Sawyer and Sawyer, *Tao of Spycraft*, pp. 1–3.

34. Although an English language history of the Warring States remains to be written, *The Cambridge History of Ancient China: From the Origins of Civilization to 221 B.C.*, ed. Michael Loewe and Edward L. Shaughnessy (Cambridge: Cambridge University Press, 1999) contains a useful overview.

35. Although Mao Zedong compared strategy with a game of *wei-ch'i*, David Lai has recently expanded the analogy with a well-known publication *Learning from the Stones: A Go Approach to Mastering China's Strategic Concept*, Shi (Washington: Strategic Studies Institute, 2004). China's quest for world domination has been widely discussed in recent years, including by Ross Terrill in *The New Chinese Empire and What It Means for the United States* (New York: Basic Books, 2003), and several authors have charted possible programs for world conquest, the latest being an eight-stage PRC strategy projection unfolded by Constantine Menges in *China: The Gathering Threat* (Nashville: Nelson Current, 2005).

36. "Ch'in-yü," 3 and 4, *Chan-kuo Ts'e.*

37. "Chao-yü," *Chan-kuo Ts'e.*

38. A translation of the book attributed to Wei Liao-tzu will be found in our *Seven Military Classics.*

39. *Shih Chi,* "Li Ssu Lieh-chuan." For a complete account of this episode, see our *Tao of Spycraft* or Sawyer, "Chinese Strategic Power."

40. For a recent PRC assessment of Sun-tzu's concept of balking alliances, see Yao Huai-ning and Wang Ch'en-ch'ing, "On Sun-tzu's Strategy of 'Attacking their Alliances'" ("Ye T'an *Sun-tzu Ping-fa* te 'Fa-chiao' Ssu-hsiang"), *CMS,* 2004:5, pp. 126–31. For an even earlier Warring States model, see Li Hung-ch'eng and Jen Li, "Juo Yen Niu-chuan Chan-lüeh T'ai-shih Chan-sheng Ch'iang Ch'i te Ts'e-lüeh Yün-yung" ("Strategic Application of Weak Yen in Defeating Strong Ch'i by Transforming Strategic Position"), *CMS,* 2003:1, pp. 131–37.

41. The case of a Japanese diplomat assigned to the PRC who recently committed suicide rather than succumb to blackmail efforts as a result of a *mei-jen-chi* is only the latest of many known examples.

42. Mao Zedong's heritage concept of people's war, despite being conspicuously outmoded, has been reborn as information warfare, as cyber attacks employing tens of thousands to infiltrate and manipulate, when desired, information-based capabilities.

43. The issue of influencing academic institutions and carrying forward cultural warfare was discussed in "Strategic Political Work and Strategic Psychological Warfare," *CMS,* 2005:3, pp. 144–56.

44. "Deceiving the Enemy." In the context of deceiving the enemy, Hsü speaks about "employing the unorthodox to conquer, the essential Tao of the military."

45. For a discussion of the "ruthless practice of efficient warfare"—my characterization for Sun-tzu's vision—see the introduction to *The Essential Art of War,* trans. Ralph D. Sawyer and Mei-Chün Lee Sawyer (Cambridge: Basic Books, 2005).

46. Ch'iao Liang and Wang Hsiang-sui's *Unrestricted Warfare,* originally published in Chinese by the PLA in 1999, has been translated by the Foreign Broadcast Information Service.

In addition to *Unrestricted Warfare,* two far more extreme, clearly unorthodox formulations nominally identified with the former Minister of Defense Ch'ih Hao-t'ien have recently been circulating: "The War Is Approaching Us" and "War Is Not Far from Us and Is the Midwife of the Chinese Century." Citing the lessons of the Warring States period and viewing war with the United States as inevitable, the author essentially advocates the abandonment of all restraints and the eventual implementation of a biologically based genocidal program to be implemented through clandestine means in the United States and Canada preliminary to their occupation by the ever expanding Chinese populace. (The articles are widely available in English translation on the Web. However, for a brief analysis of their content and possible implications in the contemporary geostrategic environment, see Sawyer, "Chinese Strategic Power." How such xenophobic diatribes of conquest are to be evaluated remains an open question.)

47. *Unrestricted Warfare,* pp. 206–7.

48. The idea of manipulating and controlling others by seizing what they love is briefly articulated in "Nine Terrains."

49. The critical role of unity is discussed in the first chapter of the *Art of War*, "Initial Estimations."

50. For example, the idea of war in depth is seen in Kao Heng's article "Future Military Trends" (in *Chinese Views of Future Warfare*, ed. Michael Pillsbury [Washington: National Defense University Press, 1997], pp. 85–94). Ch'en Huan also discussed the broadening of the battlefield and elimination of traditional bounds in a 1996 article that emphasizes paralyzing the enemy's fundamental capabilities. (See "The Third Military Revolution" in *Chinese Views of Future Warfare*, pp. 389–98.) Other articles have concluded that there will no longer be a distinction between combatants and non-combatants, including Pi Ts'ang-keng's "On the Soft Casualty in Modern Wars" ("Shih-che Hsien-tai Chan-cheng Juan-sha-shang"), *CMS*, 2003:5, pp. 122–26, and Niu Li and Wu Chi-feng's "On the New Concepts of Chinese Military Strategy in the 21st Century" ("Shih-lun 21 Shih-chi Chung-kuo Chün-shih Chan-lüeh Hsin-kuan-nien"), *CMS*, 2003:2, pp. 85–90. All of these of course continue the thrust of Mao's earlier military writings.

51. "Agricultural Implements."

52. "Martial Plans." The *Tao Te Ching* states: "Under Heaven there is nothing more pliant and weak than water,/ But for attacking the firm and strong nothing surpasses it,/ Nothing can be exchanged for it." (Chapter 78 of the traditionally received text, translated per Wang Chen's understanding.)

53. For a historical overview, see our *Fire and Water*.

54. "Strategic Military Power." In "Ch'i Fa," the *Kuan-tzu* likens the army's power to a flood. (For a discussion of the concept of *shih* or "strategic configuration of power" [in my terminology], see our *Art of War*, pp. 143–47. For a recent, expanded study of the concept in Chinese military history, see William H. Mott and Jae Chang Kim, *The Philosophy of Chinese Military Culture: Shih vs. Li* [New York: Palgrave, 2006].)

55. Again, for a systematic discussion, see our *Fire and Water*. Some of the scenarios envisioned for the invasion of Taiwan predict significant subversive activity and numerous, preliminary acts of sabotage that will target the infrastructure, especially the electricity grid and water supplies. See, for example, Denny Roy, "Tensions in the Taiwan Strait," *Survival* 42, no. 1, Spring 2000, pp. 76–96.

56. Recent journal articles have begun to explore the concept and value of "deterrence." However, the main coercive threat to the U.S. is likely to be from nuclear missiles launched by undetected submarines lurking in littoral waters.

57. For a translation, see "The Biographies of the Wandering Knights," in *Records of the Grand Historian of China*, vol. 2.

58. For a translation of the chapter, see "The Biographies of the Assassin-retainers," in *Records of the Grand Historian: Qin Dynasty*.

59. To which the question—"ally against whom, the Martians or the Venusians?"—might be asked.

Selected Bibliographies

Three selected (rather than comprehensive) bibliographies are provided below. The first includes a broad range of English language works relevant to Chinese history and contemporary issues; the second encompasses a number of contextual writings useful in determining the comparative nature of the unorthodox; and the third consists of fundamental Chinese language works. (Chinese character titles have not been provided for contemporary articles because citations in the text already include both Romanized and translated renditions.)

Chinese Historical and Contemporary Issues

Adshead, S. A. M. *China in World History*. 3rd ed. New York: St. Martin's Press, 2000.

Ames, Roger. *Sun-tzu: The Art of Warfare*. New York: Ballantine Books, 1993.

Barnes, R. H., Andrew Gray, and Benedict Kingsbury, eds. *Indigenous Peoples of Asia*. Monograph and Occasional Paper series, 48. Ann Arbor: Association for Asian Studies, 1995.

Bernstein, Richard and Ross H. Munro. *The Coming Conflict with China*. New York: Alfred A. Knopf, 1997.

Billingsley, Phil. *Bandits in Republican China*. Stanford: Stanford University Press, 1988.

Binnendijk, Hans and Ronald N. Montaperto, eds. *Strategic Trends in China*. Washington: Institute for National Strategic Studies, 1998.

Bishop, John L. *Studies of Governmental Institutions in Chinese History*. Cambridge: Harvard University Press, 1968.

Blasko, Dennis J. "Chinese Army Modernization: An Overview." *Military Review*, September–October 2005, pp. 68–74.

Booth, Martin. *The Triads: The Growing Global Threat from the Chinese Criminal Societies*. New York: St. Martin's Press, 1990.

Bracken, Paul. *Fire in the East: The Rise of Asian Military Power and the Second Nuclear Age*. New York: HarperCollins, 1999.

Brandauer, Frederick P. and Chun-chieh Huang, eds. *Imperial Rulership and Cultural Change in Traditional China*. Seattle: University of Washington Press, 1994.

Brooks, E. Bruce and A. Taeko Brooks. *The Original Analects: Sayings of Confucius and His Successors*. New York: Columbia University Press, 1998.

Brzezinski, Zbigniew. "Living with China." *The National Interest*, Spring 2000, pp. 5–21.

Burkitt, Laurie, Andrew Scobell, and Larry M. Wortzel, eds. *The Lessons of History: The Chinese People's Liberation Army at 75.* Washington: Strategic Studies Institute, 2003.

Burles, Mark and Abram N. Shulsky. *Patterns in China's Use of Force: Evidence from History and Doctrinal Writings.* Washington: Rand, 2000.

Caddell, Joseph W. *Deception 101—Primer on Deception.* Washington: Strategic Studies Institute, 2004.

Carpenter, William M. and David G. Wieneck, eds. *Asian Security Handbook: Terrorism and the New Security Environment.* Armonk: M. E. Sharpe, Inc., 2005.

Chai, Winberg. *Essential Works of Chinese Communism: Mao Tse-tung, Liu Shao-chi, Lin Piao, P'eng Chen.* New York: Bantam Books, 1969.

Chan, Albert. *The Glory and Fall of the Ming Dynasty.* Norman: University of Oklahoma Press, 1982.

Chang, Kwang-chih. *Art, Myth, and Ritual: The Path to Political Authority in Ancient China.* Cambridge: Harvard University Press, 1983.

Ch'i, Hsi-sheng. *Warlord Politics in China 1916–1928.* Stanford: Stanford University Press, 1976.

Ch'ü, T'ung-tsu. *Law and Society in Traditional China.* La Havre: Mouton & Co., 1965.

Cole, Bernard D. *The Great Wall at Sea: China's Navy Enters the Twenty-first Century.* Annapolis: Naval Institute Press, 2001.

Creel, Herrlee Glessner. *The Origins of Statecraft in China.* Chicago: University of Chicago Press, 1970.

Crossley, Pamela Kyle. *The Manchus.* Cambridge: Blackwell Publishers, 1997.

Currey, Cecil B. *Victory at Any Cost: The Genius of Viet Nam's Gen. Vo Nguyen Giap.* Dulles: Potomac Books, (1997) 2005.

Dardess, John W. *Conquerors and Confucians: Aspects of Political Change in Late Yüan China.* New York: Columbia University Press, 1973.

Deacon, Richard. *The Chinese Secret Service.* New York: Ballantine Books, 1974.

Deng, Yong. "Hegemon on the Offensive: Chinese Perspectives on U.S. Global Strategy." *Political Science Quarterly,* Fall 2001.

Di Cosmo, Nicola. *Ancient China and its Enemies: The Rise of Nomadic Power in East Asian History.* Cambridge: Cambridge University Press, 2002.

Di Cosmo, Nicola, ed. *Warfare in Inner Asian History (500–1800).* Leiden: E. J. Brill, 2002.

Dibb, Paul. "The Revolution in Military Affairs and Asian Security." *Survival* 39, no. 4, Winter 1997–1998, pp. 93–116.

Dien, Albert E., ed. *State and Society in Early Medieval China.* Stanford: Stanford University Press, 1990.

Dubs, Homer H. *The History of the Former Han Dynasty.* 3 vols. Baltimore: Waverly Press, 1955.

Duiker, William J. *China and Vietnam: The Roots of Conflict.* Berkeley: University of California, 1986.

Eberhard, Wolfram. *Conquerors and Rulers: Social Forces in Medieval China.* Leiden: E. J. Brill, 1970.

Eftimiades, Nicholas, *Chinese Intelligence Operations.* Annapolis: Naval Institute Press, 1994.

Eikenberry, Karl W. *Explaining and Influencing Chinese Arms Transfers.* Washington: Institute for National Strategic Studies, 1995.

Elleman, Bruce A. *Modern Chinese Warfare, 1795–1989.* New York: Routledge, 2001.

Ellis, R. Evan. *U.S. National Security Implications of Chinese Involvement in Latin America.* Washington: Strategic Studies Institute, June 2005.

Esherick, Joseph W. *The Origins of the Boxer Uprising.* Berkeley: University of California Press, 1987.

Fairbank, John King. *China: A New History.* Cambridge: Harvard University Press, 1992.

Fairbank, John K. and Kwang-Ching Liu, ed. *The Cambridge History of China.* Vols. 10–11: *Late Ch'ing, 1800–1911, Parts 1 and 2.* Cambridge: Cambridge University Press, 1978, 1980.

Faligot, Roger and Remi Kauffer. *The Chinese Secret Service: Kang Sheng and the Shadow Government in Red China.* Trans. Christine Donougher. New York: William Morrow, 1989.

Feigenbaum, Evan A. *China's Techno-warriors: National Security and Strategic Competition from the Nuclear to the Information Age.* Stanford: Stanford University Press, 2003.

Gardner, Charles S. *Chinese Traditional Historiography.* Harvard Historical Monographs, v. 11. Cambridge: Harvard University Press, 1961.

Gauthier, Kathryn L. *China as Peer Competitor? Trends in Nuclear Weapons, Space, and Information Warfare.* Maxwell Air Force Base: Air War College, 1999.

Goldman, Merle and Andrew Gordon, eds. *Historical Perspectives on Contemporary East Asia.* Cambridge: Harvard University Press, 2000.

Goldstein, Avery. *Rising to the Challenge: China's Grand Strategy and International Security.* Stanford: Stanford University Press, 2005.

Graff, David A. *Medieval Chinese Warfare, 300–900.* New York: Routledge, 2002.

Graff, David A. and Robin Higham. *A Military History of China.* Boulder: Westview Press, 2002.

Griffith, Samuel B. *Mao Tse-tung on Guerrilla Warfare.* New York: Praeger Publishers, 1961.

Griffith, Samuel B. *Sun Tzu: The Art of War.* London: Oxford University Press, (1963) 1971.

Grousset, Rene. *The Empire of the Steppes: A History of Central Asia.* Trans. Naomi Walford. New Brunswick: Rutgers University Press, 1970.

Groussett, Rene. *The Rise and Splendour of the Chinese Empire.* Trans. Anthony Watson-Gandy and Terence Gordon. Berkeley: University of California Press, 1958.

Guo Ji-wei and Xue-sen Yang. "Ultramicro, Nonlethal, and Reversible: Looking Ahead to Military Biotechnology." *Military Review,* July–August 2005, pp. 75–78.

Halloran, Richard. "Taiwan." *Parameters,* Spring 2003, pp. 22–34.

Hildinger, Erik. *Warriors of the Steppe: A Military History of Central Asia, 500 B.C. to 1700 A.D.* New York: Sarpedon, 1997.

Hsiao, Ch'i-ch'ing. *The Military Establishment of the Yuan Dynasty.* Cambridge: Harvard University Press, 1978.

Hsiung, James C., ed. *China's Bitter Victory: The War with Japan, 1937–1945.* Armonk: M. E. Sharpe, Inc., 1992.

Hsu, Cho-yun. *Ancient China in Transition: An Analysis of Social Mobility, 722–222 BC.* Stanford: Stanford University Press, 1965.

Hsu, Cho-yun and Katheryn M. Linduff. *Western Chou Civilization.* Early Chinese Civilization. New Haven: Yale University Press, 1988.

Hucker, Charles. *The Traditional Chinese State in Ming Times (1368–1644).* Tucson: University of Arizona Press, 1961.

Hui, Victoria Tin-bor. *War and State Formation in Ancient China and Early Modern Europe.* New York: Cambridge University Press, 2005.

Huters, Theodore, R. Bin Wong, and Pauline Yu, eds. *Culture & State in Chinese History: Conventions, Accommodations, and Critiques.* Stanford: Stanford University Press, 1997.

Jagchid, Sechin. *Peace, War and Trade along the Great Wall: Nomadic-Chinese Interaction through Two Millennia.* Trans. Jay Van Symons. Bloomington: Indiana University Press, 1989.

Joffe, Ellis. *The Chinese Army After Mao.* Cambridge: Harvard University Press, 1987.

Johnson-Freese, Joan, "China's Manned Space Program: Sun Tzu or Apollo Redux?" *Naval War College Review,* Summer 2003.

Johnston, Alastair Iain. *Cultural Realism: Strategic Culture and Grand Strategy in Chinese History.* Princeton: Princeton University Press, 1995.

Jullien, Francois. *A Treatise on Efficacy: Between Western and Chinese Thinking.* Trans. Janet Lloyd. Honolulu: University of Hawaii Press, 2004.

Jullien, Francois. *The Propensity of Things: Toward a History of Efficacy in China.* Trans. Janet Lloyd. New York: Urzone, Inc., 1995.

Keightley, David N. *Sources of Shang History: The Oracle-Bone Inscriptions of Bronze Age China.* Berkeley: University of California Press, 1978.

Keightley, David N., ed. *The Origins of Chinese Civilization.* Studies on China, 1. Berkeley: University of California Press, 1983.

Khalilzad, Zalmay M. et al. *The United States and a Rising China: Strategic and Military Implications.* Washington: Rand, 1999.

Kierman Jr., Frank A., ed. *Chinese Ways in Warfare.* Cambridge: Harvard University Press, 1974.

Krawitz, Howard M., "Modernizing China's Military: A High-Stakes Gamble?" *Strategic Forum,* December 2003.

Lai, David. *Learning from the Stones: A Go Approach to Mastering China's Strategic Concept,* Shi. Washington: Strategic Studies Institute, 2004.

Lam, Willy. "Beijing's Strategy to Counter U.S. Influence in Asia." *China Brief* (Jamestown Foundation), 5, no. 25, Dec. 6, 2005.

Lampton, David M., ed. *The Making of Chinese Foreign and Security Policy, in the Era of Reform, 1978–2000.* Stanford: Stanford University Press, 2001.

Langlois, Jr., John D., ed. *China Under Mongol Rule.* Princeton: Princeton University Press, 1981.

Lattimore, Owen. *Inner Asian Frontiers of China.* Boston: Beacon Press, 1962.

Legg, Stuart. *The Barbarians of Asia: The Peoples of the Steppes from 1600 B.C.* New York: Dorset Press, (1970) 1990.

Leslie, Donald D. et al. *Essays on the Sources for Chinese History.* Columbia: University of South Carolina Press, 1975.

Levathes, Louise. *When China Ruled the Seas: The Treasure Fleet of the Dragon Throne, 1405–1433*. New York: Oxford University Press, 1996.

Levenson, Joseph R. *Confucian China and Its Modern Fate: A Trilogy.* Berkeley: University of California Press, 1968.

Lewis, Mark Edward. *Sanctioned Violence in Early China.* Albany: State University of New York Press, 1990.

Li Jijun. *Traditional Military Thinking and the Defensive Strategy of China.* Letort Paper No. 1. Washington: Strategic Studies Institute, 1997.

Li Nan. "From Revolutionary Internationalism to Conservative Nationalism: The Chinese Military's Discourse on National Security and Identity in the Post–Mao Era." United States Institute of Peace, May 2001.

Li Xueqin. *Eastern Zhou and Qin Civilizations.* Trans. K. C. Chang. New Haven: Yale University Press, 1985.

Lilley, James. *China Hands: Nine Decades of Adventure, Espionage, and Diplomacy in Asia.* New York: PublicAffairs, 2004.

Liu, James J. Y. *The Chinese Knight-Errant.* Chicago: University of Chicago Press, 1967.

Liu Jikun. *Mao Zedong's Art of War.* Hong Kong: Hai Feng, 1993.

Loewe, Michael. *Crisis and Conflict in Han China: 104 BC to AD 9.* London: George Allen & Unwin Ltd., 1974.

Loewe, Michael. *Records of Han Administration: Historical Assessment.* Cambridge: Cambridge University Press, 1967.

Macdonald, Peter. *Giap: The Victor in Vietnam.* New York: W. W. Norton, 1993.

Malik, Mohan. *Dragon on Terrorism: Assessing China's Tactical Gains and Strategic Losses Post-September 11.* Washington: Strategic Studies Institute, 2002.

Mancall, Mark. *Russia and China: Their Diplomatic Relations to 1728.* Cambridge: Harvard University Press, 1971.

Manz, Beatrice F., ed. *Central Asia in Historical Perspective.* John M. Olin Critical Issues. Boulder: Westview Press, 1994.

Mao Tse-tung. *Selected Military Writings of Mao Tse-tung.* Beijing: Foreign Languages Press, 1966.

Mao Tse-tung. *Selected Works of Mao Tse-tung.* Beijing: Foreign Languages Press, 1965.

Marshall, Robert. *Storm from the East: From Genghis Khan to Khubilai Khan.* Berkeley: University of California Press, 1993.

McCready, Douglas. *Crisis Deterrence in the Taiwan Strait.* Washington, D.C.: Strategic Studies Institute, November 2003.

Medeiros, Evan S. and Bates Gill. *Chinese Arms Exports: Policy, Players, and Process.* Washington: Strategic Studies Institute, 2000.

Menges, Constantine. *China: The Gathering Threat.* Nashville: Nelson Current, 2005.

Menon, Rajan. "The New Great Game in Central Asia." *Survival* 45, no. 2, Summer 2003, pp. 187–204.

Meskill, John, ed. *The Pattern of Chinese History: Cycles, Development, or Stagnation?* Boston: D. C. Heath and Company, 1965.

Meyer, Karl E. and Shareen Blair Brysac. *Tournament of Shadows: The Great Game and the Race for Empire in Central Asia.* Washington: Counterpoint, 1999.

Miles, James. "Chinese Nationalism, US Policy and Asian Security." *Survival* 42, no. 4, Winter 2000–2001, pp. 51–71.

Miller, Jr., Frank L. *Impact of Strategic Culture on U.S. Policies for East Asia*. Washington: Strategic Studies Institute, 2003.

Mosher, Steven W. *Hegemon: China's Plan to Dominate Asia and the World*. San Francisco: Encounter Books, 2000.

Mote, F. W. *Imperial China, 900–1800*. Cambridge: Harvard University Press, 1999.

Nathan, Andrew J. and Perry Link, eds. *The Tiananmen Papers*. New York: Public-Affairs, 2002.

Needham, Joseph. *Science and Civilisation in China*. 7 vols. Cambridge: Cambridge University Press, 1974–2005.

Nienhauser Jr., William H. et al. *The Grand Scribe's Records / Ssu-ma Chien*. Vols. 1 and 2: *The Basic Annals of Pre-Han China*. Vol. 7: *The Memoirs of Pre-Han China*. Bloomington: Indiana University Press, 1994, 2000.

O'Donogue, Patrick M. *Theater Missile Defense in Japan: Implications for the U.S.-China-Japan Strategic Relationship*. Washington, D.C.: Strategic Studies Institute, September 2000.

Office of the Secretary of Defense. "The Military Power of the People's Republic of China, 2005." Washington Department of Defense.

Office of the Secretary of Defense. "The Military Power of the People's Republic of China, 2006." Washington Department of Defense.

Parsons, James B. *Peasant Rebellions of the Late Ming Dynasty*. Ann Arbor: Association for Asian Studies, (1970) 1993.

Pearce, Scott, et al. *Culture and Power in the Reconstitution of the Chinese Realm, 200–600*. Cambridge: Harvard University Press, 2001.

Pillsbury, Michael. *China Debates the Future Security Environment*. Washington: National Defense University Press, 2000.

Pillsbury, Michael, ed. *Chinese Views of Future Warfare*. Rev. ed. Washington: National Defense University Press, 1998.

Pinck, Dan. *Journey to Peking: A Secret Agent in Wartime China*. Annapolis: Naval Institute Press, 2003.

Pines, Yuri. *Foundations of Confucian Thought: Intellectual Life in the Chunqiu Period, 722–453 B.C.E.* Honolulu: University of Hawai'i Press, 2002.

Pirazzoli-t'Serstevens, Michele. *The Han Dynasty*. New York: Rizzoli International Publications, Inc., 1982.

Pumphrey, Carolyn W., ed. *The Rise of China in Asia: Security Implications*. Washington: Strategic Studies Institute, January 2002.

Pye, Lucian W. *Asian Power and Politics: The Cultural Dimensions of Authority*. Cambridge: Harvard University Press, 1985.

Pye, Lucian W. *The Spirit of Chinese Politics: A Psychocultural Study of the Authority Crisis in Political Development*. Cambridge: MIT Press, 1992.

Qiao Liang and Wang Xiangsui. *Unrestricted Warfare*. Beijing: PLA Literature and Arts Publishing House, 1999.

Ramo, Josh. *Beijing Consensus: Notes on the New Physics of Chinese Power*. London: Foreign Policy Centre, 2004.

Rand, Christopher Clark. *The Role of Military Thought in Early Chinese Intellectual History.* Ann Arbor: U.M.I. Dissertation Information Service, 1977.

Randall, Bobbie L. *Sun Tzu: The Art of Network Centric Warfare.* U.S. Army War College, 10 March 2001.

Rossabi, Morris. *China and Inner Asia: From 1368 to the Present Day.* New York: Pica Press, 1975.

Rossabi, Morris. *Khubilai Khan: His Life and Times.* Berkeley: University of California Press, 1988.

Rossabi, Morris, ed. *China Among Equals: The Middle Kingdom and Its Neighbors, 10th–14th Centuries.* Berkeley: University of California Press, 1983.

Roy, David T. and Tsuen-hsuin Tsien, eds. *Ancient China: Studies in Early Civilization.* Hong Kong: Chinese University Press, 1978.

Ryan, Mark A., David M. Finkelstein, and Michael A. McDevitt, eds. *Chinese Warfighting: The PLA Experience since 1949.* Armonk: M. E. Sharpe, Inc., 2003.

Sage, Steven F. *Ancient Sichuan and the Unification of China.* Albany: State University of New York Press, 1992.

Saunders, J. J. *The History of the Mongol Conquests.* Philadelphia: University of Pennsylvania Press, 2001.

Scales Jr., Robert H. and Larry M. Wortzel. *The Future U.S. Military Presence in Asia: Landpower and the Geostrategy of American Commitment.* Washington: Strategic Studies Institute, 1999.

Schaberg, David. *A Patterned Past: Form and Thought in Early Chinese Historiography.* Cambridge: Harvard University Asian Center, 2001.

Schell, Orville. *Mandate of Heaven: A New Generation of Entrepreneurs, Dissidents, Bohemians, and Technocrats Lays Claim to China's Future.* New York: Simon & Schuster, 1994.

Schram, Stuart R., ed. *Foundations and Limits of State Power in China.* Hong Kong: The Chinese University Press, 1987.

Schram, Stuart R., ed. *The Scope of State Power in China.* Hong Kong: The Chinese University Press, 1985.

Schurmann, Franz. *Ideology and Organization in Communist China.* Berkeley: University of California Press, 1968.

Scobell, Andrew. *China and North Korea: From Comrades-in-Arms to Allies at Arm's Length.* Washington: Strategic Studies Institute, 2004.

Scobell, Andrew. *China and Strategic Culture.* Washington: Strategic Studies Institute, 2002.

Scobell, Andrew. *China's Use of Military Force: Beyond the Great Wall and the Long March.* Cambridge: Cambridge University Press, 2003.

Scobell, Andrew. *Chinese Army Building in the Ear of Jiang Zemin.* Washington: Strategic Studies Institute, 2000.

Scobell, Andrew. *The Cost of Conflict: The Impact on China of a Future War.* Washington: Strategic Studies Institute, 2001.

Scobell, Andrew. *The U.S. Army and the Asia-Pacific.* Washington: Strategic Studies Institute, 2001.

Scobell, Andrew and Larry M. Wortzel. *The Asia-Pacific in the U.S. National Security Calculus for a New Millennium.* Washington: Strategic Studies Institute, 2000.

Scobell, Andrew and Larry M. Wortzel, eds. *China's Growing Military Power: Perspectives on Security, Ballistic Missiles, and Conventional Capabilities*. Washington, D.C.: Strategic Studies Institute, 2002.

Scobell, Andrew and Larry M. Wortzel, eds. *Civil-Military Change in China: Elites, Institutes, and Ideas After the 16th Party Congress*. Washington: Strategic Studies Institute, 2004.

Shambaugh, David. "China's Military Views the World." *International Security*, Winter 1999/2000.

Shambaugh, David, ed. *Is China Unstable?* Armonk: M. E. Sharpe, Inc., 2000.

Shaughnessy, Edward L. *Before Confucius*. Albany: State University Press of New York, 1997.

Shaughnessy, Edward L. *Sources of Western Zhou History: Inscribed Bronze Vessels*. Berkeley: University of California Press, 1991.

Shaughnessy, Edward L., ed. *China: Empire and Civilization*. Oxford: Oxford University Press, 2005.

Shaughnessy, Edward L., ed. *New Sources of Early Chinese History*. Berkeley: Society for the Study of Early China, 1997.

Shih, Vincent Y. C. *The Taiping Ideology: Its Sources, Interpretations, and Influences*. Seattle: University of Washington Press, 1967.

Shinn, James ed. *Weaving the Net: Conditional Engagement with China*. New York: Council on Foreign Relations Press, 1996.

Shulsky, Abram N. *Deterrence Theory and Chinese Behavior*. Arlington: Rand, 2000.

Sinor, Denis, ed. *The Cambridge History of Early Inner Asia*. Cambridge: Cambridge University Press, 1990.

Smith, Richard J. *Chinese Maps*. Oxford: Oxford University Press, 1996.

So, Jenny F. and Emma C. Bunker. *Traders and Raiders on China's Northern Frontier*. Seattle: University of Washington Press, 1995.

Spuler, Bertold. *History of the Mongols: Based on Eastern and Western Accounts of theThirteenth and Fourteenth Centuries*. New York: Dorset Press, (1972) 1988.

State Council Information Office, People's Republic of China. "China's National Defense in 2004." Beijing, 2004.

Stokes, Mark A. *China's Strategic Modernization: Implications for the United States*. September 1999.

Storey, Ian James. "Living with the Colossus: How Southeast Asian Countries Cope with China." *Parameters*, Winter 1999–2000, pp. 111–25.

Struve, Lynn A. *The Southern Ming 1644–1662*. New Haven: Yale University Press, 1984.

Sutter, Robert G. *China's Rise in Asia: Promises and Perils*. Lanham: Rowman & Littlefield, 2005.

Swanson, Bruce. *Eighth Voyage of the Dragon: A History of China's Quest for Seapower*. Annapolis: Naval Institute Press, 1982.

Tao, Jing-shen. *The Jurchen in Twelfth-Century China: A Study of Sinicization*. Seattle: University of Washington Press, 1976.

Teitler, Ger and Kurt W. Radke, eds. *A Dutch Spy in China*. Leiden: E. J. Brill, 1999.

Terrill, Ross. *The New Chinese Empire, and What It Means for the United States*. New York: Basic Books, 2003.

Thompson, David J. and William R. Morris. *China in Space: Civilian and Military Developments.* Maxwell Air Force Base: Air War College, August 2001.

Thorp, Robert L. *China in the Early Bronze Age: Shang Civilization.* Philadelphia: University of Pennsylvania Press, 2005.

Tregear, T. R. *A Geography of China.* Chicago: Aldine Publishing Company, 1965.

Trulock, Notra. *Code Name Kindred Spirit: Inside the Chinese Nuclear Espionage Scandal.* San Francisco: Encounter Books, 2003.

Tsien, T. H. *Written on Bamboo and Silk: The Beginnings of Chinese Books and Inscriptions.* Chicago: University of Chicago Press, 1962.

Twitchett, Denis and Michael Loewe, eds. *The Cambridge History of China.* Vol. 1: *The Ch'in and Han Empires, 221 B.C.-A.D. 220.* Vol. 3: *Sui and T'ang China, 589–906.* Vol. 6: *Alien Regimes and Border States, 907–1368.* Cambridge: Cambridge University Press, 1978–1994.

Twitchett, Denis and Frederick W. Mote, eds. *The Cambridge History of China.* Vol. 8: *The Ming Dynasty, 1368–1644.* Cambridge: Cambridge University Press, 1988.

Van de Ven, Jans J., ed. *Warfare in Chinese History.* Leiden: E. J. Brill, 2000.

Van Ness, Peter. *Revolution and Chinese Foreign Policy: Peking's Support for Wars of National Liberation.* Berkeley: University of California Press, 1973.

Van Slyke, Lyman P. *Yangtze: Nature, History and the River.* Reading: Addison-Wesley Publishing Company, Inc., 1988.

Von Senger, Harro. *The Book of Stratagems: Tactics for Triumph and Survival.* New York: Viking Penguin, 1991.

Wakeman Jr., Frederic. *Spymaster: Dai Li and the Chinese Secret Service.* Berkeley: University of California Press, 2003.

Waldron, Arthur. *From War to Nationalism: China's Turning Point, 1924–1925.* Cambridge: Cambridge University Press, 1995.

Waldron, Arthur. *The Great Wall of China: From History to Myth.* Cambridge: Cambridge University Press, 1992.

Waley, Arthur. *The Opium War through Chinese Eyes.* London: George Allen & Unwin Ltd., (1958) 1960.

Waley, Arthur. *The Secret History of the Mongols.* London: George Allen & Unwin Ltd., 1963.

Wang Gungwu. *The Structure of Power in North China during the Five Dynasties.* Stanford: Stanford University Press, 1967.

Wang Xuanming. *100 Strategies of War.* Singapore: Asiapac Books, 1994.

Wang Xuanming. *Six Strategies for War.* Singapore: Asiapac Books, 1993.

Wang Xuanming. *Thirty-six Stratagems.* Singapore: Asiapac Books, 1993.

Wang Xuanming. *Three Strategies of Huang Shi Gong.* Singapore: Asiapac Books, 1993.

Wang Zhongshu. *Han Civilization.* Trans. K. C. Chang. New Haven: Yale University Press, 1982.

Wasserstein, Bernard. *Secret War in Shanghai: An Untold Story of Espionage, Intrigue, and Treason in World War II.* New York: Houghton Mifflin, 1998.

Watson, Burton. *Courtier and Commoner in Ancient China: Selections from the History of the Former Han by Pan Ku.* New York: Columbia University Press, 1974.

Watson, Burton, trans. *Records of the Grand Historian of China.* 2 vols. New York: Columbia University Press, 1961.

Watson, Burton, trans. *Records of the Grand Historian: Qin Dynasty.* New York: Columbia University Press, 1993.

Watson, Burton, trans. *Ssu-ma Ch'ien: Grand Historian of China.* New York: Columbia University Press, 1958.

Wheatley, Paul. *The Pivot of the Four Quarters: A Preliminary Enquiry into the Origins and Character of the Ancient Chinese City.* Edinburgh: Edinburgh University Press, 1971.

Willmott, H. P. *The Second World War in the East.* London: Cassell, 1999.

Wilson, Dick. *China's Revolutionary War.* London: Weidenfeld and Nicolson Ltd., 1991.

Wittfogel, Karl A. *Oriental Despotism: A Comparative Study of Total Power.* New Haven: Yale University Press, 1957.

Wortzel, Larry M. *China's Military Potential.* Washington: Strategic Studies Institute, 1998.

Wortzel, Larry M. *Dictionary of Contemporary Chinese Military History.* Westport: Greenwood Press, 1999.

Wortzel, Larry M., ed. *The Chinese Armed Forces in the 21st Century.* Washington D.C.: Strategic Studies Institute, 1999.

Wright, Arthur F. *The Sui Dynasty: The Unification of China, A.D. 581–617.* New York: Alfred A. Knopf, 1978.

Wright, Arthur F. and Denis Twitchett, eds. *Perspectives on the T'ang.* New Haven: Yale University Press, 1973.

Wright, Richard N. J. *The Chinese Steam Navy, 1862–1945.* London: Chatham Publishing, 2000.

Wu Baiyi. *The Chinese Security Concept and Its Historical Evolution.* Washington, D.C.: Strategic Studies Institute

Yang, Dan. *Atlas of the People's Republic of China.* Beijing: Foreign Languages Press, 1989.

Yang, Lien-sheng. *Excursions in Sinology.* Cambridge: Harvard University Press, 1969.

Yang, Lien-sheng. *Studies in Chinese Institutional History.* Cambridge: Harvard University Press, 1963.

Yoshihara, Toshi. *Chinese Information Warfare: A Phantom Menace or Emerging Threat?* Washington: Strategic Studies Institute, 2001.

You Ji. *The Armed Forces of China.* New York: I. B. Tauris, 1999.

Yü Ying-shih. *Trade and Expansion in Han China: A Study in the Structure of Sino-barbarian Economic Relations.* Berkeley: University of California Press, 1967.

Yuan Gao. *Lure the Tiger Out of the Mountains: The 36 Stratagems of Ancient China.* New York: Simon & Schuster, 1991.

Yuan Jing-dong. *Asia-Pacific Security: China's Conditional Multilateralism and Great Power Entente.* Washington: Strategic Studies Institute, 2000.

Yuan Jing-dong. "Sino-US Military Relations since Tiananmen: Restoration, Progress, and Pitfalls." *Parameters,* Spring 2003, pp. 51–66.

Zarrow, Peter. *Anarchism and Chinese Political Culture.* New York: Columbia University Press, 1990.

Zeng Xianwu. *The Great Wall of China in History and Legend.* Beijing: Foreign Languages Press, 1986.

Western Warfare and Intelligence

Abella, Alex and Scott Gordon. *Shadow Enemies: Hitler's Secret Terrorist Plot against the United States.* Guilford: Globe Pequot Press, 2002.

Adcock, F. E. *The Roman Art of War Under the Republic.* New York: Barnes & Noble, (1940) 1995.

Addington, Larry H. *The Patterns of War through the Eighteenth Century.* Bloomington: Indiana University Press, 1990.

Ameringer, Charles D. *U.S. Foreign Intelligence: The Secret Side of American History.* Lexington: D. C. Heath and Company, 1990.

Aron, Raymond. *Clausewitz: Philosopher of War.* Trans. C. Booker and N. Stone. Englewood Cliffs, NJ: Prentice-Hall, 1985.

Asprey, Robert B. *War in the Shadows: Guerrilla Past and Present.* New York: William Morrow, 1994.

Austin, N.J.E. and N.B. Rankov. *Exploration: Military and Political Intelligence in the Roman World from the Second Punic War to the Battle of Adrianople.* London: Routledge, 1995.

Barber, Noel. *The War of the Running Dogs: How Malaya Defeated the Communist Guerrillas 1948–1960.* London: Cassell, 2004.

Barnett, Roger W. *Asymmetrical Warfare: Today's Challenge to U.S. Military Power.* Washington: Brassey's, 2003.

Bartlett, Merrill L. ed. *Assault from the Sea: Essays on the History of Amphibious Warfare.* Annapolis: Naval Institute Press, 1983.

Bartlett, W. B. *The Assassins: the Story of Medieval Islam's Secret Sect.* Gloucestershire: Sutton Publishing, 2001.

Bartusis, Mark C. *The Late Byzantine Army: Arms and Society, 1204–1453.* Philadelphia: University of Pennsylvania Press, 1992.

Bergerud, Eric M. *The Dynamics of Defeat: the Vietnam War in Hau Ngjia Province.* Boulder: Westview Press, 1991.

Betts, Richard K., and Thomas G. Mahnken, eds. *Paradoxes of Strategic Intelligence: Essays in Honor of Michael I. Handel.* Portland: Frank Cass, 2003.

Black, Jeremy. *Rethinking Military History.* New York: Routledge, 2004.

Blank, Stephen J. *Rethinking Asymmetric Threats.* Washington: Strategic Studies Institute, 2003.

Bond, Brian, ed. *Fallen Stars: Eleven Studies of Twentieth Century Military Disasters.* London: Brassey's, 1991.

Bozeman, Adda B. *Strategic Intelligence and Statecraft.* London: Brassey's, 1992.

Bradford, Ernle. *Hannibal.* New York: Barnes & Noble, (1981) 1993.

Bradford, Ernle. *Thermopylae: The Battle for the West.* New York: Da Capo Press, 1980.

Budiansky, Stephen. *Her Majesty's Spymaster: Elizabeth I, Sir Francis Walsingham, and the Birth of Modern Espionage.* New York: Viking, Penguin Group, 2005.

Builder, Carl H. *The Masks of War: American Military Styles in Strategy and Analysis.* Baltimore: Johns Hopkins University Press, 1989.

Bulloch, James D. *The Secret Service of the Confederate States in Europe.* New York: Modern Library, (1959) 2001.

Bundt, Thomas S. "The Painful Lessons of Chemical Warfare: Gas, Mud, and Blood at Ypres." *Military Review*, July–August 2004, pp. 81–82.

Caesar, Julius. *The Gallic War*. Trans. Carolyn Hammond. Oxford: Oxford University Press, 1996.

Caesar, Julius. *The Battle for Gaul*. Trans. Anne and Peter Wiseman. London: Chatto & Windus Ltd., 1980.

Caven, Brian. *The Punic Wars*. New York: Barnes & Noble, (1980) 1992.

Cernenko, E. V. *The Scythians 700–300 BC*. London: Osprey Publishing, 1983.

Chaliand, Gérard, ed. *Guerrilla Strategies: An Historical Anthology from the Long March to Afghanistan*. Berkeley: University of California Press, 1982.

Chandler, David. *The Art of Warfare on Land*. London: Penguin Books, (1974) 2000.

Chandler, David, *Atlas of Military Strategy: The Art, Theory, and Practice of War, 1618–1878*. London: Arms and Armour, (1980) 1996.

Choate, Pat. *Agents of Influence*. New York: Alfred A. Knopf, 1990.

Clayton, Anthony. *Forearmed—A History of the Intelligence Corps*. London: Brassey's, 1996.

Clutton-Brock, Juliet. *Horse Power: A History of the Horse and the Donkey in Human Societies*. Cambridge: Harvard University Press, 1992.

Cohen, Eliot A. and John Gooch. *Military Misfortunes: The Anatomy of Failure in War*. New York: Random House, 1990.

Collins, John M. *America's Small Wars: Lessons for the Future*. New York: Brassey's, 1991.

Collins, John M. *Military Strategy: Principles, Practices, and Historical Perspectives*. Washington: Brassey's, 2002.

Connolly, Peter. *Greece and Rome at War*. London: Greenhill Books, 1998.

Cooper, H. H. A. and Lawrence J. Redlinger. *Making Spies: A Talent Spotter's Handbook*. Boulder: Paladin Press, 1986.

Corfis, Ivy A. and Michael Wolfe, eds. *The Medieval City Under Siege*. Suffolk: The Boydell Press, 1995.

Corum, James S. *The Roots of Blitzkrieg: Hans von Seeckt and German Military Reform*. Lawrence: University Press of Kansas, 1992.

Cottrell, Leonard. *The Roman Invasion of Britain*. New York: Barnes & Noble, 1992.

Cream, C. W. *The Secret of the Hittites: The Discovery of an Ancient Empire*. New York: Dorset Press, (1955) 1990.

Daraul, Arkon. *A History of Secret Societies*. New York: Citadel Press, (1961) 1995.

Darman, Peter. *Surprise Attack: Lightning Strikes of the World's Elite Forces*. New York: Barnes & Noble, 1993.

David, Saul. *Military Blunders: The How and Why of Military Failure*. New York: Carroll & Graf, 1998.

Davis, Diane E. and Anthony W. Pereira, eds. *Irregular Armed Forces and Their Role in Politics and State Formation*. Cambridge: Cambridge University Press, 2003.

Dear, Ian. *Sabotage and Subversion: The SOE and OSS at War*. London: Cassell, 2002.

Department of the Army. *U.S. Army Counterguerrilla Operations Handbook*. Guilford: The Lyons Press, 2004.

Department of the Army. *U.S. Army Desert Operations Handbook*. Guilford: The Lyons Press, 2004.

Department of the Army. *U.S. Army Reconnaissance and Surveillance Handbook.* Guilford: The Lyons Press, 2004.

Dennis, George T. *Maurice's Strategikon: Handbook of Byzantine Military Strategy.* Philadephia: University of Pennsylvania Press, 1984.

Denis, George T. *Three Byzantine Military Treatises.* Washington: Dumbarton Oaks Research Library and Collection, 1985.

DeVries, Kelly Robert. *Medieval Military Technology.* Orchard Park: Broadview Press, 1992.

Dewar, Michael. *The Art of Deception in Warfare.* Newton Abbot, UK: David & Charles, 1989.

Dikshitar, V. R. Ramachandra. *War in Ancient India.* Delhi: Motilal Banarsidass, 1987.

Dupuy, T. N. *Understanding Defeat: How to Recover from Loss in Battle to Gain Victory in War.* McLean: Nova Publications, 1995.

Dupuy, T. N. *Understanding War: History and Theory of Combat.* London: Leo Cooper, 1992.

Duyvesteyn, Isabelle and Jan Angstrom, eds. *Rethinking the Nature of War.* New York: Frank Cass, 2005.

Dvornik, Francis. *Origins of Intelligence Services.* New Brunswick: Rutgers University Press, 1974.

Dyer, Gwynne. *War.* Toronto: Stoddart Publishing, 1985.

Elton, Hugh. *Warfare in Roman Europe AD 350–425.* Oxford: Clarendon Press, 1996.

Evans, M. H. H. *Amphibious Operations.* London: Brassey's, 1990.

Farago, Ladislas. *Burn after Reading: The Espionage History of World War II.* Annapolis: Naval Institute Press, (1961) 2003.

Ferrill, Arthur. *The Fall of the Roman Empire: The Military Explanation.* New York: Thames and Hudson, (1986) 1990.

Ferrill, Arthur. *The Origins of War: From the Stone Age to Alexander the Great.* New York: Thames and Hudson, 1986.

Finnegan, John Patrick. *Military Intelligence.* Washington: Center of Military History, United States Army, 1998.

Flint, Roy K. *The Arab-Israeli War, the Chinese Civil War, and the Korean War.* Wayne: Avery Publishing Group, 1987.

Forsyth, Michael. "Finesee: A Short Theory of War," *Military Review,* July–August 2004, pp. 17–19.

Foster, Simon. *Hit the Beach! Amphibious Warfare from the Plains of Abraham to San Carlos Water.* London: Arms & Armour Press, 1995.

Freedman, Lawrence, ed. *War.* Oxford: Oxford University Press, 1994.

Fuller, J. F. C. *A Military History of the Western World.* 3 vols. New York: Da Capo Press, (1954–56) 1987.

Gabriel, Richard A. and Karen S. Metz. *From Sumer to Rome: The Military Capabilities of Ancient Armies.* New York: Greenwood Press, 1991.

Gannon, James. *Stealing Secrets, Telling Lies: How Spies and Codebreakers Helped Shape the Twentieth Century.* Washington: Brassey's, 2001.

Gardiner, Robert, ed. *The Earliest Ships: The Evolution of Boats into Ships.* Annapolis: Naval Institute Press, 1996.

Gartner, Scott Sigmund. *Strategic Assessment in War.* New Haven: Yale University Press, 1997.

Gerard, Philip. *Secret Soldiers: The Story of World War II's Heroic Army of Deception.* New York: Dutton, Penguin Putnam Inc., 2002.

Glantz, David M. *Soviet Military Deception in the Second World War.* Totowa: Frank Cass, 1989.

Glantz, David M. *Soviet Military Intelligence in War.* Portland: Frank Cass, 1990.

Goldsworthy, Adrian. *Caesar's Civil War 49–44 BC.* Oxford: Osprey Publishing, 2002.

Goldsworthy, Adrian. *Cannae.* London: Cassell, 2001.

Goldsworthy, Adrian. *The Punic Wars.* London: Cassell, 2000.

Goldsworthy, Adrian. *Roman Warfare.* London: Cassell, 2000.

Gooch, John, ed. *The Army of the Caesars.* New York: M. Evans, (1974) 1992.

Gray, Colin S. *Explorations in Strategy.* Contributions in Military Studies, 164. Westport: Praeger Publishers, 1996.

Grbasic, Z. and V. Vuksic. *The History of Cavalry.* New York: Facts on File, 1989.

Green, Peter. *Alexander of Macedon, 356–323 B.C.: A Historical Biography.* Berkeley: University of California Press, 1991.

Green, Peter. *Alexander to Actium: The Historical Evolution of the Hellenistic Age.* Berkeley: University of California Press, (1990) 1993.

Green, Peter. *The Greco-Persian Wars.* Berkeley: University of California Press, 1996.

Griffith, Paddy. *The Viking Art of War.* London: Greenhill Books, 1995.

Grossman, Dave. *On Killing.* New York: Little, Brown, 1995.

Hackett, John, ed. *The Profession of Arms.* New York: Macmillan, 1983.

Hairr, John. *Guilford Courthouse: Nathanael Greene's Victory in Defeat March 15, 1781.* Cambridge: Da Capo, 2002.

Haldon, John. *Byzantium at War AD 600–1453.* Oxford: Osprey Publishing, 2002.

Haldon, John. *Warfare, State and Society in the Byzantine World, 565–1204.* London: UCL Press, 1999.

Hall, Bert S. *Weapons and Warfare in Renaissance Europe—Gunpowder, Technology, and Tactics.* Baltimore: Johns Hopkins University Press, 1997.

Handel, Michael I. *Masters of War: Sun Tzu, Clausewitz and Jomini.* London: Frank Cass, 1992.

Handel, Michael I. *War, Strategy and Intelligence.* London: Frank Cass, 1989.

Handel, Michael I., ed. *Intelligence and Military Operations.* Portland: Frank Cass, 1990.

Hanson, Victor Davis. *A War Like No Other: How the Athenians and Spartans Fought the Peloponnesian War.* New York: Random House, 2005.

Hanson, Victor Davis. *The Western Way of War: Infantry Battle in Classical Greece.* New York: Alfred A. Knopf, 1989.

Hanson, Victor Davis, ed. *Hoplites: The Classical Greek Battle Experience.* London: Routledge, 1993.

Hart, B. H. Liddell. *Scipio Africanus: Greater than Napoleon.* Novato: Presidio Press, (1926) 1992.

Hedges, Chris. *War Is a Force that Gives Us Meaning.* New York: PublicAffairs, 2002.

Herzog, Chaim and Mordechai Gichon. *Battle of the Bible.* London: Greenhill Books, 1997, revised edition.

Hesketh, Roger. *Fortitude: The D-day Deception Campaign.* New York: The Overlook Press, 2000.

Hewitt, John. *Ancient Armour & Weapons: From the Iron Age to the Thirteenth Century.* London: Bracken Books, (1855–60) 1996.

Hoffman, Frank G. "Small Wars Revisited: The United States and Nontraditional Wars." *The Journal of Strategic Studies,* 28, no. 6, December 2005, pp. 913–940.

Hooker, Richard. D. "Beyond *Vom Krieg*: The Character and Conduct of Modern War." *Parameters,* Summer 2005, pp. 4–17.

Hooker, Richard D., ed. *Maneuver Warfare: An Anthology.* Novato: Presidio Press, 1993.

Hinsley, F. H. et al. *British Intelligence in the Second World War: Its Influence on Strategy and Operations.* London: Her Majesty's Stationery Office, 1984.

Hinsley, F. Harry and Alan Stripp, eds. *Codebreakers: The Inside Story of Bletchley Park.* Oxford: Oxford University Press, 1993.

Hodgkin, Thomas. *Huns, Vandals and the Fall of the Roman Empire.* Mechanicsburg: Stackpole Books, 1996.

Hogg, Ian V., ed. *The Weapons that Changed the World.* New York: Arbor House Publishing, 1986.

Hogg, O. F. G. *Clubs to Cannon: Warfare and Weapons before the Introduction of Gunpowder.* New York: Barnes & Noble, (1968) 1993.

Hooper, Nicholas and Matthew Bennet. *The Cambridge Illustrated Atlas of Warfare: The Middle Ages 768–1487.* Cambridge: Cambridge University Press, 1996.

Howard, Michael E. *The Causes of Wars and Other Essays.* Cambridge: Harvard University Press, 1983.

Howard, Michael E. *Clausewitz.* Oxford: Oxford University Press, 1983.

Howard, Michael E. *The Lessons of History.* New Haven: Yale University Press, 1991.

Howard, Michael E. *Strategic Deception in the Second World War.* New York: W. W. Norton, 1990, 1995.

Howard, Michael and Peter Paret, ed. and trans. *Carl von Clausewitz: On War.* Princeton: Princeton University Press, (1984) 1989.

Hughes-Wilson, John. *Military Intelligence Blunders.* New York: Carroll & Graf, 1999.

Hyland, Ann. *Equus: The Horse in the Roman World.* New Haven: Yale University Press, 1990.

Hyland, Ann. *The Medieval Warhorse from Byzantium to the Crusades.* Phoenix Mill, UK: Allan Sutton, 1994.

Hyland, Ann. *Training the Roman Cavalry.* Dover: Alan Sutton, 1993.

Isaac, Benjamin H. *The Limits of Empire: The Roman Army in the East.* Rev. ed. Oxford: Oxford University Press, 1992.

Jeffreys-Jones, Rhodri. *Cloak and Dollar: A History of American Secret Intelligence.* New Haven: Yale University Press, 2002.

Jeffreys-Jones, Rhodri and Andrew Lownie, eds. *North American Spies: New Revisionist Essays.* Lawrence: University Press of Kansas, 1991.

Jiménez, Ramon L. *Caesar Against Rome: The Great Roman Civil War.* Westport, CT: Praeger Publishers, 2000.

Jomini, Antoine Henri baron de. *The Art of War.* Trans. G. H. Mendell and W. P. Craighill. Westport, CT: Greenwood Press, 1962 (1862).

Jones, A. H. M. *Sparta*. New York: Barnes & Noble, (1967) 1993.

Jones, Archer. *The Art of War in the Western World*. Urbana: University of Illinois Press, 1987.

Jowett, Benjamin, trans. *Thucydides: The Peloponessian War*. New York: Bantam Books, 1960.

Kagan, Donald. *On the Origins of War and the Preservation of Peace*. New York: Doubleday, 1995.

Kagan, Donald and Frederick W. Kagan. *While America Sleeps: Self-delusion, Military Weakness, and the Threat to Peace Today*. New York: St. Martin's Press, 2000.

Kahn, David. *The Codebreakers: The Story of Secret Writing*. Rev. ed. New York: Scribner, 1996.

Kahn, David. *Hitler's Spies: German Military Intelligence in World War II*. Cambridge: Da Capo Press, 2000.

Kam, Ephraim. *Surprise Attack: The Victim's Perspective*. Cambridge: Harvard University Press, 1988.

Katz, Ruth Cecily. *Arjuna in the Mahabharata*. Columbia: University of South Carolina Press, 1989.

Keegan, John. *A History of Warfare*. New York: Alfred A. Knopf, 1993.

Keegan, John. *Intelligence in War: Knowledge of the Enemy from Napoleon to Al-aeda*. New York: Alfred A. Knopf, 2003.

Keegan, John and Richard Holmes. *Soldiers: A History of Men in Battle*. New York: Konecky & Konecky, 1985.

Keeley, Lawrence H. *War before Civilization: The Myth of the Peaceful Savage*. New York: Oxford University Press, 1996.

Kelly, Jack. *Gunpowder: Alchemy, Bombards, & Pyrotechnics: The History of the Explosive that Changed the World*. New York: Basic Books, 2004.

Kennedy, Hugh. *The Armies of the Caliphs: Military and Society in the Early Islamic State*. New York: Routledge, 2001.

Kennedy, Hugh. *Mongols, Huns & Vikings: Nomads at War*. London: Cassell, 2002.

Kenny, Anthony. *The Logic of Deterrence*. Chicago: University of Chicago Press, 1985.

Keppie, Lawrence. *The Making of the Roman Army: From Republic to Empire*. New York: Barnes & Noble, 1984.

Koch, H. W. *Medieval Warfare*. New York: Dorset Press, 1978.

Kwasny, Mark V. *Washington's Partisan War 1775–1783*. Kent: Kent State University Press, 1996.

Laffin, John. *Brassey's Battles*. London: Brassey's, 1986.

Laflin, John. *Brassey's Book of Espionage*. London: Brassey's, 1996.

Lanning, Michael Lee. *Senseless Secrets—The Failures of U.S. Military Intelligence, from George Washington to the Present*. New York: Carol Publishing Group, 1995.

Lazenby, J. F. *The First Punic War: A Military History*. Stanford: Stanford University Press, 1996.

Lee, Bradford A. and Karl F. Walling, eds. *Strategic Logic and Political Rationality: Essays in Honor of Michael I. Handel*. Portland: Frank Cass Publishers, 2003.

Lendon, J. E. *Soldiers & Ghosts: A History of Battle in Classical Antiquity*. New Haven: Yale University Press, 2005.

Lepore, Jill. *The Name of War: King Philip's War and the Origins of American Identity.* New York: Vintage, 1999.

Liddell Hart, B. H. *Strategy.* 2nd ed. New York: Meridian, 1991.

Lind, William S. *Maneuver Warfare Handbook.* Westview Special Studies in Military Affairs. Boulder: Westview Press, 1985.

Lloyd, Mark. *The Guinness Book of Espionage.* Middlesex: Guinness Publishing, 1994.

Lorber, Azriel. *Misguided Weapons: Technological Failure and Surprise on the Battlefield.* Dulles: Brassey's, 2002.

Lorenz, Konrad. *On Aggression.* New York: MJF Books, 1966.

Loveman, Brian and Thomas M. Davies Jr. *Che Guevara: Guerrilla Warfare.* 3rd ed. Wilmington: Scholarly Resources, 1997.

Luttwak, Edward N. *Coup d'Etat.* Cambridge: Harvard University Press, (1968) 1979.

Luvaas, Jay, ed. and trans. *Frederick the Great on the Art of War.* New York: Free Press, 1966.

Lynn, John A. *Battle: A History of Combat and Culture.* Boulder: Westview Press, 2003.

Lynn, John A. "Patterns of Insurgency and Counterinsurgency." *Military Review,* July–August 2005, pp. 22–27.

Machiavelli, Niccolo. *The Art of War: A Revised Edition of the Ellis Farnsworth Translation.* New York: Da Capo Press, (1965) 1990.

Machiavelli, Niccolo. *The Discourses.* Ed. Bernard Crick. Trans. Leslie J. Walker. London: Penguin Classics, 1983.

Machiavelli, Niccolo. *The Prince.* Trans. George Bull. London: Penguin Classics, 1995.

Mackenzie, William. *The Secret History of SOE: The Special Operations Executive 1940–1945.* London: St. Ermin's Press, 2000.

Mahaffy, John Pentland. *The Empire of Alexander the Great.* New York: Barnes & Noble, (1898) 1995.

Malone, Patrick M. *The Skulking Way of War: Technology and Tactics among the New England Indians.* Baltimore: Johns Hopkins University Press, 1993.

Manwaring, Max G. *Internal Wars: Rethinking Problem and Response.* Washington: Strategic Studies Institute, 2001.

Manwaring, Max G. "The New Master of Wizard's Chess: The Real Hugo Chavez and Asymmetric Warfare." *Military Review,* September–October 2005, pp. 40–49.

Markle, Donald E. *Spies and Spymasters of the Civil War.* New York: Hippocrene Books, 1994.

Marks, Leo. *Between Silk and Cyanide: A Codemaker's War, 1941–1945.* New York: Simon & Schuster, 1999.

Marsden, E. W. *Greek and Roman Artillery; Historical Development.* New York: Oxford University Press, 1969.

Marsden, E. W. *Greek and Roman Artillery; Technical Treatises.* New York: Oxford University Press, 1971.

Mayor, Adrienne. *Greek Fire, Poison Arrows & Scorpion Bombs: Biological and Chemical Warfare in the Ancient World.* New York: The Overlook Press, 2003.

McGeer, Eric. *Sowing the Dragon's Teeth: Byzantine Warfare in the Tenth Century.* Washington: Dumbarton Oaks, 1995.

McKercher, B. J. C. and A. Hamish Ion, eds. *Military Heretics: The Unorthodox in Policy and Strategy.* Westport: Praeger Publishers, 1994.

McNeill, William H. *Keeping Together In Time: Dance and Drill in Human History.* Cambridge: Harvard University Press, 1995.

McNeill, William H. *The Pursuit of Power: Technology, Armed Force, and Society since A.D. 1000.* Chicago: University of Chicago Press, 1984.

McNicoll, A. W. *Hellenistic Fortifications from the Aegean to the Euphrates.* Oxford: Oxford University Press, 1997.

McRandle, James H. *The Antique Drums of War.* College Station: Texas A&M University Press, 1994.

McRaven, William. *Spec Ops: Case Studies in Special Operations Warfare.* Novato: Presidio Press, 1995.

Medcalf, Peter. *War in the Shadows.* Australia: University of Queensland Press, 1986.

Mendez, Antonio and Jonna Mendez. *Spy Dust: Two Masters of Disguise Reveal the Tools and Operations that Helped Win the Cold War.* New York: Atria Books, 2002.

Metz, Steven and Douglas V. Johnson II. *Asymmetry and U.S. Military Strategy: Definition, Background, and Strategic Concepts.* Washington, D.C.: Strategic Studies Institute, January 2001.

Meyer, Herbert E. *Real World Intelligence.* New York: Weidenfeld & Nicolson, 1987.

Michael, Franz. *The Taiping Rebellion: History and Documents.* Seattle: University of Washington Press, 1966.

Miller, William I. *The Mystery of Courage.* Cambridge: Harvard University Press, 2000.

Milner, N. P., trans. *Vegetius: Epitome of Military Science.* Liverpool, UK: Liverpool University Press, 1996.

Moltke, Helmuth, Graf von. *Moltke on the Art of War: Selected Writings.* Ed. Daniel J. Hughes. Trans. Daniel J. Hughes and Harry Bell. Novato: Presidio Press, 1993.

Moran, Daniel. *Wars of National Liberation.* London: Cassell, 2001.

Munn, Mark Henderson. *The Defense of Attica: The Dema Wall and the Boiotian War of 378–375 B.C.* Berkeley: University of California Press, 1993.

Murray, Williamson, ed. *The Making of Strategy: Rulers, States, and War.* Cambridge: Cambridge University Press, 1994.

Nash, Jay Robert. *Spies: A Narrative Encyclopedia of Dirty Tricks & Double Dealing from Biblical Times to Today.* New York: M. Evans, 1997.

Neilson, Keith and B. J. C. McKercher, ed. *Go Spy the Land: Military Intelligence in History.* Westport: Praeger Publishers, 1992.

Niditch, Susan. *War in the Hebrew Bible: A Study in the Ethics of Violence.* New York: Oxford University Press, 1993.

Norman, A. V. B. *The Medieval Soldier.* New York: Barnes & Noble, (1971) 1993.

Norman, Bruce. *Secret Warfare: The Battle of Codes and Ciphers.* New York: Dorset Press, (1973) 1987.

Oakeshott, R. Ewart. *The Archaeology of Weapons: Arms and Armor from Prehistory to the Age of Chivalry.* New York: Barnes & Noble, 1960.

O'Connell, Robert L. *Of Arms and Men: A History of War, Weapons, and Aggression.* New York: Oxford University Press, 1989.

O'Connell, Robert L. *Ride of the Second Horseman: The Birth and Death of War.* New York: Oxford University Press, 1995.

O'Donnel, Patrick K. *Operatives, Spies, and Saboteurs: The Unknown Story of the Men and Women of WWII's OSS*. New York: Free Press, 2004.

Oman, Charles. *A History of the Art of War in the Middle Ages*. London: Greenhill, (1924) 1991.

O'Neill, Bard E. *Insurgency & Terrorism: Inside Modern Revolutionary Warfare*. Herndon: Brassey's, 1990.

Ostrovsky, Victor. *The Other Side of Deception*. New York: HarperCollins, 1994.

O'Sullivan, Patrick. *Terrain and Tactics*. Westport: Greenwood Press, 1991.

Owen, Denis. *Camouflage and Mimicry*. Chicago: University of Chicago Press, 1982.

Paret, Peter. *Clausewitz and the State: The Man, His Theories, and His Times*. Princeton: Princeton University Press, (1976) 1985.

Paret, Peter. *Understanding War: Essays on Clausewitz and the History of Military Power*. Princeton: Princeton University Press, 1992.

Paret, Peter, ed. *Makers of Modern Strategy: From Machiavelli to the Nuclear Age*. Princeton: Princeton University Press, 1986.

Paret, Peter and Daniel Moran, eds. and trans. *Carl von Clausewitz: Historical and Political Writings*. Princeton: Princeton University Press, 1992.

Parker, Geoffrey. *The Military Revolution: Military Innovation and the Rise of the West, 1500–1800*. Cambridge: Cambridge University Press, 1988.

Parker, H. M. D. *The Roman Legions*. New York: Barnes & Noble, 1993.

Partington, J. R. *A History of Greek Fire and Gunpowder*. Baltimore: Johns Hopkins University Press, 1999.

Payne-Gallwey, Ralph. *The Crossbow: Mediaeval and Modern Military and Sporting*. London: The Holland Press, (1903) 1990.

Peddie, John. *Hannibal's War*. Gloucestershire: Sutton Publishing, 1997.

Peddie, John. *The Roman War Machine*. Phoenix Mill, UK: Alan Sutton Publishing, 1994.

Perrett, Bryan. *Against All Odds! More Dramatic 'Last Stand' Actions*. London: Arms and Armour Press, 1995.

Perrett, Bryan. *At All Costs! Stories of Impossible Victories*. London: Arms and Armour Press, 1993.

Perrett, Bryan. *The Battle Book: Crucial Conflicts in History from 1469 BC to the Present*. London: Arms and Armour Press, 1992.

Perrett, Bryan. *Last Stand! Famous Battles Against the Odds*. London: Arms and Armour Press, 1991.

Perrett, Bryan. *Seize and Hold: Master Strokes on the Battlefield*. London: Arms and Armour Press, 1994.

Perry, James M. *Arrogant Armies: Great Military Disasters and the Generals Behind Them*. New York: John Wiley & Sons, 1996.

Persico, Joseph E. *Roosevelt's Secret War: FDR and World War II Espionage*. New York: Random House, 2001.

Phillips, T. R. ed. *Roots of Strategy*. Harrisburg: Stackpole Books, 1987.

Pimlott, John, ed. *Rommel and His Art of War: Field Marshal Erwin Rommel*. London: Wren's Park Publishing, 2003.

Polmar, Martin and Thomas B. Allen. *Spy Book: The Encyclopedia of Intelligence*. New York: Random House, 1997.

Porter, Bruce D. *War and the Rise of the State*. New York: Free Press, 1994.

Prados, John. *Lost Crusader: The Secret Wars of CIA Director William Colby: The True Story of One of America's Most Controversial Spymasters*. New York: Oxford University Press, 2003.

Pritchett, W. Kendrick. *The Greek State at War*. 5 vols. Berkeley: University of California Press, 1971, 1974, 1979, 1985, 1991.

Raaflaub, Kurt and Nathan Rosenstein, eds. *War and Society in the Ancient and Medieval Worlds, Asia, the Mediterranean, Europe, and Mesoamerica*. Cambridge: Harvard Center for Hellenic Studies, 1999.

Ralston, David B. *Importing the European Army: The Introduction of European Military Techniques and Institutions into the Extra-European World, 1600–1914*. Chicago: University of Chicago Press, 1990.

Randers-Pehrson, Justine Davis. *Barbarians and Romans: The Birth Struggle of Europe, A.D. 400–700*. Norman: University of Oklahoma Press, 1983.

Raphals, Lisa. *Knowing Words: Wisdom and Cunning in the Classical Traditions of China and Greece*. Ithaca: Cornell University Press, 1992.

Rapoport, Anatol, ed. *Carl Von Clausewitz: On War*. New York: Penguin Books, 1985.

Raviv, Dan and Yossi Melman. *Every Spy a Prince*. Boston: Houghton Mifflin, 1990.

Record, Jeffrey. "Why the Strong Lose." *Parameters*, Winter 2005–2006, pp. 17–31.

Rector, Mark. *Hans Tolhoffer, Medieval Combat*. London: Greenhill Books, 2000.

Regan, Geoffrey. *Great Military Disasters: A History of Incompetence on the Battlefield*. New York: M. Evans, 1987.

Reuer, Jeffrey J. ed. *Strategic Alliances: Theory and Evidence*. Oxford: Oxford University Press, 2004

Rich, John and Graham Shipley, eds. *War and Society in the Greek World*. London: Routledge, (1993) 1995.

Richelson, Jeffrey T. *A Century of Spies: Intelligence in the Twentieth Century*. New York: Oxford University Press, 1995.

Rodgers, William L. *Greek and Roman Naval Warfare: A Study of Strategy, Tactics, and Ship Design from Salamis (480 B.C.) to Actium (31 B.C.)*. Annapolis: Naval Institute Press, (1937) 1986.

Rommel, Erwin. *Infantry Attacks*. Trans. G. E. Kidde. Novato: Presidio Press, 1990.

Rooney, David. *Military Mavericks: Extraordinary Men of Battle*. London: Cassell, 2000.

Rose, Susan. *Medieval Naval Warfare, 1000–1500*. New York: Routledge, 2002.

Royster, Charles. *The Destructive War: William Techumseh Sherman, Stonewall Jackson, and the Americans*. New York: Alfred A. Knopf, 1991.

Rubenstein, Robert and Mary Foster, eds. *The Social Dynamics of Peace and Conflict*. Dubuque: Kendall Hunt Publishing, 1997.

Rustmann Jr., F. W. *CIA, Inc.: Espionage and the Craft of Business Intelligence*. Washington: Brassey's, 2002.

Sage, Michael M. *Warfare in Ancient Greece: A Sourcebook*. London: Routledge, 1996.

Santosuosso, Antonio. *Storming the Heavens: Soldiers, Emperors, and Civilians in the Roman Empire*. Boulder: Westview Press, 2001.

Scanlon, Charles Francis. *In Defense of the Nation—DIA at Forty Years*. Washington: Department of Defense, 2002.

Schelling, Thomas C. *The Strategy of Conflict.* Cambridge: Harvard University Press, 1980.

Schilling, William R. ed. *Nontraditional Warfare: 21st Century Threats and Responses.* Washington: Brassey's, 2002.

Schneider, James J. *The Structure of Strategic Revolution: Total War and the Roots of the Soviet Warfare State.* Novato: Presidio Press, 1994.

Seabury, Paul and Angelo Codevilla. *War: Ends and Means.* New York: Basic Books, 1989.

Seymour, William. *Great Sieges of History.* London: Brassey's, 1991.

Shulsky, Abram N. *Silent Warfare: Understanding the World of Intelligence.* Washington: Brassey's, 1993.

Shultz Jr., Richard H. *The Secret War Against Hanoi: Kennedy's and Johnson's Use of Spies, Saboteurs, and Covert Warriors in North Vietnam.* New York: HarperCollins, 1999.

Sifakis, Carl. *Encyclopedia of Assassinations.* New York: Facts on File, 1991.

Simkins, Michael. *Warriors of Rome: An Illustrated Military History of the Roman Legions.* London: Blandford, 1988.

Southern, Pat and Karen R. Dixon. *The Late Roman Army.* New Haven: Yale University Press, 1996.

Southworth, Samuel A., ed. *Great Raids in History: From Drake to Desert One.* New York: Sarpedon, 1997.

Spalinger, Anthony John. *Aspects of the Military Documents of the Ancient Egyptians.* New Haven: Yale University Press, 1982.

Spence, I. G. *The Cavalry of Classical Greece: A Social and Military History with Particular Reference to Athens.* New York: Oxford University Press, 1993.

Stafford, David. *Secret Agent: The True Story of the Covert War Against Hitler.* Woodstock: Overlook Press, 2000.

Starr, Chester G. *A History of the Ancient World.* New York: Oxford University Press, 1991.

Starr, Chester G. *The Influence of Sea Power on Ancient History.* New York: Oxford University Press, 1989.

Starr, Chester G. *The Roman Empire, 27 B.C.–A.D. 476.* New York: Oxford University Press, 1982.

Steele, Robert D. *The New Craft of Intelligence: Achieving Asymmetric Advantage in the Face of Nontraditional Threats.* Washington, D.C.: Strategic Studies Institute, February 2002.

Stern, Philip Van Doren. *Secret Missions of the Civil War: First-Hand Accounts by Men and Women Who Risked Their Lives in Underground Activities for the North and the South.* New York: Wings Books, (1959) 1990.

Stevens, Anthony. *The Roots of War: A Jungian Perspective.* New York: Paragon House, 1989.

Strassler, Robert B., ed. *The Landmark Thucydides.* New York: Free Press, 1996.

Strauss, Barry S. and Josiah Ober. *The Anatomy of Error: Ancient Military Disasters and Their Lessons for Modern Strategists.* New York: St. Martin's Press, (1990) 1992.

Sudoplatov, Pavel and Anatoli Sudoplatov. *Special Tasks: The Memoirs of an Unwanted Witness—A Soviet Spymaster.* Boston: Little, Brown, 1994.

Sullivan, Denis F., ed. *Siegecraft: Two Tenth-Century Instructional Manuals by "Heron of Byzantium".* Washington: Dumbarton Oaks Research Library and Collection, 2000.

Sumption, Jonathan. *The Hundred Years War*. Philadelphia: University of Pennsylvania Press, 1990.

Taillon, J. Paul de B. *The Evolution of Special Forces in Counter-Terrorism: The British and American Experiences*. Westport: Praeger Publishers, 2001.

Taylor, Philip M. *Munitions of the Mind: A History of Propaganda from the Ancient World to the Present Day*. Manchester: Manchester University Press, 2003.

Thompson, Julian. *The Lifeblood of War: Logistics in Armed Conflict*. London: Brassey's, 1991.

Tidwell, William A. *Come Retribution: The Confederate Secret Service and the Assassination of Lincoln*. New York: Barnes & Noble Books, (1988) 1997.

Trento, Joseph J. *The Secret History of the CIA*. New York: Carroll & Graf, 2001.

Turner, Michael A. *Why Secret Intelligence Fails*. Dulles: Potomac Books, 2005.

Turney-High, Harry Holbert. *The Military: The Theory of Land Warfare as Behavioral Science*. West Hanover: Christopher Publishing House, 1981.

United States Marine Corps. *Warfighting*. New York: Currency Doubleday, 1989.

Urbano. *Fighting in the Streets: A Manual of Urban Guerilla Warfare*. Fort Lee: Barricade Books Inc., 1991.

Van Creveld, Martin. *Command in War*. Cambridge: Harvard University Press, 1985.

Volkman, Ernest. *Espionage*. New York: John Wiley & Sons, 1995.

Wallach, Jehuda Lothar. *The Dogma of the Battle of Annihilation*. Westport: Greenwood Press, 1986.

Ward, Diane Raines. *Water Wars: Drought, Flood, Folly, and the Politics of Thirst*. New York: Riverhead Books, 2002.

Warner, Michael, ed. *The CIA under Harry Truman (CIA Cold War Records)*. Washington: History Staff Center for the Study of Intelligence, CIA, 1994.

Warner, Rex, trans. *Xenophon: The Persian Expedition*. Baltimore: Penguin Books, 1949.

Warry, John. *Alexander 334–323 BC: Conquest of the Persian Empire*. London: Osprey Publishing, 1991.

Warry, John. *Warfare in the Classical World*. London: Salamander Books, 1980.

Webber, Ralph E. ed. *Spymasters: Ten CIA Officers in Their Own Words*. Wilmington: Scholarly Resources, 1999.

Weigley, Russell F. *The Age of Battles*. Bloomington: Indiana University Press, 1991.

Weigley, Russell F. *New Dimensions in Military History*. San Rafael: Presidio Press, 1975.

West, Nigel, ed. *The Faber Book of Espionage*. Boston: Faber & Faber, 1993.

Westerfield, H. Bradford, ed. *Inside CIA's Private World: Declassified Articles from the Agency's Internal Journal, 1955–1992*. New Haven: Yale University Press, 1995.

Wheeler, Everett L. *Stratagem and the Vocabulary of Military Trickery*. Leiden: E. J. Brill, 1988.

Wimberley, Scott. *Special Forces Guerrilla Warfare Manual*. Boulder: Paladin Press, 1997.

Winters, Harold A. et al. *Battling the Elements: Weather and Terrain in the Conduct of War*. Baltimore: Johns Hopkins University Press, 1998.

Whitby, Michael. *Rome at War AD 293–696*. Oxford: Osprey Publishing, 2002.

Whitehead, David, trans. *Aineias the Tactician: How to Survive Under Siege*. Oxford: Clarendon Press, 1990.

Winks, Robert. *Cloak and Gown: Scholars in the Secret War, 1939–1996*. New York: William Morrow, 1987.

Wolf, Markus and Anne McElvoy. *Memoirs of a Spymaster: The Man Who Waged a Secret War Against the West*. London: Random House, 1998.

Woosnam-Savage, Robert and Anthony Hall. *Body Armour*. Dulles: Brassey's, 2000.

Worley, Leslie J. *Hippeis: The Cavalry of Ancient Greece*. History and Warfare. Boulder: Westview Press, 1994.

Wright, Quincy. *A Study of War*. Chicago: University of Chicago Press, 1964.

Wrixon, Fred B. *Codes and Ciphers: An A to Z of Covert Communication, From the Clay Tablet to the Microdot*. New York: Prentice Hall General Reference, 1992.

Yadin, Yigael. *Masada*. London: Weidenfeld & Nicholson, 1966.

Yalichev, Serge. *Mercenaries of the Ancient World*. London: Constable, 1997.

Zacharias, Ellis M. *Secret Missions: The Story of an Intelligence Officer*. Annapolis: Naval Institute Press, (1946) 2003.

Zagoria, Donald S., ed. *Soviet Policy in East Asia*. New Haven: Yale University Press, 1982.

Fundamental Chinese Language Works

二十五史

八陣合變圖說，龍正

十七史百將傳，張預

十大經

三十六計

三國志

三略，黃石公

大同鎮兵車操法，俞大猷

王氏新書，王基

火攻挈要，焦勖

火器略說，黃達權、王韜

火龍神器陣法

太平條規

太平軍目

太平御覽

太白陰經，李筌

六韜

公羊傳

史記

司馬法

戊笈談兵，汪紱

左傳

北洋海軍章程

古今圖書集成

老子

自強軍創制公言，沈敦和

自強軍西法類編，沈敦和

百將傳續編，何喬新

守城錄，陳規、湯君寶

行軍總要，

永樂大典

兵法，魏禧

兵法史略學，陳慶年

兵法百言，揭暄

兵要四則，

兵跡，魏禧

兵謀，魏禧

兵學新書，徐建寅

兵略對，俞大猷

兵鏡，吳惟順、吳鳴球、吳若禮編輯

兵機要訣，徐光啟

兵蠡，尹賓商

兵籌類要，綦崇禮

何博士備論，何去非

宋本十一家注孫子

投筆膚談，何守法

決勝綱目，葉夢熊

吳子

李衛公兵法輯本，李靖

防守集成，朱璐

呂氏春秋

言兵事書，晁錯

車營叩答合編，孫承宗（鹿善繼、茅元儀、杜應芳）

尚書

武侯八陣兵法輯略

武備志，茅元儀

武經七書直解

武經七書匯解，朱墉

武經總要

武編，唐順之

孟子

虎鈐經，許洞

明實錄類纂，武漢出版社

長江水師全案，

長短經，趙蕤

直隸練軍馬步營制章程

美芹十論，辛棄疾

風后握奇經

施氏七書講義，施子美

荀子

春秋

城守籌略，錢栴

草廬經略

紀效新書，戚繼光

洋防說略，徐稚蓀

訓練操法詳晰圖說，袁世凱、段祺瑞、馮國璋、王世珍

海防要覽，丁日昌、李鴻章

海防圖論，胡宗憲

海國圖志，魏源

陣紀，何良臣

鬼谷子

素書，黃石公

孫子

孫子書校解引類，趙本學

孫子參同，李贄

孫臏兵法

尉繚子

唐太宗李衛公問對，李靖

射經，王琚

淮南子，劉安

淮軍武毅各軍課程，聶士成

救命書，呂坤

乾坤大略，王餘佑

國語

商君書

曾文正公水陸行軍練兵誌，王定安

曾胡治兵語錄，蔡鍔

登壇必究，王鳴鶴

鄉約，尹耕

運籌綱目，葉夢熊

道德經論兵要義述，王真

道藏

塞語，尹耕

經法

詩經

新書

新建陸軍兵略錄存，袁世凱

資治通鑑

道德經

逸周書

稱

說苑

廣西選鋒兵操法，俞大猷

翠微北征錄，華岳

管子

閫外春秋，李筌

墨子

潛夫論，王符

練兵實紀，戚繼光

練勇芻言，王璞山

選練條格，徐光啟

諸葛忠武候文集

歷代兵制，陳傅良

戰國策

戰略，司馬彪

魏武帝集

韓非子

韓詩外傳

籌洋芻議，薛福成

籌海圖編，鄭若曾

鶡冠子

權書，蘇洵

續武經總要，趙本學

續資治通鑑

中國軍事史，解放軍出版社

中國軍事通史，軍事科學出版社

中國歷代戰爭史，黎明文化事業股份有限公司

于學彬，三十六計新解詳析，北京，中國經濟，1993.

王兆春，中國火器史，軍事科學出版社，1991.

束涵，三十六計秘本集解，台北，國家，1991.

吳井田，中國謀略大典，北京，國際文化，1993.

吳毅，畫說三十六計，北京，美术，1992.

房立中，姜太公全書，北京，學苑，1996.

房立中，鬼谷子全書，北京，學苑，1995.

房立中，縱橫家全書，北京，學苑，1995.

南闊音，中華謀略寶庫，北京，南海，1992.

馬森亮，三十六計，長沙，湖南，1991.

席龍飛，中國造船史，湖北教育出版社，2000.

徐兆仁，三國韜略，北京，中國人民大學，1995.

柴宇球，謀略庫，北京，藍天，1990.

柴宇球，謀略論，北京，藍天，1991.

柴宇球，謀略家，北京，藍天，1991.

張秀楓，中國謀略家全書，北京，國際文化，1991.

張鐵牛、高曉星，中國古代海軍史，八一出版社，1993.

郭硯溪，中外詭謀全書，哈爾濱，哈爾濱，1912.

陳維禮，歷代名臣奇謀妙計全書，長春，吉林文史，1986.

鈕先鐘，中國古代戰略思想新論，安徽，教育，2005.

靈光，文韜武略:三國智慧今用，北京，金城，2000.

Selected Index

Paradigm Battles

Martial and Other Texts

MAJOR THEORETICIANS

Also by Ralph D. Sawyer

Further discussion of the topics raised by Sun-tzu's *Art of War* and many other focal subjects in Chinese military and intelligence history may be found in the following Westview Press books, translated and authored by Ralph D. Sawyer.

The Tao of War
The Martial Tao Te Ching
0-8133-4081-0, $15.95/$25.00 CAN, paper

Wang Chen, a ninth-century military commander, was sickened by the carnage that had plagued the glorious T'ang dynasty for decades. "All within the seas were poisoned," he wrote, "and pain and disaster was rife throughout the land." Wang Chen wondered, how can we end conflicts before they begin? How can we explain and understand the dynamics of conflict? For the answer he turned to a remarkable source—the *Tao Te Ching*. Here is Wang Chen's own rendering of and commentary on the ancient text, insightfully expanded and amplified by translator Ralph D. Sawyer, a leading scholar of Chinese military history. Although the *Tao* long influenced Chinese military doctrine, Wang Chen's interpretations produced the first reading of it as a martial text—a "tao of war." Like Sun-tzu's *Art of War*, certainly the most famous study of strategy ever written, the Tao provides lessons for the struggles of contemporary life. In the way that the ancient *Art of War* provides inspiration and advice on how to succeed in competitive situations of all kinds, even in today's world, Wang Chen's *The Tao of War* uncovers action plans for managing conflict and promoting peace.

A book to put on the shelf next to *Art of War*, Wang Chen's *The Tao of War* is a reference of equally compelling and practical advice.

Sun Tzu: *Art of War*
0-8133-1951-X, $15.95/$25.00 CAN, paper

"The *Art of War* has become so accepted as a 'must read' book . . . that it need no further justification. . . . The most accurate, concise, and usable English-language translation available."— *Military Review*

The *Art of War* is almost certainly the most famous study of strategy ever written and it has had an extraordinary influence on the history of warfare. The principles Sun-tzu expounded were utilized brilliantly by such great Asian war leaders as Mao Tse-tung, Giap, and Yamamoto. First translated two hundred years ago by a French missionary, Sun Tzu's *Art of War* has been credited with influencing Napoleon, the German General Staff, and even the planning for Desert Storm. Many Japanese companies make this book required reading for their key executives. And increasingly, Western businesspeople and others are turning to the *Art of War* for inspiration and advice on how to succeed in competitive situations of all kinds.

Ralph Sawyer places this classic work of strategy in its proper historical context. Sawyer supplies a portrait of Sun-tzu's era and outlines several battles of the period that may have either influenced Sun-tzu or been conducted by him. While appreciative of the philosophical richness of the *Art of War,* his edition addresses Sun-tzu's practical origins and presents a translation that is both accurate and accessible.

The Complete Art of War

Sun-tzu Sun Pin

ISBN 0-8133-3085-8, $35.00/$52.95 CAN, cloth

"The combination of a . . . clear translation with an informative commentary makes this an essential element in the study of Chinese martial philosophy. . . . An excellent [book]."—*Military & Naval History Journal*

The only single-volume edition available of the classic essays on strategy by the great Sun-tzu and his descendant, Sun Pin. With Sawyer's thoughtful chapter-by-chapter commentaries, *The Complete Art of War* is designed to guide the reader to new insights into the nature of human conflict and a greater understanding of every field of human activity—from playing the game of politics to building a successful marriage, from closing a deal to managing a large organization, and even from making war to making peace.

The Seven Military Classics of Ancient China

ISBN 0-8133-1228-0, $37.50/$56.50 CAN, cloth

The Seven Military Classics is one of the most profound studies of warfare ever written. Here translated in their entirety for the first time, the seven separate essays in this volume (written between 500 BC and AD 700) include Sun-tzu's famous *Art of War*. This is the definitive English-language edition of a unique contribution to the military literature.

Sun Pin
Military Methods
ISBN 0-8133-8888-0, $32.00/$47.95 CAN, paper

"Sawyer's translation . . . further adds in an important way to our knowledge of the place of warfare in classical Chinese civilization."—John Keegan

In addition to translating this "eighth military classic," Sawyer has prepared insightful chapter-by-chapter commentaries and a vivid general introduction that describes Sun Pin's life and times, analyzes in detail Sun Pin's tactics in important battles, and compares Sun-tzu's strategic thinking with Sun Pin's.

One Hundred Unorthodox Strategies
Battle and Tactics of Chinese Warfare
ISBN 0-8133-2861-6, $22.00/$32.95 CAN, paper

"Not only insightful, but impeccable."—*War in History*

"Sawyer's commentary, written in language understandable to both soldiers and businessmen, is useful beyond its application to the study of military theory. . . . Enjoyable and enlightening."—*Military Review*

Beginning with Sun-tzu's *Art of War*, the anonymous author of this Sung dynasty military manual abstracted the one hundred generally paired tactical principles—such as fast/slow, unorthodox/orthodox—he felt to be essential to battlefield analysis and martial conceptualization before appending a similar number of historical examples.

The Tao of Spycraft
Intelligence Theory and Practice in Traditional China
ISBN 0-8133-3303-2, $35.00/$52.95 CAN, cloth

"Ralph Sawyer has once again written a text which combines the virtues of scholarly integrity, shrewd analysis, and plain fun. This book is not only for those interested in the history and theory of intelligence, but for those simply intent on a good read."—Robert L. O'Connell, author of *Ride of the Second Horseman*

In *The Tao of Spycraft*, for the first time anywhere Ralph Sawyer unfolds the long and venerable tradition of spycraft and intelligence work in traditional China, revealing a vast array of theoretical materials and astounding historical developments.